DOWNTOWN HONOLULU'S LOST BUILDINGS & FORGOTTEN ARCHITECTS

GARY R. COOVER

Rollston Press

Downtown Honolulu's Lost Buildings and Forgotten Architects
by Gary R. Coover

All rights reserved. No part of this book may be reproduced, scanned, transmitted, or distributed in any printed or form electronic without the prior permission of the author except in the case of brief quotations embodied in articles or reviews.

Copyright © 2023 Gary R. Coover

ISBN-13: 978-1-953208-06-4

All images are in the public domain unless otherwise noted.

Recent photographs are by the author.

Cover photo: The Chilton Block (1890), photograph by Frank Davey, courtesy Hawaii State Archives.

Also by Gary R. Coover: *Honolulu Chinatown: 200 Years of Red Lanterns & Red Lights*
(Rollston Press, 2022)

Pocket Walking Tour of Honolulu's Chinatown
(Rollston Press, 2023)

ROLLSTON PRESS
1717 Ala Wai Blvd #1703
Honolulu, HI 96815
USA
www.rollstonpress.com

TABLE OF CONTENTS

PREFACE 8
INTRODUCTION 9
THE CITY OF HONOLULU 10
DOWNTOWN STREETS 11
SELECTED FIRE INSURANCE MAPS 13
THEN & NOW 18
ADAMS LANE 42
Mutual Telephone Building 43
Knights of Pythias Lodge 45
ALAKEA STREET 46
Sailors' Home 47
Catton-Neill Building 49
Alakea Building 51
Kapiolani Building 52
Union Trust Building 55
L.B. Kerr Building 56
Masonic Temple 61
Mutual Telephone Building 64
Wm. French Residence 66
The British Club 67
McGrew Building 70
A.J. CartWright House 72
BERETANIA STREET 74
Schnack Building 75
Hustace Block 76
Sachs Building 77
Fred Harrison Block 79
Central Fire Station 84

Day Block 88
Makee Residence 93
Galen Building 95
BETHEL STREET 96
The Friend Building 97
The Seamen's Bethel 98
McCandless Building 100
Cosmopolitan Restaurant 102
Hawaii Theater 104
Hawaii Building 108
Bethel-Pauahi Building 109
Aloha Grill Building 110
BISHOP STREET 113
T.H. Davies Warehouse 114
Dillingham Transportation Building 115
Alexander & Baldwin Building 120
Theo. H. Davies Building 124
S.M. Damon Building / Bishop Bank 129
Alexander Young Building 133
Long's Drugs 141
Monsarrat Building 142
Jade Building 144
Associated Oil Service Station 149
Reynolds House / Sacred Heart Convent 150
Patten Building 151
Catholic Rectory 153
Eli Jones House 155
FORT STREET 156

Honolulu Fort	157
Custom House	162
Chayter Building	164
Pacific Mail Warehouse	165
Lucas Clock Tower	166
Honolulu Planing Mill	169
Court House	171
Hackfeld Building	175
Wilder Building	180
The Beaver Block	183
Spreckels Block	187
J.A. Cummins Building	192
W.E. Foster Building	195
Safe Deposit Building	197
Mrs. Lack Building	201
Lewers & Cooke	203
Austin Building	205
A.L. Smith Building	206
Odd Fellows Building	208
Waterhouse / Andrade Building	212
B.F. Ehlers / Campbell Building	216
Wichman Building	221
Boston Block	226
Williams / Hollister Building	230
J.J. Williams Building	233
Tregloan Building	235
Benson Smith Building	239
Pantheon Building	243
Mott-Smith Building	253
McCorriston Building	260
French Hotel	263
Kress Building	266
Club Stables Building	268
J.H. Fisher Building	272
Love Building	273
Fisher Building	275
Sacred Heart Convent School	277
Blaisdell Hotel	282
Watumull Building	286
Our Lady of Peace Cathedral	288
Model Block	293
Knights of Columbus Building	294
Progress Block	295
HOTEL STREET	297
Gray's Block	298
The Waverley Block	299
Robinson Block	302
Empire Theater	305
Warren / Canton Hotel	307
James Campbell Building	311
Palm Building	313
Arlington Block	317
Portland Building	320
Oregon Block	322
Elite Block	325
Hotel Baths	328
YMCA Building	329
Old YMCA Building	331
Snow Cottage	335
Black Cat Café	336
Hawaiian Hotel	340
Royal Hawaiian Garage	344
KA'AHUMANU STREET	346
Theo. H. Davies Buildings	347

A.B. Howe Building	349
Rhodes Building	350
KING STREET	352
Thomas / Yat Loy Building	353
Hoffschlaeger Building	356
Castle & Cooke Building	358
Damon Building	362
John Hopp Store	363
Von Holt Block	365
Metropolitan Meat Building	368
Waity Building	370
Republic Building	371
Union Grill	373
Collins Building	376
Dimond Block / Elks Building	377
Central Building	381
O'Neill Building	383
Chilton Block	389
E.O. Hall Building	394
McIntyre Building	400
Kauikeolani Building	406
Home Insurance Building	408
Haleakala / Arlington House	410
Bank of Hawaii	417
Emmeluth Building	421
First National Bank	424
Lewers & Cooke Building	426
Lincoln Block	429
Occidental Hotel	430
Burgess & Johnson Showroom	433
Advertiser Building	435
Hawaiian Electric Building	437
S.C. Allen Cottage	438
New Hawaiian Electric Building	441
MERCHANT STREET	445
Royal Saloon	446
J.T. Waterhouse Warehouse	449
Honolulu Sailors' Home	450
Kalakaua Police Station	453
Cartwright Building	456
Melchers Building	457
Kamehameha V Post Office	460
Honolulu Hale	463
Bishop Bank	467
Hawaiian Gazette / Union Saloon	469
Bishop Estate Building	472
Campbell Block	474
B.F. Snow Building	478
McInerny Block	482
Judd Building	487
Stangenwald Building	491
Star Building	494
Castle & Cooke Building	495
Daily Bulletin Building	498
Schuman Carriage Co.	499
Mutual Telephone Building	500
Magoon Building	502
Schuman Carriage Co.	503
Podmore Building	505
PAUAHI STREET	507
E.W. Quinn Building	508
QUEEN STREET	509
The Old Corner	510
J.T. Waterhouse Buildings	512

Senator Waterhouse Building 515	John L. Cliff 571
Market House 516	Herbert Cohen Cayton 571
R.W. Wood Building 519	Dahl, Conrad & Preis 572
McChesney Building 521	Louis E. Davis 574
C.L. Richards Block 524	Charles W. Dickey 575
Allen Block 527	Francis R. Dunn 576
Makee & Anthon Block 532	Emory & Webb 576
Robinson Warehouse 535	Fred Fujioka 577
Hustace-Peck Building 537	Ernest Hara 578
M.P. Robinson Building 538	Fred Harrison 578
Inter-Island Steam Navigation Building 540	Hawaiian Engineering & Construction Co. ... 579
A.W. Peirce Building 542	Isaac N. Hayden 580
Masonic Hall 543	Hoffman & Riley 580
Star-Bulletin Plant 547	Howard & Train 581
California Feed Co. 548	Harry L. Kerr 582
F.L. James Building 550	George W. Lincoln 583
RICHARDS STREET 551	Lord-Young Engineering Co. 584
The Bungalow 552	George Lucas 585
Ideal Finance Building 554	Henry W. McIntosh 586
YWCA Building 556	Merrill, Simms, & Roehrig 586
UNION STREET 558	Isaac Moore 587
Union Building 559	Louis Christian Mullgardt 587
Wolters Building 561	William Mutch 587
Dowsett House 562	E.A.P. Newcomb 588
Wood/Spalding House 564	Kenji Onodera 588
Triangle Auto Supply Building 566	J.G. Osborne 589
ARCHITECTS & BUILDERS 567	Vladimir Ossipoff 589
Thomas J. Baker 568	John Ouderkirk 590
Beardslee & Page 569	Pacific Engineering Company 590
Henry F. Bertelmann 570	Isaac A. Palmer 591
Bowler & Ingvorsen 570	Carl H. Patzig 592
Robert S. Chase 570	George W. Percy 592

Hardie Phillip	592
Mark Potter	593
Fred H. Redward	593
Clinton B. Ripley	594
Lincoln Rogers	595
Guy N. Rothwell	595
E.B. Thomas	596
George Thomas	597
Oliver G. Traphagen	597
Charles W. Vincent	598
Thomas B. Walker	599
Fred W. Williams	600
Wimberly & Cook	600
R.A.S. Wood	601
Ralph E. Woolley	601
York & Sawyer	602
J.L. Young Engineering Co.	602
SOURCES & ACKNOWLEDGEMENTS	603
THE AUTHOR	605
INDEX	606
GEOGRAPHICAL INDEX	614

PREFACE

While doing the research for *Honolulu Chinatown: 200 Years of Red Lanterns and Red Lights* (Rollston Press 2022), I kept running across interesting tidbits, stories, and photographs of buildings in downtown Honolulu that were outside my stated area of interest. But I made a strict effort to ignore them as much as possible – one has to set boundaries; you can't research everything!

But chasing after leads about a particular forgotten architect kept leading me deeper and deeper into downtown. After discovering several of his buildings, including one of my favorites (the Chilton Block), it just made sense to keep on going and eventually fill in the rest of the blanks about who built what, where, and when in the main Honolulu business district.

This research was helped immensely by the wealth of historical photographs in old newspapers and the official archives of the State of Hawaii, the Hawaiian Historical Society, and the Bishop Museum, and it is my distinct pleasure to present some of these photographs in this book, many published for the first time. Now identified, located, and often compared and contrasted with current street scenes.

The historical information was collected mostly from newspapers, historical photographs, land records, and old fire insurance maps. A gigantic jigsaw puzzle with the added dimension of different things being in different places at different times. And there's also the inevitable gaps, inaccuracies, misspellings, mistakes, biases, and lapses of information that often accompany printed historical accounts. Street numbers varied widely before 1900.

This book is mostly about buildings and builders, and about providing locations and context to historical photographs. It doesn't include *every* building in downtown Honolulu although it may feel like it. Some write-ups have additional historical information, others don't. Selected more by whim than by importance. Unfortunately, only so much can be included in a manageably sized book. Histories of the larger firms have been well-documented elsewhere, so this book concentrates more on those who are lesser-known. There is still much more waiting to be discovered, there is always more to the story.

This book also includes thumbnail bios of over 50 architects and builders who worked in downtown Honolulu. Some will be well-known, others less so, and some you may be hearing about for the first time. It is important to credit those whose designs and efforts have made such an impact on Honolulu's business center over the years.

I hope this will inspire you to learn more on your own about Honolulu's history, architecture, and the people who lived and worked in these wonderful buildings. It is their stories that bring the historical downtown streetscapes to life.

Gary R. Coover
Honolulu, Hawaii

NOTE: Please see *Honolulu Chinatown: 200 Years of Red Lanterns & Red Lights* (Rollston Press, 2022) for histories of buildings on the ewa side of downtown Honolulu.

INTRODUCTION

This is the story of downtown Honolulu's architectural heritage and the people who designed and built it. Since most of the buildings are long gone due to the vicissitudes of time and the seemingly never-ending push for progress, this is also a documentation and a celebration.

The names of the early builders and architects have mostly been lost to history. Fortunately, this new research has led to the rediscovery of many – sometimes conclusively and sometimes by conjecture as the most-likely suspect.

The first houses and buildings in Honolulu built by the original Native Hawaiians were simple one-story affairs made of pili grass over a wooden frame, *"looking like so many hay-stacks in the country"* as one writer noted in 1828.

Immigration from America and Europe and Asia in the 1800's brought new building styles to Hawaii that incorporated popular designs and materials found elsewhere.

This book documents the many buildings that have come and gone, including those that may or may not still be here in the indeterminate future. A select few have survived relatively unscathed to the present day, but most have been demolished, remodeled, covered up, even disfigured. Some were once regaled as Honolulu's most beautiful buildings, and it is a sad fact that many are no longer with us.

Some of the buildings in this book are not physically lost… yet. For some, it is their origins that have been lost. As history has shown, no building is completely safe from the ravages of man or nature – nothing lasts forever.

Is what has been built since of higher or better quality? I'll leave that to you, the reader, to decide. To assist your assessment, photographs contrasting then and now are shown in many instances.

Downtown Honolulu is constantly changing and evolving, and its built environment will continue to respond to social and market forces. Let us hope that what is built in the future are not lesser replacements but are true civic improvements in both function and beauty.

NOTE: As many corner buildings have frontages and addresses on both streets, check both streets if you are looking for a particular building. Original building names are shown where possible, but names often change through successive generations and owners. If in doubt, consult the Geographical Index.

A Word about Hawaiian Directions: The cardinal directions of north, south, east, and west do not make much sense in an island setting, so these are the directions commonly used in Hawaii and specifically in Honolulu:

Mauka (MAU-ka)	=	toward the mountains
Makai (ma-KAI)	=	toward the ocean
Ewa (EV-uh)	=	toward Ewa Beach
Waikiki (WAI-kee-kee)	=	toward Waikiki (1800's and early 1900's)

THE CITY OF HONOLULU

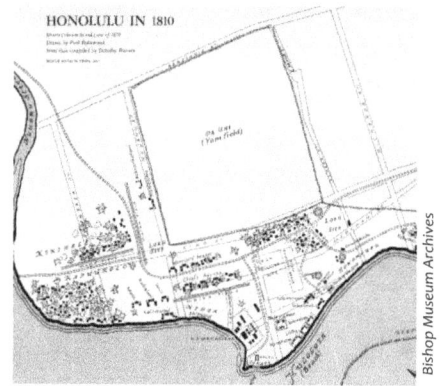

What is now downtown Honolulu started out as a small Native Hawaiian fishing community known as Kou. It had a sandy beach where canoes could easily land and the confluence and estuary with Nuʻuanu Stream plus a large shallow reef provided ample fishing opportunities for the village that was well-established long before 1800.

After King Kamehameha I's conquest of Oahu in 1795 he moved his royal compound to Kou in 1809. With Honolulu Harbor being one of the few places deep enough for European trading vessels, the area quickly turned into a major trading center.

The name "Honolulu" translates to "sheltered harbor" and early visitors called it "Fair Haven". The first foreigner to visit the harbor was Captain William Brown in 1794.

When the Russian-American Trading Company's stone building started looking too much like a fort in 1816 they were expelled and a proper fort was built in its place to protect the harbor from future threats.

Port d'Hanarourou by Louis Choris, 1816

The first wharf in 1825 was the hulk of the *Eliza Ann*, but both wooden and stone wharves were soon constructed to accommodate the ships of the sandalwood trade, then the whaling fleets, and then the many commercial vessels to and from places like San Francisco, Hong Kong, US Mainland, and Europe.

By 1838 Honolulu had a population of 6,000, including about 250 Americans, 100 English, 40 Chinese, and a few French, Spanish and Portuguese.

Honolulu became the official capital of the Hawaiian Kingdom in 1845 and has remained so through the overthrow of the monarchy in 1893, territorial annexation by the United States in 1898, and official Hawaiian statehood in 1959.

With Nuʻuanu Street being the principal road leading up from the docks, Merchant Street became the main commercial center housing the post office, newspaper, and offices for the many merchants and commission agents. As the city grew, businesses began moving up Nuʻuanu Street and then over towards Fort Street as the area closer to the docks began turning into what we now call Chinatown.

Downtown Honolulu was built and developed by mostly American and European influences, and that is readily seen by the buildings and structures built in the last 200 years.

DOWNTOWN STREETS

Early downtown streets were initially no more than simple crooked and irregular footpaths between grass houses that gradually developed over time into the broad, straight streets we see today. Many of the building changes, remodels, and demolitions over the years were due to street-widening projects as transportation needs dictated wider thoroughfares.

STREET VIEW AT HONOLULU.

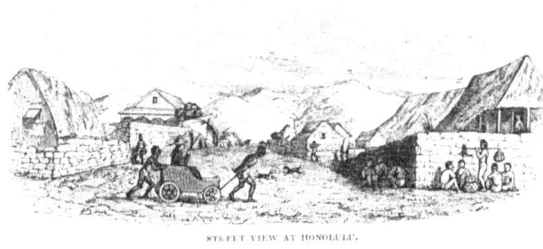

Early maps called the streets "alanui" which translates to "big path".

Governor Kekuanaoa is credited with establishing the current street layout in 1838 after much prodding by the *Sandwich Island Gazette* which suggested naming six streets: King, Queen, Merchant, Fort, Ka'ahumanu, and Garden Lane.

The first formal street survey and official map was made by German surveyor H. Ehrenberger and published in *The Friend* on October 1, 1845. The map below of downtown Honolulu was enclosed in a letter by Richard Charlton dated August 25, 1843:

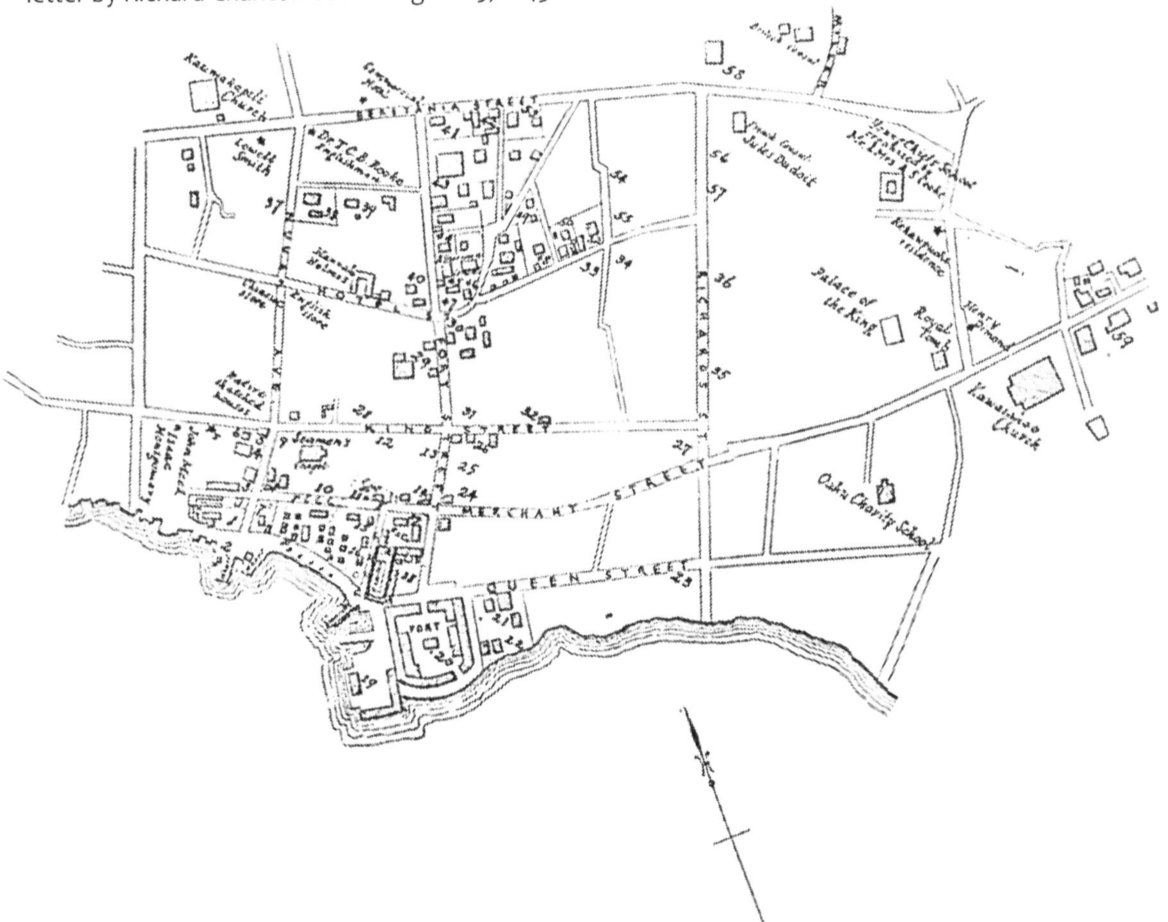

Adams Lane was known as Branch Street, later named for Alexander Adams whose house was at the mauka/ewa corner with Hotel Street.

Alakea Street was first known as Cross Street, then White Street, which translated into Hawaiian is "alakea" and presumably named for the white coral rock it was paved with.

Beretania Street was first known as Back Street since it was at the mauka boundary of the town. It was also where the British Consul lived, and "Beretania" is a corruption of "Britannia".

Bethel Street was named for the Seamen's Bethel church at King and Bethel Streets. It took over Rose Lane between King and Hotel streets in 1887, was extended to Pauahi Street in 1924, then to Beretania Street in 1927 and to Queen Street in 1931.

Bishop Street was named for Charles R. Bishop through whose property Bishop Street was constructed in 1900. It was extended to the harbor in 1918 and to Beretania Street in 1927.

Chaplain Street was named for Samuel C. Damon, the chaplain of the Seamen's Bethel Church, since the street passed in front of his house.

Fort Street extended mauka from the front gate of the Honolulu Fort, and was called Alanui Papu by the Hawaiians, roughly translating to "street by the gun enclosure".

Garden Lane was also called Kihapai Street, and it was absorbed when Bishop Street was extended to Beretania.

Hotel Street was named after the Warren Hotel owned by Major William R. Warren in the 1820's. It later became the Canton Hotel and was located where the National Building is today at the mauka/waikiki corner of Bethel and Hotel streets.

Ka'ahumanu Street was named for Queen Ka'ahumanu but was originally known as Laulau Lane and Beef Lane due to the native markets along it.

King Street was called a variety of names in the early years, including Broadway, Church Street, Chapel Street, Main Street, Kawaiahao Street, and Alanui Ali'i ("street of royalty") by the Hawaiians. It was the main ewa/waikiki thoroughfare beyond the downtown area on both sides for many years.

Merchant Street was the first financial center where many of the businesses and offices were located, and it was sometimes called Exchange Street or Alanui Kalepa and Alanue Kuai by the Hawaiians.

Nimitz Highway was built in 1951, absorbing much of Queen Street.

Nu'uanu Street translates to "cool cliff", a reference to it extending up the Nu'uanu Valley to the Pali.

Queen Street was also called Sea Street, Wharf Street, and Front Street, and was initially just a small path along the waterfront.

Richards Street was named for former missionary and later President of the Board of Commissioners, Reverend William Richards.

Union Street was initially called Alanui Maua, Alanui Huina, Ke'eke'e, Branch Street, and Crooked Lane, but was known as Union Street as early as 1851. According to Mrs. Monsarrat it was named for a street in her English hometown and was in the heart of the early mostly haole residential area. The section between Hotel and Bishop streets was turned into a pedestrian mall in 1964 and the upper portion above Bishop Street was abandoned in 1968.

SELECTED
FIRE INSURANCE MAPS

 1879 – Lion Fire Insurance Company of London, Pacific Branch

1885 – Dakin Publishing Company, San Francisco

1891 – Dakin Publishing Company, San Francisco

1899 – Dakin Publishing Company, San Francisco

1906 – Dakin Publishing Company, San Francisco

1914 – Sanborn Map & Publishing Company, New York

FORT STREET – BETWEEN KING AND HOTEL STREETS – EWA SIDE

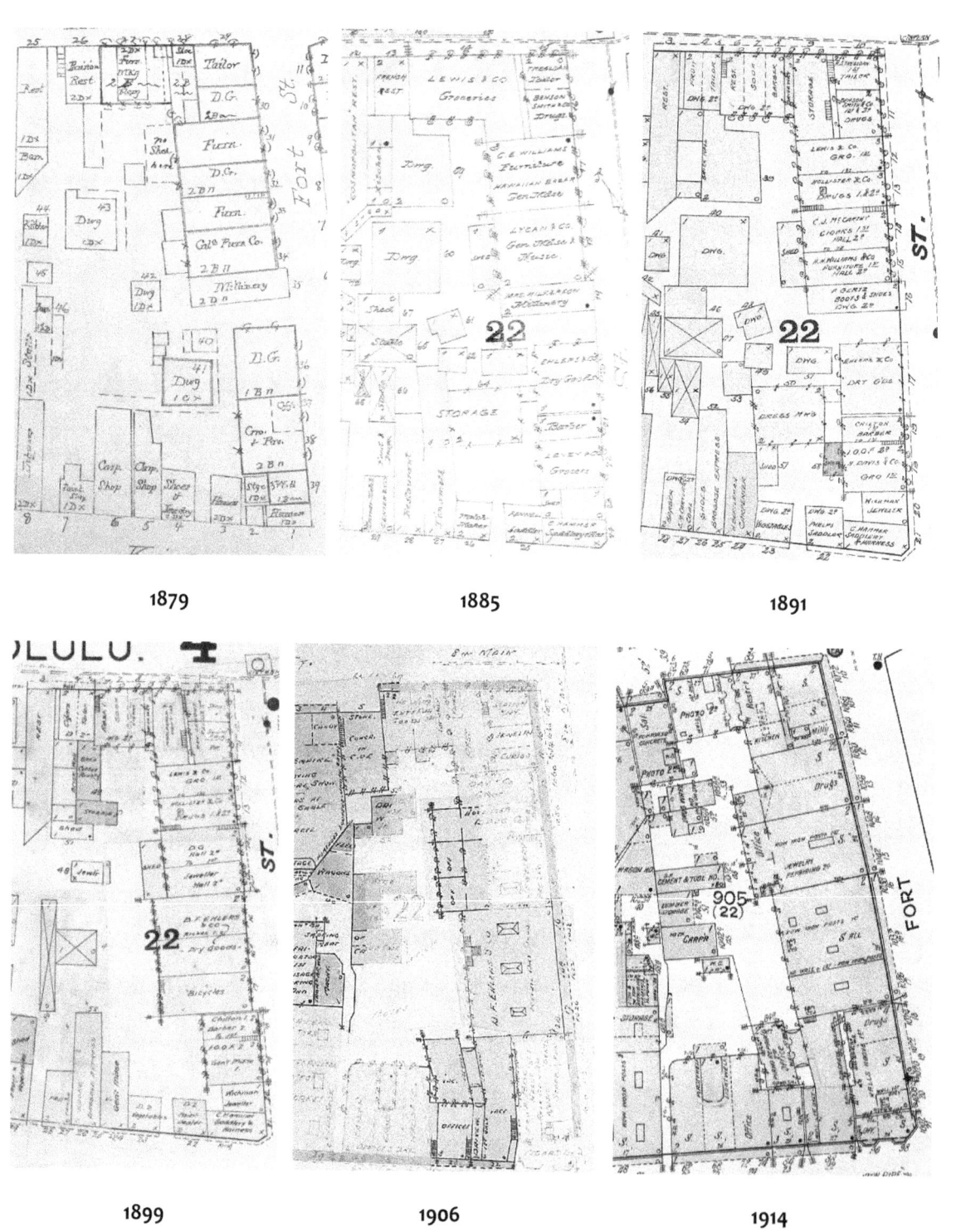

FORT STREET – BETWEEN KING AND HOTEL STREETS – WAIKIKI SIDE

FORT STREET – BETWEEN MERCHANT AND HOTEL STREETS – EWA SIDE

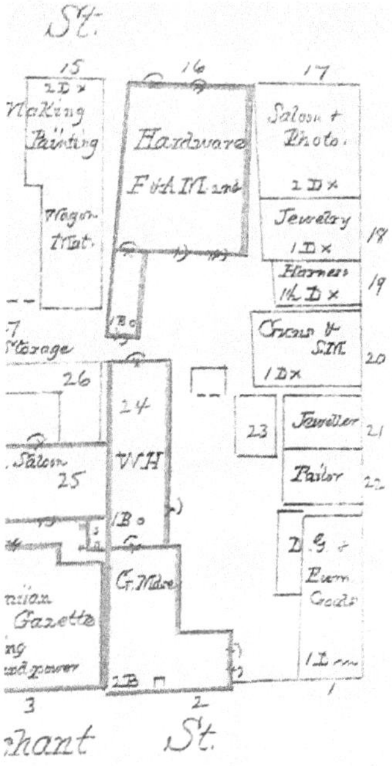

1879

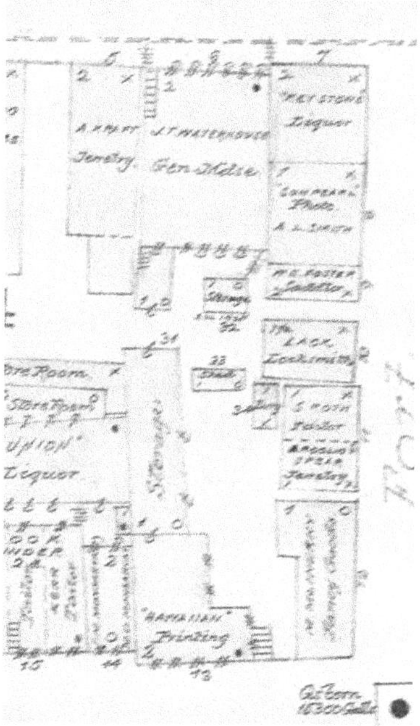

1885

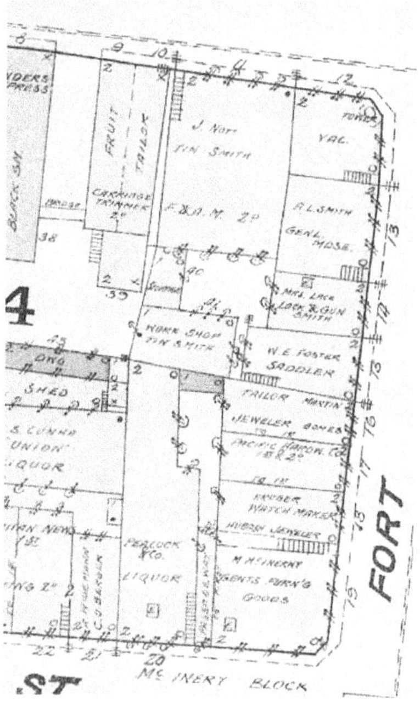

1891

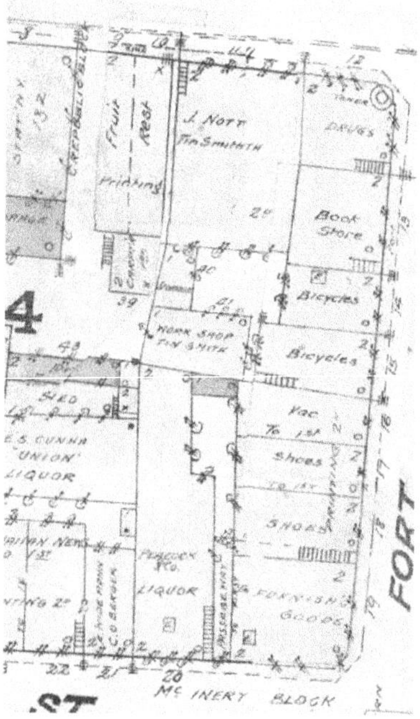

1899

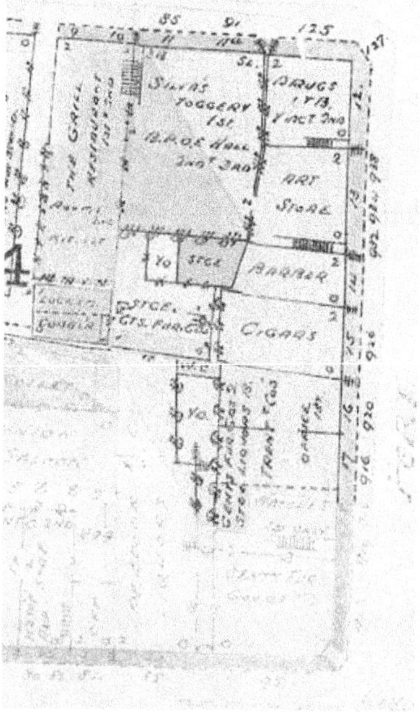

1906

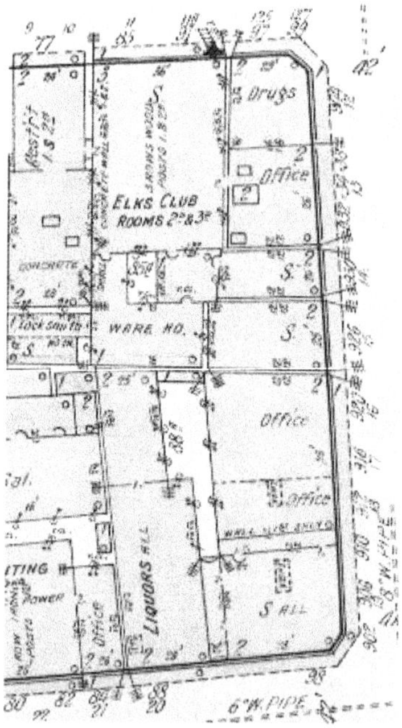

1914

FORT STREET – BETWEEN MERCHANT AND HOTEL STREETS – WAIKIKI SIDE

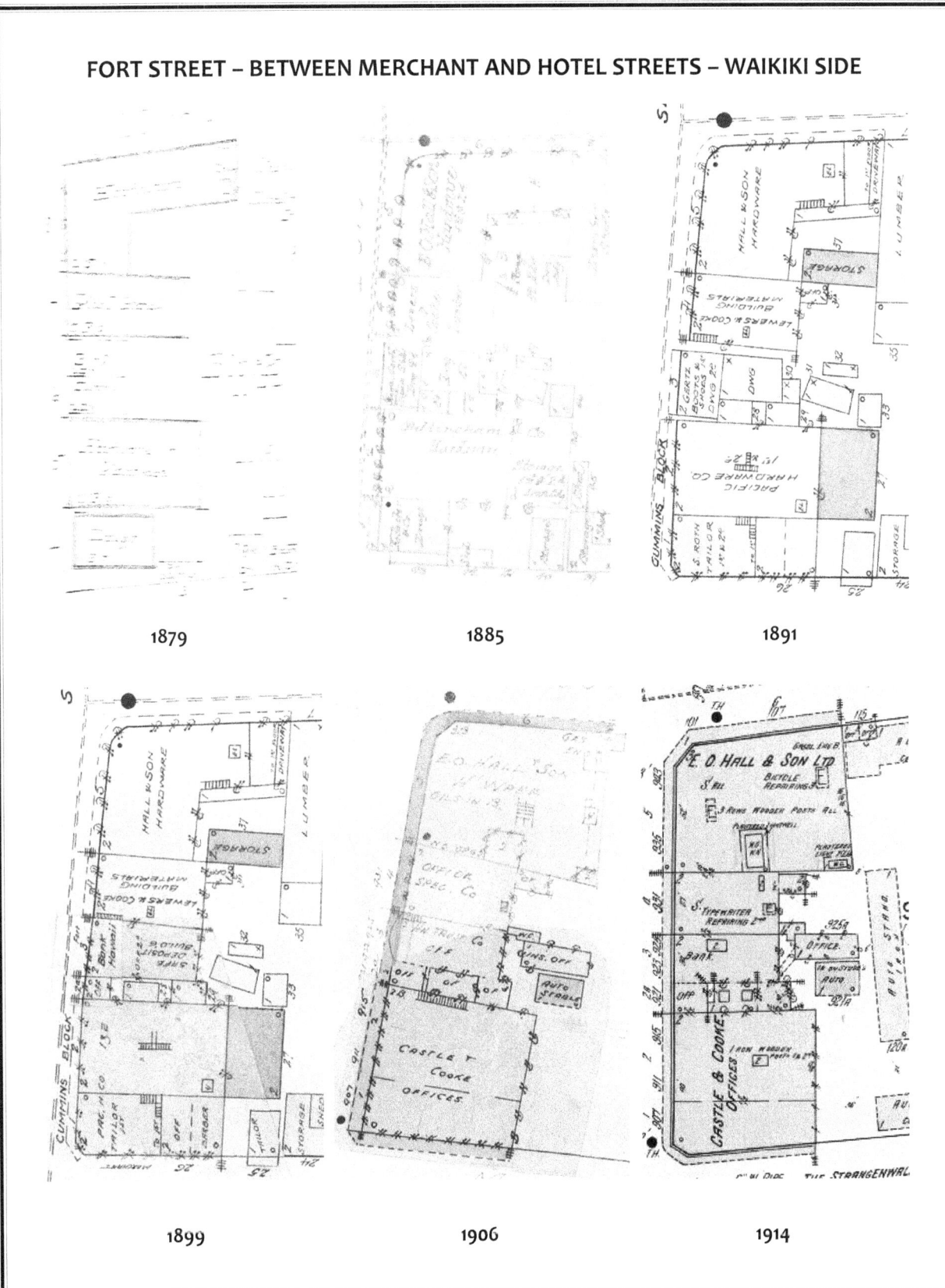

THEN & NOW

Fort Street, looking mauka from King Street

Fort Street, looking makai from King Street

Fort Street, looking makai from Hotel Street

Fort Street, looking mauka from Hotel Street

Fort Street, looking mauka from Queen Street

Fort Street, looking mauka from Merchant Street

King Street, looking ewa from Alakea Street

King Street, looking ewa from Bethel Street

King Street, looking ewa from Fort Street

Merchant Street, looking ewa from Fort Street

Merchant Street, looking waikiki from Nuʻuanu Street

Merchant Street, looking waikiki from Bethel Street

Ka'ahumanu Street, looking makai from Merchant Street

Merchant Street, looking waikiki from Kaʻahumanu Street

Alakea Street, looking mauka from Hotel Street

Hotel Street, looking ewa from Alakea Street

Merchant Street, looking ewa from Alakea Street

Union Street, looking mauka from Hotel Street

Hotel Street, looking waikiki from Bethel Street

Ka'ahumanu Street, looking mauka from Queen Street

King Street, looking mauka at Fort Street

The Honolulu Advertiser, March 28, 1926

Queen Street, looking ewa from Fort Street

Queen Street, looking waikiki from Nuʻuanu Street

Honolulu Star-Bulletin, October 20, 1924

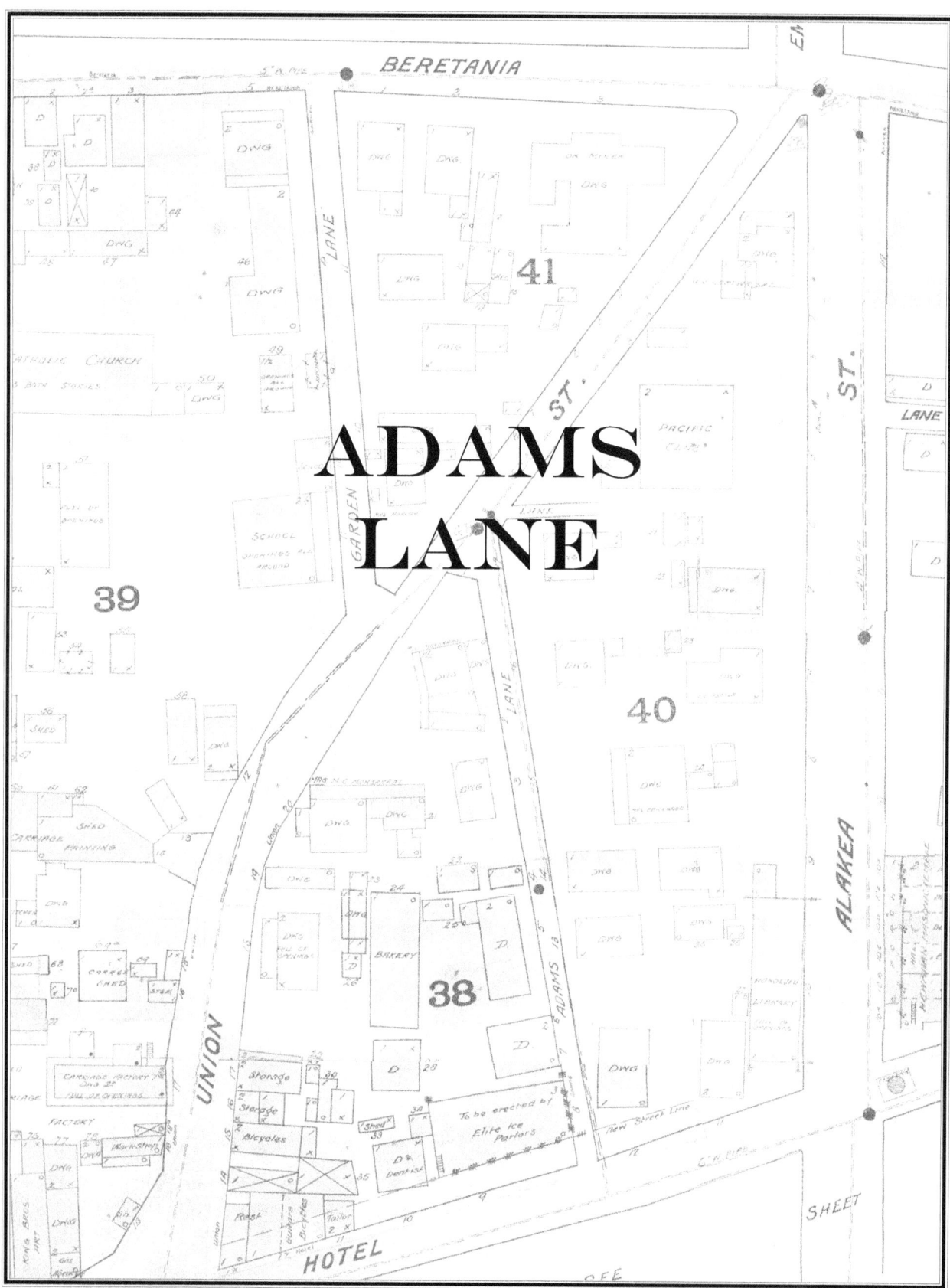

MUTUAL TELEPHONE BUILDING

1141 Adams Lane

1910 – present
Architect/Builder: Frederick G. Hummel

What started out as a small building on Adams Lane is now a massive $13M telecommunications complex towering 17-stories high, stretching from Bishop to Alakea streets.

The first Mutual Telephone Company building on this site was started in 1909 and completed in 1910 on the site of the old 2-story Brickwood house facing Adams Lane. It was designed by Mutual Telephone manager Frederick G. Hummel and had 2,500 automatic switches incased in glass cases containing 5 or 6 rows of 120 new "centrals".

> THE NEW CENTRAL.
> The old Brickwood premises in Adams' lane, which has been acquired for a central office for the Mutual Telephone Company, is situated on the Waikiki side of the lane about half way between Hotel street and Union street. The large house on the lot will be removed and a fine, fireproof building erected there. It is expected that this will be the first home of the automatic system in Honolulu.

Hawaiian Star, August 20, 1909

> The building of the company, as it stands today in Adam's lane is also the work of Hummel, the work of his brains and almost of his hands. He designed it, drew the plans and was his own contractor, personally superintending its construction.

The Honolulu Advertiser, August 28, 1910

The Honolulu Advertiser, August 28, 1910

The building is still visible today on Adams Lane, just barely.

Photo by H.L. Chase, 1870

The "large house on the lot" known as the Brickwood house facing Adams Lane was built in 1860 by Robert C. Wyllie for the huge sum of $9,500 and briefly leased to David L. Gregg, Minister of Finance. Gregg named it "Emma House" or "Hale Emma" for his daughter who was named after Queen Emma.

It replaced a house that Wyllie had previously lived in and where the British Club met from 1855 until it was torn down and the new house built in 1860.

The estate of R.C. Wyllie put the house up for sale in 1867 and it was bought by J.T. Waterhouse who rented it out for room and board, later offering it for sale or lease in 1872.

> **ROOMS and BOARD!**
> 561 4t   At EMMA HOUSE.

> **To be Sold or Let.**
> THA➤ ELEGANT AND COMMODIous family mansion, EMMA HOUSE (built two years ago, at a cost of $9,500), lately occupied by the Hon. David L. Gregg and his family.
> Parties wishing to see the House can apply to Mr. N. Fuller, who resides in the adjacent premises, lately occupied as the Government Offices.   48 tf

By the early 1880's it was the home of Postmaster General Arthur P. Brickwood from Devonshire, England, with his wife Louisa Luika Nahili "Chu Chu" Gilman Brickwood remaining in the house after he died in 1883.

> **Where Can we Get a Good, Large, Convenient House on Moderate Terms?**
> **To Let or for Sale.**
> THE "EMMA HOUSE," having been named after the Queen, and built by His late Ex. R. C. Wyllie, for a first class residence. It has just been put into thorough repair, with a new corrugated iron roof calculated to last 25 years and upwards.
> TERMS—Credit, 5 or 7 years, at the option of the purchaser, bearing interest at 8 per cent. per annum. If no deposit is made, ten per cent. of the purchase will have to be paid annually. First come, first served. Let or Sell.
> 17 1m   JOHN THOS. WATERHOUSE.

KNIGHTS OF PYTHIAS LODGE

1165 Adams Lane

1930 – c.1968

Architect/Builder: Fred W. Williams / Frank M. Dias

Honolulu Star-Bulletin, June 7, 1930

Built at a cost of $100,000 for building and land, this 2-story reinforced concrete building was designed by Fred W. Williams and built by Frank M. Dias for Mystic Lodge No.2 of the Knights of Pythias. The hall was 48' x 53' and the upstairs also included a stage, kitchen, anterooms, and trustee's offices.

The lodge was founded on January 10, 1884, at Harmony Hall on King Street and at one time had nearly 350 members. The benevolent organization was founded on principles of co-operation, friendship, and good will, "pointing the way to happiness through the path of service".

The wholesale and commission firm of Hurd-Pohlmann Co. Ltd. leased the downstairs for 25 years. They were manufacturers' representatives for various types of store fixtures and equipment and dry goods.

The Knights of Pythias sold the building to Hawaiian Telcom in 1964, and it was demolished around 1968 for the construction of the 17-story Hawaiian Telcom Building designed by Wimberly Whisenand Allison & Tong and completed in 1970 by Reed and Martin, Inc.

2022

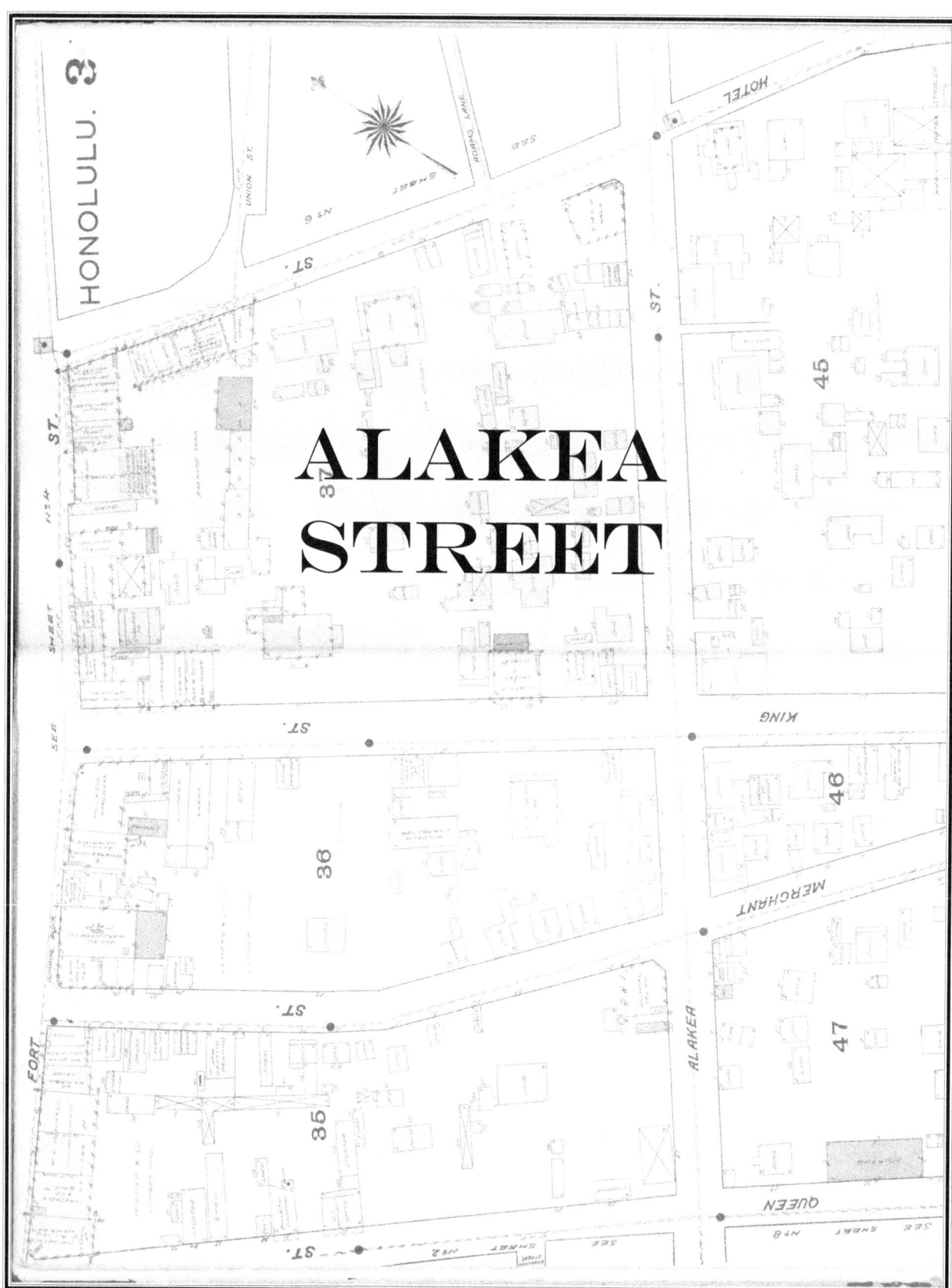

SAILORS' HOME

707 Alakea Street

1894 – 1962

Architect/Builder: C.B. Ripley / Lucas Brothers

Drawing by John K. Waiamau, assistant to C.B. Ripley, The Honolulu Advertiser, March 2, 1895

Facing Halekauwila Street on the mauka side of the new city market building, the new 2-story brick Sailors' Home was designed by C.B. Ripley and was completed by the Lucas Brothers in 1894 for $15,619.

It was the replacement for the former Sailors' Home on Merchant Street that was torn down shortly after the 1886 fire. The Honolulu Sailors' Home Society Board held a design competition in 1891 with C.B. Ripley winning first place and $200, with George L. Dall receiving the second prize of $50, and Harry Mills coming in third with $25.

NOTICE to ARCHITECTS!

GROUND and Elevation Plans for a Sailors' Home Building to be erected on the site S. E. corner of Alakea and Halekauila streets, 125 ft on Alakea street, and 100 ft. frontage respectively, are asked for, to be handed in to the undersigned on or before February 1, 1891.

A prize of $200 will be awarded for the best plan and a prize of $50 for the second best plan submitted.

For particulars apply to
F. A. SCHAEFER,
C. M. COOKE,
W. W. HALL,
720 td   Committee.

Queen Liliʻuokalani authorized the Minister of the Interior to give the society a 19,220 square foot lot at the mauka/waikiki corner of Alakea and Halekauwila streets in an official act dated August 25, 1892:

> "Such conveyance shall contain the conditions that the premises shall be used only for the purpose and uses of a Sailors' Home: that no intoxicating liquors shall be allowed to be drunk on the premises; that such Sailors' Home shall be equally available to the sailors of all nations; that if the described lot or any part thereof shall at any time cease to be used for the purposes of a Sailors' Home, the whole of said lot shall forthwith revert to the Government."

Architect Isaac Moore took public issue with the thickness of the walls, concerned about potential collapse, but the board decided to uphold Ripley's original design. Construction began in early 1893 and was completed by April 1894. The building was illuminated with electric lights and the government nursery provided 50 trees for the yard.

> Entering the new Sailors' Home by means of a flight of steps, Jack finds himself in a handsome hallway from which a double flight of stairs leads to the upper story. On his left is a nice billiard room furnished with modern table, just large enough for comfort and sociability. This is at Jack's use as long as he stays in the home. In the rear is a library room fitted with shelves and other conveniences. This room has not yet been fitted up, but the pile of books and magazines on the large table afford abundant promise for the future. In the rear of the library are the three living rooms of the superintendent and his family.
>
> On the right hand side of the hallway is the main dining room, accommodating about forty at a sitting. In the rear is the pantry and kitchen. The former is provided with every variety of crockery and other tableware, ready for instant use; the latter with a fine range with capacity enough to do the cooking for a hundred men, and the necessary cooking utensils, hot and cold water, and in fact every modern convenience. Everything is as neat and clean as a new pin. This department of the new Sailors' Home is not yet being used, pending the appointment of a steward. It is the desire of the present board of trustees to give this position to some reliable and competent white man, and until such a one is found none other will be appointed. In the meantime sailors stopping in the home are furnished with meal tickets on some prominent restaurant as they need them.
>
> Proceeding up the handsome painted and carpeted stairway Jack finds himself in very different quarters to those he is accustomed in the forecastle. If he is an able bodied seaman and wants accommodations suitable to the size of his purse, Mr. Green, the present efficient superintendent, will conduct him to the main seaman's ward. Here are sixteen iron bedsteads of the latest pattern, each fitted with wire spring mattress, double mattresses, a pair of sheets, white blanket and counterpane. So clean is the bedding that its whiteness is almost reflected in the polished floor.
>
> If Jack happens to be a second or third mate and disposed to put on airs accordingly he can be accommodated with a small room to himself at very little extra expense. These are called "mate's" rooms and are furnished in modern style with every convenience. Still better and larger rooms are those set apart for captains and their friends. These are large and handsomely furnished and front on the main upper veranda, which is liberally supplied with lounging chairs and overlooks the harbor. On this floor are bath rooms furnished with hot and cold water, water closets and lavatories for the use of those using the rooms. The entire building is lit up with incandescent lights distributed wherever needed in handsome fixtures.

The Honolulu Advertiser, March 2, 1895

In sad shape by 1959, San Francisco waterfront priest Monsignor Matthew Francis Connolly called it "a flophouse – not fit for a dog".

The building was demolished in 1962.

The Harbor Square Condominium now on the site was designed by Seattle architects Naramore Bain Brady and Johanson, with Long Beach architects Killingsworth Brady and Associates. Completed by Hawaiian Dredging & Construction in 1971, it incorporates a 4-story building that houses the current Sailors' Home.

CATTON-NEILL BUILDING

801-817 Alakea Street / 202 Queen Street
1913 – present
Architect/Builder: H.L. Kerr & Edwin C. Pettit / Lord-Young Engineering Co.

On October 26, 1912, Catton, Neill & Co. Ltd. took out a building permit for this office building at Alakea and Queen streets to cost $20,000. Founded in 1898 by Robert Catton and John Neill, the company was a large manufacturer of sugar mill machinery for 25 years.

This was their uptown office and warehouse for handling electrical and engineering supplies. Robert Catton was president, John Neill was the chief engineer.

The 150 employees held a big luau on the second floor in honor of Catton's retirement in 1915.

CATTON-NEILL CO. IS IN ITS NEW HOME

Already occupying the new building at Queen and Alakea streets which was commenced but a few months ago, the Catton-Neill Company is at last ensconced in offices up-town, built along classic models in both the Doric and Ionian modes. The building is of two stories and so planned that a third can at any time be added to it, the plans having been drawn to make possible a general enlargement, both in height and increase of floor space. The plans were drawn in the offices of H. L. Kerr, architect, under the direction of Edwin C. Pettit, his chief draughtsman.

The first story of the building is in the Doric mode with the triglyphic Doric frieze. The second story is built after the Ionian mode of nine diameters with arches and imposts, the transoms glazed with ornamental glass. The third story, when added will be in the Corinthian style with fluted columns and handsome capitols, crowned with an ornamental entablature.

The building now covers a space of forty-four by eighty-seven feet, the shorter side along Queen street, being planned to be extended to eighty feet. The first floor is devoted to show windows and the general and private offices while the second floor is a large room destined for general electrical purposes. The building cost $25,500.

Construction is of reinforced concrete with the exterior walls steel fireproofed with columns and girders carrying a fireproofed frame floor tested to carry a weight of 150 pounds to the square foot. The sidewalk is protected by a metal awning supported by handsome chains from the second story pilasters.

Honolulu Advertiser, June 23, 1913

Hawaiian Historical Society

Catton, Neill & Co.

Consulting and Contracting
Mechanical and Electrical
ENGINEERS
Works at Second and South Streets

Robert Catton was born in Aberdour, Fife, Scotland in 1847 and came to Hawaii in 1878. He laid out the foundations for the Waimanalo, Waianae, Kilauea, and Paauhau sugar mills, and lived in Maui from 1879 to 1883. When he came to Honolulu, he worked for G. W. Macfarlane & Co. and W. L. Green and sold sugar machinery and steam plows.

He opened his own office in 1893, and three years later teamed up with John Neill and William Stodart to form the Catton-Neill co-partnership to run a foundry, machine, and boiler shop. Catton, Neill & Co. was founded in 1898 and sold to the Honolulu Iron Works in 1923.

Catton became good friends with Robert Louis Stevenson in 1893 during the author's visit here. About their first meeting he remarked:

> "He (Stevenson) is the most unaffected, unconventional man imaginable, and very unlike a Scotsman till he begins to talk; then there is no mistaking the Edinburgh origin of him. He is quite modest about his books and took all my homage and hero worship very nicely."

The Cattons and Stevensons often met and dined together. Catton loaned Stevenson a copy of Carlyle's *Essays* whereupon Stevenson wrote in the margin next to Voltaire's comment about raising his income a princely sum: "800 – 3,200 pounds? I doubt ye, T.C.!" A friend's wife remarked, "Just think of it! Carlyle's Voltaire annotated by Stevenson!"

2022

ALAKEA BUILDING
918-932 Alakea Street / 193-197 S. King Street
1907 – 1957
Architect/Builder: unknown

This 2-story plastered stone building was built for William McCandless in 1907 and was known as the Alakea Building.

It replaced an old 1-story wooden house that had been added onto in 1905 in violation of the building regulations which restricted wooden construction within the fire limit line.

Known as the Camarinos property, Territorial Judge Lindsay ordered the wooden buildings demolished in 1906.

Honolulu Star-Bulletin, February 17, 1956

The Alakea Building was torn down in 1957 to make way for the 7-story $600,000 Finance Factors building owned by a large syndicate fronted by Hiram L. Fong, attorney and former Speaker of the State of Hawaii House of Representatives.

The new Finance Factors building was designed by Wimberly & Cook.

It was replaced by the $175M First Hawaiian Center designed by New York architects Kohn Pedersen Fox and completed in 1996.

Honolulu Star-Bulletin, January 9, 1957

2022

KAPIOLANI BUILDING

1004-1036 Alakea Street / 198 S. King Street

1903 – 1971
Architect/Builder: Beardsley & Page / Lucas Brothers

Honolulu Advertiser, May 10, 1902

KAPIOLANI BUILDING.

It is intended by the Kapiolani Estate to erect a building at King and Alakea streets, with 46 feet frontage on the former and 188 feet on the latter. The building will be of two stories, adaptable for adding another story, and its construction of buff brick, terra cotta and Hawaiian stone. Columns and girders are to be of iron. The ground floor will have eight stores and the second floor twenty offices. There is to be a basement under all. It is estimated the building will cost $50,000. Beardslee & Page are the architects. Queen Kapiolani's memory will be perpetuated in the structure with her name, coat-of-arms and the motto, "Kulia i kanuu" (elevated to the highest), on the corner.

Evening Bulletin, December 28, 1901

OLD LANDMARK GOING.

The old wooden store building at King and Alakea streets, belonging to the Kapiolani Estate, is being demolished to make way for a modern block. There is a lot of history connected with the shack, including an abortive suit for $20,000 damages brought by a Chinese tenant against John F. Colburn on the ground of unlawful ejectment. Some years ago the place was occupied by the Louvre of Brussels, a dry goods store kept by Mr. Michiels, one of the greatest living cornet players, holding, as he did, a gold medal presented by the King of Belgium. He occasionally contributed to charity concerts in the Hawaiian Opera House.

Evening Bulletin, May 26, 1902

> Quite an innovation was noticed this morning at the excavation now going on for the new Kapiolani Estate building. A Japanese woman with pick and shovel worked alongside of Japanese men. How's that?

The Independent, June 26, 1902

> The corner stone of the new Kapiolani building was laid yesterday. Photographs of members of the royal family with Hawaiian coins bearing the date of Prince David's birth were placed in the metal box which was deposited in the corner stone.

Honolulu Advertiser, January 21, 1903

Designed by Frank Beardslee and George W. Page, the Kapiolani Building was built by the Kapiolani Estate and replaced a 1-story house and a 1-story wooden grocery store, hat store, and barber shop.

The M. Nunes and Sons Ukulele Factory was here in 1912. Arriving from Portugal on the *Ravenscrag* in 1879, Manuel Nunes claimed to be the inventor of the ukulele.

> UKULELES.
> The celebrated strictly hand-made ukulele, invented by M. Nunes 33 years ago. Salesroom, Kapiolani Bldg. No trouble to show instruments.

Starting about 1913, various city offices started moving into the Kapiolani Building and by 1915 half of the city offices were in the McIntyre Building and half were in the Kapiolani Building. By 1916 there were discussions about buying the Kapiolani Building but they ended up leasing it in its entirety in 1920 with remodeling plans by L.S. Cain, the city's building inspector. City Hall was here until 1929.

Honolulu: The Cross-Roads of the Pacific, 1913

the downs and ups of Honolulu

There used to be an imposing concrete structure at King and Alakea streets downtown. Yesterday, the 69-year-old Kapiolani Building was gone. In its stead, The Hawaii Corp. will put up two 27-story office towers—a block-sized development set to cost $30 million.

Honolulu Advertiser, January 20, 1971

In 1971 the Kapiolani Building was demolished for the Pacific Trade Center, consisting of two 27-story towers valued at $30M. It was designed by Alex Weinstein and Joseph Farrell with Lemmon Freeth Haines Jones & Farrell and built by the Pacific Construction Company. Completed in 1972, it was the tallest office building in Hawaii at the time.

2022

UNION TRUST BUILDING

1023-1025 Alakea Street

1923 – 1956

Architect/Builder: Emory & Webb / Robert S. Chase

This building was built by the Sociedade Portugueza de St. Antonio Beneficente de Hawaii and the Sociedade Lusitana Beneficente de Hawaii, better known as the San Antonio Society and the Lusitana Society – the two leading Portuguese benevolent societies in Hawaii.

The two societies formed Union Trust Company on November 9, 1921, with president A.D. Castro, treasurer Vincent Fernandez, and secretary J.P. Dias. A.D. Castro explained: "Almost from the dates of formation of the two societies, we have been called upon by members to assist them in their investments, business dealings, in trusts of all kinds and other commercial matters".

Out of their initial capitalization they purchased the land for $30,000 and hired Emory & Webb to design a building to cost $65,000 that was described as being "of no period design or style". It was designed to be 4 stories with an additional 2 stories to be added later, and was built by Robert S. Chase.

In 1933 the Union Trust had assets of $2.8M, but it was closed by the Territorial bank examiner in 1938 for "impaired financial position" brought on by the Great Depression. The trust went into receivership and was liquidated between 1938 and 1947.

The building was sold in 1940 to the San Antonio Society for $37,100 and they sold it to the Continental Assurance Company in 1954.

It was torn down in 1956 for a parking lot and the site is now the $36M 22-story Central Pacific Bank building designed by Ernest H. Hara & Associates and completed in 1983.

2022

L.B. KERR BUILDING

1049-1061 Alakea Street

1903 – present
Architect/Builder: George A. Howard / John Walker

The Honolulu Advertiser, November 25, 1903

Laurence B. Kerr was born in Ireland and came to Hawaii in 1878. He was a merchant tailor and established the L.B. Kerr company in 1889. His large dry goods store on Queen Street near Fort Street was destroyed in a fire on January 5, 1903, which resulted in "the total destruction of the valuable and large stock of the L.B. Kerr Co., valued at $125,000".

Kerr initially considered a location on Bishop Street near Hotel Street, across from the Alexander Young Hotel, but one month after the fire ended up buying 82' x 95' of the old Dr. McWayne place on Alakea Street from Dr. and Mrs. George Herbert for $20,000.

He hired architect George A. Howard to design a 2-story brick building "to cover the entire lot, finished in stucco, with brick trimmings". The ground floor had one big room with iron pillars 27 feet apart, three entrances with double doors, and recessed show windows. The side walls were 21 inches thick to allow for a future third story. The inside boasted 150 incandescent lamps. Kerr felt that the business center of Honolulu was moving east and in five years he expected to be "in the absolute center of the city".

VISIT KERR'S TO-NIGHT, TO-NIGHT!

ALAKEA, BETWEEN KING AND HOTEL STREETS.

Doors Open at 7 o'clock.

ONE HUNDRED DOLLARS IN PRIZES GIVEN AWAY AT THE

Grand Opening of a Big Store.

The formal opening of L. B. KERR & CO.'S new store marks a forward step in the mercantile life of Honolulu. We have a great Store, new throughout. It has been built, fitted and stocked to furnish the public the highest degree of convenience comfort and satisfaction, and will be the leading store of this city.

The Public is invited to make itself at home in this beautiful new and freshly equipped store this evening. Every man, woman and child will be given the opportunity of winning one of the following prizes absolutely free:

One New Cabinet Automatic Sewing Machine. Value $70.00
Six Pairs of Shoes, either Sorosis or Walkover, to suit the winners.

Absolutely no goods will be sold tonight, but each visitor will be given a numbered ticket free. Drawing takes place tomorrow evening at 8 o'clock.
Keep your ticket—it may be a lucky number.

L. B. KERR & CO. Ltd.

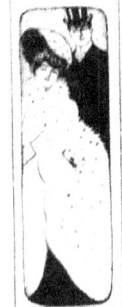

Music By Solomon's Quintet Club

Evening Bulletin, November 20, 1903

THE PACIFIC COMMERCIAL ADVERTISER, HONOLULU, NOVEMBER 25, 1903.

OPENING OF KERR'S FINE NEW STORE

Pacific Commercial Advertiser, November 25, 1903

NEW KERR SITE FAMOUS IN THE OLD ROYAL DAYS

The removal of the residence of Dr. George Herbert on Alakea street to make room for the new business structure of L. B. Kerr & Co. has more than a passing interest to the kamaainas, who remember the premises as the scene of many royal festivities during the reign of Kamehameha IV. Dr. Herbert purchased the property from Dr. McWayne, who in turn bought it from Maria Beckley, now Mrs. Kahea.

The deed to the property was given to Mrs. Kahea by her father, William Beckley, eldest son of Captain George C. Beckley. Captain Beckley was the first military commander of the old Honolulu fort, and one of the counsellors of Kamehameha the Great. The Herbert premises, as well as a large amount of property around it, including the present site of Alakea street as far as Hotel street, was given to Captain Beckley by Kamehameha I. in token of his friendship, and he was also made a chief by Kamehameha at the birth of Princess Nahienaena at Keauhou, Hawaii, in 1816. He was a close friend of Kamehameha, and his constant companion in the Holua races at Keauhou. He was one of the the few who held council with Kamehameha and the chiefs of Kailua, Hawaii, at the royal residence to determine whether the missionaries should be allowed to land there. Captain Beckley and all the other haoles there, Young, Davis, and Adams, persuaded the conqueror to grant the permission. Captain Beckley was also the designer of the Hawaiian flag.

Captain Beckley's grand-children are Admiral George Beckley, Mrs. M. Beckley Kahea, Mrs. Julia Afong, Mrs. A. A. Montano, and Mrs. Roland Wilbur. Fred W. Beckley, present speaker of the Hawaiian House of Representatives, is the great grandson of Captain Beckley.

When Drs. Herbert, Humphris and Walters built their present office on the Herbert property, the excavators encountered the old Beckley tomb. The remains of Captain Beckley were found in the vault and were removed to the Beckley burial plot in Nuuanu Valley. The remains had been enclosed in the old vault since about the year 1825, the tomb having been built about the year 1818.

When Dr. McWayne tore down the old Beckley home for the present residence on the premises, an immense grass house was also removed. It was in this old structure during the reign of Kamehameha IV. that many of the royal festivities were given. The officers of the various war ships calling here were generally entertained at the Beckley home.

Honolulu Advertiser, February 23, 1903

The Evening Bulletin and later the Honolulu Star Advertiser occupied the mauka side of the building.

For 25 years, from 1916 to 1941, it was the showroom for the largest automobile dealer in Hawaii – the von Hamm-Young Company Ltd.

The company was founded on January 30, 1899, when five men incorporated to conduct a dry goods and machinery business on Queen Street in the former John T. Waterhouse building. Archibald A. Young was the manager of the machinery department and Conrad von Hamm was in charge of the dry goods business, with Scottish engineer Alexander Young as the company president.

A correspondence about Hawaiian postage stamps led von Hamm from Bremen, Germany, to Hawaii in 1890 where he met and married the daughter of Alexander Young and went into business with Young's son Archibald.

In 1904 they added automobile sales as the agency for Buick and Oldsmobile. The following year they added Winton and Reo, and later the Haynes, Stevens-Duryea, Pope-Hartford, Thomas Flyer, White Steamer, Mitchell, Stoddard-Dayton, Buick, Anderson Electric, Paige, Kissel, Stutz, Scripps-Booth, Chandler, Packard, Nash, Cadillac, and GMC trucks.

They also had the biggest garage in the territory, across the street, with 46,500 square feet that could accommodate 400 automobiles offering "quick, efficient and thorough service to all patrons". It had a staff of 28 and 12 gasoline pumps dispensing Standard and Shell products.

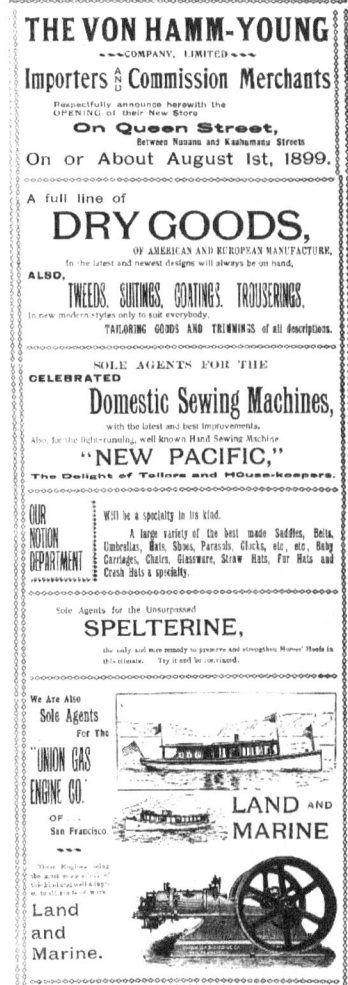

The company also managed the Alexander Young Hotel and later owned the Moana Hotel in Waikiki. The von Hamm-Young Company entered the insurance business and in 1964 became the Hawaii Corp.

The building later housed Stewarts' Alakea Pharmacy and became the Yong Sing Chinese Restaurant in 1967. It was the Mandalay Chinese restaurant from 2006 to 2022.

Although the beautiful arched-window front has either been covered up or removed, the back of the building still shows the original bricks from 1903.

2022

2022

The OLD and the NEW

The von Hamm-Young Co., Ltd., has a reputation for integrity and faithful service that extends over a period of twenty-seven years.

The company was incorporated in 1899 by Alexander Young and George W. Herrick and it first started business as agents for machinery and dry goods, and later took the representation of several insurance companies.

In 1904 this firm was able to obtain the Buick agency. Buick has upheld all its standards and traditions here, and has acquired additional merits for service and durability in these islands.

In 1908 the Cadillac agency was added to their fast-growing organization, and this car has proven to be one of the most desired automobiles in the Territory.

With the increased use of automobiles, this company has enlarged its physical plant so that it is always a step ahead. We now offer the most complete service in the Territory from one of the oldest automobile firms. It is a service built on years of experience, and extended to all the islands through branches at Hilo, Wailuku and Kapaa.

The von Hamm-Young Co., Ltd., takes a certain pride in their usefulness to the community from 1899 to the present day---in their ability to serve that community---and in the fact that they will continue to serve through their progressiveness.

The Honolulu Advertiser, February 24, 1926

MASONIC TEMPLE
1107-1117 Alakea Street / 206 S. Hotel Street
1893 – 1967
Architect/Builder: Clinton B. Ripley / E.B. Thomas, Fred H. Redward

Honolulu Advertiser, February 23, 1903

In 1892 the Hawaiian Masonic lodge purchased the lot at the mauka/Waikiki corner of Hotel and Alakea streets for $5,500 that was previously the site of the Royal Hawaiian Theatre. Immediately mauka in 1850 was "a little cottage occupied by Mr. Charles R. Bishop and his young bride Bernice Pauahi Bishop".

The Royal Hawaiian Theatre, c.1853-1881

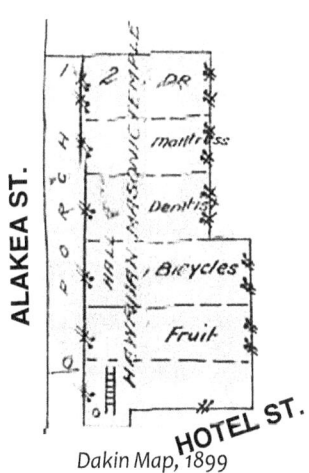

Dakin Map, 1899

The building was designed by Clinton B. Ripley with masonry by E.B. Thomas and woodwork by Fred H. Redward. The cornerstone with time capsule was laid on December 27, 1892, to much pomp and ceremony, including multiple speeches and rituals, the St. Andrews Cathedral choir, and the Hawaiian Band. Queen Liliʻuokalani was in attendance as was Governor Cleghorn and four Ministers of the Crown.

In 1913 they hired architect H.L. Kerr to design a 10-story skyscraper on the site to be built of Tenino sandstone at a cost of $250,000 to $300,000. But it never happened.

Honolulu Star-Bulletin, July 12, 1913

Honolulu Star-Bulletin, May 13, 1966

Known as the Aloha Building by the 1960's, it was demolished in 1967. There were once again big plans for a replacement – a 21-story hotel-commercial building that didn't happen either. The site is now the 11-story District Court Building "Kauikeaouli Hale" designed by Anbe Aruga & Ishizu and completed in 1982 at a cost of $24M.

2022

MUTUAL TELEPHONE BUILDING

1130-1140 Alakea Street

1919 – present (1941 remodel)

Architect/Builder: Frederick G. Hummel (1919), Guy N. Rothwell (1941)

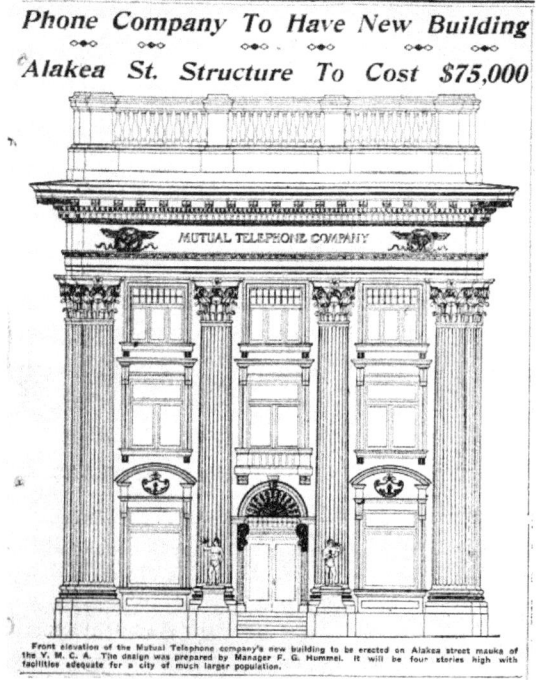

The Honolulu Advertiser, June 5, 1919

Honolulu Star-Bulletin, October 20, 1924

In 1919 Mutual Telephone added a new building on Alakea Street that backed up to the 1910 Adams Lane building. It was also designed by Mutual Telephone's Frederick G. Hummel.

The Honolulu Advertiser, December 24, 1919

Reportedly the first use of art to beautify the exterior of a building in Honolulu, a sculpture in high and low relief by Gordon Usborne adorned the front entrance: "Thought is passing from the figure on the left, which holds the transmitter, to that on the right, which has the receiver."

The interior was decorated with "large and beautiful mural paintings" by famed Hawaii artist D. Howard Hitchcock.

In 1941 they commissioned architect Guy Rothwell to design an additional building mauka of the 1910 and 1919 buildings on the Alakea Street side of the property that was previously the site of the 2-story wooden Metropole rooming house built in 1901. The Metropole at 1150 Alakea had replaced the c.1890 T.C. Porter house and Steinitz Chess Club buildings.

Honolulu Star-Bulletin, March 10, 1941

Alakea Street side, 2022. The 1919 building is hiding on the left.

The current Hawaiian Telcom Building was designed by Wimberly, Whisenand, Allison & Tong, and was constructed in 1970 by Reed and Martin, Inc.

Bishop Street side, 2002

The communications equipment inside was estimated to cost an additional $12M. It was built adjacent to the 1919 building, on the site of the old British Club, and across what was formerly Union Street.

WM. FRENCH RESIDENCE

1155 Alakea Street
Before 1838 – c.1880
Architect/Builder: unknown

Paul Emmert, 1854

Once the home of Honolulu merchant William French, it was the residence of Capt. Horatio Nelson Crabb when sketched in 1854 by Swiss artist Paul Emmert.

A native of Maine (or Vermont), French came to Hawaii about 1825 and quickly became a leading merchant in the sandalwood trade. This house was built before 1838 and was torn down about 1880 when the Hawaiian Hotel expanded its grounds.

The hotel built a 2-story 29-room annex on the site in 1901 with large rooms and wide verandas around the entire building facing a large inner courtyard. It was designed by Oliver Traphagen and built by Campbell & Pettus for $27,000.

On April 15, 1937, the annex officially re-opened as Hale Alakea, "a home for the man without a home" after extensive renovations personally overseen by owners Dr. and Mrs. C.B. Cooper. She was the daughter of Dr. J.S. McGrew who had made substantial improvements when he leased the hotel in 1882.

Hale Alakea was demolished in 1948 to expand a parking lot. The site is now the 11-story District Court Building "Kauikeaouli Hale" designed by Anbe Aruga & Ishizu and completed in 1982 at a cost of $24M.

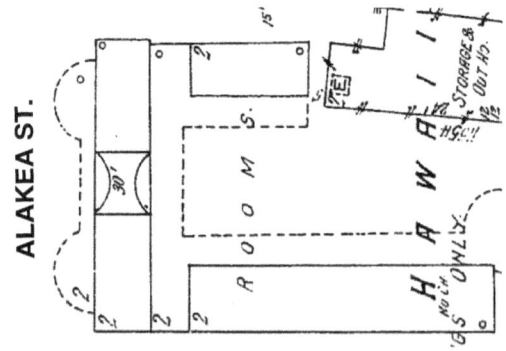

Sanborn Map, 1914

Honolulu Star-Bulletin, April 10, 1937

THE BRITISH CLUB

1160 Alakea Street

1892 – 1926

Architect/Builder: Isaac A. Palmer / E.B. Thomas

The British Club was founded by a group of 14 English businessmen, starting out in 1851 as "The Mess" in an old 1-story building behind Liberty Hall on Maunakea Street.

They purchased the William Wond house facing Union Street in 1867 for $2,000 (pictured on the left) and another facing Alakea Street in 1878.

The building on Alakea Street was built c.1835 by William French with stonework by Captain John Ebbetts. In 1854 it was the home of John Ladd.

In 1892 the British Club hired architect Isaac A. Palmer to design a new clubhouse that was built by E.B. Thomas for $10,000. Since the club had recently merged with several other clubs, they changed their name to The Pacific Club.

Paul Emmert, 1854

MANY TENANTS.

The old building on the British Club's premises, to be sold at auction by Mr. Levey to-morrow, has quite a history. Prior to 1849 it was a two-story building, occupied by Mr. Ladd. Then it became the American hospital, of which Mr. Ladd was purveyor. It was afterward occupied as a residence in turn by Bernard F. Ehlers, B. F. Bolles, Mrs. Dudoit and Capt. Babcock, with their respective families. When the British Club took the building it was cut down to one story. Mr. A. J. Cartwright, who gave these particulars to our reporter, has the history of several other notable buildings in the same quarter, from 1849 when he arrived here, at his fingers' ends.

Evening Bulletin, October 21, 1891

c.1892

THE BRITISH CLUB.

Opening of the Handsome New Building.

The British Club has taken off the hands of the contractor, Mr. E. B. Thomas, its new building situated between A'akea and Union streets, near Beretania street and opposite the Hawaiian Hotel. Luncheon was served to members for the first time in the new building at noon to-day, by Steward Mariano, whose abilities as a caterer set the standard for Honolulu.

The main building is 64 feet 6 inches by 47 feet on the ground plan. It is a combination of the Eastlake and Queen Anne styles of architecture. Mr. I. A. Palmer was the architect. The entire cost of building and new furniture will be about $10,000.

The club lot fronts 100 feet on Alakea, and about the same on Union street. As previously recorded in this paper, by an exchange of "jogs" of ground with Mr. A. J. Cartwright the club was able, before building, to square its site. The new building is a rather imposing structure of wood two stories high. Inviting-looking verandas, on both flats, 60 feet long and 12 feet wide, cover the breadth of the main front on Alakea street. Pillars and arches of verandas are ornate without any gingerbread appearance. From a wide front door a hall 10 feet wide runs to the back door. In this hall near the servants' stations is an electric bell indicator, by which calls can be made from any of the rooms by pressing a button. While on electricity it should by noted that the building is being fitted throughout with electric lights by the Hawaiian Electric Company.

Entering from Alakea to the right you are ushered into the billiard room, a wainscoted apartment 26 feet by 46 feet. It contains two tables, another to be added. There are snug lockers on the inner side for the use of members. Across the hall is a smoking and lounging room, 26 feet by 26 feet, fitted with sideboard and lockers. All the rooms above and below are 14 feet high.

A dressing room with lavatory is in rear of the smoking room. It is 12ft.x15ft., and flanked by a commodious bathroom. Then across a small hall are the sanitary requirements with modern appliances. An ice chest is placed under the stairs at the far end of the main hall. On the lower floor of a wing facing Union street are the servants' and store rooms, from which a stairway leads to kitchen and pantry upstairs.

The main stairway springs from near the middle of the hall, facing the front entrance, and has one turn at right angles from a rest midway. On the left-hand side, front, looking toward Alakea street, is the reading room, 24ft.x40ft. Rear of that are two private card rooms, each 14ft. square, connected with large swinging doors on rollers, whereby they may be thrown into one apartment. Either singly or doubly they are designed for private dinner parties when so required. A hall from front to rear divides the three rooms just mentioned from the dining room. This is spacious, being 24 feet by 46. A long table extends lengthwise of the room, surrounded with very comfortable chairs.

The British Club has survived several national clubs in Honolulu, which flourished for a time and then went under. Having a cosmopolitan constitution it admits gentlemen of other nationalities than that its name indicates. With such a handsome new home as the one now sketchily described, the British Club has apparently entered a fresh career of prosperity. The new building makes a conspicuous enhancement of appearances in that part of the town where it is situated. With Mr. Cartwright's remodeled residence adjacent, and the imposing Hawaiian Hotel, Honolulu Library, Y. M. C. A. building and Mr. T. C. Porter's graceful new cottage all within sight of the new Club, owners of property in that locality will be stimulated to arise and build fabrics in keeping with such a respectable environment.

The Daily Bulletin, October 27, 1891

In the beginning, many of the members resided at the club. They often entertained distinguished visitors including admirals and officers from ships in port. Kamehameha IV and V often visited the club as did King Kalakaua, and The Duke of Edinburgh was a guest in 1868.

In addition to fancy dinners and lavish entertainment, E.I. Spalding recalled:

> exceptionally successful affair. Another notable occasion, which will appeal feelingly to many of you, was the burial of John Barleycorn, slain by one Volstead. April, 1918. The auction of the club's store of liquors, Mr. Frank Thompson officiating as auctioneer, netted good returns for the club, as well as $1500 for the Red Cross, one bottle of champagne alone, after lively bidding between two ranchers, having been knocked down for $250 for the Red Cross. John Barleycorn, in effigy, lies buried in the cellar of the club, and his resurrection, should it ever occur, will no doubt be celebrated with appropriate ceremonies.

Honolulu Advertiser, January 2, 1924

Is the effigy of John Barleycorn still buried in the cellar, now under the Hawaiian Telcom Building? Maybe.

The club sold the land for $90,000 and the clubhouse for $630 in 1926 and moved to the old Cleghorn estate on Queen Emma Street. The building was demolished for the Burgess & Johnson car lot.

OLD PACIFIC CLUB IN ALAKEA ST. BOWS TO MARCH OF BUSINESS

Another Honolulu landmark is passing, the building of the old Pacific club in Alakea St., which is to be engulfed by the march of the city's business progress. The club has been moved to the former Colonial hotel further mauka in Emma St. and the old structure is soon to go its way.

The clubhouse, which runs from Alakea to Union St., just below the intersection of Beretania, Union and Alakea Sts., was remodeled about 12 years ago at considerable cost, but the entire structure is to be taken away.

The present owners have leased the Alakea St. frontage to Burgess & Johnson, Ltd., automobile dealers, who will use it for display of used cars and possibly for display of some of their agency cars. The firm began removing the old trees and shrubbery yesterday.

The Pacific club had its origin under British auspices, in 1851.

Honolulu Star-Bulletin, November 27, 1926

Honolulu Advertiser, November 28, 1926

2022

MCGREW BUILDING
1175-1196 Alakea Street / 209-225 S. Beretania Street
1901 – 1958
Architect/Builder: Pacific Land & Improvement Company

On March 21, 1901, the Pacific Land & Improvement Company (owned by several Chinese businessmen including C.Q. Yee Hop) took out a building permit for a 2-story brick building at Beretania and Alakea streets that had 10 stores on the ground floor and the 39-room El Premero rooming house upstairs.

The McGrew Building in 1941, the 1924 Galen Building is on the left

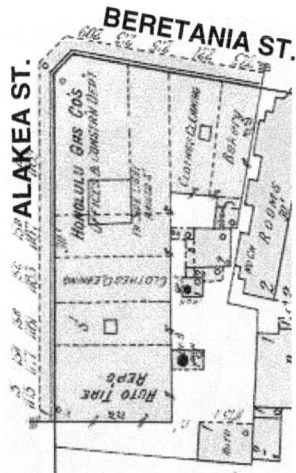

C.Q. Yee Hop had a large grocery store on the first floor corner.

El Premero is the name of the new lodging house in the Pacific Land and Improvement Company's building, corner Beretania and Alakea streets. Miss M. K. McKenzie is landlady, and can show you as fine furnished apartments as can be found in Honolulu.

The Honolulu Advertiser, October 19, 1901

The Honolulu Gas Company moved their offices here in 1910, and by the 1920's the rooming house was known as the St. Charles Hotel.

Sanborn Map, 1914   *Honolulu: Cross-Roads of the Pacific, 1913*

A large 2.5-story house was previously on the site, later known as the Dudoit premises but built in the 1850's as the Benjamin Pitman "mansion".

It was destroyed by fire in May 1892.

The vacant lot became the site of Bristol's Pavilion in 1897 featuring vaudeville, circus, boxing matches, tug-of-war-contests, acrobats from Japan, The Quaker Medicine Show, and "Kickapoos".

Dakin Map, 1885

The McGrew Building was demolished in 1958 and replaced by the American Mutual Life Building designed by Vladimir Ossipoff and completed in early 1959.

The Honolulu Advertiser, December 28, 1957

BRISTOL'S PAVILION

Corner Beretania and Alakea Sts.

SHORT SEASON

COMMENCING

Monday, March 15, 1897.

First and only Appearance in this City of the World-Famous

Prof. D. M. Bristol

And His Wonderful Performing

HORSES, PONIES AND MULES

The Original Eques-Curriculum.

The Largest and Best School of Educated Horses. The Most Expensive Equipment, and the most Prosperous Amusement Enterprise of Its Kind in the World.
For the past Ten Years "A POPULAR AND FASHIONABLE SUCCESS" in all the Large Cities of America.

Over Two Hours' Performance by these

Amazing Animal Actors.

PRICES:

Evening—50 cents. Reserved Seats, $1.00
Matinee—Adults, 50 Cts, Children, 25 Cts.

At the Matinees All Small Children Are Given a FREE PONY RIDE, and Are Admitted to Any Seat in the House for 25 Cents.
Reserved Seats at Wall-Nichols Co.
527 td

2022

The Independent, March 9, 1897

A.J. CARTWRIGHT HOUSE

1180-1196 Alakea Street
c.1888 – c.1955?
Architect/Builder: unknown

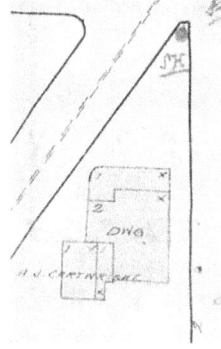

1899 Dakin Map

This little triangular lot should probably be diamond-shaped instead, in honor of the man who lived here in the late 1800's – Alexander J. Cartwright.

Captain William Blanchard (of *Thaddeus*) built two houses here in the summer of 1831, with one being for his daughter, Harriet, who later married John Townsend.

When Cartwright bought the property in the late 1880's he built a new house that he "enlarged and modernized" in 1892.

ALEX. J. CARTWRIGHT,
COMMISSION MERCHANT AND GENERAL SHIPPING AGENT,
Honolulu, Hawaiian Islands.   jy29 ly

Alexander Joy Cartwright was born in New York City in 1820 and came to Hawaii in 1849. He was a commission merchant and general shipping agent, also Chief Engineer for the Fire Department from 1851 to 1863.

An avid reader and education advocate, he donated many books to the Library and Reading room, including some dating back to as early as 1776.

But Cartwright's main claim to fame comes from his time in New York as a Major League Baseball Hall of Fame Pioneer, officially credited by the US Congress on June 3, 1953, as having invented the modern game of baseball when he was the founder and manager of the Knickerbocker Base Ball Club in Manhattan.

Hawaii State Archives

The truth of the matter is no one person invented baseball – not Alexander J. Cartwright in Manhattan, and not Abner Doubleday in Cooperstown. American baseball evolved over many years, originating mostly from a traditional English bat and ball game known as Rounders.

There were many variations of Rounders played by children, also known as three-cornered cat or town ball or roundball. In 1842, Cartwright organized and managed a "base-ball" club called the Knickerbockers in Manhattan, and in 1845 a committee from his club consisting of William R. Wheaton and William H. Tucker wrote and published the first set of rules that converted the playground game into a proper sport for adults.

Due in part to his grandson's tireless efforts to promote Cartwright as the single inventor of the game, Cartwright was inducted into the Baseball Hall of Fame and officially recognized by Congress. There were many variations of rules floating around as the game developed, but Cartwright was the first one to publish an official set of 20 rules.

Cartwright is said to have brought the game of baseball with him to Hawaii. In 1859 the *Pacific Commercial Advertiser* reported on "an impromptu game of 'bat and ball'", and the first mention of the words "base ball" was on April 7, 1860, when *The Polynesian* newspaper reported "some of the leading merchants and their clerks had a game of good old-fashioned base ball".

The large 2-story Victorian Cartwright house survived many alterations over the years, including conversion to a rooming house.

Paragon Meat Market was built adjacent to it in the corner in 1907. In December 1940 the market was replaced by Koki Makishi's 90-seat Denver Grill designed by Albert Ely Ives and built by George J. Oda for $18,000. It was the Alakea Grill from 1949 to 2004.

The Cartwright house was still around in 1955, but was eventually demolished for a parking lot.

The section of Union Street running from Bishop Street to the five-way intersection at Alakea and Beretania streets, called "an old shortcut, a worn footpath that grew by stages into the dignity of a street", was abandoned in 1968 for the construction of the new Hawaiian Telcom Building.

Construction began in 2022 on the $88M, 20-story, 222-unit Kokua Senior Living complex on the corner site.

Honolulu Star-Bulletin, December 21, 1940

It was designed by SVA Architects and built by Hawaiian Dredging & Construction Company.

2022

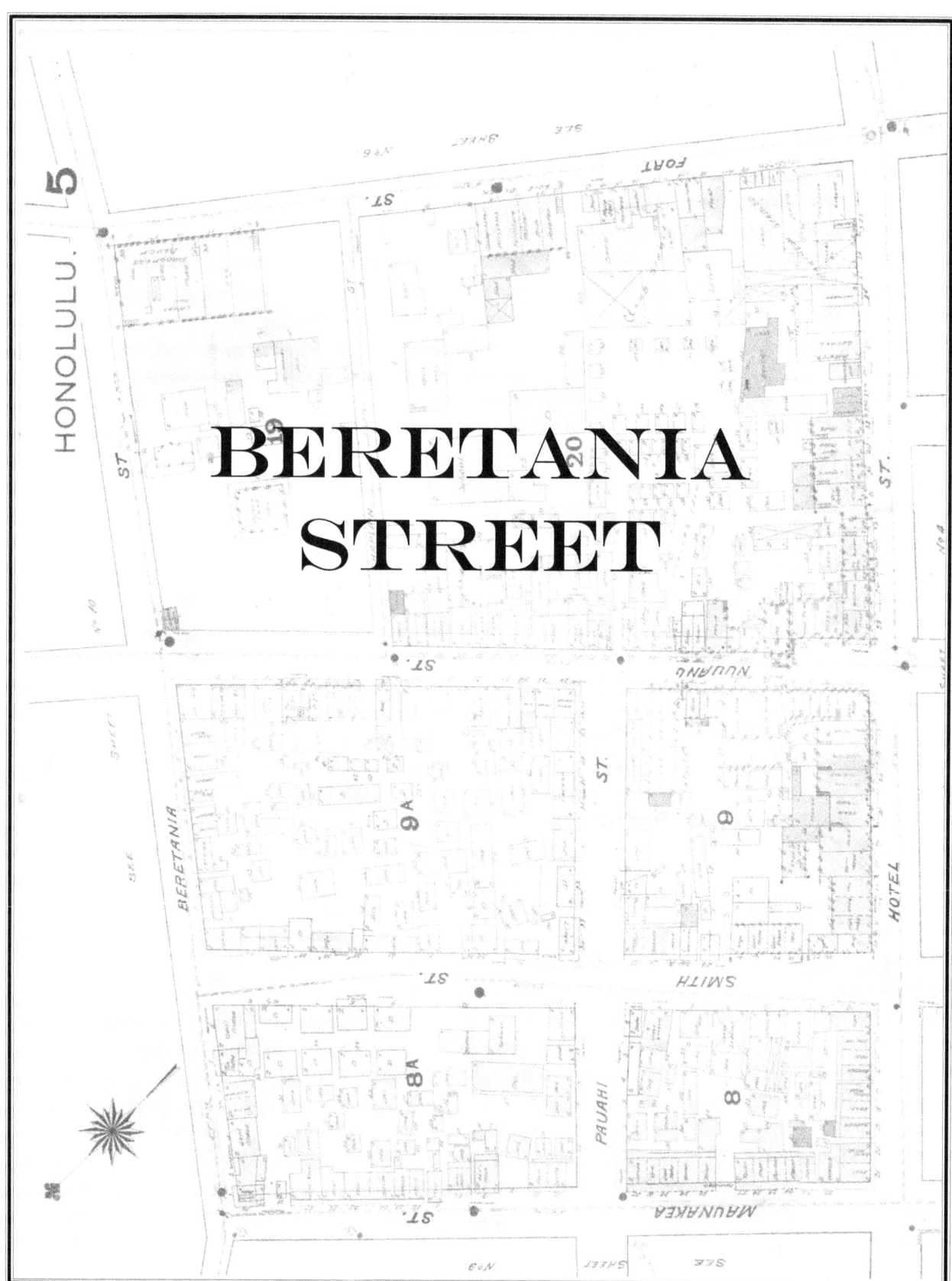

SCHNACK BUILDING

51-59 S. Beretania Street

c.1927 – present
Architect/Builder: unknown

2022

This was the site of a large 14-room house built in 1851 by R.A.S. Wood, at one time owned by R.C. Wyllie, and known in the late 1800's as the Bolles' premises. By 1906 it was "Japanese tenements" and an empty lot by 1914.

Paul Emmert, 1854

By 1927 there was a 20-car enclosed garage here made of steel trusses over a concrete floor that was possibly part of Strauch Auto Park.

The American Dispensary and the Poinsettia Flower shop moved here in 1928, and by 1955 the building contained 5 stores and had been extended makai for 2 more stores.

HUSTACE BLOCK

69-71 S. Beretania Street

1901 – present
Architect/Builder: H.L. Kerr

HUSTACE BLOCK. H. L. Kerr, Architect.

The Pacific Commercial Advertiser, January 1, 1902

ANOTHER NEW BUSINESS BLOCK TO BE CONSTRUCTED

Frank Hustace Begins the Building of a Two-Story Structure Fronting Beretania Street.

Excavating is progressing at a lively rate in the rear of Progress block for a business block to be erected by Frank Hustace. It will front 35 feet on Beretania street and have a depth of 105 feet. The building will be of brick, two stories with basement. It will have two stores, forty feet deep, with plate glass lighting, in the front, which will be of pressed brick with terra cotta trimmings. In the rear will be two warehouses, each 33 feet square, with basement eight feet in the clear. The second story will contain sixteen rooms, to be let for lodging house or office purposes. The rooms will be walled in lath and plaster and each be fitted with a lavatory. H. L. Kerr & Co. are the architects.

The Honolulu Republican, March 21, 1901

NEW HUSTACE BUILDING.

Handsome Structure on Beretania Street Nearly Completed.

A handsome new two-story building is just being completed on Beretania street, adjoining the Progress building, off Fort street, for Frank Hustace by H. L. Kerr, the architect. The ground floor contains two large stores and two spacious warehouses at the back, to which a ten-foot lane leads from Chaplain lane, Mr. Hustace having secured the exclusive use of this. The upper story contains sixteen large rooms suitable for offices or for lodging rooms, but it has not yet been decided whether it will be let to office tenants or as an apartment floor.

The building will be completed and ready for occupancy by the first of the month. Applications are in for the rental of the stores, but tenants have not yet been decided upon.

The Honolulu Republican, November 14, 1901

2022

SACHS BUILDING

72-98 S. Beretania Street / 1202-1216 Fort Street

1902 – 1962

Architect/Builder: H.L. Kerr / Hawaiian Engineering & Construction

The Honolulu Advertiser, January 1, 1902

The Sachs Building was on the ewa/mauka corner of Fort and Beretania streets and was built on the site of the 1-story wooden Waring Block completed in January 1895. The 141' x 123' property was purchased by Charles S. Desky and N.S. Sachs from Lau Chong of the Wing Wo Tai company on January 21, 1898.

Desky was in the process of completing the Progress Block across the street and he bought this property knowing that impending street widening would negatively impact the Waring Block The city plans called for widening Fort Street by 14' feet and Beretania Street by 16'.

In December of 1899 he hired H.L. Kerr & Company to prepare plans for a 3-story building similar to the Progress and Model blocks, to cost $75,000. It had 6 stores on the ground floor and 36 rooms on each of the upper floors with a bath, closet and washstand that could be used for either offices or lodging, plus a full basement. The upstairs was later known as the Majestic Hotel.

Nathaniel S. Sachs moved his N.S. Sachs store here from the Brewer Block at Fort & Hotel streets. In 1900 he sold the property to C.M. Cooke Ltd for $75,000.

The building finally opened in September 1902 after waiting for plate glass.

From 1932 to 1962, the building housed the Fair Department Store founded by Matsuemon and Masae Tanimura. It was forced out of business by the urban renewal Kukui Redevelopment Project taking over and demolishing the entire block through eminent domain. Mr. Tanimura passed away a year later at age 88.

Honolulu: The Cross-Roads of the Pacific, 1913

2022

FRED HARRISON BLOCK

101-125 S. Beretania Street / 1189-1197 Fort Street

1906 – 1953

Architect/Builder: Fred Harrison

Honolulu: The Cross-Roads of the Pacific, 1913

Prominent local contractor Fred Harrison built this large building containing eleven stores at the makai/waikiki corner of Fort and Beretania streets on land leased from the Catholic Church in 1906.

The three lodges of the Knights of Pythias took a ten-year lease on the entire second floor and Harrison changed the plans so "the place will be in all respects a model Pythian Castle".

"In addition to the usual lodge and retiring rooms there will be a fine hall suitable for concerts or assemblies, which of course will be a source of revenue. A special entrance to the Pythian quarters will be made from Fort Street."

During the laying of the cornerstone,

> "Bishop Boeynaems placed a Hawaiian coin in the cement and blessed the works, and Father Valentin put in two francs and a medal bearing the likeness of St. Anthony the patron saint of money and good fortune. Bystanders also placed a few coins and the stone was laid."

(The Hawaiian Star, March 30, 1906)

1941

By the 1940's the building was in the way of a proposed widening of Beretania street. In spite of the fact that architectural engineer Earl Stephenson with the city had developed plans to arcade the Harrison Block, the building was demolished in November 1953.

According to historian Thomas G. Thrum, the first building on the site was a grass house owned by Captain G. H. Nye.

Captain Charles Brewer purchased the property in 1831 and erected a large 2-story frame house that was first built in Boston and then dismantled and shipped around Cape Horn to Hawaii. This house was on the site for approximately 70 years.

When sketched by Paul Emmert in 1854 it was the residence of Dr George A. Lathrop.

J.M. Oat Jr. was living at the house by 1885, and Dr. Francis R. Day was here in 1887.

Paul Emmert, 1854

Sketch by Lydia Nye, 1843

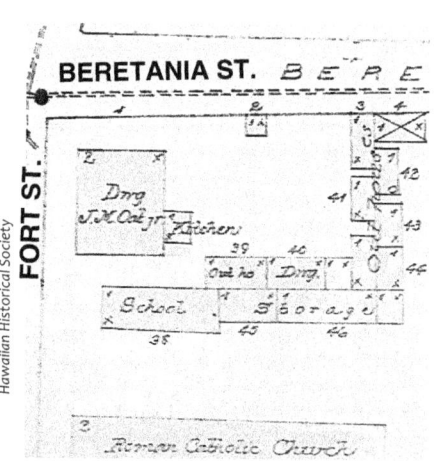

1885 Dakin Map

View along Fort Street, with algaroba tree, c. 1887

Dr. Day's parlor and dining room, c. 1887.
From the Dr. Clifford B. Wood Collection at the Hawaii State Archives.

THE ALGAROBA TREE

For nearly 100 years there was a large algaroba (kiawe) tree near the makai/waikiki corner of Fort and Beretania Streets. It was the first one planted in Hawaii, in 1828, and it was the parent of all the kiawe trees in Hawaii. It was said to have come from "the King's garden in Paris".

"WOODMAN, SPARE THAT TREE!"

THE OLD ALGEROBA TREE AT THE CORNER OF FORT AND BERETANIA STREETS WILL NOT BE ENTIRELY CUT AWAY FOR THE ERECTION OF FRED HARRISON'S NEW BUILDING—FIRST IN THE ISLANDS.

The first algeroba tree planted in the islands is not to lose its life.

The tree stands on the corner of Fort and Beretania streets and next to the new building being erected by Fred Harrison. One limb, which is nearly half of the tree, leans directly over the new building, and it was thought that the entire tree would have to come down so that the building could be erected. Many were the people who have asked that the tree be saved if possible, and today Contractor Fred Harrison promised that no more should come off of the tree than was absolutely necessary. This means that about one-half of the tree will be cut away.

"You would be surprised at the interest taken in that tree," said Mr. Harrison this morning. "Nearly every one who passes the corner has something to add in the way of a plea for the tree. I have even been asked if I would build an arch over the limb. Now that is absurd, for it would spoil the building. But I have resolved to cut away no more of the tree than is absolutely necessary. There will be over half of it left when I am through."

The tree in question is the oldest algeroba in the islands and is the ancestor of the remainder of that species here. It was planted by Father Bachelat many years ago.

Hawaiian Star, April 27, 1906

The tree survived the construction of the Harrison Block but was cut down in 1919. The stump is preserved nearby on the Catholic church site.

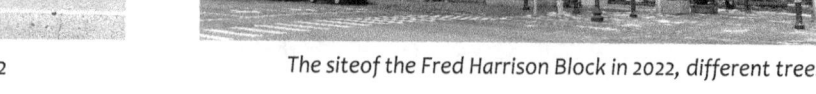

2022 — The site of the Fred Harrison Block in 2022, different tree.

In 1899, US Senator C.D. Clark and A.W. Anderson, both from Wyoming, proposed to build the Alana Block at this corner and hired Ripley and Dickey to prepare the plans. It was to be 4-stories tall and cost $70,000, but it was never finished, leaving a large open hole for the basement. January 1, 1900, is the last mention of it in the newspapers.

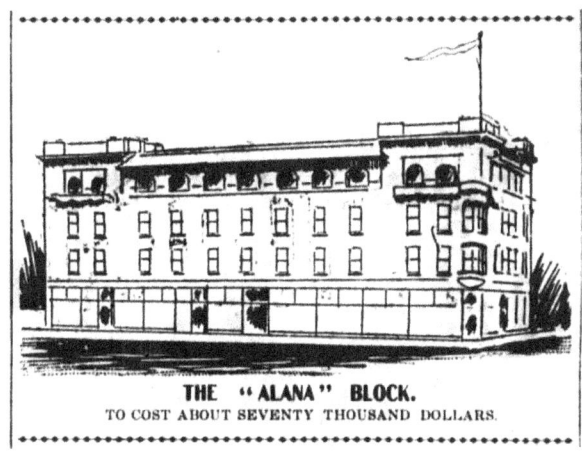

THE "ALANA" BLOCK.
TO COST ABOUT SEVENTY THOUSAND DOLLARS.

"ALANA" BLOCK

Four Story Structure for Corner of Fort and Beretania.

BACHELORS' QUARTERS A FEATURE

Large Cafe and Dining Room in Basement — Estimated Cost Seventy Thousand Dollars.

Work will soon be commenced on another addition to the buildings of upper Fort street. The new structure is to be a 4-story block put up at the corner of Fort and Beretania, now occupied by a boarding-house and several cottages. The promoters are United States Senator C. D. Clark of Wyoming and A. W. Anderson of the same State. This fact is worthy of notice, as it is the first big building to be put up entirely by outside capital. Henry Waterhouse & Co. will act as the agents for the new block.

The building will cost $70,000. A 40-year lease of the property has been obtained from the Catholic Mission, which controls quite an area in that section. The corner building, which is to be torn down, is an old structure. It was first built in Boston over sixty years ago and was then taken down and shipped around the Horn, to rise again on its present location. Another historic fact in connection with the new building is that the first algeroba tree that was planted in the Islands will have to be uprooted in order to make way for the onward march of progress.

In the style of the new building the architects, Ripley & Dickey, may be said to have produced something of the Romanesque order. The dimensions will be 74 by 146, the long way running along Beretania street. Over the main entrance will be the name of the block in large letter, "Alana," a gift from heaven. A large stone stairway leads to the basement, where will be fitted up an elegant and handsome cafe which will rival the Louvre or the Grotto of San Francisco. In the center and almost hidden under banks of ferns and potted plants will be a music stand from where a full orchestra will discourse sweet music during dining hours.

The first floor will contain seven stores. Each of these will have large show-windows fronting, some on Fort and some on Beretania streets. The second and third floors will be given up entirely to offices which will be complete in every detail with all modern improvements.

Upon the fourth floor there will be a new feature, a sort of bachelors' club. The rooms will be arranged so that they may be taken and fitted up according to the wishes of the occupants. They will be single and in suite with baths attached to each. Large, porticoed windows will admit light and air, and a wide verandah will run clear around. In addition to the regular passenger elevator there will be a dumb-waiter so that meals may be brought up from the cafe. The idea is a new one in Honolulu and the

The Hawaiian Gazette
September 8, 1899

THE "ALANA" BLOCK.

Work has long since commenced on the "Alana" Block which is to occupy the corner of Fort street and Beretania avenue, seventy-four feet front on Fort and one hundred and forty-six feet front on Beretania.

In the large stone basement there is to be fixed up a handsome cafe which will rival the Louvre or the Grotto of San Francisco.

The first floor will have seven stores, each provided with immense show-windows. The second and third floors will be given up entirely to offices which are to be complete in every detail and with all modern improvements.

Upon the fourth floor there will be a new feature in the way of a bachelors' club.

The rooms are arranged to be fitted up according to the wishes and tastes of the occupants, in single rooms and in suite with baths attached to each. Porticoed windows of large size will admit light and air and a wide veranda will run around the entire block.

There is to be a passenger elevator, and also a dumb waiter connecting with the cafe below. The young unmarried men and those whose families are not at present residing in Honolulu have been greatly attracted by this novel feature.

The promoters are U. S. Senator C. D. Clark of Wyoming and Mr. A. W. Anderson of the same State. A noteworthy fact, since all capital for this structure is furnished from non-residents of our islands.

Henry Waterhouse & Co. acts as agents for the promoters.

Ripley and Dickey, architects.

The Honolulu Advertiser
January 1, 1900

CENTRAL FIRE STATION

104-116 S. Beretania Street

1897 – 1934
Architect/Builder: Ripley & Dickey (1897) / C.H. Patzig (1897)

CENTRAL FIRE STATION.
The Hawaiian Gazette, January 5, 1897

Hawaii State Archives

OLD LANDMARK BEING RAZED

Workmen Start Tearing Down Old Fire Station To Make Way For New One

A landmark that has stood in downtown Honolulu during the 36 years since the annexation of Hawaii to the United States is now being razed by federal emergency relief administration workers. It is the great cut stone building that has housed the headquarters offices and central station companies of the Honolulu fire department.

The old stone building, which cost $30,000 in 1898, will be replaced by a modern station for which a contract has been let to E. E. Black, Ltd. at $75,566.56.

The new central fire station has been designed by C. W. Dickey, one of the architects who designed the building now being razed, and by John Mason Young, engineer.

Stone blocks, some of them weighing as much as 1,000 pounds, taken from the building are to be transported to Kaimuki park where it is planned to erect a community center. The plan for this center was advanced by the Kaimuki Improvement club which has offered to aid it financially and has requested the municipality for cooperation.

Very little material would be required for the structure, it is pointed out by the Kaimuki folk, after the fire station stone has been made available. They hope to obtain FERA workers for the labor.

James A. Stoy, FERA foreman on the central fire station project, is having each stone marked with a symbol as it is taken from place. This will enable the reassembling of the blocks with a minimum of stone cutting.

Corregated iron from the roof of the building is being sent to the city and county yards at Kewalo for use on future projects. Little of the woodwork will be salvaged because of termite infection.

Frank Dias is representing the city and county as inspector on the job.

It is expected that at least six more weeks will be required to raze the stone building as the work is extraordinarily hazardous. Forty formerly unemployed men are on the NFERA project, two crews of 20 men each working three days a week.

When the site is cleared it is expected that Mr. Black will begin at once to erect the new structure. Seventy per cent of the cost of the new building will be borne by the city and county, the remaining 30 per cent being a grant from the federal government.

The building now being demolished was designed in 1897 by Ripley & Dickey, architects. The stone masonry is an example of Mediterranean workmanship, according to Mr. Dias, who says that Portuguese workmen shaped the lava blocks from which the structure was constructed. The stone, according to Mr. Dickey was quarried near Punahou academy.

PASSING OF OLD LANDMARK

Work is now under way on the razing of the old central fire station at Fort and Beretania Sts. to provide a site for a new modern fire station, to be constructetd as an FERA project. The upper view shows preliminary work in removing the roof of the station. The lower picture, taken a day or so later, shows "the begining of the end" of the station's tower as workmen start tearing it down, stone by stone.—FERA and Star-Bulletin photos.

Honolulu Star-Bulletin, June 23, 1934

The Honolulu Advertiser, October 22, 1933

The Honolulu Advertiser, March 17, 1935

YOUNG ASSOCIATED WITH DICKEY

Editor The Advertiser:

On two recent occasions mention was made in your columns of my name as architect for the new Central Fire Station and the name of Mr. John Mason Young was omitted. This was unfortunate as we were associated in that work and he deserves full credit for his share in the final result.

May 14. C. W. DICKEY.

The Honolulu Advertiser, May 15, 1935

2022

DAY BLOCK

122-134 S. Beretania Street
1899 – c.1962
Architect/Builder: H.L. Kerr / C.S. Desky

1941

THE NEW DAY BLOCK.

To be Partly Occupied as a Carriage Repository.

Under the personal direction of the architect and contractor, H. L. Kerr, the Day block, on Beretania street, is rapidly assuming shape. It is learned that one-half of the lower floor is to be taken by a carriage company with W. W. Wright at the head. The space in the building will be used for displaying the carriages, while in the rear another large building will be put up to be used as a manufacturing shop. The other half of the building is to be occupied with stores, and on the second floor there will be about twenty nicely fitted up lodging rooms.

*The Honolulu Advertiser
September 13, 1899*

THE LATE DR. F. R. DAY.

In 1890, prominent doctor Francis R. Day built a new 1-story frame house and 1-story frame office on this site. Nine years later he moved the buildings and contracted with C.S. Desky to build this large 2-story brick building next to the 1897 Central Fire Station in late 1899.

The building was 91' x 60' with 21 rooms upstairs, 4 stores on the ground floor, with cream-colored pressed brick veneer in front.

Antoine Schnerr's store was here for 50 years from 1912 to 1962. The upstairs housed the Delmonico Hotel until 1924 and then the St. George Hotel to at least 1959. Pacific Vehicle & Supply were located in back.

The building was demolished as part of the massively destructive Kukui Redevelopment Project plus the new Pali Highway connection to Bishop Street. In 1968 the site became the Kamalii Mini Park.

The Honolulu Advertiser, March 29, 1900

It is just a long rectangle on the 1899 Dakin Fire Insurance Map, and today it would be in the middle of the Pali Highway about 100' mauka of Beretania Street, but next to Dr. Day's original office was one of Honolulu's earliest historic homes that was later a place of fine dining known as the Hotel Richelieu.

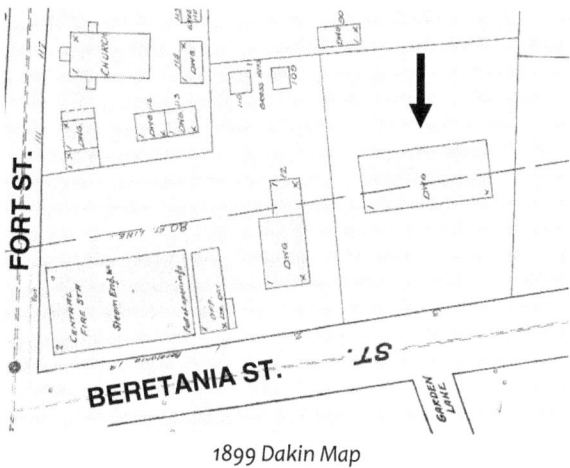

1899 Dakin Map

Known in the late 1800's as the Dickson house, it was built about 1835 by Jules Dudoit from Port Louis, Mauritius, the long-time French Consul to Hawaii. The house was prominently featured in Paul Emmert's 1854 series of sketches of Honolulu, and historian Thomas G. Thrum described it in 1898:

> *"Its spacious rooms and wide verandah running the entire length of the front made it early conspicuous by such provisions for Honolulu climate comforts, and though of reputed light construction, of wood, it bids fair to last yet many years."*

Paul Emmert, 1854

In October 1895, Mrs. B. Freimann leased the Dickson premises and opened "The Richelieu". Meals were served "a la carte or table d'hote", and a limited number of rooms with "electric lights and all modern appliances" were available single or ensuite. W.S Bartlett, formerly of the Ilaniwai seaside resort in Waikiki, was chef and caterer.

Big fancy dinners were a specialty – they were known for French, German, New England, Hawaiian, Dutch, Thanksgiving, Christmas, and New Year feasts serving up to 150 people.

These dinners often included music provided by the Quintette Club or the Kawaihau Club, with dancing afterwards.

Hotel Richelieu.

SATURDAY, NOVEMBER 1st, 1895.

Usual French Dinner

SERVED FROM 5:30 TO 7:30 P.M.

KAWAIHAU : CLUB

In Attendance.

Luncheon served daily from 12 to 2:30 p.m.
4139-1t

To Epicures.

Mrs. B Freimann wishes to announce to the public of Honolulu that she has leased the Dickson premises on Beretania street where she will open a first-class Hotel to be known as

"THE RICHELIEU."

Do you wish a first-class meal of the finest that the market affords served in such a manner as to make the edibles doubly palatable? If you do, try

"THE RICHELIEU."

The dining room will be permanently opened on SATURDAY, October 12th, for luncheon. Meals served a la carte or table d'hote.

Luncheon............12 to 2:30.
Dinner...............5:30 to 7:30
Breakfast............6 to 9.

A limited number of elegantly furnished rooms, fitted with electric lights, single or en suite, can be obtained on application.

Mrs. B. Freimann.

123-3t

The Richelieu Tonight.

The menu at the Richelieu dinner tonight was arranged by Mrs. C. N. Arnold and the dishes will be prepared under her direct supervision.

The decorations and arrangement of the tables in regular Hawaiian fashion will be also designed by her.

Following is the menu:

PAINA HAWAII MA KA RICHELIEU.
Feb. 1, 1896.

NA MEA AI:

Hee Kupaia me ka Luau me ka Nioi.
Moa Kupaia me ka Luau me ka Niu.
Amaama Lawalu.
Kumu Lawalu.
Kamano Lawalu me ka Luau.
Puaa Kalua.
Moa Laulau.
Kalo Kalua.
Uala Kalua.
Luau Pulehu.
Ia Lomi.
Ia Maloo.
Hee Maloo.
Limu, Kukui Akimona, Nioi, Akaakai, Opihi.

Dinner will be served from 5:30 to 7:30.

Quintet club in attendance.

Hotel Richelieu.

MENU.

Hors d' Oeuvre.
Olives   Pickles.   Caviar.
Soupe Tortue.
Salade Bordelaise.
Poisson
Mullet—Sauce Tartar.
Entree.
Cervelle Croquettes—Sauce Tomate.
Roman Punch.
Roti.
Dinde—Sauce Cannerge.
Legumes.
Puree de Pommes—Petits Pois a la francaise
Tomates.
Asperges a la Mayonaise.
Creme glace.   a la Vanille
Quatre mendionts.   Cafe.   Roquefort.

4250-1t

A Dutch Dinner

Hotel Richelieu invites its patrons to enjoy a German menu to-morrow instead of the usual French dishes. We invite our readers to go there and try the dinner which is most excellent—if you are not obliged to pronounce the names of the dishes:

SPEISE KARTE.
SAMSTAG, DEN 14th DECEMBER.

Caviar.
Nudeln Suppe.
Marinierte Lachs.
Wiener Bratwurst mit Sauerkraut.
Fleisch Kloesze.
Kuemmel Sherbet.
Rindsbraten.
Gebratens Huehnchen.
Kartoffeln.   Spargel.
Rothkraut.
Kartoffeln Salat.
Deutsche Pfannekuchen.
Citronen Eis.
Kase { Roquefort.
       { Limburger.
Cafe.

Mrs. E. D'Arcy, formerly in charge of the Club Hotel in Kobe, Japan, took over the lease in June 1896 and changed the name to the Club Hotel. She brought in furnishings from Japan, including blinds, screens, vases, cabinets and Takanabe ware, plus 16 large cases of tableware.

But Mrs. D'Arcy didn't last long, and the building was up for rent by August only two months later. The furnishings were purchased by Gus Froboese and Mrs. Quinn, and they became the managers of the Club Hotel.

She was the daughter of Major Edward H.F. Wolter who purchased the building in October 1896 when the Froboese's moved on to manage the Queen boarding house on Nuʻuanu Street. Major Wolter celebrated his 43rd birthday in grand style at the Club Hotel on February 22, 1897.

Meanwhile, Dr. C.B. Wood joined Dr. F.R. Day at his office next to the fire station, and they purchased the Club Hotel in April 1899, sold off the furnishings and moved Dr. Day's old house to Makiki and the doctor's office to the Club Hotel premises in preparation for building the 2-story Day Block.

The Club Hotel
[Late RICHELIEU.]
Will open under the management of Mrs. E. D'Arcy, formerly proprietor of the Club Hotel, Kobe, Japan,

On June 10th.
Excellent Table!
  Service Unequaled!
Rich fittings for Dining and Tiffin Rooms, imported direct from the Orient. Private Dinner Parties a specialty.

A limited number of persons may be accommodated with rooms, single or en suite.
322-tf

Although they talked of building a 4-story business block on the Club Hotel site, and had hired an architect, Day and Wood sold the property in 1900 to Mr. J.A. Gilman for $25,000 cash. The house was demolished in 1924.

The site of the Day Block and the Dudoit/Dickson/Richelieu/Club Hotel in 2022

MAKEE RESIDENCE

169-177 S. Beretania Street

c.1870 – 1923

Architect/Builder: Captain James Makee

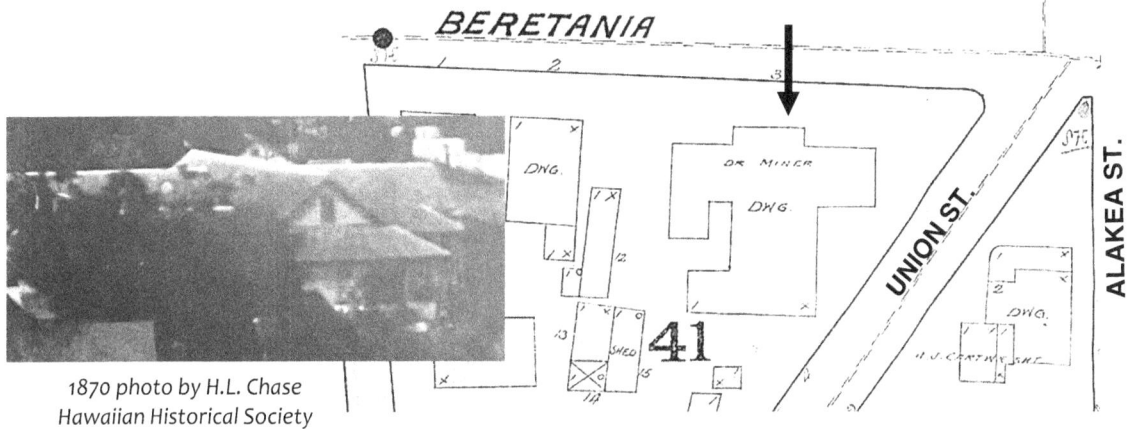

1870 photo by H.L. Chase
Hawaiian Historical Society

1899 Dakin Fire Insurance Map, before Bishop Street was extended to Beretania

Sometime around 1870 there was a sprawling 1-story house on this site that was "built by the late Captain Makee for his own use. The house is large and roomy, faithfully built, and with particular reference to the wants of our tropical climate."

Known as "the famous old Makee homestead" by the 1920's, Makee's young daughter, Rose Makee Tenney, grew up here. And it was in this house that James Makee passed away on September 16, 1879, at age 67.

Makee was born in Woburn, Massachusetts in 1812 and arrived in Lahaina in 1843 as captain of the whaling ship *Maine*. Attacked by the knife-wielding ship's steward and nearly killed, he stayed in Hawaii to recuperate and became one of Honolulu's most prosperous merchants as Jones & Makee, later Makee, Anthon & Co. He built the first 3-story building in Honolulu and owned the Ulupalakua Ranch.

In 1887, Dr. Frank L. Miner purchased the house from Makee's son-in-law, Frank.P. Hastings. Frank Leslie Miner was born in Vermont and was a graduate of McGill College in Montreal and a member of the Royal College of Physicians in London. He first came to Hawaii as the ship's physician on the German bark *Priscilla* when it brought the first Portuguese immigrants to Hawaii in 1878.

Miner added a second story in 1892, making it into "a distinguished-looking mansion". The Miner's "elegant home and office stood for many years on Beretania Street, between what is now Bishop Street and Union Street". Not so much their 14-year marriage – the divorce was front page news for months in 1900 and 1901, going all the way to the Hawaii Supreme Court.

Drs. Mori and Kobayashi moved into the former Miner premises in June of 1904, and J.J. Muller turned it into a boarding house in 1908.

In 1909, Mr. & Mrs. Hobson from Australia rented the house and opened it up as a "first class rooming hotel" renamed "The Knutsford". Four months later all the fixtures and furniture were sold at auction.

Dr. F.H. Schurmann

By 1911 the house was the clinic for the Schurmann Institute of Nature Cure and Osteopathy run by Dr. Frank H. Schurmann.

He sold it in 1918, very likely due to the international ruckus caused by the publication of his book, *The War As Seen Thru German Eyes* in 1916. Although he claimed to be pro-American, he was also fiercely and unapologetically pro-German, and in that era of rampant anti-German sentiment he was branded as "the foreign poet laureate to the Kaiser" and his US citizenship was revoked by a federal judge. Schurmann moved to Mexico and ran a hotel in Guadalajara.

By late 1918 the house was "The Lorraine" apartments with 23 rooms, managed by the Marquebielle's from France.

Renters included army private Frank Darnell who performed illusions as "The Great Darnell" which included skipping out on the rent, a young Japanese woman who committed suicide by drinking carbolic acid, ukulele and steel guitar maker and teacher Jose Marteo, and two French soldiers named Durecu and Peuchet who had both worked with Renault and De Dion of Paris and opened an automobile repair business after receiving their discharge while passing through Honolulu on their way to Vladivostok.

All furniture and furnishings were sold at auction on March 6, 1922, and Rudolph Bukeley bought the property for $45,000 and it became a Union Oil Company service station in 1923.

The 36-story Pinnacle Condominium was built on the site in 2007 and was designed by David Stringer and Hank Reese.

GALEN BUILDING

235 S. Beretania Street

1924 – 1988

Architect/Builder: Pacific Engineering Company

The Honolulu Star-Bulletin, August 23, 1924

1941

Built for the Waterhouse Investment Company and constructed by the Pacific Engineering Company in 1924, the 3-story brick Galen Building cost $100,000 and had 16 offices, an elevator, and a full basement. After much discussion they decided to name it after the renowned 2nd century physician, Claudius Galenus, more commonly known as Galen. Their decision might have been influenced by having the entire top floor rented in advance to several doctors and surgeons.

It replaced the Captain David P. Penhallow cottage built in 1846/1847 that had also been the home of the Macfarlanes and Samuel Savidge.

In 1991, the Galen Building was replaced by the State Office Tower designed by Lawton and Umemura, now called the Leiopapa A Kamehameha Building.

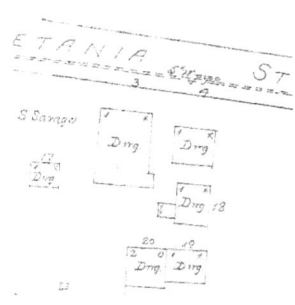

2022

1885 Dakin Map

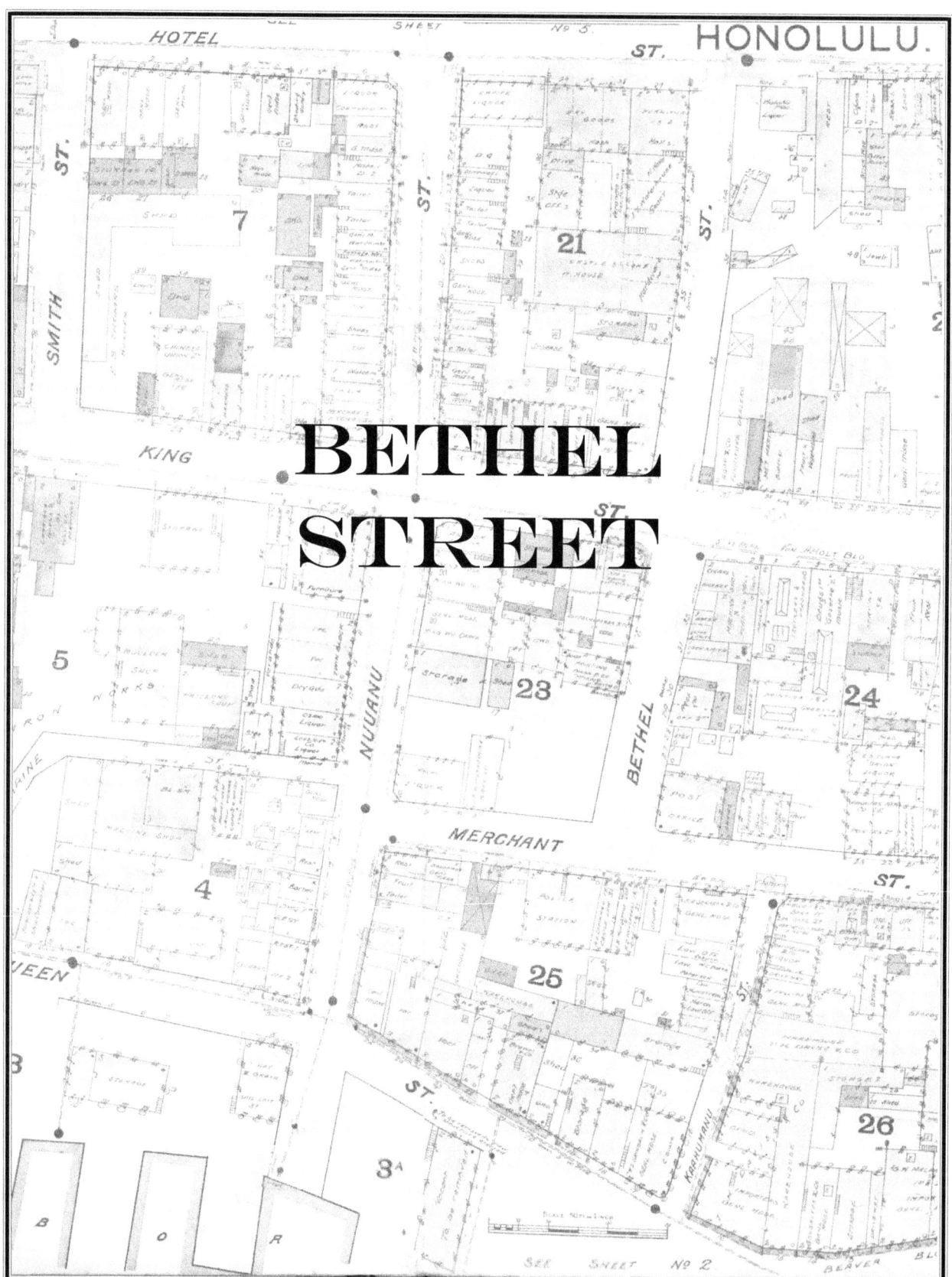

THE FRIEND BUILDING

924-928 Bethel Street

1887/1906 – present
Architect/Builder: George Lucas

2022

This 2-story tuck-pointed brick building started out as a single 25' x 50' building on the right, with the first floor occupied by the Press Publishing Company and Rev. E.C. Oggel's editorial rooms of the *Friend* upstairs.

After removing a large tamarind tree the matching section on the left was added in 1906 when S.M. Damon became a partner in the Bank of Bishop. The building housed the Bishop Trust and Bishop Insurance companies.

First published in 1843 as *Temperance Advocate*, the *Temperance Advocate and Seamen's Friend*, and then *The Friend* in 1845, it was a monthly newspaper for seamen by Rev. Samuel C. Damon. It is Hawaii's oldest continuously published periodical and said to be "the oldest newspaper west of the Rockies".

> **The "Friend" Building.**
>
> Work will shortly be commenced on a new building to be erected on Bethel street for the Hon. S. M. Damon, to be known as the "Friend" building. It will be two story, of red brick, 26x50. The lower floor will be occupied by the Press Publishing Company, while up stairs the Rev. E. C. Oggel, editor of the "Friend", will have his editorial rooms. Mr. George Lucas has the contract for the building, and it is expected to have it ready for occupancy by the 1st of March.

The Honolulu Advertiser, January 1, 1887

Born in Honolulu in 1845, Samuel Mills Damon was the son of missionary Samuel Chenery Damon who had arrived in Honolulu in 1842 and was the chaplain of the Seamen's Bethel church. Samuel M. Damon initially worked as a clerk in the W.N. Ladd store, joined the Bishop Bank in 1871, became full partner by 1881, and owned all shares by 1893.

THE SEAMEN'S BETHEL

934 Bethel Street
1833 – 1886 (remodeled 1847)
Architect/Builder: unknown

Paul Emmert, 1854

This building was originally on a large site that took up about a quarter of the block on land given to the American Seamen's Friend Society by King Kamehameha III.

The society sent Rev. John Diell to Hawaii as its first chaplain to establish a chapel near the port and this building was shipped from New London, CT, via Cape Horn in autumn of 1832.

It was the first church for public worship of English-speaking people in Polynesia and it was dedicated on November 28, 1833 in a service attended by "the king, Kīna'u, and the principal chiefs, together with a respectable number of residents, masters of vessels and seamen".

The first regular church services in Hawaii started here in 1837. Rev. Samuel C. Damon succeeded Rev. Diell in 1841. Damon founded *The Friend* newspaper which he published from the church until 1885.

The chapel was expanded in 1847 by turning the first floor into a single hall and erecting galleries, doubling its capacity. Bethel members founded the Fort Street Church in 1852.

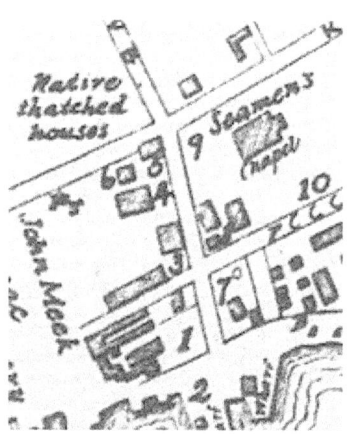

Bethel Street, 20' wide, was opened between Merchant and King streets in 1853.

The building burned in the April 18, 1886 fire.

Bethel Church with D.W. Clark's Observatory and public drinking fountain at the corner, c.1880

The day after the fire, April 19, 1886

MCCANDLESS BUILDING

919-937 Bethel Street / 43-45 S. King Street

1907 – present
Architect/Builder: H.L. Kerr / Lord-Young Engineering (1914 addition)

The Honolulu Advertiser, January 7, 1906

As early as 1905 the McCandless Brothers had architect Harry L. Kerr draw up plans for what was initially a 2-story building with basement, designed to allow for a third story. The estimated cost was $45,000. John A. McCandless, James S. McCandless, Lincoln L. McCandless, Peter C. Jones, and Ella McCandless incorporated the McCandless Building Company in January 1906. They took out a building permit on February 17, 1906, and they laid the cornerstone with tin box time capsule on June 14, 1906, having decided to go ahead and add the third floor, and then the fourth floor.

The building has a frontage of 140' on Bethel Street and 40' on King Street, and originally had 7 stores on the ground floor, two of which were leased to the Post Office and one to the Star Newspaper Association whose presses were in the basement.

There were 16 offices on the second floor and a rear setback to provide interior light. The basement was designed to extend to the curb and had 1,000 square feet of three-pointed "bar lock prisms" in the sidewalk.

The Hawaiian Star, April 1, 1907

The Commercial Club leased the fourth floor with a 36' x 40' lounging room on the King Street end and a 40' x 46' dining room on the Post Office end, with card, billiard, and reading rooms in between.

Building name over front door *Detail in elevator*

The club hired Lord-Young Engineering Company to add a fifth floor in 1914 for $27,900. It projected over the rear setback and light court "because the floor space was needed to comply with the requirements of the owners and renters of the floor space, and because there is no law prohibiting it as in other large cities".

But one hour after they started building the fifth floor the city attorney stopped the work and arrested 40 of the workers. The issue had been festering for some time, having to do with compliance of current building codes for additional stairways and fire shutters.

This corner was previously the site of a 2-story wooden building that had been Castle & Cooke's store before they moved across the street in 1854. The devastating "Varieties Theater Fire" burned it and a large portion of the block on July 3, 1855.

The burned buildings were replaced with a "motley collection of shacks" that previously housed a Chinese planing mill with blacksmith shops on King Street and a cigar store on the corner, plus the New Land Chinese restaurant next to the Post Office. In 1906 a Japanese barber shop, Chinese gunsmith, candy store, cigar store, and Japanese shoemaker shop were in the buildings.

"Another antiquated, historic but archaically encumbered spot in Honolulu is about to give evidence of the march of progress." (The Hawaiian Gazette, January 2, 1906).

2022

COSMOPOLITAN RESTAURANT

1028 Bethel Street

1887 – 1895

Architect/Builder: unknown

The Cosmopolitan Restaurant

New House,   **Bethel Street**

(Next Castle & Cooke's)

Board, $5.50 per week, 35 cts per meal.
$4.50   "   25 cts   "

The tables are supplied with every delicacy obtainable in the market.

21   Patronage solicited.   1m

This beautiful little building with the wonderfully decorative brickwork was built in 1887 when Rose Lane was converted into Bethel Street between King and Hotel streets.

It was built for Jun Hee, the owner of the Cosmopolitan Restaurant. He moved here from his previous location on Hotel Street between Fort and Nuʻuanu streets.

Cosmopolitan Restaurant.

JUN HEE,

The Best Cook in the City, has opened the above Restaurant, where everything is neat and clean, and where the table is supplied with the best the market affords.

WIRE GAUZE DOORS Make the Place Cool and Fly Proof

The · Cosmopolitan · Restaurant,

BETHEL STREET.

The Proprietors of this most popular Restaurant take pleasure in informing their patrons and the public generally that they have greatly increased their accommodations and are now prepared to seat over sixty boarders.

The tables are furnished with the best the market affords; and Meals can be obtained at any hour.

Boarding, per week, - - $4.50
Boarding, private room, per week 5.50

☞ THE COSMOPOLITAN is the coolest and most comfortable Restaurant in Honolulu.

                        YOUNG & CO.,
136-2w   Proprietors.

But it didn't last long – Jun Hee was foreclosed on for non-payment of rent in 1895 and the building was demolished for a large Castle & Cooke warehouse built in 1896 to match the adjoining Waverley Block.

MORE WAREHOUSE.

Land For the Purpose Purchased By Castle & Cooke.

The lease of the premises on Bethel street adjoining Castle & Cooke's warehouse, and on which stands the Jun Hee restaurant brick building, was sold by J. F. Morgan at noon today. The sale was for nonpayment of principal and interest. Jun Hee leased the premises for thirty years. He built a brick building on the property. The lease has twenty-two years to run.

The lease was bought at auction today by J. B. Atherton for Castle & Cooke. It is the intention of that firm to extend their warehouse. As the two buildings adjoin each other the walls alone will have to be removed and the buildings connected. Another story will be added to the Jun Hee building.

The Hawaiian Star, July 22, 1895

1966

Jun Hee's building was built on the homesite of Martin Beck, identified on the 1879 Lion Map as an "old dwelling" even then. Born in Copenhagen in 1792 and raised in England, Beck first came to Hawaii in 1815, permanently moving here in 1817, and he obtained this lot sometime after 1823.

His house was a 2-story frame building behind Castle & Cooke at the end of Rose Lane which was the side entrance of the International Hotel.

Beck passed away in the house in 1873 at 80 years of age. He had been a crew member on HMS *Bellerophon* in 1815 when Napoleon Bonaparte surrendered to the English.

1885 Dakin Map

2022

The site today is the entrance driveway to the Chinatown Gateway Municipal Parking Garage. Immediately on the lefthand side is a vestigial brick wall and outline of a gable roof that were part of the Castle & Cooke warehouse.

HAWAII THEATER

1130 Bethel Street

1922 – present

Architect/Builder: Emory & Webb / Pacific Engineering Company

Drawing by John C. Poole, based on a photograph by H.F. Hill
Honolulu Star-Bulletin, September 6, 1922

Proclaimed the "Pride of the Pacific" when it was completed in 1922 for Consolidated Amusements, the Hawaii Theater was designed by Emory & Webb with "hints of Corinthian and Byzantine" architecture and was built by the Pacific Engineering Company for close to $500,000. Construction began on June 10, 1921. It was originally to be called the Bijou Theater (which was previously on the site).

The theater was "Hawaii-designed and Hawaii-built" and seated 1,800 on the main floor and the balcony. It had 2,000 light bulbs connected with 76,000 feet of wire, with marble and tile work by J. Arthur Reed and Frank L. McAfee, sculptured decorations by Julian Rosenstein, and mosaic in the great dome by Gordon Usborne.

The theater had a "heroic-sized" painting 50' long and 20' high above the stage by Lionel Walden titled "The Glorification of the Drama" that was "allegorical to the nth degree… it represents the progress of the race, especially in so far as the finer arts are concerned, from the days of long ago down to this, the twentieth century".

The orchestra pit included a Robert Morgan Unified Orchestral pipe organ with four-manuals and 72 stops that took six months to build and was said to be one of the best ever built for theater work.

There was a "honeymoon box" way up in the balcony next to the projection room with an upholstered railing and wicker furniture. "It is more or less removed from the rest of the house, and will prove a boon to honeymooners who, in the past, have been forced to spoon under his hat or her veil while at the theater."

Honolulu Star-Bulletin, September 6, 1922

They advertised "30 pretty Chinese girls will usher you to your seat" dressed in "varied costumes of the land of their ancestors" and features included motion pictures, vaudeville, live theater, concerts, and touring acts.

The opening of the theater generated tremendous excitement and the *Honolulu Star-Bulletin* published a massive 14-page supplement especially for the Hawaii Theater on September 6, 1922.

The Hawaii Theater closed in 1984 and was threatened with demolition. Luckily, a group of concerned citizens formed a non-profit to save the building and raise money for a $32M renovation led by Malcolm Holzman of Hardy Holzman Pfeiffer from New York. It reopened in 1996, with exterior renovations completed in 2004, including replication of the original 1938 lighted marquee. The League of Historic American Theatres named it an "Outstanding Historic Theatre in America" and the National Trust for Historic Preservation gave it the highest Honor Award.

2022

2022

Before there was a Pauahi Street or a Bethel Street, the land in this area was called Pa Moʻo, and was part of an original land grant to Kamehameha III. Various land documents later referred to this tract as the "Blonde Yard" so it might have had something to do with Boki's grog house or ship of the same name.

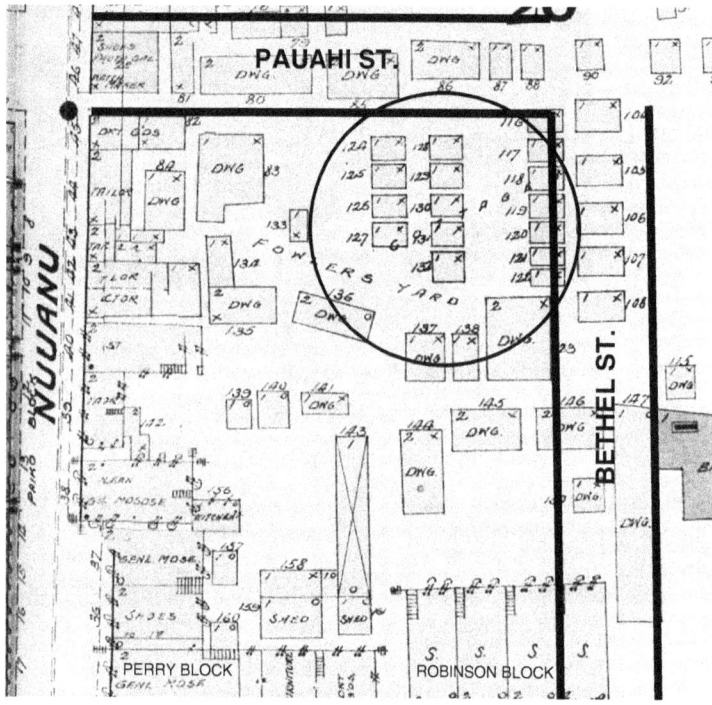
1891 Dakin Map

By 1882 there was a large collection of small workers' cottages on the site known as Fowler's Yard, owned by George W. Fowler who rented furnished rooms for 25 cents a night or $1 per week.

Described as "a village unto itself", there were 100 rooms in several dozen cottages, mostly rented to laborers, mechanics, and sailors.

It was a rough and noisy place and the *Evening Bulletin* on November 24, 1884, wrote "it is about the lowest place in town and ought to be cleaned out".

It seems it had more than the usual number of melees, rows, affrays, stabbings, robberies, and fights.

From a letter to the editor, *The Honolulu Advertiser*, June 8, 1888:

> "There is now in the very heart of the city, a court called "Fowler's Yard," where these Norwegian, German, and other families, congregate: thriftless, lazy, broken-down, men and women, with swarms of children, to be fed and clothed. Those of them who are willing to work, are unskilled and ignorant of the English language, so as to make it difficult to get employment."

From 1886 to 1889 the Government Dispensary was also located here, and in 1886 the YMCA held 10-months of temperance meetings.

The Mechanics Home was located here, providing lodging for out-of-work carpenters and builders. The access lane off Nuʻuanu Street was known as Mechanic's Lane and became Pauahi Street in 1900. The other access lane was from Hotel Street.

> Mrs. Anna Breeze Southwick, with one or two ladies to assist her has organized a Sunday school in Fowler's yard. Thirty-seven children were present last Sunday, the majority not attending any other Sunday school. This is a move in the right direction and should have the support and co-operation of all interested. Fowler's yard is a village in itself, and Mr. Fowler has provided comfortable homes for many poor but respectable people, at low rents, otherwise these people would scarcely find a place to shelter them in Honolulu. Neither are honest, industrious men or women ever turned from his doors, when misfortune visits them and are unable to pay their rent. Mrs. Southwick will also give lessons free of charge, Saturday evenings of every week at the same place, to any Germans or Norwegians, who may desire to acquire an knowledge of or perfect themselves in the English language.

Daily Honolulu Press
October 6, 1885

Joe Cohen opened the Princess Roller Skating Rink on the site on August 21, 1909. Built at a cost of $10,000 it had a 80' x 150' concrete floor that was "smooth as glass" plus a grandstand, a "semicupola" bandstand that could "accommodate a hundred musicians if necessary", dressing rooms, a main entrance off Pauahi Street, and a secondary entrance from a lane off Hotel Street. Admission was 15 cents and they had 500 pairs of skates to choose from that could be rented for an additional 15 cents.

The Honolulu Advertiser, August 21, 1909

"The electric lighting arrangements make up the most masterly effect. Over the center line of the rink there are three huge, flaring arcs that will make the rink bright as day. Should the moon be riding high in the heavens, the arcs will be switched off and a series of colored lights, arranged round the sides of the rink, will glow in effective cooperation of that big moon."

But the Princess Rink only lasted one year. The Bijou Theater was built on the site in late 1910 by contractor Angus P. McDonald in 27 days. Opening day was Thursday, December 1, 1910.

The theater was open on three sides with a large single-span corrugated steel roof with no columns. Seating was provided by more than 1,000 orchestra chairs on a gradual incline. Admission was either 10 cents or 15 cents.

Sam Kubey was the manager and vaudeville talent bookings were handled directly through the Bijou's representative on the mainland. The first performance included seven artists and a complete orchestra who arrived on the ship *Wilhelmina*.

Work crews started dismantling the Bijou theater on March 2, 1921, to make way for the new Hawaii Theater.

HAWAII BUILDING

1121-1137 Bethel Street

1925 – present
Architect/Builder: H. Richard Stettin / Robert S. Chase

Honolulu Star-Bulletin, March 3, 1925

Owned by fruit merchant Charles Akana and Liberty Bank Cashier Lau Lan, this concrete building with 6 stores was designed by H. Richard Stettin and built by Robert S. Chase for $45,000.

Local restauranteur Joseph C. Fatt opened the Silver Dragon Cabaret upstairs in 1925, reportedly the first cabaret in Honolulu.

Comes Now the Silver Dragon

The City of Los Angeles Orchestra will play at
THE SILVER DRAGON
THURSDAY AND FRIDAY NIGHTS

Through a special arrangement we have been able to secure
Johnny Noble's Famous Orchestra
TO PLAY FOR YOU
Thursday Evening May 13th
EVERYBODY WELCOME—DANCE TO THIS MUSIC
at the
SILVER DRAGON

The Silver Dragon lasted only one year, becoming the Golden Dragon which lasted less than a year, then becoming the Olympic Club in 1927.

The 25' x 40' dance floor and fixtures were for sale in 1928 with "no reasonable offer refused".

2022

BETHEL-PAUAHI BUILDING
1149 Bethel Street
1961 – present
Architect/Builder: Ernest H. Hara / Hirano Brothers, Ltd.

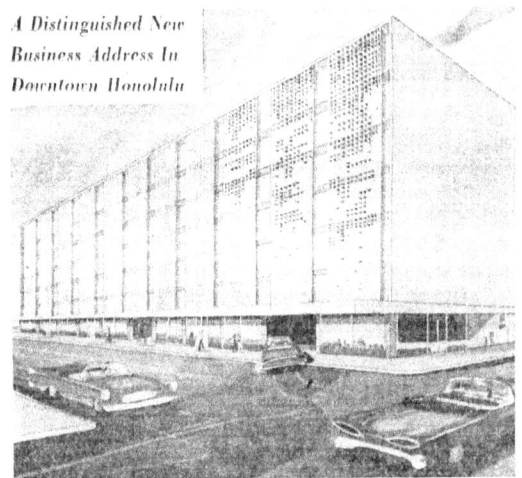

The Honolulu Advertiser, September 15, 1961   *2022*

Advertised as "the ultimate in modern beauty, convenience and flexibility", the $1.25M Bethel-Pauahi Building has 7 floors built of reinforced concrete. "ULTRA MODERN are all appointments, equipment and facilities".

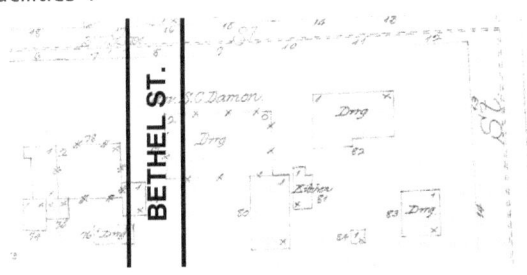

1885 Dakin Map   *1906 Dakin Map*

This was the site of Rev. Samuel C. Damon's large 2-story coral house. Damon was the pastor of the Bethel Church from 1841 to 1882, the editor and publisher of *The Friend*, and it is why the street in front of his house was called Chaplain Street. Bethel Street was extended through the property in 1927.

Mark Twain was friends with Reverend Damon and wrote in his notebook in 1866, "Went with Mr. Damon to his cool, vine shaded home. No care-worn or eager, anxious faces in the land of happy contentment – God! what a contrast with California and Washoe [County, Nevada]."

In 1892 the Mills Institute was founded in the house by Damon's son, Francis. It was torn down sometime between 1924 and 1927 when Bethel Street was extended, and the site became a parking lot.

ALOHA GRILL BUILDING

1165 Bethel Street / 44 Chaplain Lane

1952/1958 – present
Architect/Builder: Fred Fujioka / Tani Contracting Company

Matsu Teruya and sons Robert and Herbert built the first Aloha Grill Building in early 1952, which included the Aloha Grill, a cocktail lounge, a mezzanine party room, and a 12-lane bowling center in the basement.

Honolulu Star-Bulletin, January 11, 1952

In 1958 they expanded the building to 3-stories that was designed by Fred Fujioka and built by Tani Contracting Company at a cost of $200,000. The second and third stories were used for office space and parking for restaurant and bowling customers.

2022

Honolulu Star-Bulletin, January 11, 1952

Genoa Keawe and her group at Aloha Grill. A spectator plays the spoons at far left. —Photos by Bob Young

Aloha Grill, an unlikely on Bethel Street.

Genoa Keawe, Queen of Aloha Grill

Honolulu Star-Bulletin, October 27, 1975

 Staring in 1974 Auntie Genoa Keawe, one of Hawaii's first ladies of song, performed at the Aloha Grill three nights a week. Her most famous song was "Alika" where she held a high falsetto note for an incredibly long period of time. Scan the QR code to hear Genoa Keawe and her Hula Maids sing "Kealoha".

Bob and Nancy Teruya retired after 46 years, and the Aloha Grill closed in 1979.

The Aloha Grill was built on the site of a 1-story frame house constructed about 1849 or 1850 for Frederick W. Thompson. He was born in Charlestown, Massachusetts in 1819 and was a well-known auctioneer and also co-owner of the Mansion House (located on the makai side of Beretania under Bishop Street today).

F. W. THOMPSON,
AUCTIONEER,
HONOLULU, OAHU, H. I.
(Office over C. Brewer & Co.'s Retail Store,)

Paul Emmert, 1854

It was the home of Alexander J. Cartwright in the 1850's, and for many years it was the home of financier William G. Irwin.

It became Silva's Undertaking in 1910 with coffins stored in the old garage. It was later Townsend Undertaking and then Bothwick's mortuary chapel in the early 1920's before being torn down for an auto stand c.1923.

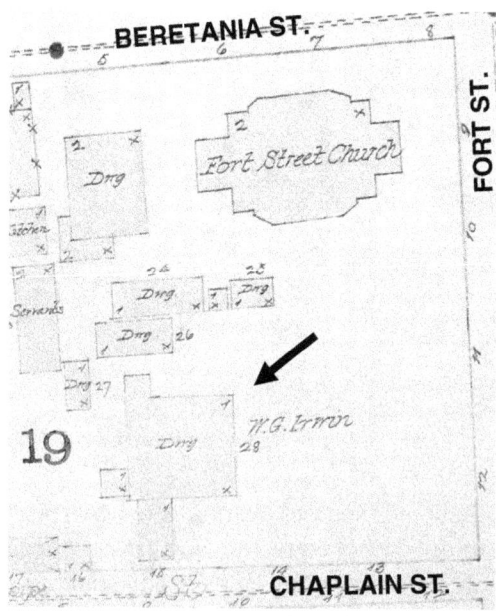

1885 Dakin Map

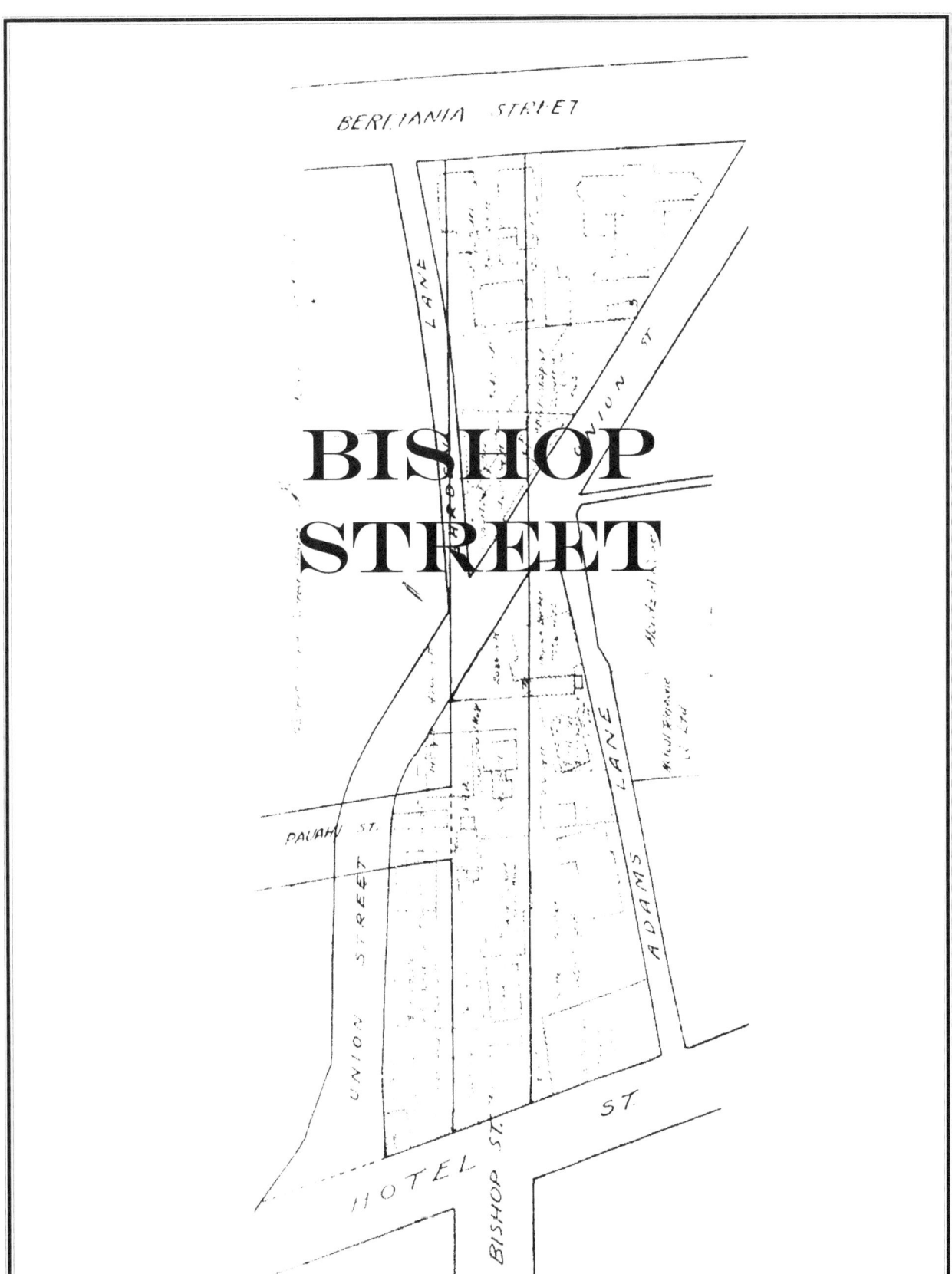

T.H. DAVIES WAREHOUSE
680 Bishop Street
1901 – 1932
Architect/Builder: Fred Harrison

ANOTHER NEW BUILDING
CONTRACTS LET FOR A LARGE WAREHOUSE.

Davies & Company to Erect a Modern Building on the Site of One of their Old Ones.

Theo. H. Davies & Company have let contracts for another large building near the water front, to be used as a warehouse. Work has already begun on the foundation and the structure is to be ready for occupation in about six months. Fred Harrison has the contract.

The building is to be at the corner of Kilauea and Halekawila streets, where Davies and Company had a small frame building. This has been torn down to make room for the new building, which is to be a large modern warehouse.

The warehouse will be a three story, brick building, with 100 feet frontage on Halekauwila street and fifty feet on Kilauea street. There will be a large freight elevator, and the structure, with large doors on the warehouse plan, will present a handsome appearance. The cost is to be over $25,000. The building is to be on leased land and may some day become the property of the government.

Contractor Harrison is expecting a lot of trouble with the water flow in the foundation. It is known that there are strong underground streams in the locality, the land being lower than at the new Hackfeld building, where there was great difficulty in keeping the water down so that the concrete foundation and cellar could be constructed.

The Hawaiian Star, October 25, 1900

This 3-story brick building was built by Fred Harrison for Theo. H. Davies in 1901, and it was originally at the corner of Halekauwila and Kilauea streets in the reclaimed land called The Esplanade.

Sixteen years later it was in the way of the extension of Bishop Street to Ala Moana Street, so in July 1917 D.J. and T. Sullivan raised the building 1" off the foundation with 8 large jacks, inserted 12" x 12" timbers and rollers, and used a donkey engine with steel cables to move it approximately 100' ewa, 10' at a time.

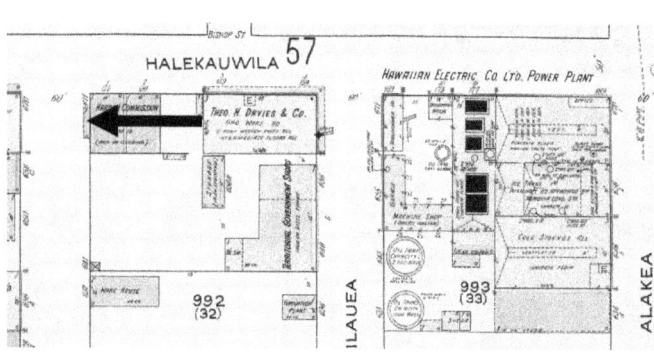

1914 Sanborn Map

The building and land were purchased in 1930 by Helene Irwin Fagan to be turned into Irwin Park in honor of her father, William G. Irwin.

The building was demolished in 1932, and the site is now in the makai lanes of Ala Moana Boulevard.

DILLINGHAM TRANSPORTATION BUILDING

701-765 Bishop Street

1930 – present
Architect/Builder: Lincoln Rogers, Marshall H. Webb / Ralph E. Woolley

Completed in 1930, this building was built as a memorial to "Hawaii's foremost figure in transportation development" – Benjamin Franklin Dillingham. It was designed by Lincoln Rogers from Los Angeles with local supervision by Marshall Webb, and it was constructed by Ralph E. Woolley for $619,368.

It was completed in 325 working days and was built with 13,000,000 pounds of concrete with 400 tons of specialty cut steel, 100 tons of wire reinforcing, and was faced with 50,000 hollow terra cotta tiles. Since the site is on reclaimed land, it required 700 reinforced concrete piles extending to bedrock. The sidewalks were tinted in "a three-tone brown" to harmonize with the building, and 10 tall palm trees were transplanted along the street by landscaper Richard C. Tongg. It also included a large parking garage for 250 cars on the back half of the lot, separated from the main building by a motor court.

The formal opening was September 4, 1930, on the 86th anniversary of Dillingham's birthday, and also 55 years to the day that Hawaii's first railroad train took a party of excursionists to the Palama rice fields.

THE FORMAL OPENING OF THE DILLINGHAM TRANSPORTATION BUILDING WILL TAKE PLACE ON THURSDAY, SEPTEMBER 4th .. YOU ARE CORDIALLY INVITED TO INSPECT THIS MODERN OFFICE BUILDING BETWEEN 8:00 A. M. AND 6:00 P. M.

Adjoining the Dillingham Transportation Building and equally as modern in design, is the Dillingham Garage . . . strategically located downtown and affording the motorist "under cover" parking space. A complete staff of expert machinists is in attendance to service your car. Rates $5.00 to $15.00 monthly, dependent on amount of service.

Honolulu Star-Bulletin, September 2, 1930

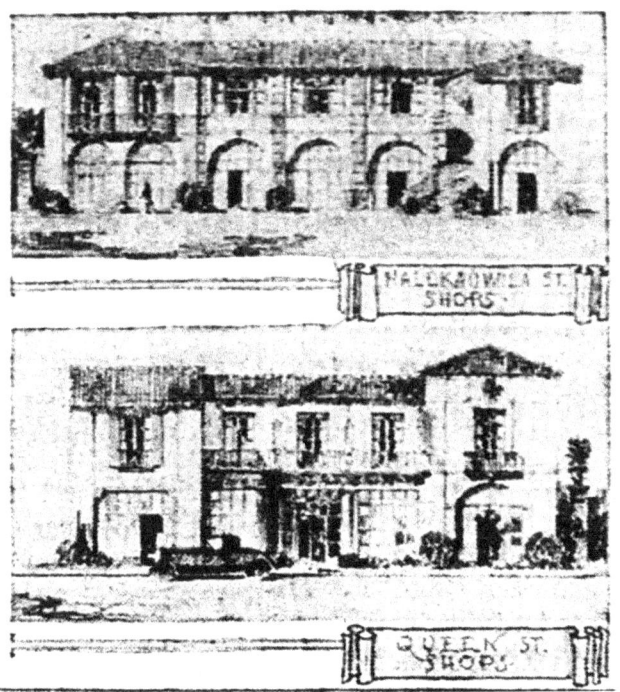

There were additionally two buildings of shops, flanking the parking garage and facing Halekauwila and Queen streets.

> "The architectural motif of all the buildings will be Mediterranean, the feeling substantial but not heavy. Italian renaissance has been selected by the architect as being in keeping with sub-tropical conditions."

> "The exterior of the main building will be stone to the second floor level and concrete stucco from there up to the sheltering overhanging eaves and the variegated burnt tile roof.'"

The decorative ceiling in the lobby of the main building was the work of Einar Peterson from Los Angeles.

Honolulu Star-Bulletin, April 17, 1929

"I think that in such a city there should be more buildings of this kind, and less of the classical type. And modern and modernistic styles are quite out of harmony with the surroundings" – Lincoln Rogers

Benjamin F. Dillingham was born at West Brewster, Massachusetts in 1844, He shipped aboard the clipper ship *Southern Cross* and sailed to places like San Francisco, Hong Kong, and Macao. He first came to Hawaii in 1862, having just made third mate at age 17, but didn't come ashore.

He was captured and imprisoned by the Confederate privateer *Florida* during the Civil War and put ashore in Brazil. While stopping in Honolulu with the bark *Whistler* in 1864, he was hurt falling from a horse and ended up staying and getting a job at Henry Dimond's store for $40/month.

In 1869 he teamed up with Charles Alfred Castle to purchase H. Dimond & Company.

Dillingham obtained an exclusive franchise in 1888 to construct a railroad on Oahu and founded the Oahu Railway & Land Company.

The Dillingham TRANSPORTATION Building

Honolulu Star-Bulletin, September 3, 1930

His son, Walter Dillingham, was a businessman and industrialist called the "Baron of Hawaii Industry." Born in Hawaii and educated at Harvard University, he was highly connected politically and served on several territorial commissions. He founded Hawaiian Dredging Company in 1901 – it is now the oldest and largest full-service construction company in Hawaii.

In addition to dredging Pearl Harbor and constructing many of the docks, Hawaiian Dredging Company also constructed the Ala Wai Canal, the King Kalakaua Building (the Main Post Office), the Honolulu Museum of Art, Phase I of the Ala Moana Shopping Center, and several 5-star hotels. The company recently restored the 1929 Honolulu Advertiser Building on Kapiolani for their current headquarters.

From 1973 to 1979 there was a popular restaurant and nightclub called The Territorial Tavern on the harborside end of the building. It helped establish the careers of many now-famous Hawaiian slack-key guitarists and musicians like Keola and Kapono Beamer, Brothers Cazimero, the Sons of Hawaii, Eddie Kamae, Dennis Kamakahi, Country Comfort, Sunday Manoa, and the comedy trio Booga Booga.

The Makaha Sons of Ni'ihau also played here, featuring the singing and ukulele playing of Israel Kamakawiwo'ole, affectionately known as Braddah Iz. You still hear his beautiful version of "Over the Rainbow" throughout Hawaii today.

ALEXANDER & BALDWIN BUILDING

822 Bishop Street

1929 – present
Architect/Builder: C.W. Dickey, Hart Wood / Ralph E. Woolley

In March 1924, the Alexander & Baldwin Company purchased 10,154 square feet of land at the corner of Bishop and Merchant streets from Bank of Bishop for $140,000, and then bought the remaining 10,838 square feet to Queen Street from the Inter-Island Steam Navigation Company in 1926.

The 1892 Daily Bulletin and 1911 Schumann Carriage Company buildings had previously been on the Merchant Street side but were demolished in 1921.

They hired Charles W. Dickey and Hart Wood to prepare the plans, and contractor Ralph E. Woolley was the lowest bidder at $706,369 with the building to be completed in 439 days. The total building cost with all furnishings was estimated to be $1.1M. Groundbreaking was in January 1928, and opening day was September 30, 1929.

The building is built of structural steel with walls of terra cotta and a tile roof. The main entrance portico on Bishop Street is 12' deep, 50' wide, and 35' high and decorated with art tile. The main room, 120' x 40' originally had a 35' ceiling that was decorated with travertine walls and art tiles. The floor is "Belgian black in Chinese design" on the public side of the counter. Landscaping was by Richard C. Tongg.

The sidewalks were stained green in a special process developed by Robert Lammens whose "Keramik" staining process was also used for Grauman's Egyptian and Chinese theaters in Los Angeles.

Editor's Note:
C. W. Dickey, architect of the Alexander & Baldwin building, in answer to many requests, describes below some of the interesting motifs and features incorporated in the architectural design of Honolulu's latest important downtown structure.

By C. W. DICKEY

There have been so many questions asked in regard to the architecture of the new Alexander & Baldwin Building that I will take this opportunity of answering some of them.

In the first place, I wish to say that I was greatly helped in the original design for this building by my former partner, Hart Wood.

My foremost thought architecturally was to produce a building suitable to the climate, environment, history and geographical position of Hawaii. The early history of the sugar industry, upon which the firm of Alexander & Baldwin, Ltd., was founded, was most closely linked with Chinese labor. It was felt that this, added to the location of Honolulu at the crossroads of the Pacific, in close touch with the Orient, gave sufficient reason for allowing Chinese architecture to clearly influence the design.

Once adopted, this idea led to fascinating results. It was found that the wide projecting roofs and balconies of China, as well as the deep window reveals of some of the fine stone structures of old Peking, were admirably adapted both artistically and practically to a building in Honolulu. It was also found that there was a wealth of Chinese architectural detail that could be used without becoming blatantly Chinese.

The problem naturally was to design an appropriate modern building to fit modern needs and yet feel the Chinese influence without making it appear that the building itself, or any part of it, was transplanted from China. To obtain this result required great self-restraint, and literally hundreds of sketches were discarded as being too strongly Chinese in flavor, and I feel that in the final building the exotic Chinese influence is so subtle that it would not be noted by a casual observer. However, it is there in every detail of the design. On the exterior it is most pronounced in the water buffalo heads and quaint Chinese faces of the window ornamentation, in the circular "Good Luck" signs at the main entrance portico on Bishop St. and the long life signs in the column capitals.

An interesting point in this connection is that many of the elements of ornament, such as wave pattern, egg and dart, lamb's tongue, etc., that occur so frequently in classic architecture are found in a somewhat modified form throughout the architecture of the old buildings of the Imperial City of Peking, and this ornament in its Chinese form is used in the Alexander & Baldwin Building.

The art tile work of the main entrance portico surrounding the panels of Hawaiian fish life is all carried out in Chinese motifs, as are the acoustical tile of the ceiling of the big room on the first floor and the decoration of the ceiling beams.

The influence of Chinese art is strongly felt in the fretwork and ornament of the bronze grilles for doors, windows, elevator fronts, elevator cars, balustrades, etc., and in the inlaid floor of black Belgian marble and Roman Travertine stone in the public space in front of the main counter on first floor.

The construction, materials and workmanship in this building are the equal of any in the United States. There is a complete steel frame clothed and protected with reinforced concrete, and the basement, which extends far below water level, is as dry as a bone.

The exterior walls on front and rear are of mat-glazed terra cotta, tied to the concrete backing by copper anchors, which in turn are bedded in concrete.

The roof is of steel and reinforced concrete covered with a built-up felt and asphalt roof over which is laid the colored roofing tile, securely anchored to the concrete slab by copper ties.

All exterior doors and windows are of bronze, and bronze is used in place of wrought iron throughout the interior wherever the latter might deteriorate.

Floors throughout are covered with marble, cork tile or battleship linoleum.

There is no woodwork in the construction or finish of the building. All interior doors and trim that are not of bronze are of steel with a grained walnut baked enamel finish.

The large main room on first floor has walls of Roman Travertine imported from Italy and on the end walls are large mural decorations executed in art tile. One of these pictures is in place and represents the Iao Valley and Kahului Harbor on Maui. The companion picture at the opposite end of the room is now being manufactured and will represent the harbor of Port Allen on Kauai, with mountains and clouds for a background and a full-rigged ship in the foreground, entering the harbor.

The special features introduced in this building that have not before been seen in Honolulu are so numerous that they cannot be here enumerated, but will be revealed by a visit to the building.

Honolulu Star-Bulletin, September 30, 1929

Alexander & Baldwin, now known as A&B, was once one of the Big Five companies in territorial Hawaii, with business in real estate, sugarcane, and in diversified agriculture. They are still one of the state's largest private landowners and still office in this building today.

The company began in 1869 when Samuel T. Alexander and Henry P. Baldwin teamed up to cultivate sugarcane in Maui. They acquired more land and sugar mill operations and even owned their own railroad lines. At one point they controlled more than 100,000 acres.

In 1905 they took control of C&H sugar, and from 1969 to 2012 they were the owners of Matson Navigation Company.

Hawaii State Archives

Hawaii State Archives

THEO. H. DAVIES BUILDING

841 Bishop Street

1921 – 1970

Architect/Builder: Louis Christian Mullgardt / Pacific Engineering Company

This building was once "the largest unitary concrete structure in the world". It was built on the site of W.G. Irwin's "immense warehouse", a 1-story brick building built by the Harrison Brothers in 1893 and later used by the Associated Garage in conjunction with the Schumann Carriage Company.

The plans for this massive 360,000 square foot building which took up the entire block were completed in 1918 by San Francisco architect Louis Christian Mullgardt, and the estimated cost with fixtures was close to $2M. Professor J.M. Young from the College of Hawaii supervised the construction.

Called "the most artistic and distinctive commercial building in any land of the Pacific", it was in the shape of a quadrangle with a large open courtyard in the center with a large fountain. Built solely of reinforced concrete, the outside was covered in enameled architectural terra cotta tile in various tints of "Pompeian red". Much of the interior was constructed of glazed tile in "French grey".

The building housed the hardware department on Merchant Street, the grocery department on Alakea Street, the offices and dry goods departments on Bishop Street, with the shipping and receiving on Queen Street. In addition to 7 electric passenger and freight elevators it had 5 spiral chute conveyors from the upper floors to the shipment area.

There was no basement, but the building did have a large flat roof garden covered with floor tile to be used as a place for employee recreation and visitor observation.

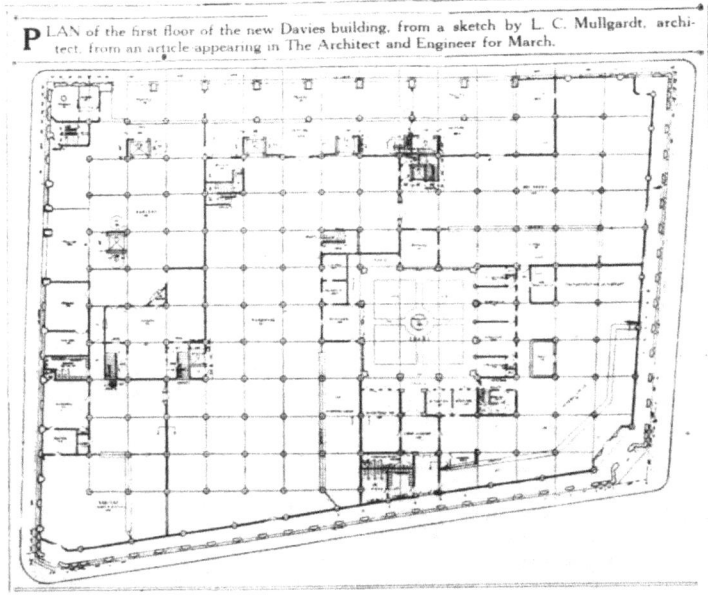

The Honolulu Advertiser, April 14, 1920

The Honolulu Star-Bulletin, November 22, 1921

The Honolulu Advertiser, December 22, 1920

The T.H. Davies Building was ready for occupancy on November 15, 1921 and was erected as memorial to the late Theopholis Harris Davies by his son, T. Clive Davies.

Theo. H. Davies & Co., Ltd.
Founded in 1845

FROM the days when Honolulu was a drowsy little village to the present time when she takes her place among the metropolitan communities of the world; from the time of whaling fleets to the days when the finest boats of the Pacific call at her door; from a tiny store in 1845 to one of the finest, largest and most modern business homes—that in a few words tells the history of Theo. H. Davies and Co., Ltd.

What is today Theo. H. Davies and Co., Ltd., had its beginning in 1845 when R. C. Janion, under the name of Starkey, Janion and Company opened in a tiny store in what was then a very thinly settled business district. This firm was really a branch of the Liverpool firm of James Starkey and Company and so continued until the year 1852 when the partnership between Mr. R. C. Janion and Mr. James Starkey was dissolved and the business was taken over by Mr. Janion in his own name, but in association with Mr. W. L. Green, who later became a partner, the firm then taking the name of Janion, Green and Company.

From the very beginning of the Honolulu branch considerable business was done, considering the times and conditions of commerce. Old records tell of the frequent shipments of large sums of money and the receiving and distributing to San Francisco and other ports, great quantities of hides, tallow, pulu, beef, sugar and other island products.

At this time the Honolulu offices were located in a small building on Kaahumanu street. In 1857 Theo. H. Davies arrived in the islands from England after a trip around the Horn and by way of San Francisco, and became affiliated with the firm of Janion, Green and Co. Later to become the dominant personality in the firm and one of the business powers of the territory. In 1865 Mr. Davies took over the business in his own name. By his personal associations he was able to secure large investments of capital for the development of different sugar enterprises in which he was interested. From this date begins the great expansion and progress of the firm.

The upper picture shows the present building of Theo. H. Davies & Co., Ltd.

Lower—The first class of the company located on the corner of Kaahumanu and Queen streets about 1888. Reading from left to right are: Rhea Lea, W. H. Baird, Alexander Cockburn, H. W. M. Mist, the center figure with derby is Theo. H. Davies, E. W. Holdsworth, W. F. Wilson, Hay Woodhouse, David Morton, Wm. Pennegelly and P. D. Kellett.

Oval picture shows the late Theo. H. Davies.

In 1882 Mr. T. R. Walker was admitted to partnership, the firm name being T. H. Davies and Co. Three years later F. M. Swanzy was admitted as a partner and in 1894 the firm was incorporated with Mr. Davies as managing director.

As sugar factors. Theo. H. Davies & Company, Limited, represent eight Hawaiian plantations. They conduct a large wholesale merchandise business and are financial agents of the Honolulu Iron Works Company, the Pearl City Fruit Company, Ltd., the Waianae Lime Company, Ltd., the Kukaiau Ranch Company. They represent various: fire, accident and marine insurance companies. The firm first introduced the fire insurance business into the Islands, as agents for the Northern Assurance Co., London. They have for many years been agents for Lloyds. The company also represents the Canadian-Australasian Royal Mail Line, the Cunard Steamship Co. and the Canadian Pacific Railway Company.

The company's staff of employees in Honolulu numbers about 400 persons, besides which it employs a considerable number at its branch establishment in Hilo, Hawaii, and in New York and San Francisco.

OFFICERS AND MEMBERS OF THEO. H. DAVIES & CO., LTD.

President and Managing Director	T. Clive Davies
Vice-Pres. and Resident Managing Director	E. H. Wodehouse
Vice-Pres. and Managing Director	Geo. F. Davies
Treasurer and Director	John E. Russell
Secretary	W. C. Shields
Director	E. D. Tenney
Director	Geo. H. Angus
Director	J. N. S. Williams
Director	L. M. Judd
Director	D. F. McGarrison
Director	Thomas Guard

Theo. H. Davies & Co.
LIMITED

The Honolulu Advertiser, February 24, 1926

"Architecture is not something one may discard as a suit of clothes out of fashion, and for that reason, the company has been extremely solicitous that the structure it is about to erect shall be of a type which will do lasting honor to the city." – Louis Christian Mullgardt

c.1965

That "lasting honor" lasted 49 years. The building was demolished to make way for the 22-story $24M Davies Pacific Center designed by Grosvenor Development with Au, Cutting & Smith, completed in 1972.

2023

S.M. DAMON BUILDING / BISHOP BANK

901-937 Bishop Street

1924 – 1993
Architect/Builder: John Mason Young / Ralph E. Woolley

Built for the headquarters of the Bank of Bishop and the Bishop Trust in 1924, the S.M. Damon building was designed by John Mason Young and built by Ralph E. Woolley for $750,000.

This was a most prestigious address, and by November 1925 it also housed the offices of architects C.W. Dickey, Robert Miller, Herbert Cohen, and contractors E.J. Lord and J.L. Young Engineering Company.

It was named for Samuel Mills Damon, who was born in Honolulu in 1845. His father was the pastor of the Seamen's Bethel and the founder of *The Friend*. During the reign of King Kalākaua, Damon was the Minister of Finance, and he was one of the founders of the Bishop Trust and was the head of Bishop Bank for many years.

THE S. M. DAMON BUILDING

The Honolulu Advertiser, November 9, 1925

The building was "classical Ionic in design" with a finish of "granitex terra cotta" in a soft tint to harmonize with the adjacent buildings of T.H. Davies, Castle & Cooke, and the Young Building.

The building was "absolutely fireproof" with doors and trimmings of hollow steel with an olive green finish. There were 6,000 safety deposit boxes in the vault behind a door that weighed 23 tons.

As one enters the main corridor from the King street entrance, the impression is one of distance and height, for this corridor is 120 feet long and 30 feet high. The interior treatment is a Corinthian style of architecture, with tall, fluted columns and heavily molded cornices. The floor of the main corridor is of grey and pink Tennessee marble and the wainscoting is of pink Tennessee marble, with a finish of verd antique. Delicately tinted art glass forms the ceiling and the whole is lighted by artistic bronze chandeliers. The color scheme throughout the main banking room is old ivory with a slightly wiped out brownish tint giving soft neutral contrasts.

The Honolulu Advertiser, November 9, 1925

In 1957 the ceiling was lowered and the massive central lobby was "modernized".

The Honolulu Advertiser, March 4, 1957

In August 1992, the First Hawaiian Bank (formerly Bishop National Bank) announced plans to demolish the building to make way for the $175M 30-story First Hawaiian Center designed by New York architects Kohn Pedersen Fox.

This created an uproar in the historic preservation community, but the bank countered by saying it was made of "plaster" and not massive stone blocks, there was no way to add parking, the new design would have 43% open space, and there would be an art gallery with local artists keeping 100% of the proceeds. The S.M. Damon building fell to the wrecking ball in 1993.

2022

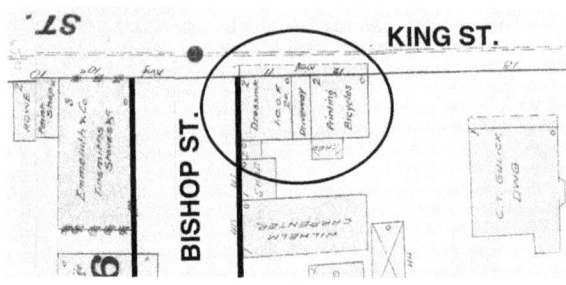

1899 Dakin Map

The S.M. Damon Building was built on the site of Way's Block, built in 1883 by Lewish Way. It was a large 2-story wooden building with a covered driveway leading back to Way's carpentry shop and some with sort of heavy coating on the wooden siding. It was demolished in 1924.

Hawaiian Historical Society

The upstairs was known as Harmony Lodge, a meeting place for Polynesian Encampment No.1 I.O.O.F, Hawaiian Council No. 689 American Legion of Honor, and the Knights of Pythias. It was also the first meeting place of the Christian Church and Honolulu Lodge No. 616 of the Benevolent and Protective Order of Elks.

The extension of Bishop Street went between the Emmeluth Building and Way's Block.

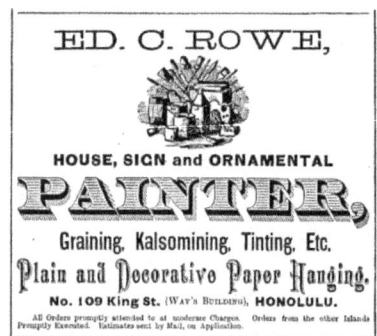

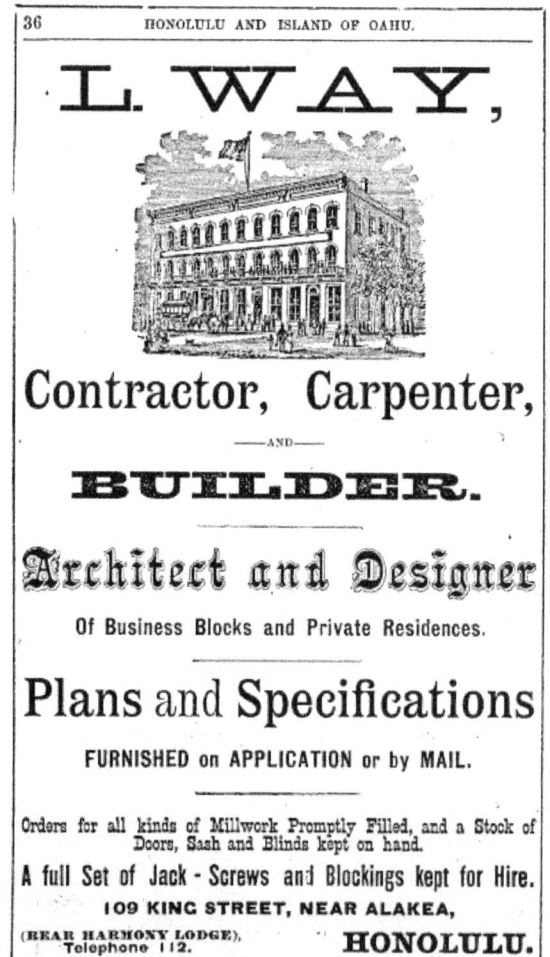

ALEXANDER YOUNG BUILDING

1001-1091 Bishop Street

1903 – 1981

Architect/Builder: George W. Percy, Henry H. Meyers, Oliver G. Traphagen / William Mutch

Designed by Oakland architects George W. Percy and Henry H. Meyers, and built by William Mutch, this was the largest building built in Hawaii up to that date, with an estimated cost of $750,000. The mauka end was a hotel and the makai end housed offices and shops. Its roof garden was known worldwide.

Construction began on October 1, 1900, with clearing and grubbing and foundation excavation by the firm of Vincent & Belcher from San Francisco. The blasting operations resulted in lots of flying coral, some of which broke windows in nearby buildings and houses, and one blast frightened a horse and upset a carriage, throwing two women into the muddy street. The excavators also uncovered a skeleton with a Kamehameha III belt buckle and some boar's teeth.

Bishop Street was created through the former Bishop property to provide a long front access to the hotel. Initially planned to be private, it was later extended to Halekauwila Street, and later to Beretania Street. The verandas and two or three feet of the Waikiki wing of the Arlington Hotel, formerly the Abner Paki and Charles Bishop residence, were shaved off to make room for the new street.

> **$176,000 LAND TRANSFER**
>
> Beautiful Town Homestead of Dr. McGrew Is Sold.
>
> Hon. Alex. Young and Bishop Estate Purchasers —Magnificent New Business Block— Sixty Foot Street
>
> The old homestead of Dr. J. S. McGrew on Hotel street has been sold to Hon. Alexander Young and the Bishop Estate for a sum aggregating $175,000; of this amount Dr. McGrew will receive $150,000. This means the passing of the old social landmarks of old Honolulu made famous in the local and political history of the past three decades. The march of improvements following annexation will soon be seen in the block bounded by Hotel, Alakea, King and Fort streets, as will be seen by the folowing brief interviews given the Bulletin by Hon. Mr. Young and Mr. Dodge.
>
> Hon. Alexander Young was seen today about the intended improvements on the McGrew property just purchased. He said: "The Bishop Estate and myself will put a street through from Hotel to King streets. The new street will be sixty feet wide. I will build on the East side of the new street, to be named hereafter, a row of buildings of the very best class, both fire and earthquake proof, with all the latest modern improvements. The buildings to be erected will have steel frames, and all the floor will be either of concrete or of tiling; they will be four stories in height and fitted with improved elevators and the block will have an electric plant of its own. The length of the street to be occupied by these buildings will be 458 feet frontage on the new street, with a frontage of 61 feet on King street and 151 feet on Hotel street.
>
> "As yet I have made no definite arrangements as to plans or style of architecture; but while at the Coast I will look into these matters very closely and prepare for the immediate erection of the buildings. Wm. Mutch will have the control and superintendence of construction and will probably visit the Coast with me in two months from now for the purpose investigating the latest methods of construction adopted on the Mainland."
>
> Mr. Dodge of the Bishop Estate said: "The Bishop estate retains control of the entire frontage on the Ewa side of the new street, amounting to 439 feet, the frontage on King street of 195 feet, and that on Hotel street of 82 feet; this land the estate proposes to subdivide in the near future. The Arlington House property will be vacated on the 31st of next August with the view to the erection of new buildings. A new hotel project is being considered, and, if proper terms can be secured, a new hotel building will be erected upon the north corner of King and the new street.
>
> *Evening Bulletin, May 15, 1900*

The 75,000 pieces of iron and steel for the building came from the Milliken Brothers in New York City and were shipped around Cape Horn on the steamship *Hawaiian* and *Oregonian*. The large stone blocks for the foundation were cut in California by John D. McGilvray and brought on the 4-masted schooner *Rosamond* and the schooner *Mary E. Foster*; some were the largest ever brought to Hawaii, weighing up to seven tons apiece.

> The Alexander Young building is designed for a hotel building and stores. Being in the heart of the town, it will make a striking appearance when finished, and from a business point of view it will be a great improvement, though the removal of old landmarks and the felling of beautiful trees must cause a pang of regret.
>
> *The Hawaiian Gazette, November 26, 1901*

Unfortunately, architect George W. Percy died suddenly on December 14, 1900. Percy had finished the plans, but they brought in Oliver Traphagen in case there was any additional work needed.

> O. G. Traphagen has been appointed contractor to complete the work on the Young building. The original contractor died in San Francisco a short time ago.
>
> *The Hawaiian Star, March 23, 1901*

The name blocks on the mauka end of the building saying "The Alexander Young Building" were raised and installed on January 17, 1902.

W.P. Fuller & Company from San Francisco was responsible for installing $50,000 worth of windows in September 1902.

The first tenant, a cigar merchant named David Lawrence, moved in on October 4, 1902, even while glaziers, painters, plasterers, and finishers were still at work.

The hotel had 192 rooms, with $25,000 in mahogany and oak furniture from Grand Rapids, Michigan, personally selected by manager H. Wingate Lake and shipped around The Horn.

Grand opening day was July 31, 1903, with the building bedecked in American and Hawaiian flags. It was a huge gala affair, with flowers, colored lights, music, food, and dancing. The *Honolulu Advertiser* declared, "New Hotel is Like a Palace".

In 1911 and 1912 Percy's former partner Henry H. Meyers, drew plans for some additions and alterations, including a new sketch of the lobby.

Alexander Young was born in Blackburn, Scotland, located about halfway between Edinburgh and Glasgow, in 1832.

Initially working for Alexander Chaplin & Company in Glasgow and Anderson & Company in London, he went to Vancouver in 1860 to build a sawmill.

In 1865 he and his family went to Hawaii where he ran a foundry and machine shop in Hilo with William Lidgate.

By 1869 Young was the manager of the Honolulu Iron Works and also the owner of several sugar companies.

From 1887 to 1892 he served in the House of Nobles and was briefly the Minister of the Interior from late 1899 to mid-1900.

> A partnership has been formed by Von Hamm & Young, who will do business in Honolulu as commission agents and brokers. The members of the new firm are C. Von Hamm, lately of the firm of E. Hoffschlaeger & Co., and Archibald Young, a son of Hon. Alexander Young, the well-known planter and capitalist.
>
> *The Independent, January 19, 1899*

In 1899 Young created a new company with his son Archibald Alfred Young and new son-in-law Conrad Carl von Hamm that was called the von Hamm-Young Company, capitalized at $100,000. They initially sold American and European dry goods, notions, saddles, glassware, carriages, crockery, hats and shoes, along with Union Gas Engines, Domestic and New Pacific sewing machines, and they were also agents for the Lancashire Insurance Company and Baloise Fire Insurance Company.

In 1904 they started selling Oldsmobile automobiles and quickly added Winton, Reo, Haynes, Stevens-Duryea, Pope-Hartford, Thomas Flyer, White Steamer, Mitchell, Stoddard-Dayton, Buick, Anderson Electric, Paige, Kissel, Stutz, Scripps-Booth, Chandler, Packard, Buick, Cadillac, and GMC. They built a large garage in back of the Young Hotel and converted the L.B. Kerr building into a showroom.

They later added Otis Elevator, Marshall Field, Frigidaire, Michelin, plus several more insurance companies including Lloyds of London. The company became the Hawaii Corporation in 1964.

Young has been called "the father of the hotel industry" in Hawaii since he later also owned the Moana Hotel and the Royal Hawaiian Hotel on Hotel Street.

The Honolulu Advertiser,
August 1, 1903

Hawaii State Archives

Hawaii State Archives

The Alexander Young Building was built on the site of Dr. R. W. Wood's large coral house on Hotel Street built in 1847. Dr. Wood came to Hawaii from Boston to practice medicine and later rented the house to Commissioner Pierce and General McCook, and then sold it to Dr. John McGrew in 1866.

The McGrews were famous for their hospitality and the mansion hosted many social events for politicians and dignitaries. It was decorated with curios from the Orient and had a suite of heavy oak furniture that had belonged to Louis XVIII.

William R. Bliss, one of the first guests of the Hawaiian Hotel, described the McGrew house and grounds:

"Here is one I admire, a large, square house, standing alone, built of gray coral blocks, pointed with white cement, two stories high, surrounded on each side by a wide veranda over which juts the peaked roof. No chimneys mar it. The rooms are large and lofty. The doors and windows open upon the verandas, and command views of grass, flowers and trees. Between the cottage and the street is a fountain of water, surrounded by large-leafed, tropical plants, sea shell and roses. A winding, tasselated pavement leads to from the gate. Jets of water are showering the grass that surrounds it, out of which large rubber trees rise higher than the roof, their thick leaves glistening like mirrors in the sun. A line of orange and banana trees hedges the yard. Aside, near the gate, is a miniature cottage with a peaked roof, porch and blinds; this is the doctor's office.

Dr. McGrew had first come to Hawaii while on a trip around the world to help recover from the Civil War and decided to stay. The McGrews lived here for 34 years until retiring and selling the property to Alexander Young for $150,000.

Young sold off the wooden buildings, temporarily kept the doctor's office for the contractors, and demolished the coral house to re-use the stone elsewhere.

Paul Emmert, 1854

The 28-story Pauahi Tower of Bishop Square is on the site of the 1847 Wood/McGrew house.

Photo by H.L. Chase, 1870

McGrew residence and doctor's office, c.1880

McGrew gardens, c.1880

In 1969 the Hawaii Corporation began converting the hotel rooms of the Alexander Young Building into offices as hotel demand moved to Waikiki.

Although listed on the National Register of Historic Places in 1980, new owners Northwest Mutual Life Insurance Company decided to demolish the building in 1981 in spite of valiant efforts and pleas from the community, including an emergency restraining order from the Hawaii Supreme Court to preserve and restore the building. Demolition began on July 7, 1981 and was completed two months later. It was replaced with Bishop Square's 28-story Pauahi Tower and Tamarind Park designed by Franklin Gray and Chapman Cobeen Desai & Sakata along with landscape architect James C. Hubbard.

c.1915

The same view in 2022

LONG'S DRUGS
1088 Bishop Street / 141 S. Hotel
1954 – 1981
Architect/Builder: Rothwell & Lester / E.E. Black

Honolulu Star-Bulletin, March 29, 1954

The Long's Drug Store building was built on the site of the former Richard W. Laine residence, a 1-story frame house here from at least 1885 to 1899. When Bishop Street was constructed in 1900 the site became a taxi stand at the corner of Bishop and Hotel streets.

Laine was born in Hallowell, Maine, in 1828 and came to Hawaii in 1872 as the purser for the steamship *Nebraska*. He became the Spanish Vice-Consul to Hawaii in 1880 and the later the consul for Mexico. He was also the Commissioner of Deeds for the State of California for the Hawaiian Islands, and General Agent for the Pacific Mutual Life Insurance Company.

Designed by Rothwell & Lester, built by E.E. Black, and opened on March 29, 1954, at a cost of $150,000 for building, fixtures and lease, this was the 10th Long's Drug store and the first one in Hawaii. Long's was founded by Joseph M. & Tom Long in Oakland, California in 1938.

The building was demolished 27 years later to make way for the Executive Center complex. Long's temporarily relocated to Union Street and then moved back into the Executive Center on Hotel Street in October 1983 where they still do business today.

2022

MONSARRAT BUILDING

1129-1141 Bishop Street

1929 – present
Architect/Builder: Fred W. Williams / John L. Cliff

Formally opened on May 8, 1929, this building was designed and constructed for the Bailey Furniture Store "embodying the latest ideas in retail display and merchandising of furniture". It had 17,400 square feet of floor space, 2-stories plus a mezzanine and a basement, and was completed in 77 days at a cost of $40,000. This was their showroom and offices; the Honolulu Brewery building was their warehouse.

The Honolulu Advertiser, May 8, 1929

Harry B. Bailey was born in Canada in 1887 and came to Hawaii with his parents in 1894 when he was 12 years old.

He attended 'Iolani School and initially worked for Theo. H. Davies and Alexander & Baldwin before becoming manager of his father's company, Bailey Furniture, in 1915.

In addition to civic work Bailey was also an avid amateur sportsman who enjoyed soccer, baseball, yachting, and rowing.

Paul Emmert, 1854

2022

Abraham Fayerweather's house was at the corner of Union and Adams Lane in the 1840's. It became the residence of Captain Thomas Spencer in the 1850's and it was later owned by Marcus Douglas Monsarrat, the son of Marcus Cumming Monsarrat and Elizabeth Jane Dowsett Monsarrat who lived immediately ewa, where the Jade Building sits today. The M.D. Monsarrat house was demolished in December 1928.

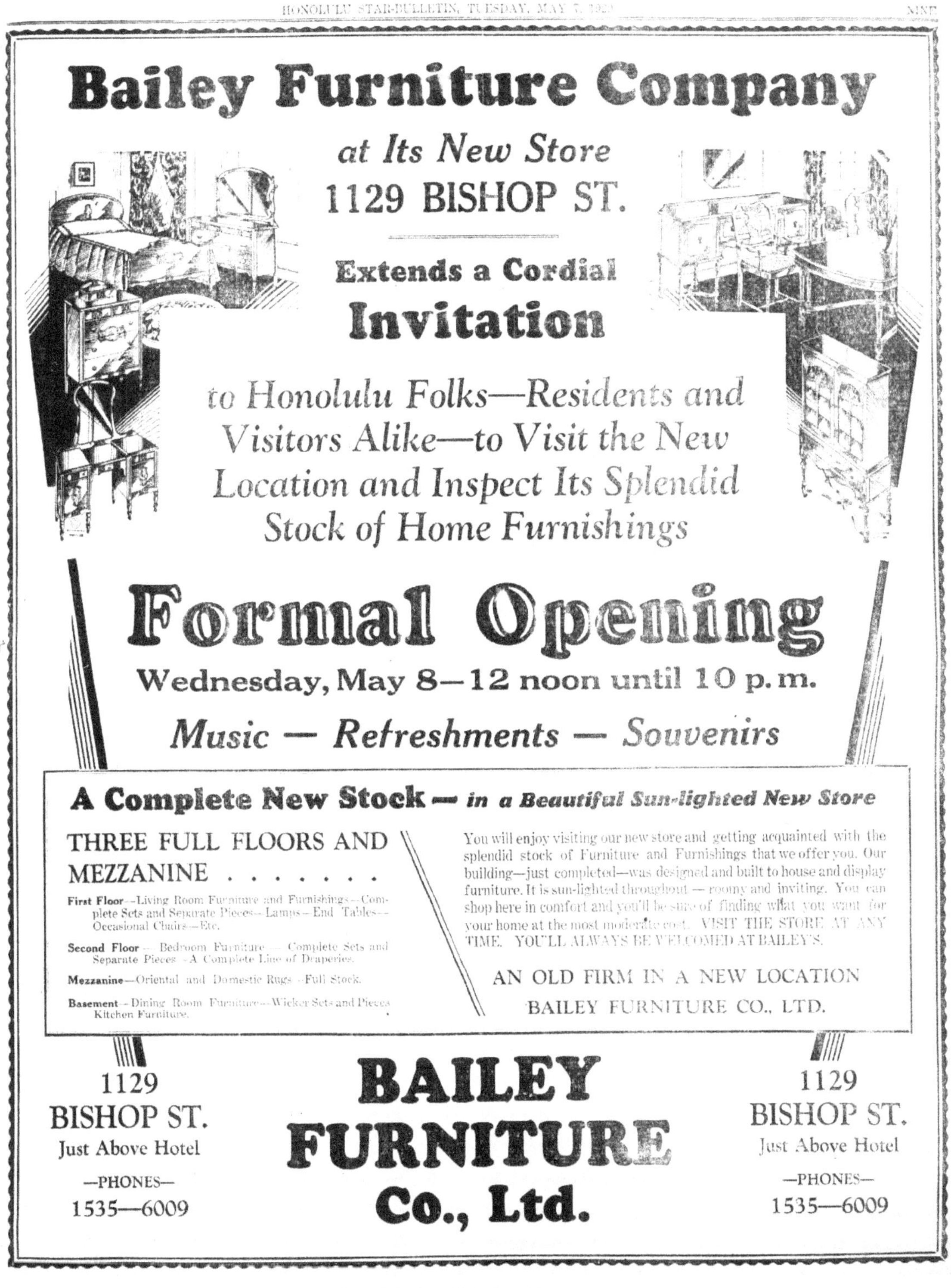

HONOLULU STAR-BULLETIN, TUESDAY, MAY 7, 1929
NINE
Bailey Furniture Company
at Its New Store
1129 BISHOP ST.
Extends a Cordial
Invitation
to Honolulu Folks—Residents and Visitors Alike—to Visit the New Location and Inspect Its Splendid Stock of Home Furnishings
Formal Opening
Wednesday, May 8—12 noon until 10 p.m.
Music — Refreshments — Souvenirs
A Complete New Stock — in a Beautiful Sun-lighted New Store
THREE FULL FLOORS AND MEZZANINE . . . .
First Floor—Living Room Furniture and Furnishings—Complete Sets and Separate Pieces—Lamps—End Tables—Occasional Chairs—Etc.
Second Floor — Bedroom Furniture — Complete Sets and Separate Pieces—A Complete Line of Draperies.
Mezzanine—Oriental and Domestic Rugs—Full Stock.
Basement—Dining Room Furniture—Wicker Sets and Pieces Kitchen Furniture.
You will enjoy visiting our new store and getting acquainted with the splendid stock of Furniture and Furnishings that we offer you. Our building—just completed—was designed and built to house and display furniture. It is sun-lighted throughout — roomy and inviting. You can shop here in comfort and you'll be sure of finding what you want for your home at the most moderate cost. VISIT THE STORE AT ANY TIME. YOU'LL ALWAYS BE WELCOMED AT BAILEY'S.
AN OLD FIRM IN A NEW LOCATION
BAILEY FURNITURE CO., LTD.
1129 BISHOP ST.
Just Above Hotel
—PHONES—
1535—6009
BAILEY FURNITURE Co., Ltd.
1129 BISHOP ST.
Just Above Hotel
—PHONES—
1535—6009

Honolulu Star-Bulletin, May 7, 1929

JADE BUILDING

1146-1150 Bishop Street

1941 – present

Architect/Builder: Alfred Preis (Dahl & Conrad) / Pacific Construction Co.

NEW DOWNTOWN BUILDING: Construction is scheduled to start next week on this new downtown office building at the corner of Bishop and Union Sts. The building, owned by Mrs. Annie Lan Nyuk Chang, will be constructed of reinforced concrete and hollow tile. Carrara glass will ornament the exterior. Verticle neons will illuminate the building's curved exterior surfaces. Each of the four offices will have two main ground floor entrances, one on the Bishop St. side, the other on Union St. Architects for the project are Dahl & Conrad, Associated. Alfred Preis.

Honolulu Star-Bulletin, February 8, 1941

This unique modern-style building was designed by 30-year-old Austrian architect Alfred Preis when he was working with Bjarne C. Dahl and Conrad W. Conrad. It was built of reinforced concrete and hollow tile by Pacific Construction Company for a cost $30,000.

The building originally had "fine woods and colors on the inside, and jade carrara glass on the outside making the base, with four offices and a roof garden on top".

It was built for Mrs. Annie Lan Nyuk Chang, the wife of Dr. Dai Yen Chang. The cornerstone was laid in May 1941, with "traditional ceremonies celebrating completion of the roof".

Designed by the Office of

DAHL & CONRAD

Associated

ALFRED PREIS

303 Stangenwald Bldg.

$30,000 Office Building To Be Open Soon

Construction is in the finishing phase on the new $30,000 office building at Bishop and Union Sts., owned by Mrs. Ann Lan Nyuk Chang, wife of Dr. Dai Yen Chang. The cornerstone was laid a week ago, with traditional ceremonies celebrating completion of the roof.

The Honolulu Advertiser, June 1, 1941

Annie Lan Nyuk Chang was born in Hawaii in 1894 and married Dr. Dai Yen Chang in 1915. Dr Chang was born in Honolulu in 1888 and obtained his DDS degree in 1911 after studying at the University of Southern California and Northwestern University in Chicago. He was reportedly the first Chinese DDS in Honolulu.

He was also president of the Union Syndicate, a $100,000 realty corporation, vice president and director of the Fidelity Investment Company, and he was also a real estate investor.

Dr. Chang was the first person of Chinese ancestry to be elected to the Honolulu Board of Supervisors in 1926. He was fluent in Chinese, Hawaiian, and English.

He worked hard to establish peaceful relations among the peoples and nations of the Pacific and was also very active in supporting medical and famine relief efforts in China.

The building was designed by the architectural firm of Dahl, Conrad & Preis – Bjarne C. Dahl, Conrad W. Conrad, and Alfred E. Preis. Starting in 1935, Dahl and Conrad designed many homes and buildings throughout Hawaii, many were in the streamlined Art Moderne style.

Bjarne C. Dahl was the architect, originally from Chicago, and had come to Hawaii to superintend the construction of the YWCA Building, and he later became the architect for the Territorial Public Works Department. Conrad W. Cornfeldt spent two years as an architecture student at the University of Southern California, and with only $100 dollars he bought a $75 ticket to Hawaii in 1933. Since people often called him "Mr. Conrad" he eventually made that his legal name. He teamed up with "Barney" Dahl and designed many houses in Waikiki plus the Queen Theater and the Kau Kau Corner.

After escaping from Austria with his wife in 1939, Alfred Preis was offered an architectural job in Hawaii with Dahl & Conrad. The Jade Building was the first commercial building designed by Preis who described it in a later interview as "something of a curiosity" being clad in green Carrara Glass, and because:

> "I was trained in the metric system. What I did not know, really, was the scale in the metric system and the yard system. So this building became rather queer. All the windows were narrower."

Preis's most famous design is the USS *Arizona* Memorial in Pearl Harbor, dedicated in 1962 by President John F. Kennedy. Although initially criticized for looking like "a squashed milk carton", Preis responded saying: *"Wherein the structure sags in the center but stands strong and vigorous at the ends, expresses initial defeat and ultimate victory.... The overall effect is one of serenity. Overtones of sadness have been omitted to permit the individual to contemplate his own personal responses... his innermost feelings."*

The USS *Arizona* memorial is a major Oahu tourist destination attracting 1.5 million visitors a year.

Paul Emmert, 1854

The Jade Building is on the site of the residence of James Dowsett, built in 1847.

Dowsett's father, Samuel, had built a house immediately makai in 1832, but he was lost at sea in 1834 when James Dowsett, the eldest child, was only 5 years old at the time.

James Isaac Dowsett was born in 1829 and was a childhood friend of Kamehameha IV, Kamehameha V, and Lunalilo.

When he was 12 years old, Dowsett went to work for the Hudson's Bay Company while still attending school.

He went on to become one of Hawaii's most beloved and trusted businessmen. He was involved in whaling, lumber, shipping, and ranching, and was the first to bring Aberdeen Angus cattle to Hawaii.

Dowsett spoke fluent Hawaiian and was called "Kimo Pelekane" (Jim the Englishman). He was also a historian and biographer, and "could always supply day and date and all required details". He was one of the founders of the British Club and was a trustee of Queen's Hospital.

Dowsett also mentored and helped young Chung Kun Ai get started in business, and Dowsett's desk is still a prized possession at City Mill.

"Mr. Dowsett was a man of kindly, genial disposition. It was a habit of his for a number of years to make a trip to Waikiki each evening in a street car. It was genuine treat to be a passenger with him... It was a study for one not acquainted with him to watch him in the car and to see all the natives and even the Chinese pay their respects to him on entering the car. Everybody knew who he was and strangers liked him in advance, while those who came to speaking terms with him valued the privilege."

This photograph was taken in 1870 by H.L. Chase from the bell tower of the fire engine house and shows the Dowsett / Monsarrat house at the lower right corner.

The large building with the dormer windows across Union Street is the former house of Stephen Reynolds.

Hawaiian Historical Society

The Dowsett House became the home of Ireland-born Marcus Cumming Monsarrat when he married James Dowsett's sister, Elizabeth Jane. Monsarrat was banished from Hawaii in 1857 for "having perpetuated a grievous injury" to the royal family. Something to do with being caught by Prince Lot in Princess Victoria Kamamalu's bedroom in a compromising position and hastily "arranging his pantaloons".

Monsarrat returned anyway and was banished again. His sentence was finally reduced to 7 years due to the King being "moved by a feeling of deep sympathy" for the Monsarrat family.

There had been talk of arranging a marriage between Victoria Kamamalu and David Kalākaua, but this incident may have been a major factor in ending those plans.

The house was poetically described by *The Advertiser* on September 25, 1921:

> "Like a leaf drifting serenely in the center of a lake whose shores hum with industry, right in the center of Honolulu, surrounded by commerce, education and art, there is a bit of rare old Honolulu, the Honolulu of the thirties of the last century."

It had beautiful Chinese tiles brought from China that were used around the foundation instead of lattice, plus Chinese flagstones.

By December of 1926, Japanese carpenters had bought the house for lumber and were ripping it apart in preparation for the extension of Bishop Street which plowed right through the property.

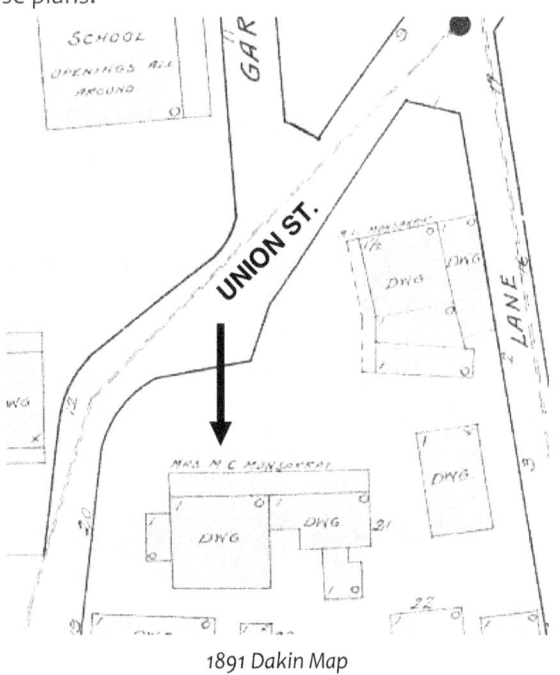

1891 Dakin Map

Union Street side, 2022

Bishop Street side, 2022

ASSOCIATED OIL SERVICE STATION

1161 Bishop Street

1934 – c.1968?
Architect/Builder: James M. Tanaka

1935

ASSOCIATED OIL WILL HAVE ANOTHER STATION

A permit has been issued to the Associated Oil Co. for the construction of a service station at Bishop St. and Adams lane, the estimated cost being $2,600. J. Tanaka is the contractor.

Honolulu Star-Bulletin, June 9, 1934

Perhaps the world's only gas station with a coconut palm tree growing through the roof?

It was built in 1934 by James Masato Tanaka for the Associated Oil Company as part of the Ben Hollinger Service Station at the corner of Bishop Street and Adams Lane.

In the photo above you can see the offices of the Catholic Church, Sacred Heart Convent, and the bell tower of the Cathedral Basilica of Our Lady of Peace across Bishop Street.

Abraham Fayerweather's house, brought around the Horn from Boston c.1840, was mostly on this triangular tract. His daughter, Julia, was married to Chinese millionaire Chun Afong with whom she had 16 children.

2022

REYNOLDS HOUSE / SACRED HEART CONVENT

1160-1164 Bishop Street

1830's – 1973

Architect/Builder: unknown

Built sometime in the 1830's by George Wood, this 1-story coral building was the office and evening dancing school of Stephen Reynolds.

Paul Emmert, 1854

A wooden second story was added after it was purchased by the Catholic Mission for $5,500 in 1860.

Photo by H.L. Chase, 1870

A new $42,000 3-story convent was designed by architect E.A.P. Newcomb and built by Bowler and Ingvorsen in 1926.

"In planning the building the walls of the original coral building, built some 50 years ago, are still retained. The old building was of coral for the first story and wood above. The new building is built around the old coral building and uses the old coral walls in its first story." – (The Honolulu Advertiser, July 31, 1919)

Honolulu Advertiser, June 14, 1926

It was demolished in 1973 for the $10M 16-story 1164 Bishop office building designed by the Grosvenor Design Group and constructed by Hawaiian Dredging & Construction Company in 1975.

PATTEN BUILDING

1177 Bishop Street

1927 – c.1966

Architect/Builder: Rothwell, Kangeter & Lester / J.L. Young Engineering Co.

YEAR END BUILDING PERMITS ARE ISSUED

The largest building permit of the week was that issued to Patten company, Ltd. for a $15,000 two-story, concrete addition to its store building at Bishop and Union streets. Rothwell, Kangeter and Lester are architects and J. L. Young Engineering Co., the contractor.

Honolulu Advertiser, January 2, 1927

Founded in 1909, Patten Co. Ltd. specialized in office supplies and writing materials. Their main store was at 117 S. Hotel Street and they built a "large, modern concrete paper warehouse" a little further up on Union Street in 1923 for wholesale paper service, replacing the St. Louis Alumni Association Building.

Adjacent Pacific Hotel / St. Louis Alumni Building, new Patten warehouse

Patten added the corner building in 1927 for their office equipment department. From 1946 to 1956 it was Weiller Furniture, known for "distinctive rattan" furniture. Famed swimmer Duke Kahanamoku was one of the directors of Weiller Corp. Ltd. It was later the Territorial Sales store, and then the Petland store. The site now the $13M 17-story Hawaiian Telephone Company (Hawaiian Telcom) Building designed by Wimberly Whisenand Allison & Tong, and built in 1971 by Reed & Martin.

A Modernized PATTEN'S

Completing Twenty Years of Service to Hawaii

—a modernized and renovated Patten's invites your inspection tomorrow. Remodelled with the thought of better, more efficient service to our customers, greater floor space has made it possible for you to shop more easily, more comfortably. We believe you will like the new Patten's—and invite you to make it your headquarters on shopping tours downtown.

In planning the new arrangement, every consideration was given to making easy your shopping requirements in Patten's. Departmentalization has been brought to a new high in this respect. Whatever your needs in Patten's, the merchandise is conveniently displayed, easily accessible.

STATIONERY DEPT.
By putting in a mezzanine, for office personnel, floor space for the Stationery and Gift department has been almost doubled. Above is the view from the front door showing mezzanine arrangement.

STATIONERY DEPT. SPECIALS
FOR ONE WEEK ONLY

Suede
BRIDGE TABLE COVERS
Regular 85c value
69c

PLAYING CARDS 20c per deck

"Smithcraft"
IMITATION LEATHER
WASTEPAPER BASKETS
FILES
CIGARETTE BOXES
TRAYS
MEMORANDUMS
and many other articles.
Regular values $1.75.
$1.00

BOOK DEPARTMENT
The Book department display space has been greatly increased, as has the Rental Library. Compact floor displays and twice as many shelves allow easy selection of your favorite books.

BOOK DEPARTMENT SPECIALS
FOR ONE WEEK ONLY

"UNDER HAWAIIAN SKIES"
A narrative history of the islands.
Regularly priced at $4.00
SPECIAL **$2.95**

POPULAR FICTION
Recent Editions
Regularly priced at 85c
SPECIAL **59c**

One Table of
FICTION and NON-FICTION
REDUCED TO **$1**

Novelty and Gift Department
Taken from the Mezzanine, showing the center display arrangement of novelties and gifts.

LEFT—Housing Patten's Office Equipment and Metal Furniture, and Wholesale Paper offices and warehouse, this building at Bishop and Union Streets is a familiar landmark.

RIGHT—Patten's Office Equipment and Metal Furniture lines are comprehensive and complete. These offices are located at Bishop and Union Streets.

The Honolulu Advertiser, November 7, 1937

CATHOLIC RECTORY

1184 Bishop Street

1928 – c.1971

Architect/Builder: Fred W. Williams / J.L. Young Engineering Company

The Honolulu Advertiser, November 27, 1927

Built by the J.L. Young Engineering Company and designed by Fred W. Williams, this 3-story presbytery was completed in 1928. The construction cost was $71,029.

The building was demolished for the $10M 16-story 1164 Bishop office building developed by Grosvenor International (Hawaii) Ltd and built by Hawaiian Dredging & Construction on behalf of the Catholic Church in 1975.

CATHOLIC MISSION TO BUILD BISHOP ST. PRESBYTERY

The Catholic Mission of Hawaii will build a three-story presbytery on Bishop street mauka of the Sacred Heart convent and back of the Fort street cathedral, it was announced yesterday.

Plans for the structure are now being drawn and will be completed within one week, according to F. W. Williams, architect for the project. Construction of the building will begin about January 1, Williams stated.

The building will front 80 feet on Bishop street and will have a depth of 127 feet. The architecture will be in the modified Mission style. Reinforced concrete construction will be used in the presbytery, which will be a Class A building. Williams estimates that it will take four or five months to build the structure.

The basement of the presbytery will have a large dining hall, a kitchen and several storage rooms. The ground floor will have twelve classrooms and parlors.

On the second floor will be the administration offices. Here will be the bishop's office, the chancellor's office and a waiting room. The second floor will have several lanais, an infirmary, and seven other rooms. On the third floor there will be 12 bedrooms. The building is also to have an elevator.

The Honolulu Advertiser
November 20, 1927

J. L. YOUNG GIVEN CONTRACT TO BUILD CATHOLIC STRUCTURE

Contract for the construction of the new home for Catholic priests which is to be built on Bishop St., mauka of the Convent of Sacred Hearts, has been awarded to the J. L. Young Engineering Co., it was announced this week by F. W. Williams, architect.

The plans call for the construction of a new three-story building. The Young company has agreed to build the structure for $71,029 and to finish the work in 130 days.

Honolulu Star-Bulletin
February 25, 1928

2022

ELI JONES HOUSE

1188 Bishop Street

1832 – 1928

Architect/Builder: unknown

Paul Emmert, 1854

According to historian Thomas G. Thrum, Eli Jones built a 2-story coral residence with 8 rooms here at the corner of Beretania Street and Garden Lane (later Bishop Street) in 1832.

James Makee and Julius Anthon obtained a royal patent to the property from King Kamehameha III in 1851. By the time Paul Emmert was sketching and painting Honolulu's buildings in 1854 it was the residence of Louis Anthon, the Danish Consul.

It changed hands several times before being sold to Bishop Louis Maigret in 1862 for $3,300. It was later incorporated into the 2-story wooden Catholic Mission building and was used as offices.

In 1928, the coral blocks were still in excellent condition but the woodwork was almost completely destroyed by termites. The building was torn down and the land was leased to Western Auto.

Honolulu Star-Bulletin, November 8, 1928

The 36-story $35M Century Square Building on the site was developed by L. Robert Allen in conjunction with the Catholic Church. Designed by Jo Paul Rognstad, it was built by Pacific Construction and completed in 1982.

2022

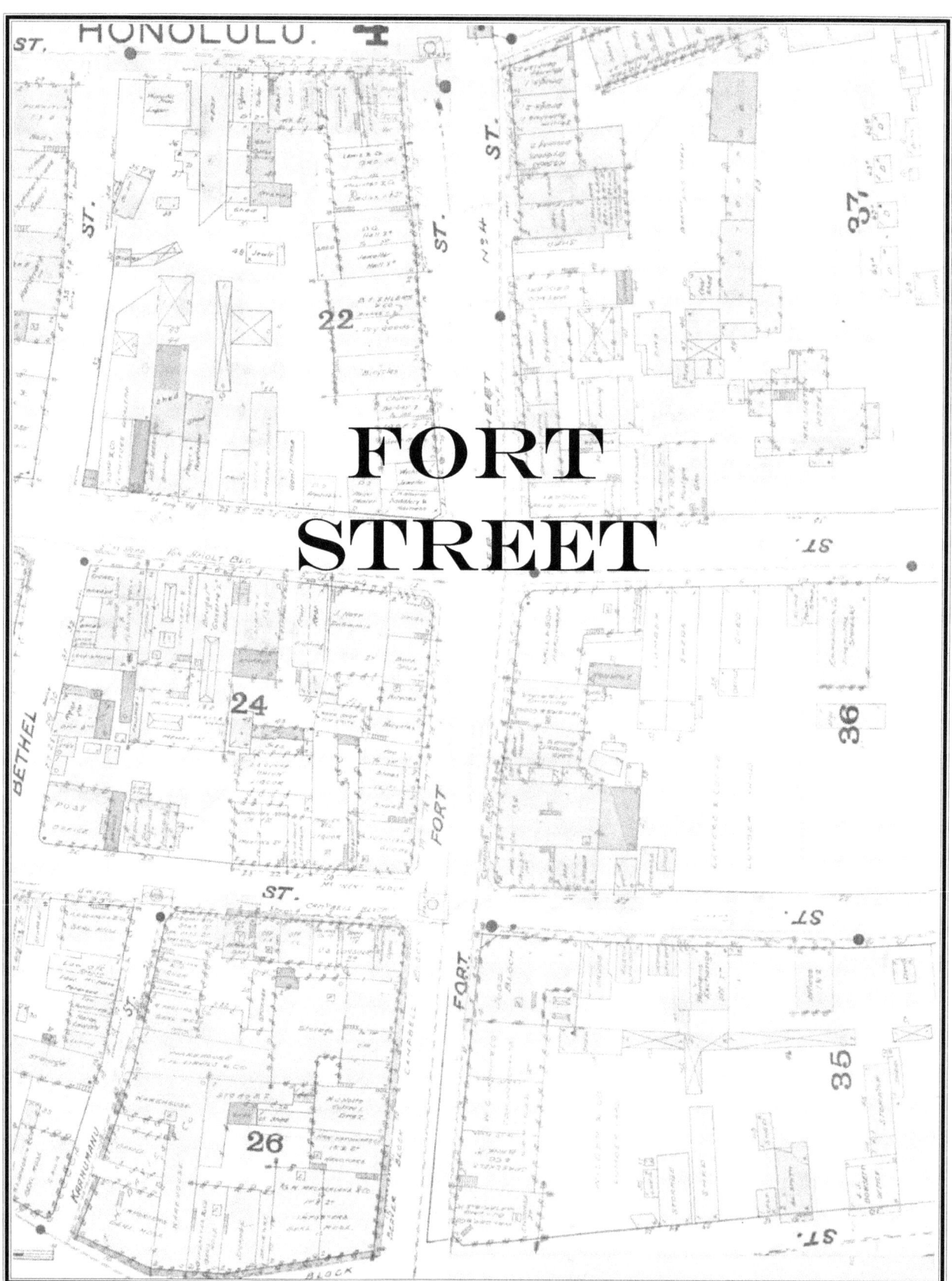

HONOLULU FORT
"Kekuanohu"

Georg Anton Schäffer was a German doctor working with the Russian-American Company and Governor Alexander A. Baranov, the chief executive of the Russian colonies in America. Schäffer was sent to Hawaii in 1815 on the American ship *Isabella* for scientific research and to negotiate compensation for the cargo of the shipwrecked *Bering* that had been seized by Kaua'i's King Kaumuali'i. He was also to determine if Russia could obtain a monopoly on the sandalwood trade. If all peaceful means failed, then a Russian invasion was an option.

Dr. Schäffer provided medical services to Kamehameha and Ka'ahumanu and was given permission to set up trading stations on parcels of land on Hawaii and Oahu. In 1816 he made a deal with Kaumuali'i for the return of the cargo, a monopoly on sandalwood, and an allegiance with Russia that included acceptance of Russian citizenship. Although Kaumualii had previously agreed to a truce with Kamehameha, he obviously had designs on greater conquest and provided 500 individuals and a "secret treaty" giving Dr. Schäffer "carte blanche for this expedition and all assistance in constructing fortresses on all islands". In return, the Russian-American Company would get half of Oahu and all of its sandalwood.

When the Russian trading station built of coral and flying the Russian flag near Kamehameha's compound in Honolulu started looking more like a fort than a storehouse, the Russians were thrown out in late 1816. The Russian government was not keen on multi-island conquests and the Kaua'i/Russian invasion of Oahu never materialized. Dr. Schäffer left Hawaii in July 1817 never to return.

Realizing the potential danger of future attacks, Kamehameha ordered a proper fort to be constructed at this location to protect his interests. Described as "a square with loopholes" it was about 340' by 300' in size with hard clay walls about 12' high and 12' thick faced with coral stone blocks, and 52 guns of various calibers facing out to sea giving it the nickname "Kekuanohu" – "back of the scorpion fish". The guns of the fort were never fired in anger, but they were often used to announce the arrival of ships in port and other celebratory occasions.

The main entrance faced mauka, giving Fort Street its name. The original shoreline was much closer, and the fort's oceanside walls were located where the makai side of Nimitz Boulevard is today. There was a long shallow reef in front of the fort that was exposed at low tide, a coral outcrop called Pākākā (or The Point) next to the fort on the ewa side, and a beach that was used for canoe landings that later became James Robinson's shipbuilding and repair yard.

In addition to protecting Honolulu Harbor, the fort housed various administrative offices including the police headquarters and the first courts. It also had barracks, officers' quarters, and powder magazines.

Drawing by Edward Belcher from H.M.S. Sulphur, July 1837

The fort was also used as a jail for prisoners and unruly sailors, and was occasionally the scene of hangings. One hanging in particular attracted a huge crowd who had been completely quiet when the trap door dropped, but then suddenly panicked fearing they might now be subject to the ghosts of the two deceased prisoners!

In 1849 the fort was captured by 140 French Marines who overpowered the two men defending it. Led by Admiral Louis Tromelin, the French were upset about past persecutions of Catholics and high tariffs on French Brandy. They issued a list of demands to King Kamehameha III, destroyed the fort's armaments and sacked the city. The local residents responded with ridicule, and realizing they could not prevail the French Marines packed up and sailed away two weeks later.

By 1857 the fort was no longer needed for harbor defense, so it was decommissioned and dismantled. The shallow reef area in front was sold off as "water lots" and filled in with the former walls of the fort and developed into wharves and warehouses. This new area was called "The Esplanade". Many of the cannons were repurposed as hitching posts – two still remain in front of the old Post Office at Merchant and Bethel streets.

Drawing by James D. Dana, geologist with Wilkes U.S. Exploring Expedition, 1840

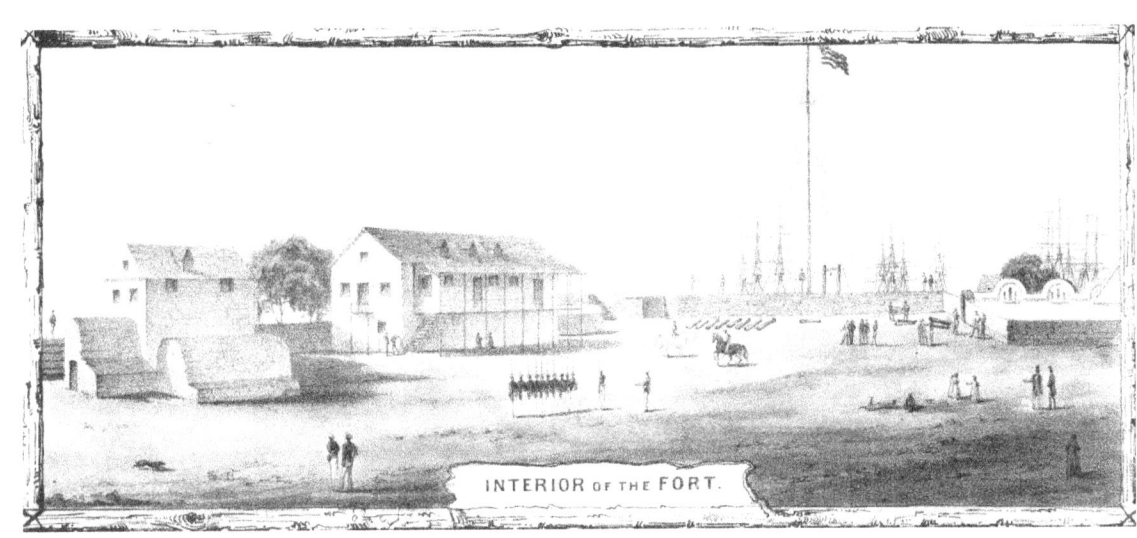

Paul Emmert, 1854

Map by Theophilus Metcalf, c.1847-1849

NOTES OF THE WEEK.

THE OLD HOUSE IN THE FORT.—In the course of demolishing the "Fort" of Honolulu, now going on, the old stone house, formerly occupied by the Governor, is sharing the fate of the surrounding walls, and fast "hiding its diminished head." It was built in 1831, by Governor John Adams Kuakini, (a High Chief, and Governor of the Island of Hawaii from 1820 till his death in 1845,) and was the residence of Governor Kekuanaoa until the French "raid" in 1849, when he gave it up to the "brave *Poursuivantes*," who amused themselves by breaking calabashes, making charcoal sketches on the walls, and recording on them their own praises. When, after wreaking their vengeance on the guns and calabashes—the French retired to their ships, the Governor disdained again to occupy his desecrated domicile, and it has been used since as a barrack and partly as a prison until the other day, when it was again evacuated for the new prison at Leleo. Many recollections cluster around "the old house in the Fort," and had we a poet laureate attached to our staff of Government officials, we should seriously recommend the composition of an elegy on this occasion. Here, in bygone days, all who intended to commit matrimony must present themselves before the stern old Governor for his consent to the bans—here taxes were paid, in poi, fish, tapas, sandal-wood and dollars—here captains came for permission to ship sailors and for help to catch runaways—here criminals and offenders of all sorts were summarily disposed of in the "good old times" when we had little law and less equity—in short, here was transacted all and every kind of Government business, for then the "Governor" was the factotum of the powers that be,—and certainly, in the matter of simplicity and economy, we cannot confidently assert that the present routine is an improvement on the old.

The Pacific Commercial Advertiser, October 1, 1857

Paintings by Paul Emmert, c.1853-1854

Paul Emmert, 1854

Looking waikiki along Queen Street, George Henry Burgess, 1857

CUSTOM HOUSE

539-549 Fort Street
1860 – 1926 (1867 addition)
Architect/Builder: R.A.S. Wood / George Thomas, Robert Lewers

Bishop Museum Archives

One of the first buildings built on the reclaimed land called the Esplanade was this coral stone Custom House completed in 1860 for $9,845.65. R.A.S. Wood supervised the work, with masonry by George Thomas and carpentry by Robert Lewers.

NEW CUSTOM HOUSE.—The first step towards the erection of the New Custom House have been taken, and the foundation is progressing. The site chosen for it, is on the New Esplanade, and is a very suitable locality. It is intended we suppose, to draw business to that vicinity, and enhance the value of the wharf property, and ere long we may find it the principal arena of active bustle and business movement. After viewing such a creditable specimen of Architecture as the New Prison, we doubt not the building now in course of erection will do ample credit to those to whom the work is entrusted, and shall expect when completed, it will, like most of its kind in nearly all foreign cities, be entitled to rank among the best and most substantial of our town edifices. The size of the building is 60 by 80 feet, and it will be two stories high.

The Pacific Commercial Advertiser, January 5, 1860

Through the doors of the customs have passed thousands of tins of opiums; fine silk dresses from China; beads from Japan; quaintly carved jewelry from mystical India; tea from Ceylon; young customs inspectors who have long ago grown gray in the service of their country, and beautiful brides who registered their names with their skipper husbands and who fared forth across the sea in tall ships.

Honolulu Star-Bulletin, February 10, 1926

An additional Government Warehouse was added on the makai side in 1867 at a cost of $20,121.84.

A large stone 1-story fire-proof bonded warehouse, 50' x 200', was added in back in 1878.

In 1926 the building was sold at public auction for $3,015 and dismantled at a cost of $20,000 "to beautify the space in front of Aloha Tower" as part of the extensive Pier 11 redevelopment project that included the new Aloha Tower.

> Across the threshold of the old structure, which is soon to be dismantled to make way for the development of Honolulu's waterfront, have strode picturesque skippers, black bowled pipes in their mouths, fresh from whaling off Hawaii; smugglers, trembling in their shoes at the fate which waited them; blackbirders and all that queer flotsam of humanity which once made Honolulu an unique and colorful sea port.

Honolulu Star-Bulletin, February 10, 1926

NOTES OF THE WEEK.

THE NEW CUSTOM HOUSE.—This public building, which has recently been completed, stands in the center of the Esplanade on the south side of Fort street. It has been erected under the supervision of R. A. S. Wood, Esq., the able superintendent of Public Works. The building is 60 by 80 feet in size, and two stories in height. It is built of coral stone, and in the most thorough manner, and entirely fire-proof, with strong iron shutters and doors, manufactured in San Francisco. Its external finish is in imitation of brown free stone. Being intended for the storage of heavy goods, the floors are heavily timbered, and its capacity for that purpose has been already well tested in the storing of forty tons dead weight in the *space of ten feet square*, on the first floor. The Collector's Office, is on the second floor, to which access is had by a broad and easy flight of stairs. The spacious accommodations for the Custom House business here provided, form a marked contrast to the pent-up quarters recently vacated. The Surveyor of the port, Mr. Miles, and the store-keeper, Mr. Ward, have their head-quarters here. The Collector has added to his department, another clerk, Mr. Levi Chamberlain, whose services will be fully required in the increasing labors of the office. In fact, the want of a second clerk has long been felt by those who have had frequent occasion to call for statistics, and other information. The building is covered with the patent fire-proof roofing, and the view from the roof is one of the finest that Honolulu affords. In every respect the building appears to be constructed in the most thorough and substantial manner, and is certainly a credit to the government. The mason-work was done by Mr. Geo. Thomas, and the carpenter-work by Mr. Lewers. The cost of the building is $10,500, and every person who visits and examines it, will admit that for once a government job has been done faithfully, and quite as economically as if it had been built for an individual. The Court House is said to have cost $46,000, and of the two buildings, we think the Custom House the finest. We congratulate the Collector on having so neat and comfortable quarters provided for him, and doubt not be will continue to fill the office with the credit and ability he has heretofore shown.

The Pacific Commercial Advertiser, April 26, 1860

CORAL BLOCKS
Clean, square dimensions, ready for your garden walls, steps and terrace walls, 50c per cubic foot
Red Bricks at $3.50 per hundred, or $32.00 per thousand.
Half bricks at $1.25 per hundred.
AT OLD CUSTOM HOUSE SITE
Phone 4981
　　　 7012
　　　 4012

CHAYTER BUILDING

601 Fort Street

1879 – 1928
Architect/Builder: unknown

This 2-story red brick building, 67' x 27', was built in 1879 as a blacksmith shop and carriage factory for John Thomas Chayter, replacing his previous 1859 brick workshop. The second story was a finishing shop for carriages and there was a wheelwright's shop in the back.

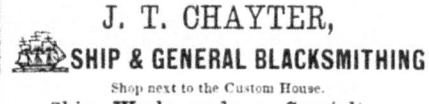

After Chayter passed away in 1880 the building became a rice mill run by a Chinese company before becoming the Hollister Soda Water Works factory in 1890.

Honolulu: The Cross-Roads of the Pacific, 1913

Hollister renamed it the Consolidated Soda Water Works in 1894 and were here until moving to Sheridan Street in 1921.

The building was torn down in 1928 for the Pier 11 redevelopment project.

PACIFIC MAIL WAREHOUSE

613-619 Fort Street

1891 – 1928

Architect/Builder: Isaac A. Palmer? / Fred Harrison

Contractor Fred Harrison obtained the lease for this lot in April 1890 for $660 per year for 25 years with the condition that he erect a fire-proof building to cost not less than $3,000 with the plans to be approved by the Superintendent of Public Works.

The architect was not identified, but the building looks to be in the Eastlake Victorian style that was a specialty of architect Isaac A. Palmer who was working at the time with Harrison on the Cummins Building (1891) further up Fort Street.

> Col. J. H. Boyd, clerk of the Land Office, Interior Department, sold at auction the lease of the Pacific Mail warehouse on the Esplanade, Messrs. H. Hackfeld & Co. buying it at the upset price of $500 a year.
>
> *Evening Bulletin, August 19, 1892*

Initially known as the Pacific Mail Warehouse, the large 2-story brick building was leased to H. Hackfeld & Co. in 1892 and they added several 1-story additions in back plus a 2-story stone and brick building (c.1899) facing Kekuanaoa Street.

It was the Hackfeld warehouse for many years, then the US Customs warehouse by 1926. Everything on the entire block was demolished in 1927 and 1928 to create a public park as part of the city's massive Pier 11 redevelopment project.

The site today is the ewa side of the parking lot in front of the Aloha Tower Marketplace facing Pier 11.

LUCAS CLOCK TOWER

637 Fort Street
1883 – 1928
Architect/Builder: George Lucas

This building was a well-known landmark in the Esplanade for 40 years until supplanted by the Aloha Tower about 500' away. Its illuminated dial was readily visible from most parts of the city to ships in the harbor, and it was said that King Kalākaua regularly set his pocket watch by the Lucas clock so he would not miss his appointments.

The building was built in 1883 for Richard W. Laine, next to the Honolulu Steam Planing Mill run by builder George Lucas. Laine was a dealer in grain, feed, and hay.

> To-day witnesses the removal of an old Honolulu landmark, Mr. R. W. Laine's old office being taken away to make room for his new building. This will consist of a brick building 100 by 50 ft. of two stories with a clock tower 80 ft. high. The office will be under the clock but in the meantime Mr. Laine's business will be transacted at Mr. Lucas'.

Evening Bulletin, September 17, 1883

> The brick turret above Messrs. Laine & Co's new building on the Esplanade is nearly completed. Above this will will be placed a wooded tower about 25 feet high for the reception of an illuminated four-faced clock. The clock is already on the premises and is in working order. When completed it will be connected by an electric wire with the Government transit instrument. It will be placed at an elevation of 80 feet from the ground and will be visible in all directions from long distances.

The Honolulu Advertiser, December 10, 1883

Richard W. Laine was born in Hallowell, Maine, in 1828. He was a Civil War and Mexican War veteran, Commissioner of Deeds for the State of California for the Hawaiian Islands, general agent for Pacific Mutual Life Insurance, and consul for Spain and Mexico.

Lucas leased the Esplanade lot in 1878 and his son Jack bought the clock for his father in New York in 1883. It was made by the Howard Watch & Clock company, the leading maker of large municipal clocks.

> Messrs. Laine & Co. have occupied their new premises on the lower part of Fort street. The clock has been placed in the tower and is now going; but arrangements have not yet been completed for the nightly illuminations. It is expected that the Government will see fit to defray the expenses of lighting up this clock, as it will be for the public benefit.

The Honolulu Advertiser, February 16, 1884

> STOCK FEED.—Laine & Co., office on Fort street, next to Mr. G. Lucas' steam planing mill, are making the grinding of feed for stock a specialty. Heretofore the dealing in these articles has been combined with the grocery business, but Laine & Co. have made arrangements to give their undivided attention to dealing in hay, oats, corn and barley. Having steam power attached to their mill, they can execute orders for ground feed or corn meal with promptness. The store-house of the firm is situated on the corner of Custom-house street, (running south from Fort street) and is a large and substantially constructed building, being 100 feet long by 50 broad. In this they keep on store large supplies of hay, (which they cut to order) oats and barley. The large and constantly increasing number of draught and carriage horses kept in this city renders an establishment like that of Laine & Co. quite a desideratum.

The Pacific Commercial Advertiser, April 12, 1879

> **LAINE & CO.**
> **No. 34 Fort St., Clock Building,**
> Have received a consignment of the most Economical and Valuable Feed for all kinds of stock, viz:
> **COOKED LINSEED MEAL.**
> It is the greatest Flesh former, Milk and Butter producer in use.
>
> Oil Cake Meal shows about 97 per cent of nutritive matter; this nearly 39 per cent.
> 100 lbs. of this meal is equal to 300 lbs. of oats, or 318 lbs. of corn, or to 767 lbs. of wheat bran.
> Also, our Unrivaled MIXED FEED, as well as our usual supply of the best kinds of
> **Hay, Oats, Wheat, Corn, Etc., Etc.,**
> Which is offered at the Lowest Market Rates, and delivered free to any part of the city.
>
> Agents for the
> **Pacific Mutual Life Insurance Co. of California.**
> Agents for the HOOTER TELEPHONE.
> Commissioner of Deeds for the State of California.
> TELEPHONE NO. 147.

> Lucas' clock on the Esplanade has been groggy for some time lately but repairs are being made. It's a godsend to the waterfront people and the government should keep it in repair.
>
> *Evening Bulletin, July 12, 1897*

Richard W. Laine moved out in 1886 and drayman Henry Hebbard moved in. From 1889 to 1894 the building housed the Union Ice Company. It was subleased by the Hawaiian Electric Company in 1898 to the US Government as a garrison commissary.

It was Dennis J. Cashman's Sail Loft in 1909, becoming Honolulu Tent & Awning in 1922.

Lucas closed off the clockface when Aloha Tower was built, and the works were removed and stored in their planing mill on Ala Moana Boulevard. It is not known what became of the clockworks after that.

The site is makai of the three flagpoles at the makai/waikiki corner of Nimitz Highway and Fort Street.

HONOLULU PLANING MILL

651 Fort Street
1879 – 1928
Architect/Builder: George Lucas

Owned by master builder George Lucas, the Honolulu Planing Mill was initially built in 1879 as a 1-story brick building, 82' x 40', with iron doors and shutters.

> time since. On the opposite side of the street is the planing mill and carpenter shop of Mr. Geo. Lucas. The building is one story, of brick, 82 by 40 feet, and 14 feet in the clear. It is to have iron doors and shutters, has an iron roof, and thus will be fire proof. Here is all the latest improved patent machinery for planing, moulding, sawing and morticing wood, and it is interesting and surprising to note how human labor and time is saved by the application of machinery, and the work better executed too than by hand. Two men with these appliances can do the work of twenty in the old style. Here a board 12 by 14 inches wide, and 60 feet in length can be smoothly planed in a very few minutes. The boiler house, of iron, in the rear of the main building, is 18 by 24 feet. The Engine which runs the machinery is of 20 horse power, capable of being worked up to 30, and has attached a Blake's patent supply pump.—Farther down on the same side of the

Pacific Commercial Advertiser, April 5, 1879

A second story was added in 1881, and the business became known as the Honolulu Steam Planing Mill due to the newly installed steam-operated machinery.

Honolulu: The Cross-Roads of the Pacific, 1913

HONOLULU STEAM PLANING MILLS.

Prominent among the principal industrial establishments of Honolulu stands the concern named in the heading to this descriptive article. It is situated on an irregularly shaped site near the foot of Fort street, almost close to the various steamship wharves. The front measures about 150 feet, and a portion of the lot is 200 feet deep, the remainder about half that depth. Everybody here, however, knows the spot, for the clock tower, visible at great distances on all sides, is one of the city's chief landmarks, and its dials, brightly illuminated at night, are the great regulators of all who make a note of time in their incomings and outgoings.

Having visited the snug and well-appointed office in a corner of the main brick building, the BULLETIN representative was escorted all over the place by Mr. J. Simmons, the genial book-keeper of the establishment, and afterward meeting the energetic and urbane proprietor, Mr. George Lucas, was shown the working of the more delicate machinery by that gentleman.

On the ground floor of the main building are band, buzz and jig saws, planer, lathe and shaper. They are making delightful music to the utilitarian ear. Indeed, the moaning of the saws yield cadences of such delicate crescendo and diminuendo as would not discredit the great Remenyi's fiddle. At the rear is the engine room, where a 70 h. p. Putnam engine, latest style, with tireless energy makes things hum all over the place. There, on the wall, is the electric bell connected with the Survey Department in the Government Building. The whistle cord depends from the ceiling, and the fireman takes hold of it a minute before twelve, noon, awaiting the signal to wake the echoes with the shrill intimation of the sun's arrival at the meridian. In a shed outside there is a band saw of so versatile a capacity that the production of veneer as thin as paper or of deals a foot or more thick is all the same to it.

On the second floor the fitting room is entered, where doors, sashes, blinds, etc., are put together. This room also contains the fine machines for making blinds, which are so ingenious that the human hand has only left to it the function of being a tender to them. Even the little wire staples hingeing the rod to the middle of the slats are put in and linked by a machine. Here is a place for melting glue by steam and there a chest where the same agent dries lumber—in fact, no labor-saving contrivance is omitted that can be supplied.

Entering the second building—that adorned with the clock—the iron street door opens into a spacious store-room for lumber, cement, corrugated iron, lime and building supplies generally, which are on sale in either wholesale or retail quantities. The most noticeable object at this visit was the handsome six-oared boat just bought by His Majesty, which rested softly on canvas cushions on the floor. This building is of cemented brick and fire-proof, on its second floor a large workshop and store-room combined, together with a smaller store-room for hardware, mountings, etc.

Ascending a flight of steps in the tower above the second story a beautiful object is encountered in the shape of a handsomely mounted telescope, which brings the grand mountain and ocean scenery close under the eye and through which, now, is seen the sublime spectacle of a gallant vessel, away in the offing, breaking her way at a furious pace through billows that enrobe her hull in ever-changing foam. From a gallery at this level a magnificent view of the land and water environs of Honolulu is obtained, which the writer has not the geographical or topographical knowledge to describe.

Up another flight and the remarkably simple as well as pretty mechanism of the Seth Thomas tower clock is seen. It is connected by cords with the other simple mechanism moving the hands over the dials on a still higher level. The clock and the various buildings are lighted with gasoline made on the premises by the most approved apparatus, an automatic device pumping the illuminant to the burners away up in the dial chamber.

These mills have been established five years, and in brisk times employ 200 hands, the present pay roll numbering about 150, about three-fourths skilled workmen. They are therefore a most important factor in the industrial and commercial life of Honolulu and a great credit to the enterprise and push of their proprietor. That his business may increase and himself have good health and every blessing is the wish of the BULLETIN.

*Evening Bulletin,
September 19, 1884*

COURT HOUSE

745 Fort Street

1852 – 1968 (1874 remodel)
Architect/Builder: William Brandon, R.A.S. Wood, Charles W. Vincent

Paul Emmert, 1854

Between 1845 and 1851 the Privy Council looked at various locations to relocate the courts, finally deciding on a site just outside the fort. William Brandon and R.A.S. Wood had prepared plans for a combined court house and jail, but these were scrapped when the government selected this site and decided to build a separate jail on the far side of the harbor. Brandon was paid $362 for providing revised plans in August of 1851.

Brandon came from Boston on the *Charles* in 1850 and was employed by the Minister of the Interior to superintend the construction of a reservoir and the cast iron water line from the "King's Spring" in Nuʻuanu to the harbor due to his recent work on the Boston water system. Wood also came from Boston, arriving in Honolulu in the very early 1840's.

Brandon and Wood "purchased the stock and stand" of Charles W. Vincent's carpenter business in September 1850 and immediately put out a call for 20 carpenters. R.A.S. Wood took over the business in September 1851.

> **BRANDON & WOOD,**
> Carpenters, Joiners, and Dealers in all kinds of Building Materials,
> At the old stand of C. W. Vincent.
> Honolulu, October 19, 1850.—23-y.

Construction on the Court House likely began in June 1851 and by October there were 60 prisoners cutting coral blocks out on the reef. The stone work was completed by the first of February 1852.

The government opted to use prison laborers thinking this would result in a cost savings, but the newspapers at the time were quick to point out the "miserable quality" of the laborers leading to many time delays and extra costs.

> NOTICE.—Sealed proposals will be received by the undersigned, at his office in Honolulu Hale, until the 10th day of June proximo, at 12 o'clock, M, for contracting to do the carpenter and joiner work for the court house about to be built in this place. Plans and specifications together with the facilities granted, and the conditions exacted by government of the contractor, will be open on Monday next, for the inspection of all whom it may concern.   T. METCALF,
> May 31, 1851.2t-3 Sup't Bureau Public Works.

The Polynesian, May 31, 1851

Richard Greer estimated the final cost of the courthouse to be $34,229.50, a "very considerable sum for that time". It was 56' x 75', 2-stories, with a classical portico at the entrance facing Fort Street.

> THE NEW COURT HOUSE.—The stone work of the New Court House is completed, and the carpenters are now at work upon the roof. There is some prospect that the building will be in readiness for the meeting of the Legislature in April.—Should such be the case, they will be better accommodated than any previous legislature has been as the Supreme Court Room, in which they will meet, is a fine one, well ventilated, and some 30 feet in height.
> The building is a very substantial one, and well adapted to the purpose for which it was designed.

The Polynesian, February 7, 1852

> ☞ The New Court House was occupied on Wednesday of this week, by Police Justice Harris, and on Thursday, the Chief Justice and clerk of the Superior Court removed into their respective offices.
> The Superior Court Room is not yet completed, but it is expected to be ready for the July term, on the 5th proximo.

The Polynesian, June 19, 1852

The Court House was the official meeting location of the Legislature and the Supreme Court from 1852 to 1874, as well as for various civic groups. The first organization to use the Court House was the Royal Hawaiian Agricultural Society, holding their second annual meeting there on June 1, 1852.

Police Justice C.C. Harris moved in on June 16, 1852, and Chief Justice W.L. Lee and the superior court clerk moved in on June 17. The court room itself was finished in time for the July term that opened on July 5, 1852.

IRON FENCE AND FOUNTAIN AT THE COURT HOUSE.—We notice that work has been commenced on the iron fence for the Court House premises, recently imported from England by the *Paraguay*. The basement will be of stone laid in cement, surmounted by the iron work. At the corner facing Queen street, will be an iron *drinking* fountain, not a constantly running one like that at the Bethel corner, but worked by touching a spring, when the water issues forth, and stops when the pressure is removed.

The Pacific Commercial Advertiser, March 5, 1870

The public drinking fountain at the front corner of the property was removed in 1899.

At the opening session, Chief Justice William Little Lee dedicated the new building, saying:

> "Justice in a grass house is as precious as justice in one of coral, but no one can fail to agree with me, that the latter with all its comforts and conveniences is greatly to be preferred, inasmuch as it tends to promote that dignity and propriety of manners so essential to secure a proper respect for the law and its administration. May this Hall ever be the temple of Justice—may its walls ever echo with the accents of truth—may its high roof ever look down upon us in the faithful discharge of our duties—and may the blessing of Him who built the Heavens and whose throne is the fountain of all justice ever rest upon us."

The Court House hosted the ball to celebrate the wedding of King Kamehameha IV to Emma Rooke (Queen Emma) and it was also where the meeting was held to formally establish Queen's Hospital in May 25, 1859.

On February 12, 1874, it was the scene of a riot after the legislature elected Kalākaua to be the new monarch by a vote of 39 to 6 over Queen Emma. An angry mob of her supporters "forced their way into the courthouse, attacked members of the legislature, and ransacked the building and its furnishings".

The building was badly damaged and was partially repaired before the government moved everything into Aliiolani Hale on April 30, 1874.

After the legislature and judiciary moved out of the Court House, the government put the building up for sale. It was purchased by H. Hackfeld & Co. at auction on September 19, 1874, for $20,000. They rebuilt the interior to be their company headquarters and a warehouse. Between 1885 and 1891 they extended the building in back and built a large warehouse on the makai side.

When Hackfeld started building their new headquarters building in front of the old Court House in 1899 they removed the front portico and put up an elaborate cast- and wrought-iron gateway between the two buildings. Each gate included medallions with number "49" on the left side for the year the company was founded (1849), and number "99" on the right side for their 50th anniversary in 1899.

Hackfeld and their successor American Factors (Amfac) continued to use the old Court House Building for office and warehouse space until 1968.

When they announced plans to build a new high-rise tower on the site in 1968, they offered to donate the old Court House Building plus up to $25,000 toward the costs of dismantling and reconstruction elsewhere. Preservationists and the state government both worked on several plans to move and save the building, but since nothing feasible had been proposed Amfac commenced demolition on December 28, 1968. They saved some of the coral blocks and the wrought iron gateway and donated them to be placed in the little triangular Walker Park in front of their new office towers.

HACKFELD BUILDING

701-745 Fort Street / 102 Queen Street

1902 – 1970

Architect/Builder: Oliver G. Traphagen / Fred Harrison

The Hackfeld Building, later known as the Amfac Building, was built on Fort Street in the former open courtyard in front of the old Court House. Construction of the foundation started on November 18, 1899. The architect was Oliver G. Traphagen and the contractor was Fred Harrison. In spite of delays due to the shipment of woodwork catching fire, the building was completed in 1902 at a cost of $482,000.

> **WORK DELAYED ON THE HACKFELD BUILDING.**
>
> Finishing work on the Hackfeld building will be delayed considerably on account of the destruction of the hardwood material which was recently burned in the bark C. D. Bryant. The bark brought a large consignment of wood for wainscoting, doorways and doors. The architect, Traphagen, will duplicate the order and hopes to have the new material here in a few weeks. The stone work has been completed and plastering is being done. The dome is being made ready for its final coating.

The Honolulu Advertiser, July 13, 1901

While the building was still being finished the offices of the German Consul were opened on January 27, 1902, for the 43rd birthday of Kaiser Wilhelm II.

The official opening day was March 21, 1902.

> The big hall in the Hackfeld building which is being fitted up for the Chamber of Commerce will be given over to that body for its use, free of rent. This concession has been made by J. F. Hackfeld and H. A. Isenberg.

Evening Bulletin, September 13, 1901

HACKFELD'S NEW BUILDING.

The Massive Structure Which will Add Beauty to Honolulu's Architecture.

The handsome new Hackfeld building, corner of Fort and Queen streets, is progressing very satisfactorily to its contractor, Fred Harrison. The building is to be very massive and substantial, and will be three stories in height. The outside walls will be of native stone, taken from Mr. Harrison's quarries in the Kaimuki tract. This will be the largest structure of native stone ever erected in these Islands.

The stonework will be richly and handsomely ornamented. Five sculptors are at work making the designs, and five carvers are engaged in chiseling them out of the native stone. A Republican reporter, in a cursory way, inspected some of the work of the sculptors' yesterday, who, by the way, are from San Francisco. An immense cap for a column was particularly imposing; also, a panel and a pediment. The work, in achievement and magnitude, compares favorably with similar work on the Claus Spreckels building, known as the Call building, in San Francisco.

A little idea may be derived of the substantial character of the new Hackfeld building from the window sills. They weigh two tons each, are 10 feet in length and are composed of a solid stone.

The architectural beauty of new Honolulu will be greatly augmented when the Hackfeld building is completed.

The Honolulu Republican, June 24, 1900

THE HOUSE BEAUTIFUL

NEW HACKFELD BUILDING TO BE OPENED.

The Public Invited to Inspect it Tomorrow—Ladies Especially Included in the Invitation.

The new Hackfeld building will be formally opened to the public tomorrow March 21. From 10 a. m. to 4 p. m., and from 7:30 p. m. to 9 p. m. the public will be received by the members and employes of the old established house, and be shown the hospitality of the house and the new building erected to mark the Semi-centennial of its establishment.

H. Hackfeld and Company wish particularly that it be known that ladies are invited to attend this public opening of the new building. During the evening hours of the reception light refreshments will be served, and the Quintet club will be in attendance.

The new Hackfeld building is probably the finest completed building in the Islands. In beauty of architecture, commanding position, adaption to use, interior and exterior finish, and superb arrangement, it would be a credit to any city. It was designed by O. G. Traphagen and built by Fred Harrison. Work on it was begun in November 1899 just fifty years after the mercantile and shipping house of H. Hackfeld & Company was established by Captain Henry Hackfeld. It occupies the entire frontage on the Waikiki side of Fort street from Halekauila to Queen streets. This is a historic locality much of the early political history of Hawaii centering right there. The legislature which elected Kalakaua king sat in a building on a spot included in the Hackfeld premises.

The building is in Italian Rennaissance. The walls are of a blue basalt stone quarried near Honolulu. The building is practically fire-proof. Marble has been extensively used in the interior. The windows are of heavy plate glass. Elevators make ascent to the upper floors easy. Interior decoration has been lavish.

The Hawaiian Star, March 20, 1902

The building also featured the Clark Automatic Telephone Switchboard system, with no operator required. "You turn the dial; it does the rest."

H. HACKFELD & CO. Ltd.

AGENTS FOR:

PACIFIC MAIL S. S. CO.'S STEAMERS:
"China," "City of Pekin," "City of Rio De Janeiro,"

OCCIDENTAL AND ORIENTAL S. S. CO.'S STEAMERS:
"Doric," "Coptic," "Gaelic,"

TOYO KISEN KAISHA'S STEAMERS:
"America Maru," "Hongkong Maru," "Nippon Maru,"

AMERICAN-HAWAIIAN S. S. CO.'S STEAMERS:
"Californian," "Oregonian," "American," "Hawaiian," "Alaskan," "Arizonan," "Nebraskan," "Nevadan," and "Texan."

BREMEN AND LIVERPOOL LINE OF PACKETS.

PACIFIC GUANO AND FERTILIZER CO.

HONOLULU REPRESENTATIVES:

Lihue Plantation Co., Kauai
Grove Farm Plantation, Kauai
Koloa Sugar Company, Kauai
Kekaha Sugar Company, Kauai
Pioneer Mill Co., Lahaina, Maui
Kipahulu Sugar Co., Kipahulu, Maui
Hawaii Mill Co., Hilo, Hawaii
Kukaiau Plantation Co., Hawaii
Oahu Sugar Co., Waipahu, Oahu

EXTENSIVE HANDLERS OF HAWAIIAN COFFEE
AND DEALERS IN GENERAL MERCHANDISE

MAIN OFFICES:
HACKFELD BUILDING
CORNER FORT AND QUEEN STREETS, HONOLULU
BRANCH HOUSES:
HILO, HAWAII   KAILUA, HAWAII   LAHAINA, MAUI

CENTERPIECE — A pillar in the main lobby is fitted with ornate lights and a counter to make a public-service desk. Note the mosaic tile floor.

UP, UP AND AWAY — This may be the largest remaining Victorian wrought iron stairway in the world.

DESIGNER'S DELIGHTS — A bit of carved exterior stonework and painstakingly detailed metalwork.

The Honolulu Star-Bulletin, November 27, 1969

The building was demolished in 1970 to make way for the $27M Amfac complex featuring two 20-story high-rise office towers. Much of the black stone was salvaged and given to the Bishop Museum while the interior features were sold at auction.

The new towers were designed by the Hadley Company and built by Center Enterprises out of Seattle.

The Honolulu Star-Bulletin, April 16, 1970

WILDER BUILDING

801 Fort Street / 102 Queen Street

1881 – 1929

Architect/Builder: E.B. Thomas

Hawaii State Archives

THE wooden building heretofore occupying the corner of Fort and Queen Streets used by Messrs. Wilder & Co. as an office and store has been removed farther up Queen Street, in the neighborhood of Mr. J. I. Dowsett's office.

Daily Honolulu Press, May 28, 1881

GROUND was broken on Wednesday for putting in the foundation of Messrs. S. G. Wilder & Co's. new store. The Queen St. frontage will be on the old line; the Fort St. frontage will be set back five feet adding that width to the street.

Daily Honolulu Press, July 16, 1881

After some delay, awaiting the arrival of pressed brick, work has been resumed on Messrs. Wilder & Co.'s new building. This building when completed will have one of the handsomest fronts of any in the city. A superior quality of brick being used for the front walls which are being laid in an artistic manner under the supervision of Mr. E. B. Thomas. The building will be two stories high, and a decided ornament to Queen and Fort streets.

The Hawaiian Gazette, September 21, 1881

WILDER & CO

(Established in 1872.)

Estate S. G. WILDER -:- W. C. WILDER.

IMPORTERS AND DEALERS IN

Lumber and Coal

Building Materials

SUCH AS

DOORS, SASH, BLINDS,

Builders' Hardware,

Paints, Oils, Glass.

WALL PAPER, ETC.

Cor. Fort and Queen Streets,

HONOLULU, H. I.

MESSRS. WILDER AND CO. are tearing down one of the old landmarks of Honolulu, the large wooden building standing in the yard adjoining their office. It was erected in the '50s by Governor M. Kekuanaoa, and used by him as an office. Afterwards the District Court held its sessions there, and finally the late C. C. Harris occupied it as an office. It is now being demolished to make room for a lumber yard.

The Honolulu Advertiser, August 17, 1882

Samuel Gardner Wilder was born June 20, 1831, in Leominster, Massachusetts and first came to Hawaii in 1856.

A year later he married Elizabeth Kinau Judd, the daughter of missionary doctor and politician Gerrit P. Judd.

The couple's honeymoon voyage was on the clipper ship *White Swallow* carrying bird guano from Jarvis Island to New York City.

Wilder partnered with E.P. Adams in the auction business for three years and later co-owned a sugar plantation with Judd that is now the Kualoa Ranch.

In 1871 he took over the lumber business of James I. Dowsett and became the agent for the steamship *Kilauea*.

He established the shipping company of Wilder & Company in 1872 with Christopher H. Lewers and they added more ships plus railroads to bring sugar to the ports, becoming the Wilder Steamship Company in 1883.

Wilder was a member of the House of Representatives, House of Nobles, and was Minister of the Interior and president of the legislature. He established the first telephone line on Oahu in 1878, running from his government office to his lumber business.

In 1905 the Wilder Steamship Company merged with the Inter-Island Steam Navigation Company, which later became Inter-Island Airways, and then Hawaiian Airlines in 1941.

On October 3, 1916, the building became the new offices of the Sumitomo Bank of Hawaii, managed by Masayuki Kawakatsu and renovated by Kikutaro Matsumoto's carpenters.

"The Sumitomo Bank of Hawaii" was written in large gold letters on the windows and doors in both Japanese and English. It was a private bank with unlimited liability that was backed by multi-millionaire Baron Kichizayemon Sumitomo from Osaka.

The Honolulu Advertiser, October 4, 1916

The Honolulu Star-Bulletin, October 20, 1924

In 1924 the building became the offices of the Los Angeles Steamship company.

The Wilder Building was demolished in 1929 to make room for the new offices of the C. Brewer Company, and the site today is the Brewer building's courtyard at the corner of Fort and Queen streets.

THE BEAVER BLOCK
802-822 Fort Street / 74-98 Queen Street
1882 – 1965
Architect/Builder: George Lucas

The Honolulu Advertiser, February 19, 1950

Started in July 1881, this large business block was built by George Lucas for James Campbell who was also building a large 2-story brick block at Fort and Hotel streets.

The city decided to widen Queen Street in 1881 after construction had started, so the foundation had to be moved back about 8'. The city paid damages versus a $4 per foot "betterment" charge along Queen Street – the resulting payment to James Campbell was $10.

An additional James Campbell building would be added immediately mauka to this one in 1883, and a new Campbell Building was built on this site in 1965. AIA Honolulu is currently located at the corner.

MESSRS. G. W. MACFARLANE & Co. have moved into their new office in the Beaver Block, at the corner of Queen and Fort streets. The counting room is handsome and spacious, measuring 55 feet on Fort street, and 45 on Queen street. The counters and rails that divide the space allotted to the employees from the customers, are made of California cedar trimmed and paneled with black walnut. Near the Queen street entrance stands the cashier's desk, and within the same enclosure are the desks of the book-keepers. These desks are very handsome, and conveniently arranged. The room is well lighted having large windows, each containing a single sheet of plate glass, and glazed doors. Adjoining the counting-house is a large room in which is stored a variety of goods, samples of those Messrs. Macfarlane & Co. import. This room communicates with the counting-house by two large arches. A broad staircase leads to the upper floor where are displayed dry and other goods, and pianos. Everything in and about the offices is complete and comfortable. We wish the firm all prosperity in their new quarters.

BEAVER SALOON
The Best Lunch in Town,
Tea and Coffee at All Hours
The Finest Brands of
Cigars, Tobacco
Always on Hand.
H. J. NOLTE, Proprietor.
1-91

The Honolulu Advertiser, February 21, 1883

The 1882 Campbell building was built on the site of the former Hudson's Bay Company premises. Since the Hudson's Bay Company mascot was the beaver, the new building was called the Beaver Block.

The Hudson's Bay Company was founded in England on May 2, 1670, and is the oldest incorporated joint-stock merchandising company in the English-speaking world.

GEORGE PELLY & GEORGE T. ALLAN,
AGENTS FOR THE
HUDSON'S BAY COMPANY,
HONOLULU, OAHU, H. I.

Its initial focus was to seek the Northwest Passage to the Pacific, operate from Hudson's Bay in Canada, and to carry on profitable commerce and trade, particularly in animal furs. The company still exists today and is active in real estate, merchandising, and natural resources, with headquarters in Toronto.

They came to Honolulu in 1832 and first opened a store on Nuʻuanu Street just above Marin Street.

In 1842 they loaned the Hawaiian Government the staggering sum of £10,000 (approx. $1.5M today).

It gives me pleasure to inform you that the debt arising under the credit for £10,000 on the Hon. Hudson's Bay Company of London in 1842, is now fully paid off. The credit was of great use to this government in the adverse circumstances which followed, and I am happy to add on behalf of the agents of that Company here, that through good report and through bad report, their confidence in the national faith has been unshaken, while by their example they have uniformly sustained His Majesty's authority, thereby promoting good will to England and to Englishmen. (Signed) G. P. JUDD, Minister of Finance.

The Polynesian, August 8, 1846

In 1846 the Hudson's Bay Company moved from Nuʻuanu Street to across from the entrance to the fort and operated out of a large 2-story coral building. The Land Commission officially gave this large tract of land to the company in 1854. It was nearly a half-acre in size, fronting 123 feet along Fort Street and 162 feet along Queen Street.

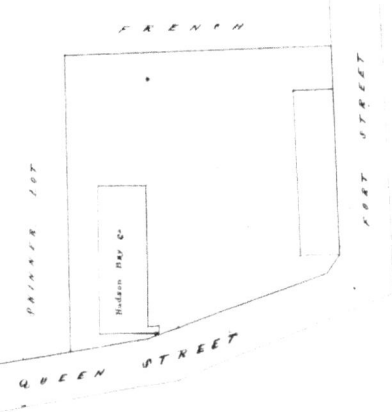

Paul Emmert, 1854

Hudson's Bay Building in foreground, Court House and Honolulu Fort on the right.
George Henry Burgess, 1857

The Hudson's Bay Company left Hawaii in 1860 and their buildings were demolished in 1881.

> "The time-honored, but not handsome buildings, which had so long been familiar to our eyes have disappeared and substantial stores are to replace them."

> The demolition of the old Hudson Bay buildings has gone on apace. The adobe store at the corner is pulled down and the bulk of it carried away; the wooden buildings behind are removed to the Esplanade, and now the coral building abutting on Queen street is amongst the things of the past.

Daily Honolulu Press, June 25, 1881

Two items remained as reminders: a large carved wooden beaver and a copper weathervane.

For many years the wooden beaver was in the Beaver Saloon. The original weathervane is now on top of the C. Brewer Building across the street.

According to an 1856 newspaper article, this was the site of Halehui, the royal residence compound of King Kamehameha between 1809 and 1812. Archibald Campbell described it in 1809:

> were along the beach and up the valleys. The King's residence was in an enclosure where the fort now stands and which included the land now occupied by the Hudson Bay Co. His house stood just where the store of the Co. is located. A grove of cocoanut trees, long since cut down, stood on the site of the fort and Robinson & Co.'s ship yard.

Pacific Commercial Advertiser, July 10, 1856

> "The king's residence, built close upon the shore, and surrounded by a pallisade upon the land side, was distinguished by the British colours and a battery of sixteen carriage guns, belonging to his ship, the Lily Bird, which at the time lay unrigged in the harbour. The palace consisted merely of a range of huts, viz. the king's eating-house, his sleeping-house, the queen's house, a store, powder-magazine, and guard-house, with a few huts for the attendants, all constructed after the fashion of the country. At a short distance were two extensive storehouses, built of stone, which contained the European articles belonging to the king."

2022

SPRECKELS BLOCK
817-835 Fort Street
1884 – 1929
Architect/Builder: George W. Lincoln

Honolulu: The Cross-Roads of the Pacific, 1913

This building was built in 1884 by George W. Lincoln for the new bank of German-born mega-industrialist Claus Spreckels. The bank was organized by Spreckels with William G. Irwin, F.F. Low, James Campbell, Samuel G. Wilder, and others.

The bank officially opened on May 4, 1885, with $200,000 in Hawaiian bonds for security. The first depositors were "Their Majesties the King and Queen".

Spreckels was one of the richest men in America, mainly from sugar, and had a huge mansion in San Francisco. William G. Irwin was his agent in Hawaii.

Irwin bought the bank and the building in 1908 and sold the building to C. Brewer & Co. for $85,000 in 1910.

William DeWitt Alexander, 1896

A Handsome Building.

Yesterday, Mr. George W. Lincoln, the well-known builder, turned over to Messrs. W. G. Irwin & Co. the handsome building adjoining the Wilder premises, and extending 160 feet along Fort street towards Merchant street. The building is of brick, finished with a cement facing, and is two storys high, the front of the ground floor being of iron, with large plate-glass lights.

The first floor is divided into three large rooms, the ceilings of which are 17 feet high. The first division, next to the stairway, which is on the *mauka* side next the Wilder building, is 40 by 60 feet in size, the heavily-corniced ceiling being supported in the centre (as are the other first floor divisions) by three handsome iron pillars. On the right-hand side as one enters this room are two large fire and burglar proof vaults, each 5 feet 6 inches deep, 12 feet long, and 8 feet high, lined throughout with iron, which has been set in brick-work 2 feet thick, the whole mass resting, as does the entire building, on a foundation of concrete built up from the coral rock. These vaults are fitted with inner and outer doors, with a wide air-space between, the outer double doors being secured by an elaborate system of bolts, controlled by a combination lock. Adjoining the vaults, on the one side, is a large closet contrived under the stairs leading to the second floor, and on the other side is a convenient wardrobe. This room is wainscoted all around to a height of 4 feet, and is finished, as are all the rest, in hard white plaster, or kalsomine.

From the rear part of this first room admittance is had to the adjoining division, which is fitted up for the use of the firm of W. G. Irwin & Co. From the front, as the visitor enters from the street, the first thing that attracts the attention is the lightness and airyness of the room, and the strong and pleasing contrast afforded to the white walls and ceiling by the handsome black walnut counter that divides the space irregularly into two parts. The top slab of this counter is of solid black walnut, very handsomely joined at the rounded angles, and highly finished throughout. Below the top the front is divided into panels, each containing a centre-piece of laural wood set in a frame of dark red. This front is grained to imitate black walnut, which it does in a remarkable degree. The work was done, as was all the paint-work on the building, by Mr. Kerr.

The rear of this room is divided from the front by a ground glass partition, swing doors affording admittance into the sanctum as well as to the banking-room on one side; and the third, and last, of the three main divisions of the first floor. This room, like the others, is about 40 x 60, and is, at present, to be occupied by Messrs. Irwin & Co. There is an archway also between these two rooms.

Leaving the ground-floor, access is had to the second story by means of a wide staircase of thirty steps, the rise of each step being about seven inches. On each side of the staircase is a round hand-rail of koa, and at the head the stair well is guarded by a balustrade of the same wood, finished with a handsome octagon newel post and wide, raised rail. The second floor is divided into twelve good-sized rooms, six looking upon the street, and six on the opposite side of the long hall running the length of the building. This hall is lit by a dome-light set in the roof, and arranged with a view to the ventilation of the building. Each room has two windows, and every adjoining pair communicate with each other. These rooms are finished in white, and provided with inside shutters, as are all in the building. The ceiling of the second story is 14 feet high.

Opposite the head of the stair are a number of water-closets fitted with the newest and best appliances for preventing any escape of foul air. Opposite these are convenient wardrobes, and in the same space is a convenient sink, where lamps, etc., can be trimmed.

The whole building is fitted throughout for gas, and thoroughly plumbed. It covers an area of nearly 20,000 square feet, having a frontage on Fort street of 160 feet, and a depth of 123 feet, and is thoroughly fire-proof throughout.

Mr. Lincoln has had the contract for the entire building from its foundation up. He commenced work on it last May, and finished it December 1st. The whole work has been done in the most thorough manner, and reflects great credit upon the builder. Particular attention has been paid to adapting the front to the grade of the street, and with the best results. Mr. Lincoln is to be congratulated upon the satisfactory completion of his contract, and the city of Honolulu can boast of its new building.

The Honolulu Advertiser, December 11, 1884

The Spreckels Block was demolished in 1929 and replaced with the C. Brewer & Co. building that formally opened to the public on November 5, 1930.

It was built by Walker & Olund for $332,000, and was designed by Hardie Phillip of Mayers Murray and Phillip, the successors to the famous New York architect Bertram Goodhue. Harry Sims Bent was the Honolulu representative and supervising architect.

Designed not as an office building but as a home for C. Brewer & Co., "the building will also be a departure in downtown Honolulu architecture." "A building that is not merely different, but that is adapted to particular conditions in an interesting way." In the words of Harry Sims Bent:

> *"You cannot call it Hawaiian, because there is no true Hawaiian architecture, but an attempt has been made to develop something purely local. It is not even such as you see in Florida or California. There will be an informal feeling in the building, and it will be more like a private home or a clubhouse than like an office structure."*

Honolulu Star-Bulletin, February 9, 1929

The design has since become known as the "Territorial Style", being a combination of Mediterranean Revival, Moorish and Spanish Colonial styles with a cut sandstone and stucco finish. "The iron grillwork on the mezzanine floor is designed to represent growing sugar cane and is painted 'cane green'".

C. Brewer was founded in 1826 by ship's officer James Hunnewell who came to Hawaii in 1817 trading sandalwood and general merchandise to Boston, China, and Russia.

Charles Brewer joined him in 1845 and C. Brewer & Company officially incorporated in 1883 with Peter Cushman Jones as president. At one point they controlled 25% of Hawaii's sugar production and were one of the island's largest corporate landholders.

C. Brewer & Co. officed here until 1998. The building is now the offices of the Hawaii Community Foundation.

If you look closely you can see a copper weathervane on top of the building with a large beaver. It came from the original 1846 Hudson's Bay Company building across the street and was placed here for all to see since it would not have been visible from the top of the 1967 Campbell Estate Building.

HAWAIIAN TOUCH GIVEN NEW HOME OF C. BREWER & CO.

A distinctive Hawaiian touch has been given the designs for the new building of C. Brewer & Co., a house now more than century old, which is to be erected on the site of the firm's present structure at Fort and Queen Sts. Two preliminary sketches of the building are reproduced herewith, the one at the top showing the Fort St.-Queen St. corner, and the one at the bottom the frontage along Queen St. Directors this week authorized the management to proceed with the preparation of plans and specifications. Hardie Phillip of Mayers, Murray & Phillip of New York is the architect, and the cost will be between $250,000 and $500,000. The structure will be a story and a half in height, the roof tiled, and wall construction of native stone finished on the exterior to have the appearance of Hawaiian adobe. There will be a stone wall along the Queen St. frontage and along a portion of the Fort St. frontage, the main entrance to be on Fort St. Spaces between the wall and building will be grassed and planted with Hawaiian shrubs and flowers.

Honolulu Star-Bulletin, November 15, 1928

J.A. CUMMINS BUILDING

907-915 Fort Street / 102-110 Merchant Street

1891 – 1966

Architect/Builder: Isaac A. Palmer / Harrison Brothers

Honolulu: The Cross-Roads of the Pacific, 1913

Hawaii State Archives

THE CUMMINS' BUILDING.

The new Cummins building situated on the corner of Fort and Merchant streets, has been turned over to Jno. A. Cummins the owner by Harrison Bros. the contractors. As we have but very few business buildings of its class, a short description might prove interesting.

The structure faces eighty feet on Fort street and about the same number on Merchant street. It is an Eastlake pattern with an entire pressed brick front and stone trimmings, two stories high; the first story being sixteen feet in clear, the second is fourteen feet.

The cellar is six feet deep and has a cement concrete floor. There are two elevators; one from the cellar to the second story, the other is something new in Honolulu—an elevator running from the side wall to the cellar that will save a great deal of labor in handling goods.

The handsome stairway that leads to the second story is appropriate and in keeping with the building. The store and show rooms upstairs are fitted with large windows thus making the interior as bright as can be.

The iron work was made by the Honolulu Iron Works—another instance of patronizing home industry. It is by far the handsomest business block in Honolulu and reflects much credit on J. A. Palmer, the architect. Harrison Bros., the builders, have cause to pride themselves for building the structure in such a solid manner. The Pacific Hardware Co. will occupy both floors with the exception of the space on the corner allotted to S. Roth.

Hawaiian Gazette, October 27, 1891

The "grand Cummins Block" was a towering Eastlake Victorian building designed by Isaac A. Palmer and built by the Harrison Brothers for $21,223 at the mauka/waikiki corner of Fort and Merchant streets in 1891.

It was built to house the Pacific Hardware Company and S. Roth, the "boss merchant tailor". The hardware company had temporarily relocated to the McInerny Block across the street, and when it came time to move to the new building they rigged up a traveling cage on a cable between the upper floors of the two buildings. James L. Torbert surprised many onlookers by personally making the first aerial passage in the cage. Just for fun, "the hauling rope was held fast a minute, keeping the passenger suspended over the middle of the street".

Wall-Nichols Co. leased the building in 1908, and Castle & Cooke moved here in 1910 from the Stangenwald Building when Wall-Nichols moved to the Republic Building. After Castle & Cooke moved to their new building next door in 1925, Allen & Robinson moved in after remodeling by Emory & Webb.

ALLEN & ROBINSON IN NEW QUARTERS—The former Castle & Cooke building, at the corner of Fort and Merchant streets, has been overhauled and redecorated and now forms the business home of Allen & Robinson, local lumber and building materials dealers.

Honolulu Star-Bulletin, June 13, 1925

John Cummins was the son of Thomas Cummins, who along with his wife Kaumaka had been granted the land by Governor Adams (Kaumaka's father) sometime between 1831 and 1833.

The new J.A. Cummins Building replaced two previous buildings – a 2-story stuccoed brick building built in 1878 by Thomas J. Baker for Dillingham & Company, and a coral building at the corner that dated back to 1842. The coral building had replaced a thatched building that was moved across the street.

NEW IMPROVEMENTS.—We notice that ground has been broken on Fort street, above Merchant, on the lot of Captain Thomas Cummins, for the erection of a large and substantial store room, to be occupied as a hardware store by the enterprising firm of Dillingham & Co. The erection of the building is to be under the supervision of Mr. Baker, whose skill and taste insures a structure that will be an ornament to the city.

The Hawaiian Gazette, June 19, 1878

ANOTHER NEW BUILDING.—Within the past few days, Mr. T. J. Baker has laid the foundations of a two-story brick building, to be 50 feet front by 82 feet in depth, on Fort street near the corner of Merchant, for T. Cummins, Esq.

The Pacific Commercial Advertiser, June 27, 1878

Hawaii State Archives

OLD LANDMARK GONE.

The coral building just taken down, on part of the site to be occupied by the Cummins block, Fort and Merchant streets, was a landmark of forty-nine years standing. It was erected in 1842 by the late Mr. Thos. Cummins, father of Hon. John A. Cummins, replacing a thatched store that was moved across Fort street to the site now occupied by the McInerny block. Into the new building Mr. Cummins transferred his ship chandlery and general merchandise business, which he closed out in 1849, when he let the building to Dr. Hunter for a drugstore. It was afterward occupied by von Holt & Heuck, importers. Later the building was tenanted by the Black Horse Saloon and, after several other occupants, Dr. Trousseau rented the building for his office and dispensary. It was finally occupied by Mr. S. Roth, tailor.

Evening Bulletin, March 28, 1891

DILLINGHAM & CO'S NEW STORE.—This fine new brick structure, on Fort street near the corner of Merchant, deserves more than a passing notice. In 96 days from the time when ground was first broken the building was completed, occupied, and the enterprising firm were selling hardware, etc. This speaks well for the quick industry of the builder, Mr. T. J. Baker, as well as the activity of the firm, who had to remove their immense stock of goods from the old stand on King street. The building is of two storys, and the front is handsomely ornamented. Its dimensions are 50 feet front by 82 feet in depth. The sales room on the ground floor—where about everything that can possibly be needed in the hardware, glassware and paint line can be found—is 50x50, with a packing and receiving room in the rear of about 30x50 feet. On the second floor is a store room, 50x55 feet, from which goods are lowered to the ground floor or sent up by a patent elevator, the first in the country. By this contrivance three men can easily raise three tons weight. Also on the second floor, fronting on the street, are three fine offices, each 25 feet deep, all of which are leased as law offices etc. In the rear of the building there is a spacious yard, affording ample room for the erection of an additional storehouse when needed. The office of the proprietor and of the book-keeper has its floor considerably elevated, and is so situated as to command, from the desk, a view of the entire salesroom and of the packing room. The arrangement of the salesroom as to the disposition of the goods, is a pattern of convenience and compactness. Altogether, the new store of Dillingham & Co., is in all respects one of the finest in the city, and in all particulars, both exteriorly and in its internal arrangements, its enterprising proprietors feel justly proud of it.

The Pacific Commercial Advertiser, October 5, 1878

W.E. FOSTER BUILDING

926 Fort Street

1887 – 1974
Architect/Builder: E.B. Thomas

This building was built by E.B. Thomas in 1887 for harness and saddle maker W.E. Foster. Formerly the location of Thomas Lack's store, it was purchased by W.E. Foster in 1885 for $6,700.

William E. Foster came to Hawaii from San Francisco in 1877 and by 1879 was advertising "saddler and harness maker" at a store next to Thomas Lack on Fort Street.

Foster was the nephew of Thomas R. Foster of the Inter-Island Steamship Navigation Company who had married the eldest daughter of James Robinson, and Foster married her sister Matilda on March 20, 1878.

> THE wooden building lately occupied by Mr. W. E. Foster, as a saddle and harness shop, on Fort street, will be sold at auction, at 12 o'clock noon to-morrow, by Messrs. E. P. Adams & Co. The sale will be on the premises.

Evening Bulletin, June 20, 1887

W. E. FOSTER,

MANUFACTURER OF   AND DEALER IN

Saddlery & Harness.

—ALSO—

SADDLE AND HARNESS LEATHER.

HARNESS

Of all kinds always on hand.

American, English, Sydney, and the well-known Mexican

SADDLES

ALWAYS ON HAND.

Also, all other Articles used about a Horse, too numerous to mention.

Orders from the Other Islands Promptly Attended to.

81 FORT STREET, HONOLULU.

Foster auctioned off the old wooden building and hired E.B. Thomas to build a new 2-story brick building with 27' frontage on Fort Street in 1887.

> It is stated that W. E. Foster has had a severe attack of the brick building fever, which will culminate in a fine building on his lot just above McInerny's, Fort Street.

The Hawaiian Gazette, March 29, 1887

Foster retired from business in 1895, sold off his stock, and moved back to California.

> Mr. W. E. Foster has removed his harness manufactory and store from Fort street to King street, next the Metropolitan Market. This is only a temporary shift, as Mr. Foster has given Mr. E. B. Thomas the contract to put up a handsome two story brick building on the old lot, on which work will begin July 1st.

The Daily Herald, June 20, 1887

Hawaii Times / Nippu Jiji

The C.M. Cooke Company, Ltd. bought the building in 1906 for $19,000. They purchased the adjoining Mrs. Lack Building in 1911, and in 1934 they hired architect Charles W. Dickey and contractor E.E. Black Ltd. to "completely remodel" and combine the two buildings into the offices of the Cooke Trust Co

SAFE DEPOSIT BUILDING

923-925 Fort Street

1893 – 1931

Architect/Builder: Clinton B. Ripley / Harrison Brothers

Designed by Clinton B. Ripley and built by the Harrison Brothers for James W. Austin in 1893, this unusual-looking building was the birthplace of the Bank of Hawaii.

> *"While it will conform to no particular style of architecture, it may be described as similar to the modern German."*

SAFE DEPOSIT BUILDING.

The New Edifice Which J. W. Austin is About to Errect.

The building which James W. Austin of Boston has decided to put up in this city will be used as a safe deposit and is to be located on the site of Gertz' shoe store on Fort street.

Work will be begun on the 15th of the present month, and it is expected the structure will be ready for its tenants in about fourteen weeks. The frontage on Fort street will be 40 feet, with a depth of 60 feet. There will be two stories and a basement. The ground floor is to be occupied by the vaults of the Safe Deposit Company and will, at first, contain 256 boxes of various sizes which will be increased with the demands of business. The second floor will contain roomy offices, and the basement will be used for storage purposes.

The Safe Deposit business will be carried on by a stock company and will probably be under the management of Edwin A. Jones, who states the Company will be ready to begin the transaction of business by the first of August.

The contract for building has been let to Messrs. Harrison Bros.

The Hawaiian Star, April 4, 1893

Peter Cushman Jones and his son, Edwin A. Jones, created the Hawaiian Safe Deposit and Investment Company on July 1, 1893, shortly after the overthrow of the monarchy. In December 1897 they incorporated the investment side of the business as the Bank of Hawaii, Ltd., which opened for business on January 1, 1898.

The "safe deposit" part of the business became the Hawaiian Trust & Investment Company and added Clarence H. Cooke and George R. Carter as partners on December 21, 1897. They officially incorporated on August 10, 1898, with an initial capitalization of $30,000 and with Edwin A. Jones as the manager.

"Hawaiian Trust Co. Ltd. was started by young men in their late 'teens and early twenties and its continuing policy has been to follow the guidance of young men, active, progressive, holding to the ideals of service before profit." By 1933 the company had over $75M in its custody.

A New Building.

J. W. Austin of Boston is planning the erection of a stone building on the site occupied by Gertz's shoe store on Fort Street. It will be used for safe deposit purposes. The building material will be blue lava rock and the structure will be an ornament to the city.

The Hawaiian Star, March 30, 1893

The Safe Deposit Company.

An announcement in another column states that the Hawaiian Safe Deposit Company expects to be ready for business about August 1st. It will do a general business in stocks, bonds, securities, real estate, loans and investments and will act as agent for the collection of rents, coupons, interest, etc. Boxes in the vault will be for hire to business men and others at a reasonable rate.

Evening Bulletin, June 20, 1887

C. B. RIPLEY, ARCHITECT !

Office—New Safe Deposit Building, Honolulu, H. I.

Plans, Specifications, and Superintendence given for every description of Building.
Old Buildings successfully remodelled and enlarged.
Designs for Interior Decorations.
Maps or Mechanical Drawing, Tracing, and Blueprinting.
Drawings for Book or Newspaper Illustration.

The Honolulu Advertiser, September 5, 1893

The cut stone for the front of the new Safe Deposit building on Fort street is being hauled in from the quarry near the Kamehameha schools to-day.

The Hawaiian Star, June 8, 1893

GREAT FALL IN GLASS.

Largest Window Pane Ever Imported Here Collapses.

The monster plate glass for the front window of the Safe Deposit building was landed safely from the barkentine Hilo and stored until this morning, when a gang of workmen under supervision of J. W. Gibbs, painter, carried it upright along Fort street to the building. They carried the precious article carefully and safely into the building, but as they were laying it flat, previous to raising it into position, the plate broke in the middle. At the same time the men let go both ends and the glass went crash on the floor, breaking into a thousand pieces. The noise made by the fall sounded like the report of a cannon, and the storekeepers in the vicinity ran out to see what the matter was. The accident is attributed to the absence of men, who should have been supporting the glass in the middle, as the plate was thin. It was the largest sheet of plate glass ever imported here, its dimensions having been 11ft. 3¼in.x7ft. 9¼in. and a quarter of an inch in thickness. It was valued at $150.

Evening Bulletin, June 20, 1887

The building was demolished in 1931 for the Austin Building.

SAFE DEPOSIT.

DESCRIPTION OF THE COMPANY'S NEW BUILDING ON FORT STREET.

Fire and Burglar Proof Vaults Which Will Hold the Wealth of the Nation.

Many residents of Honolulu have doubtless wondered at the extensive excavations which have been going on adjoining the building of the Pacific Hardware Company on Fort street, and at the massive pile of rock going up on the left hand side. This work is all being done for the foundations of the new Safe Deposit building, of which, through the courtesy of Mr. C. B. Ripley, the architect, under whose supervision the building is being erected, the following description has been obtained.

The building will be two stories in height, with cellar. The front will be of cut stone taken from the quarry near the Kamehameha schools, and will be unlike anything of the kind in Honolulu. While it will conform to no particular style of architecture, it may be described as similar to the modern German. The feature of the front will be an immense bay window in the second story, 23 feet wide, covered with burnished copper, which will be quite a novelty. The building proper will be of brick, 42 ft. 9 in. in width, 50 ft. in height from the sidewalk to the top of the coping, and extends to a depth of 60 feet. The basement is 7 ft. 6 in. in the clear, and will be occupied by Lewers & Cooke, an entrance being made from the present basement of their own store, while light and air will be obtained from glass and iron gratings at the sidewalk and rear.

The openings to the first story from the street will be entirely of plate glass and iron, as will be the window looking from the counting room to the safe deposit vault. This window will be of the heaviest plate glass manufactured, 96x132 inches, and is the largest single piece of glass ever used in the islands. Behind this immense piece of glass will be the vault, consisting of two separate and distinct steel fire and burglar proof structures, each over 7 feet square, and each provided with separate time locks. These vaults are lined with solid steel 1½ inches thick, and are the very best that can be made by the Hall Safe and Lock Company. The steel casing is to be further protected with a covering of fire-brick 20 inches thick. One of these vaults is for the use of the bank itself, and will be entered from behind the main counter, and is fitted up especially for banking purposes. The other is the safe-deposit vault, containing 250 separate boxes for use of depositors. Each of these is fitted with a double combination lock, and the depositor himself cannot open his own box until a clerk has first unlocked it with the bank's master key. No two of these locks are alike, and as, after business hours, the main door will be closed and the time lock put on, these receptacles for the deposit of money, jewels, papers, etc., will be as safe as the ingenuity of man can make them.

The main counting room will be 26x43. Passing through this and around the semi-circular wire-screened counter, the customer enters the safe deposit room in which two screened alcoves will be arranged for depositors who wish to open their boxes in complete privacy, while on the other side is a director's room 14x20. In the corner adjoining the Pacific Hardware Co. will be a handsome office room, 16 feet square, which will be for rent. The height of the ceilings of the first floor are 15 feet, while the flooring throughout the building will be of matched Oregon pine.

A handsome and capacious staircase entirely separate from the bank ascends to the second floor, which is divided into five offices, which have already been rented. The two front ones are each 17x20 and will be beyond doubt the finest in the city, taking in as they do the immense bay window before mentioned. One of the others is 14x20, and the other two 12x15 each. The height of the ceilings on this floor is 13 feet. Every room in the building is fitted with stationary wash stands, and each occupant will have his own toilet room. There are patent sliding blinds, new to this country, to every window, and in all the minor arrangements no expense has been spared to add to the comfort of the inmates.

The roof of the building will be of corrugated iron, the cornices of zinc or galvanized iron, and the building will be plastered throughout. A handsome awning will extend over the sidewalk, and is to be supported by graceful iron brackets. Harrison Bros. are the contractors, and their contract calls for the completion of the building by August 1st. The building will present a very handsome appearance and will cost not less than $16,000.

*The Honolulu Advertiser,
May 25, 1893*

There was a 2-story wooden building previously on the site, "though not an ancient landmark it nevertheless filled a niche in what may be termed the social side of Honolulu business".

It was constructed in 1859 by Christopher Lewers and was leased to Ned Burgess for a billiard hall, the first one in Hawaii that didn't have a bar associated with it. Opening day was February 1, 1860, and the *Advertiser* called it "Burgess Hall".

It had 3 billiard tables, and a few months later they added a 10-pin bowling alley that was popular with merchants, professionals, clerks, and captains and officers of ships in port. James I. Dowsett and J.O. Dominis were skilled in "ten strikes" and Dr. E. Hoffman was adept at a game called "cocked hat".

Shortly after Frederick Horn established his bakery at King and Maunakea streets in 1862, Burgess carried Horn's fine pastries and island fruit preserves in the front room and added a light refreshment room with coffee and oyster stews. "Everything was done up in first class style. The fittings and furnishings showed individuality and artistic taste."

A bar was later added and it became known as the Bank Exchange, briefly managed by Captain H.S. Howland in 1866 and James Louzada before reverting back to Burgess in 1869.

By 1885 it was the boot and shoe store of Frank Gertz, with Captain Lorenzo Marchant running a cigar stand on the makai side. Marchant's helper, Henry Grube, used to pass the time by engraving and making carvings which led to an apprenticeship in one of the first engraving establishements in Boston.

MRS. LACK BUILDING

930 Fort Street

1886 – 1974 (1934 remodel)

Architect/Builder: E.B. Thomas (1886), C.W. Dickey (1934)/ E.E. Black (1934)

Hawaii State Archives

The old wooden building occupied by Mrs. Thos. Lack, on Fort street, is to be torn down and a new brick building is to be erected in its place. It will be a good improvement on the old building and on the entire block.

Daily Honolulu Press, February 26, 1886

MRS. THOS. LACK,
No. 81 Fort Street, Honolulu,
IMPORTER AND DEALER IN

Shot Guns, Rifles, Revolvers,
AND ALL KINDS OF FIRE ARMS;
Also, Metallic Cartridges, all kinds and sizes; Brass and Paper Shot Shells, Powder, Shot and Caps, and all kinds of Sporting Goods, Etc.
IMPORTER AND DEALER IN

SEWING MACHINES

And Genuine Parts, Attachments, Oils and Accessories.
AGENT FOR THE IMPROVED
White and New Home Machine
THE WHITE AUTOMATIC MACHINE,
The New National and Peerless Hand Machine;

Sewing Machine and Hand Needles of all kinds;
Clark's, Chadwicks and Brooks' Machine Cotton Barbour's Linen Thread.

CORTICELLI SILK!
IN ALL COLORS.

Having secured the services of a first-class Gun and Locksmith and thorough mechanic, I am prepared to do all kinds of Repairs. Restocking, browning and boring Guns a specialty.
Sewing Machines, Lock, Surgical, Nautical and Surveying Instruments, cleaned and repaired with quick dispatch.
GOOD WORK GUARANTEED.

FANCY DEPARTMENT
AGENT FOR
Balls' Health Preserving Corsets,
AND
Mme Demorest's Reliable Cut Paper Patterns.
Largest and Best Assortment of
Stamping Patterns and Materials
FOR ALL KINDS OF FANCY WORK.
Lessons given, and all orders promptly filled. Island orders solicited.   1160 3m

Formerly the site of W.E. Foster's saddle and harness making shop, this building was built in 1886 by E.B. Thomas for Sophia Margaret Lack, the widow of Thomas Lack who had died in 1881.

There were not many women in those days who dealt in sewing machines and shotguns!

E. B. THOMAS,
Who has just completed a two-story fireproof building on Fort street for Mrs. Thos. Lock. This building has plate glass windows and a pressed brick front, together with a good cellar and a hand elevator. Mr. Thomas has in course of

The Honolulu Advertiser, July 13, 1886

Elegant -:- Restaurant
—— FOR ——
LADIES AND GENTLEMEN.

Mrs. Lack's Building, Fort, between King and Merchant streets.

Opening on Thursday, June 29th,
AT 10 A. M.

☞ Upstairs Room Reserved for Ladies and their Escorts.

Home Cookery. Only White Help Employed.

FRANCES M. NICOLL, : : Proprietor.

764-1m

THE LACK BUILDING.

The new building lately erected on Fort street, between Merchant and King streets, by Mrs. Thos. Lack, is an ornament to the neighborhood. It is a fire proof brick building, two stories high, and cost $6,000. The lower floor is the machine, gun, ammunition and repairing department, neatly fitted up with ornamental shelves and other fixtures. The upper floor is reached by an elevator. Upstairs is the fancy work department, where Mrs. Nicoll, assisted by Misses Tuck and Webster, attend to the sale of fancy work, or give lessons in embroidery. This department is nicely furnished and has abundance of light and ventilation. The building also contains a cellar for storage purposes.

Evening Bulletin, July 14, 1886

The C.M. Cooke Estate bought the building for $20,000 in 1911 and they hired architect Charles W. Dickey and contractor E.E. Black Ltd. to "completely remodel" the Mrs. Lack and W.E. Foster buildings in 1934 for $31,860 to become the offices of the Cooke Trust Co.

The front was cut stone and plate glass, and the interior featured an open court "decorated in the Hawaiian manner with a fountain, ferns and flowers.

When the old brick walls were being demolished a notable site was Jimmy Askham standing high on the walls wielding a pick eight hours a day. He was quoted as saying, "Everything that goes up must come down" and "You learn to love buildings. There is a poetry in a city skyline to me. And when you are perched on the skyline there is fascinating rhythm in the movement of the streets below".

The building was demolished in 1974 for Pioneer Plaza.

Honolulu Star-Bulletin, December 15, 1934

LEWERS & COOKE

931 Fort Street

1881 – 1931

Architect/Builder: Lewers & Dickson

> Messrs. Lewers & Dickson have commenced the erection of their new brick office and sales room on Fort Street. The building is to have a fine cellar.

The Hawaiian Gazette, December 1, 1880

> THE new brick building erected on Fort street by Lewers and Dickson, is one of the finest that has yet been built in Honolulu. The length of the building is 60 feet and it has a fronting on Fort street of 36 feet. Both stories are twelve feet in hight; the upper one is used for storing material, and an elevator for moving goods runs from the cellar—which is seven feet in the clear, and used also for storing—to the second story. The arrangements on the ground floor are in the most convenient form. The walls of the building to the second story are 17 inches thick and above that have a thickness of 12 inches. All of the iron work—doors, grating, &c.,—was made at the Honolulu iron works, and is equal to any imported from abroad.

Daily Honolulu Press, February 26, 1881

> Messrs. Lewers & Cooke have taken possession of their fine, new premises in Fort street. The internal fittings of the store and office are unusually handsome. Surrounded by the evidences of opulence, the firm did not forget their less fortunate fellowmen. The first check written in the new premises was for a contribution of $50 to the American Relief Fund.

The Pacific Commercial Advertiser, March 5, 1881

> We see by the *Friend* that Messrs. Lewers & Cooke, when opening business in their new store, wrote their first cheque in favor of the Stranger's Friend Society. The amount was $50.

The Hawaiian Gazette, March 2, 1881

William DeWitt Alexander, 1896

Johnson & Lewers advertised as "house carpenters" as early as 1852 and were located on Fort Street adjoining the French Hotel, later moving opposite the hotel in 1857.

In 1859, Christopher H. Lewers took over the Swinton, Reynolds, and Samsing lots on the waikiki side of Fort Street between King and Merchant streets and built a 150' x 24' machine shop, 120' x 25' carpenter shop, a large paint shop for Harvey and McClymont, and a cabinet and upholstery shop and "ware-room".

Lewers had a 12-horsepower steam engine, the first in Hawaii, that drove the saws, boring machines, lathes, grindstones, etc. The boiler and furnace-fronts were lined with tin and sheet iron and were accompanied by a 200-barrel cistern and two 60-barrel tanks served by 3 water wells.

Joshua G. Dickson partnered with Lewers in 1863. After the death of Christopher Lewers in 1877, the three partners became Joshua G. Dickson, Robert Lewers (Christopher's cousin), and C.M. Cooke.

After Dickson passed away in 1880 the old wooden store was sold for $5 and the company built this 2-story brick office and sales room on Fort Street and changed the company name to Lewers & Cooke.

The back portion of the entire block behind the buildings along Fort Street was the Lewers & Cooke lumber yard.

The brick building was demolished in 1931 for the Austin Building.

AUSTIN BUILDING

921-931 Fort Street

1931 – 1966
Architect/Builder: Louis E. Davis / Jack L. Cliff

Trim, fire-proof structure erected by the Austin Estate next to Dimond-Hall's on Fort Street, which has just been completed and is now ready for occupancy. It was built by J. L. Cliff, Honolulu contractor.

The Honolulu Advertiser, October 27, 1931

The Lewers & Cooke Building (1881) and Safe Deposit Building (1893) were demolished in 1931 for the Austin Building, designed by Louis E. Davis and built by Jack Cliff for $30,000. It had 5 stores on the first floor and 8 offices on the second floor.

Early tenants were the Mutual Building and Loan Society of Hawaii, Ltd., and realtor Charles Pietsch.

It was demolished in 1966 to make way for the Financial Plaza of the Pacific.

A.L. SMITH BUILDING

932-938 Fort Street

1890 – 1949 (1910 remodel)
Architect/Builder: Henry W. McIntosh / Fred Harrison

Hawaii State Archives

A. L. SMITH,
AGENT FOR THE
Domestic Sewing Machine,
AND THE
DOMESTIC PAPER FASHIONS,
Clocks, Watches, Jewelry, &c.
NO 83 FORT STREET, HONOLULU.

A FINE BUILDING.

Mr. A. L. Smith Opens His New Store on Fort Street to the Public—Some Particulars of the Place.

On Monday morning Mr. A. L. Smith opened to the public for the first time, his new two-story brick building on Fort street, which is a decided ornament to the city. The front is of pressed brick and the style of architecture is very neat doing credit to Mr. McIntosh who drew the plans. Mr. Fred Harrison was the contractor and he has most faithfully carried out his part of the work. On the ground floor is one large showroom fitted up with handsome showcases for displaying the numerous articles which Mr. Smith has for sale. One case is filled with beautiful fans, while another contains optical goods of every description, and still another has a large assortment of the much-sought-after domestic paper fashions. The entire fittings are extremely neat and the show windows are large. The novelties that Mr. Smith keeps on hand are really too numerous to mention, but a glance at his advertisement in another column gives fullest particulars. One side of the store is occupied by Mr. Tannatt the jeweler. There is a seven-foot cellar which will hold a large quantity of stock, while on the first floor reached by elevator and also a stairway from the street, are three offices. One is already occupied and the other two soon will be.
Mr. Smith is sole agent for the Domestic Sewing machine and purposes to add new goods and novelties from time to time. He had quite a large number of visitors on the opening day. On the front of the building in large letters is "A. L. Smith, 1890." From a flag pole was flying a red, white and blue flag with the word "Domestic" on it.

The Honolulu Advertiser, May 14, 1890

Augustus Lowell Smith purchased this property in 1885 for $6,300. In 1889 he hired Henry W. McIntosh to design a 2-story brick building that was built by Fred Harrison. The work was somewhat delayed by a shortage of bricks when the walls were only halfway up until the *W.S. Bowne* arrived with several thousand bricks ordered by Fred Harrison.

Smith was born in Honolulu in 1851, and in addition to his sewing machine and fancy goods store he was superintendent of the Sunday School programs of Kaumakapili Church parish. The church was founded by his father, Rev. Dr. Lowell Smith. His sister was married to Benjamin F. Dillingham.

> Work on Mr. A. L. Smith's new building on Fort street, is somewhat delayed on account of waiting for bricks. Mr. Harrison the contractor has several thousand on the W. S. Bowne, which will be unloaded in a day or so, and then the building will be pushed along rapidly. The second floor joists are being placed in position.

Evening Bulletin, October 3, 1889

> The title "1889, A. L. Smith" graces the top front of the new building near the corner of King and Fort streets. Why not 1890?

The Honolulu Advertiser, December 7, 1889

C.M. Cooke Ltd. bought the building in 1910 and hired Fred Harrison to add "an immense vault", renovate the interior, and build a practically new front by veneering over the brick front and installing huge plate glass windows.

An unintended side effect of the remodel gave an electric shock to anyone who touched the front, sometimes even generating an actual spark. Local newsboys enjoyed playing with it and tricking others into touching it, even playing a game by joining hands in a séance circle and being electrified when one touched the building.

It was replaced in 1949 with the 2-story First Federal Savings & Loan Association Building designed by Mark Potter and built by G.J. Oda Contracting Co. Ltd. for $400,000. The building had a "solid glass front in color" and was built for the company's 45th anniversary. It was demolished in 1974 for Pioneer Plaza.

The Honolulu Advertiser, July 31, 1949

From 1860 to 1866, C.E. Williams had a furniture showroom on this site in a wooden building that was previously a molasses warehouse owned by Utai and Ahee.

ODD FELLOWS BUILDING

1008-1024 Fort Street

1904 – 1980 (1952 remodel)
Architect/Builder: Oliver G. Traphagen / John Ouderkirk

The Pacific Commercial Advertiser, August 28, 1903

Under pressure from the territorial government wanting to widen Fort Street, the 1859 Odd Fellows building was about 5' into the proposed street line so the Excelsior Lodge asked local architects in 1901 to submit proposed plans for a new building. Four sketches were to be submitted, two with native lava rock and two with terra cotta and pressed brick.

Initially planning the new building to be at Fort Street and Chaplain Lane, they ended up accepting the government offer of $3,940 for 309 square feet along Fort Street plus $1,576 "for the damage attendant upon the removal of the building back from the street line". They selected a design by Oliver G. Traphagen and John Ouderkirk had the lowest bid of $45,733 plus $23,500 for iron and terra cotta.

The cornerstone of the new building was laid on October 25, 1903. Jacob Lando officiated as Grand Marshal and over 400 members of various fraternal societies marched in the parade.

> *"In Benevolence and Charity I lay this cornerstone, earnestly praying that as it is firmly fixed in this solid foundation, so may those cardinal virtues immutably repose in our organization, and be the constant practice of our Order."* – Lester Petrie, Noble Grand

The completed building was officially dedicated on July 31, 1904, with speeches and dancing on 2 floors.

The J. Lando clothing store returned to the new building on the mauka side (Jacob Lando was an active member of the I.O.O.F.).

The Bergstrom Music Company was located on the makai side from 1904 to 1924.

The second floor was rented to other lodges and societies, with the Odd Fellows occupying the entire third floor. The top floor was used as a reception and dance hall with a roof garden.

2022

Excelsior Lodge No.1 of the Independent Order of Odd Fellows (I.O.O.F) was the oldest lodge west of the Rocky Mountains. It was organized in 1846, and their first room was in a 1-story adobe building with a grass roof on Hotel Street in Adam's Yard.

The lodge moved to another adobe house near the mauka/waikiki corner of Hotel and Alakea streets in 1847, and later met in the old 2-story stone building built by William French that housed Hoffschlaeger & Co. They also met in another adobe building near Hotel and Nuuanu that partially collapsed one rainy night.

In 1853 they received $1,600 from the Grand Lodge of the United States to be used for a new building. Through careful investment this sum grew to $7,090 by 1859 and they decided to build on a portion of the old Oliver Holmes property on Fort Street.

> BREAKING GROUND.—The work of excavating for the foundation of the New Odd Fellows' Hall to be erected on Fort Street, was begun last last week. The building is to be 45 by 55 feet, of brick, two stories high, with cellar.

The Pacific Commercial Advertiser, March 17, 1859

The architect/builder was George Thomas and the cornerstone with time capsule box was laid on April 26, 1859, which was the 40th anniversary of the founding of the I.O.O.F in the United States.

It was the first building erected in Honolulu for a benevolent institution and cost approximately $10,000. The first tenants downstairs were the Savidge grocery store and the W.N. Ladd hardware store. L.E. Tracy's store was there from 1897 to 1898, succeeded by the J. Lando store.

The photograph above, taken between 1866 and 1870 shows the 1859 brick Odd Fellows Building and 1866 brick B.F. Ehlers store on the left, and the 1852 stone C. Brewer / May Building on the right. All the other buildings on this stretch of Fort Street were made of wood.

Honolulu Star-Bulletin, December 23, 1939

This photograph taken c.1868 shows the Tom Moore Tavern on the corner of Fort and King Streets (later the site of the 1903 O'Neill Building) next to Ichabod Bartlett's Family Grocery and Feed Store, and the 1859 Odd Fellows Building.

WATERHOUSE / ANDRADE BUILDING

1027-1031 Fort Street
1882 – 1981 (remodeled 1904, 1920, 1953)
Architect/Builder: Walker & Treadway (1882), J.F. Bowler (1904), Emory & Webb (1920), Mark Potter (1953)

Bishop Museum Archives

"No. 10."—This cabalistic sign was suddenly thrown out on the opening of Mr. Waterhouse's new store on Fort Street, on Wednesday morning. What " No. 10" means no one has been able to find out as yet, as the stores on the street are not numbered, and much curiosity exists to know. Perhaps some of our readers may be more successful in their inquiries than we have been; at all events, we recommend them to call at No. 10, where they will find Mr. J. T. Waterhouse, Jr., in attendance with the prettiest lot of goods we have seen for many a day, embracing everything from a pin or a fish-hook to a complete set of house-furnishing articles, not excepting *warming pans*.

The Pacific Commercial Advertiser, January 15, 1863

John Thomas Waterhouse had a 1-story wooden store on this site as early as 1863 which he mysteriously called "No. 10". He replaced it with a 2-story brick building in 1882.

The Ladies of Honolulu will be glad to learn that J. T. Waterhouse is about to pull down his No. 10 Store, and erect in its stead a handsome brick one. He has rented and will occupy in the meantime the Store vacated by S. Magnin.

Evening Bulletin, March 16, 1882

AT J. T. WAITERHOUSE'S No. 10 Store,

JUST RECEIVED!

— EX —

BONANZA,

— A —

Large Assortment

— OF —

STAPLE AND FANCY GOODS

Consisting in part of a Full Line of

LADIES' UNDERCLOTHING & BABY LINEN

Ladies and Children's Waterproof Cloaks.
Ladies Fancy Silk Scarfs and Bows.

GROS GRAIN AND FRINGED RIBBONS!

Hemmed, Stitched and Plain Linen Handkerchiefs,
Flowers and Feathers, Lace Curtains and Lambrequins.

A LARGE ASSORTMENT OF

DRESS GOODS

— OF THE —

Latest Styles!

Gents White Silk Handkerchiefs,
Berlin Wool, assorted colors;
Slipper and Cushion Patterns,
Smoking Caps,

REAL LACE

Honiton, Maltese,
Point Applique, and
Vallenceinnes,

Crochet and Lace Antimacassars,

EXCELSIOR, BEAU IDEAL, ECLYPSE, FAVOURITE
AND OTHER

TRIMMINGS!

Muslin and Cambric Embroideries,
Lisle and Silk Gloves and Gauntletts,

Linen Table Damask & Napkins.

Birdseye and Russia Diaper,
Black Lace Mits,
Berlin Wool Shawls,

LADIES AND GENTS SILK UMBRELLAS!

☞ Orders from the Other Islands addressed to E. W. JORDAN, will be promptly attended to.

Patterns Sent.

Satisfaction Guaranteed.

jy24 1m

J. T. Waterhouse Has Removed

HIS STOCK OF GOODS!

FROM

No. 10 Fort Street,

To Store Lately Occupied by Mr. S. Maguin,

IN ORDER TO ERECT

A New Brick Building!

On site of old Store.

s1 897 1m   JOHN THOMAS WATERHOUSE

The new brick building in process of erection on Fort street, for J. T. Waterhouse, Esq., is rapidly approaching completion. The work reflects credit on the builders Messrs. Walker and Tredway.

The Honolulu Advertiser, May 25, 1882

The new building of Mr. J. T. Waterhouse on Fort street was opened last week. It is the handsomest shop in this city. It is on the site of the old No. 10, and will continue to be known as No. 10.

The Hawaiian Gazette, July 12, 1882

MOSAIC TILES! MOSAIC TILES!! MOSAIC TILES!!!

See a Pattern Laid

By MR. H. BURNS in pavement, front of

No. 10, No. 10, No. 10 Store

REBUILT, AND

JUST OPENED

WITH A

MOST DESIRABLE LOT OF GOODS!

...... AND ......

Large Parcels on the Way Out.

Selected by MR. J. T. WATERHOUSE, JR., including

Many Novelties for Ladies

As well as many things not seen of the kind before in these Islands

☞ **FAIR DEALING** ☜

May be depended upon

In this Old-Time Store

A STOCK OF

MINTURN TILES on HAND!

Also, Orders taken for OTHER PATTERNS to be made from any pattern manufactured, as can be shown by Pattern Box. Apply to

djy14 2w   **J. T. WATERHOUSE.**

Shortly after 5pm on Wednesday, November 12, 1884, employee Leonard Patten came rushing out of the J.T. Waterhouse store with a 4' wooden stick in his hand and started beating Hiram Bridges who was walking on the other side of Fort Street.

Bridges pulled out a .38 caliber pistol, fired two shots at Patten, and then disappeared into the Horn Bakery around the corner on Hotel Street. Patten was carried into the Benson Smith Drug Store at the corner of Fort and Hotel streets where he died moments later.

MURDER IN THE STREET.

L. P. Patten Shot and Killed on Fort Street by H. A. Bridges.

The murder caused a public sensation, especially when the details came out that Patten, who was married, had been in an "intimate relationship" for several years with Frederick Horn's daughter, Lois, who had suddenly married Bridges only 3 months before. Patten was obsessed and had stalked and threatened violence to both of them on numerous occasions.

Self-defense was claimed at the trial, but the fact that Bridges had used a pistol led to a charge of second-degree manslaughter and a prison sentence of 5 years. He was pardoned on the King's birthday two years later, left for St. Louis and never returned. Lois was granted a divorce in San Francisco in June 1887 on the grounds of his felony conviction.

E. W. Jordan, No. 10 Fort St., has an announcement in this issue. He now owns the No. 10 store and intends to keep it in the front rank of local business houses.

The Hawaiian Star, April 10, 1896

In 1896, Edward Waller Jordan bought the No.10 store. He was born in Bedfordshire, England in 1849 and came to Hawaii in 1869.

NEW JORDAN BUILDING

Work on the improvements to be made in E. W. Jordan's store was begun this morning by J. F. Bowler and contractors associated with him. The back part of the present store is to be torn down and the rear of the new structure built first. When this is completed the front of the Jordan store will be cut back to the new Fort street line and a modern front put in.

Evening Bulletin, January 18, 1904

Just Received:

TABLE DAMASK and NAPKINS, new designs.
LINEN HUCKABACK and TURKISH TOWELS.
PILLOW LINEN.
GRAY AND BROWN WOOLEN BEIGE.
LADIES' HOSE in Tan and Black.
¾ SOCKS, in colors.

E. W. JORDAN,
No. 10 FORT STREET.

Work has begun on the reconstruction of E. W. Jordan's store building. The last part of it will be a modern front on the new line of Fort street. This will eliminate the last "jog" in Fort street between Beretania street and the waterfront.

The Honolulu Advertiser, January 19, 1904

Andrade & Co. was founded in 1919 by Jason, William, and Frank Andrade along with John W. Gomes. They were the successors to E.W. Jordan and opened in May 1920.

Jason Andrade was born in Honolulu in 1879 and had worked for M. McInerny & Co. for 10 years and as a partner in Silva's Toggery for 9 years before opening his own business.

In 1953, architect Mark Potter was hired to remodel the front of the building in conjunction with the modernization of the adjacent Boston Block. But surprisingly:

> "The Gay Nineties styling of Andrade's second-story façade, however, will be emphasized by the architect. He will accentuate Andrade's ornate cornices and narrow windows by adding colorful awnings and window boxes."

As for the street level, it was given an "ultra modern" look with glass doors and continuous glass display windows angled in from the sidewalk to provide a "shopping bay". The sidewalk was overlayed with coral-colored stone that was cross-hatched with brass dividers. The improvements were mostly paid for by the Brewer Estate in connection with a 10-year lease signed by Andrade's.

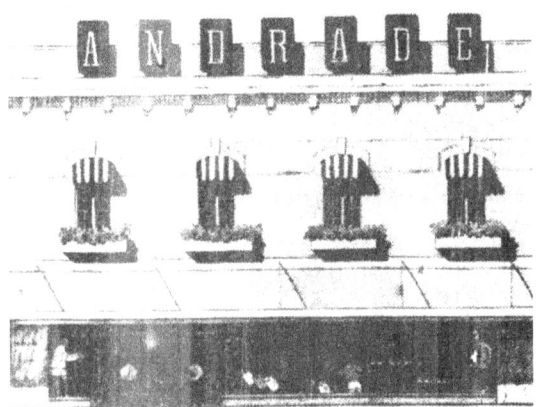

Honolulu Star-Bulletin, August 26, 1953

ANDRADE COMPANY WILL OPEN STORE

Alterations Will Be Made To Jordan Rooms In Waterhouse Building For New Concern

Emory and Webb virtually have completed plans for remodeling the old Jordan rooms in the Waterhouse building on Fort street mauka of King, and work probably will begin this week. The new corporation of Andrade & Co., Ltd., is having the alterations made and will begin a men's clothing and furnishing store between March 15 and April 1.

To Sublet Mauka Side

The work will be alterations to the inside, to divide the present rooms into two parts, each having a frontage on Fort street of 25 feet, besides basement and second-floor space; building two stairways to the second floor; remodeling the front display windows; putting in a mezzanine floor across the front and back of each of the new rooms; and setting prism glass above the display windows. These windows will be much deeper than at present (15½ feet by 5½ feet wide at the front). The front will be faced with gray Tennessee marble. The Andrade store will occupy the makai room, and the mauka will be sublet, said Jason Andrade, president of Andrade & Co.

Has Kuppenheimer Agency

Mr. Andrade is a well known Honolulan who has been in the clothing and furnishing goods business for 20 years. He has organized the company with a capital stock of $45,000. On a trip to the States, from which he recently returned, he obtained the agency for the Kuppenheimer brand of men's ready-made clothing, which, although one of the leading lines, has not been represented in Honolulu. Hats and shirts will be among the other staple goods carried, but there will be no stock of shoes; and goods for men only, not for boys, will be carried.

The Honolulu Advertiser, January 7, 1920

At one time Andrade had as many as 19 stores and resort shops in Hawaii. The Fort Street store was closed in January 1977 and the company was sold to an investment firm in 1979.

The building briefly housed a Burger King restaurant before being demolished in 1981 to make way for the $129M Executive Center complex. The site is now an open courtyard.

B.F. EHLERS / CAMPBELL BUILDING

1026-1038 Fort Street

1897 – 1980 (remodeled 1917, 1952)
Architect/Builder: Howard & Train (1897), Ripley & Davis (1916) / Fred Harrison (1897), Bowler & Ingvorsen (1917)

THE NEW CAMPBELL BLOCK.
(Designed by Howard & Train.)

The Honolulu Advertiser, August 19, 1897

After a fire destroyed the 1-story brick B.F. Ehlers store built on this site in 1866, James Campbell hired George A. Howard Jr. and Robert F. Train to design a new building with 90' of frontage along Fort Street with room for six stores on two floors.

The building was brick with a front of "iron frame and cement with ornaments" with large plate glass windows, the second story trimmed in Hawaiian stone, and "a heavy stone cornice with semicircular centre extending to considerable height".

The first tenants were B.F. Ehlers and Pacific Cyclery.

The Campbell Estate hired Ripley & Davis in 1916 to design "extensive alterations and improvements" estimated to cost $80,000 which included a new front, a third floor, and a 40' rear extension resulting in 40,000 square feet of floor space. Construction was completed by Bowler & Ingvorsen in late 1917.

The Honolulu Advertiser, April 3, 1916

1959

2022

There were two buildings previously on this site: a 2-story wooden building that was the first Hackfeld store dating to 1850 and a 1-story brick store built in 1866 by B.F. Ehlers.

A driveway in between led to Heinrich Hackfeld's 1-story wooden house (located behind the future location of the Wichman Building).

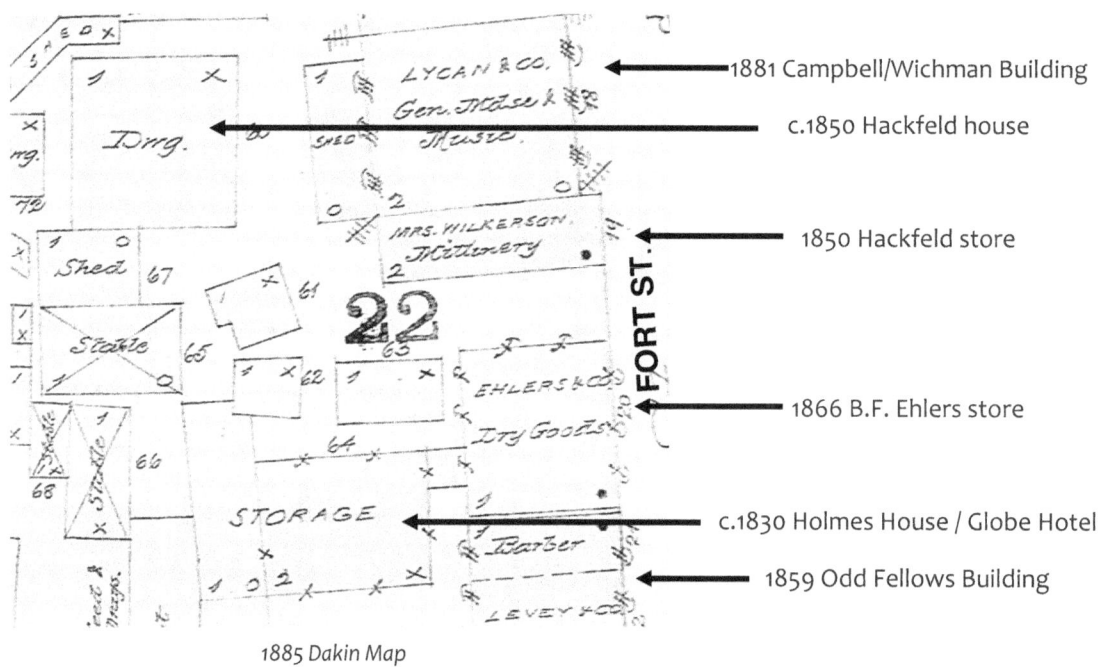

1885 Dakin Map

Called by the locals "Hale Silika" due to carrying so many silk garments, the H. Hackfeld & Co. building was on this site from 1850 to 1897. It became the retail counterpart to their main store on Queen Street.

Hackfeld's nephew Bernhard Friedrich Ehlers took over the store in April 1862 and renamed it B.F. Ehlers & Co. He built a 1-story brick building on the makai side of the property along Fort Street in 1866.

Known as the "upper store", H. Hackfeld & Co. acquired a half interest in 1878 and purchased the remainder in October 1896.

Paul Emmert, 1854

The 1866 B.F. Ehlers store and 1850 Hackfeld Building can both be seen in this photograph from the mid-1890's. The Odd Fellows Hall is on the immediate left and the Campbell/Wichman Building is on the far right. The tower of the Chilton Block and the Lucas clock tower are both visible in the background.

B. F. EHLERS,
DEALER IN DRY GOODS, SILKS, &c.
FORT STREET, HONOLULU.

The old Globe Hotel premises and the Hackfeld premises on Fort street have been purchased by Mr. James Campbell for the sum of $24,000, circa. We understand that Mr. Campbell intends erecting a number of new stores, as soon as the present leases run out, the longest lease is for a period of two years. This gentleman is certainly making a number of very excellent improvements in our city.

The Hawaiian Gazette, January 24, 1883

In 1883, James Campbell purchased the Hackfeld property and the former Globe Hotel premises located behind the Ehlers store and the Odd Fellows Building for about $24,000. He already owned all the property on the ewa side of Fort Street up to the corner of Fort and Hotel streets and in 1897 tried to buy the Odd Fellows property but they decided not to sell.

Mrs. Wilkerson's millinery shop was in the Hackfeld Building in 1885, by 1891 it was the boot and shoe store of Frank Gertz.

The brick Ehlers building burned down in the early morning hours of July 23, 1896. There were many theories as to the origin of the fire, including "a match-chewing contest on the part of some rats". Since the city was working to widen Fort Street, this presented the opportunity for a new building to be built on the new street line.

The Alien Property Custodian of the US Government seized the firm in 1918 and it was reorganized and renamed American Factors Ltd. The B.F. Ehlers department store was renamed "Liberty House" in response to widespread anti-German sentiment.

After World War I, Johann Freidrich Hackfeld, Heinrich's nephew and partner in the firm since 1881, tried to later recover the seized property and filed a suit against American Factors for "fraudulent conspiracy" that went all the way to the U.S. Supreme Court who sided with the U.S. Government in 1942.

American Factors, called Amfac since 1967, became one of Hawaii's "Big Five" landowners, and Liberty House expanded to the US Mainland with stores in 8 states. The Liberty House on Fort Street was remodeled in 1952 and demolished for a new building in 1980. The company was acquired by Federated Department Stores and became Macy's, and in 2014 the building became the downtown Walmart.

The Holmes House/Globe Hotel site is now between the Walmart escalator and frozen food section.

Honolulu Star-Bulletin, October 10, 1921

WICHMAN BUILDING

1042-1048 Fort Street

1881 – 1954, (1893, 1916 remodel)
Architect/Builder: George Lucas (1881), H.L. Kerr (1916) /
George Lucas (1881), Harrison Brothers (1893), Honolulu Planing Mill (1916)

Originally part of the large property owned by Oliver Holmes, James Campbell hired George Lucas to build this 2-story brick building in 1881.

The first tenants were the California Furniture Company owned by E.P. Adams on the makai side and the George F. Wells musical instrument store on the mauka side. The Knights of Pythias met in the hall upstairs.

Hawaii State Archives

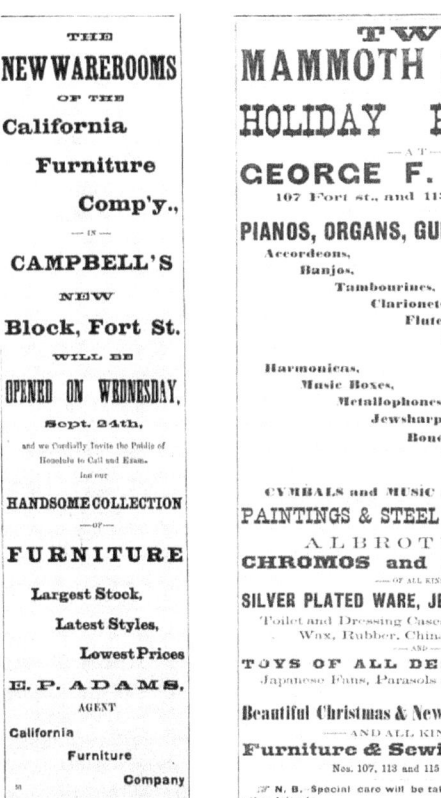

Edward Lycan & Captain James Johnson bought out George Wells in 1883, and Lycan & Johnson's Music Store was later sold to Gideon West in 1885.

In 1888 G. West & Co. sold canary birds, concertinas, baby carriages, dishes, pianos, baseballs, furniture, and jewelry, with "lambrequins a specialty".

H.H. Williams had a furniture store on the makai side in 1881 and future Hawaiian governor Charles J. McCarthy had a cigar store on the mauka side. For over 60 years, from 1893 to 1954, this was the location of the H.F. Wichman & Co. jewelry store.

Henry F. Wichman was born in Hanover, Germany, and came to New York with his family in 1866 when he was two years old. He came to Hawaii in 1886 on his way to the South Africa gold rush. Wichman initially worked as an engraver for Spears & Pfeiffer, and just as he was about to give up on the jewelry business he was asked by King Kalākaua to make some special commemorative medals and decorations.

Wichman teamed up with J.E. Gomes on August 12, 1887, to form Gomes & Wichman, which lasted 18 months until he bought out his partner.

Harrison Brothers, the contractors, are remodelling the two stores in the Campbell building on Fort street. Handsome glass fronts are to be put in each. The store formerly occupied by C. E. Williams & Co. is to be taken by H. F. Wichman, the jeweler and optician.

The Honolulu Advertiser, March 6, 1893

H.F. Wichman & Co. moved to this building in 1893 from their previous location in a 1-story wooden building a few doors down on Fort Street between the Odd Fellows Building and the Charles Hammer harness store on the corner at King Street.

"His industry and his splendid knowledge of the jewelry trade rendered his house as important in the Pacific as Shreve's to San Francisco and Tiffany's to New York." (Honolulu Advertiser, June 13, 1921)

The Lucas Brothers added a new brick addition in back in 1901 and the building was given a "complete alteration" by the Campbell Estate in 1916. It was designed by architect H.L. Kerr and built by the Honolulu Planing Mill for $7,250 less $300 for salvage.

Honolulu: The Cross-Roads of the Pacific, 1913

The large clock out front that had been a Fort Street landmark for years was given to the Outrigger Canoe Club. H.F. Wichman & Co. installed a new hand-carved wooden clock with Swiss movement on the outside of the building that was faithfully hand-wound by head watchman Joe Quientro for nearly 40 years.

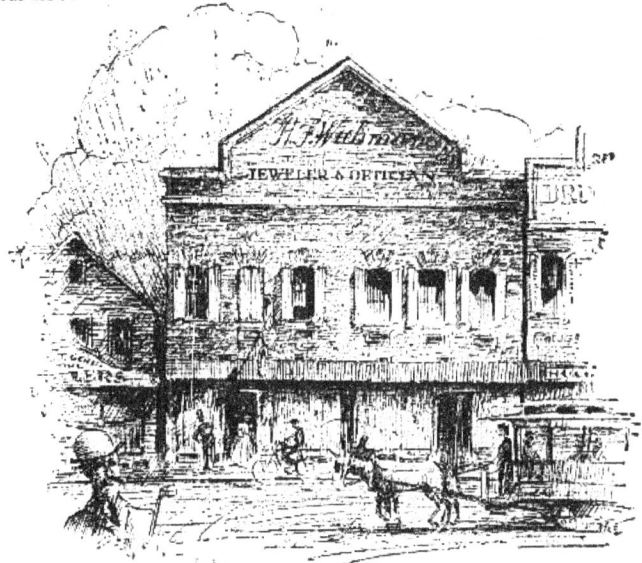

H. F. WICHMAN & COMPANY IN THE EARLY EIGHTIES

The Oldest Jewelry Store In Hawaii

H. F. WICHMAN & CO., LTD., Hawaii's oldest and most exclusive jewelry store, was established on August 12th, 1887, by H. F. Wichman, on Fort street, within several doors of its present location.

Mr. Wichman came to Honolulu as a young man, and after a number of early struggles his determination succeeded in carrying through the establishment and steady development of what is now the Territory's oldest jewelry firm.

An incident of interesting historical mention gave the struggling young jeweler a new start shortly after his early efforts in business had met with near failure. With several other business men, Mr. Wichman had about decided to leave Honolulu and seek his fortune in South Africa, when King Kalakaua awarded him the task of engraving a number of medals to be presented to the King's soldiers. This order changed the aspect of affairs for Wichman, and from that time on his business began to flourish and has continued to develop up to the present day.

The firm was incorporated in 1903, Mr. Wichman remaining the active head of the organization until his death in 1921.

Merle M. Johnson, for many years connected with the firm, now is president and manager, and has carried on the traditions of quality and integrity which this firm has always maintained.

Wichman's exhibits of jewels and objects d'art have attracted the attention of prominent visitors from all parts of the world who have expressed their surprise and commendation that a jewelry establishment worthy of the largest metropolis should be found in this mid pacific city.

H. F. Wichman & Co., Ltd.

The Honolulu Advertiser, February 24, 1926

The Honolulu Advertiser, October 12, 1916

A fire destroyed the building on June 12, 1954. It was replaced by a 3-story $400,000 building designed by Mark Potter with Hartfields clothing store on the first floor and Liberty House above. It was given a "period facelift" in 1986 designed by CSJ Group Architects Ltd.

The Honolulu Star-Bulletin, April 15, 1955

2022

According to historian Gorham Gilman, in the 1840's this was the site of Edward C. Webster's 2-story adobe store with the tailor shop of John Ballou and C.H. Nicholson on the upper floor in 1844. He described Webster as "quite small in stature, light in weight, but forcible in expression and fertile in wit".

JOHN BALLOU,
C. H. NICHOLSON, } *Tailors.*
SHOP OVER THE STORE OF MR. E. C. WEBSTER.
Honolulu, June 15.   tf

Located immediately behind the 1881 Wichman Building was the large 1-story residence of Heinrich Hackfeld, prominent merchant and Consul of Sweden.

The house was also the long-time residence of Charles E. Williams. In later years it was used as a storehouse behind the Wichman Building until demolished sometime before 1899.

Paul Emmert, 1854

BOSTON BLOCK

1035-1041 Fort Street

1900 – 1981 (1953 remodel)
Architect/Builder: Oliver G. Traphagen / Arthur Harrison

Honolulu: The Cross-Roads of the Pacific, 1913

The Honolulu Advertiser, December 18, 1899

This early 4-story "skyscraper" was built for the Charles Brewer Estate in 1900. It was designed by Oliver G. Traphagen and built by Arthur Harrison, and had a frontage of 54' on Fort Street and a depth of 93'.

The Italian Renaissance building was described as "a fine sample of the modern type of business and office structures of the eastern states. Its first floor front is of steel and glass; the front upper stories being of brown pressed brick, with cornice of stamped metal."

It was built with two wings around a large horseshoe-shaped light court in back to provide interior offices with natural light.

The basement was "thoroughly lighted with the Luxfer sidewalk prizm tiles and the Lucidux reflecting lights".

Opening day was November 17, 1900.

A fire destroyed the building on June 12, 1954. It was replaced by a 3-story $400,000 building designed by Mark Potter with Hartfields clothing store on the first floor and Liberty House above. It was given a "period facelift" in 1986 designed by CSJ Group Architects Ltd.

The Honolulu Star-Bulletin, April 15, 1955

2022

According to historian Gorham Gilman, in the 1840's this was the site of Edward C. Webster's 2-story adobe store with the tailor shop of John Ballou and C.H. Nicholson on the upper floor in 1844. He described Webster as "quite small in stature, light in weight, but forcible in expression and fertile in wit".

Located immediately behind the 1881 Wichman Building was the large 1-story residence of Heinrich Hackfeld, prominent merchant and Consul of Sweden.

The house was also the long-time residence of Charles E. Williams. In later years it was used as a storehouse behind the Wichman Building until demolished sometime before 1899.

Paul Emmert, 1854

BOSTON BLOCK

1035-1041 Fort Street

1900 – 1981 (1953 remodel)
Architect/Builder: Oliver G. Traphagen / Arthur Harrison

Honolulu: The Cross-Roads of the Pacific, 1913

The Honolulu Advertiser, December 18, 1899

This early 4-story "skyscraper" was built for the Charles Brewer Estate in 1900. It was designed by Oliver G. Traphagen and built by Arthur Harrison, and had a frontage of 54' on Fort Street and a depth of 93'.

The Italian Renaissance building was described as "a fine sample of the modern type of business and office structures of the eastern states. Its first floor front is of steel and glass; the front upper stories being of brown pressed brick, with cornice of stamped metal."

It was built with two wings around a large horseshoe-shaped light court in back to provide interior offices with natural light.

The basement was "thoroughly lighted with the Luxfer sidewalk prizm tiles and the Lucidux reflecting lights".

Opening day was November 17, 1900.

This frontage on Fort Street was originally part of the driveway for a large tract of land that extended all the way around to Hotel Street. The first recorded owner was John Gowan who sold it to Boston merchant James Hunnewell for $400 in 1826.

Hunnewell was born in Charlestown, MA, in 1794, and went to sea at age 15. He first came to Hawaii in 1817 on the brig *Bordeaux Packet*, and in 1819 as first officer and part-owner of the brig *Thaddeus* that brought the first missionaries. He lived here for 10 years as a merchant and "acquired the nucleus of an ample fortune", much of which he spent on Hawaiian charitable causes while remaining in Boston.

Hunnewell and Charles Brewer were longtime partners in the ship-owning and commission merchant business that later became C. Brewer & Co., with Brewer's nephew "Charles Brewer 2d" based in Honolulu.

C. Brewer & Co. and S.H. Williams & Co. were in the back of the lot accessed by a driveway off Fort Street, and it was known as Brewer's Yard.

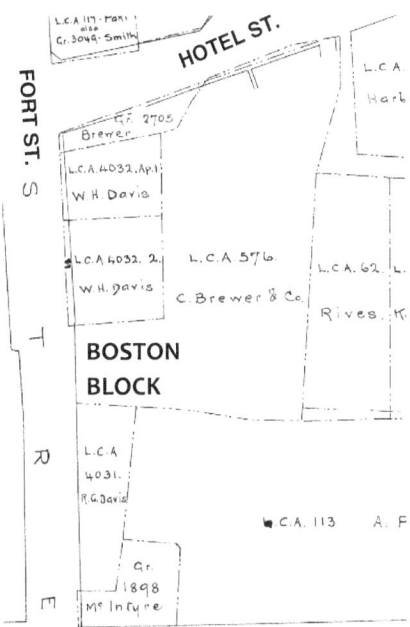

1896 Original Titles Survey Map

Paul Emmert, 1854

On the makai side of the driveway to Brewer's Yard was a 2-story coral stone building known as the May Building, built in 1852.

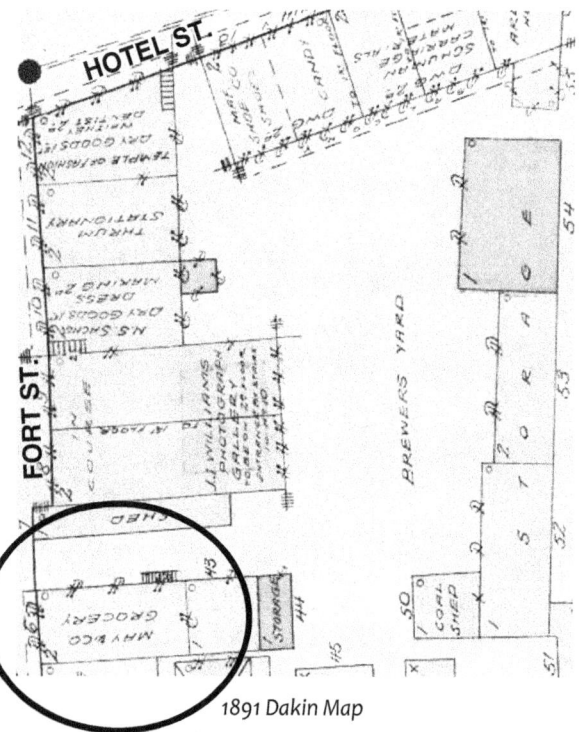

1891 Dakin Map

HISTORIC OLD STRUCTURE

MAY BUILDING, SOLD TODAY AT AUCTION.

Erected in 1852 and for a Long Time The Finest Business House in Town. Interesting Career.

Morgan sold the building of H. May & Company today at auction. The only bidder was Herman Ludloff, a German contractor, who offered $200 for the structure and was declared its owner. The house is built of rock. It will be torn down at once.

The May building, as it has been called for several years, was built in 1852 for C. Brewer, second, a son of the original Boston Brewer. At that time and for some years after it was the finest house in Honolulu. When it was opened for business John O. Dominis was bookkeeper and H. A. P. Carter was salesman.

In the early sixties Brewer moved down to Queen street into the Brewer building torn down about nine months ago. Frank Spencer, father of Mrs. Bickerton, then moved his dry goods establishment from Hotel street into the May building. Mr. Jones, well remembered to this day among Hawaiians as "Kaliopu," was manager. In 1862 or '63 Jones enlisted for the war, joining a Maine regiment, and was soon promoted to be captain.

Mr. Spencer retired from business in 1865 and Sam Savidge removed his grocery from the Odd Fellows building to the May building. In 1868 Mr. Savidge sold out to Mr. May, uncle of the present head of the concern. The May business has occupied the place ever since. Henry May had originally established the business, but retired for a number of years returning in 1868.

The May building was started in 1851, just after a big fire which swept away all the grass houses on the Arlington lot belonging to Paki, father of Mrs. C. R. Bishop. The fire started in B. F. Snow's auction room, just back of the Egan store, at night. It was checked at McIntyre's corner by buckets and a rude hose arrangement that had been fitted up. At the time Paki kept 200 men under arms in his yard. These were all burned out of their homes. The May building was the first to arise on the burnt district, where it was for many years a distinct landmark.

A five-story building will take the place of the old structure.

The Hawaiian Star, July 26, 1899

The Honolulu Advertiser, July 1, 1953

Architect Ray Morris designed new modern glass brick and vitriolite store fronts and a new lobby that was built by John Hansen in 1938.

In 1953 the Brewer Estate hired architect Mark Potter to "modernize" the Boston Block with a new front. He removed the "old-fashioned cornices" and other "gingerbread" features and added "aluminum awnings and vertical fins."

The adjoining Waterhouse/Andrade Building on the makai side was also altered at the same time.

The Honolulu Star-Bulletin, October 13, 1954

Hawaii State Archives

Store to be closed temporarily

The F.W. Woolworth store at 1045 Fort St. will close temporarily on Sept. 1 for leveling of its present home, the Boston Building.

That building will be replaced by the $126 million, 40-story Executive Centre condominium. Woolworth plans to re-open at the same location within the condominium in the spring of 1983.

In addition to changes at the downtown Woolworth, work is being completed on new Woolworth stores in Waianae, Lihue and Hilo.

The Honolulu Advertiser, August 2, 1981

The *Honolulu Star-Bulletin* described the building in 1981 as "the building no one wants to save". It was demolished that same year for the $129M Executive Center. The site is now the makai side of the Ross Dress-for-Less store.

WILLIAMS / HOLLISTER BUILDING

1056-1060 Fort Street
1871 – present? (remodeled 1918)
Architect/Builder: J.G. Osborne?

"Mr. Williams, on Fort Street, has the honor of being the first gentleman in Honolulu who has largely used concrete in the construction of a large store". It was very likely built by J.G. Osborne who was building other concrete buildings at the time such as the 1871 Post Office, the 1871 Hawaiian Hotel, and the 1872 Dimond/Dillingham Building. It replaced an earlier 1-1/2 story wooden building of similar design.

The C.E. Williams furniture business and ware rooms were in the mauka storefront, and the Criterion House dry goods store owned by the Hayselden Brothers was on the makai side. By 1876, the I.O.G.T. (Independent Order of Good Templars) were meeting in the lodge rooms upstairs.

1870

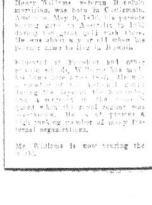

This old view of Fort Street shows the location of C. E. Williams in the building which he erected in 1872. This location is now occupied by Wichman's Jewelry Store.

67 Years of Sympathetic Service

It has been the privilege of this institution to render to Honolulu a sympathetic service for sixty-seven years. Williams Undertaking establishment takes its place among the oldest kamaaina firms of this Territory. Today, with this exceptional background of service, we find added incentive in maintaining the high standards and ideals which have always characterized this establishment.

In 1859, C. E. Williams started his undertaking service in Honolulu. He also operated a furniture store at that time, and was located in a store on Fort street, makai of Hotel street. In 1872 the building which is now occupied by Wichman's jewelry store was erected by Mr. Williams. When retail business commenced to monopolize Fort street the establishment was moved to King street where the Kauikeolani building now stands.

H. H. Williams, who grew up in his father's business, has been in charge of it over forty years; a number of years ago he acquired a sole interest. Then followed a series of moves, the establishment having at different times occupied the corner of Fort and Beretania streets, the Love building on Fort near Pauahi, and the present site of the Bank of Hawaii. Under the efficient management of the younger Mr. Williams, the establishment outgrew the combination and the furniture end of the business was discontinued.

The first modern automobile hearse in the Territory was introduced by Mr. Williams in 1915. In the same year the firm moved to its present location on Nuuanu street, where it occupies a large three-story building. H. H. Williams is proprietor and C. P. Osborne manager.

Williams Funeral Parlors

1374 Nuuanu Street ---Established 1859--- Phone 1408

C. P. OSBORNE, Manager

Night Service Phones, 2255, 2903, 1408, 8447

The Honolulu Advertiser, February 24, 1926
[wrong building!]

Charles Edward Williams was born in Hatley, a township in the Memphremagog Regional County Municipality in the Eastern Townships region of Quebec in 1825. He first came to Hawaii in 1851 but briefly left for the Australian gold rush, returning in 1857. He reportedly established the first furniture business in Honolulu in 1859 and was also the Fire Chief from 1867 to 1870.

In 1877, Williams sold all his Honolulu properties to James Campbell and in 1893 moved to San Francisco. "He was a man of sterling qualities whose word was as good as his bond".

Messrs. Hollister & Co. have removed their wholesale and retail drug store from Nuuanu street to No. 109 Fort street, in the Williams building. The new store has been elegantly fitted up and already presents a most attractive appearance, although the stock is not, as yet, entirely removed from the old stand. The new store occupies a portion of the lower floor and almost all of the upper floor of the Williams building. The display of goods in the new store is much better than it formerly was. Two of the chief attractions of the new place will be the soda water and cigar stands. The drug department reminds one of a San Francisco store.

Daily Honolulu Press, December 8, 1885

Henry Reed Hollister and Philip G. Hyland opened Hollister & Hyland in 1869 as a cigar, tobacco, and snuff shop that also sold soda water and later manufactured their own soda water. After the death of Hyland in 1871 it became Hollister & Co., and they first advertised going into the druggist and apothecary business in 1880.

They moved to this building in 1885 and became the Hollister Drug Company in 1894. By the 1930's they were the largest retail drug store in Hawaii with stores on Oahu, Maui, and Hawaii. They went out of business in 1955 and sold off all their stores, closing the Fort Street store on April 1, 1955.

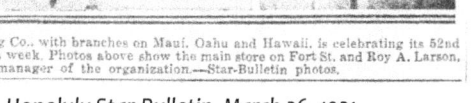

2022

Honolulu Star-Bulletin, March 26, 1931

J.J. WILLIAMS BUILDING

1045-1057 Fort Street

1891 – 1954

Architect/Builder: "Boston architect" / Henry F. Bertelmann, Thomas B. Walker

Hawaii State Archives

This building was initially called the Brewer Block (one of many) and was built by H.F. Bertelman and Thomas B. Walker for C. Brewer & Co. in 1891 at a cost of $12,200.

The plans were drawn by a Boston architect and were initially rejected for not meeting local building and fire requirements.

Photographer J.J. Williams was on the second floor, and Egan & Gunn and a shoe store were on the first floor.

The Brewer Building.

The new Brewer & Co. building on Fort street is to be turned over to-day to the company by the contractors. It is all finished with the exception of some counters, etc., to be put in by the parties renting it. The upper story is to be occupied by Mr. J. J. Williams, the two lower rooms by Messrs. Egan & Gunn, who will commence moving in to-day, and by the American Shoe Manufacture Co. represented by Mr. D. B. Smith. Large stocks of goods are to be carried by the two firms, and when stocked up will give the buying people bargains in their line.

The Honolulu Advertiser, March 14, 1891

Messrs. H. F. Bertelmann and T. B. Walker have been awarded the contract for erecting the new Brewer block on Fort street. Their tender was $12,200.

The Honolulu Advertiser, March 3, 1891

A zinc balustrade in "imitation of marble" was a first for Honolulu. The Egan & Gunn store was the first trial of electric lights in a Honolulu store, and it also featured a sewing machine and large fans run by electricity.

GRAND OPENING, MONDAY, AUG. 24.
EGAN & GUNN
Having Moved to Their New and Commodious Store
On Fort St., Brewer Block,
WILL DISPLAY A COMPLETE STOCK IN EVERY DEPARTMENT.
OPEN SAUTRDAY EVENING!

The 1891 Brewer building replaced a 1-story building that had housed the photographic studios of J.J. Williams, Meinzies Dickson, and Henry L. Chase.

1882-1890

Henry L. Chase arrived in Hawaii on *Ceylon* from Boston on August 21, 1856 and opened his first photographic gallery next to the post office in 1862. He moved to this location in 1866, and when he moved across the street in 1870 this location became the M. Dickson photographic gallery.

Meinzies Dickson was born in Charlestown, MA, and came to Hawaii in 1867 via Cincinnati after serving in the American navy in the Civil War. He was the brother of J.G. Dickson of Lewers & Dickson.

James J. "Jimmy" Williams was born in England in 1853, came to Hawaii in 1879 via Cleveland and San Francisco, and purchased the photographic gallery of M. Dickson in 1882.

Honolulu's top photographer for nearly 50 years, he was killed at age 72 when struck by a streetcar at the corner of Fort and Hotel streets.

Three generations of Williams worked in the 1891 building until it was demolished in 1954 to make way for a new Woolworth's store.

The Bergstrom Music Store was on the first floor of this building from 1931 to 1953. The building was demolished in 1954 by Walker-Moody Construction for a 3-story F.W. Woolworth Store costing $675,000. The Woolworth's store was demolished in 1981 for the $126M Executive Center development and the corner location is now the Ross Dress for Less store.

TREGLOAN BUILDING

1064-1072 Fort Street / 85 S. Hotel Street

1877, 1882 – present? (1918 reconstructed)

Architect/Builder: T.J. Baker (1877), George Lucas (1882), Emory & Webb (1918)

Isaiah W. Taber, 1880

This building started out as a 1-story brick building built by Thomas J. Baker for C.E. Williams after a fire on March 18, 1877, destroyed the previous wooden building housing the Grunwald & Schutte dry goods store and H.L. Chase's photographic studio.

> NEW CORNER STORE.—On the site of the fire of 18th March last, at the corner of Fort and Hotel streets, we noticed yesterday morning that Mr. T. J. Baker, the architect and builder, was breaking ground for a new one-story brick building, to be erected for the owners of the lot. The new building will be on a line with the adjoining brick store of Mr. C. E. Williams, thus leaving an ample side-walk, and improving the street.

Pacific Commercial Advertiser, April 21, 1877

James Campbell purchased all of C.E. Williams' Honolulu properties in October 1877 for $50,000, and it is very likely he had George Lucas add the second floor when he was constructing the adjacent 2-story building on Hotel Street in 1882.

Photograph from Bell Tower by Isaiah W. Taber, 1883

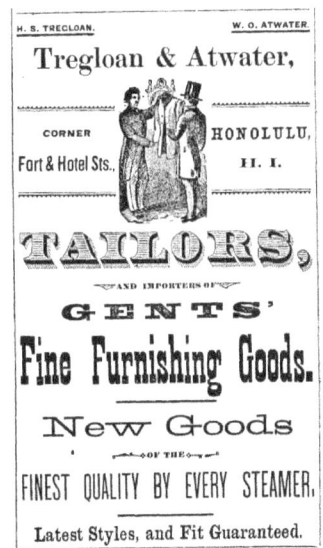

The first tenant was tailor Henry S. Tregloan, born in Cornwall, England, in 1822. Tregloan's store was a mainstay of this corner for 24 years and the building was known as the Tregloan Building.

In 1883, John A. Palmer & W.W. Kilbourn opened a drug store here which became Palmer & Thacher. Later that same year they were bought out by Benson, Smith & Co. founded by three former employees of Hollister & Co.: Captain H.M. Benson, George Waterman Smith, and David McCartney Jr.

Benson, Smith & Co. moved across the street to the Brewer Block on the corner in 1894 and were there for almost 60 years.

In 1895 the Kilohana Art League began meeting upstairs. It was created in 1894 by artists Augusta Graham, Allen Hutchinson, D. Howard Hitchcock, and Annie H. Park as a forum for local artists to meet and exhibit.

The Honolulu Photo Supply was located upstairs from 1900 to 1902.

It was also the location of the Baltimore Dairy Lunch Room, the scene of a shootout in broad daylight on November 4, 1910 between William McQuaid and Volney Driver over attentions to McQuaid's wife. Both survived, but streetcars were damaged as was a clock across the street.

This site was initially the land of John N. Colcord, an "armourer", who sold it to Stephen Reynolds in 1841 for $800. From 1860 to 1869 it was the shop of J.P. Hughes, saddle manufacturer and upholsterer.

1871-1877

From 1870 to 1877 it was H.L. Chase's Cosmopolitan Photographic Gallery and studio, adjoining the Grunwald & Schutte dry goods store. The large skylight visible in the photograph was for Chase's camera room.

The wooden building was destroyed by a disastrous fire on March 18, 1877.

REMOVAL.

HAVING OPENED A NEW PHOTO- GRAPHIC GALLERY on Fort Street, nearly opposite my old stand, next door to Grunwald & Schutte, I shall be happy to see my old patrons, and any others who wish for first-class picture. All styles taken upon the most reasonable terms. Having made arrangements with a good artist in San Francisco, I shall pay particular attention to copying and enlarging pictures for retouching or painting.

By attention to the tastes of my customers, I hope to receive a share of patronage.

Also for sale a variety of Photographic Views, Portraits, &c., and a

PANORAMIC VIEW OF HONOLULU,
The only one ever taken of the City.
d3   H. L. CHASE.

THE FIRE OF SUNDAY LAST.—Honolulu is certainly fortunate in seldom having a fire of importance. That of Sunday last, though the aggregate loss will amount to only a few thousands, was nevertheless quite an event in our community. The alarm was given at a few minutes past 3 p. m. by a printer employed in this office, named Thos. Spencer, who was passing up Fort street and detected the smell of fire from the wooden premises on the corner of Fort and Hotel streets, occupied in the upper story by Mr. H L. Chase as photographic gallery, and below by Messrs. Grunwald & Schutte, dry good dealers. The Fire Department was promptly on hand, and worked with such skill and energy that, in spite of the combustible nature of the building and its contents, in half an hour the fire was out. The upper story only was consumed, showing that the fire must have originated there,—but in what manner is yet unexplained. Mr Chase's loss is stated at $2000, and that of Grunwald & Schutte at $1000, the damage of the latter being mainly sustained by water and in removing, as none of them goods were destroyed. In fact, owing to the promptness and energy of the firemen nearly the whole lower part of the building was left standing, and adjoining wooden houses were only severely scotched. While congratulating the city on the efficiency of our volunteer Fire Department—which was so apparent to all on Sunday last—we may be thankful that the fire occurred in the day time, for had it been in the night the progress of the devouring element would probably have not been so soon stayed.

Pacific Commercial Advertiser, March 24, 1877

In 1917 the Campbell Estate embarked on a massive $160,000 reconstruction and remodeling project for this building and the adjoining buildings on Fort Street and Hotel Street. Designed by Emory & Webb, the plans included remodeling the front of the 1871 Williams/Hollister Building and adding a third story while adding a basement and completely rebuilding the 1877/1882 Tregloan Building and 1882 Campbell Building on the Hotel Street side. Designed for 5 floors, only 3 were constructed.

Completed in August 1918, tenants included Hollister Drug Co., C.J. Day & Co., A.R. Gurrey, Detor & Elie, Hub Clothiers, George B. Curtis, Mercantile Reference Agency, First Church of Jesus Christ Scientists, and architects Emory & Webb.

Hawaii State Archives

2022

BENSON SMITH BUILDING

1063-1071 Fort Street / 101-107 S. Hotel Street

1877 – 1954
Architect/Builder: Thomas J. Baker

IMPROVEMENTS IN HONOLULU.—Under the influence of better times and still better prospects, a good deal of house building of a permanent character has been going on in the city of late. The finest looking and perhaps most substantially built structure in Honolulu (aside from the Government House) is the new two-story brick store belonging to C. Brewer, Esq., of Boston, Mass., erected by T. J. Baker, architect and builder, on the corner of Fort and Hotel streets. The walls are 16 inches thick up to the second story, and 12 inches above, with fire walls all around the roof, and an ornamented ballustrade of concrete. On the ground floor are two large rooms, suitable for stores, 13 feet in the clear; on the second floor—reached by a wide stairway on Hotel street,—are three spacious rooms and a hall, all of which are 11 feet 6 inches in the clear. All the rooms are lathed and plastered and hard-finished. There are 30 openings in the building, which is thoroughly fire-proof, with iron doors and shutters. The windows on the ground floor are to be of plate glass. Altogether, it is a fine specimen of architecture, an honor to Honolulu and a credit to the builder, Mr. Baker.

The Pacific Commercial Advertiser, October 27, 1877

This corner was the site of the Robert Davis dry goods store in the 1840's, and it was the location of the Family Market by the 1860's.

The market building was moved out of the way along Hotel Street in 1868 so Archibald S. Cleghorn could build a new 26' x 36' wooden store. His dry goods store was here from 1869 to 1877. In 1878 he sold the business to his manager, Simon Grant, who renamed the fancy clothing store to Grant & Robertson.

> IMPROVEMENTS.—The well known Family Market, corner of Fort and Hotel streets, has been moved along Hotel street, to the foot of Union street, for the purpose of making room for a building, to be erected for Mr. A. S. Cleghorn, to be used as a fancy dry goods store. The building is to be of wood, twenty-six by thirty-six feet. Fort street is destined to be the Broadway of Honolulu.

Pacific Commercial Advertiser, November 21, 1868

Photograph by H.L. Chase, 1870

Grant & Robertson sold their business and entire stock to Goo Kim in 1880. Goo Kim was one the prominent leaders of the Honolulu Chinese community and was the accredited commercial agent of the Empire of China.

Goo Kim also had a store on Nuʻuanu Street in the Paiko Block (now known as the Lai Fong Building) opened in 1880. He consolidated everything at the Nuʻuanu location in 1888.

> **NEW STORE OPENED!**
>
> **A. S. CLEGHORN & CO.**
>
> Respectfully intimate that they have opened their
>
> New and Magnificent Store
>
> Corner of Fort and Hotel Streets,
>
> — WITH A —
>
> Large & Varied Assortm't
>
> — OF —
>
> **NEW STAPLE**
>
> — AND —
>
> **FANCY DRY GOODS**
>
> A large proportion of the stock just opened has been
>
> Recently Received from the United States and Europe.
>
> And will be found, upon inspection, to be of the
>
> **NEWEST FABRICS & STYLES**
>
> THE GOODS NOW OFFERED
>
> Were bought on unusually favorable terms, and the price for which they will now be sold, will be made to correspond; while much of the Stock will be disposed of at rates that will beat all former attempts at cheapness in this Market.
>
> A. S. C. & Co., have also procured the services of a
>
> **FIRST CLASS MILLINER**
>
> — AND —
>
> **DRESS MAKER!**
>
> From San Francisco, who is competent to execute work in that line of the
>
> **VERY LATEST**
>
> — AND —
>
> **Fashionable Designs.**
>
> ☞ Orders from the other Islands addressed to Mr. SIMON GRANT, Manager of A. S. C. & Co.'s
>
> **FORT STREET STORE**
>
> will receive prompt and careful attention.
>
> Honolulu, Dec. 13th, 1877.

In 1885 the three stores in the building were Goo Kim, Thomas G. Thrum, and N.S. Sachs.

Thomas G. Thrum was born in Newcastle, NSW, Australia, in 1842 and came to Hawaii in 1853.

After stints at whaling and sugar and clerking he bought the Black & Auld stationery and news business in 1870 and quickly became Honolulu's pre-eminent publisher and historian.

He began printing *Thrum's Hawaiian Annual* in 1875 and joined with J.J. Williams in 1888 to start the *Paradise of the Pacific* magazine. He moved his stationery, book and fancy goods store here from Merchant Street in early 1879.

Alfred M. Mellis moved his dry goods store here in 1880 with his wife's millinery and dressmaking shop upstairs. Previously in business with Charles J. Fishel in the California One Price Bazar, he sold his business to Nathaniel S. Sachs in 1884. The N.S. Sachs store was here until they moved to their new building at Fort & Beretania streets in 1902.

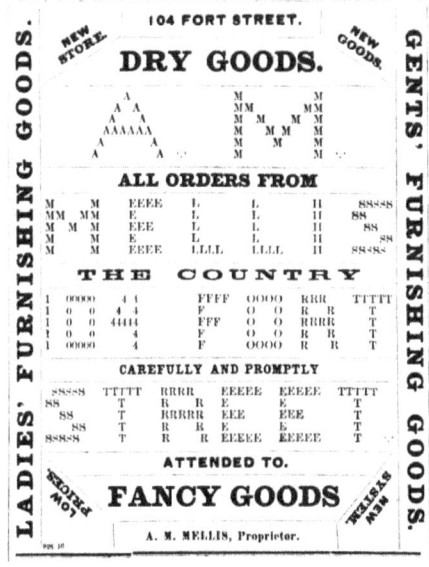

In 1888 the Temple of Fashion, owned by Samuel Ehrlich, moved from the Campbell Block across the street into the former Goo Kim space at the corner. The business closed in 1894 owing $43,000 to various creditors due to an unsuccessful investment in a Brazilian horubone (fake whalebone) factory.

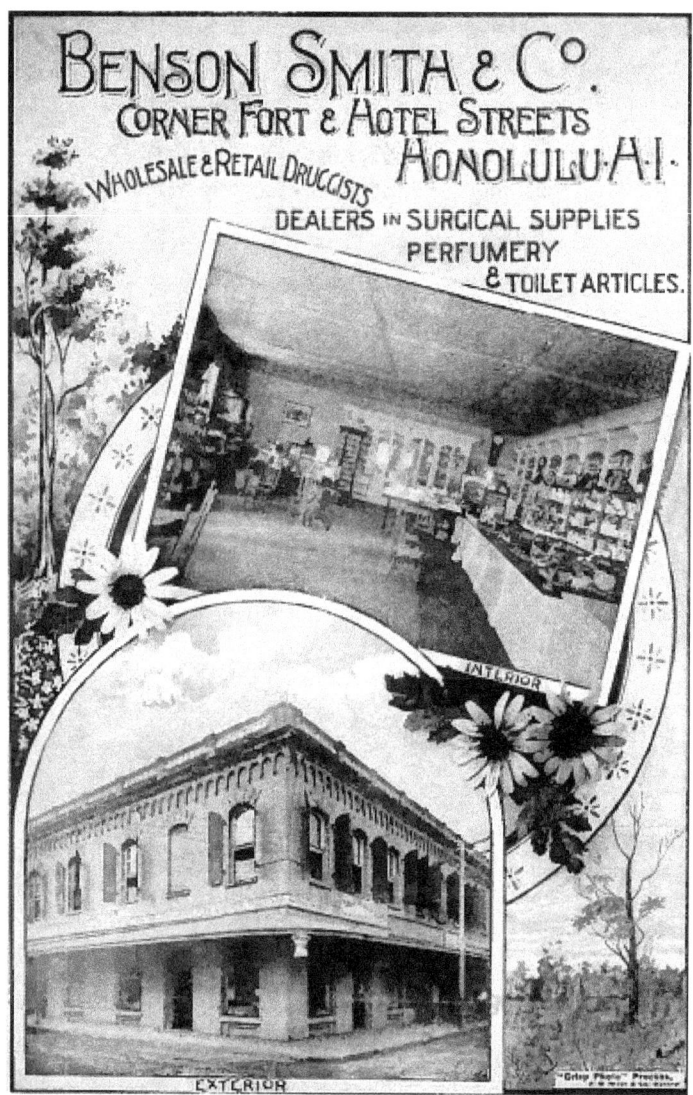

William DeWitt Alexander, 1896

For nearly 60 years, from June 1894 to December 30, 1953, the Benson Smith Drug Store was on the corner.

Benson, Smith & Company was organized in 1883 by Captain Henry M. Benson, George Waterman Smith, and David McCartney Jr. who broke off from the Hollister Company and purchased the stock and trade of Palmer & Thacher.

Born in Detroit, Smith came to Honolulu in 1880 and initially worked for the Hollister Company. Originally located across Fort Street in the Tregloan Building, they moved to this corner in 1894.

In 1923 Benson Smith opened a second location in the Chilton Block at Fort and King streets in the old Chambers Drug Store location.

The building on Fort Street was demolished in 1954 by Walker-Moody Construction, the contractors for a new 3-story F.W. Woolworth Store costing $675,000.

1966

The Woolworth's store was demolished in 1981 for the $126M Executive Center development. The corner location is now the Ross Dress for Less store.

2022

PANTHEON BUILDING

1102-1122 Fort Street / 76-92 S. Hotel Street

1911 – present (1964 remodel)
Architect/Builder: H.L. Kerr?, J.L. Young? / Lucas Brothers

The Honolulu Advertiser, July 18, 1909

Honolulu: The Cross-Roads of the Pacific, 1913

In 1909, H.L. Kerr prepared plans for a large 2-story building to be called the Pantheon Building to be built between the Art Theater on Hotel Street and the Club Stables on Fort Street. The plans called for reinforced concrete with terra cotta facings on the two main streets, an interior steel frame, basement, and spaces for 12 stores. The basement was to be lit by glass prisms in the sidewalk.

At this same time The Art Theater motion picture house started building an Auditorium in the middle of the property and this held up the plans for the Pantheon Building which was going to provide access to the Auditorium via an arcade. But the theater funds ran out and the Pantheon Building had to be redesigned.

Lucas Brothers got the 8-month $80,000 contract to build the new building, starting September 1, 1910. The newspaper at the time said J.L. Young, of Lord-Young was the architect, but it is unknown if this is correct or if he adapted H.L. Kerr's previous design. Lord-Young were the architects for the Art Theatre Auditorium previously planned behind the Pantheon Block.

The Pantheon Saloon, previously on this corner and now owned by Joseph Silva, was able to obtain permission to relocate to Nuʻuanu Street in spite of its reputation for being "the ordinary hang-out of a certain tough element, consisting largely of ne'er-do-weels, prizefight hangers-on and other undesirable citizens".

CONTRACT LET FOR BIG BLOCK

Lucas Bros. Will Build Pantheon for $80,000—Work Will Start at Once.

A contract for the construction of an $80,000 business block at the Ewa-mauka corner of Fort and Hotel streets was let yesterday by the Patheon building company, to Lucas Brothers.

Lucas Brothers will commence building operations at once, and will immediately order materials from the mainland. The tenants of the present one-story block have been notified to vacate by September 1 when the old buildings will be razed and the basement excavated.

The new building will be three stories in height with a deep basement and will be of reinforced concrete throughout. It will be strictly fireproof and there will not be a stick of wood in the block, all the doors and window sashes being of metal, similar to those in the Japanese bank building.

There will be six sidewalk elevators and the sidewalks will be set with glass prisms and the front of the first floor will also contain glass prism faces. The main cornice will be of galvanized iron and the whole will give an imposing effect.

J. L. Young of the architect and contracting firm of Lord and Young was the architect for the block. The building is to be completed by Lucas Brothers in eight months from date, which will be about April 1, 1911.

The building will extend from the Club Stables on Fort street around on Hotel street to the Art Theater, and when the lease on the Art expires the building will take in that site, placing the building alongside the Aldrich boundary. The Pantheon Block property is owned by the Wideman, Dowsett Muhlendorf and Holmes interests.

Contractor Jack Lucas states that the new building will be an ornament to the city.

The Hawaiian Gazette, August 5, 1910

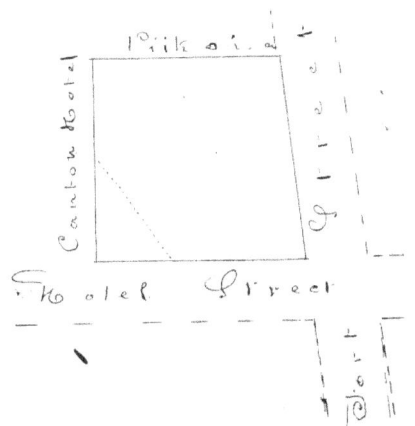

The land was initially owned by John N. Colcord, sold to John G. Munn in 1844, and officially awarded to Munn by the Land Commission in 1850 (LCA 3203). It was later owned by Judge Hermann A. Widemann who leased it to the Bartlett and Pantheon saloons.

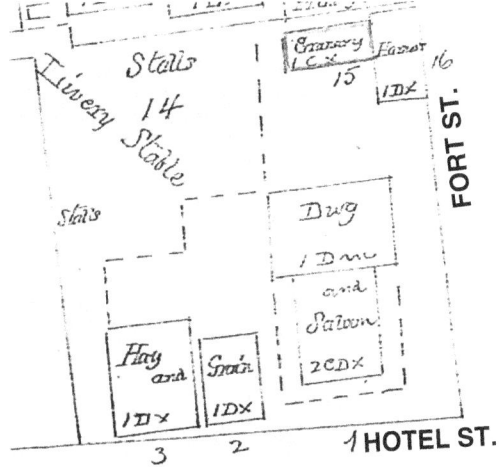

1879 Lion Map

As early as 1869 the Bartlett Saloon was on the corner in an adobe building, run by John Bartlett who was the proprietor of the Canton Hotel in the 1850's. In October 1878, James Dodd leased the Bartlett House and renamed it the Pantheon Hotel.

> OPENING.—Mr. James Dodd has leased the premises known as the Bartlett House, at the corner of Hotel and Fort streets, to be called hereafter the Pantheon Hotel. The premises have been renovated, repaired, painted and papered throughout, making them look almost as good as new. Mr. Dodd has had experience in the hotel business, and from his urbanity of manner and good business habits we doubt not but the new place will be well kept. He intends to have, in connection with the hotel, a finely arranged livery stable with a full complement of carriages and saddle horses for the accommodation of the public. This latter arrangement will be a great convenience, and we hope Mr. D. will be well supported in both undertakings.

Hawaiian Gazette, October 30, 1878

James Dodd was born in Belfast, Ireland, in 1848, and became a circus performer as the "strong man". His forté was catching cannonballs and holding ladders for two or more acrobats.

Dodd was with Lee's Circus when they came through Hawaii in 1867, and he returned in the early 1870's. He joined the police force and became captain, and he was later the manager of the Hawaiian Hotel Stables. He was a Civil War veteran and was "public spirited and charitable, a good business man".

The Bartlett Saloon is behind the white fence, c.1870

The Pantheon Saloon (on the left), c.1880

Dodd built a new building at the corner in 1883 that was lavishly decorated by two French artists, Lucien Buchmann and Fritz Rupprecht.

CARD.

Lucien Buchmann, Fritz Rupprecht

Fresco Painters,

31 Beretania Street.

d m w f

PANTHEON
LIVERY & HACK STABLES
AND
Omnibus Lines,
COR. FORT AND HOTEL STS.,
HONOLULU.

STYLISH SINGLE & DOUBLE TEAMS
And **RELIABLE SADDLE HORSES.**
SUPERIOR HACKS and CARRIAGES Furnished at all Hours.

TELEPHONE NO. 34.

PRIVATE HACK STAND:

Corner Fort and Hotel Streets.

REGULAR OMNIBUS LINES TO
KALIHI & NUUANU VALLEY; also, for the LONG BRANCH BATHS at WAIKIKI,
Where DELIGHTFUL BATHING may be Enjoyed all the year round.

JAMES DODD, Prop'r.

Frescoeing.

Messrs. Buchanan and Rupprecht, the artists who designed and executed the beautiful frescoes and other decorations of the Coronation Pavilion and Ampitheatre, have just completed the interior decorations of the Pantheon Saloon, on the corner of Fort and Hotel streets, Mr. James Dodd having erected a new building on that site. The bar-room is nearly square in shape with a lofty arched ceiling. A heavy wainscotting, grained in imitation of black walnut, with panels of koa, run around the room. Above this the walls are tinted a light brown, and finished with a heavy moulded cornice in three light shades. Below the cornice is a batten in darker brown edged with a gilt moulding. Above the cornice, where the arch of the ceiling commences, is a broad border of brown and blue. Above this is a narrower border in black, on which are painted, alternately, horse shoes and shields bearing the Hawaiian coat of arms. Above this again is a broad Rennaisance border in different colors, edged with a Grecian pattern. The ceiling proper is of a greenish blue, and set at intervals are vases on stands covered with a drapery of velvet. These vases are filled with flowers and grasses, and are very effective in design and execution. A light vine border runs around the ceiling and centre pieces, and springing from the cornice and filling up the four angles of the ceiling are stalks of sugar cane. In the billiard-room adjoining the walls and ceiling are of a much lighter tone than the room that we have just described. The walls are of a light violet shade, above a wainscoting like that in the first room. The cornice is in two light shades of gold with a bright gold moulding above. From this is a hanging border of half medallions. Above the cornice is a balustrade af light grey—in imitation of stone—on a sky blue ground. Twined in and out of the balustrade morning glories, hybiscus flowers, the blue tocama, and golden yellow blossoms. Eight vases are placed on the balustrade, two on each side of the room, and filled with exotics. A delicate vine is laid in graceful festoons along the rails of the balustrade. Around the skylight in the centre of the ceiling and the centre pieces for the light is a pretty vine pattern, and the whole effect is very elegant. The floral designs in this room are copied from flowers growing here, and the artists have shewn great originality and taste in their work.

The Honolulu Advertiser, May 28, 1883

These next five photographs were taken in February 1900 by the Board of Health and show the buildings on the Pantheon property starting on Hotel Street just ewa of Fort Street, then turning the corner and going up Fort Street to the Club Stables Building.

On February 7, 1900, the Pantheon Saloon and stables were burned by the Board of Health in an attempt to limit the spread of the bubonic plague.

After the fire, ground was broken on June 27, 1900, for a 1-story common brick building on the corner with an ornamental brick cornice, designed by Howard & Train and to be built by Isaac N. Hayden.

But construction was stopped a day later when the Board of Health said they had to wait for sewer first and not put any cesspools in potentially infected ground.

Then the government refused to allow any new saloon licenses on Fort Street.

The Board of Health relented two weeks later and allowed construction, but no occupancy until a special committee deemed it ok. Two months after construction started, they tore down part of the building to move the new Pantheon Saloon portion farther down Hotel Street away from the corner. The corner store became the Hollister Tobacco Company.

Just as the building was nearly completed, contractor Hayden suddenly died at age 48. Thomas Lucas petitioned to finish the building and settle liens and lawsuits.

Meanwhile, the *Boston Post* published a three-column sensationalist story proclaiming, "Death of Isaac Hayden in Honolulu Leaves Vast Fortune to Relatives", which caused hordes of supposed relatives and erstwhile reporters to appear, enough for a "comic opera". In actuality, a balance of $231.30 was all that remained of the Hayden estate.

Honolulu Star-Bulletin, October 20, 1924

The corner of Fort and Hotel Streets will look like this when a proposed addition to the Pantheon building is constructed. Designed by Architects Richard N. Dennis and Frank Slavsky, and Designer L. Harold Whitaker, the five-story building will be behind the present stucture.

Honolulu Star-Bulletin, January 4, 1958

Construction of the 6-story parking facility behind the Pantheon Building was completed in 1962, with access from Pauahi Street. The front of the building was "modernized" in 1964 perhaps by Dennis, Slavsky, and Whitaker.

2022

MOTT-SMITH BUILDING

1101-1103 Fort Street / 102-110 S. Hotel Street

1885 – present (remodeled 1897, 1906, 1922, 1929, 1955, 1980, 1993, 2013)
Architect/Builder: Ripley & Dickey (1897), John P. Champlin (1955) / George Lucas (1885), Peter High (1897), J.H. Craig (1906), Bert Kanzaki (1955)

The building on this site takes the grand prize for the greatest number of remodels in its 137-year history – at least eight that we know of. But has any of the original 1885 building survived?

Since so much has happened here, let's start at the very beginning and work our way up to the present time. This area was originally part of a giant yam field that helped provision visiting ships, with the first recorded building being the dentist office of John Mott-Smith.

> CARD.—DR. J. MOTT SMITH, Dentist, of Albany, N.Y., has the pleasure to inform the citizens of Honolulu that he has opened an office in Hopewell Place, corner of Beretania and Smith streets. He is now prepared to receive all who may desire his services.
> Honolulu, March 9th, 1851.—43-4t*

Born in New York City in 1824, Dr. John Mott-Smith studied dentistry in New England and practiced in Albany, NY, for three years before heading to California in 1849 for the gold rush. He came to Honolulu in 1851 and opened his first office in "Hopewell Place" across from Kaumakapili Church. He was the first dentist to set up a permanent practice in Hawaii.

Paul Emmert, 1854

Mott-Smith moved to a 2-story office at the far end of Fort Street just mauka of the French Hotel in 1852, shown in the 1854 sketch by Swiss artist Paul Emmert.

By 1856 he was in a 2-story wooden building at the corner of Hotel and Fort streets with Dr. William Hillebrand. They had an apothecary store on the first floor and a dentist office above.

In 1866, Mott-Smith became the Director of the Government Press and editor of the *Hawaiian Gazette* newspaper. He was also Vice-President of the House of Representatives (1867), Minister of Finance (1869-1872), Minister of the Interior (1878-1878), Minister of Finance (1891), and he was an initial investor in the Hawaiian Hotel and was on the first board of trustees of the Lunalilo Trust.

In 1878, Mott-Smith leased the building to the California One Price Bazar, owned by Charles J. Fishel and Alfred M. Mellis. And yes, that's how they spelled it. Fishel enlarged the building in 1882 and it became Charles J. Fishel's Popular Store. Fishel was born in Trieste, Italy, in 1853, and was one of Honolulu's most prosperous Jewish merchants.

1885 Dakin Map

Just after midnight on January 20, 1885, a fire started in the back of Fishel's store that swept through the makai end of the block and destroyed Fishel's building, George M. Raupp's Germania Market, the Elite Ice Cream Parlor, the Confectionary and Soda Water Manufactory of P. McInerny, and the Boot and Shoe Store of Frank Gertz on Fort Street.

A NEW BUILDING.

On Monday next Mr. George Lucas will commence the erection of a new building for Mr. C. J. Fishel at the corner of Fort and Hotel streets. It will be of red brick cement finished, one story, 38 by 67 ft. The height of the ceiling will be 14 feet clear. There will be three large plate glass windows, and three entrances, one at the corner, and one each on Hotel and Fort streets. The Hotel street end will be used as a millinery department and the remainder as a general store. It will be a very attractive building when completed.

Evening Bulletin, May 9, 1885

Fishel's new brick building is rising Pheonix like, from its ashes, and promises an improvement to the corner of Fort and Hotel street; it is understood that the plans have been changed and the building will be carried up two stories instead of one.

Daily Honolulu Press, June 6, 1885

Fishel quickly rebuilt, hiring George Lucas to build a 1-story brick building in 1885, but quickly deciding to make it 2-stories. It had two of the largest plate glass windows in the city, and by September the sign writer was adding the final "artistic touches".

The grand opening included Chinese lanterns, an exhibition, and a concert by the Royal Hawaiian Band.

Less than a month later, Fishel removed an interior partition and moved the inside staircase to the outside, making one large room inside.

Hawaiian Historical Society

In 1894 Fishel planned to return to New York City and sold out his stock and leased the building to L.E. Tracy who moved from his previous store on King Street. The upstairs was used by the Scottish Thistle Club and the Japanese Methodist Episcopal Church. Tracy installed an electric sign on the front of the store, perhaps the first in Hawaii.

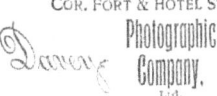

Photographer Frank Davey opened a photographic gallery upstairs in January 1897. Born in London in 1860, he had been the manager and chief operator of the Tabor Photograph Gallery in San Francisco, and previously with Wallery of Paris and Van Der Weyde of London. His father was the famous English artist and engraver William Turner Davey.

FRANK DAVEY,
President Davey Photograph Co.

The Mott-Smith estate bought back the lease in January of 1897 and hired Ripley & Dickey to design an "extensive remodeling" of the building, including removing 7 feet off the Fort Street side to accommodate the future street widening, making the exterior front and side "more modern", adding a third story, and installing the first electric passenger elevator in Hawaii. Peter High was the contractor.

STORE IMPROVEMENTS.

Mott-Smith Estate Purchases Fishel Lease to Tracy's Corner.

The Mott-Smith estate has bought back from C. J. Fishel the balance of the lease, eight years, on the Tracy store building at Fort and Hotel streets. The lease of the building was for 20 years, 12 of which had expired. Possession will be given at once.

Mr. Mott-Smith will soon proceed to make important alterations in the building. Seven feet will be taken off the Fort street front to conform to the new street line. The exterior front and side will be made more modern. Finally, a third story will be put on the building.

Mr. Tracy expects to vacate the premises shortly, unless arrangements can be made for use of side entrances while the improvements are in progress. He has not yet decided where he will go in case it is necessary to leave the house.

Hawaiian Gazette, January 22, 1897

WANTED--AN ELEVATOR BOY

NEW DEPARTURE IN HONOLULU'S BUILDINGS.

Electric Elevator Placed in the Mott-Smith Building—Similar to Those Used in San Francisco.

"Wanted—An elevator boy. Must be good looking and possess polite manners."

This is the advertisement that E. A. Mott-Smith will be obliged to insert in the newspapers in another week or so. Mr. Mott-Smith will not require experienced boys, because he well knows that his will be the first elevator ever in operation in Honolulu.

The elevator will arrive from the Coast on the 17th of the present month. It will be an electric speed affair and will be as durable and neat appearing as the elevators in the tall buildings in San Francisco and other big cities. The design will be of ribbon grill, the inside being finished off in hard wood.

The elevator will be run from the basement to the top floor. The power will be supplied by the Hawaiian Electric Company. The elevator boy will wear a bright uniform, which will advertise the Davey Photographic gallery.

The Mott-Smith building is rapidly nearing completion. It was originally intended to have the building finished on August 1, but it will be another three or four weeks before it will be opened.

Paul J. Voeller has leased the ground floor for his grocery store. Davey will have an office on this floor near the elevator. Dr. Derby will occupy the front offices on the second floor, and Dr. Howard, and possibly Dr. Ryder will occupy the other offices on this floor. The Davey Photographic gallery will be located on the third floor.

Hawaiian Star, August 6, 1897

Hawaii State Archives

The Kash store opened their second location here in 1899, specializing in "gents' furnishing goods and ready to wear clothing".

In 1906 the building underwent extensive alterations again, combining the two exterior store entrances into one on the corner, adding a "spacious stairway" between the first and second floors while keeping the elevator to the third floor, and opening up the second floor into one large showroom. The work was done by J.H. Craig for Captain Arthur Soule, proprietor of The Kash.

KASH COMPANY'S SATURDAY OPENING

An elegant gentlemen's furnishings store was opened yesterday, at the corner of Hotel and Fort streets, by the Kash Company. It was the old store remodeled, but so changed that it is hardly recognized as the same quarters. The entrance is now at the corner, a convenience which is appreciated by the Kash patrons.

The Kash store now occupies the ground floor and the second story of the Mott-Smith building. The floor is devoted to haberdashery entirely, while the second story is given over to men's and boys' clothing.

The store interior is brilliantly illuminated at night so that goods are seen to advantage. Handsome display cases are ranged about the store showing lines of hosiery, handkerchiefs, negligee and dress shirts, collars, hats underwear and small furnishings in general.

Upstairs, most of the clothing is arranged on tables, the dress suits and Tuxedos occupying hangers in glass cases. The new store is modern and up-to-date in every particular and the fixtures and display appurtenances are the very latest.

One very attractive feature of the store is the large windows fronting on Fort and Hotel streets. The backgrounds are of natural wood, and simplicity is the keynote there as elsewhere about the store. The Kash Company intends dressing the windows at frequent intervals, and never less than twice a week.

The company has a good corps of salesmen and patrons can be quickly attended to. The Kash Company has closed its former store on Hotel street and will in future conduct but the one establishment.

The Honolulu Advertiser, March 11, 1906

After 15 years as The Kash, they changed the name in 1909 to The Clarion, known as "the store for stylish dressers".

The building was completely remodeled for $20,000 in 1922 due to the widening of Hotel Street.

The Clarion Clothing Company went bankrupt in 1923 and all unsold stock was sold at auction.

Clifford Spitzer bought the building and land in late 1926 for $105,000 and on February 28, 1929 it became The Hub after an additional $7,500 remodeling.

The Hub was established in 1898 by Clifford's father, Joseph, and was formerly in the old James Campbell building diagonally opposite.

Honolulu Star-Bulletin, February 28, 1929

The Mau family bought Hub Clothing from J.S. Spitzer in 1947, and "in line with the general facelifting of downtown stores and office buildings in recent years" embarked on an ambitious remodel in 1955 that included adding a giant 8' electric outdoor clock to the building. The improvements were designed by architect John P. Champlin and were built by Bert Kanzaki for $24,954.

NEW OUTLOOK—Hub Clothiers at Fort and Hotel Sts. will look like this when a newly announced remodeling project is completed at an estimated cost of $20,000 to $25,000. Sketch is by Architect John P. Champlin.

The Honolulu Advertiser, April 12, 1955

The Honolulu Advertiser, July 4, 1956

Hub Clothing closed in 1980 and was replaced by a McDonald's restaurant. McDonald's was initially located two buildings mauka at 1113 Fort Street in 1972. The remodeling of both locations was designed by Geoffrey Patterson & Associates. For the first year this location was known as "McDonald's The Hub".

2022

2022

MCCORRISTON BUILDING

1107-1111 Fort Street

1914 – present
Architect/Builder: John Lucas

The Honolulu Advertiser, July 9, 1914

CONCRETE STORES TO REPLACE SHACKS

Contractor John Lucas has started active operations on a two-story reinforced concrete building on Fort street, mauka of Hotel street. The building is being erected for Hugh and Daniel McCorriston. It will contain three commodious stores facing on Fort street, while the upper floor will be devoted to office purposes. The building will be completed in eighty days. The new structure will be a great improvement for upper Fort street.

The Honolulu Advertiser, February 1, 1914

The McCorriston building, on the old Criterion site, Fort street, will be ready for its business tenantry on July 15. It is concrete, of two stories and is being erected by the Honolulu Planing Mill, John Lucas manager. Owned by D. and H. McCorriston, the building will cost $17,000.

Honolulu Star-Bulletin, July 3, 1914

This building was built for brothers Hugh and Daniel McCorriston who had come to Hawaii from Limvady, Londonderry, Ireland, in 1863 and 1864. By 1865 they owned and operated a rice mill in Waiau, but both later settled in Molokai and managed the Kamalo plantation.

The McCorristons, (Mc)Colgans, Loves, and Lucases were all related through marriage, and it appears this land had been in the family for some time.

A cousin, also named Daniel, had a cabinetmaking shop here as early as 1874. Hugh was married to Margaret Foster, the mother of John Lucas

This 2-story concrete building was built by John Lucas in 1914 after the previous wooden buildings had been condemned as "unsanitary".

CABINET MAKER'S SHOP!

THE UNDERSIGNED begs to notify his friends and the public generally, that he has taken
Shop on Fort Street.
one door below the Government Buildings, where he will be found hereafter, prepared to carry on the
CABINET MAKER'S BUSINESS.
in all its branches and on the most reasonable terms.
SECOND HAND FURNITURE BOUGHT AND SOLD,
—and—
Repairing Done Neatly and Expeditiously.
Please give him a Call.
ap26 tf   DANIEL McCORRISTON.

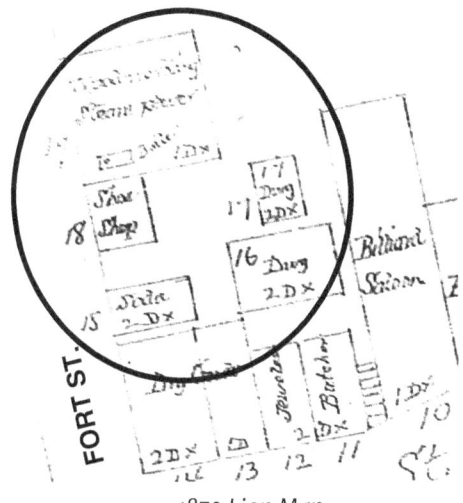

1879 Lion Map

In 1879 there was a woodworking shop here, presumably cousin Daniel McCorriston's, plus a small shoe shop and soda shop with dwellings in back. These would all have been burned in the January 20, 1885, fire that swept through the makai end of this block destroying 5 buildings and badly damaging two others.

Starting just after midnight in C.J. Fishel's store at the corner of Fort and Hotel streets, it destroyed Fishel's building, George M. Raupp's Germania Market, and the Elite Ice Cream Parlor on Hotel Street, plus the Confectionary and soda water manufactory of P. McInerny and the boot and shoe store of Frank Gertz on Fort Street.

One of the first new buildings to go up after the fire was the Criterion Saloon in 1886. It was managed by James Dodd who also managed the Pantheon Saloon across the street.

1879

The Criterion Barber Shop was located next to the saloon, and next to that was Geroge M. Raupp's Germania Market which was rebuilt after the fire.

Evening Bulletin, December 9, 1886

Shortly after the Criterion Saloon moved to the Waverley Building in 1902, the city decided to widen Fort Street so the three wooden buildings on the property had to be moved back to present a uniform appearance along the street. The old Criterion Saloon building was remodeled to have a flush front with the adjoining Mott-Smith Building on the corner.

The Criterion Saloon, c.1906

2022

FRENCH HOTEL

1115-1127 Fort Street / 1114-1120 Union Street

c.1844 – 1912

Architect/Builder: unknown

Paul Emmert, 1854

The first mention in the newspapers of the French Hotel is on August 31, 1844, when they "provided the viands" for a sumptuous dinner with the King and Governor Kekuanaoa.

Victor Chancerel had barely taken over management of the Hotel de France from Pierre Le Gueval when on the night of July 14, 1849, about sixty drunken sailors from the English frigate *Amphitrite* broke in and forced Chancerel to serve them even more drink. "In the night, a window, some bottles, some glasses, some chairs, tables and different other articles, forming a considerable damage were smashed."

FRENCH HOTEL,
BY
PETER LE GUEVAL,
HONOLULU, OAHU.

THE Subscriber begs leave to inform his friends and the public in general that he has taken this well known establishment, which is now open for the accommodation of all who may favor him with a call. His table will be furnished with the best the market can afford, and no pains will be spared to give general satisfaction. Boarders will be accommodated by the day, week or month, on the most reasonable terms. Individuals and pic nic parties will be supplied with dinners or other refreshments at the shortest notice. Persons from a distance visiting Honolvlu will be furnished with good beds and airy sleeping apartments.
Aug. 15—3w*

During French Admiral Louis Tromelin's ill-fated 2-week invasion and occupation of Honolulu in August and September of 1849 the officers of the corvette *Gassendi* and the frigate *La Poursuivante* made the French Hotel their headquarters when off-duty.

FRENCH HOTEL.

THE undersigned being about to leave the country, offers for sale the entire business, furniture and stock of this well-known and desirable establishment.

The grounds are extensive and well stocked with flowers and vegetables. The mountain-water has been laid on, and carried to several parts of the premises at great expense. The bath-houses are convenient, and the numerous suits of chambers are cool, well ventilated and comfortably furnished. The establishment is centrally situated, with three several entrances on different streets, and altogether presents a rare opportunity for persons desirous of embarking in the Hotel business.

Full particulars can be learned on application at the premises to V. CHANCEREL.
Honolulu, Dec. 12, 1856. 32-tf

Hotel de France.
(FRENCH HOTEL.)

VICTOR CHANCEREL, Proprietor, begs to inform his friends and the public generally, that he has made extensive improvements in his Hotel premises, and that he has now accommodations for parties of every desscription. Also attached, a BILLIARD SALOON, fitted up in superior style.

☞ Single rooms on the premises for families or single gentlemen.

☞ THE BAR is supplied with the choicest Wines and Liquors; and the Proprietor, grateful for the liberal patronage heretofore extended to him, begs to assure the public that no pains will be spared to entire satisfaction to residents and strangers visiting Honolulu.

COLD AND WARM BATHS!

N. B Entrance by Fort, Hotel and Union sts. 12 tf

Chancerel was originally from Canton De Vaud on the frontier between France and Switzerland and had previously lived in Tahiti before moving to Hawaii. He lived here for nearly 30 years.

> *"He indeed knew how to keep a hotel, and his unequaled breakfasts and dinners and petite soupers, in the days of Kamehameha III (who often honored the board with his genial presence) are well remembered by those who survive of the 'old hands.' M. Victor was much esteemed for his many good qualities".*

Although located on Fort Street, the premises extended all the way back to Union Street and were once owned by Dr. T.C.B. Rooke who initially had a 1-story adobe dispensary here in the 1830's.

Captain F.A. Newell added an upper wooden story with a veranda in 1848.

In July 1862, the government offices for the State of Hawaii moved from the old Pelly premises at Hotel and Alakea streets to the French Hotel buildings. The offices of the Minister of the Interior (Dr. Hutchinson) were in the large building in back, and the Minister of Foreign Affairs (R.C. Wyllie, Mons. Varigny, C.C. Harris) were in the building on Fort Street that later became P. McInerny's cigar stand.

The government offices moved to Aliʻiolani Hale in 1874.

The buildings were converted into a carriage factory by Philip Stein and later housed the W.H. Page Carriage Factory, Honolulu Carriage, and W.W. Wright & Sons Carriage Works. The buildings were demolished in 1912.

The New Government Offices.

During the past few days the offices of the executive Departments of the Government have been removed from the old Pelly premises on Hotel street, to the more roomy and much more convenient premises formerly known as the "French Hotel," bounded on the west side by Fort, and on the east, by Union streets. These premises have been put in excellent order, repaired, repainted, and rejuvenated generally. Two fire-proof vaults have been built, one for the use of the Interior Department, the other for that of Finance. These two Departments are located in the building nearest Union street, that of Finance being nearest the street, and that of the Interior in the west end. The upper story is devoted to the offices of the Ministers of the Interior and of Finance, with a room in the centre for Cabinet Councils, while the lower floor is occupied as the offices of the two principal clerks of those department, and the archives. On Fort street are the offices of the Department of Public Instruction, on the ground floor, and above, those of the Department of Foreign Relations. Water is laid on to each of the offices. The removal is a decided improvement, not only for the convenience of different departments, but as being placed in a more central position, making them more easily accessible to the public.

The Polynesian, July 12, 1862

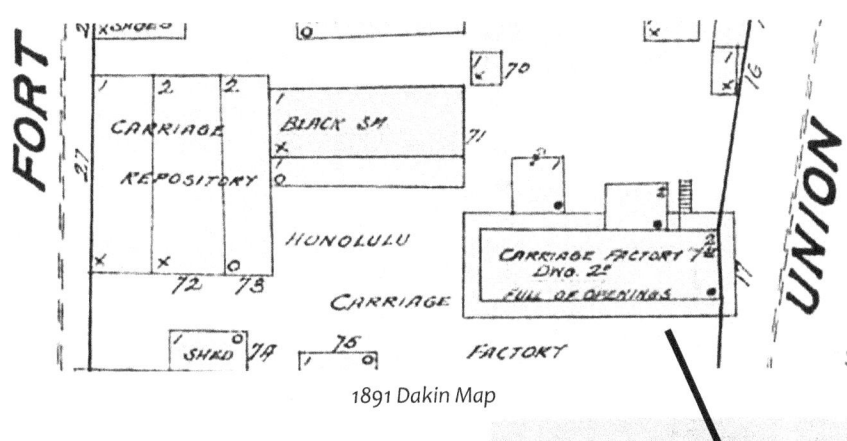

1891 Dakin Map

1868

Old Government Building About to Be Demolished

In the extensive improvements about being made by the Brewer Estate at the angle made by Hotel and Union streets, the old frame structures have been razed, and soon the old coral structure which has in its time served as everything from a residence of the royal family to a carriage factory will be a thing of the past. Mrs. Pratt, in an interview with a Star reporter this morning, told what she could remember about the old building, where many affairs of state were transacted in the early part of the last century.

"The first person that I can remember who lived in the building was Doctor Rooke, the foster-father of Queen Emma," said Mrs. Pratt.

OLD GOVERNMENT BUILDING.

The Hawaiian Star, March 9, 1912

KRESS BUILDING

1115-1127 Fort Street / 1114-1134-Union Street

1930/1935 – 1989
Architect/Builder: John G. Fleming / Ralph E. Woolley

Fort Street side

S.H. Kress & Company purchased the Fort Street side of the old French Hotel premises in 1929 for $125,000 from the Wolters Estate. The architect was John G. Fleming of New York and the 2-story reinforced concrete and steel building with basement was built by Ralph E. Woolley for $250,000.

Construction began in July 1930, and opening day was March 23, 1931. Frank M. Miller was the store manager with "150 girls and 20 men" employed.

A third story was added by Ralph E. Woolley in 1932, and in 1934 the Kress Company bought and demolished the Wolters Building on Union Street, making this the largest Kress store west of Chicago, with 24,500 square feet of floor space. The new concrete and steel 3-story addition on Union Street was built by Ralph E. Woolley for $320,000.

Opening day was October 17, 1935, and nearly 50,000 people jammed the new store for last-minute Christmas shopping. The opening featured live music, hula dancers, and was broadcast live on KGU.

The Kress Building was demolished in 1988 for a $165M 25-story skyscraper called Pan Pacific Plaza designed by Gin D. Wong, built by Pan-Pacific Construction and completed in 1992. It is now known as 1132 Bishop.

The Honolulu Advertiser, August 18, 1935

Union Street side

CLUB STABLES BUILDING

1124-1132 Fort Street

1900 – 1959
Architect/Builder: E.D. Brown / Isaac N. Hayden?

The Club Stables opened here in 1890 and built a large 2-story building along Fort Street in 1900.

Honolulu: The Cross-Roads of the Pacific, 1913

CLUB STABLES BUILDING

The new brick building in front of the Club Stables on Fort Street will be only 62 by 50 feet in dimensions. This is 44 feet less frontage than was intended. Minister Young declined to allow the corner to occupy the whole district as it is purposed to very soon extend Pauahi street over the lane.

The building will be occupied by stores. It will be two stories high and of brick.

The Hawaiian Star, April 26, 1900

Plans are ready for the Club Block. It will be a three-story brick building, to be erected at the former grounds next to the Love Block on Fort street. E. D. Brown is the architect, who is also preparing two other brick blocks, which are to be built soon. His office is No. 112, corner of Kinau and Punchbowl streets.

The Honolulu Advertiser, May 29, 1900

NEW STABLES BUILDING.

The new brick building of the Club Stables Company will be a go. It will occupy the space in front of the wooden stables on Fort street. If certain matters can be arranged it may be three or four stories high, but in any event will be at least two stories. Mr. Hayden will probably be the builder.

The Hawaiian Star, July 7, 1900

It was demolished in 1959 after being condemned as "structurally unsafe" by the City Building Department after an inspection showed it was beyond repair.

The Club Stables.

Anyone passing down Fort street cannot fail to notice the whereabouts of the new livery and boarding stables. They are known as the Club stables, and are fitted up in the neatest manner. There are forty stalls and accommodation for a large number of carriages. The stables run six hacks which are of latest style and very easy to ride in. By the bark Discovery twenty-five horses were imported from the Coast. They are all fine serviceable animals. The intention of the proprietors is to keep about thirty horses. All the carriages are new, and wagonettes, road carts, dog carts, single and double teams can always be obtained. The saddle horses are extra fine imported animals. A practical horse trainer is engaged on the premises, and is an expert in handling and breaking young stock. Horses are boarded by the day, week or month at reasonable rates. Should you keep a team there and require it any hour of the day or night, or want it fetched from your house, the Club Stables guarantee to perform this kind of work in the most satisfactory manner. The whole premises are lighted up with electricity. The stable is connected with both telephones, No. 477. Mr. S. F. Graham is the manager.

The Honolulu Advertiser, March 3, 1890

THE UNDERSIGNED

RESPECTFULLY INFORM THE public that they have purchased the establishment

NO. 127 Fort street.

KNOWN AS S. D. BURROWS'

Planing Mill,

And that we intend, and are now prepared, to carry on the business of

Contractors and Builders

Under the corporative name of

ENTERPRISE PLANING MILL,

And that by strict attention to business we shall be warranted in reducing prices to a standard that will make it an inducement for all parties wishing any work in our line to give us a call, and we shall use our best endeavors to give entire satisfaction.

C. J. HARDEE,
J. G. HAYSELDEN,
H. F. BERTELMANN.

Club Stables.

LIVERY, BOARDING & SALE STABLES!

Fort Street above Hotel Street.

477 — BOTH TELEPHONES — 477

The above Stables are now fully equipped and are prepared to furnish the public at a moment's notice with

SADDLE HORSES,
Horses & Carriages, Wagonettes,

Surreys, Dog Carts, Etc., Etc.

HORSES BOARDED
By the Day, Week or Month.

And satisfaction guaranteed. Special attention paid to the care of carriages.

Evening Bulletin, April 2, 1890

The S.D. Burrows Planing Mill was built on this site in 1879. Burrows built the Princess Ruth Keʻelikōlani mansion, the Paiko Block, and the Chinese Christian Church. It became the Enterprise Planing Mill in 1881, run by H.F. Bertelmann, J.G. Hayselden, and C.J. Hardee.

A disastrous fire destroyed the sawmill on May 3, 1885, burning several nearby buildings including The Fountain confectionary and soda shop plus Rose Cottage Lodging House on Fort Street, which resulted in the unfortunate death of a young 18-year-old English sailor who had been staying in Rose Cottage.

The Club Stables in January 1900.

Honolulu Star-Bulletin, May 31, 1961

The Hansmann Building on the site today was designed by Kenji Onodera and built by Richard M. Takeyama, Inc. in 1961 for the John F. Hansmann Estate. The design allows for four additional stories.

2022

2022

J.H. FISHER BUILDING

1133-1135 Fort Street

1901 – 1987
Architect/Builder: Howard & Train / Hoffman & Riley

Honolulu: The Cross-Roads of the Pacific, 1913

This building was built in 1901 by Hoffman & Riley for J.H. Fisher and was designed by Howard & Train.

It was Mrs. Dunn's Hat Shop in 1910, and in the 1910's and 1920's the Electric Shop was on the left with City Good Eats café on the right.

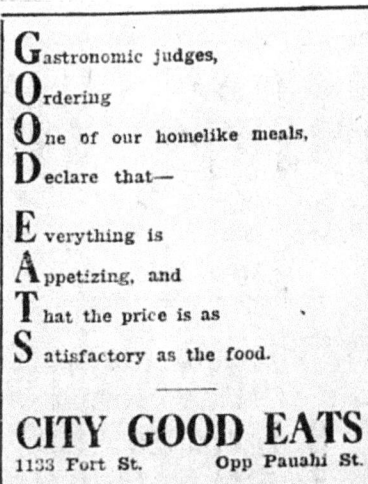

LOVE BUILDING

1138-1144 Fort Street

1896 – 1951
Architect/Builder: Ripley & Dickey / George Dall

FOR RENT.

STORES OFFICES AND APARTMENTS,
in the
NEW LOVE BUILDING.
FORT STREET.

Included in the apartments are a model suite of rooms, large and commodious. Stationary wash bowls, etc. Those wishing to take roomers can utilize other rooms well planned for such a case. This is the best appointed flat or apartment house in Honolulu.

Building now open for inspection.

For particulars as regards terms, etc., apply to.

W. A. LOVE.

Contractor George Dall will do the carpenter work on the new chapel at Kamehameha. He has practically finished at the Love building, Fort street.

The Hawaiian Star, December 30, 1896

William A. Love was the son of Robert and Fanny Love, the president of Love's Biscuit and Bread Company, a bookkeeper for Lewers & Cooke, a stockbroker, and also an accomplished violinist. He was born in 1871 and was 25 when this building was built in front of the old Love homestead.

This brick building with stone front was designed by Ripley & Dickey and built by George Dall in 1896. One of the more interesting tenants in 1917 was Madame Cleo, soothsayer.

Norman Jemal moved to Hawaii in 1932 and bought the Towne & Country Shop at Fort and Merchant in 1937 and changed the name to "Jemal's". He was a world traveler and collector who traced the sources of fine hand-made linens and was said to be "a world renowned linenist". Jemal also had a factory in Swatow, China, with other business connections in France, Italy, and Switzerland.

In February 1947 he signed a 60-year lease on the Love Building property with an agreement to erect a new building of "not less than $100,000".

Jemal's original plan was to build a 5-story building patterned after the famous May Co. store in Los Angeles, to be designed by Guy N. Rothwell and cost $400,000.

The Love Building was demolished in May 1951 and two months later architect Guy Rothwell sued Jemal for non-payment of design fees.

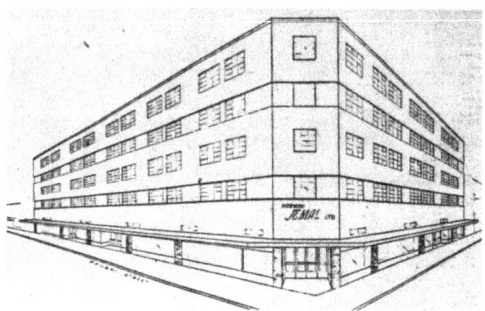

Honolulu Star-Bulletin, April 24, 1951

The building was constructed by James W. Glover, Ltd, and opening day was September 18, 1952. But it was only a 2-story concrete building with a provision for six total floors, at a cost of $200,000.

Less than a year later, Jemal's was out of business. A tight money market prevented him from borrowing $150,000 on his new building and his stock dwindled until he was forced to close.

The Honolulu Advertiser, September 21, 1952

2022

FISHER BUILDING

1139-1141 Fort Street

1897 – 1989

Architect/Builder: Ripley & Dickey / Fred Harrison

NEW BUILDING.

Will Be on Upper Fort, of Brick and to Be Occupied at Once.

Messrs. Ripley & Dickey have prepared plans for the new business house to be erected by Col. J. H. Fisher, opposite the new Love block on upper Fort street. The building will be of brick, one story and will contain two store houses. It will occupy the residence site lately vacated by Mr. D. P. Lawrence. The building is being erected for Poppleton's Home Bakery. It will be a neat structure and quite an ornament to the locality. Tenders for the work are now being received at the office of the architects.

The Hawaiian Star, October 19, 1896

Completed in 1897, this 1-story building with 2 stores was designed by Ripley & Dickey and built by Fred Harrison for $4,600. It was built on the site of the 1-story David P. Lawrence residence.

Fred Harrison is making good progress on the new Fisher building, to be occupied by the Poppleton bakery. The foundations are about completed.

Evening Bulletin, November 24, 1896

Ezra Poppleton and Oscar Moell moved their Home Bakery here in early February 1897 and James Hutchins opened a grocery store next door in November 1897.

In 1897 a fine lunch with oyster soup at Poppleton's Home Bakery was only 25 cents.

THE FISHER BUILDING.

Poppleton the Baker Will Be the Occupant.

Tomorrow morning at 10 o'clock the bids for the new Fisher building, to be erected on Fort street, opposite the Love Block, will be opened, and the work of construction will commence at once as the lease calls for the completion of the same by December 15th of this year. Mr. Poppleton, the baker on upper Fort street has leased the entire building for ten years.

In October of last year Mr. Poppleton commenced supplying families in a small way with his home made bread. He was finally forced to obtain a wagon to make his delivery on time. Since that time he has changed the capacity three times. On September 1st of this year he took into partnership Mr. Moell, a graduated baker from Germany, who was for several years connected with the best hotel in Chicago and later from Tacoma.

The new bakery will occupy the entire building and will be so constructed as to give them the most room possible. The ovens will be built at the same time as the building and will have a capacity of 4000 loaves of bread daily should their trade require it.

Their specialties are the sanitary yeast bread, made from a special yeast from which is obtained a very wholesome and strengethening bread, whole wheat bread, German black bread and the famous pompernickel bread, so much loved by the Germans.

Another feature will be a short order lunch room where can be obtained pastry of all kinds, coffee, cold meats, sandwiches. Ice cream and cakes of various make will also be served.

It is safe to say that Mr. Poppleton and his partner, Mr. Moell, are on the right road to success and most surely deserve what support they may obtain.

The Hawaiian Star, October 26, 1896

Landlord's Sale.

Public Notice is hereby given that J. H. Fisher, landlord, did on the 6th day of September, 1897, distrain and remove to a place of safe custody the following goods and chattels of his defaulting tenant, Ezra Poppleton, for rent in arrears and due the said landlord by the said Ezra Poppleton and one Oscar Moell, amounting to the sum of One Hundred ($160.00) and Sixty Dollars, being rent due the said landlord for certain premises situate on Fort street, in Honolulu, Oahu, for the months of August and September, 1897, which rent was, by covenant, payable monthly in advance, to-wit:—

Nine small restaurant tables, thirty-five restaurant chairs, twenty-two ice-cream tumblers, thirty-one water tumblers, thirty-two small glass ice-cream dishes, thirty decorated china coffee saucers, fifteen decorated china tea saucers, forty-four decorated china plates (small), twenty-eight plain white china ice-cream plates, twenty decorated china plates (medium size), twenty large decorated china platters, nine decorated china ice-cream plates, nine decorated china sugar bowls, twenty-eight decorated china butter plates, one dozen small plain white china cream pitchers, eight decorated china mush bowls, fourteen decorated china coffee cups, twenty-two decorated china tea cups, one dozen metal glass holders, one dozen ice-cream spoons, one dozen soup spoons, five dozen tea spoons, twenty-eight forks, thirty silver-plated table knives, three bone-handled knives, one bread knife, twenty-two decorated china platters (large), nine egg cups, five shirred egg dishes, one small white china pitcher, nineteen decorated china plates, one small water cooler, twenty-two cans of pie pumpkins, one large wicker bread basket, one electric fan—

And notice is hereby given that said goods and chattels will be sold at public auction at the auction rooms of Jas. F. Morgan, on Queen street, in said Honolulu, on Monday, October 11, 1897, at 12 o'clock meridian of said day, to satisfy the rent due at the time of such sale, together with the costs of such distress, removal, custody and sale.

J. H. FISHER,
By A. S. HUMPHREYS,
His Attorney.
Honolulu, September 24, 1897.
4721-td

HOME BAKERY,
Restaurant and Ice Cream Parlors,

OPEN AT 6 A. M.

The former excellence in all departments will be fully carried out.

GIVE US A TRIAL.

E. POPPLETON, Manager.

FISHER BUILDING, FORT STREET.

Poppleton's didn't last long – he faced bankruptcy and left for San Francisco in early 1899 never to return.

In 1935 the building and 35' x 66' lot was bought by Sidney Spitzer from Charles M. Cooke Ltd. for $25,000 and remodeled into the Standard Shoe Store.

Standard Shoe opened a store at Ala Moana Mall in 1959 and after 26 years moved the Fort Street store to the Blaisdell Hotel in 1961. The building was demolished in 1989 for the $100M Pan Pacific Plaza (1132 Bishop).

2022

SACRED HEART CONVENT SCHOOL

1143-1169 Fort Street

1901 – present (partial)
Architect/Builder: Dickey & Newcomb / Hawaiian Engineering & Construction

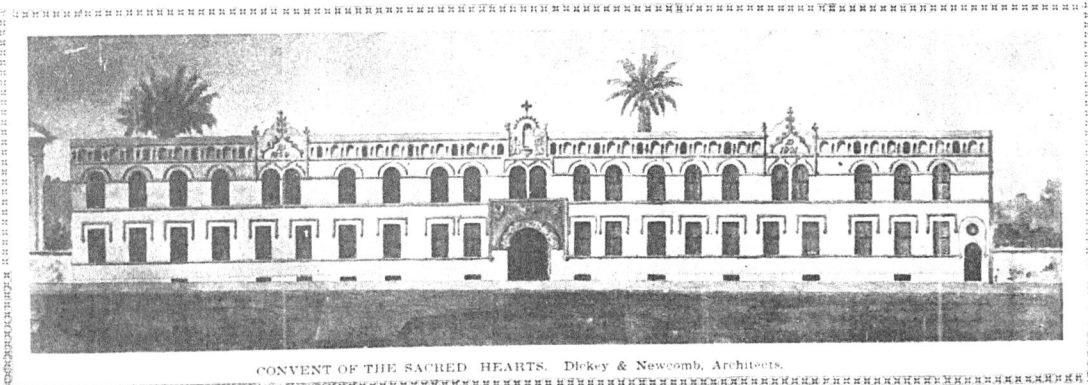

The Honolulu Advertiser, January 1, 1902

Although the parapet says, "AD 1859" don't be fooled – the building was designed by Charles W. Dickey and E.A.P. Newcomb and built by Hawaiian Engineering & Construction in 1901.

The 1859 date commemorates the arrival of the first Sacred Heart nuns in Hawaii on May 4, 1859.

The building you see today is just a fraction of what was here originally, about 70% is missing. A section with 3 windows was removed on the left, and almost 100 feet are missing on the right, including the original arched entranceway.

Due to the widening of Fort Street several large "alligator pear trees" belonging to the Catholic Mission were moved out of the way by Carl Willing. A 2-story late 1840's coral house that was likely the home of Chief Justice William L. Lee and a 1-story wooden building were also removed before they could build the new convent school.

Paul Emmert, 1854

The school was built on the house site of Captain John Dominis, located makai of the building as it exists today. When Dominis built Washington Place this building became the house of US Consul Joel Turrell.

At the time Paul Emmert painted the building in 1854 it was the residence of US Consul Alexander G. Angel. It became the Aldrich House in 1865, and was later part of the Catholic school until torn down to make way for the 1901 building.

The demolition of the coral building began on May 31, 1901, and the new building that replaced it was:

> "a fine structure of cement stucco trimmings, all of the conventional design, to cost in the neighborhood of $30,000. The building will occupy 166 feet on Fort Street and average 42.5 feet in depth. About two-thirds is two stories high. The first floor will be devoted to parlors, class rooms and rooms for the musical department, with a ten-foot cloister on the rear…. The front elevation is of pleasing design with a handsome central entrance, while directly above, over the second story niche in which a figure of the Virgin will be placed."

The architectural style was described as "Spanish Conventual" and it was built by Hawaiian Engineering & Construction for $31,384.05.

CONTRACT LET FOR ERECTION OF SACRED HEART CONVENT.
The contract for the erection of the school for the Convent of the Sacred Heart, on Fort street, has been let to the Hawaiian Engineering & Construction Company. Their bid was $31,384.05.

The Honolulu Advertiser, June 15, 1901

The building was extended between February and June 1902, making "an unbroken front from the cathedral to the billiard parlors opposite the Love Building, being continued in the same style of architecture".

The Sacred Heart Convent School.

The new school building for the Convent of the Sacred Heart, designed by Dickey & Newcomb, architects, will occupy 165 feet on Fort street with an entrance near the center of the two-story portion, from Fort street to the convent grounds. The aim of the architects has been to make a design which will harmonize with the present cathedral and at the same time be modern and convenient. The building will be about forty five feet deep, with a two story cloister on the garden side. These cloisters will be 10 feet by 105 feet. The one-story part of the building is arranged with small teaching rooms for the musical department. The first story of the main building contains two parlors and the three large rooms for school purposes, the second story five large rooms, so arranged with folding doors that they may be thrown together for social purposes.

The style of this building is Spanish Conventual. The main feature is the entrance portal with a window over it surmounted by a niche for a statue of the Virgin. The material of construction will be brick covered with concrete, the arches and certain lines of moulding being of pressed red brick. The cornice of arches across the two-story front is a feature which will add to the dignity of the building. There is a well lighted and ventilated basement for storage purposes.— P. C. A.

The Independent, June 6, 1901

The original building had a beautiful 10' x 105' arched cloister that faced the interior gardem courtyard.

The Honolulu Advertiser, January 1, 1902

The Honolulu Advertiser, January 1, 1902

Due to subsequent additions, no trace of the cloister is visible today from the exterior. Perhaps it still exists somewhere on the inside?

New Ritz Store Ready

The Honolulu Advertiser, July 29, 1938

OPENS SATURDAY.—This fine establishment, the Ritz store, at 1143-53 Fort street, will open Saturday with 100 per cent American-made merchandise stated as a policy of the organization, it is announced today.

The Ritz Store started as an electrical appliance business called Standard Sales Company, founded by Nenichi Kamuri.

After the convent moved out in 1938, Kamuri leased the makai portion of the former school for 99 years, at the time the longest lease any individual had transacted.

He hired C.J. Oda Contracting to renovate the building, with new millwork and fixtures by the Nuuanu Carpenter Shop.

Opening day was Saturday, July 30, 1938, with "25 attractive salesgirls and clerks".

The Ritz specialized in ladies' and children's ready-to-wear clothing that was "100 per cent American-made merchandise".

Kamuri claimed, "you will always find it for less at the Ritz".

They purchased the building in 1956 and embarked on an ambitious $1M expansion in 1960 that included "a new steel and concrete building in back and complete remodeling of the present building" designed by Burke Kober and Nicholas and built by Walker-Moody Construction.

In 1989 they talked of replacing the building with an extension of the $100M Pan Pacific Plaza (1132 Bishop) but decided to keep the land and concentrate on their Ala Moana Store. This section was demolished in 1989.

November has been set as the expected completion date for the million dollar expansion program now under way at the Ritz Store on Fort Street. Architects for the project are Burke, Kober and Nicholas, store-planning specialists, of Los Angeles.

Honolulu Star-Bulletin, February 24, 1960

1966

2022

2022

BLAISDELL HOTEL

1148-1160 Fort Street

1913 – present
Architect/Builder: Emory & Webb / Pacific Engineering Co.

"THE BLAISDELL"

Honolulu's Newest and Most Modern Hotel
Absolutely Fire-Resisting

Hawaii's Handsomest Hostelry

Outside View of the Blaisdell Hotel

64 Rooms

Cool, Convenient, Comfortable

27 Baths

Entrance to Elevator---The Blaisdell

Conveniences in the Hotel Building

Millinery Shop
Grocery Store
Barber Shop
Manicure and Hairdressing Parlors
Hatter
Tailor

Attractive Waiting Room in the Blaisdell

Telephone Communications with City and Country in Every Room
A Reasonable Priced Hotel in the Very Heart of the City

The Honolulu Star-Bulletin, February 22, 1913

This was originally called the Excelsior Building, and it was initially going to be 3 stories tall. It was built for the C.M. Cooke Estate by the Pacific Engineering Company for $90,000 and was designed by Emory & Webb. The upstairs was a rooms-only hotel run by Mrs. Cora Blaisdell and the first floor had stores.

GET CONTRACT FOR BIG BUILDING

One more big building contract was let yesterday, when the Pacific Engineering Company, Ltd., was awarded the contract for the construction of the Excelsior building, which will be erected at the corner of Chaplain lane and Fort street.

The work will commence at once on plans prepared by Emory & Webb for Charles M. Cooke, Ltd., the owners. The building will cost $90,000, will be of reinforced concrete and must be ready for occupancy December 1. It will be occupied by stores on the ground floor, with apartments above and will be four stories in height.

The Hawaiian Gazette, April 30, 1912

The Honolulu Advertiser, August 17, 1912

The Pacific Engineering Company had a goal of building one floor per week and had as many as 75 workers onsite at one time.

Workers on the excavation of the C. M. Cooke, Ltd., building at Fort street and Chaplain lane yesterday found the remains of a skeleton believed to be that of a woman.

Evening Bulletin, May 4, 1912

Mrs. Cora Ammie Shaw Blaisdell, originally from Minnesota, was the widow of the luna of the Keālia Sugar Plantation in Kauai. Since 1909 she had been the proprietoress of the Majestic Hotel, located in the Sachs Building at Fort and Beretania, and she leased the top 3 floors for the Blaisdell Hotel and traveled to San Francisco in 1912 to purchase furnishings and supplies. She was the grandmother of future Mayor Neal S. Blaisdell who supposedly cleaned floors here as a young boy.

The building contained "64 rooms, 27 baths, millinery shop, grocery store, barbershop, manicure and hairdressing parlors, hatter, and tailor, and had telephones in every room." From the *Honolulu Star-Bulletin*, November 28, 1914:

> "Modern to its last degree, equipped with every convenience for the comfort of its guests, and, centrally located the Blaisdell hotel represents the last word in Honolulu hostelries, for with all its up-to-date advantages, it is built to suit the climate. Occupying a new concrete building in the very heart of Honolulu, any section of the city may be reached by stepping from its palm hedged lobby to the street cars which pass its door."

Originally upstairs rooms only, the hotel added a kitchen and large dining room in 1920. The Garden Court was located in the back of the hotel, a "surprise oasis" of palm trees, potted plants and an aviary.

The building is famous for its magnificent "birdcage" elevator from West Coast Iron & Wire Works that was installed by the von Hamm-Young Company. Manually operated and still working over a hundred years later (with some updates and alterations).

The Architect & Engineer of California, November 1913

BLAISDELL HOTEL OPENS TO PUBLIC

New Hostelry on Fort Street Will Fill a Long-felt Want in Honolulu.

The Blaisdell, Honolulu's new moderate-priced modern hotel has been opened to the public. The hotel occupies all of the three upper floors of the new Excelsior building at the corner of Fort and Chaplain streets. The Blaisdell has been established to fill a long-felt want in Honolulu in providing a hotel conducted on the modern European plan, where first-class rooms and service can be secured at reasonable rates.

Mrs. C. A. Blaisdell, who owns the Majestic Hotel, controls the Blaisdell. Her long experience in the hotel business here enabled her to know what is needed here and she has set about to accomplish this purpose.

There are sixty rooms or more in the Blaisdell. The inside rooms open on large, cool lanais. Both outside and inside rooms are well lighted and cool and airy. Nearly all the rooms are connected, to be used as suites or singly as conditions warrant. Hot and cold running water and telephones have been installed in each room. Tile bathrooms, fitted with porcelain tubs and showers, connect each suite. Additional baths are located on each floor for the single rooms.

Much care has been taken by Mrs. Blaisdell in selecting the mission furnishings. There is not an old article of furniture or bedding in the hotel.

An elevator service is maintained until midnight. Bellboys and attendants are in readiness at all hours.

"We have endeavored to provide Honolulu with a modern European hotel," said Mrs. Blaisdell, yesterday. "It will be a few days yet before we have the place entirely completed to allow us to invite patrons, but this is not keeping people away. The rooms are filling rapidly. We intend to cater to those who want a good hotel with first-class service at moderate rate. The day rate will range from $1.50 to $2.50. The monthly rate will range from $25 upward."

The Honolulu Advertiser, February 3, 1913

Honolulu: The Cross-Roads of the Pacific, 1913

The hotel originally had three bronze bells on the roof to summon guests to meals. The bells were donated to the Calvary Episcopal Church in 1962.

The Blaisdell was reportedly the first business in Hawaii to obtain a liquor license after the repeal of Prohibition in 1933.

The hotel was built on the site of the residence and office of Dr. Samuel Tucker who moved here in 1886. A homeopathic doctor from Oakland, California, he was also the Superintendent of the Insane Asylum.

WATUMULL BUILDING

1162-1166 Fort Street

1937 – present
Architect/Builder: Claude A. Stiehl & Harold S. Johnson / Ralph Woolley

The Honolulu Advertiser, June 3, 1937

Jhamandas Watumull, originally from Hyderabad, India, first opened a small import store in Manila with his partner Rochirdas Dharamdas when he was 24 years old.

After a stop in Honolulu on the way back from San Francisco, Dharamdas decided to open a branch on Hotel Street in 1913, moving a year later to the Blaisdell Hotel.

They sold exotic goods from East and South Asia, China, Japan and other countries along the Pacific Rim, and were reportedly the first business in Hawaii started by someone from India.

When Dharamdas suddenly died of cholera, Watumull convinced his younger brother, Gobindram (known as "G.J."), to leave his job with the government engineering service in India to come manage the Honolulu store which they had renamed to The East India Store.

The business prospered and they built this building in 1937 for $75,000 including store and fixtures, designed by Claude Albon Stiehl and Harold S. Johnson.

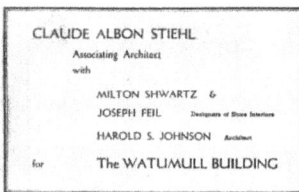

By the 1970's they had 29 stores and were the first to sell matching coordinated Aloha wear for every member of the family. They were also one of the first tenants in the new Ala Moana Center in 1959.

The Watumull companies became one of the largest family businesses in Hawaii and they invested heavily in real estate and were big promoters of the arts. They created the Watumull Foundation to promote cultural and artistic relations between US and India, provide scholarships, invest in research, and award travel grants and prizes for scholarly works.

Gulab Watumull sold the company headquarters building in 1990 and invested in strip malls and warehouses, changing the company's focus from retail to real estate.

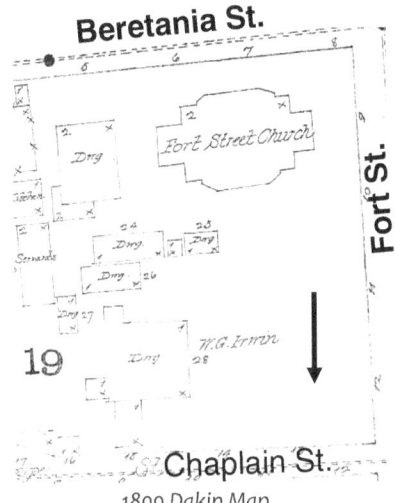
1899 Dakin Map

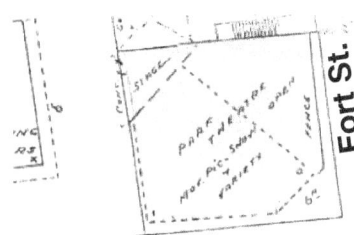
1906 Dakin Map (with update)

Hawaii State Archives

Before Watumull, this corner had been undeveloped for many years, being the side yard of the Thompson/Irwin homestead.

On February 9, 1909, it became the open-air Park Theatre with films like "The Amateur Acrobat", voted most popular because "it is just bubbling over with mirth". It also featured live music from groups like the little Melnotte Sisters and George Milne, plus sing-alongs with colored slides with words for such songs as "In Dear Old Georgia" and "There's a Room to Rent in My Heart for You".

It even had a searchlight which was played along Fort Street during intermissions. But it closed for good on July 12, 1911, due to too much rain plus competition from Hotel Street, "Honolulu's Great White Way". The site later became a Rosecrans Service Station.

NEW PARK THEATRE

Work has commenced on the Werner new "Park" Theatre which will be opened a week from tonight.

The theatre which will be an open air affair promises to afford much entertaining to the pleasure seeking people of Honolulu. There will be no stifling uncomfortableness that is in all inside theatres.

Harry Werner is confident of great success. Lucas Bros. have started today on the erection of the theatre.

The Hawaiian Star, January 30, 1909

Tonight!

Grand Opening

Park Theatre

FORT STREET and CHAPLAIN LANE

New and up to date

MOVING PICTURES

and ILLUSTRATED SONGS

Admission: 10 and 15cts.
Children, 5cts

2022

OUR LADY OF PEACE CATHEDRAL

1175 Fort Street

1840/43 – present

Architect/Builder: Monsigneur Rouchouze? / Francis J. Greenway, Mr. Forest

Paul Emmert, 1854

The Honolulu Republican, October 13, 1901

The first Catholic priest in the Hawaiian Islands was a French Jesuit on board the French corvette *Uranie* in 1819. He converted and baptized Kalaimoku and Governor Boki, among others.

When Kamehameha II visited England in 1823, he took with him Jean Reeves, a Frenchman, who left the royal party and went to Paris to visit the headquarters of the Sacred Heart, requesting they send mission workers to Hawaii.

Three priests were appointed by Pope Leo XII to come to Hawaii – Father Alexis Bachelot and Father Abraham Armand from France and Father Patrick Short from Ireland. All three were members of the Congregation of the Sacred Hearts of Jesus and Mary. They arrived in Honolulu on the *La Comete* on July 7, 1827.

Due to persecution and expulsion fomented by Hawaii's Protestant missionaries, they left the islands for California in 1831, but returned in 1837 and built the first adobe church that stood immediately behind the current cathedral. After years as a school lhouse it was demolished in 1892, "being too old and dilapidated for further use". For many years a fountain marked the location of the first church.

1843, with algaroba tree

Under the leadership of Apostolic Vicar Étienne Rouchouze, ground was broken on July 9, 1840, for the "Cathédrale de Notre Dame de la Paix" and the cornerstone was laid on August 6, 1840.

They utilized "native converts" to harvest coral blocks and completed the building three years later.

The church was dedicated on August 15, 1843, by Monseigneur Louis-Désiré Maigret, and it is said to be the oldest cathedral in continuous use in the United States. It is also the oldest building in the downtown area of Honolulu.

Drawing by Lydia Nye, 1843

The church clock was ordered from France, but the Father Superior in Valparaiso took it for the cathedral there, sending his old clock to Honolulu instead.

Father/Saint Damien (Jozef De Veuster) of Molokai was ordained here on May 21, 1864.

In 1866, Father Maigret replaced the domed square bell tower with an octagonal wooden steeple topped with a cross. Sometime around 1871 the walls were raised higher and a new roof and vaulted redwood ceiling were added.

The bronze statue of "Our Lady Queen of Peace" was unveiled by the Bishop of Panopolis in 1893, representing the Virgin Mary holding an olive branch in her right hand and the "child Jesus" in her left hand.

Bishop Libert Hubert John Louis Boeyneams envisioned the cathedral as a Gothic counterpart to other Catholic cathedrals and hired H.L. Kerr to design a large Gothic Fort Street entrance in 1910. Bishop Stephen Peter Alencastre assumed the episcopacy of the Hawaiian Islands in 1926, and he paid contractor Henry Freitas $21,500 to replace the arches with Doric columns in November 1929.

Due to termite damage the old frame steeple was torn down and replaced with a "handsome one of hollow concrete tile" in 1918 at a cost of $2,000. The new steeple was built around the existing bell.

There was a Cross and a gilded rooster on top, symbolizing Christ's words, "Watch and Pray". Father Valentin said, "the rooster symbolizes early rising and watchfulness, while the Cross indicates prayer".

c.1890

c.1900

c.1910

1921

c.1945

2022

1967

2022

MODEL BLOCK

1178-1184 Fort Street

1899 – present
Architect/Builder: Ripley & Dickey / William Mutch

After Charles S. Desky purchased the large Irwin tract bounded by Queen Emma's house, Fort, Beretania, and Chaplain streets, he sold this portion to Bruce Cartwright on April 25, 1898 for $12,000 with plans to erect an extension to the adjacent Progress Block built in 1898.

PROGRESS ANNEX.

Work Started on Bruce Cartwright's Building.

C. S. Desky is superintending for Bruce Cartwright the erection of an annex to the new Progress Block on Fort and Beretania. Ground was broken yesterday morning with a force of 20 men and 12 teams. Material is being gotten out from the quarries and work will proceed with good speed. Mr. Cartwright's building will have a frontage of 63 feet on Fort street and will have a depth of 80 feet. It will be three stories, of Island stone and brick and iron, with plate glass store fronts. The makai wall of the present Progress Block will serve as the mauka wall of the new building. Arches will be made in this point wall and for the upper floors of the two blocks there will be used the same electric elevator. Mr. Cartwright had for some time contemplated the offer of Mr. Desky for a piece of the big property at the corner of Fort and Beretania. A structure that will be handsome and well appointed in every way will go up as a companion to the Progress building.

The Honolulu Advertiser, May 4, 1898

Called the Model Block and also known as the Cartwright Block, it was based on plans previously prepared for an annex and was connected to the Progress Block with a common elevator. The building has 63' frontage on Fort Street and is 80' deep. It was built of "island stone", brick and iron, with plate glass storefronts. Construction cost $30,000 and it was completed by William Murch in 1899.

The Kilohana Art League moved into a 36' x 45' exhibition room upstairs in March 1899 that was painted by noted Honolulu artist D. Howard Hitchcock in "a terra cotta hue, the color most popular now for art exhibition rooms". Hitchcock also had a studio in the building.

The other major tenant was the Pacific Import Company of San Francisco, specializing in ready-made garments.

KNIGHTS OF COLUMBUS BUILDING

1183 Fort Street

1920 – 1961

Architect/Builder: E.A.P. Newcomb / Bowler & Ingvorsen

This building was built by the Knights of Columbus Catholic fraternal organization "for recreational and social purposes for all men of the army, navy and marine corps, the enlisted personnel especially".

The programs consisted of dancing on Wednesday and Saturday nights with dance lessons on Thursdays. Tea and other refreshments were served on Sunday afternoons and evenings.

The 3- and 4-story concrete building was designed by E.A.P. Newcomb and built by Bowler and Ingvorsen for $39,500.

ALGAROBA TREE DOOMED

Work was commenced yesterday afternoon on cutting down the algaroba tree in the Catholic Mission yard on Fort street. This is the oldest algaroba tree in the islands. It is to be removed to make room for the construction of a clubhouse for the Knights of Columbus.

The Honolulu Advertiser, October 24, 1919

Hawaiian Forester & Agriculturist, 1916

The first and oldest algaroba (kiawe) tree in Hawaii, planted by Father Alexis Bachelot in 1828 was cut down in 1919 to make room for the new building. A section of the trunk was preserved and can still be seen nearby today.

The building was demolished in 1961 and is now an open courtyard next to the 8-story Roman Catholic Diocese Chancery Office building.

2022

PROGRESS BLOCK

1188-1198 Fort Street / 79-89 S. Beretania Street
1898 – present
Architect/Builder: Ripley & Dickey / Carl H. Patzig

Charles S. Desky with the Bruce Waring Company from San Francisco purchased almost half a block of property at this corner in 1897 – 180' on Beretania, 36' on Fort Street, and 200' on Chaplain Lane. It included the old Irwin homestead, the site of old Fort Street Church, and the Bowles property.

Desky hired Ripley & Dickey to design a 3-story stone business block with 83' frontage on Fort Street and 80' frontage on Beretania Street.

The building cost $32,600, and included 3 storefronts on the first floor, 10 suites of offices on the second, and a large octagonal ballroom on the third floor that was 63' across with a 23' tall domed ceiling, capable of seating 600 people.

The dome had a 23' diameter fan and there were two 8' x 26' open-air loggias on the third floor.

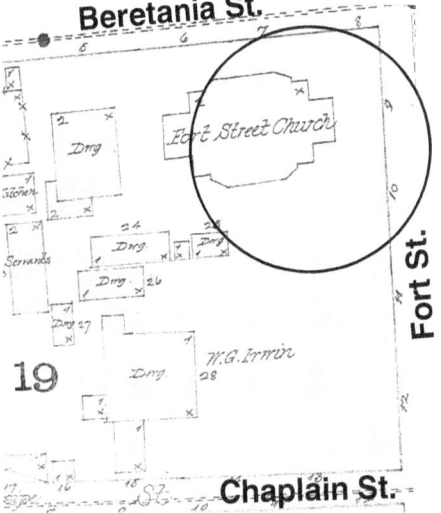

1885 Dakin Map

In the early 1900's the building was owned by the Empire of Japan and contained the offices of its consul general and a commercial museum.

The Fort Street Church was previously located at this corner of Beretania and Fort streets for 36 years.

The Second Foreign Church was established in Honolulu in 1852 as an outgrowth of the Seamen's Bethel Chapel and they built this church in 1856 and called it the Fort Street Church of Honolulu.

It was designed by Theodore C. Heuck, "perfected" by R.A.S. Wood, and built by Christopher H. Lewers for $10,575 with the church ladies raising $360 additional for a spire.

The building was officially dedicated on December 28, 1856.

After the Seamen's Bethel was destroyed in the 1886 fire, the Fort Street Church united with the Bethel to become the Central Union Church.

The church moved to a new stone building at Beretania and Richards streets across from Queen Liliʻuokalani's house (Washington Place) in 1892, and in 1924 moved to its present location at Beretania and Punahou streets.

2022

2022

HOTEL STREET, c.1944

GRAY'S BLOCK

14-24 S. Hotel Street

1882 – 1988

Architect/Builder: unknown

The Pacific Commercial Advertiser, April 1, 1882

The Honolulu Advertiser, August 4, 1882

Evening Bulletin, August 4, 1887

Built by Robert Gray in 1882, this was the M.A. Gonsalves Dry Goods Store. Born in Funchal, Madeira, Portugal, in 1856, Manuel Augusto Gonsalves came to Hawaii on the *Ravenscrag* via Cape Horn in 1879.

It was built on the site of a 2-story wooden building, the photograph on the right was taken on April 19, 1886.

Gray's Block was demolished in 1988 for Chinatown Gateway Park.

THE WAVERLEY BLOCK

15-35 S. Hotel Street / 1018-1058 Bethel Street

1896 – 1970

Architect/Builder: Ripley & Dickey / Carl H. Patzig

THE WAVERLEY BLOCK.

The Hawaiian Gazette, January 5, 1897

William Mutch had this large building built with 121' frontage on Bethel Street and 91' frontage on Hotel Street on the former site of the National Hotel. It had two stories and a cellar and was built of native grey stone with an interior of varnished natural wood.

H. Patzig is the head builder of the Mutch block. Mr. Mutch thinks of giving his building another name, but it is doubtful if he can improve *much* on it thereby.

Ordway & Porter had a large furniture store here, other stores included S. Ozaki, "The Kash", and Medeiros & Decker, and B.F. Ehlers. The Waverley Club met upstairs in Waverley Hall. In 1902 a gasoline engine and dynamo were installed to furnish the building with its own electric lighting plant.

After Ordway & Porter moved out in 1902, C.J. McCarthy's Criterion Saloon moved in, and in 1905 the *Paradise of the Pacific* established its office on the first floor with printing plant on the second floor.

While other buildings on Nuʻuanu Street were being demolished in 1970 for a city parking lot, a 21-year-old vagrant started a fire in the Waverley Block that burned 2/3 of the block.

The land was a surface parking lot for nearly twenty years until construction of the $25M, 27-story, 200-unit Chinatown Gateway Plaza project designed by Norman Lacayo and completed in 1990.

In 1840, Joseph Booth leased the 0.25-acre Eagle Tavern tract in the middle of this block, accessed from Nuʻuanu Street, from a man named Kapihi. When Kapihi died in 1844 he willed the land to Kamehameha III who sold it to Dr. T.C.B. Rooke who the same day sold it to Joseph Booth for $200. Booth was also the owner of The Blonde hotel at the corner of King and Nuʻuanu streets.

In 1847 Booth built the 2-story coral and wood National House Hotel for the enormous sum of $10,000. it was 70' x 24' with 7 bedrooms upstairs and a restaurant below. He hired James F. Lewis to manage it.

Big mistake. Lewis was an American, "about 35 years of age, dark swarthy complexion, black eyes and hair, roman nose, stout, well built, and about 6 feet tall…[with] small gold earrings in both ears". How do we know this? From the ad posted by Joseph Booth after Lewis stole over $8,000 in gold and silver and escaped on the ship *Henry Tuke* in 1848 and was never seen or heard from again, in spite of the $500 reward for his capture posted for two years.

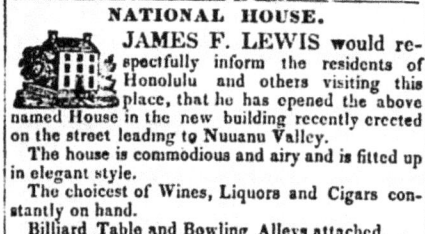

Paul Emmert, 1854

Photo by H.L. Chase, 1870

By 1868 it was known as the International Hotel. Its walls were badly cracked in the 1871 earthquake, and during the 1886 fire it was stripped and the veranda pulled down to prevent it catching fire. Already in poor condition, this damaged it beyond repair. But being of stone construction with a slate roof it stopped the progress of the fire and saved the buildings on Fort Street. Less than a month after the fire it was auctioned and sold for $150 to W.R. Scale who pulled it down for the materials.

> The new merry-go-round, at Bethel and Hotel streets drew an enormous crowd on Sasurday evening. It was estimated that the patronage amounted to a dollar a minute throughout the evening. The whirligig will be taken on to the Colonies on the next through steamer.
>
> *Evening Bulletin, August 7, 1893*

The site was vacant for 10 years after the fire and was the location for a popular steam-powered merry-go-round until the Waverley Block was built.

KA HALE POHAKU WAVELA

E KA MAKAMAKA: O kela kii e puka aku nei oia no ke kii o ka hale pohaku e ku nei ma ke kihi o na alanui Hotelo ame Betela a I kapaia ka "Hale Wavela," (Waverly Building), a ma ka hale maluna malaila e olii nau ai KA LANAKILA i kela ame keia Poaha o na hebedoma apau. Ma ke alanui Betela makai o ke kihi o alanui Hotelo ke alapii e hiki ai no ka hale maluna. O keia ke Keena Pa'i o ka Paredaiso o ka Pakipika.

2022

ROBINSON BLOCK

28-42 S. Hotel Street

1891 – 1988 (altered 1924)
Architect/Builder: Isaac A. Palmer / George Lucas

Honolulu: The Crossroads of the Pacific, 1913. Photo by L.E. Edgeworth.

On the waikiki side of Bijou Lane leading to the Bijou Theater, the Robinson Block was built for the James Robinson estate and was designed in classic Eastlake Victorian style by Isaac A. Palmer. It was constructed by George Lucas for $19,350 and completed in 1891. "Iron pilasters are at the corners and dividing the store fronts, and iron columns with reveilles frame the doorways. The whole front is of iron and plaste glass. All of the iron work was done at the Union Iron Works, being the first work of the kind ever done in Honolulu… nothing has been imported for this building which could be made here."

The righthand ¼ of the building was demolished in January 1924 to make way for the extension of Bethel Street and the building was redesigned by Guy N. Rothwell to have stores facing the new street. It was the home of the Japanese-owned Hawaiian Drug Company.

The remainder of the Robinson Block was "modernized" in 1950 with architects Cyril W. Lemmon and Douglas W. Freeth making the storefronts "largely of plate glass, corrugated asbestos cement, and opaque colored glass". The work was done by Thomas T. Tanaka for $14,600.

JAPANESE BAZAAR.

THE STOCK OF

Japanese Goods & Curios

Lately on exhibition over Gonsalves & Co.'s Store has been removed to the

Robinson Block, Hotel Street,

(Opposite Bethel Street),

Where the Proprietor will be glad to see his friends.

New Goods Opened!

☞ The Stock is on the ground floor, no staircase to climb. 340 tf

---

GRAND OPENING
—OF THE—
NEW FURNITURE STORE

Robinson Block, Hotel Street, oppo. Bethel Street.

Furniture, Upholstery AND Cabinet Making

ON HAND AN EXTENSIVE ASSORTMENT OF

Wicker Ware,   Chiffoniers,
Antique Oak   Sideboards,
Bedroom Suits,   Etc., Etc., Etc.

Wardrobes, Mattrasses, Pillows, Etc., Made to Order.

— NO SECOND-HAND OR DAMAGED GOODS KEPT ON HAND —

ORDWAY & PORTER,

Robinson Block, Hotel Street, oppo. Bethel Street.

BELL TELEPHONE 525.   MUTUAL TELEPHONE 618.

New Goods
—IN—
All Lines!

Lowest Prices
—AT—
IWAKAMI'S Robinson Block, Hotel St.

ASADA,

Hotel Street - - - - Robinson Block.

P. O. Box 215.   Telephone 973.

LADIES' AND GENTS' SILK HANDKERCHIEFS.

JUST RECEIVED EX "COPTIC."

Pajamas, Shirts, Fans, Neckties, Suspenders;
. . . White Vests, Etc. . . .

SILKS, SASHES, BLANKETS, STYLISH GOLF SHIRTS, JEWELRY.

Wholesale and Retail Japanese Goods and Provision Merchants.

The remainder of the Robinson Block was demolished in 1988 for Chinatown Gateway Park.

Before 1885 there were 9 wooden stores on this site between the Gonsalves store in Gray's Block and Frederick Horn's store in the old Canton Hotel: W. Miller (cabinet maker), barber shop (owned by Portuguese), shoe store, barber shop, Chinese coffee shop, furniture store (owned by Portuguese), Loo Joe (tailor), Wo Hop coffee saloon, and Ramsey's grocery store. This all changed just before midnight on May 10, 1890, when a huge fire started in the back of the Portuguese furniture store, destroying 8 of the buildings. There was one fatality, a former express driver with two wooden legs who was unable to escape.

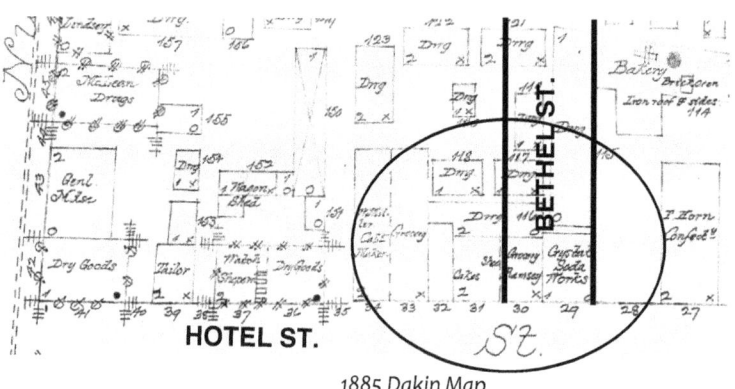

1885 Dakin Map

c.1890

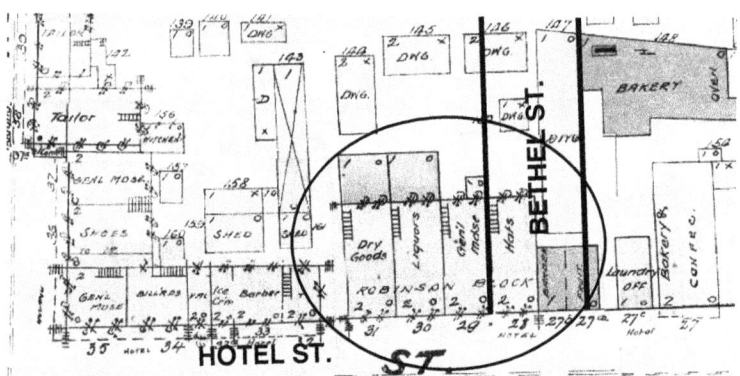

1899 Dakin Map

2022

EMPIRE THEATER
41-49 S Hotel Street / 1041-1051 Bethel Street
1909 – 1950
Architect/Builder: H.L. Kerr

Honolulu: The Cross-Roads of the Pacific, 1913

Honolulu: The Cross-Roads of the Pacific, 1913

When the Favorite Grotto Saloon's license was turned down in 1907, two young San Franciscans named Messrs. Werner and Tait opened the Empire Theater on January 14, 1908, immediately behind the Chinese restaurant at the makai/waikiki corner of Bethel and Hotel streets.

In February 1909, Frank Richardson and Robert M. Overend closed the Empire Theater and started construction on a new Empire Theater in a large concrete building designed by H.L. Kerr to cost $20,000. It was completely fire-proof with concrete walls and a galvanized iron roof allowing for unobstructed views.

> Architect H. L. Kerr is designing a number of houses to be erected in the residence sections, and is also preparing the plans for the new Empire theater, to be built on the site of the present structure.

The Honolulu Advertiser, January 27, 1909

The theater seated 1,000 people with an entrance on Bethel Street for the 10¢ and 15¢ seats and an entrance on Hotel Street for the 25¢ gallery seats upstairs. Opening day was Saturday, May 15, 1909.

In 1950, the Empire Amusement Corporation built a 3-story building with 6 stores, 36 offices, and a modern billiard parlor to replace the earlier Empire Theater. The new building was designed by Y.T. Char and built by the Pacific Construction Corporation for $180,000.

Empire's Big Opening.

Saturday night was lively downtown, particularly in the vicinity of the moving-picture theaters, and in spite of the fact that the new Empire Theater was opening up for the first time and taking in patrons who filled every seat up to the end of the performance, all the other theaters had "crush" houses. It was a very satisfactory night to all the picture shows.

The Empire was all that Manager Overend had claimed it would be. The ticket-office lobby was crowded early, and in a short time the entire theater was filled. When the lights were turned out, save the green globes, and the pictures were thrown on the screen, there was general satisfaction, for the views not only had good subjects, but were shown clearly and without flicker. Some of the pictures were so realistic, especially in a Graeco-Turkish scene, that the audience cheered as the hero saved the captive Greek princess. The orchestrelle was a pleasing feature, and the interior arrangements of the house were praised. Both Messrs. R. M. Overend and Frank Richardson were congratulated for the thorough manner in which they had built and finished what is probably the finest moving-picture theater in the Territory.

The Honolulu Advertiser, May 17, 1909

Honolulu Star-Bulletin, May 30, 1950

2022

George W. Houghtailing's Bay Horse Saloon was on the corner from 1855 to 1895, becoming the Palace Restaurant in 1896 run by Ah Hee & Co. when the government refused to renew the Bay Horse liquor license.

Bay Horse Saloon.
G. S. HOUGHTAILING, Prop'r.
Cor. Hotel St. and Rose Lane,
HONOLULU, H. I.
The Best of WINES, LIQUORS and CIGARS always on Hand.

WARREN / CANTON HOTEL

52-58 S. Hotel Street

c.1825 – 1909

Architect/Builder: unknown.

There's a lot of history on this site dating back 200 years. It was the site of the Warren Hotel opened in the 1820's by Major William R. Warren on the mauka side of Hotel Street and from whence Hotel Street gets its name.

Known as "The Major" with a "big paunch, red face, and blonde eyebrows", Warren came to Hawaii before the missionaries arrived and was in the hotel business by 1817. Warren obtained the lot sometime before 1819, and reportedly built the Warren Hotel sometime around 1825.

Warren House was renowned for its food, and a poem in honor of Major Warren was composed and published upon his impending departure to California in 1838:

> Cups of coffee quaff'd at ease,
>
> Legs of mutton, eat with peas.
>
> Good corn'd beef, with cabbage boil'd
>
> Table cloth (with gravy soil'd),
>
> Spread with pisco-punch so fine,
>
> Beer, champagne, and first rate wine,
>
> Turkeys, chickens, turtle soup,
>
> Roasted plover—quite a troop!
>
> Onions, craw-fish, pigeons, salad—
>
> Then the Major's favorite ballad!

Sandwich Islands Gazette, March 3, 1838

Major Warren was described on his departure as "a gentleman with a smiling visage, a rotund figure, a disposition like a sunbeam, and a heart as big as the Island of Hawaii". He sold the hotel to Dr. Edward Espener on December 21, 1837, for $1,600. William French purchased the hotel in December 1841 for $10,000, and it was purchased by James Robinson, Robert Laurence, and Robert W. Holt at auction for $4,620 from the estate of William French. It was one of four hotels in Honolulu in 1847.

In 1844 William French brought in a Chinese partner, Ahung, who brought in three Chinese co-partners (Atai, Ahsing, Ahlan) doing business under the name Hungtai.

Upon the death of Ahung, Hungwa bought into the business and became the proprietor.

Samuel Thompson briefly ran the hotel in 1849, being succeeded by John Bartlett for the next 10 years.

CANTON HOTEL.

THE undersigned having taken the premises formerly known as the "Warren Hotel," begs to assure the public that he has spared no expense in fitting up the same for the comfort and convenience of residents and visitors, and solicits a share of the public patronage.

BILLIARD ROOM and newly fitted BOWLING ALLEYS attached to the premises.

The services of superior *Chinese Cooks* and *Waiters* have been secured.

Residents may have their meals sent to their homes, or pic-nic parties provided for at the shortest notice.

BREAD and PASTRY made at the establishment, constantly on hand, and will be supplied in any required quantity.   HUNGWA.

Aug 24.   tf

May 30th, died John Bartlett, a resident for over twenty years, and much respected for his sterling probity of character and genial disposition. He was, during the last ten years of his life, proprietor of the "Canton Hotel," (now Horn's bakery,) a noted resort for officers of whaleships. All through the "flush" whaling seasons from 1849 to 1858, the mates and boat-steerers made a great deal of money, frequently their season's work running into thousands of dollars per man; and then, when shipping again, a good whaleman commanded from $260 to $500 advance, besides a "bonus" of an equal amount. "Jack Bartlett" was cash-keeper for most of this class, and although they squandered their means with lavish folly, no complaint was ever heard impugning Jack's honest dealing.

Daily Honolulu Press, March 24, 1883

Canton Hotel and Restaurant!

HOTEL STREET, BETWEEN FORT and Nuuanu Streets, will be

Opened on Sunday Morning, March 19th.

TERMS:

Board, per Week..............................$4.00 to $5.00
Board, per Week, sent out.................................$6 00
Board per Day...$1 00
Lodging per Week...$2.50

All Board Bills must be Settled Weekly.

m18 1m   ACHONG & AKIM, Proprietors.

It became the Eureka Restaurant in 1865.

EUREKA RESTAURANT.

SAMUEL LOLLER WOULD INFORM the Public that it is his intention to

Open a First Class Restaurant!

On the late Canton Hotel Premises,

Where Meals may be had at any Hour of the Day or Night!

Served in the Best Style the Market will Afford.

The patronage of Residents and Visitors is respectfully solicited.   500-3t

PIONEER
Steam CANDY Factory,
BAKERY and
Ice Cream Parlors!

PRACTICAL
CONFECTIONER
AND ORNAMENTER

In all branches of the business on these islands.

American, English, German and French PASTRIES Made to Order.

BIRTH-DAY AND WEDDING CAKES

Made of the Very Best Material and at Reasonable Rates.

Family Graham & Fancy Bread
Always on Hand.

ALL CONFECTIONERY

Manufactured at My Establishment Are Guaranteed to be Positively Pure and Sold at Prices no other establishment can compete with.

FACTORY AND STORE,
No. 71 Hotel Street, Honolulu.
Both Telephones No. 74.   jy26

REMOVAL.
HORN'S
Elegant Dining and Ice Cream Rooms,
Removed to No. 45 Hotel Street.

THE UNDERSIGNED BEGS TO NOTIFY his customers and the public generally that he has taken the commodious premises directly opposite his old stand, formerly known as the "Canton Hotel," where he is prepared to carry on the business of

A First Class Restaurant,

WILL OPEN ON MONDAY, JUNE 4th, and will serve the Choicest Viands and Refreshments that the market affords, with perfect cleanliness and neatness. Single meals served at any hour of the day or evening.

....ALWAYS ON HAND....

Iced Ginger Beer, Soda Water & Lemonade

Honolulu, June 3d, 1877.   **F. HORN.**
                                          648 3m

For over 20 years, starting in 1877, this was the site of Frederick Horn's bakery and confectionary business, known as the Pioneer Steam Candy Manufactory and Bakery.

Frederick Horn was born in 1819 in Dresden, Saxony. He studied confectionary and fruit preserving and worked in Hull and Manchester in England and in Sydney, Australia, and later with Swain's in San Francisco. He came to Honolulu in 1862 and opened his first business at King and Maunakea streets. Horn was the first to preserve and sell Hawaiian fruits for export.

From 1898 to 1909 it was the New England Bakery and Honolulu Candy Company.

NEW ENGLAND BAKERY.

Horn's Pioneer bakery, on Hotel street, is now known as the New England Bakery. Under the management of C. W. Eccles it is achieving great popularity.

The Hawaiian Star, September 3, 1898

1900

```
AT AUCTION
——
At the NEW ENGLAND BAKERY,
Tuesday, March 30, '09
At 12 o'clock noon.
Ice boxes, refrigerators,
Electric piano, in first-class order,
Showcases, cash registers, glass jars,
Glass dishes, large coffee urn, nickel
plated, fancy soda fountain, soda gen-
erator and ten gallon copper container
for making your own soda water,
   Tables, Vienna chairs, oak chairs,
Silverware, matting, carpets,
Table cloths, dishes, cooking stove,
Cooking utensils,
  Mirrors, ice cream freezers,
Bread troughs, baking pans,
Candy, marble coolers.
Coffee kettles, etc., etc.
——
           J. W. SMITHIES,
           Manager C. A. Co.
```

1911

The buildings were demolished in 1909 and the larger site became home to the Gem Theater, Savoy Theater, Highland Park amusement center, and the Fashion Saloon.

A 1-story brick building was built on the corner when Bethel was extended to Pauahi Street in 1924.

The National Building designed by Ray Akagi and built by Ben Hayashi Ltd. in 1949 is on the site today.

The Honolulu Advertiser, May 10, 1924

2022

JAMES CAMPBELL BUILDING

73-81 S. Hotel Street

1882 – present? (1918 reconstructed)
Architect/Builder: George Lucas (1882), Emory & Webb (1918)

Another brick building is about to be erected on Hotel street, near the corner of Fort. Mr. Geo. Lucas is the builder, for James Campbell, Esq. The site is that occupied for many years as a Cabinet maker's shop by Mr. C. E. Williams.

Evening Bulletin, April 6, 1882

The retail store of S. Magnin moved in by December 1882, and the grocery firm of Kennedy & Co. was in "Campbell's fire-proof building" by June 1883.

T.F. Kennedy became Lewis & Co. grocers in 1884.

This building was built on Hotel Street in 1882 by George Lucas for James Campbell, who very likely also added the second floor to the adjoining Tregloan Building (on the left) at the same time.

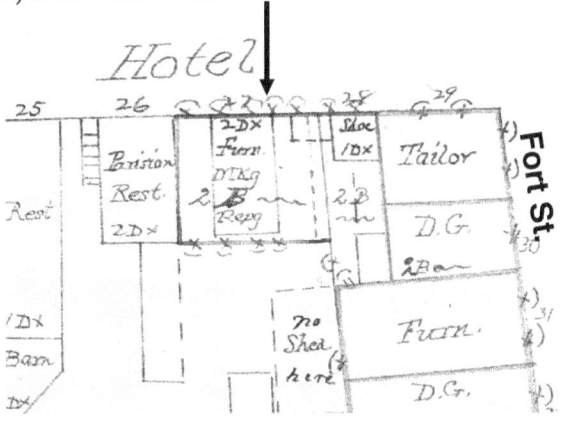

1885 Dukin Map

This new Campbell building was on the site of the cabinet-making shop of R.A.S. Wood and William C. Parke that was here as early as 1847. Wood became sole owner in 1850 and sold the business to William Henry Stuart and Gustave W. Rahe in 1851.

Paul Emmert, 1854

William H. Stuart took over the business in 1856, and after he passed away a year later, Charles W. Fox ran a cabinet-making shop here.

It became Charles E. Williams cabinet-making shop in 1859.

Thomas G. Thrum wrote in 1898 that it "served them many years till the march of progress demanded its site for the brick block now existing".

In October 1877, C.E. Williams sold all of his Honolulu property, including several buildings, to James Campbell.

The 1882 building was later incorporated into the 1918 James Campbell Building that also encompassed the Tregloan Building and the Williams/Hollister building.

PALM BUILDING

116-118 S. Hotel Street

1912 – present

Architect/Builder: Ripley & Reynolds / Lord-Young Engineering Company

Honolulu Star-Bulletin, October 20, 1924

By 1879 there was a billiard saloon and a plumber here in two 1-story wooden buildings. The Hart Brothers' Astor House dining and lunch parlor was here in 1880.

But that all changed on January 20, 1885, when a disastrous fire swept through the makai end of this block, destroying 5 buildings and badly damaging two others.

It started just after midnight in C.J. Fishel's store at the corner of Fort and Hotel streets, presumably due to workmen failing to extinguish heating irons in the Tregloan tailor shop on the second floor.

It destroyed Fishel's building, George M. Raupp's Germania Market, and the Elite Ice Cream Parlor on Hotel Street, and the Confectionary and Soda Water Manufactory of P. McInerny and the Boot and Shoe Store of Frank Gertz on Fort Street. The Elite Ice Cream Parlor building was owned by Queen Emma but had no insurance.

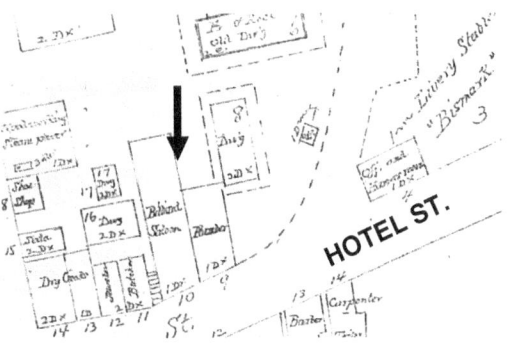

1879 Lion Map, before the 1885 fire

By the first of April 1885, William T. Rhoads was building two new wooden buildings for M.W. McChesney for the Elite Ice Cream Parlor and the King Brothers who were art and picture frame dealers.

Honolulu: The Cross-Roads of the Pacific, 1913

When the Elite Ice Cream Parlors moved to the new Elite Building in 1900, it became Miller's Restaurant and Candy Factory, owned by E.A.G. Miller. In 1906 it was bought by Charles J. Ludwigsen, a former Hart & Company employee who in partnership with Alfred H. Jungclaus renamed it the Palm Restaurant.

After giving up waiting for the city to decide whether it was going to widen or close Union Street, the Brewer Estate erected a 2-story concrete building in 1912 for $33,000 specifically designed by Ripley & Reynolds to house the Palm Café.

The first floor housed the confectionary and bakery business in front with a dining room at the back, plus a broad stairway leading to more restaurant space upstairs. Al Jungclaus traveled to New York and Chicago to buy over 40 tons of new restaurant, baking, and confectionary equipment. Opening day was September 21, 1912.

From 1914 to 1921 the building was the Sachs Dry Goods store and in 1927 it became Thayer's Piano Company and music store.

Leonard E. Thayer came to Hawaii in 1905 with 30 years' experience in the piano business plus a stock of Steinways and opened his first store in the Oregon Block. Thayer's were in the Palm Building for over 50 years.

In 1964 a new "modern" front was put on both the Palm Building and the Union Building.

Palm Building on the left, Union Building on the right, 2022

William DeWitt Alexander, 1896

ARLINGTON BLOCK

117-133 S. Hotel Street

1888 – 1981

Architect/Builder: George Lucas (1888), Mark Potter (1937) / John Hansen (1937)

Hawaii State Archives

A NEW CAKE AND CANDY STORE.

Messrs. Hart & Co. of the Elite Ice Cream Parlors, Hotel street, have recently removed, in part, to the Brewer block, on the opposite side of the street; that is, a part of their business has been removed. The ice cream parlors remain where they were, but the candy factory and candy shop are in the new building referred to. The manufacturing is done in the cellar below, and on the ground floor is the shop, where the manufactured articles are exhibited and sold. This shop presents a remarkably neat, pretty and enticing appearance. There is plenty of space for advantageous exhibition and room for customers to move around without crushing and crowding. The large windows are decorated with an interminable variety of candies, and show cases inside are also filled with the same class of sweets. Other show cases are occupied with cakes of variegated ornamentation and varying sizes shapes. There is not a prettier or a sweeter shop in this little town than the new candy and cake shop of Hart & Co.

Evening Bulletin, July 9, 1888

Built by the C. Brewer Estate for $26,216 this 2-story brick building had five stores in 1891: candy store, shoe store, Schumann Carriage Co., barber shop, plus the Arlington Hotel upstairs.

THE ARLINGTON,
Hotel St., : Honolulu.
J. H. FISHER, Prop.

TERMS:
Board and Lodging, per week, (according to location of rooms... $10.00 to $12.00
Transient, per day........ 2 00
Table Board, per week........ 7 00
Single Meals.................. 50

☞ Visitors will find this one of the most comfortable and convenient houses in the city, the rooms being large, light and airy. Hot and cold water baths.
683 tf

The new Brewer block, on Hotel street, near Fort street, is gradually nearing completion.

The block is of brick, two stories high. The ground floor contains four store rooms of various sizes, and each has a cellar. The cellars are lighted in front by iron gratings, which open on the sidewalk.

The second story of the block is reached by a winding stair case, about six feet wide. A hall, also about six feet wide, runs the entire length of the building, in the center. This hall is lighted by two large skylights. On both sides of the hall are rooms, each about 16x12 feet in size. There are 19 rooms on the second floor, nine on the back side of the main passage way and ten on the front side. The front and back of the house have balconies, about 4½ feet wide running the length of the block, and ornamented in each case, with an iron railing. Another hall connects both balconies in the center of the house, running at right angles to the main hall.

The upper floor will be well supplied with bath and toilet rooms, and arrangements for gas lighting have been put in every room and in the halls. The side walk in front of the house is of stone.

Evening Bulletin, June 2, 1888

"RING 'EM ALL UP!"

Ring up the Ladies & Gentlemen of Honolulu!
Ring up the Boys & Girls!!
Ring up the Babies!!!
Ring up Everybody all over Hawaii Nei!!!!

HELLO, HELLO, HELLO,
Tell 'Em All, that

HART & CO'Y
HAVE OPENED THEIR

New Candy Factory & Elegant Candy Store
On Hotel Street, New Brewer Block,
Where they will manufacture and sell the FINEST and CHOICE

FRENCH AND HOME-MADE CANDIES!
Fresh Candies made every day.

An Elegant Assortment of FANCY CANDY BON-BON BOXES & NOVELTIES always on hand.

Ice Cream Soda & Iced Drinks
Of all kinds served from the most unique soda fountain in the city
☞ Candies carefully packed for shipment to the other islands.
━━━ WHOLESALE & RETAIL ━━━
Ring! Ring!! Keep on Ringing and call at

"The New Candy Factory."
62 1m

From 1897 to 1956 this was the home of the Silent Barber Shop. Founded by Portuguese barbers Frank Pacheco and Joe Fernandes who started with four barber chairs and added two more within the year.

"Never before has Honolulu possessed such costly and handsome arrangements in a tonsorial establishment."

It had a "great complex mirror arrangement" with a fancy carved frame that stretched almost the full length of the shop, plus three chandeliers in the middle with three and four electric lamps each, the center one having a large electric fan.

The origin of the name is a bit of a mystery, with the folklore saying two windjammer sailors walked into the previous shop and heard only the clicking of scissors and scrape of razors, exclaiming: "What a silent barber shop this place is!"

Judge Samuel King claimed it was a joke based on a lyric from the 1891 song "The Bowery": *I went to a barbershop, he talk'd till I thought that he'd never stop.* King said the shop was anything but silent, and one always got "the latest poop on every issue in there".

In 1915 Fernandez began renting rooms upstairs calling it the Silent Hotel. "Clean, convenient, cheap, running water in each room".

The shoeshine boy was Han Choon Duk from Korea, who came to Hawaii in 1904 as a plantation laborer and ended up working at the Silent Barber shop for over 50 years, shining about 25 pairs of shoes a day.

SILENT BARBER SHOP.
The New Establishment Will Be Open at 7 This Morning.

Messrs. Pacheco and Fernandes who have had charge of the Criterion barber shop for the space of about two years and who have there carried on a business that has been second to none in town, have moved into their new and elegant quarters in the Arlington block and will open up for business at that stand at 7 o'clock this morning.

The shop on Hotel street is one to be proud of. The exterior in itself is inviting. Large plate glass windows confront the man whose whiskers have had a two days' growth and a boot black's stand, gotten up according to the latest style, is there for accommodation. A stone walk to the barber shop will soon be laid from the other side of the street.

The interior is a pleasure to behold. Everything is done in light wood highly polished and mouding with the latest designs grace the walls.

Four barber chairs stand each in front of a fine mirror and another one will be added by the first of December. The cases to the sides of these mirrors, are filled with the usual perfumes, etc. that go to make up a barber's outfit. Near each chair is an electric bell to call the boy outside for a brush down.

In the center of the room is a large circular washstand provided with three wash bowls where hot and cold water will be provided.

At the back part of the room is a large mirror on each side of which is a case for the shaving cups of the customers, while above is a large clock that is guaranteed to keep correct time.

At the side are chairs for the "nexts" and a table that will be provided with the last periodicals and papers.

The whole establishment is provided with electric lights and running down the center of the room are three chandeliers, the middle one of which is provided with a large electric fan for hot weather.

Tropical plants are scattered about in places calculated to give an artistic effect.

The work of fixing up the "Silent Barber Shop" was done by Lucas Bros. and a right fine job has been the result. A great deal of money has been spent by Messrs. Pacheco & Fernandes but they intend to give the shaving and hair cutting public a first class place.

The Honolulu Advertiser, November 27, 1897

The C. Brewer Estate hired architect Mark Potter and contractor John Hansen to "modernize" the building in 1937. The balcony with wooden floor and iron railing was removed and replaced with a sheet metal marquee "lowered to add to the attractiveness of the large plate glass windows of the stores on the ground floor".

Colored vitrolite facings were added at the waikiki corner of the building and around the store entrances. The interior was also completely changed with "modern decoration and arrangement".

Honolulu Star-Bulletin, December 16, 1937

"The building is a good example of what can be done to modernize an old building" – Mark Potter.

The Arlington Building was demolished in 1981 for the multi-million-dollar Executive Center complex. Long's Drug Store is on the site today.

Honolulu Star-Bulletin, December 16, 1937

PORTLAND BUILDING

134 S. Hotel Street / 1109 Union Street

1903 – present
Architect/Builder: unknown

After waiting for a Chinese store's lease to run out, auditor and stockbroker J.H. Fisher was finally able to build on this tiny lot in 1903. Named the "Portland" building, it nestled into the corner of the Oregon Building. Its first tenant was a cigar store with a private room above.

1966

This corner lot at Hotel and Union streets was previously the location of the Fashion Stables.

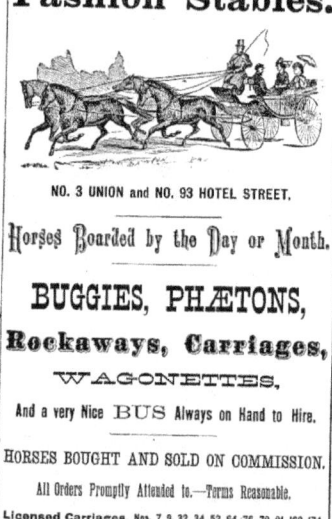

Union Street from Hotel Street, 1870

Oregon Block and Portland Building, 2022

OREGON BLOCK

148-162 S. Hotel Street / 1113-1119 Union Street

1901 – present (reconfigured 1927)
Architect/Builder: Hoffman & Riley (1901), Herbert Cohen Cayton (1927) /
Hawaiian Engineering & Construction Co. (1901)

The building here today is a mere remnant of a much larger structure that was mostly demolished when the new Bishop Street plowed right through it in late 1926.

The original Oregon Block was a 2-story brick building with 7 stores built in 1901 by Victor Hoffman and John F. Riley for about $40,000.

Hoffman and Riley were also owners along with A.V. Gear, J. Lando, and L.A. Rostin. Jacob Lando owned a clothing store on Fort Street and moved here along with Mrs. Hanna the milliner, Pearson & Potter, Rice & Perkins photographers, and the Golden Rule Bazaar.

New Building on Hotel Street.

Another business block is to be erected at once on Hotel street, adjoining the "Elite." Contracts have been let to Messrs. Hoffman and Relley for a modern two-story brick building, containing seven stores on Hotel and Union streets, and offices, and probably lodge rooms up stairs. The building is to be completed by September 1st, and is to cost about $40,000. The building will be known as the "Oregon Block." The owners are A. V. Gear, J. Lando, V. Hoffman, J. F. Relley and L. A. Rostin.

Hawaiian Gazette, April 26, 1901

Initially called the Hibernia Block, it was built on the site of the Fashion Stables and Fire Engine House No.2. The Portland Building was added in the corner at Hotel and Union streets in 1903.

1902 (no Portland Building yet)

In 1920 the Board of Supervisors approved the extension of Bishop Street from Hotel to Beretania. Tenants were given 60 days to move out of the Oregon Block in 1926.

James Steiner, owner of the adjacent Elite Block, purchased the remnants of the Oregon Block at auction in 1927. He hired architect Herbert Cohen Cayton to reconstruct the ewa remainder with 4 stores on the first floor and 9 offices on the second floor, with 76 feet of frontage on Bishop Street.

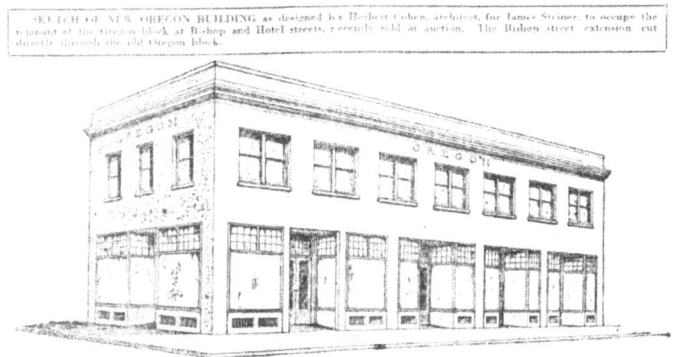

The Honolulu Advertiser, August 7, 1927

STEINER PLANS NEW BUILDING ON BISHOP STREET

James Steiner who recently purchased at auction at record prices the remnants of the Oregon block, cut in two by Bishop street extension will reconstruct and repair the ewa remnant so as to effect a two-story and basement stucco building with a front of 76 feet on Bishop street.

The first floor will be divided into four stores, three with entrances and windows both on Bishop and Union streets and one on Hotel and Bishop streets.

The second story will contain nine offices. The basement will be used as a commercial sample display room.

"The Oregon Building" will be retained as the name of the reconstruced building. Herbert Cohen, architect, has drawn the plans for the structure. Work will start at once.

The Honolulu Advertiser, August 5, 1927

2022

The Fire Engine House of Mechanic Company No.2 was located on Union Street, and in 1857 they erected a tall flagpole "surmounted with a gilt Vulcan's arm" displaying a new red flag with the words "Mechanic 2" in white letters. The landmark 75' hexagonal Alarm Bell Tower was added in 1870, designed and built by James Renton. The bell was cast in Troy, New York, weighed 1,018 pounds, and cost $500.

The property was leased from Mrs. M.C. Monsarrat. When an appropriations bill in 1884 was delayed, her son, J.M. Monsarrat, seized the property and angered the fireman by putting a lock on the building. By the 1890's the building was "a decrepit structure…rotten from the ground up and worm-eaten". It was returned to the Monsarrat family when the new Central Fire Station was completed in 1897.

OLD BELL TOWER BEING TORN DOWN

Building Housed Honolulu's Fire Department in Olden Days. Hibernia Block.

The old Bell Tower building on Union street is being demolished. The tumble-down structures, weatherbeaten and dilapidated, have been standing for the last thirty years, unoccupied of late except as a carpenter shop. In their time the buildings, and especially the one surmounted by a towering fire belfry, were quite an ornament to old Honolulu.

When first erected the buildings were used by the volunteer fire department and the hook and ladder and an engine were housed there. In the tall tower the fire bell was hung and a watchman gazed from its heights during the night-time to detect the first signs of a fire. Later, when the building began to show signs of age, the steeple became unsafe and was cut down to the proportions of a small-sized cupola and the bell was removed, fire signals being given by a deep-voiced siren along the waterfront.

As soon as the buildings are razed, excavation work will be commenced on the site. The residence cottage now standing on the Ewa side of the new Elite building, on Hotel street, will also be razed. The new Hibernia building, when erected, will thus have the advantage of two fine frontages, one on Hotel street and the other where the Bell Tower buildings now are. The corner property will not be touched for the present. The Hibernia block will be a fitting companion to the artistic Elite block, just finished.

The Honolulu Advertiser, May 4, 1900

Bell Tower site, 2022

ELITE BLOCK

170-174 S. Hotel Street

1899 – 1964

Architect/Builder: Oliver G. Traphagen / Carl H. Patzig

JAS. STEINER'S NEW BUILDING, CORNER HOTEL STREET AND ADAMS LANE. PLANS BY TRAPHAGEN.
The Honolulu Advertiser, February 3, 1899

This was the site of the coolest (and sweetest) building in downtown Honolulu – the Elite Ice Cream Parlor and Candy Factory.

Originally founded by Henry Hart from Kingston, Jamaica, the Elite Ice Cream Parlors were first located on Hotel Street closer to Nuʻuanu Street. They rebuilt in 1885 after a fire and had "16 magnificent rooms, each fitted with a marble center table, handsome curtains and comfortable chairs…lit by a pretty chandelier". In a clever bit of marketing, anyone who made a purchase had a chance to win a fancy Christmas cake. They moved to the new Brewer's Block (Arlington Building) in 1888.

In 1899, James Steiner tore down the wooden dentist office of Drs. Anderson and Lundt and hired Oliver Traphagen to design three versions of an ornate new 3-story building – terra cotta and pressed brick, same design but with galvanized cornice and stucco, or blue stone and stucco.

The selected design was pressed brick and terra cotta imported from Italy, in a highly ornamented Italian Renaissance style with "Elite 1899" incorporated on the main cornice. The contractor was Carl H. Patzig and the building cost $37,900.

The first floor and basement was the Elite Restaurant run by Hart & Co., 12 offices were on the second floor, and the third floor was a large meeting hall with a 15-foot ceiling with three ornamental domes 12 feet in diameter.

The blasting for the foundation was done by a Japanese firm and on two separate occasions showers of rock rained down over the neighborhood, including "several big coral meteors". Luckily, no one was injured. The quarried foundation stones were provided by Fred Harrison.

In 1907 James Steiner divided the downstairs into three stores to accommodate his growing Island Curios business.

This was also the first home of the YWCA in Hawaii. They initially rented a room upstairs "as a place away from work where young women could eat from their lunch boxes, perhaps make a cup of tea or maybe take a nap". It had one rest couch, a small collection of borrowed books, and a secretary who worked four hours each day. They outgrew the space six months later and moved to the Progress Block.

From 1903 to 1909 it housed the Christian Science Reading Room, and it was also the home of the Portuguese Consulate.

The Honolulu Advertiser, January 1, 1901

In the early 1950's, Gibson's Bar was on the second floor of the "tawdry, fancy-fronted Elite Building". It had "murals in circus colors of sailors chasing hula girls in grass skirts, of Princess Pupule with plenty papaya, of Manuela Boy with a big opu", and it also featured live Dixieland jazz.

Located immediately behind the building were the Helen's Court apartments from 1901 to 1927, along with the original house of Captain Alexander Adams likely built sometime before 1850.

In 1961, Investors Finance, Inc. obtained a 60-year lease on the property from the James Steiner Trust Estate. They hired Hawaiian Dredging & Construction Company to build a 6-story $1.2M office and retail center in 1964 that included a sunken mall garden with restaurants and shops, designed by Ernest Hara

2022

James Steiner was born in Austria in 1860 and came to Hawaii when he was 22 years old. He worked for candy makers Hart Brothers, caterers to Hawaiian royalty. Working his way up he became partner and sole owner.

Steiner lived in Waikiki for nearly 50 years and made the 2-hour commute by horse and carriage. Laughed at by his friends at the time, he wisely invested in many Waikiki properties.

JAMES STEINER

Honolulu Star-Bulletin, April 4, 1964

The Honolulu Advertiser, February 22, 1963

Bishop Street side, 2022

HOTEL BATHS

179 S. Hotel Street
1906 – 1916 (remodeled 1909)
Architect/Builder: unknown

The Honolulu Advertiser, February 17, 1907

Originally the site of Dr. John F. Cowes' 1-story house and dentist office, the land was vacant by 1905 and became the Hotel Baths in 1906.

This was the first-ever concrete plunge pool in Honolulu, 75' x 45' in size, from 3.5' to 10' in depth, holding 158,000 gallons of pure artesian water along with springboards, chutes, trapezes, high dives and traveling rings plus Turkish baths, bowling alleys, and exercise rooms.

Two mornings a week were set aside for ladies only.

But the baths were not financially successful, so the building was converted into a moving picture theater by Robert K. Bonine in 1909. Bonine came to Hawaii in 1901 on his way to China for the Biograph Company of New York after working with Gaumont in France, Thomas A. Edison in Orange, NJ, and Pathé in Paris.

He covered the pool and created seating for about 700 people and showed many of his own films including the first-moving pictures of Kilauea volcano by day and by night.

The Orpheum Theater moved here from Fort Street after it was destroyed by fire on April 28, 1910. They enlarged the stage and added dressing rooms.

In 1913 Ah Chuck tried running motion pictures but sold out to Henry Bredhoff and Sam Blair who renamed it the Popular, home of Paramount movies. They sold out to Phil J. Byrne in 1916 who renamed it the National Theater.

When the Alexander Young Hotel decided to build a $30,000 3-story annex in 1916, the Honolulu Construction and Draying Company spent 6 weeks using a 20-ton chain tackle and lots of manpower to remove the huge amount of concrete that had been the plunge pool built only 10 years before.

YMCA BUILDING

188-198 S. Hotel Street / 1102-1122 Alakea Street

1911 – 1989 (remodeled 1945)
Architect/Builder: Ripley & Reynolds

c.1911

Based on the tentative design of the interior room arrangements prepared by the YMCA Secretary Super, the YMCA building committee held a design competition and selected Ripley & Reynolds because they proposed a dramatic corner entrance at the mauka/ewa corner of Hotel and Alakea streets.

It was built of reinforced concrete with a budgeted cost of $112,000 plus another $20,000 for furnishings.

The building was "designed for tropical life" and was built around an interior court with the outer frontages being built on the property lines. Along Adams Lane they allowed for a 5-foot cement sidewalk "thus preserving for the future a wider thoroughfare for what will soon become an important artery in the business district". That didn't quite happen – Adams Lane today is only a short alleyway.

George Pelly of the Hudson's Bay Company bought the lot at the corner of Adams Lane and Hotel in 1835 and built a large adobe residence. It was later owned by R.C. Wyllie, and then leased as government offices from 1854 until 1862.

In 1883 the Honolulu Library and Reading Room was built on the corner by E.B. Thomas from plans prepared by Isaac Moore. It was sold at auction to be cleared away in 1910.

The new YMCA building had two cornerstones. The cornerstone time capsule of the old YMCA across the street was removed and opened in 1911 and then combined with the contents of the new cornerstone. The new stone was inscribed with the territorial motto, "Ua ma uke ea o ka aina i ka pono" ("The life of the land is preserved by its righteousness"). Moving day was October 5, 1911.

In 1945 the building was sold for $353,000 at public auction to R.A. Howe & Co. They renamed it the Austin Davis Building in honor of the manager of the Honolulu office of Universal Carloading Corporation and repurposed the building to provide office and display space for manufacturers' agents and wholesalers. They called it Merchandise Mart and remodeled and "modernized" the building.

By the 1980's Merchandise Mart was owned by automobile dealer James Pflueger.

THE HONOLULU LIBRARY AND READING ROOM.

A Description of the New Building.

An improvement to Hotel Street will shortly be made by the erection of a new building, which has been already commenced for the Honolulu Library and Reading Room Association.

The main entrance will be from Hotel street the building extending back along Alakea Street for almost one hundred feet. On entering the door one comes into a hall twenty feet by ten feet three inches, with a window facing Alakea Street. On the left of the hall is a parlor 20x20 feet, looking on to Hotel Street, and behind the hall and parlor is the reading room, 32x38 feet. Behind this again will be the library 22x30 feet over which is a large skylight, and all round the library a gallery in which the books will be arranged on shelves or in cases. Behind the library are out houses with a side entrance from Alakea Street.

The building will all be on the ground floor, its front appearance being very neat with its Corinthian columns and Doric lintels. It will have a frontage of thirty-three feet two inches to Hotel Street and a depth of ninety-nine feet five inches on Alakea. There is to be special attention paid to ventilation, there being no less than twelve ventilators to be placed in the reading room with others in the parlor and library in accordance with their size and requirements. The front doors will be of plate glass and the transoms hung on pivots, while at the right of the door a refrigerator will supply the needs of the thirsty. The floors of the reading room, hall, parlor, and library are to be worked specially out of one by three inch, clear, seasoned, picked, vertical grained North-west lumber, which is to be smoothed off when laid and subsequently to be waxed. All the doors are to be of a good height and width, while between the library and reading rooms, sliding doors twelve by thirteen feet are to be placed. The sill of the windows will be seven feet from the floor and evidently there will be plenty of light and fresh air. The building is to be made of bricks, and roofed with slates and will be completed in a few months. Mr. E. B. Thomas has the contract for its erection and Mr. Isaac Moore is the architect. This building, when completed, will be in a most central and convenient locality and there can be no doubt but that the Honolulu Library will then be more utilized than it is at present.

The Honolulu Advertiser, August 4, 1883

Pflueger announced plans in 1989 to build a 31-story tower with 195,580 square feet of space to be known as 1100 Alakea, designed by Stringer, Tusher & Associates.

The old YMCA/Merchandise Mart was demolished in 1989.

1967

2022

OLD YMCA BUILDING
185-195 S. Hotel Street / 1092 Alakea Street
1883 – 1946 (addition, 1895)
Architect/Builder: Isaac Moore / George Lucas

c.1883

c.1895

C.M. Cooke provided the financial assistance so the YMCA could move out of the Boston Block to a new building started in 1882 and completed in early 1883 at a cost of $14,600, plus another $2,000 "for furniture, lighting and the apparatus, etc. required in the gymnasium". It was officially dedicated on April 21, 1883.

> "May the elements not prevail against it. May its walls rise in symmetry, beauty and strength, and may it stand for generations a haven for the tempted, the tempest-tossed and the friendless, and a monument to the generosity of the people of Hawaii nei." – Professor Amasa Pratt, YMCA President

In 1895 they added a new gymnasium on the Hotel Street side for $18,500.

The first building on this site was the "fine large straw house" of Judge George Morison Robertson. An 8-room 1-story wooden house was built here in December 1853 at a cost of $5,400. When sketched by Paul Emmert in 1853/544 it was the residence of David L. Gregg, appointed U.S. Commissioner in 1853.

> "In entering upon the discharge of my functions as the Representative of the United States near the Government of Your Majesty, I cannot fail to be deeply gratified by the favorable auspices under which I am received. The friendly courtesies by which my arrival has been greeted, demand the sincerest acknowledgment, and a constant effort to deserve their continuance. Such an effort, I may safely promise, will always be, not only a pleasing duty to be rendered to Your Majesty, but also a source of peculiar satisfaction, on account of the friendly relations existing between Your Majesty's Government, and that of which I have the honor to be accredited as the Representative."

After his term as Commissioner Gregg was appointed by Kamehameha IV as Minister of Finance.

The house was torn down in 1882 to build the YMCA building.

Paul Emmert, 1854

With a headline on February 18, 1911, stating "Antlered Herd Purchases A Site For Home In The Future", the *Evening Bulletin* announced the purchase of the former YMCA building by Elks Lodge B.P.O.E 616. The Elks had plans to replace the building with a 4-story reinforced concrete structure to cost $60,000, and they commissioned Emory and Webb to prepare preliminary plans, but ended up building on a different site.

In 1914 the building housed The Christian Church, with David Cary as minister.

The YWCA leased the building from the Elks Lodge in 1915 and hired Ripley & Davis to design interior alterations such as enlarging the gymnasium and rearranging the interior stairs. Although the lease had an option to purchase, the YWCA moved to a new building on Richards Street that was built in 1926.

In stark contrast to its YMCA beginnings, it became the Wines & Spirits (Hawaii, Ltd) store in 1935.

The Honolulu Advertiser
January 9, 1911

In 1943, William & Zella Anderson along with J. Bailey Hinkle opened Hawaiian Midway, one of many recreation and amusement centers that sprang up to cater to the hordes of servicemen in town during World War II.

Hawaiian Midway was only a block from the Army Navy YMCA and the taxi stand to Schofield Barracks. The amusement center included a wide variety of games and entertainments, including the Russo Rifle Range, Harry's Photo Booth with hula girls, and the Capitol Recording Company.

The building was gone by 1946 when the site became the Uptown Taxi Stand, and later Capitol Cab Company. The site is now the 1,144-space parking garage for the Pacific Trade Center built in 1972.

2022

Honolulu Merry-Go-Round

These attractive girls help the soldiers, sailors, war-workers and others find amusement, tossing away care and cash along the streets jammed with servicemen seeking diversion.

NO. 1: ALMA LITTORIN

Alma's heart is in the sky with a lad who wears a pair of silver wings.

Alma is Mrs. Littorin, whose husband, Irving, is an army air corps lieutenant stationed at an air field on Oahu. She is the former Miss Alma Holbron who attended St. Andrew's priory and then spent two years at a local business school.

In a concession at 195 S. Hotel St., she operates a rabbit race track. Mechanical rabbits hop forward each time the player manages to roll a wooden ball into a series of holes.

* * *

She got her job, her first one in any sort of concession, by answering a newspaper advertisement. Before taking her present job, Alma did hula dancing for a USO troupe.

* * *

Alma, who is 22 years old, says she is saving most of her salary for a trip that she and her husband are planning to his home in Massachusetts. She is saving her money because she believes the end of the war will bring the Hotel St. amusement businesses "down to nothing."

Honolulu Star-Bulletin, June 13, 1944

Honolulu Merry-Go-Round

These attractive girls help the soldiers, sailors, war-workers and others find amusement, tossing away care and cash along the streets jammed with servicemen seeking diversion.

NO. 4: IRENE NEWBERRY

Although she poses with service men in front of the usual Diamond Head background for photos, Irene is not a Hula girl. She is a Sarong girl. In comparison to the hula skirt, she says the sarong is more modern than the old fashioned grass skirt.

Irene, who works at 195 S. Hotel St., is Mrs. Irene Newberry, 22-year-old brunette. Her husband is serving in the navy with the U. S. Atlantic fleet, while she and her two daughters, Phyllis, five years old, and Patricia, eight months old, are living in Honolulu.

* * *

Irene was born in Honolulu, and in 1935 was graduated from the Kalakaua Intermediate school.

In order to keep extra busy she has two jobs. After six hours a day as a Sarong girl, she is employed as hostess in a local ballroom.

The two jobs give Irene two salaries. She has made a $100 a month war bond allotment and the remaining part of her salary is put in the bank.

Honolulu Star-Bulletin, June 17, 1944

SNOW COTTAGE

244 S. Hotel Street
c.1850 – 1928
Architect/Builder: unknown

Paul Emmert, 1854

Captain Benjamin F. Snow first came to Hawaii as the second mate of the brig *Active* in 1825 and returned with his family in 1848. The house was likely built sometime around 1850 and had a frontage of 140 feet on Hotel Street. The current property line runs through the middle of the old Snow lot.

Being close to the Palace, the house hosted numerous guests, captains, ministers, socialites, and dignitaries, plus meetings, weddings, and funerals. The Snow Cottage was where Commissioner ("Paramount") Blount stayed in 1893 when sent by President Cleveland to investigate the cause of the overthrow of the monarchy. When he was recalled, the new US Minister, Albert S. Willis, also stayed here and this is where he personally interviewed Queen Lili'uokalani.

In 1898 architect Traphagen reported that the building was "fully as good as new" and it was offered for sale to be moved offsite, but it was too wide for the narrow streets in the neighborhood. Instead, the hotel enlarged it and added a new roof with gables.

The Snow Cottage was the first home of the University Club in 1905. Including the main house and adjoining cottages, it had over two dozen bedrooms and the main building contained the billiard, reading, smoking, and lounging rooms.

2022

The house was demolished in 1928 during the construction of the Army and Navy YMCA.

BLACK CAT CAFÉ

239 S. Hotel Street

1901 – c.1968
Architect/Builder: unknown

This 2-story wooden building was built in 1901 as the Hotel Stables with stalls for 54 horses. It became the Royal Hawaiian Garage in 1908 with Stevens-Duryea, Stoddard-Dayton, Studebaker, Pope-Hartford, and Buick automobiles for sale and for hire. They built a new garage next door on the left in 1918.

In 1930 Donald F. Darrow and Stanley Shaughnessy opened the Black Cat Café, known by virtually every G.I. in Hawaii in World War II. It was directly across the street from the Army and Navy YMCA and next to the bus and taxi stands connecting downtown Honolulu with Schofield Barracks and Pearl Harbor. Sailors lined up for blocks to see the hula girls and pretty waitresses, and to enjoy the menu featuring:

- Hamburgers – 15-cents
- Hotcakes – 10 cents
- Hot Dogs – 10 cents
- Oyster omelet – 45 cents
- Liver and onions – 30 cents
- Porterhouse steak with mushrooms – $1

The Pla-Mor-bowling alley was on the second floor, with 10 lanes available for 15 cents a game.

AUTOMOBILE SERVICE — ROYAL HAWAIIAN GARAGE — Opposite Hawaiian Hotel

ELEGANTLY EQUIPPED IN EVERY PARTICULAR. NOTHING BETTER IN THE TERRITORY. MODERN, POWERFUL MACHINES AT PUBLIC SERVICE AT REASONABLE RATES IN CHARGE OF CAREFUL, RESPONSIBLE CHAUFFEURS ACQUAINTED WITH THE CITY AND CAPABLE OF DIRECTING TO ALL POINTS OF INTEREST.

TELEPHONE 191.

This Island contains much of interest to the tourist.

These machines carry you quickly, giving you long time at objective points.

We know the where and how of automobiling. Our services are at your disposal at all hours, day or night.

Seven Seated Studebaker.

Five Seated Pope Hartford.

Our Battery of Thoroughbreds

One Seven Seated Stoddard-Dayton.
One Five Seated Buick.
One Seven Seated Studebaker.
One Five Seated Pope Hartford.
Record bearers for Pacemakers and Hill climbers.
Nothing better has ever been run over these roads.

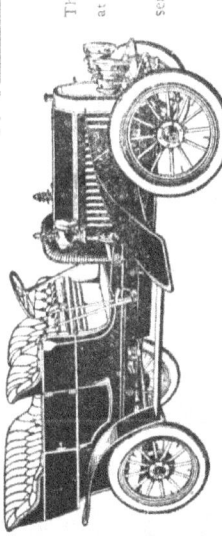

Seven Seated Stoddard-Dayton.

Five Seated Buick.

Our Chauffeurs have grown with Honolulu and know every nook and crannie of the place from the viewpoint of the tourist. Special rates for long distance runs or to Haleiwa. Visits to Kapiolani Park, Diamond Head Light, Aquarium and the beach hotels at nominal cost. A magnificent panoramic view of both sides of the Island may be obtained from this point. No one should miss this grand scene. The cost of the trip is small, compared with the satisfaction; the time is short.

Fort Shafter, Bishop Museum, Kamehameha Schools and Moanalua are objects of special interest to visitors and should not be overlooked.

——— NUUANU PALI ———

One of the finest bits of scenery on this Island. The spot where Kamehameha conquered his enemies and drove them to their death.

FULLEST INFORMATION AS TO ITINERARY ON APPLICATION.

REPAIR DEPARTMENT . . . .

This is in charge of expert mechanics thoroughly familiar with automobile construction. Repairs made quickly. Greatest attention paid at this Garage to the care of private machines. Compensation for this service on application.

GEORGE S. WELLS, Manager.

The Honolulu Advertiser, July 10, 1908

Darrow sold The Black Cat in 1943 to Thomas Awai, James Hoon Luke, Mildred S.K. Luke, Beatrice S.Y. Luke, and Senator William H. Heen for $60,000. It moved next door to 225 Hotel in 1957, and in 1962 relocated to 1704 Kanakanui Street.

Sometime after 1955 the site became a municipal parking lot until the $91M 23-story One Ali'i Place office tower was designed by Daniel Mann Johnson & Mendenhall and completed by Nordic/Mortenson in 1992.

In the late 1800's this was the site of the extensive Hawaiian Hotel Stables, and later the large 175-car Von Hamm-Young garage (which surrounded the Black Cat).

Warning, Hosts!
BEWARE BOND
He's a Menace

Honolulu has a candidate for these "Strange as it Seems" honors that are described daily in the columns of The Advertiser by Hix. He is Harry Bond, manager of the Schofield Transportation service who has established an eating record that should hold the average diner for a while.

As the result of a friendly wager the other evening, and in the presence of a dozen witnesses, Bond took aboard the following snacks, at one sitting:

1 order ham and eggs with toast.
37 doughnuts, balloon type.
7 sections of coconut cake, full grown
10 cups of coffee.

He then collected his wager from the management of the Black Cat cafe and strolled down the street to get something substantial.

The record was verified by the witnesses yesterday.

The Honolulu Advertiser, January 30, 1931

2022

This tract was first occupied "by Chin, alias Aaiana, a Chinaman, in or previous to the year 1825". In a most extraordinary Land Commission act, the land was given to the widow of Amow who had drowned.

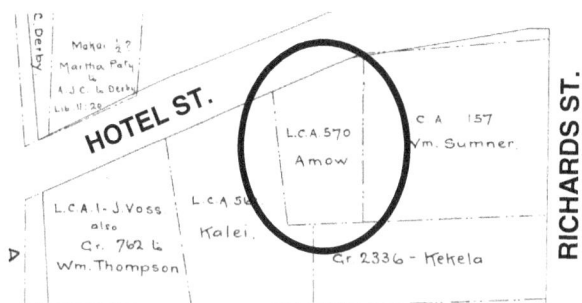
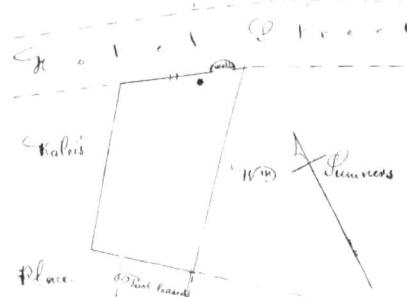

Claim No 570. Amow.

This is a claim to a house lot in Honolulu. From the Evidence taken it appears, that this land was obtained by Chin, alias Aaiana, a Chinaman, in, or previous to the Year 1825, And that he, in Company with the Claimant, and other Chinamen, occupied the same in peace, until 1st day of September A.D. 1846. When he sold all his Rights in said land to the Claimant, and went to reside on Hawaii. Amow occupied the same in peace until his death, which happened by drowning on 1st of September 1847.

According to the Rules which govern the Board the Rights of Amow in this land ceased with his death; he having nothing more than a life estate in said land; but the Claimant having been a worthy and exemplary Citizen; and having left a Widow and two Children, We would earnestly recommend to his Majesty in Privy Council, that he bestow on said Widow, named Debola, and her two children Ahoy a son, and Kaielele Ponuoole a daughter, a fee-simple or life-estate in said Land.

While such a Gift on the part of his Majesty would be generous; we consider that it would be nothing more than just; and therefore we urge the bestowment of this favor with no small degree of Earnestness.

Land Commission Award LCA 570, September 1848

HAWAIIAN HOTEL

250 S. Hotel Street
1871 – 1927 (remodeled 1892, 1899)
Architect/Builder: J.G. Osborne

"His Majesty's cabinet took the initiative and on December 5, 1870, adopted a resolution authorizing the erection of the hotel and the issue of bonds to the amount of $100,000 for this object." Local citizens raised an additional $42,500 and foundation excavation work began on May 15, 1870.

The building had two wings, each 75' x 32', connected by a central section 50' x 42', and with 10-foot-wide "verandahs" on the mauka and makai sides. The basement was four feet below ground level with a 12-foot ceiling. The upper stories had 14' and 12' ceilings with 8' and 10' hallways. It had 48 sleeping rooms and 10 other general rooms, with concrete walls in a "rustic finish, similar to that of the new Post Office". It was built by J.G. Osborne with direction and oversight provided by C.H. Lewers.

Hawaii State Archives

The building was completed by the end of 1871 but was not formally opened until February 1872 due to delays in getting furniture. Total costs were:

Land, including iron fence	$10,331.00
Erection of building	$93,544.69
Furniture and fixtures	$12,651.96
Bedding, etc.	$17,500.00
TOTAL	$134,027.65

In the first 14 months of operation over 2,000 names were recorded in the hotel registry "from nearly every country in the world".

THE NEW HOTEL BUILDING

For Lease

FOR A TERM OF YEARS

 This Handsome Three-story Building, now being erected in Honolulu, will be ready for occupancy on **The 1st of January next,** And will be Leased from that Date **On Favorable Terms.**

It is Built Expressly

For a First - Class Hotel!

And to this end,

Is Fitted with all the Appliances necessary to the Business.

THE PREMISES

Are in the central part of the City; are spacious, and well shaded with trees, and but a short distance from the steamers' wharves.

IT HAS ENTRANCES FROM THE FOUR STREETS

That Bound the Block;

And, beside the main building, there are several Cottages which will be leased, if desired, to enlarge the Lodgings.

THE HOTEL IS BUILT OF CONCRETE

120 feet by 170 feet, with broad Verandahs on the front and rear sides.

And Contains 58 Rooms.

The Dining and Billiard Rooms are each 55 by 32, Ladies' Parlor, 22 by 32, Gents' Parlor, 15 by 32, and the Bed-rooms can be used singly or in suites.

Water, from the Government pipes, is laid on in all the rooms, and mains for gas have been laid to be distributed to gas burners, when gas may be introduced.

THIS HOTEL WILL BE LEASED

For a Term of Years!

And it offers a first-rate chance for the establishing of a

Profitable and Permanent Business.

Parties desiring to Lease may apply at the FINANCE OFFICE. 31 4m

---

THE improvements at the Hotel mentioned in the BULLETIN a few days ago, as contemplated by Manager Johnson, have taken shape. Messrs Palmer & Richardson, architects, have drawn plans which have been accepted, for enclosing and roofing the large veranda on the Richards street side. There will be a hip roof topped with an ornate cupola. The sides will be partly walled with colored glass, surmounted with a row of short turned spindles under the eaves. Within will be stands of tropical plants and the floor will be prepared for dancing purposes. A staircase for a ladies' entrance will spring from the ground. This sort of bungalow annex to the hotel will be available for cafe purposes.

Evening Bulletin, November 3, 1891

The Hawaiian Gazette, January 31, 1872

A new bandstand and fancy lanai designed by Palmer & Richardson were added in 1892, and the distinctive circular lanais 42' in diameter were added in 1899 and were designed by A. T. Large with H.L. Kerr & Co.

On November 25, 1917, it became the Army and Navy YMCA.

The building was torn down in 1927, demolished for $1500 by E.K. Sugihara's Japanese workmen.

It was replaced with a 5-story concrete building designed by Lincoln Rogers from San Diego along with Emory & Webb. The architectural details were inspired by the Davanzatti Palace in Florence, Italy, and the design also included an homage to the previous hotel's large circular lanais.

The Campbell Building Company built it for $600,000 and it was officially dedicated on March 16, 1928. It had 268 sleeping rooms, swimming pool, billiard hall, cafeteria, barbershop, gymnasium, auditorium, tailor, and curio shops. It was the major R&R hub for Pacific military personnel during World War II.

2022

The building was purchased by Christopher Hemmeter in 1988, who remodeled it into the Hemmeter Corporation offices and renamed it the No. 1 Capitol District Building.

In 2002 it became the Hawaii State Art Museum.

ROYAL HAWAIIAN GARAGE

259-269 S. Hotel Street
1918 – c.1968
Architect/Builder: Emil F. Cykler (Lord Young Engineering) / H. Knaack & Co.

Honolulu Star-Bulletin, October 20, 1924

This building was built in 1918 by contractor H. Knaack & Co. for $17,500 on the site of the 1883 Hawaiian Hotel stables at the ewa/makai corner of Hotel and Richards streets.

The Royal Hawaiian Garage was incorporated in 1909 with F. W. Macfarlane as the first president. They sold Reo, Saxon, Moreland, Cole, Stanley Steamer, McFarlan, Chalmers, and Mercer automobiles.

They changed their name to Royal Hawaiian Sales Company in 1918 and were distributors for the General Motors Export Company, selling Oldsmobile, Chevrolet, and Oakland automobiles in Hawaii. They also carried International trucks and Goodyear tires.

Honolulu Star-Bulletin, October 20, 1924

The Royal Hawaiian Garage was built on the site of the Hotel Stables which were burned by the Board of Health on February 27, 1900, after a Chinese worker and a Japanese worker died of bubonic plague.

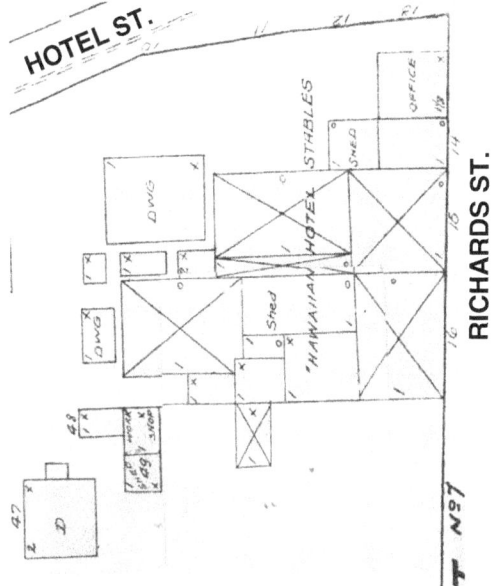

1899 Dakin Map

In the golden days, under the reign of the Merry Monarch, the Hawaiian Hotel stable, destroyed by fire this week, was the greatest money-making proposition extant. It had the exclusive patronage of the court circle and everybody else that was good. The hackmen on the stand wore dazzling diamonds and would take nothing less than dollar loads. The stable equipages were for the wealth, the beauty and the fashion.

Austin's Hawaiian Weekly, March 3, 1900

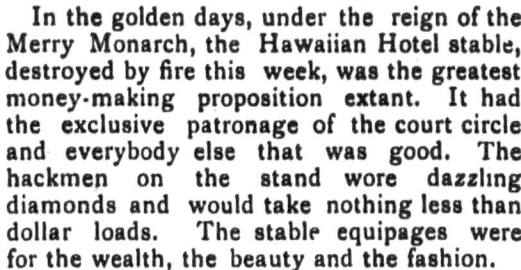

Hawaiian Hotel Stables, opposite Royal Hawaiian Hotel, Miles & Macfarlane, proprietors; they furnish buggies, phaetons, wagonettes, etc., with stylish, gentle horses.

The Honolulu Advertiser, May 31, 1885

Board of Health photographs, February 1900

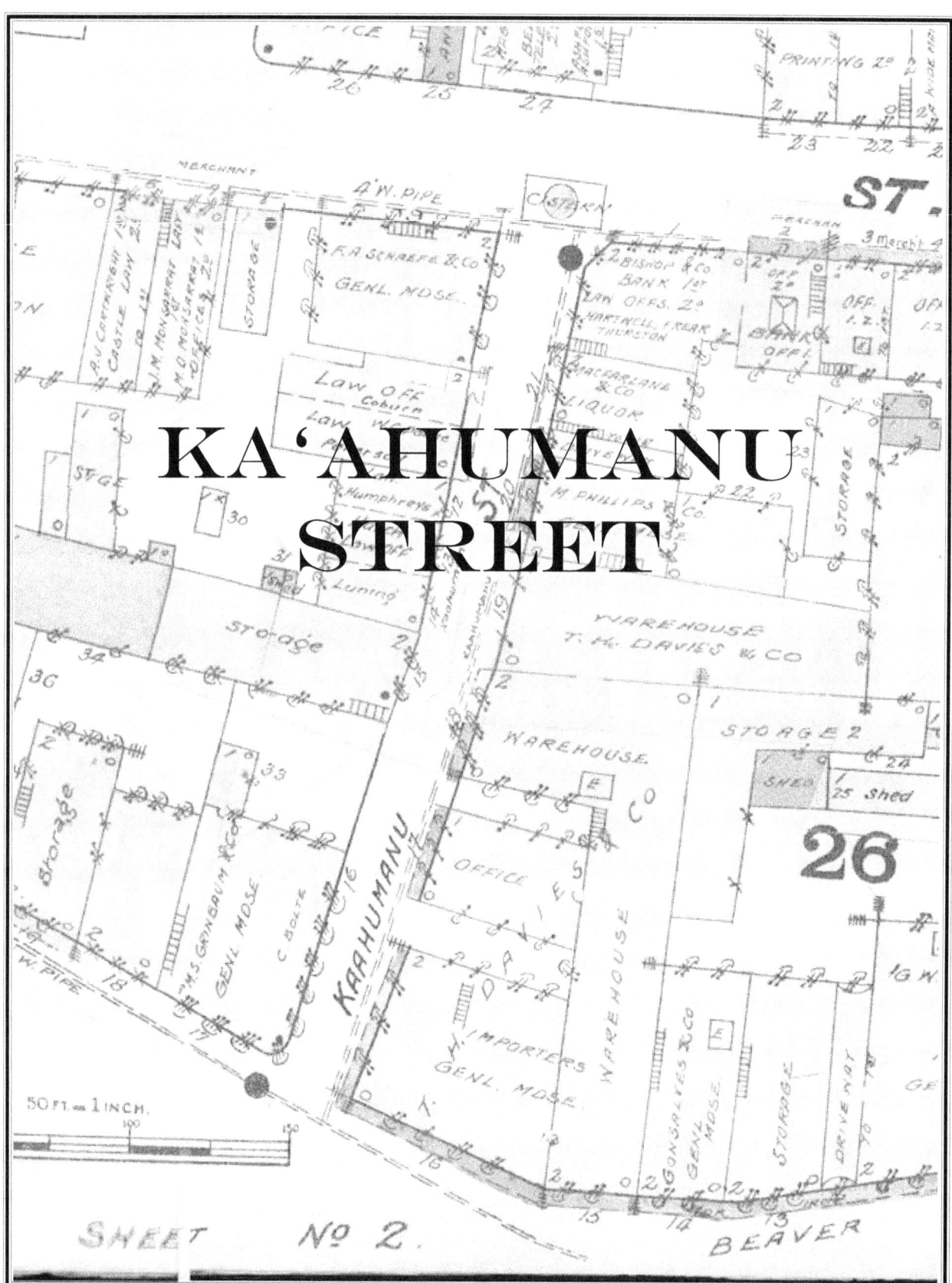

KA‘AHUMANU STREET

THEO. H. DAVIES BUILDINGS

801-843 Ka'ahumanu Street / 58 Queen Street

1858 – 1888

Architect/Builder: unknown

c.1880's

1925

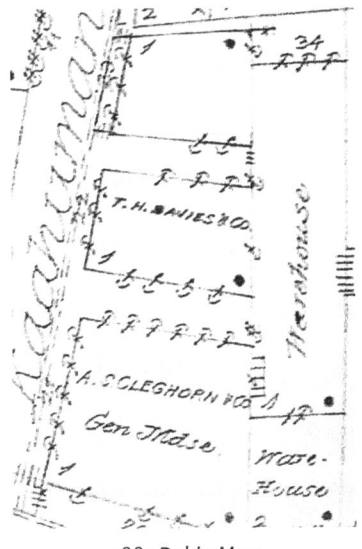

1885 Dakin Map

There are not many photographs of the buildings on this corner, but the Dakin Fire Insurance Maps from 1885 (on the left) and 1891 (on the right) show a large office and warehouse complex.

It was the location of the T.H. Davies company before building their massive new building at 841 Bishop Street in 1921.

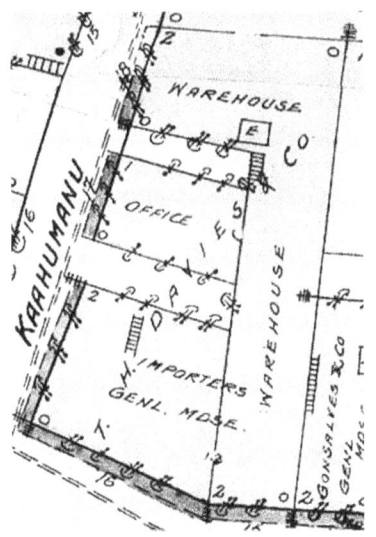

1891 Dakin Map

According to Richard Greer, James Hunnewell had the first retail store in Honolulu at this corner in 1817.

British Consul Richard Charlton hired Andrew Auld and Jame Ruddack to build an "adobie" building on the site, but after a heavy rain collapsed one of the walls they built with coral stone instead.

This was Charlton's store and consular office until 1837 when it became the store of English merchant Henry Skinner. It was later the Leidesdorff, Robson, Thompson & Howe, C.A. Williams and W.F. Allen, premises until it was demolished by Robert C. Janion in 1858 and replaced with three new stone buildings.

> DEMOLISHED.—The old Charlton House, at the corner of Queen and Kaahumanu streets, is now quite leveled with the ground to make room for the new buildings of R. C. Janion.

The Pacific Commercial Advertiser, April 8, 1858

One of the buildings was "an immense warehouse" 40' x 150' with 2-stories in front, the one on the corner was an auction room for A.P. Everett, and the third building on Kaʻahumanu Street contained two stores.

> Removal.—We wish to call the attention of our readers to Mr. Archie Cleghorn's advertisement in another column. He has removed to the spacious fire-proof store on the corner of Queen and Kaahumanu streets, with an entrance for ladies at the upper end of the store in Kaahumanu street, so as to avoid the throng on the corner. With a stock of dry goods unrivalled in Honolulu for quality and variety, and with tempting prices to suit, Mr. C.'s store opens under the most flattering auspices.

The Polynesian, May 17, 1862

> **NOTES OF THE WEEK.**
>
> THIRTY YEARS AGO.—We casually mentioned last week the demolition of the "Old Charlton House" at the foot of Kaahumanu street, and in conversation since with some of the old residents we have learned some interesting facts respecting the history of that old house—old for this country,—where civilization itself dates back but a few years before its foundation walls were laid. It was in 1827, when Mr. Andrew Auld and Mr. James Ruddack (the last named over ten years deceased) undertook to build an adobie house for Mr. Charlton, the then British Consul for these islands, on the same spot where the stone building recently stood. After getting the walls up, a heavy rain set in and one side of the house fell, when Mr. Charlton concluded to pull down the adobies and build of stone, which was done by Messrs. Auld and Ruddack. "I little thought," said Mr. Auld to us, while superintending the pulling down of the old house, "that I should live thirty-one years, to take down these same walls." Mr. Charlton occupied the building as a store and consular office until 1837, when Mr. Skinner succeeded him. He was followed for a short time by Mr. Leidesdorff, one of the pioneers of San Francisco, and latterly came Mr. Robson, and then Messrs. Thompson & Howe, auctioneers, and last of all it was occupied by Messrs. C. A. Williams & Co. and W. F. Allen. When the old house was first erected on the beach, Honolulu was a straggling village of straw huts, with here and there an adobie or stone house, topped with wood. Kamehameha III. had one year before come to the throne, a youthful king, but fifteen years of age, surrounded by a numerous train of chiefs, and idolized by 100,000 subjects. But the old house has outlived king, nobles, and people of that generation, and at last has itself succumbed to the march of improvement; following its long-time neighbor, the old fort, it has become one of the things that were, and of which, ere long, old residents will talk when recalling reminiscences of "old times." But its place will be worthily occupied. Mr. R. C. Janion has commenced the erection on the Charlton lot of a large stone building, or rather block of buildings, on a scale of magnitude that will compare advantageously with Makee's block on the opposite corner, and will be another material guarantee of Honolulu's commercial progress.

The Pacific Commercial Advertiser, April 15, 1858

The corner building was demolished in 1888 and replaced with a 2-story "coral brick building" with a plastered front and corrugated iron roof that was designed by Isaac A. Palmer and built by E.B. Thomas. The sales and show room was 50' x 100' with a shipping room 50' x 30', upstairs was 50' x 130' with a 14' ceiling "and no pillars or obstructions of any kind". It was demolished for a city parking lot in 1952, the site became a 2-story parking garage in 1962, and it is now part of the $91M Harbor Court Condominium designed by Norman Lacayao, completed in 1994.

A.B. HOWE BUILDING

848-850 Kaʻahumanu Street
1850 – 1918 (1873 remodel)
Architect/Builder: unknown

Paul Emmert, 1854

Auctioneer Aaron B. Howe bought this property from Robert C. Janion on October 23, 1850, for $4,500 and erected a large 3-story wooden building that had been imported "in the frame" by Captain James Makee. Howe officed upstairs and ship chandlers R. Coady & Co. were downstairs.

The Chamber of Commerce met upstairs in the auction rooms which also hosted the first meeting to establish an Episcopal Church in 1851.

Henry Sea moved his auction house here in late 1851.

> ABBREVIATED.—The large three-story wooden building on Kaahumanu street, adjoining the stone store of F. A. Schaefer, has, during the past week, undergone the operation of being razeed, the lower story having been taken out and the building lowered with jack-screws to a more modest attitude. During these dull times, boss-carpenter Geo. Lucas, who had the job, and his men, have been the observed of all observers. The old building was imported in the frame by Captain Jas. Makee, and put up by the late Richard Coady and others in 1850-51, twenty odd years ago. The lower story was a ship-chandlery store for several years, while A. B. Howe, Commission Merchant and Auctioneer, occupied the second story. J. F. Colburn, Auctioneer, subsequently occupied the lower part of the building. All three of the last named persons have been dead some years.

The Pacific Commercial Advertiser, August 23, 1873

The Howe Building was replaced in 1918 with a $15,000 building of blue lava and reinforced concrete designed by Emory & Webb and constructed by Woolley & Beaton for offices of the Bishop Estate. The building housed the drafting room and vault for all the maps and plans of the estate's buildings and had a small garden in the back.

The building was demolished in 1956 for a parking lot.

The Honolulu Advertiser, September 12, 1918

RHODES BUILDING

847-857 Ka'ahumanu Street

1868 – 1956

Architect/Builder: J.G. Osborne

Hawaii State Archives

Godfrey Rhodes was born in England and initially worked for the Hudson's Bay Company out of Vancouver, coming to Hawaii by the mid-1840's. He was a member of the Privy Council and House of Nobles and was later president of the legislative assembly.

J.G. Osborne built this 65' x 40' mixed stone and brick building for Rhodes in 1868 which included an archway leading to a yard and sheds in back. The roof was made of 30" x 6'-8" corrugated iron panels from Victoria, something new in Honolulu.

Rhodes had a wholesale wine and spirits store on one side with the other being the Marks & Bernard wholesale clothing store.

The site was originally part of the William French premises and the store of Porter & Ogden built before 1838.

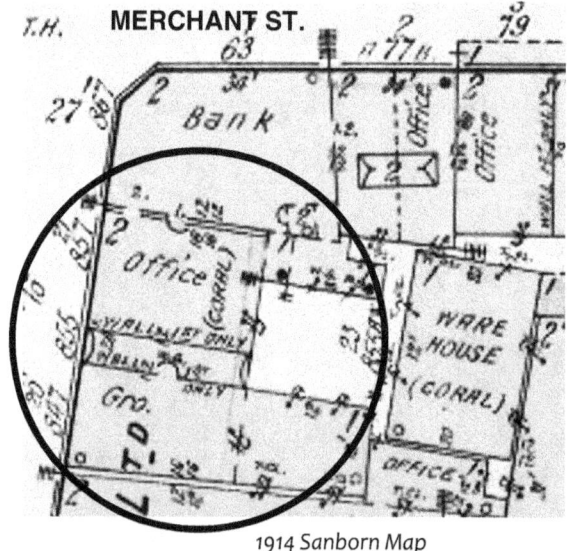

1914 Sanborn Map

Paul Emmert, 1854

AN OLD LAND MARK GONE.—The building recently occupied by Mr. Godfrey Rhodes, to old residents known as the store of William French, is being torn down to make room for a fine building of mixed stone and brick. We do not know when it was erected; but one party says it was standing when he first arrived in 1838. Some of the timbers are in an excellent state of preservation. In this connection we may say we are glad to see Mr. Osborne about again after his late mishap. Stirring, intelligent master-mechanics are not so plenty, particularly in his branch of business, that we can afford to lose them. Mr. Osborne will direct the erection of the new building.

The Pacific Commercial Advertiser, April 18, 1868

In 1912, Bishop Bank took over the adjoining portion of the Rhodes Building and Theo. H. Davies took over the other half, adding a new front. The iron shutters were removed and the building was painted silver-gray along with the Bishop Bank and Schaefer (Melchers) building.

The building was demolished in 1956 for a city parking lot. The site is now part of the 1994 Harbor Court office and condominium project.

2022

NEW BUILDING.—The handsome fire-proof building on Kaahumanu street, which has been in process of erection for some months past by Mr. G. Rhodes, has been completed, and the occupants will move in this week. The building is two stories, 65 feet front by 40 feet deep. The first story has two large stores, with a cart-way between, to the yard in the rear. One of these, with a cement floor, will be occupied by Mr. Rhodes, as a wholesale wine and spirit store, and the other by Marks & Bernard, as a wholesale clothing store.

The upper story reached by a stair-way from the street, is divided into seven large, airy rooms, admirably adapted for offices. A hall through the length of the building gives access to these rooms. It is finished throughout with lath and plaster, and there is a fine cellar for storage beneath the makai store. The walls are of the lava stone, found in exhaustible quantities at the rear of the town, and of imported brick. Of the quality of this stone, the builder says it is an excellent material, and well adapted for building purposes.

The front of the building is ornamented with cornices, pilasters and mouldings around the windows and doors, in plain stucco, giving to it a finished and handsome appearance, and adding much to the improvements in that part of the town. The roofs is of corrugated iron, a new material to us, and having good claims to public favor. The ventilation has been carefully attended to. A series of perforations through the walls, covered with gratings, open into the stores and the rooms, both at the floor and the ceiling, and the rooms on the upper floor have ventilators communicating with the garret. The temperature within, therefore, day or night, will be no higher than the air without, so that goods will be in no danger from heat, while the comfort of the occupants will be materially increased. In tropical countries, the comfort of stone buildings, and their value as stores, depend very much upon free circulation of air; and a well-ventilated structure will command tenants in preference to one that is not planned with judicious reference to this point.

The building was planned and the mason work done by Mr. J. G. Osborne, and the iron work by Crockett & Harper. It is one of the best constructed buildings in the town. Kaahumanu street with the exception of three buildings, is now built up with fire-proof stores. As these increase in the town, there will be an increasing disposition among tenants to rent only such buildings, so that capital will hereafter be obliged to erect them, if desirous of receiving an income from its investments.—*Gazette*.

In addition to the above, it should be stated that the front ornamental work was executed solely by native Hawaiian masons, and is certainly creditable to them and all concerned.

The Pacific Commercial Advertiser, September 11, 1868

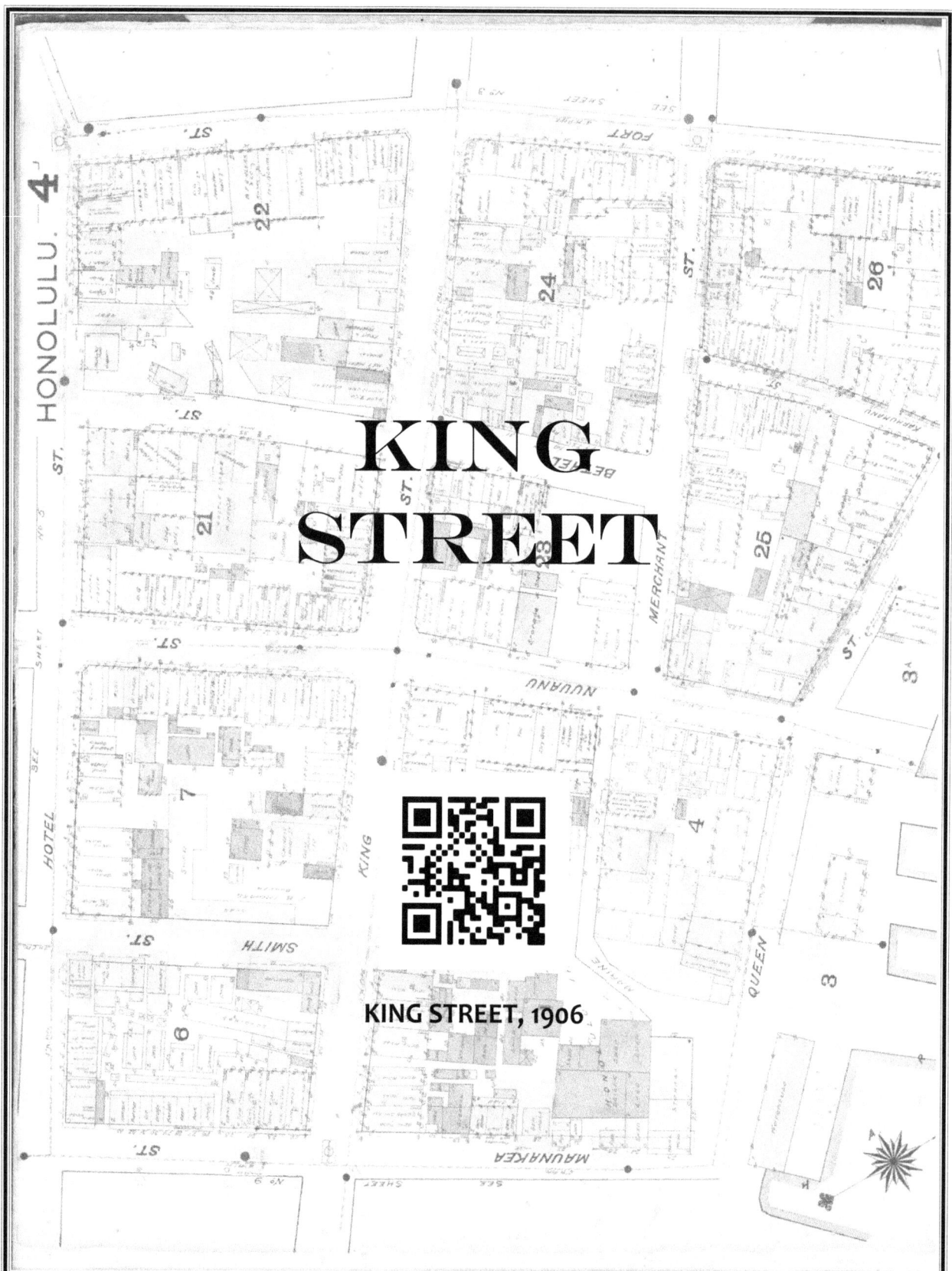

KING STREET

KING STREET, 1906

THOMAS / YAT LOY BUILDING

12-30 S. King Street

1883 – present (rebuilt 1887, remodeled 1950, 1974)
Architect/Builder: Thomas B. Walker (1883), E.B. Thomas (1887),
Ray Akagi (1950), George Johnson (1974) / Shuji Miura (1950)

The new brick buildings on King-street, adjoining Messrs. Castle & Cooke's premises, are now receiving that artistic and ornamental finish for which the builder, Mr. T. B. Walker, has justly earned such a high reputation.

The Honolulu Advertiser, January 23, 1883

This building was built in 1883 by contractor, saloon keeper, and former Indian fighter Thomas B. Walker.

But it was so badly damaged in the 1886 fire it was almost completely rebuilt by E.B. Thomas who purchased it in 1887.

On Wednesday, April 28th
at 12 o'clock, noon, at our Salesroom, Queen street, by order of Messrs. T. H. Davies & Co.,

The Brick Buildings
situated on King street, adjoining the store of Messrs. Castle & Cooke.
The Buildings were partially destroyed by the fire of the 18th instant, and can be put in order at small expense.
The Ground is leased for a term of 20 years, expiring July 1, 1902. Rent, $70 per month.
Three-fourths of purchase money can remain on mortgage for 3 years.
☞ Papers at expense of purchaser.

E. P. ADAMS & Co.,
311   Auctioneers

The original building front looked like this before the 1886 fire.

> By order of Messrs. Theo. H. Davies & Co., the brick building adjoining Messrs. Castle & Cooke's, King street, partially destroyed in the late fire, was sold by Messrs. E. P. Adams & Co., to-day, and bought by Mr. E. B. Thomas, builder, for $5,100.

The Daily Bulletin, April 28, 1886

E.B. Thomas built the Pacific Saloon Building on the left (now called the Flores Building) in 1887 and he completely rebuilt the Walker Building to match. It then became known as the Thomas Block.

> Mr. E. B. Thomas was the purchaser of the partially destroyed brick building sold at auction, Wednesday last, adjoining Messrs. Castle & Cooke's store. He has already commenced putting on a new roof and will shortly rebuild the portion which was most exposed to the fierce fire which raged on that corner.

The Hawaiian Gazette, May 4, 1886

> Mr. E. B. Thomas has taken the old fire damaged front out of the building next Messrs. Castle & Cooke's, to combine that structure with a new one that he is erecting on the lot adjoining, formerly occupied by the Merchants' Exchange saloon. When completed there will be a handsome two-storey block of five stores, with iron and plate glass fronts. Mr. Thomas himself is owner of the property.

The Daily Herald, April 12, 1887

The 1883 building was built on the site the Rising Sun saloon owned by Henry Zupplein who was called "Dutch Harry". Born in 1784, he came to Hawaii in 1808, and Kalaimoku gave him this land in 1823 "as a place for selling liquor". Zupplein was known to be a miser with considerable money and real estate.

Originally from Amsterdam and married to a Hawaiian woman for over 50 years, Zupplein must have been miserable since he shot himself with a pistol in 1860 at 72 years of age and only his wife Napua, son William, and Rev. Lowell Smith attended his funeral. Rumored to have buried much of his fortune, his son searched the Zupplein homestead and found an old powder can with $17,000 in Spanish and Mexican gold coins (worth $600,000 today).

Before the Walker/Thomas Building this was the site of Frederick Horn's confectionary saloon in 1866, specializing in pastry, cakes, preserves, candies, and ice cream. Horn's first location was the makai/waikiki corner of King and Maunakea streets. By 1879 the site was used for storage of carriages and buggies with a large 1-story brick Castle & Cooke warehouse in back.

Honolulu Star-Bulletin, March 21, 1967

For over 50 years, from 1914 to 1967, this was the popular Yat Loy clothing store founded by Doo Wai Sing. The name "Yat Loy" means "welcome" in Cantonese.

The building was remodeled and "modernized" in 1950 for their 50th anniversary, designed by architect Ray Akagi with Jules Masse of Grand Rapids Store Equipment Co. and constructed by Shuji Miura.

But this wasn't enough to overcome the movement of retail and customers out of downtown and the store closed in 1967.

In 1974 a group of local architects headed by George Johnson along with Henry Reese of Johnson-Reese and Associates plus Frank Gray and Associates decided to "recycle" the old building by renovating it to compete with new downtown office space. They obtained a 30-year lease from the Bishop Estate, renamed the building "King's Court" and removed the 1950's façade.

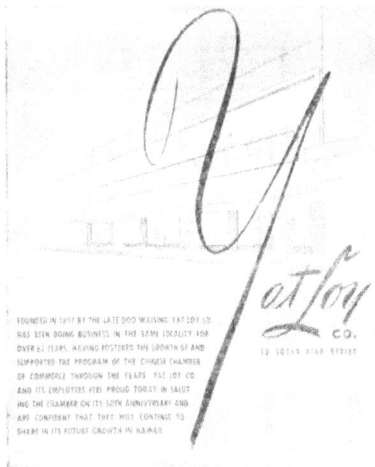

HOFFSCHLAEGER BUILDING

29 S. King Street / 934 Bethel Street
1887 – 1962
Architect/Builder: Isaac A. Palmer / E.B. Thomas

Built on the site of the Bethel Church which burned in the 1886 fire, the Hoffschlaeger Building had frontages on both King and Bethel streets, wrapping around the Damon Building on the corner. It was designed by Isaac A. Palmer in the Eastlake Victorian style and built by contractor E.B. Thomas in 1887 for Elard Hoffschlaeger.

Messrs. E I. Hoffschlaeger & Co.'s New Premises.

Yesterday a representative of the ADVERTISER was afforded an opportunity of making a thorough inspection of the commodious premises, having frontages to King and Bethel streets, lately erected for the old established firm of Messrs. Ed. Hoffschlaeger & Co. The want of more room has for some time past been felt by them, and the confidence with which the firm has uniformly inspired its clients has been the means of so far extending its business connections that latterly this need had become imperative. The new building could scarcely have been better adapted to the requirements. Constructed of brick, the outer walls being eighteen inches in thickness, it has handsome frontages, both of similar designs, of iron and glass. That on King street has a width of 33 feet and a depth of 76 feet, whilst the Bethel street frontage, of necessity at right angles to the other, is 30 feet wide and 60 feet deep, taking the measurement to the further extremity of the other width. The area of the premises, therefore, is in form that of a double rectangle. The corner lots being occupied by other firms. The ground floor is devoted to the principal show rooms and the office; miscellaneous goods, some of which are in bulk, consume the space on the upper floor, which is of similar dimensions. Both are as spacious, light and airy as they could possibly be and communicate by an easy staircase. A large attic affords additional storage room, as also does an extensive cellar, which has the merit of being well lighted from the street front and perfectly dry. A ready means of transit between the cellar and both floors is obtained by a patent elevator, situated near the King street entrance. The premises throughout are replete with every convenience and form a striking addition to the architecture of this city. They stand on freehold property of the firm (who also own the adjoining vacant lot on King street with a 57-feet frontage); they were built by Mr. E. B. Thomas, contractor, from designs prepared by Mr. J. A. Palmer.

The nature of Messrs. Ed. Hoffschlaeger & Co.'s business is well known. It is confined within no special limits, but embraces almost every article for which a wholesale market exists in these islands. Their importations are principally derived from England, Germany, France and the United States. They are also agents for the North British and Mercantile Insurance Company of London.

The Honolulu Advertiser, January 27, 1888

1885 Dakin Map

2022

CASTLE & COOKE BUILDING

32-36 S. King Street / 1002-1012 Bethel

1861 – 1930 (remodeled 1869, 1907)
Architect/Builder: George Thomas, Samuel Johnson (1861),
J.G. Osborne (1869)

This was the first substantial business house built on the mauka side of King Street, not counting the Globe Hotel which was converted from the coral residence of Hannah Holmes built between 1826 and 1832 by John Coffin Jones.

According to historian Thomas G. Thrum, the first building on this site was occupied by the Dixon Brothers, general merchants, becoming the tailor shop of Charles H. Nicholson in 1844.

> C. H. NICHOLSON,
> Merchant Tailor.
> [Establishment opposite Seamen's Chapel,]
> Honolulu, Oahu, H. I.
> A large assortment of Broadcloths, Cassimeres and Linen Drillings, constantly for sale. Garments made at short notice, in latest fashion. 35-tf

Paul Emmert, 1854

> SAMUEL N. CASTLE.   AMOS S. COOKE
> CASTLE & COOKE,
> **IMPORTERS**
> AND WHOLESALE AND RETAIL DEALERS IN
> GENERAL MERCHANDISE,
> At the old stand, corner of King and School streets,
> near the large Stone Church,
> Also, at the NEW STORE, corner of King and
> Bethel streets, near the Seamen's Chapel.
> Feb. 4—1yr-39

> There was no other conspicuous building on this side of the street up to Fort street; only some few native houses where fish and poi were sold. Opposite the Bethel on the mauka side of the street was a one-story, white-plastered adobe building, standing end to the street, which was occupied as a tailor's shop by one C. H. Nicholson, a man of large size but finely proportioned, dressed immaculately in the finest of white linen, but to use a common expression, "as black as the ace of spades." When he and his Hawaiian wife, who matched him well in size, took their promenades they attracted general attention. The shop was the favorite rendezvous for the gossips of the village, who generally gathered there in the evening, to discuss the events of the day. This building had the same location which for so many years has been occupied by Castle & Cooke.

The Hawaiian Gazette, September 9, 1904

Samuel N. Castle and Amos S. Cooke started their business in a stone building near Kawaiahao Church in 1851. They opened a branch store on the makai side of King Street across from the Bethel in 1853 and by February of 1854 they had moved into Nicholson's building.

In 1861 they hired George Thomas and Samuel Johnson to build a 1-story stone building with a basement that required blasting through 3' of coral. All of the other buildings along that part of King Street were made of wood.

William DeWitt Alexander, 1896

NOTES OF THE WEEK.

CASTLE & COOKE'S FIREPROOF BUILDING.—In times like these, of great depression of what has, for many years past, been accustomed to be looked upon as the chief source of revenue and prosperity to this Kingdom, viz: the whaling trade—it is pleasant to witness, that there are yet among us men of substantial means, whose business foresight and acumen to be of our few west'nsmen, who have had the satisfaction of trading with them, ever could doubt, who have had the nerve, in view of coming events, which it is said cast their shadows before, to erect during the past few months, on King Street, opposite the Bethel, a warehouse, which for the roughness of construction, and adaptability of means to an end, is equaled but by one or two and surpassed by none of the erections which the heyday of Island prosperity called into existence. The building, which is only one story high, brings forcibly to the recollection of the former resident of San Francisco, in the fiery era of 1850-1852, those that were erected in that city, intended to be *fireproof*, and which were fireproof. The cellar is however so thoroughly finished, that the capacity obtained is equal to that of two-story buildings whose cellars, as is customary here, are not put to use as show-rooms. It is seven feet in the clear, and has a rock bottom. To obtain this depth, it was necessary to blast to a depth of three feet through the solid rock. The dimensions are 80 ft. in length by 48 ft. 10 inches in width, and has a storage capacity of 600 tons. The light is obtained by six windows, each three feet wide by four feet high, secured by iron shutters, which fold in the jambs, when opened. The jambs are of brick. Iron gratings on the sidewalks, give through their bars desirable and sufficient light. The case goods are stored on skids raised a foot from bottom of cellar. Room enough is left for passage way among the merchandise to get around easily among it, and read distinctly the titles of the goods. The cellar way has also grated iron doors. The skids for taking in or discharging loaded packages by, are permanent. A broad and capacious stairway runs from the center of the store to the cellar. The capacious sales room is splendidly lighted, and the arrangements of counters and shelves for the display and shelving of the thousand and one articles which the general trade of this worthy mercantile firm require, shows that they possess a practical knowledge of its details. The ware-house and salesroom are ceiled with half inch white cedar, which, although much more expensive than other descriptions, is said to be a preventive against insects. The floor and roof are both of one and a quarter inch tongued and grooved Puget Sound lumber. The roof is a self-sustaining truss, one with a patent covering, like that of the Custom House and Queen's Hospital. The dimensions of the ware house are 50 ft. length by 18 ft. width; that of the sales-room, 77 ft. length by 27 ft. width. These irregular dimensions of front and rear are owing to a jog in the building, caused by the irregularity of the topography of the ground upon which the structure is built. The walls are of coral, 18 inches, dressed with Portland cement. To the worthy mechanics, under whose skillful guidance this fine edifice has leaped into life, great praise is due. Theodore Heuck, Esq., of Messrs. Von Holt & Heuck, was the architect of the roof, and the owners are greatly indebted to him for valuable suggestions in various other matters about the building. The iron work of the shutters was manufactured by J. Kettredge, of San Francisco, and they were hung by our townsmen, Messrs. Thompson & Neville. The mason work was done by Mr. Geo. Thomas and the carpenter work by Mr. S. Johnson.

The Pacific Commercial Advertiser, October 31, 1861

J.G. Osborne expanded the building in 1869 and added a second story plus concrete quoins in the corners. Castle & Cooke were at this location for 50 years until moving to the first floor of the Stangenwald Building in 1904.

CASTLE & COOKE'S STORE.—We notice that the addition and improvements to the store of Messrs. Castle & Cooke, are about completed. The new sign has been elevated to its place on the eaves, and the store adds greatly to the appearance of King Street. The building now, makes one of the largest and roomiest stores in town, and will all be needed, to accommodate their business; it has been made thoroughly fire-proof, in order to give greater assurance of safety, to the large stocks of sugars, which occasionally are in hand awaiting shipment, as also to protect their own stock of general merchandise. We regard with gratification, this growing disposition of our merchants, to put up substantial and fire-proof buildings. Messrs. Castle & Cooke, are one of the oldest firms in our town, having formed their co-partnership in June 1851. They located themselves first, in the stone building, near the Kawaiahao Church, but as they deemed themselves too far away from the centre of the town, in 1853 they established a branch store on King St., near the Bethel, on the premises now owned and occupied by J. L. Lewis, as a cooperage. The following year, they moved this branch over to their present location, into another wooden, though more commodious building, than the one they left. In 1855, their old branch store building, which they had rented to a Chinaman, was burned down, in the fire that destroyed the Varieties Theatre, the Police Station House, and other buildings in that neighborhood. This fire was a most threatening one, and was only stayed from a large spreading, by the fire-proof store of Mr. Dimond on the East, and the Government House on the makai or leeward side of it. In 1861 they built their present fire-proof store, with a main floor and basement containing an area of about 6000 feet, of store and storage room, and located there, their whole business. The present enlargement consists of extending the west wing to King St., giving 50 feet frontage, and covering the whole with another story, which gives about 4500 more square feet of additional room, and something more than 10,500 feet in all. The original building, was built of coral stone with a brick front, the coral exterior being finished with Portland cement, the addition is of black stone laid in lime, and will be cemented outside, to correspond with the former outside finish. The corners are laid with blocks of concrete. A slate roof covers the building. The work has been done in a substantial and workman-like manner, by Mr. Osborne, who on this, as on other buildings, has proved his abilities as a master mechanic. Five weeks has sufficed to put up this addition, the business meanwhile, being kept on, with no more inconvenience than the litter and rubbish in the street, and the noise of the masons and carpenters. The original flat roof was not removed, until after the present roof had been finished. Mr. Osborne, we understand, will immediately go on with the new Post Office building, that is to be erected, which will be made fire-proof, and will be another sightly and substantial edifice, added to those which now adorn our town.

The Hawaiian Gazette, November 24, 1869

Hawaiian Historical Society

Yee Chan & Co. Dry Goods moved here in 1907 and they "remodelled and fitted this new store with modern fixtures and an entire new stock of dry goods, novelties, gents' furnishing goods, etc."

The business was destroyed by a fire in 1930 that caused an estimated $170,000 in damage. Sumitomo Bank, the building owners, were ordered by the city to raze the building.

Honolulu Star-Bulletin, April 12, 1930

After the fire, the site was vacant for many years. A large 3-story building with a stage and 200-300-person hall plus Japanese rock garden was proposed in 1939 to be the Honolulu store of Tokyo's Mitsukoshi department store.

In 1940, Honolulu architect Fred Fujioka revised the original plans from Tokyo "which were along Oriental lines, to conform to modern Occidental style to meet local conditions and needs."

The Honolulu Advertiser, May 14, 1939

The House of Mitsukoshi bought the site from the bank for $85,000 in 1939. The first-class reinforced concrete building cost $150,000 for over 50,000 square feet of floor space. It was built by Honolulu contractors Keizo Nagata and Shigeru Horita.

Grand opening day was November 4, 1940.

In addition to three special "Tokonoma" Sukiya display stands built in Japan without nails, the store had the first escalator in Hawaii, which only went one way from the first floor to the second floor.

The building was confiscated during World War II and became a U.S.O. Center.

Later owned by the National Mortgage and Finance Company, it underwent a $1M facelift in 1960 that was designed by William F. Cann from St. Louis along with the original architect, Fred Fujioka.

Honolulu Star-Bulletin, February 14, 1967

2022

DAMON BUILDING

33-39 S. King Street / 942 Bethel Street

1887 – 1962

Architect/Builder: Walker & Redward

After the 1886 fire destroyed the Bethel Church, the property was divided into 4 lots and sold at auction in September 1886 with this 1,940 square foot lot purchased by the S.C. Damon Estate for $3,800. Thomas B. Walker and Fred Redward built this 2-story brick building in 1887.

This corner was previously the site of the public drinking fountain in front of the Seamen's Bethel.

2022

JOHN HOPP STORE

44 S. King Street
1882 – 1930
Architect/Builder: John Hopp

John Hopp was born in Holstein, Germany, in 1828, and came to Hawaii via Cape Horn on the ship *Carl Melches* in 1855 to build frame houses that were in the ship's cargo. He worked as a carpenter and his family joined him three years later. His son William built furniture and opened a shop on this corner in 1878.

L. W. HOPP,
Cabinet Maker, Upholsterer, Dealer in Furniture.
No. 88 King Street, between Nuuanu and Fort Streets.
Mattresses constantly on hand or made to order.

When William died in 1881 at age 26, John Hopp and son-in-law E.M. Marshall tore down the former building on the site, built a new 2-story wooden building in May 1882, and renamed the business J. Hopp & Co. They later moved to the Young Building in 1904.

The Hopp Building was the last wooden building on King Street in downtown. It was torn down in 1930.

This was previously the site of the furniture shop of Major T. Donnell from 1869 to 1876.

Originally from Maine, Donnell was a 22-year-old carpenter when he was briefly caught up in the aborted 1859 slave-trading voyage of the schooner *Wanderer*.

The Hawaii Attorney General's exquisitely crafted koa desk is believed to have been made by Donnell in 1870.

William DeWitt Alexander, 1896

NEW STORE! NEW GOODS!

J. HOPP & CO.,
74 King Street.

Having secured the Services of an

EMINENT UPHOLSTERER

From Paris and London, and recently in San Francisco, we are prepared to furnish Designs and Estimates for New and Original Styles of

HIGH CLASS UPHOLSTERING

More suited to the Climate, Elegant and Cheaper than

Interior Importations!

Parlor, Bedroom
AND
BOUDIOR SETS!

In Stock and to Order.

SOFAS, LOUNGES, CHAIRS, CHIFFONIERS, WARDROBES, DESKS, CRIBS, &c., &c.,

At the LOWEST possible Cash Prices.

MATTRESSES!

In every material, Hair, Moss, Eureka and Straw.

Celebrated NE PLUS ULTRA

Spring BEDS!

And a variety of other styles, at the LOWEST possible Prices.

Window Cornices and Lambrequins, in New and Elegant Sale. J. HOPP & Co., No. 74 King street

Over twenty-five years ago the late John Hopp opened up a small business as a furniture dealer and repairer at the corner of King and Bethel. At that time King street was a shaby locality. The block now occupied by the Chambers Drug Co., Woods & Sheldon, John Nott, the Union Grill, the Wall, Nichols Co., The Advertiser, Dimond, and other firms was at that time a row of small shacks. On the mauka side of the street the Metropolitan Meat Co. occupied a wooden building, and the coral building recently vacated by Castle & Cooke was classed as one of the most conspicuous structures on the street. Hopp's business prospered. As he needed more room he built additions to the older buildings so that today the lot is covered by one wooden building and a half dozen additions to the old structure. Mr. Hopp died in 1899 and his son-in-law, E. M. Marshall, has carried on an ever increasing business since that time. The business has spread to such an extent that it has outgrown the buildings.

The Honolulu Advertiser, October 1, 1904

J. Hopp & Co.,

74 King st.  74 King st

Importers of
Rattan & Reed Furniture.

Pianos & Furniture
Moved with Care.

Matting and Carpets Laid.

CORNICE POLES.

Fine Upholstering & Bedding
A Speciality.

CHAIRS TO RENT.

apr-10 8f

VON HOLT BLOCK
53-61 S. King Street
1895 – 1935
Architect/Builder: Ripley & Reynolds / Lucas Brothers

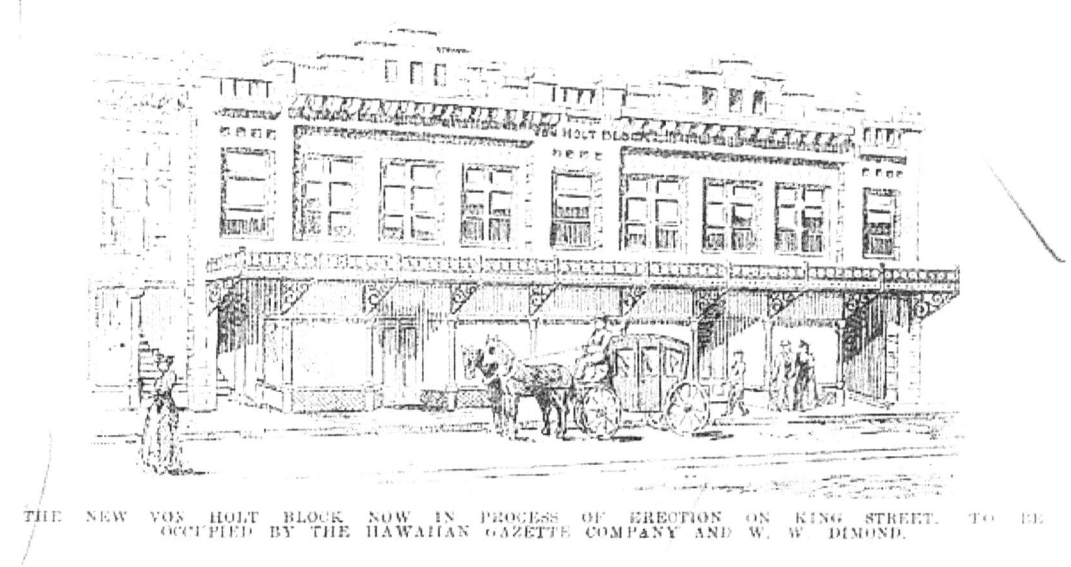

The Honolulu Advertiser, August 7, 1895

This was the site of the Varieties Theater built in 1853. It was a wood and canvas building attached to the makai side of a long wooden building owned by Governor Kekuanaoa. On Saturday night, July 3, 1855, about 8:30 pm the "unusually combustible materials" of the theater caught fire and burned the Police Station House and the stores of Mr. Cohn, Afong, and Watts & Co. on this side of the street between Bethel Street and Dimond's coral store.

The new wooden fence around the Bethel was laid flat and the building was given up for lost by the chaplain but luckily the front door was only charred by the heat. The other stone buildings nearby were threatened by "sparks flying seaward in every direction" but the heroic efforts of many kept roofs from igniting. This was the largest fire ever seen in Honolulu up to this time and was suspected to be the work of "an incendiary". The estimated damage was $25,000.

There was another fire here in 1894 that started in Kubey's tobacco store next door and destroyed 6 businesses including W.W. Wright's carriage manufactory. The *Hawaii Holomua Progress* wrote:

> "The willingness to 'save' that is so characteristic of any crowd around a fire was also prominent yesterday. As a result, several "saviors" will have cigars and cigarettes, fruits and tools for the coming week. The owners will probably have nothing."

VON HOLT BLOCK.

It Will Add Very Much to King Street.

Ripley & Reynolds are now completing for Harry Von Holt plans for the new block to go up on the makai side of King street, between Fort and Bethel. The lot is 80x140 and all of it will be used. There will be a passageway from King street to the postoffice. This will have a track for handling goods.

The building will be two stories, of brick, with stone and plate-glass front. On the Ewa side W. W. Dimond will have for his crockery business forty feet of the width and ninety-five feet of the depth, cellar and two floors.

All the rest of the building will be used by the *Gazette* Company. The business office will be in front on the first floor. Back will be presses on concrete floor. In its space on the second floor the *Gazette* Company will have its editorial and composing rooms and job printing and book binding departments.

The building will be one of the handsomest in the city and a notable addition to the business quarter. It will replace some low tin and wooden structures.

The Hawaiian Star, June 20, 1895

A big iron try pot of the pattern formerly used by whalers was unearthed to-day on the Von Holt premises where ground is now being broken for a new building. The pot was *not* full of dubloons but Mr. Cunha intends to plough up *his* lot before erecting his nine story building, and see if he can't find a pot with dubloons.

Hawaii Holomua, July 7, 1894

It is pleasing, in spite of the alleged hard times, to see a new building on King street go up. The von Holt estate has given the contract to the Lucas Brothers, and ground was broken to-day. The new building adjoins the Republic and Cunha, and will be an ornament to the city. The building is supposed to be finished by November next, and before Christmas W. W. Dimond and The Hawaiian Gazette Company will have possession and be in their new quarters.

The Independent, July 1, 1895

Lucas Bros. have sixty-three workmen employed on the Von Holt building at present. Immense quantities of brick are being piled up in the rear of the site of the building, ready for immediate use when the excavations are completed.

Evening Bulletin, August 7, 1895

Built for Harry Von Holt, the brickwork was by E.B. Thomas and George W. Lincoln plus Archibald Sinclair.

Arthur Harrison provided the cut stone for the front from his quarry in Punahou.

The Honolulu Advertiser, January 1, 1902

The Von Holt Block was torn down in 1935 for the King Theater designed by Herbert C. Cayton and built by Kobayashi & Sons for $50,000. The King advertised "the latest talkies at popular prices". The grand opening featured Rube Wolf and his band along with a Fanchon and Marco show featuring a dozen chorus girls known as the Fanchonettes. The first movie shown was "Cappy Ricks Returns" which was based on the fictionalized story of Captain Ralph Peasley of City Mill's schooner *Vigilant*.

The new King Theater, which is to open on December 14, will be a striking example of modern architecture. Its modern lines growing forcibly upward from an effective silhouette from which a striking panel of white light emerges, exhibiting the name of the theater in blue enameled letters in red Neon tribing. At the top of the panel will appear a bold silhouette of King Kamehameha's head, and at the base an illuminated coat of arms, which in turn forms a transition to a most spectacular marquee of blue and gold. The entire composition of marquee and sign will be striped in blue Neon tribing. Innovations in the building are the three sets of projectors, the Peerless lamps, the microscopic screen, the new ventilation system, refrigerated drinking fountains, special earphones for deaf persons, luxurious seats and carpets designed and woven especially for the theater, and the latest wide range Western Electric sound and public address systems. Herbert C. Cayton was architect for this building and the above drawing was made by Conrad W. Conrad.

The Honolulu Advertiser, December 8, 1935

Elvis Presley's *Blue Hawaii* had its world premiere at The King on November 8, 1961. But by the 1980's the theater had become "a slum with seats" according to newspaper columnist Phil Mayer. The theater closed in 1986 and the building was demolished in 1987.

Atoz, a joint venture between Maeda Hawaii and Itoz Inc. built an 8-story 192-space parking garage on the site that was completed in 1994 by Maeda (Hawaii) Construction and purchased by the Bank of Hawaii. The underlying land was still owned by the Von Holt family of Kaua'i.

2022

METROPOLITAN MEAT BUILDING

50-60 S. King Street
1901 – 1978 (remodeled 1917)
Architect/Builder: Fred Redward (1901), Frank Loehr (1917)

Honolulu: The Cross-Roads of the Pacific, 1913

The Honolulu Advertiser, February 24, 1926

The Metropolitan Meat Market was founded in 1872 by Gilbert Waller. His son Gilbert J. Waller later partnered with James Campbell, James I. Dowsett, and T.R. Foster and built this building in 1901. It was completely remodeled in 1917 for $80,000 by Frank Loehr from Oakland who raised it 20' to permit a double ceiling for the ventilation system and new brick walls with matte green terra cotta. The floors were white and green tile, and all counters were grained Italian marble.

It was later the home of Sato Clothiers and American Jewelry before being demolished in 1978 for the expansion of Liberty House, where Walmart is today.

The Honolulu Advertiser, June 1, 1917

Honolulu Star-Bulletin, June 30, 1917

WAITY BUILDING

62-74 S. King Street
1902 – 1978 (1936 remodel)
Architect/Builder: Oliver G. Traphagen (1902), Claude A. Stiehl (1936) /
Hawaiian Engineering & Construction Co. (1902)

The Waity Building was designed by Oliver G. Traphagen and built for Bishop Bank partner Henry E. Waity in 1902. Originally proposed as a 3-story building, it was built as a 2-story with the provision to add 2 extra stories later if needed.

The original design was "highly ornamental", similar to the other Italian Renaissance buildings nearby by Traphagen. It was remodeled and "modernized" in 1936 by architect Claude A. Stiehl.

During the foundation work one of the blasts sent coral rocks upwards of 100 pounds into the air with many crashing through the skylights of the Metropolitan Meat Market next door, resulting in the arrest of the three Japanese contractors: Morimito, Iwahe, and Chubawai.

> ANOTHER NEW BUILDING.
> H. E. Waity will erect a three-story brick and stone business building on the lot Waikiki of the Metropolitan Meat Market on King street. Plans are now being prepared by Architect Traphagen. It is expected that the building will be finished by next April

The Hawaiian Star, August 17, 1901

The building was completed on September 9, 1902 and replaced several 2-story wooden buildings.

On election night in 1917 the Star-Bulletin newspaper across the street mounted a large illuminated screen on the Waity building to broadcast the results.

> Architect Traphagen is receiving bids from contractors for the erection of the Waity block, adjoining the new Collins block in King street between Fort and Bethel. The block will be seventy-five feet on the street line. The building is to be of brick with a stucco front. The present height is to be two stories and the walls are designed to bear the weight of four stories which will be the ultimate size of the block. This building will be highly ornamental and will add greatly to the appearance of the street.

The Honolulu Advertiser, November 16, 1901

The building was demolished in 1978 for the expansion of Liberty House, where Walmart is now.

REPUBLIC BUILDING

67-71 S. King Street
1895 – 1976 (remodeled 1936, 1955)
Architect/Builder: Isaac A. Palmer? (1895), Clifford Young (1955) /
Fred Harrison (1895), Stanley Haraga (1955)

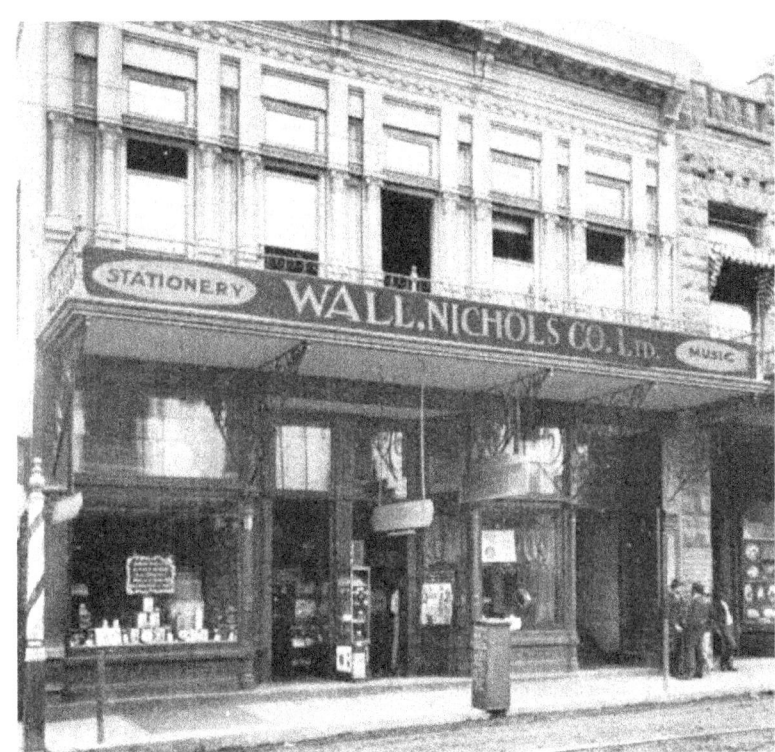

Honolulu: The Cross-Roads of the Pacific, 1913

This was the site of Benzler's Restaurant in 1857, and G. Wilhelm's German Ocean Restaurant from 1858 to 1862 where food could be ordered in English, French or German. In 1894, W.W. Wright's carriage shop, 10 carriages, and everything else including the building owned by E.S. Cunha burned in a fire that started at Kubey's cigar store.

Cunha hired Fred Harrison to build a new 2-story brick building in late 1894. The architect is unknown but was possibly Isaac A. Palmer who designed many other Eastlake Victorian buildings in Honolulu. Cunha put a large flagpole with a Hawaiian flag on top of his building and named it "The Republic".

Emanuel S. Cunha was a native of the island of St. George in the Azores where he was born in 1851. He first came to Honolulu in 1865 at age 14 on a whaling ship and stayed two years later. He was "a man of lovable disposition and made friends of all whom he met". He amassed a respectable fortune and was worth $300,000 when he passed away in 1918.

The first major tenant in 1895 was the Wall, Nichols Co. music, book, and stationary business that was here for over 50 years.

> Another sign of modernization is the Wall, Nichols building having its face lifted. King St. is getting more and more dressed up each year.

Honolulu Star-Bulletin, September 26, 1936

Although they remodeled the front in 1936, as late as 1939 there was still a horse hitching post on the curb in front of the building.

Honolulu Star-Bulletin, December 9, 1936

Wall-Nichols Co. sold their retail operations to Young's Department Store in 1947 and they remodeled the front in 1955.

Honolulu Star-Bulletin, 12/16/1936

The building was demolished in 1976 to make way for the $21M Pioneer Plaza development designed by Gerald E. Kremkow. The site is now an open space and exit driveway for the parking garage.

Site of Union Grill (left) and Republic Building (right), 2022

UNION GRILL

75-81 S. King Street
c.1855 – 1921 (remodeled 1910)
Architect/Builder: unknown

This building was perhaps built shortly after the 1855 Varieties Theater fire that destroyed the 1-story wooden building housing a general retail store owned by a man named Watts.

Hawaii State Archives

From 1855 to 1862 this was the store of wholesale merchants Utai & Ahee, and briefly the grocery store of Bartow & Stillman in 1864.

From 1885 to 1889 it was the jewelry and watchmaking store of August Kraft who was born in Germany in 1824. He also sold violins and guitars of all sizes. Sign and house painter George C. Stratemeyer rented upstairs.

After Kraft retired in 1889 it became Hans Petersen's cigar store.

In 1900, George Lycurgus opened "an elaborate and modern grill room" called the Union Grill.

Born in Vassara, Sparta, Greece, in 1859, Lycurgus was the former owner of Sans Souci in Waikiki and the Oyster Grotto in San Francisco.

By 1911 he also owned the Hilo Hotel, the Demosthenes Café, and the Volcano House. Called the "dean of Hawaiian hospitality", Lycurgus lived to be 101 years old.

MODERN GRILL ROOM.

George Lycurgus, formerly the popular host at Sans Souci, will next Saturday open in the building between John Nott's and Cunha's Lane an elaborate and modern grill room. The concern will be after the order of such institutions in the big cities, and will meet an immense want. Mr. Lycurgus takes with him into the place his famous chef and assistants from Sans Souci.

The new grill room will cater to the best trade, especially to theater parties and the like.

The Hawaiian Star, June 4, 1900

NEW UNION GRILL.

An interesting permit issued by the building and plumbing inspector today was to Fred Harrison, and was for the first section of the new Union Grill. This half of the new building will start where the kitchen now is and run back 52 feet almost to the Union Saloon. It will be of concrete and have four rooms on the first floor and eight on the second. As soon as this is finished the Grill will be moved into it, and then the front or King street end will be constructed. When the building is entirely finished it will be considerable of an ornament to the locality. George Lycurgus stated this morning that the work will not begin until after the Pacific fleet has sailed for the coast, as he expects a rush during fleet week.

The Hawaiian Star, January 25, 1910

HAWAIIAN STORE TO BE HOUSED IN OLD GRILL

A real Hawaiian store, owned and operated by real Hawaiians, is to open in Honolulu October 1. Arrangements have just been completed whereby Princess Kawananakoa acquires, on behalf of the Hale o na Alii, the old Union grill, as a location for the shop.

Members of the Hale o na Alii will be in charge of the store and will act as saleswomen in selling typical Hawaiian articles, including Hawaiian food and curios.

Half of the ground floor and all of the upper floor will be occupied by the society. Ernest Parker will conduct a florist shop in the other half of the ground floor.

Honolulu Star-Bulletin, September 6, 1920

The Union Grill.

George Lycurgus, whose fame is in many lands as the manager of Sans Souci at Waikiki, will open a high class restaurant in town on Saturday morning. He has had rooms prepared for the purpose, under his own supervision, on the makai side of King street, between Fort and Bethel streets. French cooks arrived in the Australia to prepare the viands, and they have the best kind of ranges and other utensils to work with. Mons. Arnaud is the chef. An experienced caterer from New York has also been engaged, to take charge of outside orders for family and picnic parties, etc. Fresh oysters and game will be specialties in the bills of fare. The ground floor is furnished with tables for short order custom, while the second floor is adapted for more leisure meals, social and family parties. A dumb waiter is fitted between the floors. Electric fans and lights are provided. The place will be open all night, thus being available for theater parties. There is an ample stock of linen, all stamped with the name of the house. An entrance for ladies opens direct upon an easy flight of carpeted stairs. "The Union Grill" is the name chosen by Mr. Lycurgus.

Evening Bulletin, June 6, 1900

UNION GRILL FRONT TO BE RECONSTRUCTED

George Lycurgus, controlling owner of most of the hotel business at Hilo and the Volcano House, stated this morning that the front half of the old Union Grill premises on King street will be rebuilt to conform to the rear half which was modernized some years ago.

"My intention," said Mr. Lycurgus this morning, "is to prepare for reopening of the grill, but whether or not that will actually be done may depend on future liquor regulation. If light wine and beer should be permitted by Congress the grill would be reopened as quickly as possible. Otherwise, however, I have doubts that the venture would justify the expense and risk, and the building might be turned to other uses."

The Hawaiian Star, June 4, 1900

The Union Grill was demolished in 1921 for the Commercial Trust & Bank Building. It was designed by Emory & Webb and built by Charles Ingvorsen out of concrete and had a white marble front. The main banking floor was Columbia marble and counters were of Texas marble. The real estate and trust company was on one side of the first floor and the Hawaii Bank of Commerce on the other. Opening day was January 3, 1922. It was demolished in 1976 to make way for the $21M Pioneer Plaza development.

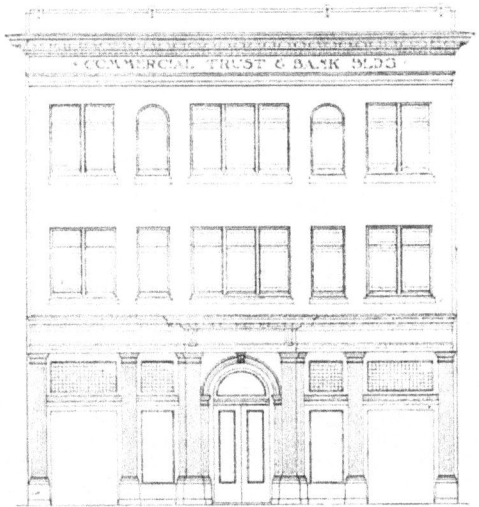

Honolulu Star-Bulletin, May 4, 1921

Honolulu Star-Bulletin, January 7, 1922

Late 1880's

COLLINS BUILDING

78 S. King Street
1901 – 1978
Architect/Builder: Oliver G. Traphagen / Hoffman & Riley

This 3-story building was designed by Oliver G. Traphagen and built by Hoffman & Riley for saddler and harness-maker Charles R. Collins. Originally from Bourne, Lincolnshire, in England, Collins' previous shop was located next to the Hocking Building on King Street just past Nuʻuanu Street.

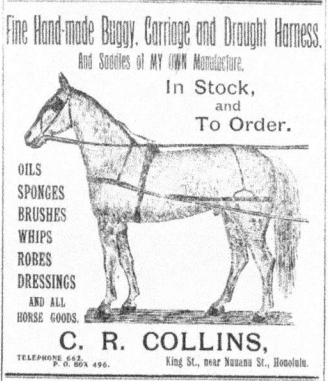

Sonny Cunha's music store was here from 1915 until purchased by Bergstrom Music in 1917. Meyer Drug Store opened here in 1919.

Noted landscape painter D. Howard Hitchcock had his studio on the third floor from 1913 to 1916. The building was demolished in 1978 for the expansion of Liberty House.

TO REPLACE AN OLD EYE-SORE.

Architect Traphagen has prepared plans for a three-story building of brick and stone which is to be built by Collins, the harness dealer, on King street near Fort, opposite the Advertiser office. The building will occupy a portion of the Austin estate, and it is believed that within a short time terms will be arrived at with the Austin heirs whereby all the open space on King street opposite the Advertiser building will be built upon as intended some months since, when it was planned to construct a three-story, arcade affair. Mr. Collins will occupy the ground and upper floors, while the second story will be used for public office purposes.

The Hawaiian Gazette, April 23, 1901

Hoffmann and Riley, 3-story brick building, No. 82, King Street.

The Honolulu Republican, June 30, 1901

Mr. C. R. Collins, the well known harness manufacturer opens to-morrow in his fine new brick store on King street, just opposite The Grill.

The Honolulu Republican, December 15, 1901

This was very likely the location of J.S. Dickson's paint shop from 1870 to 1872.

DIMOND BLOCK / ELKS BUILDING

85-91 S. King Street
1872 – 1949 (1906 remodel)
Architect/Builder: J.G. Osborne (1872), H.L. Kerr (1906) / John Ouderkirk (1906)

Bookbinder turned commission merchant Henry Dimond from Fairfield, Connecticut, had this building constructed for Dillingham & Co. in 1872.

It was the last concrete building built in Honolulu by J.G. Osborne before he sailed off to San Francisco. Osborne also built the Post Office on Merchant Street and the Hawaiian Hotel.

Dillingham & Company's first newspaper ad appeared in 1859, and the next mention of the company is at this location in April 1869 when they bought out Henry Dimond's hardware and dry goods business.

Dillingham temporarily moved to the Odd Fellows Building on Fort Street while this building was being built. During construction of the foundation an ancient stone poi beater was unearthed, and the site was said to have been the residence of one of the Hawaiian chiefs thirty years previous.

"The building which is constructed principally of concrete – part of the side walls being coral – is of two stories, with a well ventilated cellar of 70 by 50 feet. The first floor 14 feet between joints, and the second 12 feet. The cellar is 7-1/2 feet in the clear. There are 12 openings in front of the building, and ten in the rear.

The lower floor is divided through the centre from front to rear by a partition, through which are three large archways, the centre one of which is 28 feet across, partly railed off for an office, giving a view of the interior of the store to the book keeper. The entire Waikiki half of the store is devoted to shelves for hardware, with no counter, but a ledge at the front of the shelves. Under the ledge are bins for nails, etc. The opposite half of the store is fitted with deep shelves for hollow wooden-ware, etc.

Access to the second floor is by a broad stair-case on the Ewa side of the store. A convenient and powerful hoisting apparatus enables heavy goods to be sent from cellar to garret, and vice versa. The building is fireproof, with slated roof, and all the openings are secured with iron doors and shutters, made at the Honolulu Iron Works.

"The mason work of the building was by Osborne, builder and architect; the carpenter work by Hayselden & Son, and King & Co., and the painting by Phillips."
Hawaiian Gazette, July 17, 1872

The concrete building replaced a 2-story coral building built in 1849 for the firm of Wm. S. Anner & Co., comprised of William S. Anner, Edwin O. Hall, and Henry Dimond.

Anner left the islands in 1850 and the partnership of Hall & Dimond dissolved in 1853. Henry Dimond continued in this location, adding his son in 1861.

When Dillingham & Co. moved to a larger building on the Cummins property on Fort Street around the corner in 1878, John Thomas Waterhouse moved his dry goods business here. From 1889 to 1909 it was the plumbing shop of John Nott who also sold cast iron stoves. Nott was originally from Bristol, England, and came to Hawaii from New York in 1854.

Alexander & Baldwin's first home was upstairs over John Nott's store from 1898 to 1899.

In 1901 it was the temporary location for E.O. Hall & Son after their building at Fort and King streets burned.

From 1900 to 1904 it housed the bicycle and sporting goods store of Whitman & Co. which became Woods & Sheldon from 1904 to 1906, run by J.L. Woods and F.C. Sheldon.

JOHN NOTT,
Dimond Block, Nos. 95 & 97 King Street,

TIN, COPPER and SHEET IRON WORKER

Plumbing, in all its branches;
—— Artesian Well Pipe, all sizes; ——

STOVES AND RANGES,

Uncle Sam, Medallion, Richmond, Tip Top, Palace, Flora, May, Contest, Grand Prize, New Rival, Opal, Derby, Wren, Dolly, Gypsy Queen, Pansey, & Army Ranges, Magee Chester, Buck, Superior, Magnet, Osceola, Alameda, Eclipse, Charter Oak, Nimble, Invicta and Leandre Stoves, Galvanized Iron and Copper Boilers for Ranges, Granite Iron Ware, Nickel Plated and Plain.

Galvanized Iron Water Pipe, all sizes,
—— AND LAID ON AT LOWEST RATES ——
Cast Iron and Lead Soil Pipe,

House Furnishing Goods,
—— ALL KINDS. ——

RUBBER HOSE—ALL SIZES AND GRADES;
Lift and Force Pumps, Cistern Pumps, Galvanized Iron, Sheet Copper, Sheet Lead, Lead Pipe, Tin Plate, Water Closets, Marble Slabs and Bowls, Enameled Wash Stands

Chandeliers Lamps and Lanterns, Etc.

In 1906 the Honolulu Lodge of the Elks, No. 616, B.P.O.E, leased the building from C.M. Cooke and it became the new "home for the herd" after outgrowing their building at Beretania and Miller streets.

They hired architect H.L. Kerr and contractor John Ouderkirk to undertake a massive remodel over the stores of John Nott and Woods & Sheldon, taking over the entire second floor and adding a third floor with three large fancy windows.

Opening day was January 1, 1907.

Screenshot from 1906 Edison film

The downstairs became Silva's Toggery in 1907. Alfred Cezar Silva was born in Funchal, Madeira, in 1872 and came to Hawaii in 1879. He started out as a cash boy for Honolulu merchant Charles J. Fishel and continued working there after it was bought by L. E. Tracy in 1898, later working for The Kash retail clothing store.

Silva's Toggery was at this location for over 20 years until he sold it in December 1928 to George H. Vicars of George's Ltd.

On May 9, 1929, Silva sold his house in Manoa to his two children. On May 11, the 57-year-old Silva married 33-year-old Sylvia Anjo Eckert. The following day he took poison and died. Both the marriage and his sudden death caught his acquaintances and family by surprise. There had been no quarrel or foul play.

Honolulu Star-Bulletin, August 11, 1949

In 1949 the Cooke Trust hired Hego Fuchino & Robert Toshio Katsuyoshi to design a new building to be built by contractor G.J. Oda for the Easy Appliance Company.

> "An outstanding feature of the building will be a modern glass window front for complete view of the ground floor display and second story music rooms."

Easy Appliance became Servco-Pacific in 1968. Choosing to not participate in the Pioneer Plaza redevelopment, they later remodeled the building in 1978.

There was briefly a Chinatown Museum on the first floor in 2001.

Hawaii State Archives

2022

CENTRAL BUILDING

88 S. King Street

1909 – 1979 (remodeled 1929)
Architect/Builder: Fred Harrison (1909), Emory & Webb (1929)

Hawaii State Archives

> Fred Harrison, the contractor, asked the Board for a permit for blasting in the basement of a new building to be erected on King street adjoining the O'Neill building. After some discussion it was decided to grant the permit on condition that Harrison put up a bond of $10,000.
>
> *Evening Bulletin, December 12, 1908*

> **NEW BUILDING STARTS.**
>
> Excavation for a two-story business building has been started next to the O'Neill building on the corner of Fort and King streets. The building is being erected by Fred Harrison but he stated that he was not yet certain to what use it would be put. He said that a number of offers had been made for it already but none accepted.
>
> *The Hawaiian Star, December 28, 1908*

This building was constructed in 1909 by developer and contractor Fred Harrison who called it the Central Building.

Jeweler Joseph Schwartz occupied the upper floor for many years, with James Bergstrom's and Sonny Cunha's Honolulu Music Store on the first floor.

In 1929, Emory & Webb designed a new front as the King Street entrance for Liberty House that cost $85,000. The building was demolished in an expansion in 1979.

Honolulu Star-Bulletin, March 16, 1929

FRED. PHILP,
Successor to Peter Dalton,
SADDLE & HARNESS
MANUFACTURER,
92 KING STREET, HONOLULU
—Bell Telephone No. 111.—

Begs to inform his friends and the public that having bought the good will, stock and fixtures of his predecessor he bespeaks a share of the patronage of the public in Honolulu, and the Hawaiian Islands, and that notwithstanding the depression of trade and all the annoyances that the consumer has to submit to by the introduction of CHEAP IMPORTED HARNESS and machine-made work, he is able to supply to his customers as heretofore, a FIRST-CLASS

Hand-Made Harness!

Guaranteed to give Satisfaction, at a fair remunerative price. He uses only the Best Materials in

Gold, Silver, Nickel
—AND—
Rubber Mountings

And every article is made by Experienced Workmen under his personal supervision.
In ordering the above Harness the measure of the horse about the neck and girth should be sent to insure entire satisfaction as to fit and durability.
☞ If any article does not please the buyer it shall be replaced by new goods or the cash returned.

—— HE IMPORTS DIRECT ——

Sydney Saddles,
—Especially made to suit the Islands.—

Double Plate, Spring Bars and every improvement, and all Saddles purchased of him will be restuffed within six months free of charge. He desires to inform Planters, Teamsters and others that

Cart, Wagon and Plow Harness!

Can be supplied here with better Workmanship and Material and guarantee to give greater satisfaction than anything that can be imported from the Coast.

—A FULL LINE OF—

Whips, Spurs, Sponges,
Chamois, Combs,
Oils and Dressings,

Brushes, and every necessary for Stable use always on hand.
☞ What he sells he will warrant as represented, and would sooner lose a sale than misrepresent an article. 1139 3m

---

HOTEL DU GLOBE.
RESTAURANT FRANCAIS!!
JARDIN, terrasse, cabinets, particuliers, etc, service à la carte, vins, liqueurs, rafraichisements, patisserie, etc.
Par L. FRANCONI & A. MEDAILLE.
Honolulu, entries par King et Fort streets. 1y-46

Globe Hotel, French Restaurant,
HONOLULU.
SPACIOUS YARD and garden, pleasant Terrace, nice private rooms, &c. Charges as per bill of fare. Wines, Spirits, Liquors, Pastry and general Refreshments of the best choice, by
L. FRANCONI & A. MEDAILLE.
Double entrance by King and Fort streets. 1y-46

Hawaii State Archives

From 1886 to 1897 the saddle and harness shop of Fred Philp was on this site. Philp sold the business in 1897 and went to work with C.R. Collins.

The driveway on the left led back to a 2-story coral building housing a dressmaking shop in 1891 that was originally the "pretentious house" built c.1830 by John Coffin Jones for his wife Hannah Holmes.

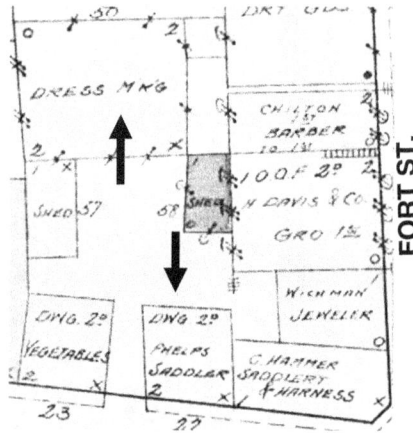
1891 Dakin Map

By 1852 the house was the Globe Hotel run by L. Franconi and A. Medaille with 13 rooms, 3 detached cottage rooms, bathroom, stable, coach house, henhouse, and kitchen. H. Hackfeld & Co. bought it in 1875 for $3,000 and sold it to James Campbell in 1883. It was demolished in 1897 for the construction of the Ehler's Block.

Paul Emmert, 1854

O'NEILL BUILDING

96-98 S. King Street / 1002 Fort Street

1903 – 1983 (remodeled 1916, 1938, 1953)
Architect/Builder: Oliver G. Traphagen (1903), Ripley & Dickey (1916), Conrad & Dahl (1938), Conrad (1953) / Fred Harrison (1903), Bowen & Ingvorsen (1916), Arthur Freitas (1938), Mutual Contracting (1953)

Designed by Oliver G. Traphagen and completed by Fred Harrison in 1903, this was the long-time home of the Gunst-Eakin cigar company out of San Francisco. From their charter:

> "To engage in, conduct and carry on the business of wholesale and retail cigars, tobacco and smokers materials in the Territory of Hawaii and to import the same. To manufacture, buy and sell cigars and smokers articles in the said Territory and generally to deal in all kinds of merchandise.

The property was only 851 square feet, with 46' on King Street and 21' on Fort Street. Built 2-stories high with iron and steel and decorative terra cotta, it was designed to have five stories with a basement.

A 1-story wooden building previously on the corner was torn down in September 1902. Work was delayed on the new building until the iron arrived by ship in January of 1903.

WILL ERECT FINE BUILDING

O'Neill Structure at Fort and King Streets Now Assured.

Pressed brick and terra cotta soon will replace the old frame buildings which now occupy the corner of Fort and King streets, the only one of the four which has not a structure which is a credit to the center of the business portion of the city.

Contractors have been at work figuring on the construction for some time past and the bids are expected to be put in either today or the first of the week. The plans which are by O. G. Traphagen, have been kept very quiet and the agreement between the various interests to take up the matter of an improvement there was reached recently after more than a year's discussion. It is understood that the plans contemplate the financing of the proposition by the securing of money on a long time mortgage, as soon as the contractors' figures are in.

The O'Neill building will be of two stories in height at the present time, although the steel cage will be put up on the basis of five stories in the completed structure. The building is planned for offices. There will be two fine rooms on the ground floor and the upper story may be subdivided into a greater number although the plans show only the same as on the ground. The rooms will be finely lighted and the front will be one of the most attractive in the city.

The building takes in all the frontage on Fort street from the corner to the Odd Fellows' building, and is to extend back to the frame building which occupies the corner on the alley on King street. The property long has been in such shape that nothing could be done in the matter of its being improved. Three-sixths of the holding rests with Thomas Douglass, two-sixths with Mrs. Cooper and one-sixth with Bruce Cartwright.

The intention to erect the building two stories is in line with some recent structures which have had their foundations made for higher buildings, so that when business reaches the limit demanding more accommodation it may be given without great trouble.

The Honolulu Advertiser, August 16, 1902

O'Neill Building Contract.

The contract for the construction of the O'Neill building at Fort and King streets has been secured by the Honolulu Engineering and Construction Company. The successful bidders are to do the work for $16,699. The iron and terra cotta, which are not included in this bid, have been ordered and are expected to arrive from the Coast about the middle of November. As soon as the contract has been signed the work of removing the present building will begin and the foundations be put down ready for the superstructure.

The Honolulu Advertiser, August 19, 1902

The contract for the new O'Neill building, instead of going to the Hawaiian Engineering Company, has been let to Fred Harrison, who will take over all contracts for iron and steel and the terra cotta work as well. Progress will be made on the work at once.

The Honolulu Advertiser, August 29, 1902

As early as July 1868 the Tom Moore Tavern was on this corner, owned by Jeremiah O'Neill from Dublin, Ireland. O'Neill started out as a painter and paper hanger on King Street in 1862, and named his pub for the famous Irish writer, poet, and lyricist Thomas Moore.

Honolulu Star Bulletin, October 20, 1924

O'Neill renovated the building in 1880 and leased it to importers and commission agent Joseph F. Pickering who sold everything from cigarettes to bedspreads, but mostly musical instruments and pianos, also offering in-store violin lessons.

The Pacific Commercial Advertiser, October 16, 1880

William DeWitt Alexander, 1896

In 1882 it became the saddlery and harness store of Charles Hammer. He was born in Grue Kommune, Hedmark fylke, Norway, in 1831 and came to Hawaii in 1879. Shop foreman Alexander Chisholm took over the business when Hammer retired in 1895.

Chisholm was from Pictou, Nova Scotia, and came to Hawaii in 1882. He was described as "a giant in strength joined with the mildest manners".

On May 23, 1900, he became very sick and was taken to Queen's Hospital where he died two days later of a "remittent fever". Some thought it to be malaria, others suspected bubonic plague.

Hawaii State Archives

REMODEL GUNST BLOCK

The entire building occupied by M. A. Gunst & Company, at the mauka ewa corner of King and Fort streets is to be altered and improved for the tenants in the near future, the changes costing probably $10,000. The main floor is to be remodelled and the second floor, until lately occupied by the Home Insurance Company, will be altered for use as a storeroom by the cigar dealers.

The Honolulu Advertiser, June 29, 1916

M. A. Gunst & Co., owners. Location, King and Fort streets. Alterations. Ripley & Davis, architects. Bowen & Ingrorsen, builders. Estimated cost, $5000.

Honolulu Star-Bulletin, August 30, 1916

Home Insurance Company of Hawaii, Ltd.

96 King Street.   O'Neill Building.   Telephone 3529

Liberty Bank vice president Kim Tong Ho purchased the building in 1929 for Jessie Ho's Smart Shoppe.

Royal Credit Jewelers leased the building in 1938 and spent $20,000 on "modernizing" and remodeling. Owned by Max Cornfeldt, his son Conrad (Dahl and Conrad) drew the plans. The contractor was Arthur Freitas with William D. Kirkpatrick responsible for masonry and plastering.

Conrad Wilfred Cornfeldt was born in Minneapolis, Minnesota, in 1910, and spent two years in architecture school at the University of Southern California before coming to Hawaii with $25 in his pocket. He went to work with architect Bjarne Dahl as a drafter and illustrator, and due to so many people calling him "Mr. Conrad" he legally changed his name to Conrad W. Conrad.

His father owned Royal Credit Jewelers, and when his parents decided to leave during World War II, Connie took over the business and opened Security Diamond at Nuʻuanu and Pauahi in 1945. In 1953 he opened the third store for Security Diamond Company in the O'Neill Building.

The Honolulu Advertiser, June 12, 1938

The Honolulu Advertiser, June 14, 1953

Designed once again by Conrad W. Conrad, it was remodeled in 1953 to "reflect modern contemporary architecture in a spirited tempo, using Hawaiian sandstone, koa, glass, split brick and plaster, and the cool green of tropical plants. The company's name and trade mark individualize the design and give interesting pattern to the entire composition". The interior featured "carefully blended mirrored walls, bleached and natural koa, and wrought iron furniture". Security Diamond closed this store in 1966 and consolidated it with their main store in the Ala Moana Center.

Although Liberty House had tried to buy the building, it remained while they built their new store behind it in 1980.

Honolulu Star-Bulletin, January 7, 1980

An unusual dilemma: due to zoning requirements it could never be modified or rebuilt.

Consequently, no one was willing to go to the expense of tearing it down just to replace it with a piece of sidewalk.

The Honolulu Advertiser
October 22, 1980

In 1983 the city finally paid $275,000 to condemn and demolish the little building.

Few remember this blank piece of sidewalk was once the site of one of Honolulu's most beautiful buildings.

2022

CHILTON BLOCK

97-99 S. King Street / 944 Fort Street

1890 – 1977

Architect/Builder: Isaac A. Palmer (1891), Mark Potter (1937), Wimberly & Cook (1961) / George Lucas (1890), John Hansen (1937)

Hawaii State Archives

Once one of Honolulu's most iconic and beautiful Eastlake Victorian buildings, the Chilton Block suffered a series of remodeling indignities during its 87-year history. There have also been a lot of drugs at this corner, including alcohol, opium, sugar, and three pharmaceutical drug stores. By the 1970's it had become unrecognizable, and today the site is an empty courtyard.

It was built for William R. Chilton by George Lucas who was, awarded the construction contract January 1890 for $6,545. The architect was undoubtedly Isaac A. Palmer, a specialist in Queen Anne and Eastlake styles who officed on the second floor.

The Hobron, Neuman & Co. drug store was here from November 1891 to May 1902 and the Chambers Drug Co. was here from 1903 to 1923 until bought out by the Benson, Smith & Co. drug store in December 1923.

> HOBRON, Newman & Co. opened business as druggists in the Chilton block to-day. Palmer & Richardson, architects, whose office is upstairs in the same building, designed the store fittings. These are very elegant, being in Eastlake style, made of redwood and nor'-west, finished in oil. Many people dropped into the store to take a look around.
>
> *Evening Bulletin November 16, 1891*

PALMER & RICHARDSON

ARCHITECTS.

Styles of Architecture:
Eastlake, Queen Anne.
Renaissance, Gothic, Italian,
Classic and Norman,

In Stone, Brick, Iron or Wood

Best Modern Designs in Residences.
Cheap Artistic Cottages a Specialty.

☞ Complete plans and specifications given; also superintendence of construction.

—OFFICE—
Chilton Block, — *Up-stairs,*
Entranc on Fort St. 2867-q

The confectionary branch of Wall Nicholls opened the Kandy Kafe at the corner in 1902 with the name selected by a contest for $10 in gold.

The building narrowly missed destruction in 1905 when Chilton sold it to the Hawaiian Trust Company for $36,500. "President J.R. Galt of the Hawaiian Trust Company stated that it was the intention of the corporation to replace the building, which is only fifteen or eighteen years old, with a modern office structure, for its own occupancy". They were unable to acquire the adjoining properties and the project fell through.

> When the Chilton block was erected it was a real acquisition to the architecture of Honolulu. It replaced a low, squabbly-looking shack occupied by the Keystone saloon—the first liquor joint eliminated from Fort street of the Honolulu of a quarter century ago. Now, under the policy inaugurated by President Dole in the time of the Republic, there is no saloon on that retail thoroughfare between Beretania street and the waterfront.

The Hawaiian Gazette, October 10, 1905

1937   *The Honolulu Advertiser, February 13, 1962*   1962

Benson, Smith & Company removed the cupola on top of the tower (technically a turret) in January 1924, and hired Mark Potter and contractor John Hansen to drastically "modernize" the building in 1937. The Honolulu Star-Bulletin claimed it was "one of the outstanding examples of remodeling that Honolulu has seen in many a day."

The British Overseas Airways Corporation hired Wimberly & Cook to design a major $100,000 remodel of the building in 1961. The BOAC officed here until 1971.

The building's last incarnation was the temporary downtown branch office of Pioneer Federal Savings and Loan Association while the Pioneer Plaza tower was being built. It was demolished in 1977.

Honolulu Star-Bulletin, July 30, 1976   *Open courtyard, 2022*

The first building on the site that we know of was a 2-story wooden building that was the barber shop of Henry Bradley in 1870. Bradley had previously worked with Jacob Wilkerson at King Barber on Fort Street and left in 1869 to open his first shop across the street from the Bethel Church.

> A DESIDERATUM SUPPLIED.—In connection with the fine hair cutting and shaving establishment of Mr. Henry Bradley, corner of King and Fort streets, can be had a warm or cold bath at any hour of the day, the former requiring fifteen minutes notice. Quite a change has been wrought in the appearance of this corner, showing what a little thrift and enterprise can accomplish.

Pacific Commercial Advertiser, May 28, 1870

"Perhaps it might be as well to call it, after the style of some of the aspiring knights of the razor and shears in the East, 'The Honolulu Emporium of Fashion and the Tonsorial Art'. But we will simply say that Henry Bradley opened yesterday, in the premises lately purchased by him on the corner of Fort and King Streets, a shaving and hair-dressing establishment, which in every respect is far the best ever seen in Honolulu. The large and airy room is filled up with taste and elegance, and provided with five luxurious chairs and as many accomplished operators. The luxury of a clean shave and a vigorous rubbing of the head in the morning, makes a man feel in good humor with himself and his neighbor, and better qualifies him for the duties of the day than everybody suspects."

Hawaiian Gazette, May 18, 1870.

There was a room at the corner, 28' x 22', a storefront on King Street, 16' x 38', and room upstairs, 18' x 38', that was used as a photographic studio. Bradley put the premises up for sale in 1876 but there were apparently no takers, so instead he opened the Keystone Saloon in 1878.

> THE KEYSTONE SALOON.—This is the name of the new and elegant saloon, corner of Fort and King street, to be opened to-morrow, by Mr. Henry Bradley, proprietor. This saloon has been fitted up in a style equal to the best in San Francisco. The workmanship of the inside fittings, under the supervision of Mr. George Lucas, is of a high style of art, reflecting great credit upon the mechanical attainments of the workmen engaged, and displaying good taste in its arrangements. The painting was done by Mr. Lenhart and reflects great credit upon him, evidencing his superiority as a workman thoroughly acquainted with his business. A principle feature of this saloon, will be the daily lunches set out for its patrons. It is the intention of the proprietor to have the management of the saloon conducted in a manner to please the most fastidious, thereby hoping to command a liberal proportion of the patronage of the public.

The Hawaiian Gazette, August 21, 1878

In 1883, the bar was run by contractor Thomas B. Walker.

In addition to owning the Keystone Saloon, Bradley was also an opium smuggler who was sent to prison in 1878 and caught with 99 tins in 1885.

In 1888, over $10,000 was found buried in his yard.

> Auction Sales by James F. Morgan,
>
> **Wooden Building**
>
> —AND—
>
> **Store Fixtures--At Auction**
>
> On SATURDAY, Nov. 23,
> AT 12 O'CLOCK NOON.
>
> On the premises, corner of Fort & King streets, I will sell at Public Auction,
>
> **The Wooden Building,**
>
> Formerly occupied by the "Keystone Saloon" and Photograph Gallery. The Building contains a large lot of window glass and is partly covered with galvanized iron. At the same time will be sold a lot of Fixtures, comprising:
>
> **1 Fine MacNeal & Urban Safe,**
>
> Large Bevelled Mirror,
> Chairs, Oil Painting, and
>
> **1 Fine LONG COUNTER.**
>
> ☞ Buildings to be removed within 7 days from date of sale.
>
> JAS. F. MORGAN,
> 407 4t   Auctioneer.

Bradley and his son-in-law, William R. Chilton, became embroiled in a license renewal lawsuit with the government in 1888 that went all the way to the Hawaii Supreme Court.

Losing the lawsuit, along with the proposed widening of Fort Street, led them to erecting a new building. On November 23, 1889, the "dilapidated and weather-stained" building was sold to contractor John Ouderkirk to be removed for $125.

Fort Street at King Street, looking mauka, 1884-1885

King Street at Fort Street, looking ewa, 1886

E.O. HALL BUILDING
101-107 S. King Street / 935-943 Fort Street
1869 – 1900
Architect/Builder: J.G. Osborne

There have been four E.O. Hall buildings on this site, starting with a wooden building in 1852 that was replaced with this 2-story "fire-proof" brick building built by J.G. Osborne in 1869.

AN OLD LANDMARK GONE.—The wooden store on the corner of King and Fort Streets, long occupied by E. O. Hall & Son, was sold at auction yesterday by Adams & Wilder, (to be removed) for the sum of $108, to L. L. Torbert. It is the intention of the Messrs. Hall to erect on the lot a substantial fire-proof store.

The Hawaiian Gazette, April 21, 1869

E. O. HALL & SON
Have Removed to their
New Brick Fire - Proof Store,
WHERE THEY INTEND TO KEEP
A Full Assortment of Merchandise
IN THEIR LINE.
NEW GOODS ARE SOON EXPECTED
Both from the United States and England,
Which, together with Stock on hand,
Will be Sold at Prices to Suit the Times!
692 1m

The first building we know of on this site was a grist mill in 1849, one of two in Hawaii, the other being in Maui and both used for handling the wheat harvest from Maui.

> *"The flour made here was not only enough to supply the home demand but ship loads of it were sent to Herba Buena, which in time has become the mighty city of San Francisco."*
>
> *The Hawaiian, March 5, 1898*

Edwin Oscar Hall was born in Walpole, NH, in 1810 and trained in Detroit and New York City to become a printer. He and his wife came to Hawaii in 1835 as part of the Seventh Company of missionaries sent by the American Board of Commissioners for Foreign Missions (ABCFM).

After serving with the mission for 15 years he became head of the government printing office responsible for printing *The Polynesian* newspaper. Along with fellow shipmate Henry Dimond, a bookbinder, he joined Wm. S. Anner & Co. in 1849.

Edwin O. Hall

The business became Hall & Dimond in 1850, E.O. Hall in 1852, and E.O. Hall & Son in 1865 and concentrated mostly on hardware, paints, oils, agricultural implements, tools, and ships supplies.

William DeWitt Alexander, 1896

> **A NEW STORE.**—We have recently looked in at the new brick fire proof building of Messrs. E. O. Hall & Son, on the corner of Fort and King streets, and for neatness and convenience it quite comes up to our notions of a first class establishment, for the business for which it was designed. Starting from a solid stone foundation, the walls are of brick and rising two stories, of good height, it is covered by a substantial slate roof, with nothing but metal, brick and stone, exposed to fire from the outside. The building is fifty-four feet on Fort street and fifty-two feet on King street, in the shape of an L. The principal sales room is fifty feet by thirty feet, on Fort street, and is remarkably cool and well ventilated. The fittings up are convenient, and do great credit to the taste and skill of the designer. The painting and graining is the neatest we have seen in Honolulu, and fully attest the ability of Mr. Dickson, the artist who did the work. On the whole this new building is a credit to the city, and to Mr. Osborne the architect ; and we trust it will stimulate others to emulate the example of this business firm, who, in securing for themselves more secure and convenient accommodations, have by no means been unmindful of the public taste in planning and executing their purpose. We trust their endeavors in this regard will meet with the approval of the public, and we bespeak for them a continuance of that patronage with which they have been favored during the sixteen years they have occupied this stand.

The Pacific Commercial Advertiser, August 28, 1869

E.O. Hall & Son were in this brick building for 30 thirty years. In addition to hardware, they were also early suppliers of electric light systems for many busineeses.

> **The Electric Light System.**
> The attention of readers is called to the notice of E. O. Hall & Son in another column, and more particularly to the fact that this firm is now paying special attention to the installation of electric light plants in sugar mills and other buildings. Among those who have received electric light plants from this firm, which are now in use and working satisfactorily, are the following: Remond Grove Pavilion, Kekaha Mill, Kauai, Union Iron Works, Honolulu, the sugar mills at Waihee and Hana on Maui, and Paauhau, Waiakea, Honokaa, and Hilo Mills on Hawaii, and the Honolulu Iron Works of this city. Mr. Wm. V. Lockwood has charge of the department of their business, and besides the above he has installed lights in several other establishments. Satisfaction in every case is guaranteed.

The Honolulu Advertiser, February 9, 1891

In 1898 E.O. Hall & Son submitted plans by Ripley and Dickey to the landowners, the Austin brothers, in Boston for a new building, 65' x 95', of gray pressed brick with terra cotta trimmings to be up to 5 stories tall.

> **HALL BUILDING SALE.**
>
> J. F. Morgan, auctioneer, sold the E. O. Hall & Son building at noon. The Hall corporation bought in the brickwork at $1,500. H. Ludloff took the woodwork for $80, the roof $32.50 and the iron veranda $32.50. Lucas Bros. got the plate glass at $56. E. B. Thomas bought 26 iron shutters at $2.50 each, and the flagpole at $5. Some little merchandise was also sold.

Evening Bulletin, February 7, 1900

They sold off bits and pieces of the old building and while the new building was being built by Victor Hoffman, they temporarily relocated to the Dimond Block two buildings ewa along King Street, on the site of their first store in 1850.

Described as "a handsome two-story terra cotta front building" in the Italian Renaissance style, it ended up being only 2-stories tall since the Austin Estate refused to grant a lease longer than 20 more years. The construction cost was $35,000.

The cornerstone was laid on July 5, 1900, and contained a history of the business, a set of Hawaiian coins and Hawaiian stamps, local newspapers, Thrum's Annual for 1900, a company calendar, and photographs of E.O. Hall, W.W. Hall, E.O. White, and Governor S.B. Dole.

The Honolulu Advertiser, January 1, 1901

Eight months after they moved in, the building was gutted in a devastating fire that started at 3:45am on August 6, 1901, resulting in a loss of $200,000. There were large amounts of paint, oil, gasoline, and gunpowder in the building and spontaneous combustion was the suspected origin of the fire.

Hawaiian Gazette, August 9, 1901

E. O. Hall & Son, Ltd., will erect a three-story building on the site of that which was burned.

The Hawaiian Gazette, August 30, 1901

They hired architect Oliver G. Traphagen to design a new 3-story building that was built in 6 months by contractor Fred Harrison.

Unfortunately, at 10:45 pm on March 16, 1929, a fire believed started by spontaneous combustion in the paint department once again destroyed the E.O. Hall Building, causing about $300,000 worth of damage.

PREMISES OCCUPIED UNTIL 1900

BUILT 1901. BURNED SAME YEAR

BUILDING NOW OCCUPIED. E. O. HALL & SON, LTD. HARDWARE. ESTABLISHED 1850.

Honolulu: The Cross-Roads of the Pacific

The Honolulu Advertiser, August 11, 1929

Louis E. Davis was hired to design a radically modern Class A 3-story concrete, terra cotta, and tile building in the Art Deco style that was built by Henry Freitas in seven months for $130,000.

Opening day was June 3, 1930. The exterior was jet black with gold stripes, with 60% of the wall surface being glass. Wrought iron ornaments embellished the windows on the first floor.

"It has the brilliant coloring and luster of a Chinese porcelain temple" and was known as the Dimond-Hall Building.

E.O. Hall & Son moved to 850 Richards Street in 1947 and a Chinese-owned and operated company from San Francisco called National Dollar Stores, Ltd. moved in.

Honolulu Star Bulletin, June 14, 1930

2022

The building was demolished in 1966 for the Financial Plaza of the Pacific designed by Wou & Partners, Inc.

The site is now a landscaped courtyard designed by Lawrence Halprin that features three modern sculptures by Arnaldo Pomodoro.

MCINTYRE BUILDING

102-110 S. King Street / 1001-1021 Fort Street

1902 – 1968 (remodeled 1926, 1948)
Architect/Builder: Oliver G. Traphagen (1902), Charles W. Dickey (1948) / John Ouderkirk (1902), Charles Ingvorsen (1926), Pacific Construction (1948)

The Pacific Commercial Advertiser, June 30, 1905

One of three buildings at this intersection designed by Oliver G. Traphagen, the building permit for the McIntyre Building was announced in the newspaper on May 2, 1901. It was built by John Ouderkirk for $55,000, with construction completed in 10 months.

The McIntyre Building had a frontage of 112' on Fort Street and 63' on King Street, with foundation walls of native blue stone, piers of cut blue stone, and with iron and steel girders.

> "The building is a most modern one in every respect and is constructed of pressed brick and terra cotta in the Richardsonian Romanesque style of architecture, and so constructed that an additional story or two can be added on at any time."
>
> *Evening Bulletin, September 30, 1901*

[Note: the style is actually Italian Renaissance]

The First National Bank was on the makai side, with McInerny Bros. on the mauka side. The second story was divided into 14 offices accessed by "a commanding entrance on the Fort Street side" that led to the offices through a large tiled hallway.

Honolulu: The Cross-Roads of the Pacific, 1913

On July 1, 1905, the Board of Supervisors rented 4 rooms for county offices. Fifteen years later in 1920, City Hall moved from the second floor of the McIntyre Building to the Kapiolani Building at King and Alakea streets.

Fort Street looking mauka from King Street

Hugh McIntyre shows up in Honolulu newspapers as early as 1854 and is running a grocery store the corner of King and Fort streets from at least 1859.

HAWAIIAN BACON.
SUPERIOR QUALITY, for sale at
H. McINTYRE'S,
39-tf   Corner King and Fort sts.

c.1856

In January 1868 it became H.E. McIntyre & Brother.

His son, Hugh E. McIntyre, joined the business around 1863 and on December 31, 1864, they announced they were closing the business. And this is where it starts to get a little murky...

In March 1865, D.C. McCandless & John Paty announce that they have taken over the business of H. McIntyre & Son, but this was contested in four separate lawsuits by E.O. Hall and Son, T.C. Heuck, J.M. Smith, and B.F. Bolles & Co. in a case that went to the Hawaii Supreme Court in 1868 that ruled against McCandless, Paty, and McIntyre. "The question being whether Mr. McIntyre was a member of the firm."

H. E. McINTYRE & BROTHER,
GROCERY AND FEED STORE.
Corner of King and Fort Streets,
o7 ly   Honolulu, H. I.

Fort Street looking mauka from King Street, c.1865

Messrs. H. McIntyre and Brother have, within a few weeks, removed the old wooden structure which has been occupied for many years past as a grocery store, on the corner of King and Fort streets, together with some of the adjacent buildings, and will soon erect in their place a fine brick edifice.

The Hawaiian Gazette, June 20, 1877

In 1877, the McIntyre brothers hired Thomas J. Baker to build a 1-story brick building on the site, with 63' frontage on King Street and 112' frontage on Fort Street. All rooms had 14' ceilings and were 25' deep with 10' cellars underneath.

Hawaii State Archives

...appearance of that part of the city. The brick store of Messrs. H. McIntyre and Brother on the corner of King and Fort streets is progressing rapidly, the walls being nearly completed, and the iron door and window frames being in place.

The Hawaiian Gazette, August 1, 1877

—On Fort street also, Mr. McIntyre's new brick building, corner of King, has been completed and occupied. It is of one story, fire-proof, and in the form of an L, 62.8 feet on King street and 112 feet on Fort. The King street portion is occupied by H. E. McIntyre & Bro., the well known grocery firm, and on Fort street there are three commodious, airy rooms. All the rooms are 14 feet in the clear, and 25 feet deep. Under each room there is a roomy cellar. That under the King streets store is 60 by 25 feet, and 10 feet in the clear. Fort street between King and Hotel street it may be observed, bids fair to be erelong built up entirely with fireproof structures.

The Pacific Commercial Advertiser, October 27, 1877

On May 18, 1899, H.E. McIntyre & Brothers and J.T. Waterhouse merged their grocery operations with Henry May & Company who built a new building two doors up on Fort Street known as the Boston Block.

The 1-story brick building on the corner was demolished in November 1900.

H. E. McINTYRE & BRO.,
Grocery and Feed Store,
Cor. of FORT & KING Sts., HONOLULU.

Goods Received by Every Steamer from the United States and Europe.

All Orders Faithfully Attended to, and Goods Delivered FREE of Charge to any Part of the City.

> It seems almost a pity that any of the beautiful shade trees in town should be cut down; but, to make room for fine buildings in the business part of the town, they must go. The two venerable hao trees on either side of McIntyre's store-yard, on King-street, should be preserved, provided the awkward little step-up in the side-walk beneath their shade is graded off in some manner.

The Honolulu Advertiser, March 14, 1883

Hau Tree Slips.

When the hau tree outside the excavations at the corner of King and Fort streets, was being cut down the other day, several kamaainas gathered around and, taking out their pocket knives, cut off slips for planting at their homes. The tree is an old landmark and had reached its seventy-eighth year when felled by the woodman's axe. Mrs. Nakuina was one of those who took a slip and E. Faxon Bishop was another. Mr. Bishop took a slip on account of his wife who was a Walker and one of the owners of the property upon which the new block is soon to be erected.

Charles Brewer. I recall distinctly, at this period, the planting of the hau trees along the sides of the roads. They were cut up in the mountains, some ten or twelve feet long, destitute of any branches, and the trunks were about the thickness of a man's arm. These were stuck in the ground, and the earth filled in around them. To what size they may have grown since then your reader can tell better than I. (The last succumbed with the erection of the McIntyre Building.—Ed.)

The Hawaiian Gazette, September 23, 1904

Evening Bulletin, December 8, 1900

The large hau tree on the King Street side of the McIntyre corner, "an old landmark", was cut down in December 1900.

McInerny's shoe department moved into the McIntyre Building in 1926 and hired contractor Charles Ingvorsen to do $20,000 in "extensive repairs".

The building was "modernized and enlarged" in 1948 at a cost of nearly $1M. The cost included adding a third floor plus $200,00 for fixtures, furniture, elevator, air conditioning, 40 new mannequins, and a Muzak sound system. The original terra cotta exterior was covered with corrugated asbestos. Two large "laupahoehoe" or "leaves of lava" columns from Puna, Hawaii, flanked the front entrance.

Honolulu Star-Bulletin, March 6, 1948

Hawaiian sculptor Roy E. King was commissioned to create "four full-sized authentic ancient Hawaiian gods on two stone columns in the men's clothing department" carved out of blue rock. King also carved the 15' x 8' koa shield weighing 2 tons that was featured prominently on the front of the building.

The interior also featured inlaid ceramic tiles "with authentic Hawaiian designs" created by California ceramic artist William Meyer. The completely remodeled store opened on March 8, 1948.

Honolulu Star-Bulletin, February 25, 1948

The building was condemned by the City and County of Honolulu for $933,760 as part of the Fort Street Mall project, and Tajiri Lumber Ltd. demolished it in June 1968. The site today is an open courtyard.

2022

KAUIKEOLANI BUILDING

120 S. King Street
1914 – 1983 (1922 addition, 1960 remodel)
Architect/Builder: Ripley & Davis (1914), Ripley, Davis & Fishbourne (1922) /
Lord-Young Engineering Company (1914), Charles Ingvorsen (1922)

The Kauikeolani Building was built on the site of two 2-story brick buildings built between 1885 and 1890 that were warehouses for Lewers & Cooke that later housed the Hustace Grocery and Evening Bulletin offices.

Anticipating the new federal building would be built across the street on the Mahuka tract (Lewers & Cooke lumberyard), the Charles Brewer Estate, represented by the Hawaiian Trust Company Ltd, hired Ripley and Davis to design a building that was "four-story, class A, reinforced concrete, with an up-to-date elevator".

"The intention in fact is to make it the most modern business edifice, both in appearance and convenience, in the Pacific west of San Francisco".

They named the building "Kauikeolani" the same name as the children's hospital, and it was named after the wife of one of the principal stockholders, Mrs. A.S. Wilcox.

Honolulu Star-Bulletin, April 26, 1913

It was built by the Lord-Young Engineering Company at a cost of $110,000 and had 14,700 square feet of floor space. The basement held a 70-ton "five-play chrome steel" vault with a 12-ton steel door that had two combination locks and a 72-hour triple time lock.

"The whole construction is a guarantee against dynamite, fire or mob violence, and will defy earthquakes".

A 5th floor designed by Ripley, Davis & Fishbourne was added in 1922 by Charles Ingvorsen. Mark Potter designed a 2-story addition in back in 1948 built by Walker-Moody.

The Bank of Hawaii leased the building in 1960 and "modernized" it at a cost of $200,000 which included a gold screen that completely covered up the front façade and Doric columns.

Hawaii State Archives

Honolulu Star-Bulletin, January 24, 1960

The building was demolished in 1983 for the $126M Executive Center project designed by Jo Paul Rognstad and built by Charles Pankow Associates for developer L Robert Allen.

The site today is an open courtyard plus the exit driveway from the Executive Center Parking Garage.

2022

HOME INSURANCE BUILDING

115-129 S. King Street

1930 – 1966
Architect/Builder: Charles W. Dickey / John L. Cliff

Honolulu Star-Bulletin, June 1, 1929

The structure will be two stories in height of modernistic type of architecture that will conform with its neighbor on the ewa side, the new E O. Hall building. There will be a four-foot alley on each side, and a ten-foot alley next the Castle & Cooke building, thus providing for ample light and air circulation. Ventilation will be increased by an arcade in the center of the building, leading back to an open court, 24 feet square. This court will be beautified with a tile pyramid and an abundance of vegetation.

A black and gold color scheme will be carried out on the exterior of the building The walls will be cream and white stucco with broad fluted black terra cotta columns with gold tile in the flutes. The cornice will be of terra cotta with sawtoothed bottom edge with gold leaf on the edge. The marquise across the front will be black and gold.

The whole building will be of reinforced concrete with steel windows and hollow tile partitions.

The Honolulu Advertiser, September 1, 1929

Designed by Charles W. Dickey, this building was built by John L. Cliff for $75,354. It was built at the same time as the adjoining new E.O. Hall Building and was planned as a "tax-payer" with only 2 floors and no basement until a larger more permanent building could be built on the site. The building permit was obtained on October 16, 1929.

As Dickey described it, "The exterior is of real marble, real terra cotta and real tile with gold burned in. The grilles are copper, painted black and inlaid with gold leaf". The grand opening was April 2, 1930.

Home Insurance was founded in 1911 and managed by Zeno K. Myers with Cecil Brown from First National Bank as president, John A. McCandless as vice-president, along with Norman Watkins, F.D. Lowyer, A.S. Wilcox, and Chu Gem. Their first location was across the street in the O'Neill Building.

Honolulu Star-Bulletin, April 1, 1930

The site was previously the lumber yard and lumber sheds of the Lewers & Cooke Company for many years in the late 1800's. It was the site of the "290 Hack Stand" in the days of King Kalākaua, later E.H. Lewis's taxi stand from 1919 to 1929.

The Home Insurance Building was demolished in 1966 by Ken Brady Construction to make way for the $21M Financial Plaza of the Pacific that was designed by Leo S. Wou and Victor Gruen Associates and built by Hawaiian Dredging & Construction Co., Pacific Construction Co., and Swinerton & Walberg Co.

2022

HALEAKALA / ARLINGTON HOUSE

140 S. King Street
1850 – 1900
Architect/Builder: Abner Pākī

Hawaii State Archives

Abner Kuhoʻoheiheipahu Pākī, the King's Chamberlain, and his wife Kōnia officially opened this "splendid new house" on July 31, 1850, on the 7th anniversary of the restoration of the islands by Vice Admiral Richard Thomas.

This was a day of great celebration and Pākī entertained "Her Majesty the Queen, the King's Ministers and high Judicial Officers with their ladies, High Chiefs, Members of His Majesty's Privy Council, their Excellencies, the Governors of Islands, and other personages to the number of about fifty".

Pākī, said to be about 6'-4" and weighing 300 pounds was born around 1808 on Molokai and was a high chief during the reign of Kamehameha III. He and Kōnia had a daughter, Bernice Pauahi Pākī, who later married Charles Reed Bishop. Their *hānai* daughter, Lydia Pākī, would later become Queen Liliʻuokalani.

The grounds were known as Haleakalā and the house was called ʻAikupika, which translates to "Egypt".

☞ IMPROVEMENTS.—Notwithstanding the exceedingly high price of lumber just now, we notice several new buildings going up, and others undergoing the process of repair and alteration.

Among the former, the mansion of Mr. Paki, a large and well-built stone edifice, takes the precedence, and will be an ornament and a great improvement to that part of the town. We know

The Polynesian, November 10, 1849

His Excellency, A. Paki, had postponed the opening of his splendid new house, until that day. At three o'clock he entertained at dinner, Her Majesty the Queen, the King's Ministers and high Judicial Officers, with their ladies, the High Chiefs, Members of His Majesty's Privy Council, their Excellencies, the Governors of Islands, and other personages to the number of about fifty.

The Polynesian, August 3, 1850

Paul Emmert, 1854

Liliʻuokalani and John Dominis were married at Haleakala on September 16, 1862.

Bernice Pauahi Bishop inherited the property and the Bishops lived here until her death in 1884. She left the property to her husband, Charles R. Bishop. Liliʻuokalani wrote, "I could not help feeling it ought to have been left to me... This wish of my heart was not gratified, and at the present day strangers stroll through the grounds or lounge on the piazzas of that home once so dear to me."

Charles Reed Bishop came to Hawaii in 1846 and although he only had an 8th grade education he quickly became one of the wealthiest men in the islands from banking, real estate, agriculture, and other investments. He met Bernice Pauahi Pākī in 1847 while she was a student at the Chiefs' Children's School.

In spite of her parents wanting her to marry Prince Lot instead, Bernice married Bishop in 1850. Her parents boycotted the wedding but later consented and let them live in the big house.

King Street, looking waikiki from Fort Street, c.1855

From 1886 to 1889 the building was rented out as Mrs. Dudoit's boarding house.

Hon. C. R. Bishop's residence, on King street, has been let to Mrs. Dudoit, and will shortly be opened as a first-class boarding house.

Daily Honolulu Press, February 27. 1886

THE DUDOIT HOUSE.

"The Dudoit House" is an appellation familiar to most people in this town. But it sometimes misleads, on account of being applied to two different houses, which have no connection with each other. There is a cottage on the Hawaiian Hotel grounds, fronting on Beretania street, known as the Old Dudoit House, but by "the Dudoit House" is usually meant the private hotel kept by Mrs. Dudoit. It is situate on King street, and was formerly the residence of Hon. C. R. Bishop.

Evening Bulletin, November 20, 1888

COMPLIMENTARY CONCERT AND DANCE.

At the residence of Mrs. Dudoit, King street, last evening, there was a fashionable assembly of about sixty persons, the occasion being a complimentary concert by the Royal Hawaiian Band to Mrs. W. E. Breton, and a dance given by Miss A. Dudoit, who recently returned from the States. The evening being admirable, promenading about the spacious grounds and verandahs during the music, was most enjoyable. Following is the programme of the concert:

March—Old England..........Rappey
Overture—Festival.............Bach
Waltz—My Queen.............Coote
Selection—Robert Bruce....Bonniseau
   Ai; Hiki Mai Ipo Lauae,
Selection—The Bohemian Girl....Balfe
Gavotte—Queen's Own........Amilton
Waltz—Jubilee..................Coote
Polka—Royal Hussars..........Hertel
   God Save the Queen.
   Hawaii Ponoi.

Dancing followed to the music of a string band, and was continued until after midnight. Refreshments were served at 11 o'clock.

The house was nicely decorated with lanterns and flowers.

Evening Bulletin, November 30, 1889

THE HAMILTON HOUSE.

The Hamilton House, conducted by Hamilton Johnson, is almost full of boarders. On taking the place, formerly the Dudoit House, Mr. Johnson had it renovated and refurnished throughout, and fitted with thirty-eight incandescent electric lights from the Government system. The bedrooms are large, airy, opening on wide verandas, and furnished with old oak sets, the beds being peculiarly fitted to woo "nature's sweet restorer." The cuisine is conducted on the principle of giving a choice home table. Not only is the best staple diet, cooked in the varied styles one would relish at home, served, but the market is ransacked for seasonable delicacies. Yesterday evening the writer dropped in on the host and was regaled with real turtle soup as the starter of a substantial dinner the dessert comprising a variety of the finest California and Hawaiian fresh fruits. Even choice grapes are not considered too good for the Hamilton household's board. Many of the present complement of the house are visitors from abroad, who find there besides good fare the comforts of a quiet domestic circle. The proprietor has made great improvements in the spacious grounds surrounding the house. His residence hotel, Waikiki Villa, has continued to be well patronized since the close of the out-of-town season, which speaks well for the management of it by Mrs. Johnson.

Evening Bulletin, February 21, 1890

In early 1890 it became Hamilton House, owned by Hamilton Johnson who also owned the Waikiki Villa.

The Hamilton House was a first-class lodging establishment well known for its fancy menus and elaborate dinners.

Madame Sarah Bernhardt was a guest in May 1891 during the steamer *Monowai*'s stay in port, with "a suite of rooms specially fitted up for the occasion".

On August 31, 1891, they hosted an unusual "Cobweb Party" with cords of twine "woven and interwoven" throughout the building with prizes attached to the ends.

The hotel temporarily closed on October 5, 1891, when Hamilton Johnson bought 50% of the Hawaiian Hotel from G.W. Macfarlane.

The menu comprised:

Soup.
Consomme aux Asperges. Creme de la Creme.
Fish.
Pond Mullet, Sauce aux Capres.
Entrees.
Squab, Sauce Choud de Volaille, Fricasse, Shrimp Curry, Orange Ice.
Roast.
Turkey, Bread Sauce.
Filet de Boeuf, Sauce Madero.
Ham aux Epinard.
Salad Russe.
Fresh Asparagus Hawaiienness, Sauce Hollandaise.
Vegetables.
Cauliflower, Stewed Tomatoes.
Pomme de Terre au Beurre et aux Fines Herbes.
Entremets.
Vanilla Ice Cream. Snow Pudding.
Strawberry Short Cake.
Fruit Cake. Chocolate Cake. Sponge Cake.
Macarooons. Confectionery.
Dessert.
Apples. Grapes. Bananas. Pine Apples.
Assorted Nuts. Raisins.
Tea and Coffee.

During the progress of the repast conversation flowed in natural and easy channels. Savory viands appeased each sharpened appetite, and softened music filtered through leafy environments fell with enchanting effect on each ear. The following programme was rendered:

March—Honolulu................Berger
Overture—Fra Diavolo..........Auber
Waltz—My Queen................Coote
Selection—Bohemian Girl.......Balfe
Gavotte—Welcome...............Kluss
Polka—The Royal Hussars......Hertel
Selection—Pinafore...........Sullivan
Galop—Come Again..............Faust
God Save the Queen,
Hawaii Ponoi.

Evening Bulletin, March 15, 1890

Cob-webs.

The guests of the Hamilton House and Waikiki Villa amused themselves Monday evening at the latter named place unraveling cobwebs. The webs consisted of many cords of twine woven and interwoven, passed through every keyhole, knothole and crevice, over and around and tangled every way imaginable. At one end of each cord was attached a prize, at the other end an entangler; the object being to trace the string to the end tied to the prize, which was done with considerable amusement to all who took part or looked on. Dancing was enjoyed by a few and other amusements tended to make the evening one of the many pleasant occasions at the Villa. Light refreshments were served to the taste of those present.

Honolulu Advertiser, September 1, 1891

Col. G. W. Macfarlane has sold a half interest in the Hawaiian Hotel to Mr. Hamilton Johnson, proprietor of the Hamilton House. Waikiki Villa, hitherto a branch of the Hamilton House, becomes the same to the Hotel. The Hamilton House is to be closed forthwith, but its lease retained by the Hotel proprietors, so that the house may be reopened when business warrants. Mr. Johnson will assume the management of the Hawaiian Hotel to-morrow.

Evening Bulletin, September 30, 1891

They auctioned off all the household furniture on Ocrober 9, 1891, including wicker sofas and rockers, parlor chairs, rugs, oak and ash bedroom sets, mattresses, mosquito nets, crocker, glassware, and a fine Westermayer piano.

On January 19, 1893, the former Hamilton House became known as "Camp Boston" – the headquarters for the blue jackets from the USS Boston who were brought in as a show of force during the overthrow of the Hawaiian monarchy.

> The battalion from the United States cruiser Boston on duty on shore have been at last domiciled in decent quarters, in the late Hamilton House. They marched to their new quarters this afternoon and their pleasure, at change of quarters, was noticeable.

Evening Bulletin, January 19, 1893

BRANCHING OUT.

Mr. T. E. Krouse Leases the Bishop Premises.

Mr. T. E. Krouse, the manager of the Eagle and Arlington hotels, has leased the Hamilton house on King street for a term of years. Mr. Krouse's rapidly increasing business is the cause of his new departure. His new acquisition will be known as the Arlington. The building will be entirely renovated, both inside and outside. Painters and paper hangers are at work now, and Mr. Krouse expects to have the house open by June 1st. It will be newly furnished throughout.

A force of men will be put to work on the grounds today and the handsome lawns and flower beds will be put in perfect order.

Mr. Krouse will retain the present Arlington premises, but when the new house is opened it will contain dining rooms for both places.

The Hawaiian Gazette, May 16, 1893

On May 16, 1893, Thomas (Tommy) E. Krouse leased the house and incorporated it into his adjoining Arlington Hotel premises on Hotel Street. Krouse also owned the Eagle House on Nuʻuanu Street above Beretania Street.

The house was officially reopened on June 1, 1893, with additional cottages, lawns for tennis and croquet, plus cages of birds and animals.

A New Hotel.

Manager T. E. Krouse, of the Arlington hotel, has everything in readiness for the opening of the Bishop premises today. It will be known as the Arlington annex. The main entrance for both houses will be on King street. The dining room is situated in the annex.

The Honolulu Advertiser, June 1, 1893

> The invitation extended, to be present at the private exhibition of the loud-talking phonograph, in the parlor of the Arlington House, last evening was generally accepted and a couple of hours was spent pleasantly in listening to various songs and speeches.

Hawaii Holumua Progress, February 9, 1894

After the purchase of the McGrew premises by Alexander Young in early 1900, the Bishop Estate coordinated with them on a new 60' wide street through both properties to be called Bishop Street.

The Arlington Hotel closed on September 1, 1900, and all the furnishings and grounds and outbuildings were auctioned off over several days beginning on September 6, 1900.

> "Before the echoes of the auctioneer's mallet have died away the wreckers will have begun the work of tearing to pieces the building and dismantling the beautiful grounds so long the home of charming hospitality and in which so many comers to Hawaiian shores have looked their first on the foliage and exquisite growths of the Islands."
>
> The Honolulu Advertiser, September 6, 1900

The Arlington Hotel building was purchased for $180 by contractor John Ouderkirk who was required to remove the material in the building within 30 days. It was estimated Ouderkirk would clear $2,500 from the salvage.

The private zoo on the grounds was also auctioned off, and included squirrels, cockatoos, Java sparrows, fan tail pigeons, and a dozen other animals.

But by far the most unusual item sold was a cage containing two monkeys.

> "The monkeys seemed to know by instinct that something working for their harm was brewing. They ran nervously about the cage and mounted to their armchairs when Auctioneer Fisher began the sale".

At first there were no bids, but they finally sold for $15. "The broken-hearted apes clasped each other and wept. This is when the Advertiser artist caught them with Will E. Fisher nearby."

The Honolulu Advertiser, September 8, 1900

PASSING OF A LANDMARK

OLD BISHOP PLACE PRACTICALLY DEMOLISHED.

Gangs of men are Busy removing the Rubbish and material from the Grounds.

Time and the march of improvement level all things. What was but yesterday the cradle of a dynasty is today a pile of rubbish, a mass of broken timbers. The demolition of the old Arlington hotel has been progressing at such a rapid rate ever since the sale of the property was effected, that practically nothing but a memory is left of that famous place. The hotel building proper, the famous home of the Bishops is no more and but for a few small cottages which the purchasers have failed to remove, the entire lot from King to Hotel street, has been cleared of buildings.

While the buildings may be practically gone the extensive tract is strewn with piles of wood and lumber, heaps of plater, bricks and coral building rock and it will be some weeks before the gang of men can clear all of this stuff away. The ruin which is every where visible impresses one strikingly of a battle field, such a battle field as Stephen Crane would have imagined before he really viewed the place of actuality, so great and gaunt is the ruin that stalks about. No better conception of the extensive enterprise contemplated by Alexander Young can be secured than by a view of the property as it exists at the present time. It looks big enough to be the site for the Waldorf-Astoria.

"There was a time when the haole would have thought it an honor to visit this place," sighed a loyal royalist, "but now—look at it." Truly the place seems as desolate as the Walls of Balclutha and no wonder it is that none of the older Hawaiians can pass the spot without feeling a lump come into their throats for old, primative as the place was, it stood for much to them. It was once the gathering place of loyal people, the early home of their last Queen the center of a famous and fast disappearing hospitality. The old Bishop residence was to Hawaiians the link which bound society with the state for it was there that the powerful chieftains and their consorts mingled with other leaders in the nation's affairs and watched a queen that was to be, developed in sprightly womanhood.

Old Paki the biggest and one of the most powerful chieftains of the group was the father of the house. He built it for his home and for a time he held almost regal sway there. He maintained an establishment which was feudal in character. He scarce knew how many servants he had to serve him but the King knew that Paki could summoned 1000 armed fighting men at a moment's notice and the favor of the old chief was courted by the reigning monarchs. They realized too well his power. Strong enough to be a king-maker, they knew his indomitable will, and feared it. But as Paki grew old and the house passed from his possession, he was content to distribute justice as district magistrate where Judge Wilcox now holds court, and a memorial tablet in Kawaiahao church perpetuates his memory.

A hole in the ground, a dozen heavy beams, a few bricks, a pile of stone is all that can be seen of the once famous house. Nothing has been respected, everything profaned, but what matters it in these days of progression what the former owner was or what the present owner was. The spirit of the Nineteenth Century is no respector of sentiment. He throttles sentiment, he scorns reproach, he triumphs over the traditions of a passing race.

The tall, red hued wall is rapidly disappearing and within a few days it will be but a broken mass to litter the grounds. Cords of fire wood have been cut from the grand old trees which once helped make the grounds among the most beautiful in the Islands. The vines are torn down and trampled under foot, the plants are overturned and demolished. And where only the carriages of wealth were permitted to travel heavy teams of work horses are busy carting away the stuff to every part of the town. Well may the Hawaiian race pause to shed a tear and say with Shakespeare, as it takes a long last look at the ruin "Tis true, 'tis pity and pity 'tis, 'tis true." But the old house has run its course. It has served its purpose and now in the days of its decadence it can serve no nobler purpose than to adorn a tale and paint the moral of a fading race.

The Hawaiian Star, October 4, 1900

BANK OF HAWAII

140 S. King Street

1927 – 1968
Architect/Builder: Hardie Phillip / Hawaiian Contracting Co.

The Bank of Hawaii was started on December 17, 1897, by P.C. Jones, E.A. Jones, Charles M. Cooke, and J.B. Atherton in the Safe Deposit Building on Fort Street. They moved to the Judd Building in March of 1899 and later purchased the land at this corner in 1922 for $250,000 to build their own building.

The bank hired architect Hardie Phillip from the New York firm of Mayers, Murray & Phillip, Bertram Grosvenor Goodhue Associates to design this building. James Hopkins was the supervising architect. As the architects explained it, "the exterior architecture is an Hawaiian adaptation of the Spanish". The roof was dull green Granada tile and Davis sandstone from Molokai was used for the exterior finishing.

The lobby featured two large maps designed by cartographer Ernest Clegg and a tapa ceiling designed by Ludmila Timotheff and Julian Berla based on rare works in the Bishop Museum.

It was built on the site of the Arlington House by the Hawaiian Contracting Co. Ltd. for $491,000, but with extras the final cost was closer to $600,000. Opening day was March 28, 1927, and the Honolulu Star-Bulletin celebrated by publishing a special 15-page supplement.

Pineapples, sugar cane tops and other Hawaiian motifs are noticeable in this charming solid Bronze Grill, left in its natural Verde Antique Patina finish. This finish is noticeable also in the other Wm. H. Jackson Co's bronze gates, doors, windows, check desks, counter screens, cases, mail chute, clock, ceiling light and sidewalk lights.

Honolulu Star-Bulletin, March 28, 1927

The Honolulu Star-Bulletin, March 28, 1927

BANK OF HAWAII ANNEX ON BISHOP STREET SITE

The building in the center of the group pictured herewith is the new Bank of Hawaii annex which will be constructed in Bishop St. adjoining the bank premises. Construction is to begin early this fall. In the group shown here the bank building is at the left, while the building at the right was blocked in by the architect to illustrate how the new structure will fit into future building in that vicinity.

Honolulu Star-Bulletin, August 18, 1928

Hardie Phillip designed a new annex along Bishop Street in 1928, but it was never built.

The Bank of Hawaii Building was demolished in 1968 and replaced by the $7.5M 15-story Bishop Trust Building designed by William F. Cann of the Bank Building and Equipment Corporation of St. Louis that was completed in 1970.

The six 4' x 8' bronze bas-relief plaques commissioned by Clarence Hyde Cooke and designed and cast by New York sculptor Lee Lawrie were salvaged, with four going in the new Bank of Hawaii building across King Street and two in the new 15-story Bishop Trust Company building.

> *The two plaques which faced King Street depict Hawaiians shaping a canoe and casting a fish net. The four on the Bishop Street side portray ancient and modern means of transportation and livelihood.*

The heavy green-bronze doors and expensive koa and monkeypod furnishings were also salvaged.

Honolulu Star-Bulletin, April 6, 1969 2022

EMMELUTH BUILDING

141-145 S. King Street

1897 – 1923

Architect/Builder: Ripley & Dickey / Thomas B. Walker

Paradise of the Pacific, 1902

This building was designed by Ripley & Dickey and built by Thomas B. Walker. It had two stories with an iron and pressed brick front and a third floor with a mansard roof covered by Spanish copper tiles.

There was 40' frontage on King Street and it was 80' deep with a concrete basement. It had the first metal ceiling in a business "in panels, beautiful in design and painted in light shades".

It also had an electric elevator, one of the first in Honolulu, used as a freight elevator along with a dumb waiter for smaller items. The first floor was the showroom which showcased an "assortment of zinc and enamel bath tubs in various sizes" and the second and third floors were used as repair shops and manufacturing with the plumbing department in the basement.

John Emmeluth came to Hawaii from Cincinnati in 1879 and quickly became Honolulu's principal supplier of plumbing and household furnishings.

He was one of the leaders of the Reform Party who forced King Kalākaua to sign the Bayonet Constitution, and he was also a prominent member of the Committee of Public Safety which overthrew the monarchy in 1893. He was elected to the Territorial Legislature in 1900 as a member of the Home Rule Party and became known as "Boss Emmeluth" by some, and the "drainpipe statesman" by others.

"EMMELUTH BLOCK."

Vill Appear at Top of Fine Brick Building Soon.

"Emmeluth Block" will, in about four months, appear at the top of a fine three-story brick building, to be erected opposite the Arlington Hotel grounds on King street.

Work on the foundation has already begun. The building has been talked of for sometime, but there was delay in arranging details. Messrs. Ripley & Dickey prepared the plans for it. Suggestions for making it one of the prettiest business houses in town were received from abroad and also from local authorities. That is, as to details—after the building proper has been finished by the masons.

The Emmeluth Block will have a street frontage of 40 feet, and a depth of 80 feet. It will contain three full stories and a basement. The latter will be so extensive as to be practically a fourth floor. Brick will be used in the building. The front will be highly ornamented. The following description has been furnished a reporter for the Advertiser by Mr. Emmeluth:

First floor, iron front, with granite piers. Second floor, stone front. Third floor, copper Spanish tile in squares. Above the first story there will be an iron frame balcony with glazed floor, and copper apron and balustrade. Above this, lighting the second story, will be three triple Mullion windows. The side lights will be fixed, the center ones fastened at the top. For the mansard three handsome dormers, with fancy hoods have been planned.

The interior will also be quite attractive. Two huge girders will span the lower story from front to rear, giving the building great strength. The ceiling will be of the pretty steel material used in the Hawaiian Opera House, save that it will be of a different pattern. Ventilator pieces will be set here and there. The squares, girders and false girders will be fancy in design.

In the building will be an elevator, as well as stairs. The former will run by hydraulic pressure. It will be used for all purposes—moving freight and transporting customers from floor to floor. A light well will follow the elevator shaft from the ceiling. It will be a wide affair, and will open upon the office on the lower floor. The stairway will also follow the elevator. Each floor will have two flights or runs, and will each time open alongside the elevator doors.

The basement of the building will be used for heavy storage, and the plumbing business of Emmeluth & Co. On the first floor the general business of the concern will be carried on, and there, too, the office will be located.

The second floor will be reserved for light storage, and on the third the general workshops of the company will be located.

Altogether, the building will be one of the handsomest business structures in Honolulu, and will be a permanent improvement to this quarters of the town. Emmelth & Co. expect to get into it next summer.

The Honolulu Advertiser, January 13, 1897

The Emmeluth Building.

Tom Walker has the contract to put up the stone foundations and brick walls of the new Emmeluth building on King street, and is rushing the work. The owner furnishes all materials and Tom does the rest.

Evening Bulletin, February 10, 1897

There was some major drama during construction when Thomas B. Walker took a rifle and fired a shot at John Emmeluth from behind the stone wall on the Arlington grounds.

The bullet went through a window sash on the third floor and lodged in some timbers, only 4' over the heads of Emmeluth, Walker's brother-in-law Tommy Cummins, and two carpenters.

Emmeluth and Walker had apparently had a discussion earlier in the day about the schedule, and the fact that Walker had been paid but hadn't finished yet.

After the shooting, Walker calmly walked across the street, leaned the rifle against the building, and turned himself in at the Police Station saying, "I want to deliver myself up, I have just shot John Emmeluth." He was sentenced to "one year in prison with hard labor" and was pardoned nine months later.

Many were surprised that Walker had missed, considering he was an excellent marksman who had fought with the British in Abyssinia and with the US Cavalry at the Battle of Powder River.

Emmeluth appeared to take it all in stride and had initially thought the noise was from the adjoining lumber yard. Walker had apparently been drinking.

2022

Immediately adjacent on the ewa side of the Emmeluth Building was the house and sign-painting business of Stanley Stephenson. In addition to painting and wallpapering, in 1901 he was appointed by the Territory of Hawaii's Treasurer's Office to be in charge of renumbering all the streets and buildings in Honolulu.

Honolulu: The Cross-Roads of the Pacific, 1913

EVERYTHING = = =
---THAT IS ARTISTIC IN---
WALL DECORATION

Our business calls for the display of good taste, a thorough knowledge of color values, and artistic harmony. Our experience and training enables us to offer suggestions in Artistic Wall Papers. We make sketches if you wish.

STANLEY STEPHENSON,
WALL PAPER ARTIST, KING ST.

FIRST NATIONAL BANK

141 S. King Street

1925 – 1966

Architect/Builder: York & Sawyer / Charles Ingvorsen

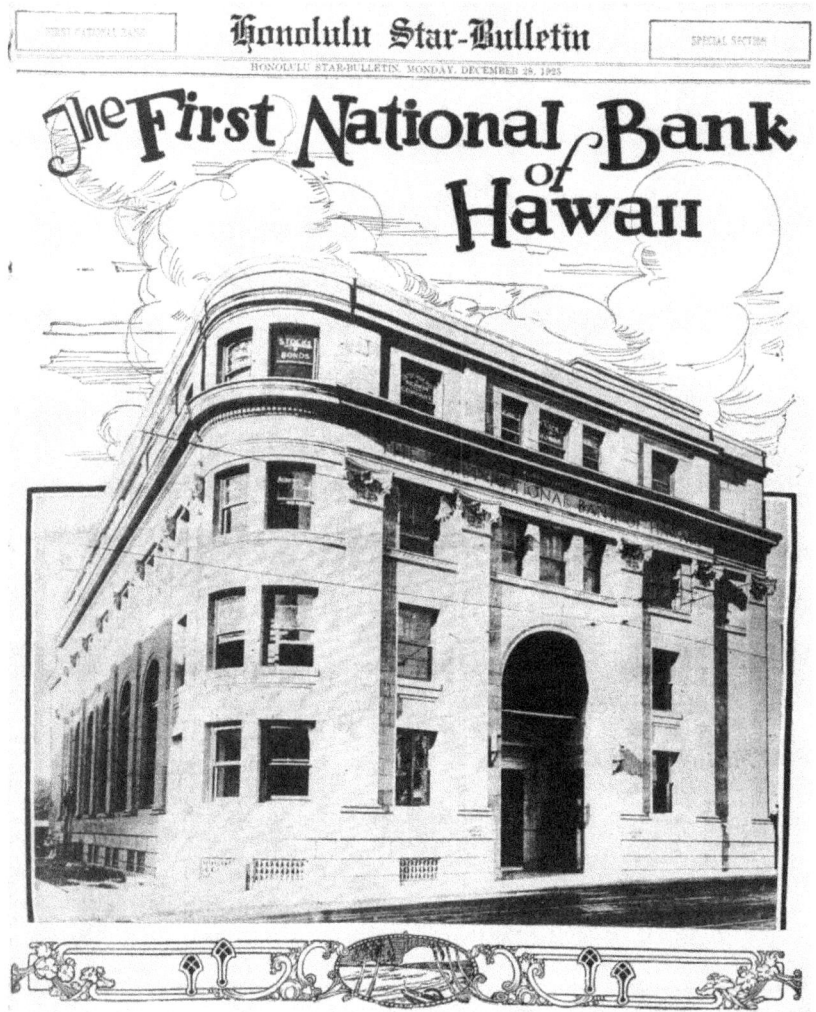

Honolulu Star-Bulletin, December 28, 1925

After 25 years in the McIntyre Building at Fort and Hotel, the First National Bank demolished the Emmeluth Building in 1923 and built this building designed by New York architects York & Sawyer with local supervision by Rothwell Kangeter & Lester and construction by Charles Ingvorsen for $400,000.

But it took a complicated three-way land deal to make it happen. First National Bank traded their vacant lot at the mauka/waikiki corner of Bishop and Merchant streets for this lot which was owned by the Bank of Bishop. James D. McInerny, who owned the makai/waikiki lot at King and Bishop streets, gave the Bank of Bishop a 30-year lease with option to purchase so they could acquire the entire half block to build their new building, to be called the S.M. Damon Building.

"Architecturally, the new bank building is a composite, with the forms and columns following classical precedent, and with much suggestive of Italian Renaissance." The exterior walls were covered in stucco, a first for Hawaii, made of Sacramento River sand and mortar mixed on the mainland to imitate Indiana limestone. Napoleon gray marble was used for the interior wainscotting, with Lepanto or Tennessee marble for the floors and bases, constructed by local tile contractor J.A. Reed.

Sculptor Julius Rosenstein was responsible for the interior and exterior ornamentation, utilizing models created by New York artists.

The vault weighed 200,000 pounds and came from Mosler Safe Company in Baltimore via the Panama Canal on the *Tuscaloosa* whose captain coincidentally attended the same school in Brooklyn, New York, as bank president L. Tenney Peck.

The bank officially opened for business in their new location on December 28, 1925.

The Honolulu Advertiser, February 24, 1926

Although architect Guy N. Rothwell said the stucco finish "would last for centuries", the building was demolished 41 years later in 1966 for the Financial Plaza of the Pacific.

LEWERS & COOKE BUILDING

169-185 S. King Street

1902 – 1960
Architect/Builder: Oliver G. Traphagen / Hawaiian Engineering & Construction

The Honolulu Advertiser, January 1, 1902

Completed in September 1902, this new headquarters for Lewers & Cooke was designed by Oliver G. Traphagen and built by the Hawaiian Engineering & Construction Company.

It had a frontage of 154' on King Street and was 80' deep. The front was "a beautiful shade of pressed brick and terra cotta" with ornamental iron work, mosaic floors, and electric elevators for three stores.

The concrete foundation was 18" thick to account for a layer of black volcanic sand about 2' deep that was subject to tidal flows.

During the attack on Pearl Harbor on December 7, 1941, a shell exploded on the third floor of the building, ostensibly fired by one of the American ships shooting at the Japanese planes.

The building was built on the site of the "very pretentious" 1-story "ornamental villa" of Charles T. Gulick which replaced a previous house that burned on June 28, 1883.

Gulick was born in Forked River, NJ, in 1841 to a family of missionaries, and attended Punahou School where he played baseball with the sons of Alexander J. Cartwright.

From 1883 to 1886 he was the Minister of the Interior, appointed by King Kalākaua, and was also acting Minister of Finance. He was briefly Minister of the Interior under Queen Liliʻuokalani in 1892.

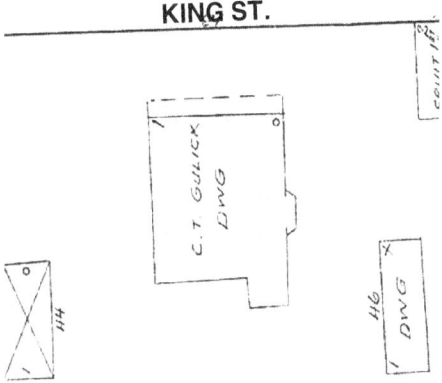

1891 Dakin Map

He would have been Minister of Finance if the 1895 Wilcox Rebellion had succeeded, but he was arrested and tried for treason since the plotters had met at this house. Gulick was convicted and sentenced to death, later reduced to 35 years in prison plus a fine, and then pardoned and released in 1896.

> ing chair on the upper lanai. Where the Lewers & Cooke block now stands on King street was the residence of Charles T. Gulick at, or about that time minister of the Interior. That residence was burned in the early 80's, and (for Honolulu) a very pretentious house erected on its site. This latter house was later removed to the site where it now stands, on the makai side of King street, a short distance waikiki of Piikoi street.

Honolulu Star-Bulletin, June 30, 1917

The house was cut into two pieces and moved near Independence Park in late 1899.

> **A LUMBER YARD.**
>
> The fine homestead of the late Charles T. Gulick, on King street near Alakea, has been purchased by Senator Northrop, of Hawaii, and will be moved via Merchant and King streets to a new lot bought by the Senator in the tract at the corner of Sheridan and King, just Ewa of Independence park.
>
> The Gulick premises, which were purchased by C. M. Cooke for Lewers & Cooke, will be added to the lumber yard of the firm named. It was the first intention to improve the fine property but the business of the owners has increased to such dimensions that yard room is now the most important consideration.

The Hawaiian Star, December 7, 1899

> The old Gulick house is moving toward Independence park at the rate of a mile in two weeks. From last Saturday to now it has reached Alapai street

The Hawaiian Star, December 14, 1899

> **Mr. YOUNG INTERFERES.**
>
> Minister Young has interfered in the slow moving of the old Gulick house to Independence park. He yesterday told the contractors that the street had been blocked too long and that the house must be gotten out of the way at once. Work was kept up all day and all night with the result that the first half of the building has reached its destination and the second half will arrive there this afternoon. Last night the steam roller took the second half in tow and carried it as far as Union Square.

The Hawaiian Star, December 16, 1899

The Lewers & Cooke Building was demolished in 1960 for the Bishop National Bank designed by Lemmon Freeth Haines & Jones and completed in 1962. It in turn was demolished in 1993 for the $175M First Hawaiian Center designed by William Pedersen of the New York architectural firm of Kohn Pedersen Fox (designers of the World Bank Building in Washington, D.C.).

Honolulu Star-Bulletin, June 20, 1959

2022

LINCOLN BLOCK

174-180 S. King Street

1884 – 1982

Architect/Builder: George W. Lincoln (1884), Herbert C. Cayton (1936) / George W. Lincoln (1884), Naotishi Monji & Sengo Tsutsumi (1936)

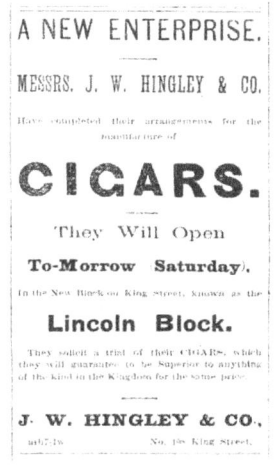
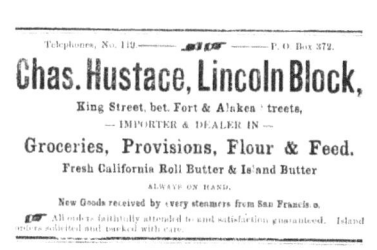

This 2-story brick building with two stores was designed and built by George W. Lincoln in 1884. At the time it was one of the few brick buildings past Fort Street.

From 1911 to 1916 it was the home of the Baron School of Physical Culture, later Baron's Gymnasium run by Frenchman Pierre Baron. In 1925 it became the Young Laundry, and they hired architect Herbert C. Cayton, Naotoshi Monji, and Sengo Tsutsumi to do "extensive alterations" for $13,000 in 1936.

Honolulu Star-Bulletin, October 3, 1936

OCCIDENTAL HOTEL

201-203 S. King Street / 919-929 Alakea Street
1897 – 1950
Architect/Builder: Francis R. Dunn / Peter High & Co.

c.1899

Named after the Occidental Hotel in San Francisco, construction of this building, owned by Edward H.F. Wolter, was the scene of much controversy. Begun in 1896, construction was temporarily halted by the government who claimed it was "not nearly fire proof as it should be". There was a claim that Wolter's title was defective. The contractor, Peter High, had to file suit for final payment of $2,812. And the *Honolulu Advertiser* wrote "while it may not be remarkable for its architectural beauty it at least puts in the shade the buildings further east in the same block".

Mrs. Adolf Shmeden and George Cavanagh were hired to run the hotel with restaurant veteran Cavanagh in charge of catering.

> *"The crowning feature of the whole place is the roof garden, where bananas, palms and vines of all kinds have been started in tubs and boxes. The view from this place is a good one, and the atmosphere delightful."*

Lunch featured "chicken, currie and rice, roast pig and apple sauce, peach pie and other luxuries".

OCCIDENTAL HOTEL,
Cor., King and Alakea Streets,
HONOLULU, H. I.
Mrs. A. Schmeden, Proprietress.

Rooms en suite and single, with board from $5.50 per week, according to requirements of the guests.

The only Roof Promenade Garden in the city.   GEO. CAVENAGH,
Telephone 654,   Manager.

On Friday, January 12, 1900, a military guard was placed around the entire block consisting of men carrying bayonets placed ten feet apart with no one allowed to approach within 10 feet of the guards, all due to a Chinese boy found to have contracted plague that morning. This was the first instance of plaque reported outside of the previously cordoned-off Chinatown.

Approximately 200 people were suddenly under quarantine, including many who had been having lunch at the Occidental Hotel and others who were in the government dispensary on the same block. Fire Engine House No. 1 was also affected but luckily the men and equipment were out fighting a fire.

The entire block except for the Occidental Hotel was set on fire by the Board of Health on Monday, January 15, 1900.

> "As enthusiastic as the Board of Health were in their treatment of bacteriology they had the wisdom to spare the Occidental Hotel, which stands as a most remarkable specimen of architecture that guides show to tourists."

January 15, 1900

In 1950, Henry B. "Heinie" Wolter, son of Edward H.F. Wolter, completed plans on his mother's birthday (September 15) for a new $80,000 building to be completed on his father's birthday (February 22, 1951).

The Honolulu Advertiser, October 5, 1950

The architect was Al Tom and it was built by Oahu Builders (Paul C. Tanigawa and Charles K. Tanigawa). Built of "hollow stone" and originally planned for two stories with provision for three more, only one story was built due to an increase in building costs.

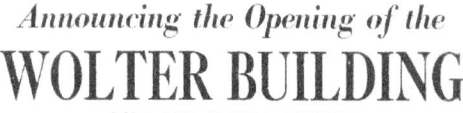

The Honolulu Advertiser, March 3, 1951

Sometime between 1903 and 1911

2022

BURGESS & JOHNSON SHOWROOM

202-210 S. King Street / 1001-1007 Alakea

1928 – 1956

Architect/Builder: Rothwell, Kangeter & Lester / J.L. Young Engineering Co.

The Honolulu Advertiser, July 6, 1928

After outgrowing their two previous locations in six years, J.A. Johnson and Eric W. Burgess hired Rothwell Kangeter & Lester to design a fancy new showroom with parking spaces and a gasoline service station on the King Street side – the first one inside the city's fire limit line.

The *Honolulu Star-Bulletin* ran a 3-page spread on opening day, July 6, 1928, and *The Honolulu Advertiser* published a special 6-page supplement. Burgess & Johnson carried REO, Hupmobile, Marmon automobiles and Moreland trucks along with Red Crown gasoline and Zeroline oil.

The Honolulu Advertiser, July 6, 1928

SITE OF NEW BURGESS & JOHNSON SALESROOM

The Honolulu Advertiser, July 6, 1928 2022

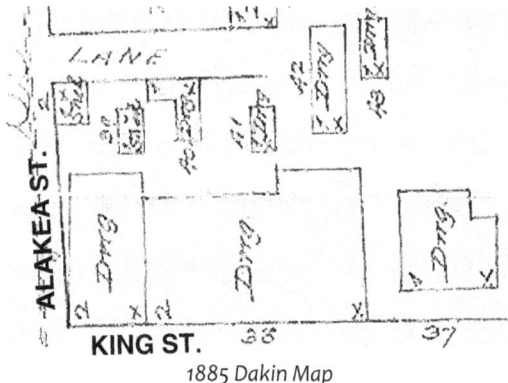

1885 Dakin Map

There was a large 2-story wooden house on this corner in 1885. It was gone shortly after 1899 and the corner was vacant and used as a garden until built on by Burgess & Johnson. The photo above shows a 1-story building that had been a Christian Church.

The land was previously owned by Samuel C. Allen who had built three houses closer to Richards Street.

In May of 1932 Burgess & Johnson added on to their building, but by October the company was bankrupt, likely one of many victims of the Great Depression.

The building later housed a marine supply store selling Evinrude outboard motors and then briefly a restaurant until becoming the offices of the Honolulu Finance & Thrift Company from 1936 to 1950. It was the Trading Center Store until the building was demolished in 1956 for a parking lot.

The site is now the $36M 22-story Central Pacific Bank building designed by Ernest H. Hara & Associates and completed in 1983.

2022

ADVERTISER BUILDING

213-215 S. King Street

1913 – present
Architect/Builder: Emory & Webb / Pacific Engineering Company

Sunday Advertiser, December 8, 1912

Extending 153' all the way to Merchant Street and with a frontage on King Street of 53', the Advertiser Building was designed by Walter Emory and Marshall Webb and constructed by the Pacific Engineering Company in 1913 for $38,390.

General offices were on the ground floor along with the press room, stock rooms and mailing department. The editorial offices were upstairs and included rooms for the *Kuokoa* and *O Luso* newspapers. The art department, engraving plant, and photograph gallery were on the third floor.

Eventually needing more space, they later took over the Podmore Building at the corner of Merchant and Alakea streets. They moved to a new building at Kapiolani, South, and King streets in 1930.

The building was remodeled in 1931 by Rothwell & Lester and renamed the Arcade Building since they added an internal hallway with space for 18 shops.

The Advertiser Building was built on the site of painters and paperhangers Spanton & Lund, the Hawaiian Marble Works owned by contractor Fred Harrison, plus a grocery and a restaurant.

These buildings were burned along with the rest of the block on January 15, 1900. Harrison removed the tombstones beforehand and had them fumigated. Joseph R. Mills' grocery was on Merchant Street.

King Street side, January 1900

Merchant Street side, January 1900

King Street side, 2022

Merchant Street side, 2022

HAWAIIAN ELECTRIC BUILDING

223-227 S. King Street

1901 – present
Architect/Builder: H.L. Kerr

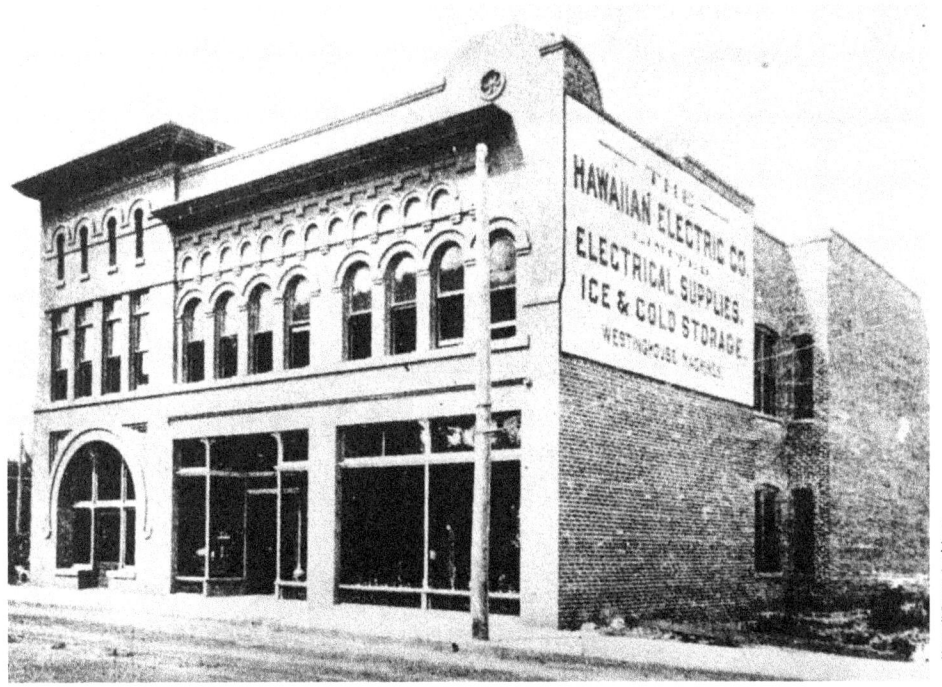

Hawaii State Archives

The Hawaiian Electric Company was incorporated under a franchise from the Hawaiian Government, and their first office in 1891 was at 186 S. King Street. It was a 1-story brick building, 20' x 30' in size, which they quickly outgrew. They hired architect Harry L. Kerr to design a new office, and they laid the foundation in December 1900.

> The Hawaiian Electric Co.'s new office building has a picturesque facade on King street. It is of the most fanciful brickwork seen here. There are different series of windows, arched, rectangular and semi-circular, also a grandly arched doorway.

Honolulu Republican, February 16, 1901

January 1900 (burned by the Board of Health)

1967

2022

Covered up in December 1966 with a louvered metal façade in an attempt at "modernization", the building was restored in 1987 by architect James K. Tsugawa along with contractor Mouse Builders.

S.C. ALLEN COTTAGE

254 S. King Street

1891 – 1928

Architect/Builder: unknown, possibly Lucas Brothers

An Old Landmark Soon to Go In Cause of Progress

With the removal of the old two story house on the corner of King and Richards streets Honolulu will contribute another landmark to the cause of Progress.

The house, built some 40 years ago by the late S. C. Allen was located in the city's residential district and was occupied by families who are well known in the community today. Other occupants have long since passed into the beyond. At one time the family of the late Thomas Wall lived there.

Back in 1897 and '98 it became the rendezvous of the Honolulu newspaper fraternity. During that period it was the home of the late James T. Stacker and his family. Stacker, who was a member of The Advertiser staff, and other scribes congregated around the luncheon table where all problems political and otherwise were threshed out. It was before the days of annexation and government affairs were more or less intriguing.

Though not one of the "newspaper crowd" Dr. James T. Wayson who opened his first office in Honolulu in that home was frequently a member of the discussion group.

Ed Towse, president of the Mercantile Printing Co., and general club member yesterday spent half an hour reminiscing about the old house and the men who gathered there. Among the men were Robert W. Shingle, at that time a reporter on the old Hawaiian Star, and at present an outstanding figure in island politics; Joseph Cranwell with the Hawaiian Star; Archie Steel, who later died in Hilo; Ed Dekum, for many years connected with The Advertiser, now in San Francisco; Will Coney, William Getz, a printer, and the late C. C. Coonley, an artist with The Advertiser.

In those days the house was newly painted and there were flowers in the tiny garden where children played. Many persons have occupied it in the last 28 years, and its last coat of paint has become worn and tired looking. Signs advertising everything from a dress shop to a restaurant removed every vestige of the home aspect and in recent years made it look entirely commercial.

All of the buildings in the block are to be sold at auction on April 9 and will be removed shortly after that date. In the future there will be another building in harmony with the architectural scheme of the Civic Center.

The Honolulu Advertiser, April 4, 1928

This large Victorian "cottage" built by Samuel C. Allen in late 1891 and was one of four built on the mauka/ewa corner property that had been a vacant lot previously owned by John Moanauli.

Allen started a house on King Street in July 1891, and the house on the corner in October 1891.

The cottage on the Richards Street side was built in 1894 by the Lucas Brothers for S.C. Allen. In 1897 it became the office of Dr. James T. Wayson who previously officed in the house on the corner. Dr. Wayson came to Hawaii from San Jose, CA, in 1894 and had been the physician with the Bering Sea whaling fleet.

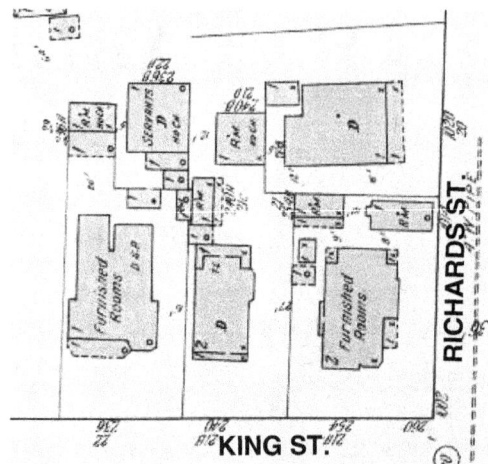

1914 Sanborn Map

The houses were demolished for a parking lot in 1928. The Hawaiian Trust Building designed by Wimberly & Cook with Paul D. Jones was built on the site by Pacific Construction Co. in 1957.

When completed in 1957 it was the tallest building in downtown Honolulu. It was also the first steel-framed building constructed downtown since the 1929 Alexander and Baldwin Building.

The Star-Bulletin called it "Hawaii's largest and most modern business structure… (that) represents everything that is new and progressive in architecture, yet successfully retains much of the Hawaiian flavor of its neighboring Palace and the general art and culture of the islands."

Ben Norris, professor of arts at the University of Hawaii, supervised the color selections and designs for the decorative mural tiles, hand-made wall tiles, and terrazzo flooring. The building's original colors were "predominantly white in coloration for the stucco and concrete walls, with tones of gray, brown and green, and natural lava rock and cast stone for variation".

It was purchased by the State in 1968 and is now known as the Princess Victoria Kamamalu Building.

2022

NEW HAWAIIAN ELECTRIC BUILDING

255 S. King Street / 250 Merchant Street / 916 Richards Street

1927 – present
Architect/Builder: York & Sawyer / Ralph E. Woolley

Considered for the site of a new Federal Building in 1900 and a City Hall in 1915, instead this trapezoidal tract facing Palace Square became the site of the new Hawaiian Electric Building. The building permit was granted on January 28, 1926, for an estimated cost of $578,897, one of the largest ever in Honolulu at the time.

It was designed by Edward York & Philip Sawyer from New York City, with local firm Emory & Webb as supervising architects. York & Sawyer had also designed the US Post Office across the street.

The building has a structural steel frame with reinforced concrete walls on the exterior, hollow tile walls on the interior, and is covered with buff-colored California stucco. Julian Garnsey from Los Angeles painted the Hawaiian murals and decorations, and Julius Rosenstein was the sculptor responsible for the ornamentation of the ceiling in the main hall. The decorative tower conceals a fire escape.

The final cost was $600,000 plus $150,000 for equipment and furnishings. The *Honolulu Star-Bulletin* published a 10-page special supplement on July 23, 1927, and opening day was July 25, 1927.

MONKEYPOD TREES FELLED TO MAKE WAY FOR H. E. BUILDING

Before a large group of spectators the work of felling two large monkeypod trees which have furnished shade at the corner of Richards and King Sts for almost a half century, was brought under way. The trees were removed to make way for the new Hawaiian Electric Co. building.

Approximately one hour for every five years of growth was taken up in removing the trees. Saws, hatchets and pulleys were used by the workmen to accomplish their purpose.

Removal of the old trees marked the passing of a Honolulu landmark as they stood on the property once claimed by "Princess" Theresa who lived there for several years as a squatter.

Honolulu Star-Bulletin, January 25, 1926

HAWAIIAN ELECTRIC PERMIT $578,897

One of the largest applications for a building permit filed recently was presented at the office of City Building Inspector Harry K. Stewart for the erection of the new Hawaiian Electric building on the corner of Richards and Merchant Sts. at a cost of $578,897.

Plans and specifications were submitted with the application. Ralph E. Woolley is to be the builder and York & Sawyer are the architects.

Honolulu Star-Bulletin, January 28, 1926

PROGRESS RAPID ON NEW HAWAIIAN ELECTRIC BUILDING

Work is progressing rapidly on the new Hawaiian Electric building and builders started setting the travertine a few days ago, according to M. H. Webb of Emory and Webb, architects, who is superintending the building.

Travertine as a base course is new to Hawaii, although it is used extensively on the mainland. An imported Italian stone, resembling pumice in texture, it is good in appearance, has qualities of durability and is consistant with the Italian design of the building. It is being laid from the Merchant street ewa end of the building.

Workmen have also started filling the outside walls, and the concrete work is practically all finished. When finished the exterior will resemble the postoffice building which was designed by the same firm, York and Sawyer. Above the travertine base course will be stucco; terra cotta will be laid around the windows; a band of marble will bear the name of the building; stucco will then extend to the cornice which will be of terra cotta. The roof will be red tile.

The building will be complete in April or May.

The Honolulu Advertiser, October 10, 1926

Here is what was previously on the site, burned by the Board of Health on January 15, 1900:

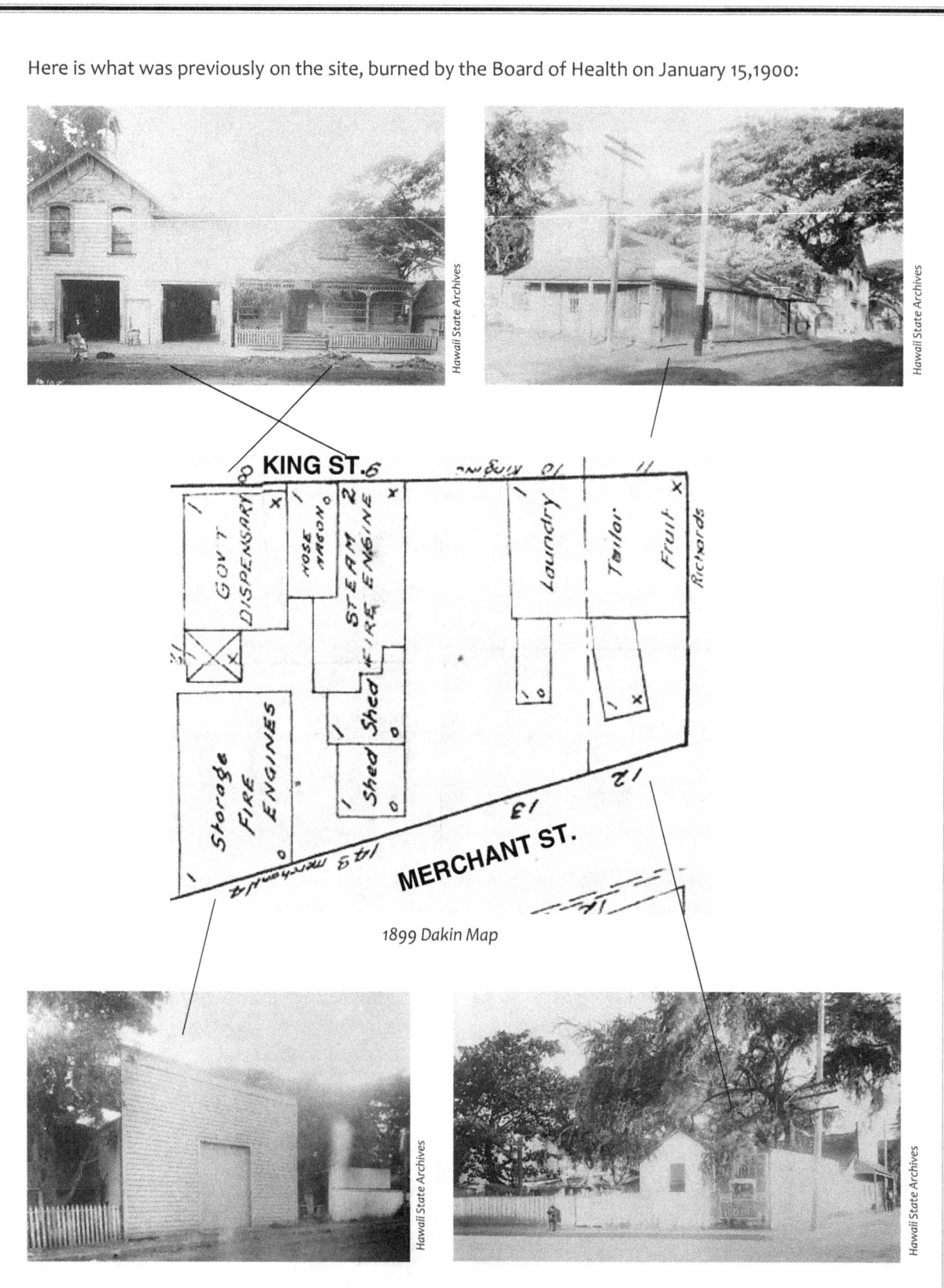

1899 Dakin Map

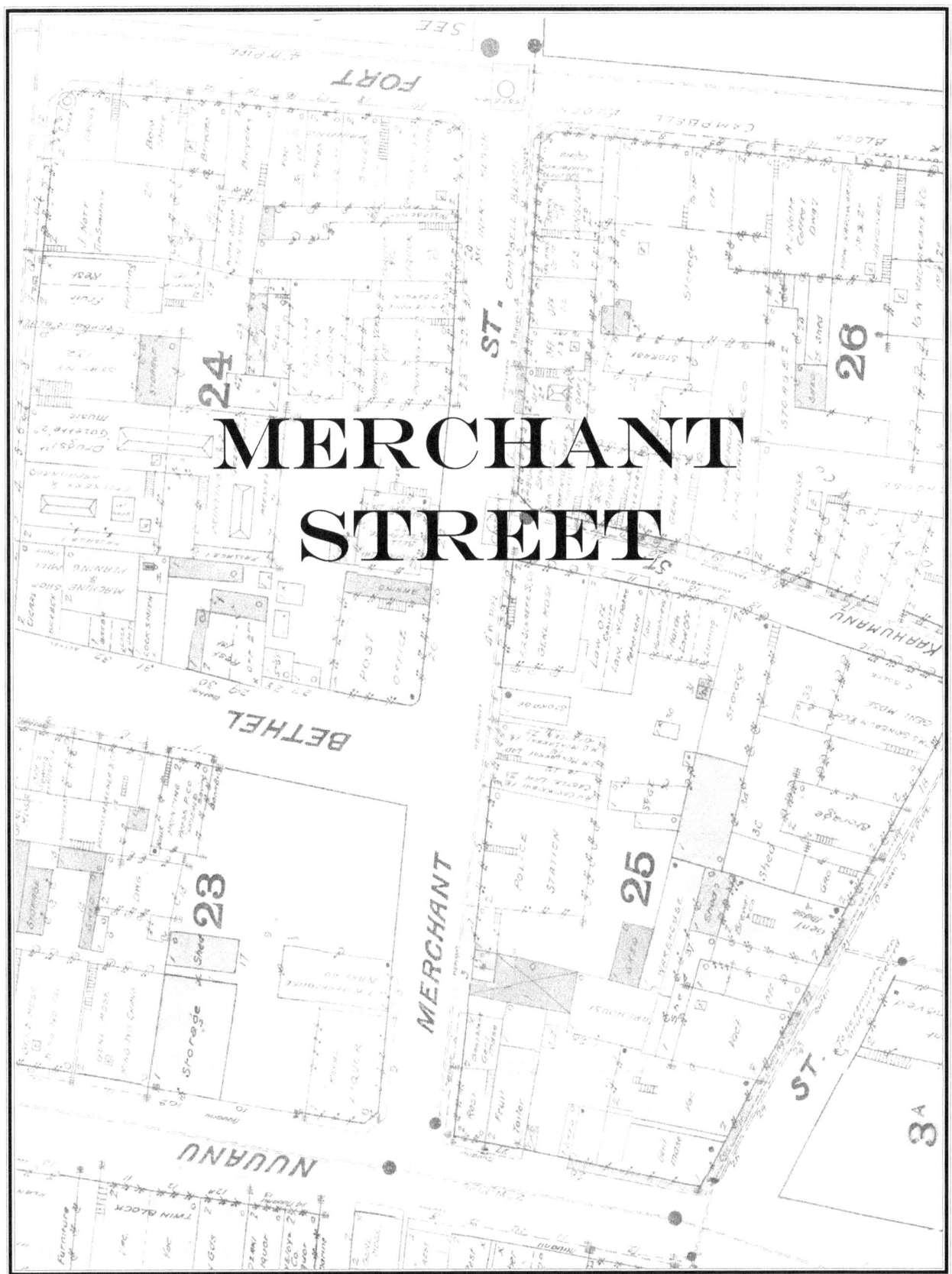

MERCHANT STREET

ROYAL SALOON

2-10 Merchant Street / 901 Nu'uanu Street

1890 – present
Architect/Builder: Isaac A. Palmer / Walker & Redward

According to Paul Rockwood's and Dorothy Barrere's map "Honolulu in 1810" the houses of Hawaiian chiefs were once on this corner and along Merchant Street.

Stephen Reynolds, prominent merchant and chronicler, had a store at this corner in 1829 made of grass. He replaced it sometime in the 1830's with a 2-story coral building that was torn down in 1855.

The first drinking establishment on this corner was the 2-story wooden Royal Hawaiian Hotel built by John Maxey. Opening day was July 2, 1855, and it featured live music three nights a week "for the lovers of music and good fellowship".

Paul Emmert, 1854

Hawaii State Archives

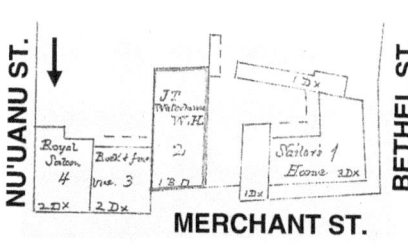

1885 Dakin Map

Maxey was also proprietor of the White Swan Hotel on the mauka/ewa corner of King and Nuʻuanu streets and had purchased the land on this corner from Stephen Reynolds with the understanding he would be able to build a saloon.

But the construction of the Sailors' Home that same year on the waikiki/makai corner of the "Bethel Block" led to much rancorous debate about whether spirits being sold a few doors away would "thwart its usefulness".

ROYAL HAWAIIAN HOTEL,
JOHN MAXEY, PROPRIETOR.

THIS NEW AND SPLENDID ESTABLISHMENT is now open to the Public, and the proprietor has spared no cost in providing every convenience for his friends and customers.

The supplies for this house will be found abundant and varied, and of that sterling quality which the most noted European markets can furnish. Those kind patrons who have so long known the proprietor, as landlord of the White Swan Hotel, will now find him, as of old, a successful caterer, for their comfort and enjoyment. One of the most attractive features connected with this hotel, is the Vocal and Instrumental Entertainments, which will be given on three evenings in each week, and the talented band lately arrived per "Kingfisher," have been engaged at a tremendous cost, which is evidence that the proprietor will not study expense in his resolve to constitute the "Royal Hotel" by far the most attractive resort in Honolulu, for the lovers of music and good fellowship.

Honolulu, July 6th, 1855.   9-tf

By 1856 it was simply known as the Royal Hotel, with the Varieties Theater upstairs featuring "Tragedies, Comedies, Farces, Singing, Dancing, Burlesque Operas, Ballads, Violin Solos, &c." (A completely different business called the Hawaiian Hotel opened downtown in 1872, becoming the Royal Hawaiian Hotel in 1880).

The building at Nuʻuanu and Merchant streets was called the Royal Hotel Saloon by 1883, or just the Royal Saloon, managed by E.H.F. Wolter.

By the late 1880's saloonkeeper and liquor dealer Walter Chamberlain Peacock, originally from Lancaster, England, had bought the Royal Saloon, and on November 7, 1889, W.C. Peacock & Company announced they would be erecting a new building on the site due to the upcoming widening of Merchant Street. Contractors Thomas Walker and Fred Redward paid $100 on November 14 at auction to remove the old 2-story wooden building.

In addition to a wholesale liquor business Peacock also owned at least two other saloons in town, the Pacific and the Cosmopolitan, both further up Nuʻuanu Street.

The new 1-story brick building was built by Walker & Redward for $6,127, and the new Royal Saloon opened on March 25, 1890.

> Messrs. W. S. Peacock & Co. received the following tenders for the erection of a new building for them on the site of the old Royal Hotel premises: George Lucas, $10,800; Bowler & McKenzie, $7,275; Fred. Harrison, $7,269 50; Walker & Redward, $6,127. The last named tender was accepted.

The Honolulu Advertiser, November 20, 1889

The design is classic Eastlake Victorian with cast iron decorations and stucco pilasters, balustrades, and cornices, and shares many similar design elements with the 1888 Perry Block at the corner of Nuʻuanu and Hotel Streets and the 1891/1892 T.R. Foster Building across the street. Isaac A. Palmer was undoubtedly the architect of all three.

THE NEW ROYAL SALOON.

The new Royal Saloon building nearing completion is a beauty. It occupies the site of the old building at the corner of Nuuanu and Merchant streets. The structure is of one story and is built of brick. The street facings are relieved and ornamented by nine stuccoed pilasters. Skew backs, for the imparting of correct arches above the tops of the doors and windows, project from these. Commencing with the top of the verandah is the cornice, composed of series of stop blocks of beautiful architectural design surmounted by a stucco railing of semi-mullions against a background of brickwork. This railing is crowned with a fitting cap of stucco. The summits of the pilasters are appropriately topped with ornamental heads. The corner of the building on Nuuanu and Merchant streets is splayed sufficiently to allow of large double doors. There are double doors also in the front and on the Merchant street side. The windows are large and tastefully arched. The verandah extends along the street facings covering the stone pavement in width.

The interior is graced with wainscoting and finish of Eastlake style. The saloon room has dimensions of 37 by 35 feet. In the rear of this is a store-room 21 feet by 22 feet. Separated from this by a partition are a hall room 16 feet by 22 feet and two card rooms taking up the balance of the building. The contract for the construction of the building is in the hands of Walker & Redward. It will probably be ready for occupancy the last of this week.

Daily Bulletin, March 3, 1890

Peacock bottled his own liquors in clear and amber bottles that are still very collectible today. He sold three grades of gin, but his nephew who once worked filling bottles said all three came from the same barrel!

The Royal Saloon closed during prohibition and the building later housed a print shop, real estate office, stockbrokers, a warehouse, and a furniture store, with George's Diner on the Merchant Street side from 1950 to 1970.

In 1969, Alan C. Beall and William R. Lahmann Jr. proposed developing a Hawaiian version of San Francisco's Ghirardelli Square to be called Merchant Square. The plan was to recreate the romantic gaslight Old World charm of the late 1800's and called for the restoration of up to 12 buildings on Merchant Street.

Tom and Gipsy Norton, with Mary Louise Walker, restored the building in 1971, turning it into the Royal Spaghetti House with 1890's melodramas on Monday nights.

In 1973 it was purchased by Lin Comito who wanted to use the original Royal Saloon name but the liquor commission refused due to the word "saloon". It became the Golden Guinea instead.

Richard Gusman and Duncan MacNaughton hired architect Spencer Leineweber to convert it into Matteo's Royal Tavern in 1976. They also bought and restored the adjacent J.T. Waterhouse building for Jamieson's Irish Coffee House.

San Francisco native Don Murphy opened the popular Murphy's Bar and Grill at the corner in 1987. The Murphy's St. Patrick's Day block party has been a major downtown event for over 34 years.

During the filming of the *Lost* TV series the street in front of Murphy's and O'Toole's was used to film a snowy scene supposedly taking place in Boston. A local ice company provided the snow, which lasted about five minutes, but that was enough to get the shot.

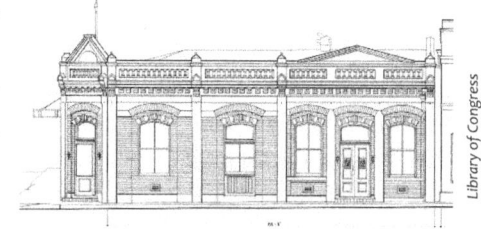

J.T. WATERHOUSE WAREHOUSE

16 Merchant Street
1871 – present (1912 remodel)
Architect/Builder: unknown

Honolulu: The Cross-Roads of the Pacific, 1913

This building was likely one of "the two fine fire-proof brick stores" built by John T. Waterhouse in 1871. Initially a 1-story warehouse, a building permit on October 19, 1912, for $3,500 for "store and office" added the second story and distinctive "Alamo" parapet. At the time it housed the McChesney Coffee Company.

This building was one of several owned by John Thomas Waterhouse, a leading 19th century merchant who established Hawaii's first mail-order business.

Waterhouse came to Honolulu from Tasmania in 1851 and became a very successful importer and local merchant who issued his own silver dollar-sized payment tokens that were redeemable only at his establishments. Their original value was 50 cents – today they are very rare and worth several thousand dollars each.

2022

HONOLULU SAILORS' HOME

24-32 Merchant Street

1855 – 1886

Architect/Builder: Thomas G. Harding / Charles W. Vincent

Hawaii State Archives

Damon Memorial, 1882

In November the first steps were taken at a public meeting for the establishment of a "Sailors' Home." Prominent in the movement were—Rev. S. C. Damon, Hon. S. N. Castle, Hon. G. M. Robertson, J. T. Waterhouse, Rev. A. Armstrong, and Captains Walker, Elliot and Neil. The outcome of this was the erection of the building which stands on the corner of Merchant and Bethel streets. At the date mentioned there were over one hundred foreign vessels in the harbor of Honolulu.

It may be interesting to note here, that the the lot on which the Home stands was donated by the King in Privy Council, by the following resolution:

"*Resolved*, That the petition for a lot of land for a Sailors' Home be granted, provided it shall be a rule established in such Home, and strictly enforced, that no intoxicating liquors shall be drank on the premises; no woman of lewd character admitted; no gambling allowed; nor any disorder tolerated. This resolution shall not be binding on the King's Government unless the sum of $5000 be raised by subscription for the purpose aforesaid, within 16 months, and on the further condition that such Sailors' Home shall be equally available to the sailors of all nations, including those of this Kingdom,—and when said lot ceases to be used for the purpose of a Sailor's Home, the same shall revert to the Government.

By order of the Privy Council, Nov. 20, 1854.
LORRIN ANDREWS, Sec'ry.

Daily Honolulu Press, October 21, 1882

The 3-story wooden Honolulu Sailors' Home was built in 1855 to provide a wholesome refuge for the tremendous number of foreign sailors who came through the Port of Honolulu every year. It also housed the offices of the Hawaiian Board and Bible Society, *The Friend*, and the YMCA Reading Room.

The cornerstone was laid by Kamehameha IV on July 31, 1855, on the anniversary of the restoration of the Hawaiian flag by Admiral Thomas of the British Navy. Kamehameha IV gave a speech, concluding with:

> "I congratulate you on this event, auspicious for the better conditions of seamen at our port. A regard for the foreigners who visit us, an interest in the prosperity of the port and the Kingdom, and the higher and holier regard for humanity, should urge us on to the most vigorous efforts for the success of this enterprise. May this corner stone long remain as the support of a cheerful, happy home, for all those who come from 'old Ocean's gray and melancholy waste.'"

The building was designed by Road Supervisor Thomas G. Harding and built by Charles W. Vincent in 60 days at a cost of $13,000. The first managers of the home were Thomas and Elizabeth Thrum.

The Sailors' Home.

The Sailors' Home building, to which a correspondent refers in another column, was commenced in 1855, the corner stone being laid on Restoration Day, July 31st of that year, and the building was finished in September of the following year. The main building is three storeys high, and with its wings covers an area of about 65 by 80 feet. There is a broad front staircase and two in the rear, of the ordinary width, but the chances all are, that in case of fire commencing on the ground floor, they would be inaccessible in a few minutes. The building is entirely of wood, has been repainted a number of times, and having a large stock of paper, etc., on the ground floor, is likely, if once on fire, to burn very rapidly.

The roof of the main building is slated. There is no kerosene (nothing but peanut oil) burned on the upper floor, and the rest of the lights are all hanging lamps. The only fire used on the premises is in a stove in a small kitchen, and Mr. Dunscombe, the manager, uses every precaution to guard against accidents of all kinds. The principal danger to which the Home is subjected is that arising from its being burned by flying coals from some other burning building in its vicinity.

The Honolulu Advertiser, January 27, 1885

The building was greatly threatened during the 1886 fire and preparations were made to blow it up to provide a fire break. Sailors from the British warships *Satellite* and *Heroine* helped pull down adjoining wooden buildings and when a wind shift looked like the Home could be saved, one daring sailor dashed in and cut off the burning fuse with only 8" to spare.

By July 30, 1886, the *Evening Bulletin* called it a "magnificent firetrap" and advocated it should be torn down with as little delay as possible due to its proximity to important civic buildings like the General Post Office and the new Police Court.

The contents and building were auctioned off for cash on October 13, 1886, with the purchaser of the building given 45 days to remove it. Nathaniel Kaiaikawaha bought the building and outbuildings for $432. The furniture inside sold for $600.

On October 30, 1886, George Lucas raised the old cornerstone. The 10" x 6.5" x 5.5" copper time capsule contained a Bible in the Hawaiian language, a copy of J.J. Jarves' *History of the Hawaiian Islands*, daguerreotypes of Kamehameha I, II, III, and IV, copies of newspapers and various publications relating to the Home, and several copper coins with the impression of Kamehameha III.

A new Sailor's Home was designed by Clinton B. Ripley and built by the Lucas Brothers in 1894 on the block bounded by Richards and Alakea streets, facing Halekauwila Street.

The site lay vacant for 21 years until the Yokohama Specie Bank bought the corner in 1907 for their new bank. The Yokohama Specie Bank was Japan's largest bank, founded in 1880, and this was their first branch in the Hawaiian Islands to cater to the many Japanese immigrants who comprised 40% of the population of Hawaii by 1908.

The cornerstone for was laid on October 20, 1908, and the bank opened for business on April 18, 1910. The iron rails and stairways came from Chicago and the marble window casings and stairs came from Yokohama, Japan. The exterior of the building is faced with terra cotta. Harry L. Kerr was the architect and contractor with Fred H. Redward as construction foreman.

In response to the December 7, 1941, Japanese attack on Pearl Harbor, the Alien Custodian Agency seized this building later that same day. It was used to store confiscated goods and the basement was converted into a cellblock for intoxicated soldiers. The building was owned by the US government until 1954. Final claims for impounded money and property were not settled until 1967.

Honolulu: The Cross-Roads of the Pacific
1913

2022

KALAKAUA POLICE STATION

27-31 Merchant Street
1886 – 1930
Architect/Builder: Fred Harrison

Plans for a new Police Station House at this location were well underway before the disastrous 1886 fire that destroyed the Station House on King Street and most of Chinatown.

The cost of the lot and the brick building was $75,519.20. Fred Harrison was the contractor and George Lucas and E.B. Thomas also worked on the building. E.B. Thomas also did additional improvements to the station in 1899 for $5,849.

John F. Bowler was the low bidder for the foundation and basement at $10.40 per cubic yard, and a gang of prisoners cleared away the earth on the site in June 1884.

The station house was opened in 1886, the jubilee year of King Kalākaua, who celebrated his 50th birthday that same year. The parapet had the name "Kalākaua" plus a raised crown and the year "1886" in gold letters. King Kamehameha III organized the first police force in the Hawaiian Islands in 1834 – this was twelve years before any American city and only four years after London, England.

Old Police Station In Wreckers' Hands

Last week workmen started razing the old police station on Merchant street to clear the site for the fine new modern structure that is to rise in its place. The old building is a survivor of monarchy days.

The Honolulu Advertiser, April 28, 1930

The new station was designed by Louis E. Davis and completed in 1931 by Frank M. Dias for $239,000.

Honolulu Star-Bulletin, September 30, 1931

Bethel Street was extended to Queen Street in 1931 and the new building replaced the earlier 1886 police station on this site. The Spanish Colonial architectural style was very popular in Honolulu at this time and local architect Louis E. Davis combined this style with elements of Art Deco.

The sandstone for the walls came from Waianae, 11 tons of the Roja Alicante marble were imported from France, and the doors are made of mahogany from the Philippines.

The cell block was in the basement, offices were on the first floor, and the courtroom was on the second floor. During World War II the building housed the Alien Property Custodian Office which seized property owned by foreign citizens (mostly Japanese but a few Germans as well).

> *"So great is the contrast between the old police jail and the new that someone has remarked that prisoners will be fighting to stay in jail rather than to get out."*

In 1989 the building was named after Walter Murray Gibson. Gibson had been a gunrunning ship captain in the Caribbean who later escaped from a jail in the East Indies after being charged with fomenting rebellion. He joined the Mormon Church in Utah and was sent to Hawaii by Brigham Young to open a new colony on the island of Lanai but was excommunicated for embezzlement and preaching false doctrine. His supporters deserted him and founded a new colony at Laie where the first Mormon temple outside of Utah was later dedicated in 1915.

Wanting to create his own Pacific empire as savior of the island races, Gibson stayed in Hawaii and started his own newspaper and became a confidant of King David Kalākaua who eventually named him Prime Minister of the Kingdom of Hawaii in 1886. Gibson was forced out during the turmoil of the 1887 Hawaiian Constitution and nearly lynched. Fearing for his life he fled to San Francisco where he died penniless in 1888. He was called a "brilliant, audacious imposter" yet still had the main police station named after him!

It served as the headquarters of the Honolulu Police Department until 1967. It was renovated in the 1980's and now houses other city offices.

2022

2022

CARTWRIGHT BUILDING

35-37 Merchant Street
1889 – 1931
Architect/Builder: Isaac A. Palmer / E.B. Thomas

A HANDSOME BUILDING.

The new building adjoining the Station house for the Messrs. Cartwright, is about completed and will be occupied next week. It is a two-story building, with pressed brick front, concrete trimmings, plastered and hard finished inside. The front windows are of Queen Anne style. It is fitted up with sash doors, movable transomes and safe vaults 7x10 feet. Mr. A. J. Cartwright will occupy one side and the Messrs. Monsarrat the other. The upstairs, approached by a spacious hallway, will be let for lawyer's offices. The plans were drawn by Mr. J. A. Palmer. Mr. E. B. Thomas was contractor and superintendent, and the work is a credit to him.

Evening Bulletin, January 18, 1889

This building was designed by Isaac A. Palmer and built by E.B. Thomas for Alexander J. Cartwright.

It replaced a 1-story wooden liquor store owned by Brown & Co. that was built sometime before 1879, and it covered up a small lane that had extended from Merchant Street to the waterfront.

The Oahu Railway Company officed upstairs in 1889, and James B. Castle officed here in 1890.

The city paid $37,500 for the building in 1930 and demolished it in 1931 to extend Bethel Street.

2022

MELCHERS BUILDING
41-55 Merchant Street
1854 – present
Architect/Builder: unknown

Paul Emmert, 1854

"Melchers & Co. (a heavy German house) have built a splendid coral store just on the corner of Merchant & Kaahumanu Streets, adjoining the large Wooden Establishment of Coady & Co. at a cost of over $18,000." (Letter from William L. Lee to J. Turrill dated December 17, 1853).

This is the oldest surviving commercial building in Honolulu. It was built by German importers Gustave C. Melchers and Gustave Reiners and was made with coral stone blocks covered in stucco, and it had koa wood shelves and glass cabinets.

City Improvements.

A fine stone store is building at the corner of Kaahumanu and Merchant streets, by Messrs. Melchers & Co. and the walls are already up to the second story. Having a good dry cellar, and being built in a most substantial manner, this will be one of the best stores in Honolulu, and nearly fire-proof.

The Polynesian, October 15, 1853

☞ The fine new stone store of Messrs. Melchers & Co was formally opened to the public on Monday last, on which occasion an abundant and tastefully arranged lunch was set out, to which ample justice was done by a large number of the gentlemen of Honolulu.

This is one of the most substantial stores in town, and is nearly fire proof. Messrs. M. & Co. commence operations in their new building with a cargo from Hamburg in addition to their old stock of China and European goods. See advertisement in another column.

The Polynesian, February 25, 1854

Opening day was February 20, 1854. Melchers specialized in fancy European fabrics, cigars, and china goods.

Gustave Melchers was based in Bremen, with John D. Wicke and Frederick A. Schaefer replacing Gustave Reiners in the partnership in 1861.

Thirty-one-year-old Wicke and twenty-five-year-old Schaefer were also from Bremen, and Schaefer was the "Vice Consul of H.I.M. the Emperor of all the Russias".

Schaefer bought the business in 1867 and continued as F.A. Schaefer & Co. until 1919.

The iron shutters were removed in 1913 and the building was painted a light gray to match the Bishop & Co. bank building on the opposite corner.

Located here for over 50 years, F.A. Schaefer & Co. sold the building to the Dillingham interests in October 1919 for $35,000, and they remodeled it to house the Hawaiian Dredging Company and the Hawaiian Contracting Company.

The Hawaiian Dredging & Construction Company took out a building permit for $14,000 on November 4, 1936, to double the size of the building with two reinforced concrete bays on the Bethel Street side that matched the style of the original building.

Rough coral blocks can still be seen in the back of the building on the Ka'ahumanu Street side.

There is a crest above the door on Ka'ahumanu Street commemorating the founding of the Hawaiian Dredging and Hawaiian Construction companies in 1901.

The building was sold to the City of Honolulu in 1950.

2022

2022

KAMEHAMEHA V POST OFFICE

44-50 Merchant Street
1871 – present
Architect/Builder: J.G. Osborne

According to the 1957 Rockwood-Barrere map titled "Honolulu in 1810" the first buildings on this site were chief's houses facing an ulu maika (Hawaiian bowling game) field where Merchant Street is today.

A 2-story coral building costing $3,785.12 was built here in 1847 for the Government Printing Office. They imported a press from Boston to print all of Hawaii's statutes and official documents, but the building was better known as the office of The *Polynesian*, Hawaii's principal weekly government newspaper.

They started keeping a letter bag as a courtesy and in 1850 this became the kingdom's first Post Office with Henry Whitney as the first Postmaster.

Paul Emmert, 1854

Whitney was born in Hawaii of missionary parents and initially worked in the Government Printing Office. He designed Hawaii's famous Missionary stamps as well the 5-cent and 13-cent stamps in 1851 featuring King Kamehameha III. He was the first to establish carrier routes and post offices on all the other islands.

In 1854 he moved the Post Office to the Honolulu Hale building next door and opened a stationery and book store. In 1856 he published *The Pacific Commercial Advertiser* which became Hawaii's principal independent newspaper. The first issues had four pages and were printed on a hand press that could produce 600 papers an hour. Through various changes in name and ownership that newspaper is now known as *The Honolulu Star-Advertiser*.

David Kalākaua (later to become King Kalākaua) was the postmaster from 1863 to 1865, and the only clerk was William G. Irwin who would go on to become one of Honolulu's richest merchants.

DEMOLITION OF THE GOVERNMENT PRINTING OFFICE.—This building, on the corner of Merchant and Bethel streets, has been demolished during the past week, to make room for a new stone three-story building, on the ground floor of which is to be located the Post Office, the upper part to be devoted to the Government printing establishment. The *Gazette* is astray in its figures again, when it says the old building was erected in 1846, and that J. J. Jarves "thought and wrote in its editorial room." The facts as near as we can gather them are these: At the time the Government purchased the Polynesian paper and printing office from Mr. Jarves, it was located in a small building near the theatre, and continued there till the new building was ready for it. This was erected during 1847, and occupied early in 1848, Mr. Hitchcock being in charge at the time of the removal. In the spring of 1849, Mr. E. O. Hall was appointed director. Mr. Jarves was engaged as merchant with A. P. Everett & Co. at this time, and we believe had nothing to do with the paper, after its transfer to the new premises. He left these islands for the last time, early in 1848. The French soldiers had charge of the building for a short time in the summer of 1849, during the French rumpus here, and probably occupied the editorial rooms as military head-quarters, which may account for the pugnacious tendencies of some of the editorials which originated in that sanctum.

Pacific Commercial Advertiser, December 4, 1869

The old Polynesian Building was torn down in 1869 and this new building was constructed in 1871 at a cost of $18,363.

The contractor was J.G. Osborne, a brickmason from Yorkshire, England, and the cornerstone with a tin box of documents was laid by King Kamehameha V on March 2, 1870. This was the first building in Hawaii built of blocks of concrete reinforced with steel and is the oldest building of its type in America. Opening day was March 21, 1871.

The Postal Department took over the entire building in 1894 and this was the official Post Office until 1922. It was later used by the Territorial Tax Office overflow quarters.

The building was expanded along Bethel Street in 1900 at a cost of $13,000.

It was designated a National Civil Engineering Historic Landmark in 1987.

The city renovated the building in 1993 for use by the Kumu Kahua Theater and as offices for the State Foundation on Culture and the Arts.

Often used as a backdrop for wedding photographers, the exterior was featured in a Hawaii 5-0 TV episode in 2015 about pirates supposedly raiding Hawaii in the 1880's.

2022

"Seeing two twenty-four pounder cannon lying in front of the new Post Office Building, a stranger inquired what they were intended for. He was gravely informed that they were for the use of the Postmaster General to announce the arrival and departure of the mails. One to be fired ten minutes before the opening of the general delivery and the other ten minutes before the closing of the office. The stranger walked away musing on the queer customs of Hawaii, never dreaming that the old guns were intended for corner posts."

Pacific Commercial Advertiser, January 11, 1871

The two cannons in front have always attracted graffiti and handbills ever since they were first installed as hitching posts in 1871.

Most likely coming from the old fort when it was demolished in 1857, there was a third cannon located directly in front of the Bishop Bank across the street.

2022

HONOLULU HALE

52-56 Merchant Street

c.1835 – 1917

Architect/Builder: unknown

Paul Emmert, 1854

A little pocket park today, this site was the first Honolulu government office, known as Honolulu House, or Honolulu Hale. It was a 2-story coral building with 4 rooms on each floor that was built c.1835 by Kamehameha III at a cost of about $10,000.

Officially declared the private property of the king in 1850, he relinquished all back rent in exchange for $4,500 improvements made in 1847, and then rented the building to the government for $1,000 per year. The Custom House, Department of Education, Treasury Department and Department of Interior were on the first floor, and the Department of Foreign Affairs was on the second floor.

Situated at the head of Ka'ahumanu Street and with a direct view of the harbor it was "the business and official center of Honolulu".

When the government offices moved out in 1854, Henry M. Whitney relocated the post office here and opened a bookstore and printing shop along with the first editorial rooms of the *Advertiser* newspaper.

Whitney built a wooden building in back in 1861 that had "twelve or fifteen Sea-island cotton gins at work preparing cotton grown on the four principal islands for the English Market". The buildings in back were removed in 1884 when Honolulu Hale was renovated and partitioned into offices.

BOOK & STATIONARY DEPARTMENT.

H. M. WHITNEY,
—AT THE—
Old Honolulu Hale Building, Merchant St.,
(ADJOINING THE POST OFFICE,)

Importer and Dealer in

BOOKS, STATIONERY,
ACCOUNT BOOKS,

And every article of utility and fancy connected with the line, adapted to the Counting House and Office, and to Artists, Teachers, Professional Gentlemen, Travelers, etc., on as reasonable terms as can be had here or in San Francisco, among which are the following Staple Goods:

English and French Letter Papers, satin surface and extra fine, plain and gilt edges
Do. Billet and Note do. do. do., in boxes.
Do. Letter and Note Envelopes, to match the above
Mourning Paper and Envelopes, an assortment constantly on hand
American Cap, Letter, and Note Papers, from the best makers, of almost every description
Enamelled surface and pearl surface Cards
Embossed and Friendship Cards
Perforated Boards, for Chenile's work and Mottoes
Tissue and Fancy colored Papers
Moroccos and Embossed, and Gold and Silver Papers
Best London Quills and Quill Pens
1,000 Gross of Steel Pens, from the best makers
English Red and Colored Wafers, and Seals
English Sealing Wax, red and fancy
Kidder's and Payson's Indelible Ink
Glass Pens, for marking with Indian ink
Blue, Black and Red Writing Inks, and Carmine
Thermometers, Tooth-picks
Maps of Hawaiian Islands, Charts
Portable Writing Desks, from 12 to 22 inches, Mahogany and Rosewood, adapted for ladies' and gentlemen's use
School Books, of all kinds in general use
Family and Pocket Bibles, Testaments, etc.
Teachers' new Reference Bibles, Prayer Books
5,000 Standard English and American Books
Paper cover Books, Song and Music Books
English and American Juvenile and Toy Books, of every description
Best Drawing Paper, all sizes, from demy to double elephant, and in rolls of 36 and 40 yards
Bristol Boards, of every size and thickness
Fern Board and Mounting Board
Choice Chromos of American and European Scenery, framed or unframed
Stereoscopes and Stereoscope Views
All the late Piano Music, Songs, and Song Books
Tracing Papers and Tracing Cambric, in rolls
Newman's Water Colors, in boxes
Best Sable and Camel's Hair Brushes
Faber's superior Drawing Pencils, in boxes
Colored Pencils, Creta levis do., Copying do.
Mathematical or Drawing Instruments, in cases, from $1 to $10 each
Chess Men, wood and ivory
Backgammon and Chess Boards
Intellectual Card Games, Playing Cards
Dominoes, of various patterns
Gold and Silver Pencil Cases
Gold Pens, with Gold Cases
Gold Pens, with Silver Cases and Diamond Points, from $1.50 to $3.50 each
Steel Penknives, 1 to 4 blades, of pearl, shell, ivory, buck and buffalo handles, of rich and beautiful patterns, imported expressly to order
Porcelain Slates and Drawing Slates
Photograph Albums, card and cabinet sizes, in great variety, from $1 to $20.

Ivory Tablets, Paper Cutters, etc.
Cash and Deed Boxes, Check Cutters and Cancellers
Croquet Sets, School Satchels
Inkstands, in great variety
Elastic Bands and Rings, Alphabet Books
Pen Wipers and Racks, Rulers
School Slates and Slate Pencils
All kinds of Tin goods and Cash Boxes
Post-office and Envelope Tin Racks
Children's Sets Tenpins
Children's Drawing Cards and Toys, in great variety
Copying Presses, Oil Sheets and Brushes
Crayons, white and colored
Desk Folios, Pads and Weights
White and Colored Blotting Papers
Drawing, Drafts, Note, Order and Receipt Books
250,000 Envelopes, of all sizes and variety, from No. 1 to 15.
Eyelets and Eyelet Machines
Herbariums and Scrap Books
Autograph Albums, of all sizes and prices
Initial Paper and Envelopes

LEATHER GOODS.

A large and more complete assortment than can be found at any other establishment, such as:

Memorandum Books, Postage Stamp Albums
Pocket Books, Wallets and Portmonnaies
Traveling Desks, Reticules
Bankers' Wallets, folio and cap sizes
Ladies' and Gent's Portfolios, etc., etc.
Colored Morocco Skins
Sheep Skins, Morocco Cloth, etc.

BLANK BOOKS.

A very full and extensive assortment of superior quality, comprising every variety of form and style, adapted to all kinds of business, namely:

Ledgers, Journals, Day Books, Cash Books, Sales Books, Waste Books, Invoice Books, Note Books, Note and Bill Books, Letter Books, etc., etc.
Writing Books, of all the various rulings, long and broad, quarto form
Quarto Account Books
Blank Drawing Books
Albums, great variety of elegant styles
Fine Record Books, for Societies, Clubs, etc.
Workmen's Time Books, Weekly and Monthly.

PHOTOGRAPH PICTURES.

Including Stereoscopes of Hawaiian, American, English and European Scenery, cabinet and full size Photographs of public men and noted places.
☞ My collection of Photograph Pictures will always be found worth inspecting.

PICTURE FRAMES.

In great variety, from cabinet size 4 x 6 inches to heavy gilt 4-inch mouldings, for largest size pictures. Rustic and Gilt Oval Frames, of all sizes and prices.

All New Articles of Fancy Stationery Received by the earliest arrivals from London and New York.

ACCOUNT BOOKS FOR BANKS, PLANTATIONS, INCORPORATED COMPANIES, Etc., MADE TO ORDER WITH DESPATCH.

PRINTING of Bill Heads, Circulars, Cards, Etc., Etc.,
EXECUTED WITH DESPATCH AT LOWEST RATES.

New Stock Received by every Steamer.

☞ Country Merchants and Dealers will find it for their interest to call and examine my Stock before purchasing elsewhere. ☞ All orders will be filled with promptness and despatch.

From 1862 to 1865, David Kalākaua was the Postmaster General at this location with William G. Irwin as the only clerk. Kalākaua was elected King of Hawaii nine years later.

Whitney started a Hawaiian language newspaper in 1861 that lasted until 1927. In 1865 he published one of the first Hawaiian language dictionaries and in 1875 he published the first tourist guidebook to Hawaii.

By 1866 it had a wooden tower that was used to send and broadcast semaphore messages about the ships in the harbor.

Hawaii State Archives

A young reporter named Samuel Clemens came here in 1866 and asked Whitney for a job but there were no openings. However, the two became good friends and sparring partners for years.

Clemens spent several months hanging out in Whitney's offices. He would go on to become one of America's most famous and beloved writers under the name of Mark Twain.

The 25 letters Twain wrote about Hawaii for the *Sacramento Daily Union* newspaper helped launch his literary career and are still delightful reading today.

PRAYING TO DEATH.

The coral stone building, standing on the lot which adjourns the post office, on its southerly side was formerly the Government House, and within it were all of the executive offices. After these offices were removed, one part of the lower floor of the building was used as a post office, and the other part was used as a book store by Mr. H. M. Whitney, who used the book store also as the office of the Commercial Advertiser, of which he was editor. The postmaster in the year 1860 was the late King Kalakaua, and his chief and only clerk was Mr. W. G. Irwin, both of whom, owing to the advantages offered by the post office in furnishing reading materials achieved remarkable success in life, the one as a monarch, and the other as a merchant.

The Advertiser in those days took shots occasionally at the flying follies and wrongs of the day. On one occasion, Mr. Whitney criticized in the paper the native boat men because of their outrageous charges for boat services, and he threatened to place a boat in competition with their boats, unless the abuses were stopped.

The native boat men, enraged at Mr. Whitney's conduct, organized and determined to kill him. In order to avoid committing the crime of murder, as it was defined by law, they, with true pagan sagacity, resolved to cause his death by means of the anaana (the process of praying one to death) through the medium of a Kahuna, or priest of the ancient faith. Even at this period the natives, in spite of religious instruction, had much faith in this superstitious power. As killing by anaana was not forbidden by statute, the cunning natives engaged a Kahuna to act in their behalf, and place Mr. Whitney where he would cease from troubling. The Kahuna, having made his contract for compensation dependent upon the death of the editor, proceeded to gather the usual articles for this solemn ceremony, one of them, and of the utmost importance, being some substance from Mr. Whitney's person, such as a hair or finger nail. Mr. Whitney does not know how the article was obtained, and at no time did he suspect the Postmaster Kalakaua or his chief clerk of having secretly abstracted it from his person and furnished it for this horrid purpose.

In front of this building, now used for law offices, there was a fence, and a gate that was locked at night. The Kahuna approached the place at night. He carried in his arms the white pig that is a very important part of the ceremonial. Finding the gate locked, he leaned over the fence, and deposited the pig, whose feet were securely tied, on the stone steps within the gate.

Having made the most suitable disposition of his tangible machinery for affecting spiritual murder, the Kahuna, at midnight began his incantations in a weird and minor key. His voice could be heard at the distance of a few feet only. Towards morning, his language and voice became more fervid. The white pig, an involuntary assistant, gave a grunt from time to time. As the daylight broke, the Kahuna discharged at the building a series of heathenish imprecations and retired leaving the helpless pig on the stone steps.

Mr. Whitney opened his office as usual the next morning. Noticing the white pig, he inquired into the cause of its being placed before his door and was confidentially informed by a native friend that the boat men were engaged in killing him, by the anaana process. Mr. Whitney at once directed that the pig should be taken to the wharf, and thrown into the harbor, as his signal of defiance. It was done. The native boat men were utterly surprised at the outcome of their scheme. The Kahuna in his official report on the failure to kill the editor, laid the blame on the gods and spirits who in the most cowardly manner refused to tackle the haole (white man).

In this connection, the Advertiser cordially invites its enemies, especially its angry contemporaries, to make another and perhaps more successful treat of the anaana upon the representatives of this paper, especially upon its business manager. Seats for their Kahunas will be placed in front of the building occupied by the paper. A cage will be furnished for the white pig. And whenever the Kahunas become weary of repeating the weird incantations composed of our contemporaries' editorials upon the wickedness of the Advertiser, the proximity of Mr. Cunha's establishment may enable them to "work the growler" with happy facility, and make the proceeding doubly interesting.

*The Honolulu Advertiser,
November 5, 1898*

Hawaii State Archives

In 1883, Major James W. Robertson rigged up a "time ball" on the signal pole of the adjoining tower. It was 12 inches in diameter, painted black with a white band around the equator, and upon a telephone call from the Survey Office the ball was dropped each day to indicate the exact hour of noon.

The Hawaiian Government bought the land at auction in 1884 for $27,600 from Queen Emma and Mrs. Bernice Pauahi Bishop. The sale included Honolulu Hale, the Pacific Commercial Advertiser Office, the former store of J.W. Robertson & Co., and the premises occupied by W.R. Castle. The government purchased Diamond Head (729 acres) that same year for $3,300.

Although the stone wall along the street was torn down in the 1850's, its foundation of coral blocks was rediscovered during a sewer project in 1899.

Talk of demolishing "the ramshackle old building" had been going on for years when the *Honolulu Advertiser* wrote in 1917: "during the past several years, the slates have taken a fancy to slide off the roof in obedience to the law of gravitation and wholly indifferent as to whom might be passing on the street below".

c. 1917

Although there were plans for the site to become a park, the building was sold for $10 in 1917 and demolished for a parking lot.

In 1976 it was redeveloped into Alan Sanford Davis Park at a cost of $120,000 by the Outdoor Circle and the Garden Club of Honolulu as a bicentennial gift to the people of Honolulu, designed by landscape architects EDAW Inc.

HONOLULU HALE NOW ALMOST DESTROYED

Honolulu Hale, old landmark of old Honolulu is all but gone. Less than half of its crumbling walls are still standing and those are rapidly being felled. Within the next few days only a heap of debris will be left. The rear of King Street buildings, formerly obscured from view to Merchant Street passers-by, are now visible. Old timers sigh with regret as they pass the ruins, another step in the passing of the old Honolulu.

Soon there will be a splendid available site for new buildings and in time some modern building or buildings will grow up on this site. The old is merely making way for the new, and the business section of Honolulu cannot be kept back in its growth and progress by sentiment. It is, as in all other progressive cities, the old must go as the new advances, yet will many regret the passing of the old landmark.

Honolulu Advertiser,
October 10, 1917

Site of Honolulu Hale & Pacific Commercial Advertiser Building, 2022

BISHOP BANK

63 Merchant Street

1878 – present
Architect/Builder: Thomas J. Baker

This Italian Renaissance Revival and Second Empire styled building was designed and built by Australian-born Thomas J. Baker and completed in 1878. He had been a bricklayer in San Francisco and was one of the three designers of the 'Iolani Palace which started construction a year later in 1879.

The building was built for the Bishop Bank founded by Charles Reed Bishop in 1858. Having outgrown the little basement room in the Makee Block where they first started, this became the first home they could call their own. One of the old Honolulu Fort cannons was placed in front for a hitching post, similar to the two cannons in front of the Post Office Building.

When completed, this building was "the finest looking and perhaps most substantially built structure in Honolulu (aside from the Government House)".

Bishop Bank eventually became what is now known as First Hawaiian Bank.

COMMENCING OPERATIONS.—The work of demolishing the old coral stone building on "the corner" (Kaahumanu and Merchant streets) about which still hover so many pleasant memories of by-gone gossip and Dr. Hoffmann's sage utterances on passing events—has begun this week, and it may now be reckoned with the things of the past. But under the skillful manipulation of Mr. Baker, the architect and builder, we expect shortly to see arise in the place of the old building a structure which shall be an honor to Bishop & Co., and an ornament to the town.

The Pacific Commercial Advertiser
September 29, 1877

PRAISEWORTHY.—The banking firm of Bishop & Co. have moved into their new building this week, and have inaugurated the change by a most praiseworthy and sensible departure from the usual routine upon such occasions. Instead of a " spread" for the public, generally, as a "house-warming," they placed the money where it will be likely to do much more good, viz.: by sending a check to the different benevolent and charitable societies of the city. The structure erected by Bishop & Co. is, beyond controversy, the finest brick building ever erected in this kingdom, and would be considered an ornament to the street in any city. The corner of Merchant and Kaahumanu streets presents quite a different appearance from what it did in the days of "Billy French," thirty years ago.

The Pacific Commercial Advertiser
May 25, 1878

Paul Emmert, 1854

According to Thomas G. Thrum, it was built on the site of a 2-story coral store built by Dr. Robert W. Wood about 1845 or 1846.

In January 1851, that building became the offices and drug store of Dr. B.F. Hardy and Dr. C. Hoffman. E.S. Ruggles and A.G. Thurston took over the business in March 1854.

Dr. Edward Hoffman was here from about 1865 to 1877 when the building was torn down to make way for the new Bishop Bank building.

Born in Glen Falls, New York, in 1822, Charles Reed Bishop came to Honolulu in 1846 and married Bernice Pauahi Pāki in 1850. He partnered with William A. Aldrich selling supplies for the California gold rush and founded Bishop & Co. in 1858 as the first chartered bank in Hawaii. The bank moved to new headquarters on Bishop Street in 1925.

The building later became known as the Harriet Bouslog Building, housing the offices of famed socialist attorney Harriet Bouslog. Architect James K. Tsugawa bought and restored the building in 1979.

2022

HAWAIIAN GAZETTE / UNION SALOON

76-84 Merchant Street

1879/1882 – 1972

Architect/Builder: Isaac Moore (1882) / George Lincoln (1879), George Lucas (1882)

1882 – 1887

This building is actually two buildings – the first one was built on the right side in 1879 for watchmaker and jeweler D.W. Clark, and its façade was incorporated into the 1881 Hawaiian Gazette building designed by Isaac Moore and built by George Lucas.

Clark moved in the first week of October 1879, but a month later announced he was selling off everything including the building due to plans to leave the kingdom in January 1880.

Boot and shoemaker Frank Gertz moved into Clark's store in November 1879 and L.B. Kerr moved his fabric and clothing store here in March 1880.

Clark ended up staying in town and was later located at 55 Hotel Street in 1883.

> A PERMANENT IMPROVEMENT.—Mr. D. W. Clark, watchmaker and jeweler, has this week removed from his old stand nearly opposite this office to the new brick building recently erected by him on the east side of the street. The new structure has a very tasty decorated front and is a decided ornament to Merchant street. It is 42 feet deep by 18 feet front, is of two stories, respectively 12 and 11 feet high. The lower story is occupied by Mr. Clark in his business, and is provided with two large plate glass windows. The building stands back 5½ feet from the line of the old Snow building, which forms a rather unsightly contrast to its new and trim-looking neighbor. There is room for a good deal of similar improvement on Merchant street—the most frequented thoroughfare in the city.

The Pacific Commercial Advertiser, October 4, 1879

The Hawaiian Gazette Building was built on the site of a building called the Pagoda. It wasn't really a pagoda but had 7 rooms, double veranda and stone cellar and was built in the early 1830's by W.S. Hinckley and William French. It had a large 20' x 27' room on each floor flanked by rooms 10' x 27'.

It was sold to Hung and Tai of Hungwa & Co. in 1838, and later sold to Starkey, Janion & Co. in 1845.

By 1856 William E. "Peck" Cutrell ran the Merchant's Exchange saloon downstairs and Abraham Fornander printed the *New Era and Weekly Argus* newspaper upstairs.

The Merchant's Exchange was famous for "sumptuous repasts" and Cutrell was called "The Prince of Publicans".

In 1856 the Merchant's Exchange featured a "leviathan new year's cake" that was 4-1/2 feet high and 8 feet in circumference.

As a novelty they once brought in a reindeer from the Ochotsk Sea, courtesy of Captain Allen of the *Charles Phelps*. "Those who have never seen a Reindeer, the bosom-friend, the servant and God of the Lapp and the Samojede, would do well to call at the Merchant's Exchange Hotel".

One Fourth of July celebration included toasts by A.J. Cartwright, speeches, singing the Star-Spangled Banner, and a reading of the Declaration of Independence by Charles W. Vincent (whose grandparents had given him a mahogany table where General Washington and the Marquis de Lafayette often had tea).

Merchant's Exchange
BOWLING SALOON!

THE PROPRIETOR OF THE MERchant's Exchange Hotel begs to inform the Public that he has erected two superior

MARBLE BOWLING ALLEYS!

Mr. W. B. CARROLL, will have charge of the Alleys, and all those wishing to engage in this health-giving game are invited to give him a call, the Proprietor pledging himself that nothing shall be wanting on his part to render his Alleys the most agreeable place of resort for recreation and amusement in Honolulu.
20 tf

MERCHANT'S EXCHANGE BILLIARD SALOON,
W. E. CUTRELL, Proprietor.

W. E. CUTRELL would inform the Public that he is now Proprietor of the splendid Billiard Saloon attached to his premises. It will be open day and evening; everything will be conducted on the most approved plan, and Mr. C. pledges himself that nothing shall be wanting to render this Saloon a popular place of resort for all who are inclined to while away an hour in the delightful and healthy exercise of Billiard playing.
The Room will be under the sole charge of Mr. H. K. SWORE whose present popularity is a sufficient guarantee of his future success in catering in this particular department, for the amusement of the citizens of Honolulu.
39 tf

In 1860 they added two marble bowling alleys and a "first class billiards table, fitted with Phelan's patent combination cushions and marble bed". When the Backus Minstrels came through in 1862 on their way to Shanghai, they gave a billiard tournament that featured the first time 77 points had been scored at a four-ball carom game in Honolulu.

Emanuel S. Cunha opened the Union Saloon here in 1874. The building was sold at auction in 1881 for "something over $100" to be removed but had to be pulled down since it was too large and too frail to relocate elsewhere. When it was being demolished a one-cent coin from the days of Kamehameha III "tumbled out from among the beams".

Cunha built a new building in back of the former location and immediately behind the proposed Gazette Building, opening for business on July 4, 1881. George W. Lincoln was the contractor. The private lane leading to the Union Saloon was known as Cunha's Alley.

> On Monday Mr. Cunha formally opened his new saloon. He has erected a fine fire-proof building at the back of the old Union Saloon building, and has spared no expense in fitting it up. The wood work is imitation oak and laurel, the counters of koa. The decorations are handsome: a large mirror with the motto "The Union Forever" being especially striking. The room is airy and cool; two small private parlors are partitioned off from the main saloon, and are comfortably fitted with chairs and tables. The facilities for lighting are capital. Outside the bar the arrangements are good; there is a large store-room in which supplies are ready at hand, and underneath a fine and well-stocked cellar. There is also a comfortable little office. Mr. Lincoln was the builder and designer. Mr. Rowe did the painting, and Mr. Jarman, who arrived recently from California with the intention of working upon Col. Spreckel's house, which is not ready for him yet, did the decorating and graining. The result reflects credit upon all engaged on the building.

The Hawaiian Gazette, July 6, 1881

The Union Saloon was no mere beer joint – it had koa furniture, a library, plush carpeting, marble-topped tables, gilt-framed paintings of Hawaiian royalty, some of the best food in town, and catered strictly to the top of Honolulu's business class. All the lavish furnishings were auctioned off in 1918 during Prohibition.

> E. S. CUNHA,
> RETAIL WINE DEALER
> UNION SALOON,
> IN THE REAR OF HAWAIIAN GAZETTE BUILD-
> ING, NO. 23 MERCHANT STREET.
> Jan 1 81

The 2-story brick Gazette Building was completed in January 1882 with stores downstairs and Robert Grieve's newspaper and printing business upstairs for the *Hawaiian Gazette*. The bricklaying was by John Carden, plastering and cementing by John Bowler, and painting by A. Kerr.

Although it was to have been included in a list of historic 19th century Merchant Street buildings, the Pioneer Federal Savings and Loan Association of Hawaii suddenly demolished the building over a weekend in June 1972.

The bank claimed it was "an eyesore" that was "infested with termites and rats", and that no one had approached them about saving it. The reality was they had long been planning on building the Pioneer Plaza parking garage on the site.

2022

BISHOP ESTATE BUILDING

77 Merchant Street
1896 – present
Architect/Builder: Ripley & Dickey

The Honolulu Advertiser, January 2, 1897

When Princess Bernice Pauahi Bishop died in 1884 she left behind an estate of 378,500 acres of land, the largest private landownership in the Hawaiian Islands.

Her estate was managed by her husband, Charles Reed Bishop. He was originally from Boston and was on his way to Oregon around Cape Horn when he decided to stay in Honolulu.

They were married in 1850 and Bishop became one of the top bankers in Hawaii. After his wife's death he founded the Bishop Museum in 1891, renowned worldwide for its research library and collection of Polynesian and Hawaiian historical artifacts.

According to her will, the revenues from the estate lands were to be used to establish a school for native Hawaiian children from preschool through twelfth grade. Today Kamehameha Schools operates 31 preschools statewide and three K through 12 campuses, the largest being in Honolulu. The current enrollment is over 5,000 students.

Scandals in the 1990's led them to change the name from The Bishop Estate to Kamehameha Schools. They still own thousands of acres of land as well as the ground lease to Windward Mall, Pearlridge Mall, Kahala Mall, the Kahala Hotel & Resort, and the Royal Hawaiian Hotel.

This building was built in 1896 and designed by the architectural office of Clinton B. Ripley and Charles Dickey in the fashionable Richardsonian Romanesque style using a type of basalt known as blue stone from the estate's own quarries. The Bishop Estate officed here for over twenty years and this was also the first home of the offices of the world-famous Bishop Museum.

2022

The site was previously part of the larger William French premises and the 1-story brick building of Dr. Edward Hoffman built by Thomas J. Baker in 1876.

QUICK WORK.—During the past week a good many people have paused to admire the celerity and dexterity with which Mr. Baker, engaged in putting up Dr. Hoffman's new building, has handled the bricks. One could actually see the walls rise; and it is not customary to find people working that way in our tropical clime.

Pacific Commercial Advertiser, September 30, 1876

AN OLD BUILDING.

History of a Merchant Street Structure Now Passing.

The old building back of Bishop's Bank, now being torn down, was built by Dr. Hoffman twenty years ago. The magnigcent blue brick used in its construction were brought from China. They are still nearly as solid as stone. They were not wet when put in and separate with ease from the mortar. The building was used several years as a drug store by Dr. Hoffman. Afterward C. O. Berger occupied it, and it came into possession of the Bishop estate.

In the early '70s the Hoffman lot was occupied by Kenney Rawson's watch shop. It was a wooden shanty with a garden and picket fence in front. Before Godfrey Rhodes built the Macfarlane building on Kaahumanu street, there was a restaurant back of Rawson's shop, operated by Joe Roderick. In those days the French Consulate occupied a little house that stood on the bank corner.

The Hawaiian Star, March 4, 1896

MORE BUILDING.

Bishop Bank Structure to Be Extended at Once.

Bishop & Co.'s bank building will be extended back against the Campbell block. Work will begin Monday. The old building (Hoffman's drug store) occupied by the trustees of the Bishop estate will be torn down at once.

The addition to the bank building, extending over this lot, will be two stories and of like design. On the lower floor the vaults for the bank and for the Bishop estate will be kept. There will also be ample office room for officials of both concerns. The second story will be converted into offices and rented.

The Hawaiian Star, February 27, 1896

CAMPBELL BLOCK

79-99 Merchant Street / 828-852 Fort Street
1883 – 1965
Architect/Builder: Isaac M. Moore / Thomas Lucas

1887

This large corner building was built in 1883 for James Campbell and was designed by Isaac M. Moore and built by Thomas Lucas.

James Campbell was born in Londonderry, Ireland, in 1826. At age 13 he sailed to Canada and worked as a carpenter until joining a whaling crew at age 15. Shipwrecked in the South Pacific, he was one of three survivors and was almost killed by natives but finally managed to escape to Tahiti. From there he joined a whaling ship that took him to Lahaina on the island of Maui.

In 1860 he started working in the sugar industry and became one of the wealthiest people in Lahaina, using his profits to buy land throughout Hawaii. Everyone thought he was crazy for buying 41,000 acres of barren land on the western side of Oahu, but he dug the first artesian well in Hawaii and made the land productive and very profitable. **Part of that land is now the new city of Kapolei.**

The James Campbell Company is still very active today with a portfolio valued at $3 billion including 20 million square feet of buildings and 3,000 acres of land.

The two-story coral building lately occupied by E. Hoffschlaeger & Co., now being demolished, is among the last of the early business houses of Honolulu, having being erected about 1842 or 3 by Wm. French, and long used by him as a store during the palmy days of the "China trade," and even sharing it in 1847 with H. N. Crabbe, as United States Naval Store Agent. This was but a portion of what was known as the "French premises," which included the corner now occupied by the Bank, Godfrey Rhodes' building and the premises occupied by J. Nott, on Kaahumanu street, about one-half of the entire block. We have not been able to trace successively the various old firms that have held forth in this stand, but prior to its occupancy by F. Stapenhorst in 1869,—whom E. Hoffschlaeger & Co. succeeded—it remained idle for some time, excepting a few offices occupied up-stairs. The building has therefore been used by the late tenants longer than any firm that had preceded them.

Daily Honolulu Press, March 10, 1883

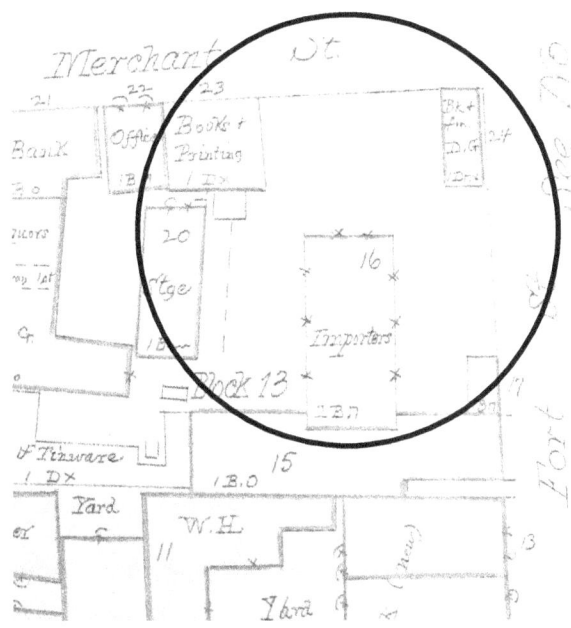

1879 Lion Map

The old buildings occupied by Messrs. Hoffschlaeger & Co., A. W. Richardson & Co. and Thos. G. Thrum are to give way to the march of improvements; the occupants having moved out the buildings will all be torn down, to be replaced by a substantial and handsome block, a prospective sketch of which by Mr. Isaac Moore, the architect, is now on view in the window of J. M. Oat Jr. & Co's store in the GAZETTE building.

The Hawaiian Gazette, March 7, 1883

Campbell's new building, now in process of erection on the corner of Merchant and Fort streets, is rapidly assuming shape under the enterprising supervision of Mr. Thomas Lucas and Mr. I. M. Moore, the architect. It will probable be ready for occupation in November next, and will be when finished, one of the most showy buildings in town.

Daily Honolulu Press, April 28, 1883

Paul Emmert, 1854

Built in 1842 or 1843 by William French, the 2-story coral building previously on this site was set back a little from the street, and it was sketched by Paul Emmert in 1854 when it was the store of ship chandler and commission agent J.C. Spalding, successor to Crabb & Spalding.

Spalding relocated to Kaʻahumanu Street and it became the office and store of German merchants Elard Hoffschlaeger and Florens Stapenhorst.

ED. HOFFSCHLAEGER & CO.,
Importers and Commission Merchants,
Corner of Fort and Merchant Streets.
720 1y

HOFFSCHLAEGER'S old establishment is being pulled down, and gradually the whole corner will be made ready for the new buildings to be erected for Mr. Jas. Campbell.

Evening Bulletin, March 3, 1883

The first brick building in Honolulu was built on this corner in 1847 by John H. Wood for his shoe store. The *Polynesian* called it "rather a novel edifice for Honolulu".

Merchant Street looking ewa from Fort Street, 1882-1884
The J.H. Wood "Brick Shoe Store" is on the left and the Snow and McInerny buildings are the right.

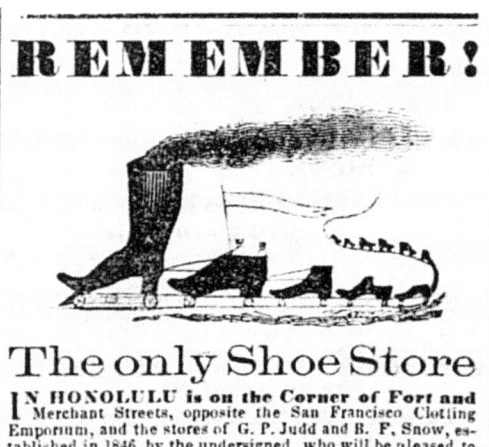

The 1883 Campbell Block was demolished in 1965 by the Campbell Estate and replaced by a new $2M office building designed by Leo S. Wou that was completed in 1967.

Honolulu Star-Bulletin, September 15, 1965

Honolulu Star-Bulletin, October 12, 1964

2022

In the photo on the right, the only surviving remnant of the 1883 Campbell Block.

B.F. SNOW BUILDING

88 Merchant Street
c.1846/47 – 1887
Architect/Builder: unknown

Paul Emmert, 1854

Called the B.F. Snow Building in Paul Emmert's 1854 sketch, this 2-story coral building was Makee & Anthon's "two story stone warehouse" that was built in 1846 or 1847 on the site of a wooden building constructed by Captain William S. Hinckley sometime in the 1830's.

Hinckley had obtained the land from John Adams, Governor of Oahu, but "being unable to pay for the buildings erected upon it by him" sold it to William French "who having built upon it and improved it" sold it to Thomas Cummins, who sold it to Eli Jones on July 27, 1841.

The firm of Jones & Slade dissolved in 1841 and by 1844 was known as Jones & Makee. The company became Makee & Anthon in 1846.

According to historian Warren Goodale, Captain Benjamin F. Snow moved into the building in 1852. Snow had partnered with Stephen H. Williams in 1848 and took over the business after Williams lost $40,000 in the 1850 San Francisco fire. The business began in 1835 as Peirce & Brewer, becoming C. Brewer in 1844, and then S.H. Williams in 1847.

1882 – 1884

The incredible accuracy of Paul Emmert's 1854 painting is evident in this photograph of the building when it was occupied by the Hyman Brothers from 1867 to 1884. The view is looking ewa along Merchant Street from Fort Street. The 1867 McInerny store is on the right.

HYMAN BROTHERS,
IMPORTERS. WHOLESALE AND RETAIL
DEALERS IN
Dry Goods, Clothing, Hats Furnishing Goods, Ladies' and Gents' Boots and Shoes Yankee Notions, &c., &c,
Capt. Snow's Building. No. 20 Merchant St. Honolulu. ap26 79

NEW AND LATEST STYLE
—OF—
GOODS
By Every Steamer,

The Finest and
Largest Assortment on the Islands.

HYMAN BROTHERS,
Importers,
WHOLESALE AND RETAIL
DEALERS IN

American Clothing,
Gent's Furnishing Goods,
Boots, Shoes, Hats, Caps,
Yankee Notions,
&c., &c., &c., &c.

Consisting of the Following:

PLAIN AND FANCY CASSIMERE SUITS,
Light and heavy grades.
Fine Blue Flannel Suits,
White Linen Deck Suits,
Brown Linen Drill Suits,
FINE SILK ALPACA COATS:
Fine Tweed Coats,
Fine Milton Cloth Coats,
Fine White Linen Coats,
Fine Brown Linen Coats,
Fine Black Dress Coats,
Frocks and Sacks.
Fine Black Doeskin Pants, Fine Beaver Pants,
Fine Blue Flannel Pants,
Fine White Linen Pants,
PLAIN AND FANCY CASSIMERE PANTS,
Light and heavy grades.
Fine Black Doeskin Vests,
Plain and Fancy Silk Vests,
Plain and Fancy Silk Velvet Vests,
White and Fancy Marseilles Vests,
Plain Cassimere Vests,
WHITE SHIRTS of all DESCRIPTIONS.
Fancy Calico Shirts of all descriptions,
Linen Collars, assorted sizes,
Fancy and Plain Woolen Overshirts, all descriptions,
Undershirts and Drawers, all descriptions,
Black and Fancy Neck Ties, all descriptions,
Together with an Endless Variety of
BOOTS, SHOES,
HATS, CAPS,
YANKEE NOTIONS, &c.

Messrs. Hyman Brothers
Would beg respectfully to call the attention of
THE PUBLIC AND COUNTRY DEALERS AT LARGE,
To their large and varied assortment of
AMERICAN READY MADE
Fashionable Clothing,
BOOTS, SHOES,
HATS, CAPS, YANKEE NOTIONS, &c.
Masters of Whaleships,
—And—
DEALERS FROM THE OTHER ISLANDS,
Would do well to call on us before purchasing elsewhere.

Capt. Snow's Building, Merchant St.,
Honolulu, Oahu, H. I.

Captain B.F. Snow's store, a spacious two-story coral building that stood on Merchant Street, near the corner of Fort, gave way only in 1887 for the McInerny Block, which occupies the whole of the "Snow Premises." The building was erected probably in the "forties," and for some time was occupied by Makee & Jones, afterwards Makee & Anthon. It was moved into by Captain Snow, following his fire in the Brewer premises on Fort Street in 1852, near the site of the building now occupied by H. May & Co. Upon his death in 1866 the business was wound up. Captain Snow was laid to rest, December 20th, on the fortieth anniversary of his arrival in Honolulu from Boston in the brig Active.

(Thomas G. Thrum, "Honolulu in 1853, Supplementary Article", *Papers of the Hawaiian Historical Society No. 10*, 1898.)

Another Old Land Mark Gone.

Another old land mark in Honolulu has disappeared from the public gaze—the Snow building on Merchant street. In its day it was regarded as one of the finest and most substantial buildings to be found here or elsewhere, and was erected by the late Capt. B. F. Snow, in 1844, for his place of business, and which he continued to occupy until his failing health compelled him to relinquish active pursuits. The walls of this building were composed of huge blocks of coral, and the roof was covered with slate, and when pulled down the whole structure was found to be in a good state of preservation, and capable of enduring the storms for many years to come, but this strong old building has to give way to the march of improvement, and its place will be supplied with a modern structure, in keeping with the demands of the times. The work of demolition set in promptly on Tuesday morning, and soon the first section of what will be known as the "McInerny Block" will rear its front to the public gaze. Mr. Thomas has the work in hand.

The Hawaiian Gazette
March 8, 1887

The photograph on the right was taken on Merchant Street in late March of 1887 looking ewa and shows the workers removing the last of the coral blocks from the B.F. Snow building.

The B.F. Snow Building was replaced by the large McInerny Block in 1887.

The site is now part of Pioneer Plaza, completed in 1977.

2022

MCINERNY BLOCK
88-98 Merchant Street / 902-920 Fort Street
1887 – 1969
Architect/Builder: Henry W. McIntosh / E.B. Thomas

This large 2-story brick building was built by E.B. Thomas in 1887 for Michael McInerny and replaced the much smaller 1-story wooden McInerny store built sometime before 1860.

> On the first of March, Mr. Thomas commences on Mr. McInerny's new building which will extend from the GAZETTE Block on Merchant street, to Mr. W. E. Foster's, on Fort Street. The first portion will be commenced where now stands the "Snow building," which will be immediately removed. This promises to be one of the finest structures in the city—the lower portion will be composed of iron and plate glass.

The Hawaiian Gazette, March 1, 1887

Patrick Michael McInerny was born in 1831 in County Clare on the west coast of Ireland and came to Hawaii in 1857 from New York via Panama. He initially worked as a ship caulker for Mr. Foster until the latter part of 1862 when he opened a small retail grocery and cigar store on Beretania Street just ewa of the Nuʻuanu Stream bridge.

McInerny obtained a retail license in 1864 and moved here in 1867, advertising his "furnishing goods" store at Fort and Merchant streets by 1869.

McInerny purchased the large "Snow Lot" where his store was located for $35,000 in 1883 with the intent of emulating the example of the James Campbell building across the street.

Architect Isaac Moore (from Balgriggan, County Dublin), working with George Lucas, prepared plans in March of 1884 for a building with 5 stores, 107' on Fort Street and 82' on Merchant Street.

But the plans for widening of Fort Street led to a delay and these plans didn't happen. Henry W. McIntosh drew new plans for the building and E.B. Thomas began removing the B.F. Snow building on March 1, 1887. In mid-July Thomas demolished the old wooden McInerny building and built the new brick McInerny block.

In 1915, H.L. Kerr was hired to make alterations for "a light, cool and airy store" with all-new store fronts, expanded floor space, new fixtures from the Lutke Manufacturing Company of Portland Oregon, adding an elevator and mezzanine office floor and "so many mirrors that the main floor will be likened unto a crystal maze."

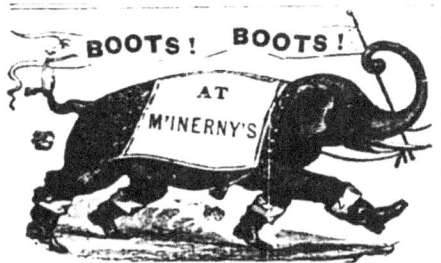

BOOTS, BOOTS, BOOTS!

JUST RECEIVED!

EX D. C. MURRAY.

BOYS SCREWED CALF BOOTS,
Boys Screwed Calf Oxford Ties,
Boys Screwed Calf Balmorals,
Misses Calf Balmoral, (screwed)
Men's Calf Balmorals, (screwed)

ALSO, A FINE LINE OF

BENKERT'S SHOE-WARE!

Also, a full Assortment of

GENT'S CLOTHING!

—AND—

SUPERIOR FURNISHING GOODS!

Which will be Sold at Prices to Suit the Times!

At M. McINERNY'S,
o5 3m   Corner of Fort and Merchant Streets.

A NEW HALL.

Over Mr. McInerny's block of buildings, corner of Fort and Merchant streets, is a new hall which is reached by a broad stairway on Fort street side. This hall is 50 by 46 feet in size, well lighted and ventilated on both sides by many large windows. The ceiling, 14 feet high, has a grated ventilator and arrangements for lighting the place. An anteroom, 12 by 18 feet in dimension, adjoins the hall. Mr. McInerny has had this large room made for social clubs, dancing parties, local minstrel companies, etc.

Evening Bulletin, January 5, 1888

THE M'INERNY BLOCK.

One of the finest blocks of buildings in Honolulu, known as the McInerny block, at the corner of Fort and Merchant streets, and which has been in progress for a long time, is now completed.

The block has a frontage of 106 feet on Fort street, and 84 feet on Merchant street. The Fort street frontage has three stores, in addition to the portion of the corner store on that side. Each of these stores has a width of about 20 feet, with a depth of 46 feet.

One large store occupies the Merchant street side, with a width of about 30 and depth of 65 feet. Behind this and belonging to it is a large warehouse, accessible from the store by a large doorway, and an outside connection with the street by a tramway.

The dimensions of the corner store are about 38 x 44 feet.

There are capacious cellars underneath all the stores. Goods are raised to the upper story and lowered to the cellars by means of elevators.

The windows are all large and of plate glass. Light and ventilation are abundant, and the facilities for exhibiting goods are excellent.

There is large storage space on the second floor of the corner store and the one fronting Merchant street; but over the three stores fronting Fort street is a large hall, intended for meeting purposes, etc., measuring 46 x 60 feet, with 14 feet ceiling. It is reached by a wide and easy grade stairway.

The arrangements for drainage, carrying off filth, etc., are of the best.

The walls of the building are of brick, plastered inside, and covered on the outside. The roof is of heavy corrugated iron. Mr. H. McIntosh was the architect and Mr. E. B. Thomas the builder.

The corner is occupied by the proprietor of the block, Mr. M. McInerny, as a general furnishing goods store, and was opened this morning. The display in the windows is elegant in the superlative degree. To each window is allotted a distinctive line of articles—in one hats, another shoes, and so on. Everything within the store is arranged to the best advantage for inspection, and customers are promptly attended to by polite and obliging clerks.

Evening Bulletin, March 10, 1888

A HANDSOME PRESENT.

Yesterday Mr. H. McIntosh, architect of the McInerny block, was presented by Mr. W. McInerny, for his father, Mr. M. McInerny, with a magnificent gold watch and chain, in recognition of the architect's efficient work on the new block, and as a token of esteem and friendship. The watch, one of the American Watch Co.'s Crescent street movement, cases 18k, contained the following inscription:

Mr. McInerny, to his esteemed friend H. McIntosh, April 17th, 188.

Evening Bulletin, April 4, 1888

The first wooden store here was a "one story frame construction with a gable, corrugated iron roof and corrugated iron lanai projecting over a narrow strip of dirt sidewalk." It was the Star Store in 1860. Its 23-year-old owner, Peter Cushman Jones, came to Hawaii in 1857 with 16 cents in his pocket. He would later become the Minister of Finance, president of C. Brewer & Co., and co-founder of the Bank of Hawaii.

Fort Street, looking mauka from Merchant Street, c.1878
Honolulu Star-Bulletin, April 14, 1959

McInerny initially specialized in clothing for whalers and later catered to a more upscale clientele. They were the first to introduce the Stetson hat to Honolulu.

Robert Lewers of Lewers & Cooke had his first job working in the McInerny store.

WOODEN BUILDINGS!
AT AUCTION!

On Wednesday, July 13th,

At 12 o'clock noon,

On the premises corner of Fort and Merchant Streets, we will sell at Public Auction,

The Wooden Buildings

At present occupied by M. McInerny, J. S. Spear, and building premises of W. E. Foster.

Part of the Buildings are covered with Corrugated Iron.

Buildings to be removed.

☞ TERMS CASH.

E. P. ADAMS & Co., Auct'rs.

The Hawaiian Gazette, June 28, 1887

M. McINERNY.

The Finest Gentlemen's Outfitting Establishment in Honolulu.

Who doesn't know McInerny? Who that is a man that hasn't either outfitted himself there or wanted to? From the old days of the coral building to the present palatial structure, where is the man who wanted fine clothing or underwear and didn't go to McInerny's? For years when you met a man with some style about him and asked him where he got it, the answer invariably was—McInerny's. And they still keep up the old reputation. The boys run the store now, but they are worthy chips of the old block, and the one object is to keep up the business reputation their father attained. Everything in the line of men's furnishing goods in the latest styles from New York, London and Paris is kept in stock. Specialties in these lines are to be found in neck wear, silk shirts, silk umbrellas, and Stetson's hats. A new and separate establishment next door has been opened for foot wear exclusively. Every purse can be suited. Rich and poor will find here the best value for their money and styles to suit every extreme of pocket book. Suspenders and gloves, bath robes and hemstitched handkerchiefs are here in profusion and of the finest styles at the lowest prices in town. Valises and bags for travelers are here in every style, suitable for everyone, from the wayback hayseed to the latest dude in town. Both floors "upstairs and downstairs" are occupied with every variety of stock, and if you want to make a Christmas present, the McInerny boys will supply you. Business men and those interested in recent inventions will want to see their sliding ladders fitted to the shelves and counters so that without exertion assistants can remove anything from the shelves, from the 20 foot ceiling down to the floor, without keeping customers waiting.

Evening Bulletin, December 22, 1894

The Pioneer Savings and Loan Association took out a 65-year lease on the property in 1968, initially saying a parking building might be built while keeping the 80-year-old façade. That didn't happen – they demolished the building that same year to make way for the Pioneer Plaza development.

2022

JUDD BUILDING

101-107 Merchant Street / 843-851 Fort Street

1899 – present (remodeled 1912, 1922, 1979)
Architect/Builder: Oliver G. Traphagen (1899), H.L. Kerr (1912),
Ripley & Davis (1922), Francis Oda (1979) / Fred Harrison (1899),
Pacific Engineering Co. (1912), Charles Ingvorsen (1922)

The Hawaiian Gazette, July 19, 1898

This Italian Renaissance style building was designed by Oliver G. Traphagen and was constructed of stone, brick, terra cotta, iron, and steel by Fred Harrison in 1899 for $44,375.

"The superstructure of the building is a façade of rare beauty, with its ornate features elaborated and embellished with great architectural skill, relieved and emphasized by the beautiful plain Roman brick, the predominating material of the fronts. Terra cotta, on account of its extreme susceptibility to a delicate finish, as well as its well known resistance to climatic influence and extreme temperature, has entered into the ornamental portions of the building."

The Honolulu Advertiser, July 16, 1898

Fight With Water.

Fred. Harrison, the contractor to lay the concrete foundation for the Judd building at Fort and Merchant streets, has a herculean task on hand. On the makai corner of the lot on Fort street a spring of water was struck which has met the full power of a pump with a capacity of 5000 gallons an hour for several days, and the volume of water has not been apparently decreased. From Merchant to Queen street there is a steady stream of water continuously flowing, of such volume and force as may be found in mountain streams after a storm. The presence of this obstruction may cause a serious change in the original plans of the contemplated building.

Evening Bulletin, April 18, 1898

Fred. Harrison Gets the Job — Tenders Vary Greatly.

The contract for the four story Judd building at Queen and Merchant streets was let at noon to-day. Fred. Harrison was the successful bidder among the following:

Patzig	$58,400
W. Mutch	54,750
J. Ouderkirk	51,339
Lucas Bros.	48,765
Enterprise Mill Co.	48,500
Arthur Harrison	46,520
Fred. Harrison	44,375

There is the large difference of $14,025 between the highest and lowest bids. The contractor in his bid engaged to complete the building in eight months from date of contract.

Evening Bulletin, May 19, 1898

The building was officially completed and handed over to its owners on March 15, 1899 and was opened for public inspection on March 20, 1899. It was the first 4-story building erected in Hawaii and its construction attracted dozens of curious spectators. The newspaper claimed it "marked an epoch in the history of these islands".

An electric elevator made by the Crane Company of Chicago was installed on February 3, 1899, and although many have claimed it was the first in Honolulu, it was actually the fourth – the first electric passenger elevator was installed in the Mott-Smith Building in 1897 to serve the Davey Photographic Gallery on the third floor. The Progress Block and Queens Hospital both installed electric passenger elevators in 1898. But the Judd Building did have the first mail chute in Hawaii!

The name "Judd Building" was carved on the lintel of the main entrance on October 4, 1898.

The painting and decorative work was done by H. McKechnie who had recently moved to Hawaii from Oakland, CA.

Hawaii State Archives

The Judd Building was one of the first office buildings in Honolulu to be built for commercial rental office space. It replaced a wooden 2-story building that had been the office of Dr. Gerrit P. Judd, an American physician and missionary who became a trusted advisor and cabinet minister to King Kamehameha III. Dr. Judd was the first person to translate medical journals into the Hawaiian language and he founded Hawaii's first medical school in 1870.

The first ground floor tenant was the Bank of Hawaii, incorporated only one year earlier on December 17, 1897, by Peter Cushman Jones, Edwin Austin Jones, George R. Carter, and Clarence Hyde Cooke. The bank purchased the building in 1910 and officed here until building a new bank in 1927.

Architect H.L. Kerr was hired in 1912 to make $80,000 in alterations for the Bank of Hawaii which included moving the elevator to the makai end of the building and creating a main entrance for the bank in the middle of the Fort Street side.

In the photograph on the left, the new front door of the Bank of Hawaii (from *Honolulu: The Cross-Roads of the Pacific*, 1913).

The stairways to the second, third and fourth floors were altered in 1920 as it was claimed that "the present stairways are unnecessarily wide and rambling."

The Bank of Hawaii hired Ripley & Davis in 1921 to design a fifth floor, built by Charles Ingvorsen for $26,000 in 1922.

The building was further altered in 1979 by First Federal Savings and Loan, hiring architect Francis Oda to turn the 5th floor into a "solarium" and converting the square entranceways and windows on the first floor into arches.

According to Oda, "We did not try to restore the building in an historically authentic way, but to recognize the essential qualities of the building and adapt these to current uses."

2022

Dr. Gerrit P. Judd arrived in Hawaii in 1826 and purchased this lot at the corner of Merchant and Fort Streets.

DOCTOR'S SHOP.

G. P. JUDD, AT THE CORNER OF FORT and Merchant Streets, reminds the public that he continues to devote himself to the treatment of DISEASES of all kinds, having for sale a great variety of DRUGS and MEDICINES of the best quality. He sells also

Poisons.
Arsenic, strichnine, veratrine, corrosive sublimate, Oxalic acid, St. Ignasius beans, nux vomica, opium, Prussic acid, alcohol.

Perfumery.
Musk, extract musk, cologne, lavender water, Windsor, honey and other soaps.

Miscellaneous.
Sago, pearl barley, oat meal, gum shellac, Writing and marking ink, Sands sarsaparilla, Soda water, and other articles too numerous to mention. Easily found when wanted. 6-tf.

Three buildings were later built here: a "rude, dusty brown, two-story frame shack with a pitched roof" known as the "Bible House" at the corner that was put up by Dr. Judd in 1852 after the eastern pine frame was shipped around the Horn, a brick building on the Fort Street side built by E.B. Thomas in 1887 for Dr. Robert McKibbin's drug store, and a 1-story wooden building on the Merchant Street side that was the office of the Annexation Club.

Hawaii State Archives

A Landmark Sold.

The old buildings on the Judd premises, corner of Merchant and Fort Streets, were sold at noon today to make room for a new five story building that will shortly go up on the site for the Bank of Hawaii and other concerns. The two-story wooden building at the corner was knocked down to Ludloff for $170; the one on Merchant street lately occupied by the Annexation Club, &c., was sold to Ho Yen Kee for $200; the outhouses in the rear to Ludloff for $48; and the brick buildings on Fort Street to Fred Harrison for $530.

The Independent, February 12, 1898

At the time this photograph was taken c.1897, the store of Henry Davis & Co. was on the corner. They were "grocers, provision and feed dealers".

OLD BUILDINGS.

Frame That Was Brought Around the Horn.

In speaking of the buildings that have been razed at the corner of Fort and Merchant for the new sky-scraper, Chief Justice Judd recalls that the corner building was put up by his father, Dr. G. P. Judd, in the year 1852. The frame was of eastern pine, shipped around the Horn. The brick building was put up by E. B. Thomas in 1886. M. Louissen says that when he came to Honolulu the two-story structure was one of the notable "blocks" of the town. Before the brick building went up there was a frame house on the site. The long frame structure which was on Merchant street, was built on the order of the Chief Justice. One of the carpenters on the corner frame buildings was Jas. Campbell, the capitalist. Lucas brothers were the contractors for the Merchant street house. Among the tenants of the corner and adjacent buildings at times during the last thirty or forty years were:

Caterer Bessie, Judge Preston, Attorney O'Halloren, Dr. Strangenwald, Attorneys L. A. Thurston, W. A. Kinney, A. S. Hartwell, A. F. Judd, Judge Bickerton, Hawaiian Board, Dr. McKibbin with drug store, Chas. T. Gulick, Tailor W. Johnson, Merchant Sam Lederer, Attorney W. Claude Jones, Jeweler M. Eckardt, Kuokoa newspaper, J. J. Egan and S. Cohn, dry goods, Attorney Chas. Achi, S. E. Pierce, Hawaiian Abstract and Title Company, Louis Marks, "Jack" Waibel.

The brick building which was next to the corner has an especially important historical association. It was here that the first meetings of the '93 Committee of Safety were held.

The Chief Justice had several photographs of the buildings made a couple of weeks ago. They have now entirely disappeared and excavation for the Judd building, four-stories, Roman brick, with electric elevator, has been commenced.

Hawaiian Gazette, March 4, 1898

STANGENWALD BUILDING

113-119 Merchant Street

1901 – present
Architect/Builder: Ripley & Dickey / Fred Harrison

Evening Bulletin, December 6, 1899

Owned by L.A. Thurston, A.W. Carter, and the Castle Estate Ltd., the Stangenwald Building was Honolulu's first 6-story "skyscraper" and was the tallest office building in the city for 50 years.

It was designed by noted architect Charles W. Dickey in the Beaux Arts / Italian Renaissance classical style that would not look out of place on the streets of Paris. It was built by contractor Fred Harrison and almost had a 7th floor to be used as a Business Men's Club. Dickey obtained a building permit for a "6-story steel and brick building" on July 31, 1900.

It was built with concrete walls and steel girders laid on a stone foundation – a first for Hawaii. "One feature, which appeals to the architect is the saving in space, as the concrete walls do not require the width of the brick or stone walls." The front is pressed brick and terra cotta. The construction was supervised by Frederick J. Amweg.

The foundation stones were the largest ever used in Honolulu up to that time and came from a quarry at Waialua. While digging the foundation they hit a well of flowing water and since they couldn't pump it dry, they decided to wall it and add a tap on top to be used for fire and other purposes.

A view of the Hawaiian Star, Stangenwald, and Judd buildings, c.1912-1921, from across the "Mahuka Tract" – the former lumberyard of Lewers & Cooke and later the site of the neo-classical Castle & Cooke building was built on the site in 1924.

Dr. Hugo Stangenwald was born in 1829 and was a "student revolutionist, Austrian émigré, able practicing physician and recognized early-day daguerreotype artist" who came to Honolulu in 1853 after trying his hand in the California gold rush. He was married to Mary Dimond, daughter of Henry Dimond, and after her death he married her sister, Anne.

He bought this property in 1869 for $905 and leased it in 1899 to a limited partnership who planned to erect a building in his name, but he unfortunately died on June 1, 1899, before construction started.

The Stangenwald Building claimed to be Honolulu's first truly fire-proof building due to its steel frame, concrete and brick construction, built-in fire hoses, and flameproof vaults on every floor.

Early tenants included the Henry Waterhouse Trust Company, B.F. Dillingham, Castle and Cooke, Alexander & Baldwin, and C. Brewer companies.

The building was restored by architect James K. Tsugawa in 1980.

Honolulu: The Cross-Roads of the Pacific, 1913

2002

2022

STAR BUILDING

125-131 Merchant Street

1912 – present (remodeled 1963, 1980)
Architect/Builder: Ripley & Reynolds / Lord-Young Engineering Co. Ltd.

The Hawaiian Star, November 25, 1911

Honolulu Star-Bulletin, September 7, 2003

Remodeled many times over the years, this building started out in 1912 as the administrative headquarters for the *Hawaiian Star* newspaper. It was designed by Ripley & Reynolds and was built by the Lord-Young Engineering Company for $14,000, on land leased from the Claus Spreckels estate.

Downstairs housed the office, stock room, and bindery, with the reporters' room, art room, editor rooms, library, linotype and makeup room upstairs. The newspaper was here from 1912 to 1962 with their printing plant on Queen Street in back.

Security Title Corporation moved into the building in 1963 and hired architect Harold L. Cook and Nordic Construction Company to do a major remodel costing $60,000.

Smith Development and Mouse Builders renovated it again in 1980.

1963

2022

CASTLE & COOKE BUILDING

130 Merchant Street

1924 – 1966

Architect/Builder: Charles W. Dickey / A.A. Brown

Honolulu Star-Bulletin, September 30, 1924

Surprisingly, this is the first building built on this site – for over sixty years it was part of the Lewers & Cooke lumberyard. Planning began in 1922 with architect Charles W. Dickey, formerly of Hawaii but now living in Oakland, CA, plus superintendent of construction A.A. Brown who had just completed the Matson Building in San Francisco. The estimated construction cost was $350,000 to $400,000.

The building featured a beautifully grained counter of Tavernelle marble from Italy that rested on a black and gold marble base, designed by J. Arthur Reed. The side walls and ceilings were finished in scagliola, an imitation marble, the floors were inlaid cork tile, the steps were granite, and the entrance doors, cashiers' cages, office partitions, and balcony railings were of solid bronze.

Samuel Northrup Castle was born in New York in 1808 and Amos Starr Cooke was born in Connecticut in 1810. Both came to Hawaii in 1837 and opened a general store in 1851. They invested in the sugar industry and at one point owned the Dole Food Company. Once one of the "Big Five" companies in Hawaii, they are now based in Los Angeles and concentrate on real estate and commercial development.

The building was demolished in 1966 to make way for the $22M Financial Plaza of the Pacific designed by Wou & Partners that was completed in 1968.

2022

DAILY BULLETIN BUILDING

137-139 Merchant Street

1892 – 1921

Architect/Builder: Palmer & Richardson / E.B. Thomas

The Honolulu Advertiser, April 15, 1921

Messrs. W. G. Irwin & Co. are putting material on the ground for a two-story brick building adjoining the Advertiser office on Merchant street. It will be occupied when built by the Daily Bulletin Publishing Co., for its newspaper and printing business. The plans have been drawn by Messrs. Palmer & Richardson, architects, and show a handsome front elevation.

Daily Bulletin, February 5, 1892

Architect Oliver G. Traphagen's first Hawaii office was in this building in 1897.

The building was demolished in 1922 along with the adjoining Schuman Carriage Co. building.

Mr. E. B. Thomas has been awarded the contract for erecting the Bulletin building by Messrs. W. G. Irwin & Co., the landlords.

Evening Bulletin, March 1, 1892

The front of the new Bulletin building, on Merchant street, is about completed, and makes a "monkey" of buildings in its neighborhood.

Evening Bulletin, May 24, 1892

SCHUMAN CARRIAGE CO.

143 Merchant Street / 820-840 Bishop Street

1911 – 1921

Architect/Builder: Emory & Webb / John Ouderkirk

Due to the extension of Bishop Street from Merchant Street to Queen Street, the Schuman Carriage Company had to replace their existing building in this location with this new one built in 1911 by John Ouderkirk. Schuman sold Locomobile, E.M.F., Mitchell, Stoddard-Dayton, and Flanders automobiles.

The building was demolished in 1922, and the Alexander & Baldwin Building was built here in 1929.

THE SCHUMAN BUILDINGS.

John Ouderkirk, contractor, yesterday started work on the Merchant street end of the Schuman Carriage Company's reconstruction. What was the old garage part, being on the line of Bishop street extension, will be cut away, with the exception of the office side. Concrete walls will be erected on the front, rear and side, completing a new office building 20x65 feet in dimensions. A concrete building of fifty feet frontage on Queen street and sixty feet deep, for the carriage department, has been erected. Between this and the office building, completing the series of structures from Queen to Merchant street, will be the garage, 75x135 feet in dimensions.

The Hawaiian Star, May 6, 1911

MUTUAL TELEPHONE BUILDING

185 Merchant Street / 840-848 Alakea Street
1884 – 1919
Architect/Builder: George Lucas

THE old buildings at the corner of Merchant and Alakea streets were sold yesterday for $30. The Mutual Telephone Co. has secured the site and intends to erect new buildings in which to conduct their business.

Evening Bulletin, January 24, 1884

The result of the meeting of the Mutual Telephone Stockholders last week has been the forwarding of work on a new building for the offices of the company. Mr George Lucas has the work in charge.

The Hawaiian Gazette, April 23, 1884

Located on the ewa/makai corner of Merchant and Alakea streets, the Mutual Telephone Company opened for business on March 16, 1885, with three operators – "two ladies and one young man".

This was one of the first buildings captured during the overthrow of the Hawaiian Kingdom in 1893 since it allowed for easy eavesdropping on local telephone calls.

The building was demolished in 1919 to make way for the massive Theo H. Davies building which covered the entire block. Mutual Telephone bought Hawaiian Bell in 1894 and is now Hawaiian Telcom.

At the time of this photo there was no Bishop Street. The 1892 Daily Bulletin Building and 1900 Stangenwald Building are visible in the distance. The 1900 Magoon Building is on the right.

2022

MAGOON BUILDING

180-188 Merchant Street
1900 – 1964
Architect/Builder: H.L. Kerr

Honolulu: The Cross-Roads of the Pacific, 1913

The first structures on this site were several 1-story frame houses that were built sometime before 1885.

This 2-story brick office building was designed by architect H.L. Kerr and built for local attorney J. Alfred Magoon in early 1900.

In 1966 it was replaced by the 8-story Honolulu Savings and Loan Building designed by Island Architects and Engineers and built by the Walker-Moody Construction Company.

This newer building was subsequently demolished in 1993 for the $175M First Hawaiian Center designed by New York architects Kohn Pedersen Fox and completed in 1996.

The Honolulu Advertiser, October 14, 1964

2022

SCHUMAN CARRIAGE CO.

201-221 Merchant Street / 753-763 Alakea Street
1916 – c.1985
Architect/Builder: Fred H. Redward & Mervin Carson / Fred H. Redward

Honolulu Advertiser, April 6, 1916

This building was designed by contractor Fred H. Redward along with Mervin Carson and was built for $75,000 in 1916 for the Schuman Carriage Company.

Gustav Adolph Schuman was born in Dresden, Germany, in 1867 and came to Hawaii in 1884 as an 18-year-old wheelwright and worked as a carriage trimmer at W. Wright & Sons before founding Schuman Carriage Co. in 1892, selling wagons and carts.

Schuman also owned the Club Stables on Fort Street and later the Territorial Stables on King Street.

G. SCHUMAN'S Carriage and Harness House
Club Stables Block, 1 door above Stables' Entrance. Telephone 477.

SCHUMAN COMPANY WILL SPEND $75,000 ON HOME

A fireproof brick and concrete structure to cost about $75,000 will be built this summer by the Schuman Carriage Company on the L-shaped lot fronting on Alakea, Merchant and Richard streets, which Gustave Schuman recently purchased at a cost approximating $35,000. Fred Redward and Mervin Carson, architects, are now busy on specifications.

The Alakea and Merchant street frontages will be two stories in height and will house the offices and show room departments. The rear structure, one story in height, will be an immense garage and repair shop. November or December should see the new building ready for occupancy.

Honolulu Star-Bulletin, May 6, 1915

Seeing "horseless carriages" at the 1904 World's Fair in St. Louis, Schuman subsequently shipped the first automobile to Hawaii – a Pope Tribune. The following year he brought in the first Ford Model T.

By 1916 they had "upward of 100 employees" when they built this large building at the corner of Merchant and Alakea streets that took up almost half of the entire block. They were the agents for Ford, Lincoln, Hudson, Essex, Willys-Overland, Buick, and Cadillac cars, along with Federal and White trucks, and sold on average one new automobile a day. They also sold motorcycles and bicycles and farming implements.

They bought the Central Union Church at Beretania and Richards streets in 1924 and turned it into their showroom. Probably the first automobile showroom anywhere with beautiful stained-glass windows!

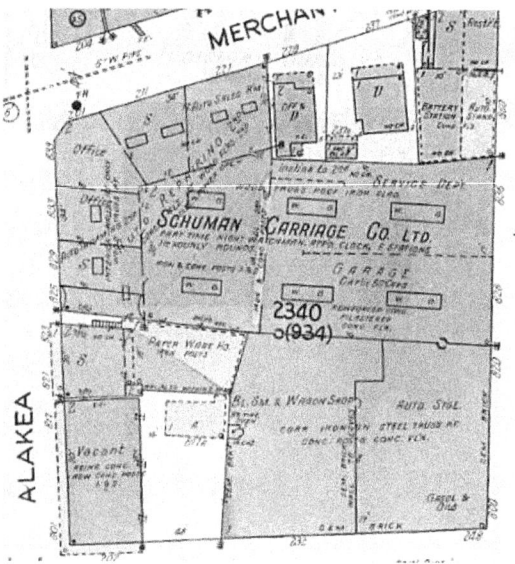

The Schuman Company closed the automobile business in 2004 after 111 years and are now in the airplane and helicopter business.

Mervin B. Carson was Gus Schuman's son-in-law. By 1938 he was the secretary of the Inter-Island Steam Navigation Company and was president of the Honolulu Chamber of Commerce in 1946.

The site is now the 24-story $30M City Financial Tower designed by Minoru Yamasaki and completed in 1989 by Hawaiian Dredging and Construction. Yamasaki also designed the infamous Pruitt-Igoe public housing project in St. Louis and the 110-story twin towers of the World Trade Center in New York City.

1967

2022

PODMORE BUILDING

202-206 Merchant Street / 901-913 Alakea Street

1902 – present
Architect/Builder: Lee Wai

2022

Peter Cushman Jones leased this property to Joseph William Podmore for 25 years in 1902 provided he "within six months from April 1, 1902, at his own cost and charge, erect and complete a good and substantial building" to cost not less than $7,000. Lee Wai obtained a building permit for this 2-story store at 901 Alakea on April 17, 1902.

The entire building was constructed of local cut lava stone with mortar joints decorated with a thin red line.

Joseph W. Podmore was an English sailor who initially clerked for the J.T. Waterhouse Company before opening his own firm specializing as an insurance and commission agent in addition to real estate investment and rental. The first tenants in this building were a tailor and a decorator with the Mercantile Printing Company upstairs.

The land and building was donated to the local Board of Missions in 1907 who officed here and printed *The Friend* until moving to the Mission Memorial Building in 1916. The *Honolulu Advertiser* also had offices here, and it was the first Honolulu office of DHL Air Cargo. It also housed the Bon Ton Café.

As early as 1885 there was a 1-story wooden house on the site, in what was known as the Union Square Block.

The entire block except for the Occidental Hotel (on the far left) was deliberately burned by the Board of Health on January 15, 1900, after a Chinese boy living in a tailor shop near the corner of King and Richards became sick with bubonic plague. White families were quarantined in the Occidental Hotel while Hawaiians and Chinese were sent to the detention camp.

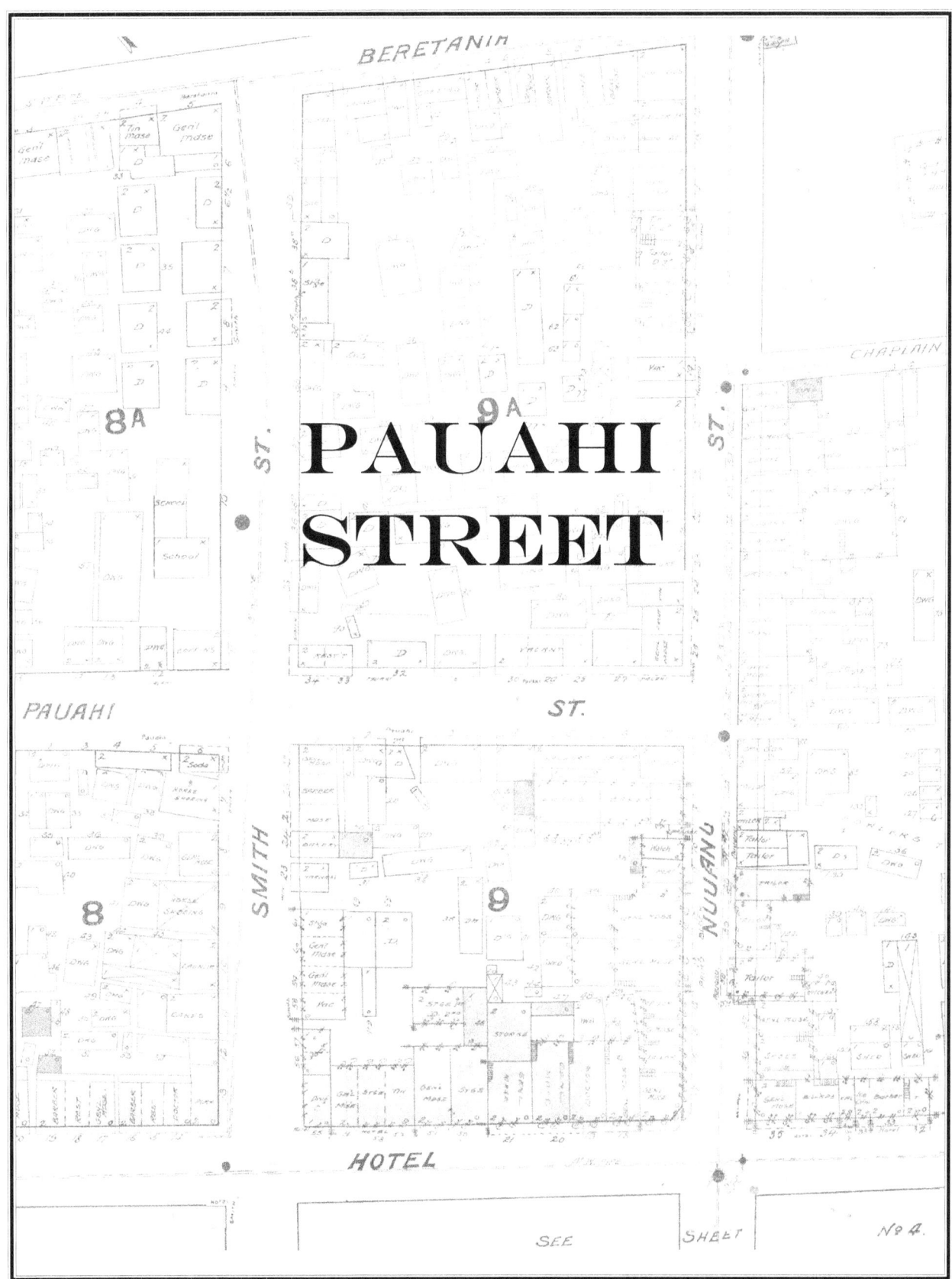

E.W. QUINN BUILDING
28-34-42 S. Pauahi Street
1913 – 1956
Architect/Builder: Lord-Young Engineering Company

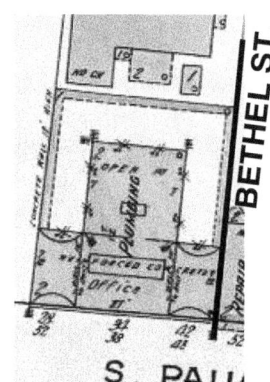

1914 Sanborn Map

This reinforced concrete building was built on Pauahi Street behind the Mills Institute for the E. W. Quinn Plumbing Company in 1913. The contractor was the Lord-Young Engineering Company, and they might have also been the designers.

Born in Benicia, CA, in 1866, Edward W. Quinn came to Hawaii in 1899 and established himself as a merchant plumber. In addition to providing plumbing services for major buildings like the Castle & Cooke Building, First National Bank, Hawaii Theater, and the YWCA, Quinn was a former Hawaii representative, senator, and supervisor.

Quinn was also known as "The Father of Sunday Baseball" for authoring a bill in 1905 allowing the game to be played on Sunday.

In 1933 the building became the store of florist Walter T. Fujikama, founded in 1919. Fujikama Florist is still in business a few blocks away, run by the third generation of the family.

Altered slightly in 1925 for the extension of Bethel Street to Beretania Street, the E.W. Quinn Building was demolished in 1956 for Marks Garage.

2022

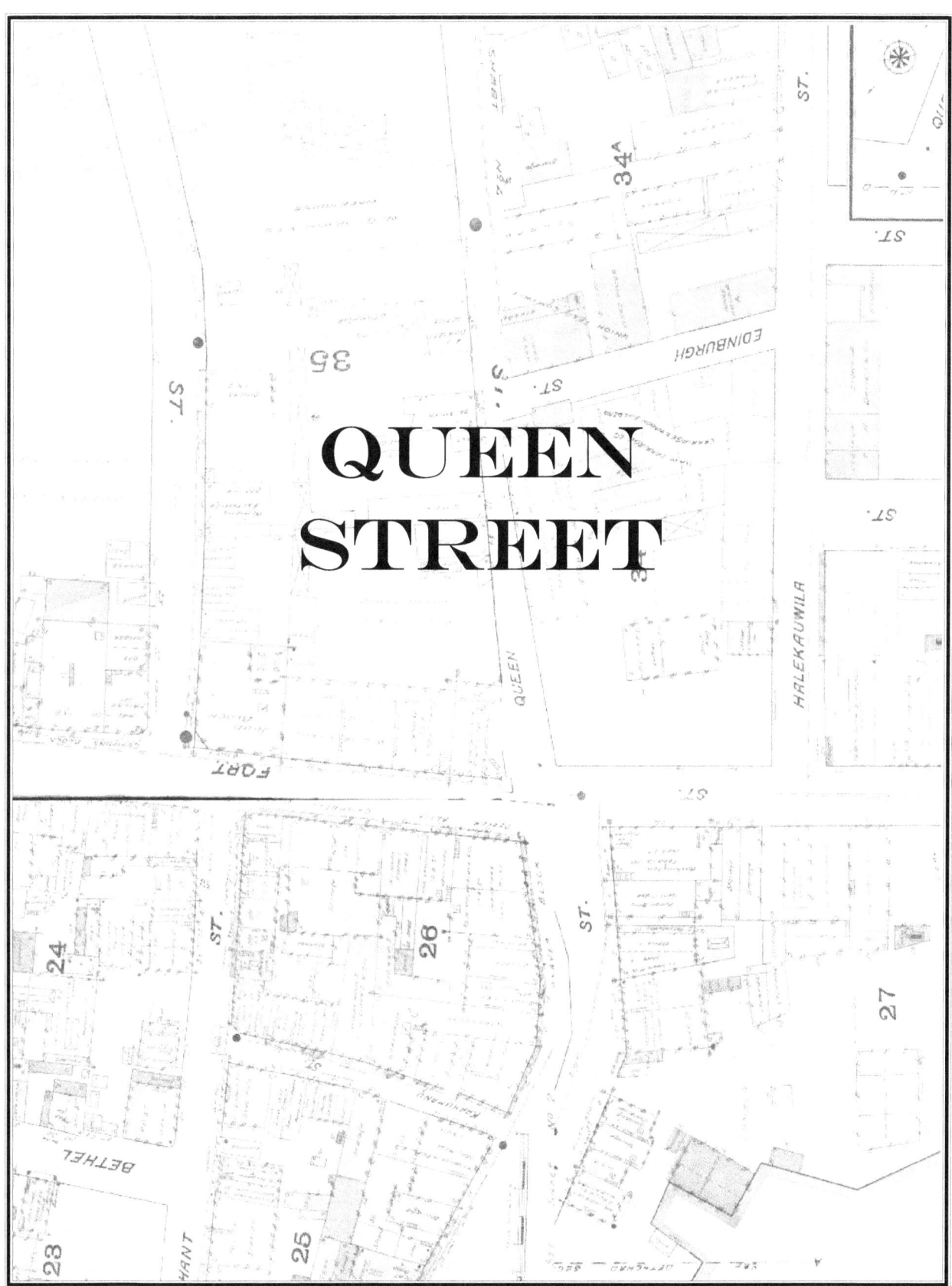

THE OLD CORNER

2-6 S. Queen Street
1846/1847 – 1948 (1857 remodel)
Architect/Builder: unknown

This building was initially George W. Punchard's 1-story coral store built in 1846 or 1847.

The Polynesian, May 9, 1857

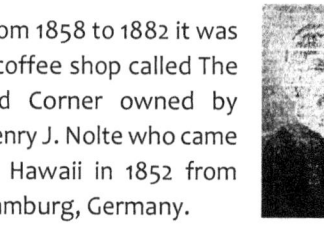

From 1858 to 1882 it was a coffee shop called The Old Corner owned by Henry J. Nolte who came to Hawaii in 1852 from Hamburg, Germany.

Famous for dispensing "the Arabian stimulant", the Old Corner also carried a wide variety of American and European newspapers and Cuban cigars.

In 1881 it was renovated into a full-service restaurant.

COFFEE SALOONS.—These popular resorts for supplying the wants of the inner man, have become great institutions in this, our city of Honolulu. They have, in a great measure, supplanted the Bar Rooms of former days, and minister to the same tendencies of human nature to congregate together. As a morning resort, the establishment of Messrs. Kruger & Nolte, on the corner of Nuuanu and Queen streets, appears to be the best patronized. Here, from 5 to 8 o'clock, A. M., may be gathered, by the eager listener, the gossip of the business portion of the town, or the patient waiter will be able to meet with any one whom he is desirous of falling in with, of those who pursue avocations which require them to be up betimes. Although not so well filled as in the matutinal hours, the current of droppers in continues vigorous during the remainder of the day and evening, and the tables are well covered with the latest European and American illustrated papers, among which, as diamonds among gems of lesser value, can always be found files of the *Commercial Advertiser* and *Polynesian*, in loving proximity, tempting the person of elegant leisure, to linger a little longer over his cup of coffee, bottle of Dashaway Beer, slice of California Cheese and a bit of ham, or whatever else, with which he is regaling the inner man. Success to these gentlemen, who have, we are glad to know, acquired a competency in administering to the wants of poor bachelors, who cannot marry, and must, perchance, go somewhere to eat.

Pacific Commercial Advertiser, November 15, 1860

After Nolte moved to Fort Street to open the Beaver Saloon in 1882, The Old Corner was run by the Hart Brothers and later by Hop Lee.

By 1905 it was known as the "The Old Corner Saloon" run by William Lishman and Charles T. Day, but in 1910 the Liquor Board refused to renew the license saying "the place has long had an unsavory reputation".

Hawaii State Archives

From 1916 to 1943 it was the Wo Hop Hing Kee store owned by Fong Hing and Fong Kui Lam, providing sailors outfits and cold drinks. Fong Hing came to Hawaii in 1895 from Canton (Guangzhou), China, and eventually opened the first Chinese steam laundry in Hawaii. He also owned the Honolulu Chop Sui House, Bow Wo Jewelry, the New York Shoe Store, Tai Loy Jewelry, and the Kai Kau Real Estate Company.

Badly damaged by termites, the building was demolished for a police parking lot in 1948.

In 1994 the 44,000 square foot Nuʻuanu Court condominium/office building was built on the site of the police station parking lot and the City and County Tax Office. It was developed by Harbor Court Developers, a joint partnership between Mike McCormack and Dick Bradley with financial partners C. Itoh and Mitsui Trust and Banking Company of Japan. It was designed by James M. Severson (Lacayo Architects) and built by the M.A. Mortenson Company.

Completed at the tail-end of the big 1990's Japanese investment boom and bust, Nuʻuanu Court (also known as Queen's Court) sat vacant for 9 years until bought in 2003 by Richard Emery of Hawaii First Inc. along with Richard Weiser.

2022

J.T. WATERHOUSE BUILDINGS

8-14 S. Queen Street
1871/1886 – c.1969 (remodeled 1928)
Architect/Builder: George Lucas (1886)

Photograph by Isaiah Taber, 1880 *c.1907-1917*

These two photographs were taken roughly 30 years apart. The brick building on the left side was built in 1871 and the brick building on the right side was built in 1886, both for importer John T. Waterhouse, replacing wooden buildings previously on the site.

IMPROVEMENTS.—Mr. J. T. Waterhouse has removed the wooden building which he has occupied for a number of years as a store near the corner of Queen and Nuuanu streets, to the lot next mauka of the first bridge on Nuuanu avenue. On the old lot, we understand that a new brick fire-proof two-story building will be erected at once. This will add not a little towards beautifying and giving a business-like appearance to the city front.

The Pacific Commercial Advertiser, May 13, 1871

The new brick building belonging to J. T. Waterhouse, on Queen street, is almost completed. When finished it will be occupied by Mr. Waterhouse, as an addition to his former store.

Daily Honolulu Press, January 18, 1886

This site was originally part of Pulaholaho, a Native Hawaiian community of straw houses. Governor Kekuanaoa built a thatched "new market place" near here in 1845.

In 1840 British Consul Richard Charlton claimed he had an exclusive 299-year lease on Pulaholaho based on a document Kalanimoku signed in 1826. It was the source of much contention with the Hawaiian government saying Kalanimoku lacked the authority to sign such a lease. In 1843 the claim was taken to the Earl of Aberdeen, the British Minister of Foreign Affairs, who naturally sided with Charlton.

Charlton evicted 156 residents and removed 23 houses, opened up the land for redevelopment, and sold it to Robert Janion who auctioned it off in six large lots. Robert Wyllie said Charlton was "the most incorrigible man I ever knew" and George Pelly publicly proclaimed Charlton to be a "Liar, Slanderer, and Contemptible Coward."

In 1854, J. Fuller built a 2-story building "on the site of the old thatched market" that housed commission merchants Feldheim & Company. In 1857 it was also the likely location of Paul Emmert's "paint shop" and the workshop of builder George Thomas.

William DeWitt Alexander, 1896

From 1907 to 1911 the building on the left was the warehouse of Macfarlane & Co., and then the offices of importers E. Langer Company from 1917 to 1920. It housed the Hurd & Pohlman Company from 1923 to 1930. The right side was the offices of the Hawaiian Fertilizer Company in 1916, and it was combined with the left side in 1917 by the E. Langer Company.

The Honolulu Star-Bulletin, June 18, 1926

From 1922 to 1947 it was the office and plant of Fred Makino's *Hawaii Hochi Sha* (*Hawaii Herald*) newspaper.

Initially starting in the building at 14 S. Queen on the right, the newspaper purchased both buildings in 1927 for $50,000 and remodeled them into one building in 1928 at a cost of $60,000.

The Honolulu Advertiser, April 15, 1928

The city condemned and took over the building in 1946 and renovated it in 1948 to house the crime prevention division of the Honolulu police department.

The building was demolished for a parking lot by 1969, and the Nu'uanu Court (Queen's Court) Building designed by Norman Lacayo was built on the site in 1994.

SENATOR WATERHOUSE BUILDING

20 S. Queen Street
1895 – 1940
Architect/Builder: Ripley & Reynolds / William Mutch

Honolulu: The Cross-Roads of the Pacific, 1913

This little 1-story stone building was built in 1895 by William Mutch and was designed in "the most modern style" by Ripley & Reynolds as new offices for Senator Henry Waterhouse. He was born in 1845 in Hobart, Tasmania, Australia, and was the son of John T. Waterhouse.

From 1901 to 1937 this building was the office of stevedore company McCabe, Hamilton & Renny, Ltd.

The building was purchased by the police department in 1939 and demolished for a parking lot.

MARKET HOUSE

21 S. Queen Street
1850 – 1899 (1866 remodel)
Architect/Builder: unknown

Paul Emmert, 1854

Paul Emmert, 1854

This site was formerly the old Pulaholaho waterfront, the only place in the harbor where Native Hawaiians could safely beach canoes. Kekuanaoa built a thatched "new market place" near here in 1845.

The government replaced it with a substantial coral stone Market House in 1850. *The Polynesian wrote in September 7, 1850:*

> "The new market house... is not only an honor to the government, but supplies a want long felt at this port, and we hope will soon supersede the miserable, filthy, thatched apologies, that have so long annoyed all the five senses."

C. Brewer & Co. moved to the old Market House in 1860 and they were located here for 50 years.

Changes and Improvements.

During the past week Messrs. C. Brewer & Co. have completed their alterations in the makai end of the Market House recently vacated by Mr. James I. Dowsett—knocked down the partition formerly dividing the two portions of the lower part, and thrown the whole length of the building open as a store-house, making one of the largest, most commodious and convenient business places in town.

The Polynesian, August 18, 1860

RENOVATED.—The large stone building on Market Wharf, now occupied by Messrs. C. Brewer & Co., has lately been thoroughly repaired and improved internally. The cumbrous stone columns and arches have been removed, making a large and elegant room—the most spacious in town—affording a roomy and delightful counting room, with plenty of space for goods. The stone steps on the south side of the building leading to the Harbor Master's office, have been removed, and firm wooden ones put up instead, improving its outward appearance exceedingly. Here we may also add, that a lookout has been erected just over the steps, so that Officer Woods can keep a detective eye on smugglers.

The Pacific Commercial Advertiser, September 22, 1866

Hawaii State Archives

OLD LANDMARK GONE.

The work of tearing down the old building preparatory to the new one Brewer & Co. are to be build, began yesterday. The old building is one of the oldest in the city.

The Hawaiian Star, February 3, 1899

Destroying a Landmark.

An old landmark is disappearing in the demolition of the C. Brewer & Co. block in Queen street. Its upper floor was the armory of the native volunteer forces under King Kalakaua, and the chief place for holding election meetings. When the crowd was too great for the interior, and sometimes after a meeting had adjourned, orators would harangue vast assemblies in the square below from the landing at top of the stairs on the outside. A modern building will take the place of the gray old fabric.

Evening Bulletin, February 2, 1899

NEW HOME OF C. BREWER & CO., LTD.

By the 1st of August of this year the big new building of the Brewer Co. will be completed. The work of placing the foundation is already going rapidly forward.

The building, which will be situated on Queen street, will consist of two stories. The first floor will be occupied entirely by the Brewer company, and here they will have their vaults and offices of the directors. The second floor will be divided into offices, with all the most modern appliances. The second floor, however, is subject to change according to the desires of patrons.

The building will have a frontage of forty-one feet on Queen street and will extend eighty-four feet toward the water. The front of the building is treated in classic style, all the first story openings being a series of arches.

The whole structure, with the exception of the cornices and mouldings, will be of brick, and will be a worthy addition to the other new business blocks in the course of construction. The plans are by Ripley & Dickey architects. The site is the location of the Brewer & Co.'s old stand.

The Honolulu Advertiser, February 21, 1899

The Honolulu Advertiser, February 13, 1910

Designed by Ripley & Dickey and built by John Ouderkirk for $19,133 in 1899, the Brewer Building was demolished 11 years later in 1910 for the widening of Queen Street.

R.W. WOOD BUILDING

26 S. Queen Street

1856 – 1940
Architect/Builder: unknown

Dr. Robert W. Wood had this building built on his lot in 1856 for H. Hackfeld & Company.

It had pressed brick, granite trimmings, and a slate roof with a hip roof only on one side, apparently planning for a future addition that never happened. Opening day was July 9, 1856.

Captain Heinrich Hackfeld was born in the village of Almsloh near Bremen, Germany, in 1816 and went to sea at age 16. He became a master mariner with his own ship and first came to Honolulu in 1844 when a war in Mexico prevented him from delivering his cargo in Mazatlan.

After several Pacific voyages that included being shipwrecked in the Philippines, Hackfeld purchased the brig *Wilhelmine* in 1848 and returned to Honolulu via Lisbon, Valdivia (Chile), and Tahiti with his wife, 16-year-old brother-in-law Carl Pflüger, and 21-year-old nephew Bernhard Friedrich Ehlers.

He sold the ship to James Makee, sold its cargo through Cornelius Bartow's store, and started his own commission and ship chandlery business.

Hackfeld worked closely with businessman Dr. Robert W. Wood and became the shipping agent for the Koloa and East Maui sugar plantations as well as the Russian government. In 1850 Hackfeld opened a retail store on Fort Street later known as B.F. Ehlers & Co., and their commission and wholesale business was located here as early as 1854. Twenty years later they moved into the old Court House in 1874.

> Messrs. H. Hackfeld & Co. opened their new store on Wenesday, with a lunch, which was numerously attended, the firm being as much respected as any in town. The building, just erected by Dr. R. W. Wood, is of brick, and built in a very superior manner.

The Polynesian, July 12, 1856

Robert Love operated a bakery and grocery store in a building adjoining the waikiki side in 1854 which was replaced by Dr. Edward Hoffman's brick drug store in 1857.

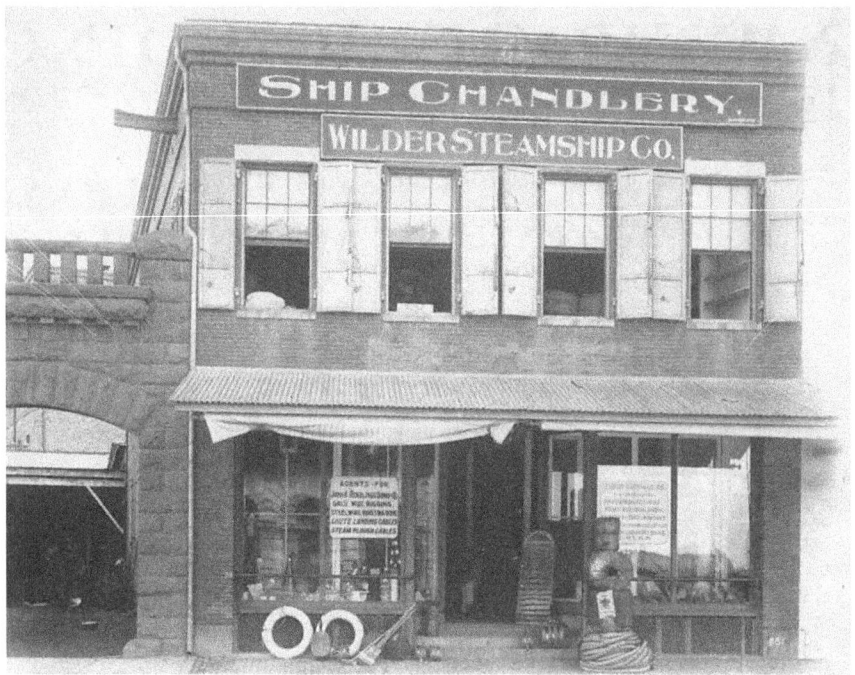

c.1901-1905

Honolulu Ship Chandlery.

The old Waterhouse store on Queen street has been secured for the business of a ship chandlery. The business will be going in full swing before long and besides proving a prosperous and enterprising affair will no doubt become, as is generally the case with a well-conducted ship chandlery, the headquarters of all the sea captains in the port, where they will congregate to boast of their respective ships, swap interesting tales of the sea, smoke strong, well-flavored pipes and long cigars, and chew tobacco to their hearts' content, as well as to do business.

Honolulu Advertiser, January 4, 1901

Wilder's Ship Chandlery.

The ship chandlery department of the Wilder Steamship Company on Queen street is being rapidly put in shape. Goods in large quantities have arrived by steamers and sailing vessels, and in a short time the various steam and sailing craft entering this port can obtain anything from a sail needle to an anchor. The management of this important branch of the extensive operations of the Wilder Steamship Company has been placed in the hands of Captain C. J. Campbell who is well known among sea-faring men. M. J. Homan who was formerly purser of the wrecked steamer Kilauea Hou, has been given a position in the house.

Evening Bulletin, January 22, 1901

It was also known as "Dr. R.W. Wood's Building" and was the general merchandise store of John T. Waterhouse from 1879 to 1901. It then became the ship chandlery for the Wilder Steamship Company from 1901 to 1905 until they merged with the Inter-Island Steam Navigation Company in 1905.

In 1931 it housed the paint and merchandise department of the Honolulu Construction & Draying Company.

It was purchased by the city police department in 1939 and became the navy shore patrol and police radio department offices in January 1940. A month later they decided to tear it down and sell the bricks to make a parking lot.

Today the site is the makai/waikiki corner of the Queen's (Nuʻuanu) Court Building built in 1994 at the corner of Queen and Bethel streets.

Old Hackfeld Building Razed

The oldest structure in downtown Honolulu, the old Hackfeld building at Bethel and Queen Sts., had been demolished by city-county workers Monday.

The two story brick building was erected in 1855 by Dr. Robert W. Wood who rented it to Hackfeld & Co. up to 1874 when Hackfeld moved to Fort and Queen Sts. where the American Factors building now stands.

After Hackfeld moved out, Dr Wood sold the building to John Thomas Waterhouse, who at one time used it as a ship chandlery.

The building, which has been unoccupied for a long time, was bought recently by the city-county at the request of the police commission which has need of the site.

Honolulu Star-Bulletin, May 21, 1940

MCCHESNEY BUILDING

36-42 S. Queen Street

1878, 1899 – 1931

Architect/Builder: Thomas J. Baker (1878), Oliver G. Traphagen (1899) / Lucas Brothers (1899)

Hawaii State Archives

This was originally two buildings – the left side was built in 1878 and the right side was added in 1899 when W.M. McChesney & Sons leased the property.

They first added a large iron warehouse in back and then hired Oliver G. Traphagen to design the building on the right to match the existing building on the left.

BUILDING CONTRACT.

Lucas Will Build the Second of the McChesney Warehouses.

Lucas Brothers have been awarded the contract for building the new brick offices and warehouse for McChesney & Sons, in Queen street. O. G. Traphagen is the architect. The bids were: Lucas Bros., $2,988; Arthur Harrison, $3,541; John Ouderkirk, $4,344.

The new building will go between Grinbaum's and the old office of the I. I. S. N. Co. It has been decided to let the latter stand, to be incorporated in the new structure. The building is in good condition and to preserve it will save both time and expense.

The Hawaiian Star, February 7, 1899

The building on the left was built in 1878 by Thomas J. Baker for Bolles & Co. and replaced the 1849 wooden building built for F.R. Vida & Co. that was the ship chandlery of Capt. Thomas Spencer when sketched by Paul Emmert in 1854.

Bolles & Co. were here until the death of Benjamin F. Bolles in 1884. A.W. Peirce & Co. was the next tenant, followed by the Inter-Island Steam Navigation Company from 1888 to 1931.

McCHESNEY & SONS' BLOCK.

This is a two-story structure of brick throughout, 27 feet by 59 feet, the entire first floor is retained as office space by the firm. The second story is especially adapted for heavy storage. Ceiling of first story is panelled and beamed, painted and decorated; plate glass front windows. Fire-proof doors connect from the Ewa side with a warehouse.

Behind this new structure is a new building entirely of iron and steel, some 36ft.x55ft. These are commodious structures in every way.

O. G. Traphagen, Architect.

The Honolulu Advertiser, January 1, 1900

W.M. McChesney & Sons were here from 1899 to at least 1907, followed by Grace Brothers in the 1930's.

Paul Emmert, 1854

It was demolished for the extension of Bethel Street in 1931.

AN OLD LANDMARK GONE.—The wooden building on Queen Street so long in the occupancy of Bolles & Co., ship chandlers, was this week sold at auction, to be removed, and in its place is to be erected a two-story fire-proof brick store. The old building is about 30 years old, having been erected in 1848–9 by Messrs. Vida & Co., an old-time business firm of the then "beach" of Honolulu. They were succeeded in its occupancy by Captain Thomas Spencer, now a sugar planter at Hilo. During his time the front store was a favorite place of resort for whaling skippers, and many was the tough yarn there spun in the "fifties," when the whaling business was "high hook," and as many as a hundred and fifty ships lay in Honolulu harbor at one time at the close of a season North. Oil was King then, and nobody bothered their heads about sugar.

The Pacific Commercial Advertiser, August 17, 1878

MORE IMPROVEMENTS.—We note preparations by the well-known house of Bolles & Co. for the erection of a two-story fire-proof brick store on the site of their old stand, Queen street. During the construction of the new building—which is in the hands of Mr. Baker, the builder and architect—Bolles & Co. will occupy the store next door to the north.

The Pacific Commercial Advertiser, August 10, 1878

REMOVAL!
BOLLES & CO.,

WOULD INFORM THEIR FRIENDS and the public generally, that they have

Removed to their New Fire-proof Store,

Which has just been completed, situated at the Old Stand, 34 Queen Street, where they have been making large additions to their stock of Ship Chandlery, Ship and Plantation Stores, which make their assortment large and varied.

Will be happy to have a call from their patrons, and they will assure them that no pains will be spared to attend to their wants in a satisfactory manner.

We have now in Stock: Cordage, hemp and Manila, an assortment of sizes; Cotton Duck, Flax Canvas, Hemp Canvas, Cotton Sail Twine, 5, 6, 7 and 8 ply; Flax Sail Twine, 3 and 5 ply; Blocks, Oars, Shieves, Hooks and Thimbles, &c., &c., all of which will be sold at Bed Rock Prices.

Honolulu, Nov. 23d, 1878.   ja1 '79

STOCKHOLM TAR,

WILMINGTON TAR, WILMINGTON PITCH.   For Sale by
ja1 '79   BOLLES & CO.

PROVISIONS,

BEEF, PORK, HAMS, BACON, CHEESE, Lard, &c., &c.   For Sale by
ja1 '79   BOLLES & CO.

☞ Messrs. Bolles & Co. are now located in their new building, and have opened with a large assortment of fresh groceries, ship stores and other requisites for sea-faring customers. Our citizens will also find there a stock of goods well suited to their wants. See their advertisement in another column.

The Hawaiian Gazette, November 27, 1878

A GENERAL ASSORTMENT OF
GROCERIES & SHIP STORES
Always on Hand!

AND WILL BE SOLD AT THE LOWEST Prices, by
ja28   BOLLES & CO.

Owing to the death of Mr. B. F. Bolles, Sr. the old established ship chandlery firm of Bolles & Co. have closed their business, the balance of the stock being sold off at cost prices.

The Honolulu Advertiser, May 17, 1884

An Old Ship Chandlery Stand.

A new floor and other improvements are being made in the store lately occupied by A. W. Peirce & Co. on Queen street, who have recently sold their stock in trade to the Inter-island Navigation Co., and give notice to their friends in our advertising columns. This building will be fitted up with a large and commodious office, into which when ready the company will move and make it their headquarters—a much more convenient stand for business than the place on the Esplanade now occupied by them. This old ship chandlery has for some forty years been a favorite resort for seafaring men, and will probably continue to be so. Early in the fifties Captain Thos. Spencer occupied it, and was succeeded about 1862 by Bolles & Co., and later by Peirce & Co., who retire after a business career of eighteen years. Captain Peirce tells us that his first visit to Honolulu was in 1843, in a whaler. Since that time he visited the islands frequently till he quit the whaling business in 1870 and located here.

The Honolulu Advertiser, June 8, 1888

The 1899 building on the right replaced a 2-story wooden building that was the drug store of Dr. George A. Lathrop in late 1853 when painted by Swiss artist Paul Emmert.

From 1858 to 1876 it was the office of Dr. Robert McKibbin from Belfast.

By the late 1890's it was a Chinese coffee shop and one of the last of the old wooden structures on Queen Street.

Paul Emmert, 1854

The Thomas Spencer and Dr. Robert McKibbin (Lathrop) buildings can both be seen in this photograph taken c.1865. The 1856 R.W. Wood Building (Hackfeld) is on the left side with the 2-story 1857 Hoffman Drug Store adjoining, and with the 1854 Makee & Anthon Block on the right.

C.L. RICHARDS BLOCK

43 S. Queen Street

1859 – 1925

Architect/Builder: Charles W. Vincent, George Thomas

James Robinson Building (1855), Swan & Clifford Building "Hale Mahoe" (1854), and C.L. Richards Block, c.1893

This 2-story coral stone building was built in 1859 by Charles W. Vincent and George Thomas on wharf land leased from the government by Charles L. Richards. The estimated cost was $8,000 to $10,000.

Richards had a ship chandlery store downstairs and C.A. Williams & Company were on the second floor where the Phenix and United States Guano Companies also had their headquarters.

> **C. L. RICHARDS & CO.,**
> Ship Chandlers and Commission Merchants, and Dealers in General Merchandise,
> Keep constantly on hand a full assortment of merchandise, for the supply of Whalers and Merchant vessels.
> 566 1y

> The stone store of Mr. Richards on the wharf, is also progressing, and promises to be completed by the opening of the fall season. The granting of the wharf space by the government, for building purposes was and is still considered to be in contravention of express statute, which had to be repealed to allow its being done, and was likewise an infringement of the vested rights of land holders in proximity. Yet the store that is being erected on it will possess an eligible site for the business of ship chandlery, for which it is designed, and when completed will be one of the most substantial buildings in the town. Its cost will probably be from $8,000 to $10,000.

The Pacific Commercial Advertiser, June 23, 1859

> **New Buildings.**
> Since we noticed the erection of the Odd Fellows' Hall in Fort street, two other buildings have gone up and been completed, which add not a little to the respectable appearance of the quarters wherein they are situated, and reflect great credit on their builders, Messrs. C. W. Vincent and G. Thomas. We refer to the addition to the Steam Co.'s flour mill and the new coral building of Mr. C. L. Richards in Queen street, opposite the Makee block.

The Polynesian, August 6, 1859

> **REMOVED.**—Mr. C. L. Richards last week moved into the new stone store recently erected by him, adjoining his old stand. The second floor will be occupied by Messrs. C. A. Williams & Co. Here will probably be also located our inter-island steamboat office.

The Pacific Commercial Advertiser, August 4, 1859

"May you live a thousand years and your shadow never be less."

Passing along Queen Street yesterday about meridian, we heard the well-known hip, hip, hip and a tiger, of our friend Capt. T. Spencer, issuing from the door of Messrs. C. L. Richards & Co., and stepping in, found it was a little festal meeting to commemorate the birth-day of the Senior, C. L. Richards, Esq., or "Charley," as he is better known to the merchants. Approving of the fine flavor of the "Rosy," and the sentiments offered, we wish him, in addition, many happy returns of his natal day, and a successful business career in the new coral "Richards' Block."

The Polynesian, August 27, 1859

By the arrival of the Mariposa we learn of the sudden death of Mr. Charles L. Richards, who was the founder of the business in this city now carried on by Messrs. A. W. Peirce & Co. For nearly twenty years past Mr. Richards has been a resident in Norwich, Connecticut. He died rather suddenly at a late hour on Sunday, 21st October, from the effects of an accidental injury sustained so far back as the fall of 1879. The *Bulletin*, a newspaper, says of him: "Charles L. Richards was born in Waterford, August 23d, 1830. In 1860 he went to California and thence to the Sandwich Islands, where he did a successful business as a ship chandler. He was engaged in business at the Sandwich Islands for a dozen years and was part owner in several whaling vessels. During the war he suffered some losses from the seizure of his vessels and still has an unsettled claim of $25,000 or more against the government for a whale ship impressed into the service of the government during the rebellion, to return the sailors of the whaling fleet destroyed by the Confederate war-ship Shenendoah, to their homes. During Mr. Richards' residence in the Sandwich Islands he became the intimate friend of King Kalakaua and accompanied him on many excursions. He returned in 1864 and settled in Norwich. In 1867 he returned to the Sandwich Islands and settled up his business affairs then returning to Norwich in 1868 and settling here permanently. The same year he married Miss Ada Pollard of this place, who, with six children—four sons and two daughters—still survive him. Mr. Richards personally was a gentleman of exact habits, fine feelings and agreeable social qualities. He made a wide circle of friend who will sympathize with his family and sincerely mourn his death." There are many here who knew him who will feel keen sympathy with his family.

*The Pacific Commercial Advertiser
November 10, 1883*

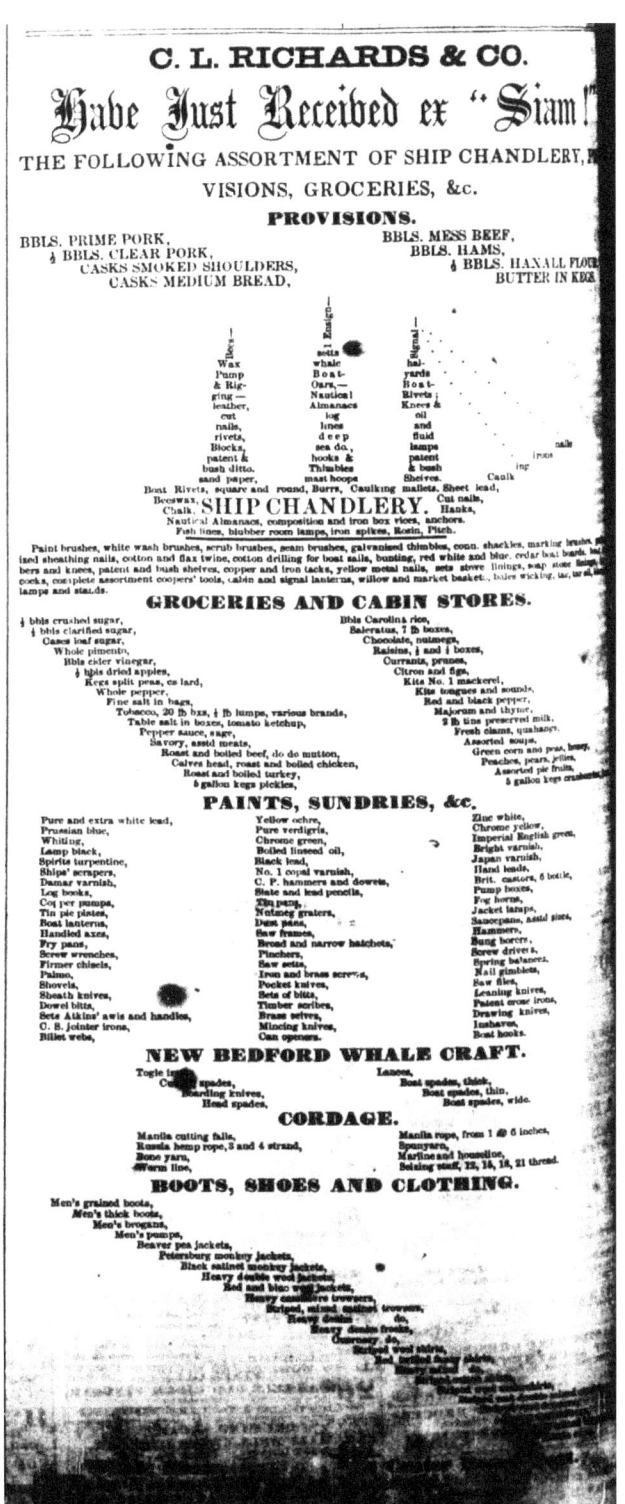

The Pacific Commercial Advertiser, September 24, 1859

Former whaling ship captain Abraham W. Peirce purchased an interest in C.L. Richards & Co. in 1870 and a year later bought out the company, renaming it A.W. Peirce & Co.

A.W. Peirce & Co. were in this building from 1871 to 1885.

They built a new building next to the Masonic Hall at Fort and Queen Streets in 1879 that was briefly a second location and perhaps a hedge against the lease on the C.L. Richards Block coming up for auction in 1878.

In March 1885 they moved across the street to the Bolles Building on the site of Thomas Spencer's ship chandlery store.

CAPTAIN PIERCE.

Captain and Mrs. A. W. Pierce depart for the States by the S. S. Australia to-morrow. Captain Pierce made his first visit to these Islands in 1844 as second officer of a whale ship. In 1864 he came here again as chief officer of the ship William Hamilton. Subsequently he paid a visit here as master of the ships Dartmouth, Cutusoff, Emerald and Lagoda, sending home the last named vessel in 1863, after a very successful season north, Captain Pierce going home by the way of San Francisco and Panama. For some years after the Captain was employed in fitting out whale ships at San Francisco for the New Bedford company. In the latter part of '69 he again came to these Islands and purchased an interest in the ship chandlery business of C. J. Richards & Co. Later he became sole owner of the business, which he conducted successfully until June 1st of this year when he sold out to the Inter-Island Steam Navigation Co. Captain Pierce will remain for some time in California where he has large landed interests. Aloha Captain.

Evening Bulletin, July 30, 1888

Auctioneer Lewis J. Levey moved into the C. L. Richards building on October 1, 1885.

Wholesale grocers McChesney & Sons were in the building from 1889 to 1899.

HONOLULU AND ISLAND OF OAHU. 11

A. W. PEIRCE & CO.

SHIP CHANDLERS

AND

COMMISSION MERCHANTS,

No. 40 Queen Street, Honolulu.

DEALERS IN

SPERM OIL,	WHALING GEAR	YELLOW
POLAR OIL,	OF ALL KINDS.	METAL,
KEROSENE OIL.	WHALE BOATS, BOAT STOCK, ANCHORS, CHAINS, HEMP CORDAGE, MANILLA CORDAGE,	SHEATHING AND NAILS, SUGAR,
The Largest Assortment of SHIP CHANDLERY AND MARINE HARDWARE ON THE Sandwich Islands.	ARTESIAN WELL ROPE, COTTON DUCK, HEMP DUCK, NAVAL STORES, ALL KINDS PAINTS AND OILS, BRASS & GALVANIZED MARINE HARDWARE, SAILMAKERS' GOODS, BOAT BUILDERS' HARDWARE, Wire Rope, all Sizes, Etc.	RICE, COFFEE, Etc., Etc. Additions to which we are constantly receiving from the United States AND Europe.

Agents for Brand's Bomb Guns and Lances.
Also for Peirce's Bomb Guns and Lances.
Also for PERRY DAVIS' PAIN KILLER.

As will be seen by an advertisement in another column, Messrs. M. W. McChesney & Sons, wholesale grocers, have removed to their new and commodious premises No. 40 Queen street. The entire building, which was formerly occupied by Capt. A. W. Pearce as a ship chandlery store, has been substantially remodelled and finely fitted up, both on the lower flat and upstairs. The business of this wholesale firm has now every store facility, and their stock is replete with every article needed in the grocery and leather finding departments; while the store is in a favorable position for shipping.

The Honolulu Advertiser, June 15, 1889

The C.L. Richards Block was here for 66 years until demolished in 1925 for the Pier 11 project.

ALLEN BLOCK

45-55 S. Queen Street

1894 – 1925

Architect/Builder: Charles H. Geddes / Lucas Brothers

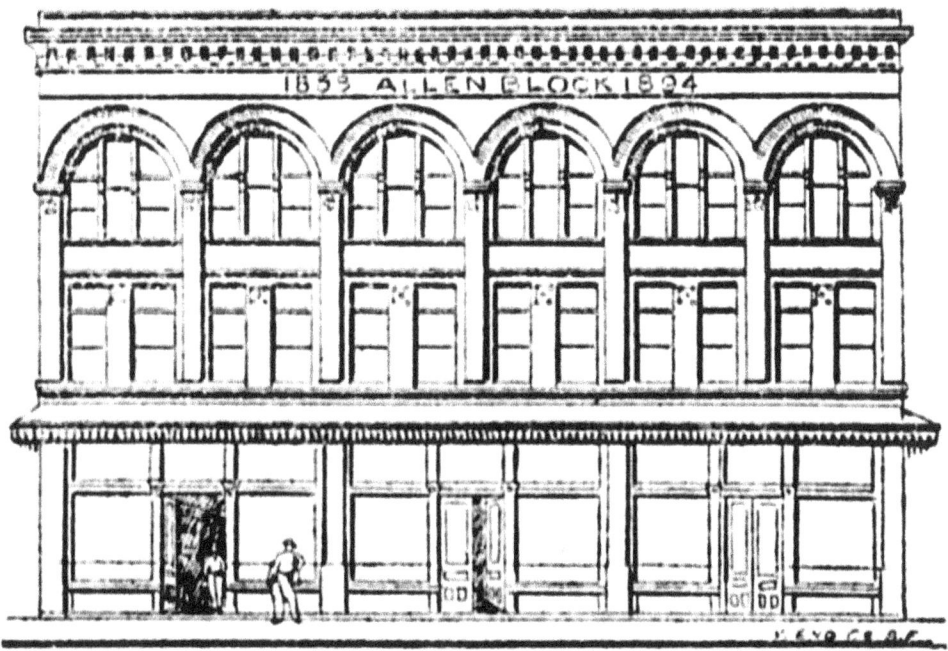

Evening Bulletin, December 12, 1894

The Allen Block was a new headquarters for the lumber firm of Allen & Robinson. It was designed by San Francisco architect Charles Herbert Geddes and built by the Lucas Brothers for $21,000.

The US Army Quartermaster Depot was here in 1898, and the Theo. H. Davies grocery department moved here in 1899.

The building was demolished in 1925 by the Hawaiian Ballasting Company as part of the government's Pier 11 waterfront improvements that wiped out four other buildings adjacent to the Allen Block.

> The old wooden building which has been occupied by Allen & Robinson for so long, will be sold at auction today and then removed or demolished. In its place a handsome brick building, three stories high, will be erected. It will have a frontage of seventy-two feet on Queen street.

The Hawaiian Gazette, May 1, 1894

> The New Allen Block.
> The Allen block, on Queen street, is fast nearing completion and will be a handsome structure. It is three stories and will present an artistic front. The windows are being put in, and today a splendid sign, cast in gilt, was laid on the front at the top. It is lettered as follows: "1853. Allen Block. 1894."

The Hawaiian Star, October 16, 1894

1853. ALLEN BLOCK. 1894.

Noble Addition to the Mercantile Architecture of Honolulu

Description of the New Quarters of the Old Firm of Allen & Robinson.

Honolulu has received an addition to its mercantile architecture which is an ornament to the business quarter. This is the Allen block on Queen street, upon the site of the lately demolished wooden building, which for a great many years was a landmark on the city front. It is of three stories with a height of fifty-six feet and ground dimensions, in round numbers, of 70 feet front by 60 and 50 feet depth. The different depths are due to the rear corners being cut out, making the middle part of the building project back. There are three self-contained divisions in the structure, each having three floors connected by both stairs and elevator. Each division is thus designed for a large mercantile establishment, having salesroom and offices on the ground floor and two warerooms on the upper floors.

The building is of brick with 17-inch walls. Its front is very handsome, being of plate glass with iron pilasters for the first story, and pressed brick with terra cotta trimmings for the upper stories, the windows of the third one being circular-headed. Steel girders are used in the front and the stability of the structure is further assured by concrete foundations, three feet wide and five feet deep, resting on the solid coral. The double doors of ¾ inch plate glass are 10 feet high by 6 feet wide, and are fitted with real bronze locks costing $8 and hinges $2.50 each, also having a concealed bolt that will hold the door in any position desired. The front windows of the store on the south side are 8ft. high by 6ft. wide, with a transom 4ft by 6ft. Those of the other stores are 8ft. by 8 feet, with transom 4ft. by 8ft. There is an awning over the first story front, with moulded gutter of galvanized iron.

The ornamental work on the front is elaborate, as may be understood by those acquainted with architecture from the following particulars: In terra cotta there are moulded cornice, scroll stop block, jack arches, scroll panel, sill course and ornamental frieze. There are besides moulded medallions, scroll capital, pressed brick pilasters and piers. The illustration accompanying this article will explain more to the ordinary reader than technical details. The terra cotta was furnished by Gladding, McBean & Co. of San Francisco. Charles Geddes was the architect of the building. He has had thirty years' experience in his profession at San Francisco, in that long period making the plans of a large proportion of the finest buildings in that metropolis of the Golden West.

Allen & Robinson, dealers in coal, lumber and builders' supplies, occupy the south store. The others are not yet occupied. A description of this store will suit that on the north side, excepting that the latter is wider by three feet. The store is 21ft. 6in. front by 50ft. deep, with a 10ft. long hallway leading to the rear entrance, an arched door with iron shutters. This hallway is in the projection before mentioned, and the corresponding spaces in the upper stories form recesses, each with a window in the side and one in the rear, back of the head of the stairs. There is a window in the side of the hallway, so that it has plenty of light when the rear door is closed. An arched door gives a side entrance to the store, and is fitted with iron shutters. There are two safe stands built of concrete resting on the solid coral inside of the office space, which is separated from the store space by counters. The elevator is on the inner side and not enclosed, but in the other stores the elevators run in shafts. Recesses under the store counter on the outside are used to hold assorted nails. Shelving and wall paper racks occupy all the available space on the sides of the store, and are designed to afford the greatest possible facilities for assorting the goods. Besides the plate glass front the lighting of the store is amply effected by one mullion and one single window on the side and the same on the rear. Under the stairs in the office is a marble wash basin, which is also provided in the corresponding place in each of the other divisions. The counters are of tasteful designs in Spanish cedar and nor'west pine, the same woods being used in all the other fittings. A speaking tube communicates with the upper flats.

Winding stairs four feet wide, built of Spanish cedar, with moulded rail 4in.x5in., and 2½in. turned balusters, make connection between the different stories. On the second floor is the wall paper wareroom. Its woodwork is finished in oil. The flat is flooded with light from two spur-headed windows with transoms in the front, one mullion and two single windows in the side, and one mullion and one single window in the rear, besides a window on the side of the recess back of the stairs.

Hardware, paints and oils are stored on the third flat. Its lighting is similar to that of the second flat, excepting that the front windows are circular-headed, 9ft.x11ft. in size. The single windows are 3ft.x9ft. Ascending a ladder through a narrow space under the roof a hatch gives access to the outside of the roof.

From here a splendid expanse of scenery is opened to the view, taking in Barber's Point, Ewa plantation, Pearl Harbor, the various mountain ranges, Punchbowl, Diamond Head, the Pacific Ocean, and every part of the city. Six fantail ventilators thrust their swinging mouths through the roof, there being two of them for each division of the block. It is said to be the best ventilated as well as the best lighted building in Honolulu.

A minute description of the two unoccupied divisions of the building is unnecessary after the foregoing details. The middle division is the largest and of course has no sunlight from the sides. In other respect its arrangements and equipments, excepting the variations already noted, are the same as those of the others. The ceiling of all the first story is of 1in.x4in. tongued and grooved redwood, while that of the other stories is of lath and plaster. The building is wired for both light and power, and the elevators are geared for running by electric motor, although workable by hand.

From top to bottom of the building there is not a flaw discernible in either material or construction. Everything seems to be well-seasoned and of the best selection in the one case, and well and truly fashioned and joined in the other. There is no gingerbread work but there is a finished appearance about every part of the construction. Lucas Brothers, proprietors of the Honolulu Planing Mill, erected the building, Thomas R. Lucas having been in constant supervision of all the details. That establishment has for a great many years been famous for the quality of its work in the building line, but it is doubtful if it has ever produced a fabric superior to the Allen block.

Evening Bulletin, December 12, 1894

The Allen Block was built on the site of the prominent Swan & Clifford building constructed by Charles W. Vincent in 1854 and known as Hale Mahoe. The building itself came from Boston and was shipped in pieces around The Horn. It was built on land owned by Englishman Robert Charlton whose supposed 299-year lease was contested all the way to the British courts, unsuccessfully.

Paul Emmert, 1854

Building.

Within a few days the frame of a fine large building at the foot of Kaahumanu street has been raised, and the busy hands of a large gang of carpenters, under the direction of Mr. Vincent, are rapidly completing a store for Messrs. Swan & Clifford. This will be one of the largest buildings in Honolulu, for mercantile purposes.

The Polynesian, January 14, 1854

Auspicious.—The fine new store of Messrs Swan & Clifford, at the foot of Kaahumanu st., was opened with a Lunch on Thursday last, on which occasion the tables fairly groaned under the weight of good things provided by M. V. Chancerel, mine host of the Hotel de France. Beverly people were around, and found their local dish in abundance and perfection; they are quite numerous in Honolulu, much more so than we imagined.

The Polynesian, March 4, 1854

Lyman Swan was born in 1823 in Watertown, New York, and was married to Antoinette Marín, a daughter of Don Francisco de Paula Marín. Ornan G. Clifford came to Honolulu in 1848 and initially partnered with Lyman Swan in the baking business at the corner of Fort and King streets.

In 1854, Swan and Clifford brought the first cargo of ice to the Islands, from Sitka in the brig *Noble*.

They later became ship chandlers but while Clifford was in China, Swan forged $40,000 in promissory notes and left for California on the bark *George* with over $80,000 in unpaid bills. When his ship docked in San Francisco it was seized and sold, and although Swan was arrested, he was never extradited to Hawaii. After years of both civil and criminal charges, he eventually returned to baking and became an upstanding member of the Santa Cruz business community.

After Swan & Clifford, the building was owned by a Mr. Luddington from Germany who kept a liquor store until his license renewal was refused when he was caught smuggling. Alexander J. Cartwright had an office in the building for more than 20 years and the United States Consulate also officed upstairs.

Henry W. Severence, the former Hawaiian Consul-General and American Consul-General kept an auction house on the lower floor. Lumber and shipping firm Allen & Robinson bought the building in the 1870's.

A LANDMARK.

HALE-MAHOE.

A Historical Building Disappears.

While everybody who believes in and admires the progress of Hawaii, ought to feel proud wherever one of the signs of infancy of this rising country is removed the feeling is mingled, as far as the kamaainas are concerned with regret, and with a sympathetic thought towards the "days of old," "the men of old," and the "memories dear." The removal of the old wooden building on Queen street at the foot of Kaahumanu street, and lately occupied by the well-known firm of Allen and Robinson, is a good instance of the ever restless hand of progress. Few of our present citizens remember the history of that building. A few lines from our feeble pen may awake memories in the hearts of some of the "old ones" that may induce them to give—if not a tear—at least a regretful thought to the cirumstances and people connected with the now destroyed old building. It was in the early fifties when the material all fixed and all fitted for the Queen street house was brought here from Boston. Honolulu then did not resemble Honolulu of to-day and the building now sold and torn down as "out of season" at that time was a palace or at least a most magnificent structure. The building was put up and Honolulu felt proud. The firm of Swan and Clifford took possession of the new house and ran successfully a ship-chandlery business. This was in the early fities—long before brother Smith and brother Castle (from Leipzig) had any idea of "cutting faces."

Mr. Clifford, who, praise to the gods is dead, went to China at one time and left the building, (and the business) in the hands of Mr. Swan. The last-named gentleman "saw" Clifford and raised him—that is, he raised h—. He disappeared and Clifford was looking for him until a few years ago when he died an aged, broken up man, existing on the charity and friendship of the never-failing helper J. I. Dowsett. The last this community heard of Mr. Swan was that he was running a bakery somewhere in California, but things in that State are evidently run in a peculiar manner. If W. G. Smith could be the "Savior" why couldn't Mr. Swan be a baker.

The next party who occupied the historical building was Mr. Luddington. He kept a liquor store and was for a while successful. He was too successful for his own good. His business was too near the water-front and he actually went into the smuggling business. If he had been alive now and doing the business he would have known enough to divide or at least pay "snorting Jim" a dividend. He didn't, and consequently Billy Smith's predecessor in office, refused him a license and poor Luddington had to be "glade" enough to go home to "Yarmany" and die. He was one of the wittiest and best known characters around town—and in those days there was some humor, wit, and ridicule knocking around, even if they didn't have an Advisory Council and W. O. S. was only *infuturo* or *in unibibus*. Well, after they got rid of Luddington, the building was occupied by a number of different people. A. J. Cartwright had his office there for more than twenty years. The United States Consulate had an office upstairs for many years. H. W. Severance ex-Hawaiian-Consul-General, and ex-American-Consul-General wielded at one time the auctioneer's hammer on the lower floor. Sailmakers and provision dealers and other business men and firms have occupied the old structure, but to the present generation it is best known as the business place and office of the great lumber firm of Allen and Robinson. It was in the seventies when this firm took possession and bought the desirable property. For a number of years the pilot office had found room there, and the great lumber and shipping firm was known here and abroad. The doom of the old wooden structure has come. Another old landmark has gone into oblivion Under the efficient management of Mr. P. Muhlendorf, the firm of Allen and Robinson erects a structure becoming the importance of the firm and the business, and the kamaainas throw their last and regretful looks at the old building originally owned by "Bob" Charlton, the cause of so much trouble to Hawaii and now disappearing as a witness of the prosperity that Hawaii's adopted sons gained under the much maligned much blackguarded and much misrepresented Hawaiian Monarchy.

Hawaii Holomua Progress
May 4, 1894

MAKEE & ANTHON BLOCK

52 S. Queen Street / 814 Kaʻahumanu Street

1854 – 1951 (remodeled 1909, 1926)
Architect/Builder: unknown (1854), John Ouderkirk (1909), Hart Wood (1926)

Paul Emmert, 1854

Built on the site of Henry Downton's adobe building built in 1846 or 1847, this was the first 3-story brick building in Honolulu.

Captain James Makee purchased the land from Swan & Clifford in 1853 for $8,055. The pressed bricks and granite trimmings arrived from Boston via Cape Horn on the clipper ship *Waverly* on February 25, 1854. The schooner *Ka Moi* brought additional building stone in July 1854.

The building officially opened on August 5, 1854, "inaugurated by a lunch to all the town" catered by Franconi & Co. of the Globe Hotel.

Something New in Honolulu.

A fine new Fire-Proof Store, three stories high, erecting at the corner of Kaahumanu and Queen streets, by Capt. Makee, built of brick, with a *granite* front, is something new in Honolulu, and consequently excites considerable attention. No granite has before been used in the erection of buildings, at the islands, although fence and gate posts, and a few door-steps, have been imported from China, of a quality, however, far inferior to the Massachusetts granite now used by Capt. Makee, in the construction of his Store. This block will be of the most substantial character, and an ornament to the city.

The Polynesian, April 1, 1854

Dr. Edward Hoffman was the first tenant on the corner. Called "a genial little doctor", he was also known for his "eminence as a pianist".

In 1857 Hoffman built a 2-story building next to the R.W. Wood Building and D.N. Flitner moved into this corner, but Hoffman returned in 1858 for 10 more years.

Captain Makee had an office on the second floor, as did Julius Anthon.

Aldrich & Bishop, importers and dealers in general merchandise were on the Queen Street side. On August 17, 1857, Charles R. Bishop and William A. Aldrich founded the Bank of Bishop & Co. in a small 10' x 10' office. This was the first bank in Hawaii, and it is known today as First Hawaiian Bank.

M.S. Grinbaum & Co., general commission merchants and sugar factors moved here in 1862 and Alexander J. Cartwright relocated here in 1878 from the Mahoe building across the street. Cartwright officed here the Cartwright Building was constructed on Merchant Street in 1887. Grinbaum expanded the building in 1909 and T.H. Davies faced it with cement in 1910.

> The first bank safe ever brought to Honolulu, which was for Bishop & Co.'s bank, is in possession of the Honolulu Scrap Iron Co. as part of the junk from the Grinbaum building now being demolished.

The Hawaiian Star, May 19, 1909

> The contract for remodeling the old Grinbaum building, at the corner of Keeaumoku and Queen streets, and erecting a two-story addition to it on Kaahumanu street, the whole to form a uniform structure two stories in height, was let yesterday to Contractor Ouderkirk, his bid being the lowest by over $3000.

The Honolulu Advertiser, March 30, 1909

The building was gutted in a fire on November 18, 1924, that collapsed the roof but left the walls unharmed. Julie Grinbaum rebuilt it in 1926 at a cost of $27,166.

> Application for permission to make alterations and repairs to the structure at a total cost of $27,166 was filed yesterday with Harry K. Stewart, building inspector, by Julie Grinbaum. Hart Wood is named as the architect on the project and S. Ito as the builder.

The Honolulu Advertiser, January 7, 1926

1925

The Armand Weill Co. was here from 1926 to 1946. Weill was a general merchandise and commission agent born in Alsace Lorraine in 1876 who came to Hawaii in 1898.

In 1947 it was the Castle & Cooke Terminals building.

The Honolulu Advertiser, June 11, 1950

There was another devastating fire on June 9, 1950, where 25 out of the 75 firemen that responded and fought the blaze for five hours were overcome with smoke.

The site was sold to the city to become a parking lot.

The $91M Harbor Court Condominium was built on the site in 1994, and Kaʻahumanu Street was turned into a pedestrian walkway.

2022

ROBINSON WAREHOUSE

59 S. Queen Street
c.1840 – 1911 (remodeled 1873)
Architect/Builder: James Robinson

Paul Emmert, 1854

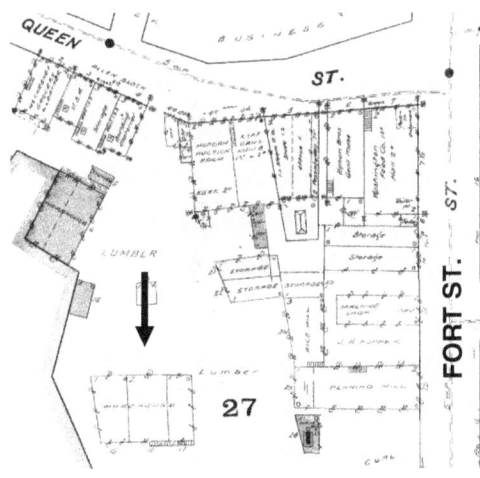

1899 Dakin Map

Located about 300' makai from Queen Street on a portion of what had been the King's Wharf adjacent to the walls of the old fort, James Robinson's Warehouse was one of Honolulu's famous landmarks for many years.

It was built sometime around 1840 and was enlarged 30' in width and 60' in length in 1873.

The most distinctive feature about the warehouse was the ship's figurehead from the *Alderman Wood*, mounted on the pulley beam keeping watch over the harbor.

The HDOT Harbors Division Building is on the site today.

John James Robinson was born in 1799 in Purfleet, Thurrock, Essex, England, and came to Hawaii via the whaling ship *Hermes* which ran aground and wrecked in the leeward Hawaiian islands in 1822 on its way to Japan. He spent four months building a small schooner from the wreckage that he named *Deliverance*, and after a voyage of 10 weeks he was able to reach Honolulu.

A ship carpenter by trade, he and shipmate Robert Lawrence sold *Deliverance* for $2,000 and started the James Robinson & Co. ship repair business. With the assistance of Kamehameha II and John Young, they established their shipyard beside Pākākā Point in 1827 in the shadow of the fort. They were later joined by Robert W. Holt who had come to Hawaii from Boston. They could repair two ships at a time, and in 1840 were the only ship chandlers and carpenters in the Pacific.

> "Honest, industrious, economical, temperate, and intelligent, they are living illustrations of what these virtues can secure to men. ... Their yard is situated in the most convenient part of the harbor, has a stone butment and where two vessels of six hundred tons burthen can be berthed, hove out, and undergo repairs at one and the same time. There is fourteen feet of water along side of the butment. The proprietors generally keep on hand all kinds of material for repairing vessels. Also those things requisite for heaving out, such as blocks, falls, etc. On the establishment are fourteen excellent workmen, among whom are Ship Carpenters, Caulkers and Gravers, Ship Joiners, Block-makers, Spar-makers, Boatbuilders, etc."

In 1824, the British ship *Alderman Wood*, owned by Sir Matthew Wood (former Lord Mayor of London), wrecked off the coast of Molokai and was salvaged by Robinson. The captain gave him the figurehead and he installed it on the pulley beam of the warehouse where it greeted sailors and customers for 87 years.

Robinson married Rebecca Kaikilani Prever in 1843 and they had 3 sons and 6 daughters. They were one of the wealthiest and most prominent families in Honolulu. Their daughter Victoria became Victoria Ward (her "Old Plantation" house was where the Blaisdell Center is today), their son Mark was Minister of Foreign Affairs in Queen Liliʻuokalani's cabinet, and daughter Mary married Thomas Foster (the founder of the Inter-Island Steam Navigation Company, better known today as Hawaiian Airlines).

The Honolulu Advertiser, February 8, 1903

The business lasted until the death of Robert Lawrence in 1868. James Robinson died in 1876 at the age of 76.

The grand ball celebrating the restoration of the Hawaiian Kingdom by British Admiral Thomas was held in the sail loft of the warehouse. The Duke of Edinburg and King Kamehameha V danced in this loft in 1869.

The slate roof collapsed in 1911, breaking the massive ridge beam and causing the coral blocks on the façade to give way. No one knows what happened to the figurehead – Judge Sanford B. Dole went looking for it in 1921 to no avail.

HUSTACE-PECK BUILDING

63 S. Queen Street
1886 – c.1926
Architect/Builder: unknown

Honolulu: The Cross-Roads of the Pacific, 1913

Frank Hustace & George H. Robertson formed a partnership in 1885 "for the purpose of carrying on the Draying Business in Honolulu" and built this small brick office in 1886.

They became Hustace, Peck & Co. in 1903 and were purchased by Honolulu Construction & Draying Co. in 1908.

Honolulu Construction & Draying moved to a new building at Bishop and Halekauwila in 1922 and this little building was gone by 1926 when all the buildings on this side of Queen Street were cleared off for the Pier 11 redevelopment project.

It was located just beyond the tip of what is now Walker Park, in the middle of Nimitz Highway.

M.P. ROBINSON BUILDING

65-71 S. Queen Street

1903 – 1926

Architect/Builder: Frederick W. Beardslee

Honolulu: The Cross-Roads of the Pacific, 1913

Completed in November of 1903, this building replaced a previous building that was "completely gutted" by fire on January 3, 1903. The fire destroyed the auction house of James F. Morgan and the store of L.B. Kerr. Firemen and bystanders were able to move most of Morgan's property into adjoining buildings, but the entire stock of L.B. Kerr was lost at a value of $125,000 (about $4M today).

Frederick W. Beardslee designed this new building for Mark Prever Robinson, the son of James Robinson. The contractor had promised to only use Portuguese and Hawaiian workers but ended up hiring Japanese stonecutters.

The building was demolished in 1926 for the Pier 11 redevelopment project.

> The plans for Mr. M. P. Robinson's new building to replace that which was burned while occupied by L. B. Kerr & Company, have been approved and the building as contemplated in Architect Beardslee's drawing will be a decided addition to the street. The building will be two stories, running from the Inter-Island to the Hustace office. The front will be ornately finished with terra cotta and the walls will be of terra cotta and brick. The entrance to the second story will be by a center stairway and the two store rooms will be entered by recessed doors at either end of the building. The interior arrangements have not been fixed owing to the fact that Mr. Robinson wants the prospective tenants to have their own convenience consulted in this matter. He has asked any one looking for quarters to investigate and the results will determine the decision.

The Honolulu Advertiser, February 8, 1903

The 1903 building was built on the site of a coral stone building that was built adjacent to the walls of the old fort in 1855 under the supervision of Thomas Harding. It was billed as "fire-proof" since it was built of stone with iron shutters, but that only protected it from fire from without.

The first tenants were R. Coady & Co. and Robert C. Janion. In 1885 it housed auctioneer E.P. Adams and the Hoffschlaeger Company, and later auctioneer James F. Morgan and the L.B. Kerr company when it was destroyed by fire on January 3, 1903.

☞ At a time when cheap lumber is filling every nook and corner of the town with houses of the most combustible description, it does one's eyes good to observe the fine stone building now in the course of erection on Queen street by Messrs James Robinson &c. It is extensive and substantial, intended we believe to be let for stores, and will be fire proof, the materials necessary to finish it in a superior way, having been imported expressly. Such houses as it is destined to be are a credit to the place and may be counted amongst the substantial marks of progress, and prove besides that there is a little capital accumulating here in the hands of people who mean to invest it permanently in the country where it was acquired.

The Polynesian, September 8, 1855

R. COADY & CO.
HAVE REMOVED THEIR OFFICE to the room directly over the store recently occupied by them, in the new building of J. Robinson & Co., on Queen street.   1t

☞ The large fire-proof building lately erected by Messrs. James Robinson & Co., under the superintendence of Mr. T. Harding, was opened on Thursday, with a lunch provided by Messrs. Franconi and Medaille such as one does not have an opportunity to partake of very often. All the arrangements were on the most liberal style, and speak volumes for the genuine hospitality of our friends at the "Point." Toasts were drunk and responded to, sentiments given, songs sang, etc., etc. The "hip-hip-hurrahs" almost vied with the thunder that ushered in the morning, and would have shook the walls if they were not too solid to be acted upon in that way. Such ice-punch and such a punch-bowl do not frequently come together—a punch-bowl from Japan, and capable of containing 15 gallons. Mr. Bullions very neatly (in allusion to the profession of Messrs. J. Robinson & Co.) compared the building to a ship, copper-fastened, no leak, and so on. Upon this, one gentlemen with a dandified voice, whispered distinctly in the ear of our reporter, that few vessels now-a-days are "lunched" with so much *eclat*. One half of the building is to be occupied by Messrs. Coady & Co. and the other half by Mr. R. C. Janion. May the house prove a lucky one to all interested it.

The Polynesian, November 3, 1855

The site is now located at the tip of the little triangular Walker Park in front of the Topa Tower, and would be mostly in the ewa-bound lane of Nimitz Highway.

INTER-ISLAND STEAM NAVIGATION BUILDING

75 S. Queen Street

1898 – 1928 (1913 remodel)
Architect/Builder: Howard & Train (1898), H.L. Kerr (1913) /
Pacific Engineering Company (1913)

Bishop Museum Archives

The Honolulu Advertiser, March 28, 1926

Designed by Howard & Train for the Inter-Island Steam Navigation Company, this building was built on the site of a 1-story iron storage shed that was built sometime before 1879.

> Howard & Train are the architects for the new Inter-Island offices on Queen street. A glance at the plans gives assurance of a very fine building.
>
> *The Hawaiian Star, December 15, 1897*

The site was previously the mauka/ewa corner of the old fort that was demolished in 1857.

This building was 2-stories high, built of native stone and pressed brick, and cost over $20,000. Heavy bronze gates "beautifully designed" fronted a covered passageway on the waikiki side that led to a large 1-story room with skylights in the back.

H.L. Kerr designed major alterations that were made by Pacific Engineering Company in early 1913.

> Inter-Island Steam Navigation Co., office alterations, Queen street; H. L. Kerr, architect; Pacific Engineering Co., builder, $20,000.
>
> *The Honolulu Star-Bulletin, December 5, 1912*

The building was sold at auction in late 1927 for $800 and demolished for the Pier 11 redevelopment project. The site is now part of the little triangular Walker Park in front of the Topa Tower.

INTER ISLAND WILL BUILD

HANDSOME OFFICE BUILDING IN PROSPECT.

Ground to Be Broken Next Week—Island Stone Will Be Used in Its Erection—Fine Carved Work.

Ground will be broken early next week for the new Inter Island Company office building on the makai side of Queen street, about 100 feet from Fort. The building is to be of native stone and pressed brick, two stories in height, and will cost when completed something over $20,000. The architects are Howard & Train, and they have designed what is destined to be the handsomest exclusive office building in town.

The building is to be occupied exclusively by the Inter Island Steamship Company, and has been planned especially to meet the needs of a growing business. The front of the structure, extending a distance of 60 feet on Queen street, will be of native stone and pressed brick. The main entrance in the center, opening into a broad corridor leading to the main offices, will be a very handsome affair, supported by polished stone columns. The second floor front is broken by a number of polished stone columns with carved capitals, and a picturesque stone balcony, finely carved, extends almost across the front of the building.

The lower floor is divided by a broad corridor into two splendidly lighted rooms, each 22x60 feet. The offices will be on the Ewa side, the general office in front lighted by a plate glass window that takes up almost the entire office in front lighted by a plate glass the rear, well lighted. The counter in the general office will be of hard wood, highly polished, and protected by polished plate glass, set in bronze gilt work. The store room on the Waikiki side will be occupied by the chandlery department, as will also the entire second floor, connected with the lower floor by a winding iron stairway, and in the rear by an elevator.

A covered driveway will extend along the Ewa side of the building to an open space in the rear. This driveway opens from the street through heavy bronze gates, beautifully designed. The building will present a very handsome appearance from the outside, and within will be furnished with the best of material. Work upon it will probably be pushed rapidly, as the present quarters of the company are rather cramped.

The Hawaiian Star, July 8, 1897

NEW OFFICE.

Inter-Island Company to Put up Another Building.

The Inter-Island Steam Navigation Company will soon have a new and elegant up-town office, in place of their present somewhat crowded quarters. The new building is to be put up where the warehouse now stands, between L. B. Kerr's and Hyman Bros., on Queen street. It is to be two stories high and built of island stone. The ground floor will be divided into two parts—one for the office proper and the other for the chandlery. It is understood that the building will be a handsome affair, and a place that the Inter-Island people will be proud of. At the present time an architect is busy getting up plans for the building. These will be completed during the early part of next week.

The Honolulu Advertiser, July 8, 1897

Good Stone Work.

The new sign, "1883-Inter-Island Steam Navigation Co.-1897," done in stone and placed just above the first story of the new I. I. S. N. Co. building, is undoubtedly the most artistic work of the kind in the city.

The Honolulu Advertiser, February 5, 1898

Handsome New Building.

Outside work on the new office building of the Inter-Island Steam Navigation Company on Queen street is about completed. The scaffolding in front will come down in a day or two now. This house is a signally handsome structure of brick with a front of native smoothed stone and plate glass. In the interior there is already in place a large vault, burglar and fire-proof and a spiral iron stairway.

The Honolulu Advertiser, March 26, 1898

A.W. PEIRCE BUILDING

85 S. Queen Street
1879 – 1926
Architect/Builder: unknown

The Honolulu Advertiser, March 28, 1926

This lot and the adjoining Masonic lot were first offered for sale by the government in July 1878. This building was built as an additional store of ship chandlery A.W. Peirce & Co. but housed the auction firm of Bartow & Tucker by March 1881, and then the California Furniture Company in July 1882. It became the home of the Hyman Brothers in 1884. They were founded in 1862 with the Honolulu branch started by two of the brothers with two other brothers in San Francisco and one in New York.

Isodor Rubinstein bought out the Hyman Brothers in 1904 and Rubinstein & Co. were here until the building was demolished in 1926 for the Pier 11 redevelopment project.

MASONIC HALL

95-97 Queen Street, 732 Fort Street

1879 – 1926

Architect/Builder: George W. Page / J.H. Styles, George Lucas, T.J. Baker

Hawaii State Archives

NEW MASONIC HALL.—The following were the successful bids for the erection of the new Hall for Hawaiian Lodge, No. 21, F. & A. M.: Masonry and Plasterer's work, J. H. Styles, $8,750; Carpenter's work, etc., G. Lucas, $6,650—total contract cost, $15,400.

The Pacific Commercial Advertiser, November 23, 1878

Built by Hawaiian Lodge No.21 of the F. & A.M. (Free and Accepted Masons) in 1879 on land that was once inside the old fort, it was likely designed by George W. Page.

☞ The foundation for the new Masonic Hall, located at the corner of Queen and Fort street, is rapidly approaching completion, and after the ceremonies usual at the laying of the corner-stone of all Masonic buildings are over, Mr. J. T. Baker will, we doubt not, with his usual energy, complete the masonwork. From the well-known reputation this gentleman has of being a skillful, rapid and finished workman, it is reasonable to look for the completion of this building at an early day.

The Hawaiian Gazette, December 25, 1878

The King and Queen attended the dedication of the cornerstone that was led by Deputy Grand Master Alexander J. Cartwright, with music by the Hawaiian Band.

William G. Irwin officed downstairs.

The building was demolished in 1926 for the Pier 11 redevelopment project and the site is now part of Walker Park in front of the Topa Tower.

MASONIC DEDICATION.—The formal and public dedication of the new Hall of Hawaiian Lodge No. 21, F. & A M., in the upper story of the building erected on the corner of Queen and Fort streets, will take place on Tuesday evening next, at the hour of 7.30 P. M. when the brethren expect to see their friends and acquaintances. The Hall is a roomy and airy one, the best and most comfortable for large gatherings in the city—outside of church buildings—and is a decided credit to the enterprise and management of the Lodge to which it belongs. This institution, under its late and present officers, has been a useful conservator of public morals in this community—as have also several other kindred organization.

The Pacific Commercial Advertiser, September 27, 1879

THE NEW MASONIC TEMPLE.—Through the politeness of the chairman of the building committee of the new Masonic Temple, Hon. E. P. Adams, we were permitted to visit the interior of the above building on Tuesday the 24th inst. The upper portion of the temple is finished and ready for the furniture, and is really a fine piece of workmanship throughout. The large room is 32 by 54 feet, with ceiling 17 feet in the clear. This is a splendid and spacious room, well lighted and ventilated. On the same floor there are rooms for the secretary and library, ante and preparing room, examination room, and a large banqueting room. The upper story is gained by a spacious and easy stairway on both sides of which there are hand rails. The lower story on the ground floor is divided into two large rooms, one of which fronts on Fort and Queen streets which will be occupied by Messrs. Irwin & Co., commission merchants. In the rear of the main building there is a brick storehouse, and in the space between the main building and the storehouse are located the water closets and the gas apparatus. The whole building will be lighted with gas and throughout there are conveniently located in the corners of the several rooms except the lodge room, wash basins for the convenience and comfort of members and guests. The building is well supplied with water for all purposes. The window lights are of plate glass of American manufacture. Take it all in all, the new Masonic Temple is a building alike creditable to the taste and skill of the architect and the builders, as well as to the Masonic fraternity of Honolulu, and is an ornament as well as an improvement to the city. Too much praise cannot be awarded to the building committee under whose supervision this beautiful and substantial building has been commenced and completed. The inauguration ball will be given on Friday evening next when the temple will be occupied for the first time. When finished and furnished it will be a pleasure to behold it, as neither money nor care have been spared to make it worthy the object for which it was erected. The work was commenced Dec. 14, 1878, and the building will be completed this week as the mechanics are now engaged on the last finishing touches. The following names comprise the list of the building committee, etc., etc., viz: Building committee—Hon. E. P. Adams, chairman, H. J. Nolte, A. F. Judd, and G. F. Luce, Esq.; Architect—George W. Page, Esq.; Carpenter—George Lucas; Mason—J. H. Lytle; Painter—W. Gibbs.

Hawaiian Gazette, June 25, 1879

The Pier 11 Terminal Building was built on the site in 1927.

The Honolulu Star-Bulletin, March 16, 1950

The Honolulu Star-Bulletin, December 16, 1950

The Honolulu Star-Bulletin, July 12, 1952

Due to the alignment of Nimitz Highway slicing through the Pier 11 Terminal Building in 1950, the building was demolished for a new building designed by Charles F. Wagner to be occupied by Matson Navigation Company. Moving-in day was July 21, 1952.

The building is now the offices of the Hawaii Department of Transportation (HDOT) Harbors Division.

The Honolulu Advertiser, October 31, 1962

STAR-BULLETIN PLANT

126-132 S. Queen Street

1916 – present
Architect/Builder: Ripley & Davis / Spalding Construction

The Honolulu Star-Bulletin, November 27, 1915

BEGIN WORK SOON ON NEW $55,000 BUILDING

Work will be commenced in a few days on the new Star-Bulletin building on Merchant street between Fort and Bishop and running through to Queen street. When completed the structure will cost $55,000. Plans and specifications have been completed by Architects Ripley & Davis. The Spalding Construction Company has been awarded the contract.

The Honolulu Advertiser, July 15, 1915

Built on what was once the S.G. Wilder lumber yard, this 3-story concrete building was designed by Ripley & Davis to be added onto the back of the existing Hawaiian Star Building on Merchant Street.

The two upper stories were used for stock rooms and housed the engraving plant and job printing plant.

The Merchant Street building was remodeled for the business office and editorial rooms, and the Queen Street building was used for the composing room and printing presses.

In spite of encountering lots of groundwater, it was built in 7 months by Spalding Construction Co.

While excavating the foundation, workers found a 50-pound cannonball, an 1859 American half-dollar, a pair of 4"-long boar's tusks, stone ginger ale bottles with a Sydney trademark, a half-dozen pearl oyster shells, and a heavy brass key 6" long "of the type mentioned in pirate stories".

The building was remodeled in 1957 for $75,000.

2022

CALIFORNIA FEED CO.

195 S. Queen Street

1913 – 1962
Architect/Builder: H.L. Kerr / John Ouderkirk

Honolulu: The Cross-Roads of the Pacific, 1913

California Feed Co., warehouse and office, Queen and Alakea streets. H. L. Kerr, architect; John Ouderkirk, builder; $15,000.

The Honolulu Star-Bulletin, July 20, 1912

California Feed Company Moves to New Home

Alakea street is welcoming still another addition to its business ranks, for the California Feed Company has just got settled in its new home at the corner of Queen street.

Moving from the long-established location on Queen near Nuuanu, this company is marking another red stroke on the calendar of progress, not only for itself, but for the business community generally. A fine new concrete building houses the office and warerooms for stock feed and poultry supplies; there is light, air and storage space in abundance.

T. J. King, who founded the business and who is still the head of it, is to be congratulated on securing such a favorable location and for making such a progressive step. The California Feed Company is the most harborward of the firms who, by moving there, are making Alakea street the newest thoroughfare of business activity.

The Honolulu Advertiser, April 27, 1913

"HOW ABOUT DYNAMITE?" IS THE STARTLING QUESTION "BILLBOARDED" FOR CONTRATOR

Has the Amalgamated Association of Dynamiters established a branch in Honolul, or is the threat received by Contractor John Ouderkirk yesterday, which hints at blowing up the building he is erecting for the California Feed Company at Alakea and Queen streets, some one's idea of a joke?

When Ouderkirk went to work yesterday morning he discovered that some time Friday night, the following inscription in large letters had been placed on a window sill of the structure:

"HOW ABOUT DYNAMITE! OUDERKIRK WHOP. WE WILL GET YOU YET."

Ouderkirk didn't know last night, whether the threat is something meant seriously, or as a poor jest. "I am employing some Japanese labor on the job," he said, "and of course, I know that there is objection to this from some people, but it is the first threat of the kind I have received. No demands have ever been made that I should stop using Japanese on the building.

"I am chiefly mystified by the letters 'whop' after my name."

While it is understood that there has been some feeling against the employment of Japanese by contractors, in the past, there is no organization known to exist here for the purpose of combatting the employment of Japanese, such as exists in San Francisco, and for this reason Contractor Ouderkirk is not inclined to take the threat seriously.

However, to guard against accidents, a night watchman has been placed at the building.

The Honolulu Advertiser, February 2, 1913

HOLLINGER & CO. NEW LOCATION

California Feed Co. Building Purchased and To Be Occupied

The Ben Hollinger & Co., Ltd., will assume new quarters at the California Feed Co. building May 1, it was announced today by Ben Hollinger.

According to Hollinger, his company has purchased the California Feed Co. building and site. The plans of the California Feed Co. have not been announced, but it is understood that the concern is to discontinue business.

The Hollinger company will install a storage garage and a service station. Offices of the Honolulu Rubber Works also will be located in the building.

The Honolulu Star-Bulletin, April 6, 1925

In 1925 the building became a storage garage for Ben Hollinger & Co., later becoming the Auto Service Garage until the building was torn down in 1962 for a parking lot.

The $50M 30-story Grosvenor Center was later built on this site. Designed by Architects Hawaii Ltd. and completed in 1979 by DMA/Hawaii Inc. and Tecon Corp. The site is now the mauka tower of the Pacific Guardian Center.

2022

F.L. JAMES BUILDING

219-231 S. Queen Street

1925 – c.1959
Architect/Builder: Davis & Fishbourne / R.S. Chase

The Honolulu Star-Bulletin, December 4, 1925

Built of "heavy concrete construction" by R.S. Chase in 1925 for real estate man Frank L. James, this building was designed by Davis & Fishbourne (Lou Davis and Ralph Fishbourne).

Frank James came to Hawaii in 1904 and was a graduate of McKinley High School. He worked with the Waterhouse Company from 1909 to 1914 and later became president of Pan-Pacific Traders.

In 1925 he partnered with Samuel Wilder King in the realty business as King & James and they officed at 82 Merchant Street in J.M. Dowsett's former office. Victor C. Baker had a battery and brake lining business on the first floor, and the second floor was divided into three offices.

The 7-story Title Guaranty Building is on the site today at 235 Queen Street, built in 1960 as the $1.1M Queen Street Corporation Building designed by Lemmon Freeth Haines and Jones and built by the Hawaiian Dredging and Construction Company.

2022

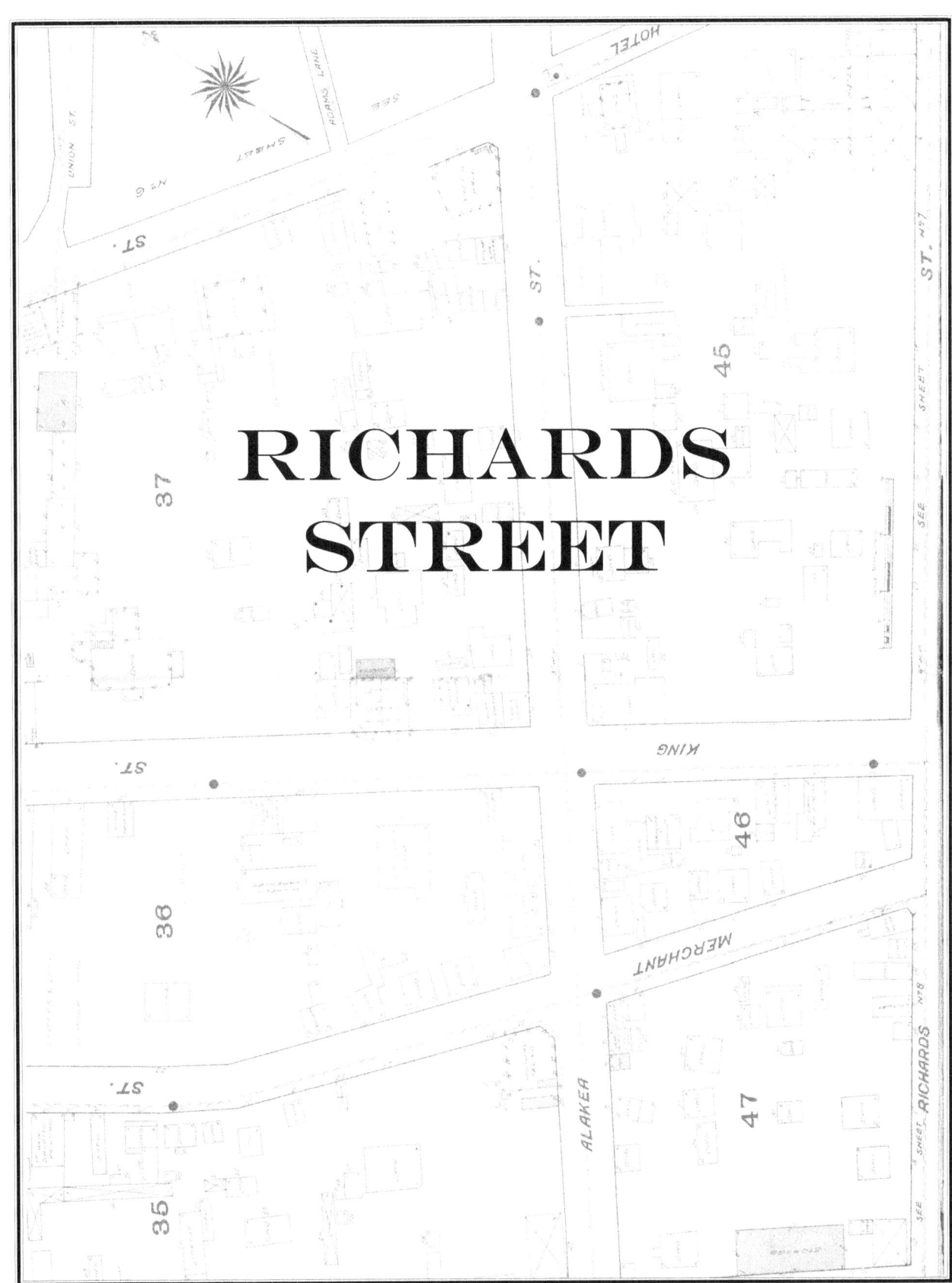

THE BUNGALOW
845-855 Richards Street
1847 – 1874
Architect/Builder: Charles W. Vincent, Samuel Jones (Johnson?)

Paul Emmert, 1854

Not a cozy little cottage, but a "pretentious and costly coral stone mansion built in the East Indian style" by "Mr. Charles Vincent, house-carpenter and Mr. Samuel Jones, stone-mason" for San Francisco businessman Theodore Shillaber. Over 60' wide and 80' deep, it had 3'-diameter Corinthian columns, 20' ceilings, and cost over $30,000. The cornerstone was laid on June 20, 1847.

Originally from New York, by the late 1840's Shillaber was trading between California, Mexico, China, and Hawaii. He was proclaimed a "Denizen of Hawaii" by the King in 1849 and was appointed King's Commissioner to the governor of Alta California to negotiate a treaty of reciprocity. But shortly after he arrived he resigned his commission claiming the "open, liberal, attractive allurements of the Republic" to be far superior to the "griping policy of the Hawaiian government". Many felt he had tricked the government into letting him sail to California for free on the King's yacht *Kamehameha*.

Reportedly "desirous of procuring a duplicate of Aladdin's lamp to transport his 'Bungaro'" (as he called it) to California, instead he traded it in a land deal with his business partner Samuel Brannan in 1850, claiming a value of $22,000.

Brannan was a former Mormon and California's first millionaire who made a fortune having the main store providing supplies for the California gold rush. He came to Hawaii in 1851 with 24 associates with the intent of buying out Kamehameha III and taking over the Islands, with The Bungalow as his base of operations. Not meeting with success, he returned to San Francisco in January 1852.

The house was rented out after the aborted takeover, mostly for fancy balls for organizations like the Odd Fellows and the Masons.

> **BUNGALOW ASSEMBLY ROOMS.**
>
> THE UNDERSIGNED WOULD RESpectfully state that he is now prepared to furnish the above Rooms for Balls, Private Parties, Picnics, Exhibitions, Fairs, Meetings, etc., on the most reasonable terms.
> Music for Processions and Balls can be had. Address
> J. F. A. PICKERING,
> (Polynesian copy.) 156-tf   Post-office, Honolulu.

Pacific Commercial Advertiser, June 30, 1859

It became a gymnasium in 1859, later operated by the German Turn Verein society in 1860. But by 1871 the building was in ruins and was sold for $2,000.

> —The "Bungalow Premises," built by Mr. Shillaber some 25 years ago, and which have been lying in ruins for several years past unoccupied, have been sold for $2,000. The coral stones on the place are said to be worth half that sum.

Pacific Commercial Advertiser, April 29, 1871

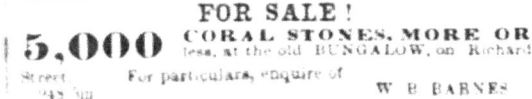

Pacific Commercial Advertiser, August 15, 1874

When the pile of coral stones was removed in 1874, they uncovered a cornerstone with a tin box time capsule. It included two newspapers, the *Sandwich Island News* of April 7, 1847, and *The Polynesian* of June 12, 1847.

It also included a handwritten note by George Pelly of the Hudson Bay Company identifying the builders as "Mr. Charles Vincent, house-carpenter, and Mr. Samuel Jones, stone mason."

By 1891 the site was used by the Pacific Tennis Club for tennis courts.

It is now the site of the "Spanish Mission Colonial" US Post Office designed by New York architects York & Sawyer, completed in 1922. The columns along Richards Street echo those of The Bungalow.

Sam Brannan's Palace.

While I am on the subject of scenery, I might as well speak of Sam Brannan's palace, or "the Bungalow," as it is popularly called. Years ago it was built and handsomely furnished by Shillaber, now of San Francisco, at a cost of between thirty and forty thousand dollars, and in the day of its glory must have considerably outshone its regal neighbor, the palace of the king. It was a large mansion, with compact walls of coral; dimensions, say, 60 or 70 feet front and 80 feet depth, perhaps, including the ample verandah or portico in front; this portico was supported by six or eight tall fluted Corinthian columns, some three feet in diameter; a dozen coral steps led up to the portico from the ground, and these extended the whole length of the front; there were four rooms on the main floor, some twenty-four feet square, each, and about twenty feet high, besides a room or so of smaller dimensions. When its white paint was new, this must have been a very stately edifice. But finally it passed into Brannan's hands—for the sum of thirty thousand dollars (never mind the particulars of the transaction)—and it has been going to decay for the past ten years. It has arrived there now, and it is the completest ruin I ever saw. One or two of the pillars have fallen, and lie like grand Theban ruins, diagonally across the wide portico; part of the roof of the portico has caved down, and a huge gridiron of plasterless lathing droops from above and threatens the head of the apostrophizing stranger; the windows are dirty, and some of them broken; the shutters are unhinged; the elegant doors are marred and splintered; within, the floors are strewn with *debris* from the shattered ceilings, weeds grow in damp mold in obscure corners; lizards peep curiously out from unsuspected hiding-places and then skurry along the walls and disappear in gaping crevices; the Summer breeze sighs fittully through the desolate chambers, and the unforbidden sun looks down through many a liberal vent in roof and ceiling. The spacious grounds without are rank with weeds, and the fences are crazy with age and chronic debility. No more complete and picturesque ruin than the Bungalow exists to-day in the old world or the new. It is the most discouraged-looking pile the sun visits on its daily round, perhaps. In the sorrowful expression of its deserted halls, its fallen columns and its decayed magnificence, it seems to proclaim, in the homely phrase of California, that it has "got enough pie."

*Mark Twain, Sacramento Daily Union,
May 24, 1866*

IDEAL FINANCE BUILDING
860 Richards Street / 253 Merchant Street
1940 – 1954
Architect/Builder: Mark Potter / Pacific Construction Co.

The Honolulu Star-Bulletin, January 31, 1940

The 2-story Ideal Finance Company building was designed by Mark Potter and built by the Pacific Construction Company for $50,000 on this corner in 1940. Glass brick was used on the second floor "to provide excellent natural lighting" and special "Aklo" sun-protective glass was used on the first-floor windows. Equipping the building with air-conditioning cost more than $10,000.

Founded by Joseph P. Medeiros in 1926, Ideal Finance & Mortgage Co. Ltd. specialized in "personal, character, and auto loans" plus real estate mortgages.

The building was demolished in 1954 by Chinn Ho's Capital Investment Company for a new building designed by Merrill Simms & Roehrig and built by Harry Kobayashi at a cost of $259,930 in 1955. It featured air-conditioned offices and "glare-proof windows shaded by aluminum sun-breaks".

Initial tenants were the Capital Investment Company, Title Guaranty Company of Hawaii, H.A.R. Austin Engineers, plus auditors and tax consultants Baker & Gillette. Hawaiian Airlines later officed here too.

The Honolulu Star-Bulletin, May 29, 1954

2022

"Charles the Lascar" built two white adobe houses on this site in 1827, surrounded by a stick fence.

In 1885 this was the site of a general store and the home of Abraham S. Bolster. He was born in 1809 in Mallow, County Cork, Ireland, and was heading to the California Gold Rush in 1849 from Tasmania but decided to stay in Honolulu due to seasickness. He bought a horse from J.T. Waterhouse and started the first draying business in Hawaii. Both buildings were gone by 1899 due to the widening of Richards Street.

1885 Dakin Map

John F. Bowler built a 2-story wooden building on the corner in July 1903, and the Palace Café opened here in February 1905. They served sandwiches, light lunch, and had fountain service. The Anti-Saloon League crusaded against the Palace Café and successfully protested the renewal of its license in 1909.

Honolulu: The Cross-Roads of the Pacific, 1913.

David O. Hammans' California Harness Shop founded in 1897 was here from 1910 to 1919. Changing with the times from saddlery to carriage and automobile trimming, they were the first in Hawaii to paint cars with lacquer. The wooden building was demolished in 1939 for the new Ideal Finance Building.

YWCA BUILDING

1040 Richards Street

1927 – present
Architect/Builder: Julia Morgan / J.L. Young Engineering Co.

The Honolulu Advertiser, January 25, 1925

Described at the time as "rarely beautiful and thoroughly practical" the Woman's Center of Honolulu and the new home of the Young Women's Christian Association was designed by New York architect "Miss Julia Morgan" as "a three-story semi-colonial structure adapted to the needs and climate of the Islands" on land purchased in 1924 by the YWCA from the Allen estate for $238,566.

Born in San Francisco in 1872, Julia Morgan was a cousin of J. Pierpont Morgan and was considered the leading female architect in America. She designed more the 700 buildings including the Berkeley Women's City Club, Hearst Castle in San Simeon, CA, and 12 YWCA's across the country.

The building has a frontage of 170' along Richards Street facing 'Iolani Palace, and has an open-air court next to the cafeteria and a 60-foot open-air swimming pool with a "picturesque and spacious runway about the pool". There was also a games room with a capacity of 500 on the first floor, a community room seating 200 on the second floor and a gymnasium. Classrooms for millinery, cooking, sewing, public speaking, languages, and art courses were on the third floor.

Built by J.L. Young Engineering Company for a cost of $425,000, Edward B. Hussey, Jr., was the supervising architect, assisted by Bjarne C. Dahl. The building was officially dedicated on June 18, 1927.

The YWCA was built on the site of the Bathsheba M. Allen home, later the Laniakea Tea Rooms founded by Miss Helen Alexander in 1916 as "a place where one could go when tired out and have a cheery cup of tea and for the out-of-town woman the pleasant rest room with an inviting punee (day bead) where an hour of more may be spent after a strenuous morning of shopping, will prove a boon". It had artist quarters, a gift shop, and a grass hut with Hawaiian women weaving lauhala mats and baskets.

As early as 1885, Frederick W. Wundenberg had a 1-story house on the mauka end of this site. He was born in Hanalei in 1850, and after working for Castle & Cooke and T.H. Davies & Co. became the Postmaster General from 1886 to 1891. His father had been the Registrar of Public Accounts under Kamehameha V, and his grandfather was a Prussian officer who fought at the Battle of Waterloo.

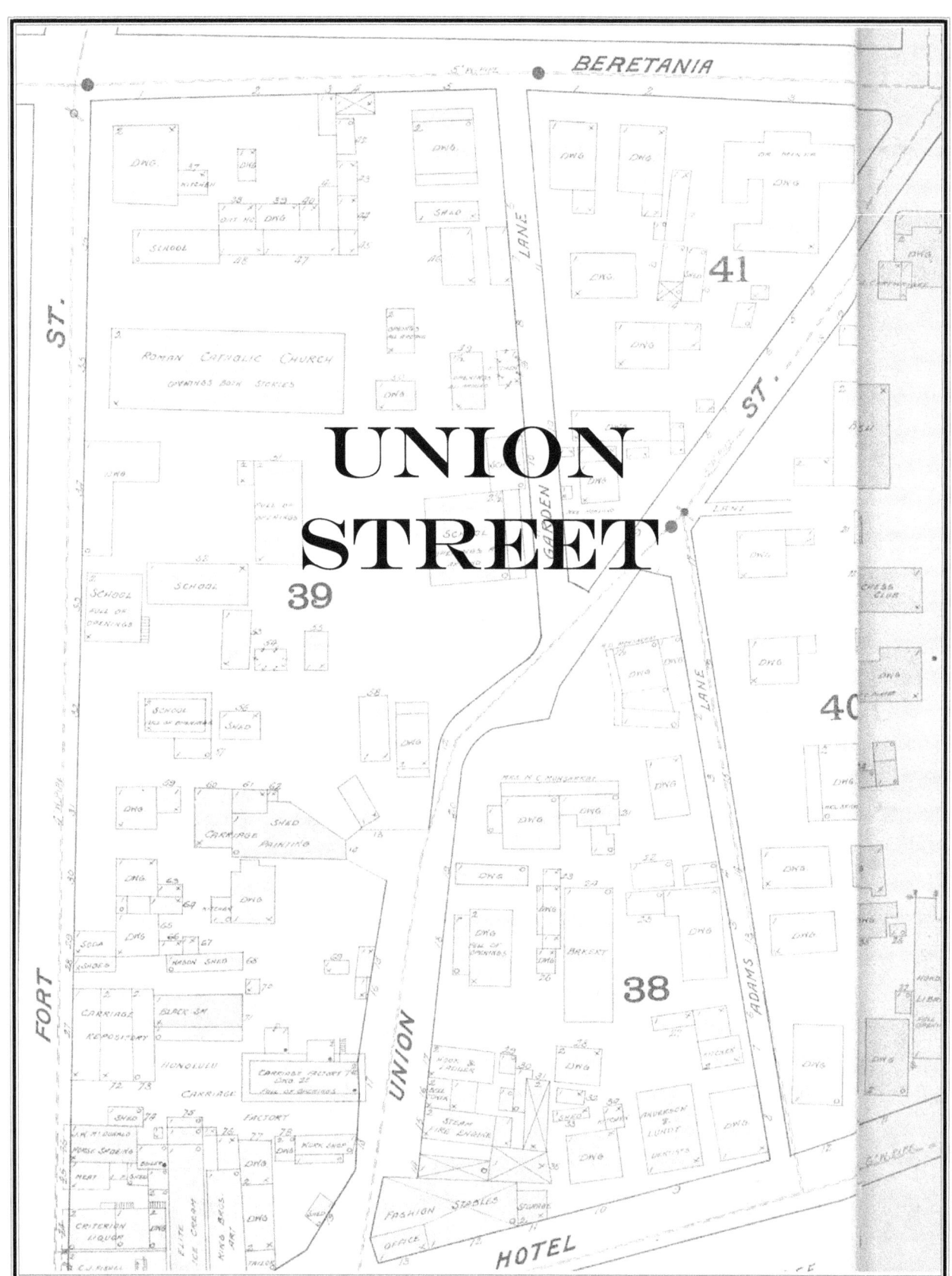

UNION BUILDING

1104-1112 Union Street

1912 – present (1922 remodel, 1964 remodel)
Architect/Builder: Ripley & Reynolds / Lord-Young Engineering Company

Built at the same time as the Palm Building on Hotel Street, the Union Building was also designed by Ripley & Reynolds and built by the Lord-Young Company for the Brewer Estate.

There had been a lot of discussion about the city widening or closing Union Street, or even making this triangular tract a park, so they built only 1-story initially, then adding a second story in 1922 when it was clear the city was not going to abandon or sell back any portion of the Union Street right-of-way.

The Union Building was built on the site of E.H. Boardman's watchmaking and jewelry store built perhaps as early as 1841.

Described as "a sprightly and somewhat irascible little person", Boardman was known as "Ticktick" by the Native Hawaiians due to his occupation.

Boardman left Hawaii for the mainland in 1849 and sold the business to David N. Flitner who continued as watchmaker, jeweler, and chronometer-rater. Flitner was here until 1857, later moving into the new Makee & Anthon Building on Queen Street.

The wooden building at Hotel and Union was still there in 1899 as part of the rear portion of the King Brothers art store. A transit installed by Flitner on the eastern corner of the lot was later used by the Government Survey Office.

Paul Emmert, 1854

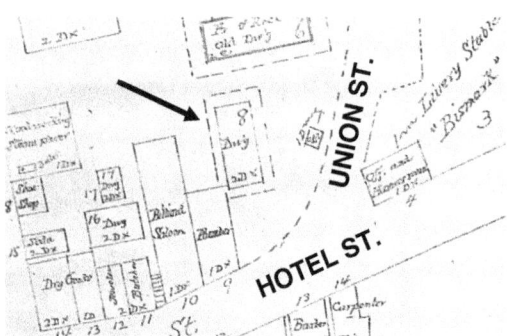

1879 Lion Map

Photo by H.L. Chase, 1870

A matching new "modern" front was put on both the Palm and Union buildings in 1964.

2022

WOLTERS BUILDING

1114-1134-Union Street

1916 – 1935

Architect/Builder: H.L. Kerr / Henry J. Freitas (Freitas & Fernandez)

No, this is not the Kress Building – it's the 3-story Wolters Building on Union Street. It was designed by Harry L. Kerr for William Wolters and completed by Henry J. Freitas in 1916 for $75,000.

It was built on the site of the French Hotel which had later been adapted for use as the government offices.

Construction was slightly delayed due to landslides in the Panama Canal forcing steel shipments to go all the way around Cape Horn.

It was a reinforced concrete building, 50' x 170', with basement. The lower floors housed 8 stores and the upper floors were for apartments with 20 on each floor. Some were plain guest rooms and some had kitchenettes. The first shop, Hartie's Good Eats, moved in on November 1, 1916.

It was a beautiful building but it didn't last long. Sidney Spitzer, the owner of the Standard Shoe Store on Fort Street bought it in 1929 and then sold it to the S.H. Kress & Company in 1934.

The building was demolished in 1935, only 19 years after it was built, to make room for the expansion of the Kress Building.

Honolulu Star-Bulletin, January 26, 1935

The Kress Building was replaced in 1991 by the Pan Pacific Plaza (1132 Bishop) designed by Gin D. Wong.

DOWSETT HOUSE

1131 Union Street / 1132 Bishop Street

1832 – 1925
Architect/Builder: unknown

Paul Emmert, 1854

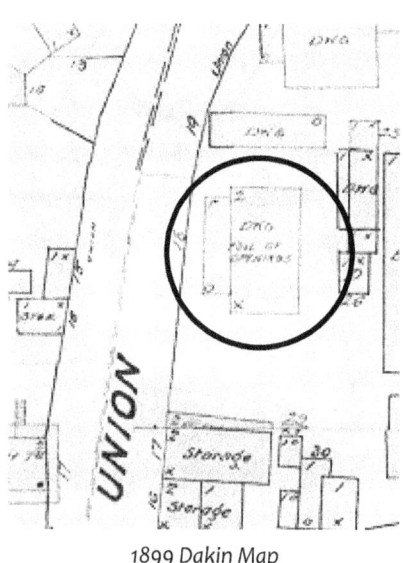

1899 Dakin Map

This was Dr. Ford's residence when painted by Paul Emmert in 1854, but it was built in 1832 by Captain Samuel Dowsett as the family homestead. The lower story was coral and the upper was wood, with much of the wood and many of the features coming from old sailing ships.

Samuel Dowsett was born in Rochester, England in 1794, became a ship captain, and settled in Hawaii in 1828. He disappeared at sea in 1834 while on a pearl-fishing expedition to the Pescadores Islands (Penghu). The Hawaiian government sent out a search party on the brig *Waverly* in 1835 but all were killed on Strong's Island (Kosrae). Captain Dowsett was never found.

His son, prominent Hawaii businessman James Isaac Dowsett was born in this house in 1829.

In 1926 the Auto Rental Company Ltd. constructed a concrete block gas station on the site as part of their large parking lot.

Harry Uehara's Evergreen Coffee shop was here from 1949 to 1962, with the exterior and interior designed and planned by the Von Hamm-Young store planning section.

The site today is an open landscaped courtyard with fountains.

2022

Honolulu Advertiser, August 15, 1949

WOOD/SPALDING HOUSE

1136 Union Street

1830's – 1938
Architect/Builder: unknown

Said to have been built back in the 1830's by George Wood, by 1854 this 2-story coral building was the residence of Josiah Chapman Spalding.

Spalding was a native of Salem, MA, and first went to sea as a clerk on one of his father's ships. In Hawaii he was in the retail and general commission business, briefly teaming with Cornelius S. Bartow in 1847 and later with Capt. Horatio Nelson Crabb.

He was appointed Captain in the Hawaiian Army and during the Civil War was the Acting Assistant Paymaster in the US Navy serving in Mississippi on the gunboat *Paw Paw*. Spalding was later chief clerk of the Brooklyn Navy Yard.

After Spalding left Hawaii the house became part of the Catholic Mission and was used as an infirmary.

Paul Emmert, 1854

In 1938, Drs. Clarence E. Fronk and William H. Wynn remodeled the 1926 building immediately adjacent into their office and clinic and tore down the coral building to make room for a driveway from Union Street.

Pioneer Tower, now called Union Plaza, was built on the site in 1967 for $2M. It was designed by architect Robert E. Wiese and was the first commercial condominium on Oahu.

Scale model, 1964

2022

The Honolulu Star-Bulletin, July 2, 1962

LANDMARK RAZED: This 90 year old coral block building on Union St. in the grounds of the former Catholic convent is being torn down to provide an approach to the two story convent auditorium that has been purchased by Drs. Clarence E. Fronk and William H. Wynn as headquarters of the Fronk-Wynn clinic.—Star-Bulletin photo.

Honolulu Star-Bulletin, September 17, 1938

$50,000 Clinic Designed for Union Street

Erection of the Fronk-Wynn clinic, to be cooperatively run by Drs. Clarence E. Fronk and William H. Wynn, will begin shortly on Union street on the site of the old Catholic convent. The two-story building formerly used by the convent will be remodeled and air-conditioned to be utilized as the clinic.

The old coral structure in the grounds of the convent, a familiar landmark of Honolulu, will be torn down to make room for a Union street approach to the clinic. The old building was the former residence of J. C. Spalding, grandfather of Irwin Spalding, vice president of Bishop National bank. The building is said to be 90 years old.

The clinic will cost $50,000, including purchase price of the property from the Sisters of the Sacred Hearts, remodeling and new equipment. The property has a 40-foot frontage on Union street and 6,000 square feet in area.

Albert E. Ives is architect.

The Honolulu Advertiser
September 18, 1938

TRIANGLE AUTO SUPPLY BUILDING

1192 Union Street

1924 – c.1955
Architect/Builder: unknown / M. Ohta

The Honolulu Advertiser, January 27, 1924

The Triangle Auto Supply Company opened on January 23, 1924, in this new building on Union Street near the corner with Beretania Street. It housed their tire department, battery department, and electric plating department.

This was possibly the first building in Honolulu built of concrete with a welded steel frame – the building "has not a single bolt in it".

Reynold McGrew bought Triangle Auto Supply in December 1924 and renamed it McGrew & Co.

The building was gone by 1955.

ARCHITECTS & BUILDERS

THOMAS J. BAKER

Originally from Australia, Thomas Baker came to Honolulu in 1876 after working as a bricklayer and builder in San Francisco for several years. His first newspaper ad appeared in October 1876.

T. J. BAKER, ARCHITECT and BUILDER
Plans and specifications furnished at reasonable rates.
Address, Post Office, Honolulu, H. I.   oc7 3m

In 1877 he built a 2-story brick building that was faced with concrete at the corner of Fort & Hotel streets for C. Brewer, "the finest looking and perhaps most substantially built structure in Honolulu (aside from the Government House)". [Brewer Block, 1063-1071 Fort Street / 101-107 S. Hotel Street].

That same year he also built a 63' x 112' brick building at the corner of Fort and King streets for grocery firm H.E. McIntyre & Bro. In September he demolished the old William French coral stone building at Ka'ahumanu and Merchant streets to make room for the new 2-story brick bank for Bishop & Co. completed in 1879.

In 1878 he built a "splendid two-story brick mansion" on Beretania Street near Punchbowl Street for Henry May, and a 50' x 82' 2-story brick building on Fort Street near Merchant Street for T. Cummins for the Dillingham & Co. store. It had the first elevator in Hawaii – "by this contrivance three men can easily raise three tons weight".

He built a large 30' x 40' "fireproof" 2-story brick building for Mr. Aswan on Nu'uanu Street near King Street in 1878, and in 1879 a 2-story brick addition to the main Queens Hospital building.

But his really big commission was in 1879 when he was one of two architects asked to draw plans for King Kalākaua's new palace. The King preferred his plan, in the ornate style called as "American Florentine". The plans called for a 4-story building, 120' x 140', with a central 80' tower plus towers at each corner, and the cornerstone was laid on the King's birthday, December 31, 1879. The brick masonry was by E.B. Thomas.

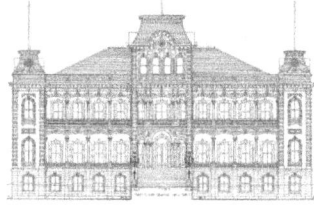

But all did not go well. The Minister of the Interior, Samuel C. Wilder, was supposed to be in charge of purchases and contracts but also claimed that he and not Baker should control the work. Baker responded saying that would be "a procedure unprecedented in the history of Architecture". Aspersions were cast on the accuracy of the foundation plans. His Majesty's Cabinet Council passed a resolution supporting Wilder, and Baker's response was said to be "insulting in tone".

Baker was paid $1,000 for plans and services on January 17, 1880, and it was announced on February 11 that he had been succeeded by Charles J. Wall, an architect from San Francisco. Baker sailed for Australia on February 25 and apparently never came back.

BEARDSLEE & PAGE

Frederick Wheeler Beardslee (1855-1919) was born in Kingston, Jamaica, in 1855 and was very active in the real estate and land development business in the San Francisco Bay area in the mid 1880's.

In addition to designing and building he was also briefly the publisher of the *San Pedro Advocate* newspaper.

Beardslee left his wife and moved to Honolulu in November of 1898, and in 1899 partnered with George W. Page who had previously worked with Howard & Train.

Beardslee & Page officed in the Arlington Annex on Hotel Street and later in the Elite Building, and they designed and built a large house for Edgar Halstead at Piikoi & Wilder in 1899, the E. Faxon Bishop house in 1900, the Honolulu Stockyards Building in 1901, and a bungalow for Carrie Castle in 1901. They also designed and built many of the buildings on Quarantine Island in 1901.

In late 1901 they designed the Kapiolani Building at King and Alakea Streets. After Page returned to California, Beardslee designed the M.P. Robinson Building on Queen Street in 1903, and teamed up with Thomas Gill to design the Insane Asylum in 1904. In 1906 he returned to California and became the supervising architect of the Realty Syndicate Company.

Beardslee was a guitar player with a bass voice that was "deep and full, yet peculiarly attractive", and he was also the organizer of the popular Tuxedo Quartette. In 1918 he was granted a patent for a separating and dewatering clarifier for the mining industry.

George W. Page (1850-1924) was originally from Boston, worked on the Grand Union Hotel in Saratoga Springs, NY, and came to California in 1876. He worked as an architect in Honolulu in 1878 and 1879.

Page briefly returned to Boston and then moved to San Jose in 1885 where he designed many residences, hotels, and churches. He returned to Honolulu in 1898 to partner with Howard & Train, and then with F.W. Beardslee in 1899, until moving back to San Jose about 1903.

Page had previously designed the Lick Observatory with John G. Howard in 1880, the Knox Goodrich Building at 34-36 S. 1st Street in San Jose in 1889, and the First Unitarian Church in 1892.

In 1904 he designed 62-room Spanish Colonial style Hayes Mansion at 200 Edenvale in San Jose that is considered to be one of the finest examples of late 19th-century architecture in the Santa Clara Valley.

HENRY F. BERTELMANN

Born in Koloa, Kauai, Henry Franz Bertelmann (1859-1921) had a carpenter shop on King Street and was a key member of Queen Liliʻuokalani's staff. He built the J.J. Williams Building on Fort Street with Thomas B. Walker, the A.P. Fernandez House, and the Government Dispensary.

A major player in the 1895 Wilcox Rebellion, he was initially sentenced to be hanged, but was later fined $10,000 and given a 35-year suspended sentence.

BOWLER & INGVORSEN

John Francis Bowler (1853-1925) was born in Blackstone, MA, and came to Hawaii in 1877. By 1880 he was advertising plastering and cement contracting services. Bowler helped build the Judiciary Building and ʻIolani Palace.

On February 17, 1895, Bowler was found guilty of "misprision of treason" and sentenced to 5 years in Oahu jail and a $5,000 fine for his part in the Wilcox Rebellion. He was released January 1, 1896.

Charles Ingvorsen (1877-1946) was born in Copenhagen, Denmark, and came to Hawaii in 1912. He teamed up with John F. Bowler in 1915 and their first project was the new YMCA swimming pool. In 1916 they built the Charles S. Judd house in Manoa.

They built the Knights of Columbus Building in 1920, the Commercial Trust & Bank Building in 1922, and the First National Bank Building and two wings of the Sacred Heart Convent in 1925. Ingvorsen built a new auditorium and classroom for the convent in 1926, and he built his own home, Hibiscus Place, on the side of Diamond Head in 1929.

ROBERT S. CHASE

Robert Sherman Chase (1879-1949) was born in Chicago and first came to Hawaii in 1911 as a tourist and stayed to become a construction contractor. After working for other firms including Lord-Young Engineering Company, Volcano Stables Ltd, and Spalding Construction Company, he started his own business in 1917. He briefly partnered with F.P. Pierce, forming Chase & Pierce.

Chase built the Union Trust Building, the Philip Brothers building, Love's Bakery (Iwilei), The Hawaii Building, Dr. H.T. Hollmann's office on Miller Street, and Mrs. Charles H. Wilcox's home in Nuuanu Valley. Chase was also the assistant treasurer of the University of Hawaii and former principal of Punahou.

JOHN L. CLIFF

Born in St. Charles, Missouri, John Lewellyn Cliff (1880-1954) moved to California with his family, went to school in Paso Robles, and initially worked as a carpenter in San Francisco.

He lived in Honolulu from 1917 to 1937 and built the War Memorial Natatorium, the Kona sea pool, the Home Insurance Building, Palolo Golf Course, the Monsarrat Building on Bishop Street, and Ala Wai Park. He was also the head of construction for the Princess Theater.

HERBERT COHEN CAYTON

Herbert Cohen (1882-1947) was born in Pottsville, PA. He graduated from the University of Chicago in 1902 and in 1907 went to work as an architect for the U.S. Treasury Department as superintendent of construction for federal buildings in Kansas, Missouri, Louisiana, and South Dakota. In 1908 he married a woman from Honolulu and relocated to Hawaii in 1914 as the supervising architect for the Hilo Federal Building.

He went into private practice in 1919 and designed the Luke Field aviation base, the 1926 Lum Yip Kee Building, the King Theater, Central Market in Kaimuki, the Furneux Building in Hilo, the Edgewater Apartments in Waikiki, the Community Church in Ewa Beach, and the U.S. Immigration Station with C.W. Dickey. He also redesigned the Oregon Block due to the extension of Bishop Street. He designed many residences including the homes of George E. Lake and Albert F. Afong.

Herbert Cohen
Architect

Rooms 323-324, S. M. Damon Bldg.
Tel. 4476

Cohen officially changed his name to Herbert Cohen Cayton in 1928, taking his mother's last name as his other siblings had recently done the same.

DAHL, CONRAD & PREIS

Although in business for only five years, Dahl & Conrad and later Dahl, Conrad & Preis, were incredibly prolific designers of residences, apartments, commercial buildings, and interiors, many with Oriental and classic Art Moderne streamline characteristics.

Dahl & Conrad was founded in Honolulu by Bjarne C. Dahl and Conrad W. Conrad in 1936 and disbanded I 1941 three weeks after the Japanese attack on Pearl Harbor when all architectural offices were closed by the government.

Dahl was the architect and Conrad was the designer and illustrator. Recent Austrian immigrant Alfred Preis joined the firm in 1939, and they often advertised as Dahl & Conrad, Associated Alfred Preis.

Renderings of their designs were a regular feature in the newspapers, and in 1938 they were selected to design the first fully-air-conditioned house in Honolulu, the Advertiser-Kelvin House in Diamond Head Estates. In addition to many houses and apartments in Waikiki, they also designed Kau Kau Korner, the original Waikiki Theatre block, and even a $600 doghouse.

Bjarne Cato Dahl (1897-1989) was born in Chicago and graduated from Chicago Technical College in 1918. He was hired by architect Julia Morgan in 1921 and came to Honolulu in January 1926 to superintend the construction of the new YWCA building on Richards Street. After it was completed, he decided to stay in Hawaii, worked for Charles Dickey for two years, and for seven years was the architect for the Engineering Division of the Territorial Department of Public Works.

Conrad Wilfred Conrad (1910-2000) was originally from Minneapolis, MN, studied art at USC for two years, traveled through Europe, and was a landscape gardener and interior decorator in Los Angeles before coming to Hawaii in 1933 at age 23 with only $25 in his pocket. Working briefly for Charles Dickey and Harry Bent, he teamed up with Dahl in 1935 and they formed Dahl & Conrad in 1936. Connie's last name was originally Cornfeldt, but since so many locals called him "Mr. Conrad" he officially changed his name before getting married in 1936.

Born in Austria, **Alfred Preis** (1911-1994) graduated from the Vienna University of Technology and was married the same day Hitler arrived in Vienna. Well aware of the danger of having a Jewish father they eventually managed to escape to America, making their way to Hawaii after falling in love with the images in South Seas movies.

Before the war Preis designed at least 20 residences with Dahl & Conrad, plus the modern-style Jade Building in 1941. He was offered the position of partner but he declined, feeling he was not yet ready. He had just passed his AIA certification exam when the Japanese attacked Pearl Harbor. That same night he and his wife were picked up and sent to the Sand Island detention camp. He was finally released on parole on March 28, 1942, through the efforts of Connie Conrad.

During World War II, Bjarne Dahl joined the U.S. Army Corps of Engineers and afterwards moved to California and along with George Benedict bought the Cardinal Hotel in Palo Alto.

Connie Conrad joined his father's jewelry business, Security Diamond, in 1942, building it into one of the top 25 jewelry stores in the country. Many of his best customers were workers in the nearby brothels in Chinatown.

As a formerly interned enemy alien, Alfred Preis was unable to find work so he opened his own architectural practice in 1943 after briefly working with a quarry and also on a project with Hart Wood. In business for twenty years, his most famous work is the Arizona Memorial, designed in 1962. Although criticized as looking like a "squashed milk carton", Elvis Presley helped support the memorial with a fundraising concert in 1961. Preis also designed the entrance to the Honolulu Zoo and the First United Methodist Church on Beretania Street. He was Hawaii's first state planning coordinator and founder of the Hawaii State Foundation on Culture and the Arts.

LOUIS E. DAVIS

Louis Edward Davis (1884-1963) was born in Oregon and was a graduate of the Wilmerding School of Architecture. He came to Hawaii in 1910 from San Francisco to join C.B. Ripley's architecture firm. Davis was most known in Hawaii for his work in the Spanish Colonial/Mission Revival style.

The architecture firm of Ripley & Reynolds was founded in 1892, and with Davis becoming partner in 1912 the firm was known as Ripley Reynolds & Davis. With the departure of Arthur Reynolds later that same year they became Ripley & Davis.

Ralph A. Fishbourne came to Hawaii in 1917 and when he made partner in 1921 the firm became Ripley, Davis & Fishbourne. Ripley passed away in 1922 and they kept his name for one year before becoming Davis & Fishbourne. Fishbourne later had his own private practice from 1926 to 1936.

In 1915 Davis took his automobile with him on board the *Wilhelmina* and went to California to attend the Panama-Pacific International Exposition and to take an extended tour of Spanish-California architecture.

Ripley & Davis designed the National Guard Armory (1914), Kauikeolani Building (1914), Hocking Building (1914), Honolulu Iron Works (1914), Territorial Prison (1915), Star-Bulletin Plant (1916), Love's Bakery (1917), Hoffschlaeger Building (1918), and the University of Hawaii main building known as Hawaii Hall.

Ripley Davis & Fishbourne designed the Princess Theatre (1922), Robinson Building Extension (1923), McKinley High School (1924), F.L. James Building (1925), and St. Francis Hospital (1927).

On his own, Davis designed the Liberty Theater (1926/1929 remodels), Kapahulu Fire Station (1927), Waikiki Tavern (1928), Kapiolani Maternity Home (1929), E.O. Hall Building (1929), New Pawaa Theatre (1929), New Palama Theatre (1930), Waipahu Theatre (1930), Territorial Board of Agriculture and Forestry Building (1930), Honolulu Police Station (1931), Austin Estate Building (1931), Lihue Theatre (1931), Schuman Building (1932), the Bird of Paradise Cocktail Bar at the Young Hotel (1935), several homes in Kahala, and the private residence in Waimanolo known as Pahonu for Mrs. Ormond E. Wall that was featured in the original Magnum PI television series.

Along with Ernest Hara he designed the 1951 expansion of Honolulu Hale (City Hall).

CHARLES W. DICKEY

Hawaii's most prominent architect, Charles William Dickey (1871-1942), was born in Alameda, CA, the grandson of missionary William Alexander and the nephew of the founders of Alexander and Baldwin. Dickey grew up in Haiku, Maui, and graduated with a degree in architecture from M.I.T. He was known informally as "C.W." or "Will" and more formerly as "Hawaii's Dean of Architecture".

After working briefly in California, he came back to Hawaii in 1894 and partnered with Clinton B. Ripley from 1896 to 1900. They designed the Hawaiian Hotel Music Pavilion (1892), Safe Deposit Building (1893), Healani Boat Club House (1895), Von Holt Building (1895), Pauahi Hall (1896), Bishop Estate Building (1896), Love Building (1896), Central Fire Station (1896), Sailor's Home (1896), Irwin Block (1897), Fishel/Mott Smith Building (1897), Fisher Building (1897), Emmeluth Building (1897), E.O. Hall Building (1898), Progress Block (1898), Brewer Warehouse (1899), Alana Block (1899, not built), Honolulu Brewery (1900), Austin Block (1900, not built), and the Stangenwald Building (1901).

Ripley & Dickey also built houses for L.A. Thurston, S. Wilder, Harold Mott-Smith, William G. Ashley, Paul R. Isenberg, F.R. Day, H.P. Baldwin, E. Kopke, S.N. Castle, H. Von Holt, E.D. Tenney, F.B. Auerbach, G.P. Castle, and the Kamehameha Alumni Association.

After Ripley left to concentrate on concrete construction, Dickey teamed with E.A.P. Newcomb from 1901 to 1904. They designed the Sacred Heart Convent School on Fort Street in 1901, the $21,000 F.M. Swanzy House in 1902, a 2-story brick building at Nuʻuanu and Beretania streets, and the Royal School on Emma Street in 1904. They were one of two firms to submit plans for a proposed major expansion of the Capitol Building ('Iolani Palace) in 1903.

Dickey moved to Oakland, CA, in 1904 but still worked for clients in Hawaii. In 1919 he formed Dickey & Wood with Hart Wood, and they designed the Castle & Cooke Building, the campus for Kamehameha Schools, and the Alexander & Baldwin Building.

Dickey moved back to Hawaii in 1924 and designed Honolulu Hale (1926), Honolulu Pineapple Cannery (1927), Kona Inn (1928), Brewer Estate Building (1929), First National Bank in Hilo (1929), UH Wist Hall (1929), Halekulani Hotel (1930), Harkness Nurses Dormitory at Queens Hospital (1931), US Immigration Office (1931, with Herbert Cohen Cayton), Alexander Hall at Punahou (1933), Cooke Trust Building (1934), Waikiki Theater (1934), Central Fire Station (1934), Kula Sanitarium (1935), Montague and Wilcox halls at Punahou (1936), Kamehameha Boy's School (1936), Nuuanu YMCA (1937), Kodak Building (1939), Farrington High School (1939), Volcano House (1940), Mayor Wright Housing Project (1940, with Stiehl, Rothwell, and Wood).

Long out of print: *The Architecture of Charles W. Dickey: Hawaii and California*, by Robert Jay (University of Hawaii Press, 1992), and *The Architectural Work of Charles William Dickey*, 1907.

FRANCIS R. DUNN

Very little is known about architect Francis R. Dunn. He was said to be from New York and first appears in the Honolulu newspapers in October 1896.

> **FRANCIS R. DUNN,**
> **ARCHITECT and SUPERINTENDENT**
> OFFICE—Spreckel's Building.
> RESIDENCE—Hawaiian Hotel.

Dunn designed the Chilton residence and the Occidental Hotel in 1896, and in 1897 he designed the $40,000 Lieut. William Edwin Safford house in Washington, D.C.

He also designed a 2-story colonial residence for John Grace in Honolulu in 1897.

The last mention of Dunn in any newspaper in the United States is this curious article in the *Hawaiian Star* dated August 27, 1897:

> **DUNN IN SAN FRANCISCO.**
>
> *The Young Architect Apparently in Clover Again.*
>
> Francis Dunn, the architect who during his brief residence in this city, built palaces on paper, but only small frame houses and but a few of them for his clients, has been heard from. He disappeared rather suddenly from his usual haunts a few weeks ago, and although he was sought high and low by numerous small creditors, no trace of him could be found.
>
> It was a bright, sunshiny morning during the last voyage of the Australia that a business man of this city, whom Dunn had but a few months before looked upon as a rival, left his stateroom for an early stroll on deck. The crew was busy scrubbing down. The traveler glanced at them curiously as he leaned over the rail to avoid the wash from their brooms. He was surprised to see Dunn there, but there was no mistaking him. Barefooted, and with his shirt sleeves rolled up, he was handling a broom like a veteran. Dunn did not attempt to conceal his identity. As he passed his erstwhile rival in business, he worked solemnly without a shadow of a smile on his face. A few days after he landed in San Francisco the traveler again saw Dunn, on Market street. This time the youthful architect was dressed in a new suit of fashionable cut, with patent leather shoes, and the latest thing in hats, ties, etc. As he passed the Honolulu man, Dunn removed a choice Havana from the corner of his mouth, and again executed the solemn wink that he had done on the steamer.

The Hawaiian Star, August 27, 1897

EMORY & WEBB

Walter Leavitt Emory (1868-1929) was born in Fitchburg, Massachusetts and studied at the Massachusetts Institute of Technology before coming to Hawaii in 1898 in hopes of making a fortune growing coffee. Finding coffee plantations to be not as profitable as advertised, he moved to Honolulu and became the assistant superintendent of construction on the Alexander Young Hotel Building.

He worked on a variety of private construction projects between 1901 to 1908 until 1909 when he formed a partnership with Marshall H. Webb. Emory & Webb were the pre-eminent architects in Hawaii for the next 10 years.

Marshall Hickman Webb (1879-1931) was born in Philadelphia, PA, and studied at the Drexel Institute, Spring Garden Institute, and the Academy of Design. The story is told that he first came to Honolulu in 1900 with fifty cents in his pocket and a camera to photograph "the beauties of Hawaii" but was accidently left behind when the steamer *Ventura*, on which he was a junior engineer, sailed off without him.

After completing his marine engineering apprenticeship he returned to Hawaii and worked as a draftsman for the Board of Public Works. In 1907 he joined the staff of the United States Engineer's Office and worked on forts DeRussy, Ruger, Armstrong, and Kamehameha plus several harbor projects.

Emory & Webb designed the Union Trust Company, Commercial Trust & Bank Building, Bishop Estate Building on Ka'ahumanu Street, new Palama Theater, Blaisdell Hotel, Hawaii Theater, new Central Union Church, Love's Bakery, Liberty House annex, Castle Hall dormitory at Punahou, Cooke Art Gallery at Punahou, the Elizabeth Waterhouse Memorial Tank at Punahou, James Campbell Building, Advertiser Building, new St. Louis College buildings, Hawaiian Electric Building, Salvation Army Boys' Home in Kaimuki, Salvation Army Girls' Home in Manoa, J.H. Schnack Building, Honpa Hongwanji Temple, Masonic Temple, Wing Wo Tai Building, and the residence of J.P. Erdman in Punahou. They were also the supervising architects for the Dillingham Transportation Building and the Army Navy YMCA.

FRED FUJIOKA

Fred Yoshimi Fujioka (1903-1983) was born in Olaa and was the first Hawaiian-born person of Japanese ancestry to become a registered professional architect in Honolulu.

He graduated from Honolulu Business College in 1922 and after working with Emory & Webb for nearly 10 years he opened his own practice in 1931.

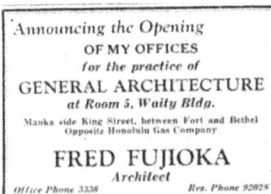

Fujioka designed houses for Arthur Robinson, Allan Bush Jr., Harold Rockwell, Edith and Katherine Phillips, along with the Kunahisa Building in Wahiawa, Union Supply Factory and Warehouse, and the Pacific Market in 1932.

In 1936 he designed the Kauai County Jail, Koloaa School Assembly Hall, and the Aloha Theater at Hanapepe; the M. Masaki Store in Waimea, Kawakami Store, addition to Nippu Jiji Building, John F. Rosa house in 1937; and the Yamashiro Hotel, Waimea Theater, and 20-house Osoria subdivision in Maikiki in 1938.

Fujioka designed the House of Mitsukoshi at King and Bethel streets in 1940 which featured the first escalator in Hawaii. He also participated in its remodel in 1960.

Other designs included the Kokusai Theater (1941), Aloha Grill (1952, 1958), and the Lester McCoy Pavilion in Ala Moana Park (1960).

ERNEST HARA

Ernest Hideo Hara (1909-2006) was born in Honolulu, went to Punahou, and graduated from the University of Southern California in 1935 with a degree in architecture.

He first worked with Claude Stiehl and went to work with C.W. Dickey in 1941. Initially refusing their job offer since it paid $20 less per week than what "mainland" architects were being paid, they finally relented and offered him full wages.

After World War II, Hara opened Ernest H. Hara & Associates in 1945. He was a founding member of Central Pacific Bank in 1950 and served on its board from 1954 to 1980.

Hara designed at least 43 schools, 36 apartments/hotels, and 32 commercial projects, including Robert Louis Stevenson School (1950), Central Pacific Bank (1955), Lee & Young Building (1957), Waikiki Grand Hotel (1962), Queen Kapiolani Hotel (1968), Waikiki Shopping Plaza (1975), Hilo Hawaiian Hotel (1976), and the new Central Pacific Bank (1981).

FRED HARRISON

Fred Harrison (1859-1946) was born in Sneinton, Nottingham, England, and came to Honolulu in 1879 with his father Samuel who was also a contractor and builder.

He was one of the most prolific building contractors in Honolulu and was the first to use cut lava blocks in construction. Highly respected by all, it was said "he mixed reputation with his mortar".

Harrison was arrested in 1895 and exiled for two years for his part in the Wilcox Rebellion to restore the monarchy.

In addition to several sugar mills, Harrison built the second brick tower on the Kaumakapili Church (1885), Chinese Engine House No.5 (1889), Lower Nuʻuanu Stream bridge (1889), Custom House (1889), Oahu Railway Depot (1889), A.L. Smith Building (1890), Cummins Building (1891), Progress Block (1897), Judd Building (1898), J.B. Castle's palatial "Kainalu" residence (1899), Elite Block (1899), Brewery addition (1901), O'Neill Building (1902), Hackfeld Building (1902), Odd Fellows Building (1903), McLean Block (1903), Harrison Block (1906), Central Building (1908), and the Union Grill remodel (1910).

HAWAIIAN ENGINEERING & CONSTRUCTION CO.

Frederick James Amweg (1856-1933) was born in Harrisburg, PA and began engineering in 1873. The Market Street Cantilever Bridge over the Schuylkill River and the City Avenue Bridge, the New River Bridge at Radford, VA, the Terry Building and Roanoke Academy of Music in Roanoke, VA, YMCA Building in Germantown, PA, the Engine #29 Fire Station in Philadelphia, and the million-dollar Insane Asylum in Wernersville, PA were all designed and built under his supervision.

Amweg was also the chief engineer of the Toledo & Monroe Electric Railroad, and he came to Honolulu in 1899 to become the chief engineer of the Honolulu Rapid Transit & Land Co. Amweg also supervised the construction of the Stangenwald Building in 1901.

On March 11, 1901, Amweg founded the Hawaiian Engineering & Construction Co. with Charles H. Atherton, William R. Castle Jr., Clarence H. Cooke, Philip M. Lansdale and Philip L. Weaver. Their first major projects were the Sacred Heart Convent, the J.P. Mendonça Building, the Sachs Building, and the Lewers & Cooke Building. They also built the Oregon Block and the Waity Building.

In the summer of 1903 they changed the name to the American-Hawaiian Engineering & Construction Company and opened a second office in the Rialto Building in San Francisco. Their first big project was building the $18,000 Carnegie Library in Vallejo, CA. In 1903 they were also awarded the contract to build the $135,000 courthouse in Redwood, CA, and the $65,000 Red Men's Hall in San Francisco.

In 1904 they proposed developing Honolulu's Pacific Heights subdivision with streetcar tracks, and they were also the successful bidder for the Hawaii Insane Asylum project that became mired in controversy over the specifications calling for a type of concrete block to be made with "a machine that hadn't been invented yet".

After completing the State Archives Building in early 1906 the company left Hawaii to concentrate on work in the San Francisco area. Amweg was appointed Lieutenant Colonel by Governor Gillette in 1907.

Amweg also built the $340,000 Kern County Courthouse in Bakersfield, CA, completed in 1912.

ISAAC N. HAYDEN

Not much is known about contractor Isaac Newton Hayden (1851-1900) who was born at St. Peter's Bay in Prince Edward Island, Canada. He was said to have gone to Boston around 1880, later going to the gold district of Kootenay in British Columbia two years later to build mining camps.

He first shows up in the newspapers in Honolulu in 1897. In 1899 he built the 2-story residence for self-proclaimed "Irish Consul" Thomas McTighe on Young Street for $3,145 that was designed by Oliver G. Traphagen. That same year he also built a 2-story stable for G. Schumann's store on Fort Street.

But his main claim to fame occurred after he suddenly died while building a 1-story brick replacement of the Pantheon Saloon after it was burned by the Board of Health. The *Boston Post* published a story in February 1901 with the headline:

> "New England Family Heirs to $2,250,000. Death of Isaac Hayden in Honolulu Leaves Vast Fortune to Relatives. Contractor Dies in Honolulu Leaving Millions to Heirs".

The amount would have been worth $80M in today's money. The story was apparently the product of "some graceless romanticist of yellow stripe" and it caused a nationwide sensation.

The actual value of the estate? After expenses, $231.30 to be distributed to creditors at 30 cents on the dollar.

MAY BE HEIRS TO A FORTUNE

Two Somerville Men Hear That a Brother Has Died Recently in Honolulu, Leaving an Estate of Over Two Millions and No Children

Word recently has come to Somerville of the death in Honolulu of Isaac Newton Hayden, and it is rumored that he left $2,250,000, which will be divided among his brothers and sisters and their children. Two brothers of the deceased are John and James Hayden of 17 Hinckley street, and while they are anxiously awaiting confirmation of the statement of their brother's death they accept the statement that he died a millionaire with a large grain of salt.

Isaac Newton Hayden was born in Prince Edwards Island. About twenty years ago he left there and came to Boston. He was a carpenter by trade and soon found employment. After remaining about Boston for a time, Mr. Hayden went to the mining lands in British Columbia, and was successful as a builder. He was not entirely satisfied with this place, however, and took passage for the Hawaiian Islands. Here he took up the trade of carpentry and soon became a leading contractor. Last October he was taken ill, and died after a short illness. He had no family, and the authorities immediately began a search for his relatives, which resulted successfully only a short time ago.

Besides John and James Hayden of Somerville, those who are entitled to a share of the assumed millions of Mr. Hayden of Honolulu are a brother, Cyrus Hayden, a contractor of Cleveland, O.; a sister, Jemima, wife of S. E. O'Brery of Portsmouth, N. H.; another sister, Elizabeth, wife of Frank Powell of Portland, and four daughters of Hannah, another sister, who died about eight years ago in Prince Edward's Island. The whereabouts of Mary, the eldest sister, are unknown. The deceased had another brother, Douglas Hayden.

Boston Evening Transcript
February 25, 1901

HOFFMAN & RILEY

Described as "an ill-mannered sort of person", Victor Hoffman was a contentious and litigious contractor from San Francisco who came to Honolulu in 1899 teamed up with John F. Riley.

They won the bid for the Beretania Street school in 1899 but backed out. They subsequently built the Queen Street Brewery (1900), E.O. Hall Building (1900), J.H. Fisher Building (1901), Oregon Block (1901), and Collins Building (1901).

V. HOFFMANN.   J. F. RILEY.
Hoffman & Riley
GENERAL CONTRACTORS AND BUILDERS.
Estimates Furnished.   P. O. Box 160

Hoffman & Riley were sued and countersued by J.H. Fishel and the Honolulu Brewing and Malt Company for shoddy work and excessive delays.

They dissolved the partnership in 1902 and Hoffman skipped town in December 1905 to avoid a judgment against him in the dispute with Honolulu Brewing and Malt Company and never came back.

HOWARD & TRAIN

George Augustus Howard (1835-1912) spent two years in Honolulu between 1889 and 1891 and designed buildings for the Oahu Railway, residences for Chief Justice Judd and R.D. Walbridge in Wailuku, plus the Volcano Hotel. He also remodeled the residences of W.G. Irwin and B.F. Dillingham.

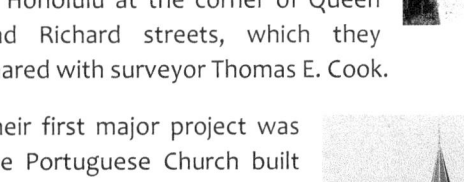

His son, George Augustus Howard (1873-1957) formed Howard & Train architects in 1895 with English-born Robert F. Train (1869-1951) after Train became a US citizen in 1894.

In 1896 they opened a second office in Honolulu at the corner of Queen and Richard streets, which they shared with surveyor Thomas E. Cook.

Their first major project was the Portuguese Church built in 1896 at the mauka corner of Punchbowl and Miller streets

Howard & Train designed the new Campbell Block on Fort Street next to the Odd Fellows Building in 1896, and in 1897 they designed houses for J.J. Egan and T.P. Harris, C.G. Ballentyne, and S.M. Ballou.

In 1898 they were the architects for the Inter-Island Steamship Company Building on Queen Street, the F.M. Wakefield Building in Hilo, and they also provided early designs for the Model Block and Sachs Block.

George W. Page joined the firm in 1898, and David Kalauokalani Jr. worked at Howard & Train between 1897 and 1899 before becoming a district court judge and leader of the Home Rule Party.

The company designed houses for Norman Halstead, Emmet May, and 11 cottages for E.C. Peck in 1899, the Territory Stables and Pantheon Saloon building in 1900, and the J.H. Fisher Building in 1901. In 1903 they were in a design competition with Newcomb & Dickey to design extensions to the Capitol Building ('Iolani Palace).

After designing the L.B. Kerr Buildling on Alakea Street and the Baseball Grandstand in 1903, Howard returned to California. Train had left previously and by 1903 was working in Los Angeles as Train & Williams.

Howard might have also designed the McLean Building on Nu'uanu Street. Oliver Traphagen is mentioned as being the supervising architect in late 1903, about the time Howard would have already returned to Los Angeles.

HARRY L. KERR

Born in Port Ewen, NY, Harry Livingston Kerr (1863-1937) attended Kingston Academy and a private architectural school, and worked for 2 years in New York City. In 1887 he moved to San Diego, then 3 years later to the state of Washington, and finally to Portland, Oregon, where he opened his own architectural office in 1892.

Kerr arrived in Honolulu on December 7, 1897, just one month after Minnesota architect Oliver Traphagen. He initially officed in the Love Building on Fort Street, later moving to the Progress Block also on Fort Street.

In addition to his architectural work, in 1900 he formed the Honolulu Clay Company with three partners to make local bricks in response to the need for more building materials after the 1900 fires.

When Ripley, Dickey, and Traphagen left Hawaii in 1907, that left Kerr as the most prominent Honolulu architect.

It is said he designed over 1,000 buildings in Honolulu, including the Orpheum Block (1899), C.J. Ludwigsen House (1899), Carl Widemann House (1899), Charles Booth House (1899), Mrs G.A. Hendricks House (1899), Hawaiian Hotel Improvements (1899), JR Wilson/ W.H. Shipman House in Hilo (1899), Day Block (1899), Magoon Block (1900), Sachs Building (1901), Y. Anin Block (1901), Hustace Building (1901), Hawaiian Electric Building (1901), C. Ahi Building (1901), United Chinese Society Building (1903), McCandless Building (1906), Maui County Courthouse (1907), Honolulu High School (1908, now the Honolulu Museum of Art School), Yokohama Specie Bank (1908), Pantheon Building (1909), L.L. McCandless Block (1910), Mid-Pacific Institute (1910), Judd Building Remodel (1912), California Feed Warehouse (1913), Mendonça Building (1913), Wolters Building (1915), McInerny Building Remodel (1915), Mission Memorial Building (1916), Wichman Building Remodel (1916), Alexander Young Annex (1916), Moana Hotel Expansion (1917), Sumitomo Bank renovation (1919), Tan Sing (Mendonça) Building (1920).

The distinctive large round lanais of the Hawaiian Hotel were designed by A.T. Large in 1899 while working for H.L. Kerr & Co.

In 1919 Kerr promoted Edwin C. Pettit to partner, and the firm became Kerr & Pettit.

After 1920 he specialized in apartment buildings, mostly in Waikiki, and was the owner of the Kerr Apartments at Kalākaua and Liliʻuokalani streets.

Kerr was a member of the Kaneohe Yacht Club and was a huge fan of transpacific yacht races.

GEORGE W. LINCOLN

Born in New York and said to be a grand nephew of Abraham Lincoln, George Walter Lincoln (1832-1924) was a Civil War veteran who came to Hawaii about 1876 or shortly before.

His first newspaper ad in 1881 offered contracting and building services as well as being the sole agent for the Housekeeper's Kitchen Cabinet, plus offering reconditioning and retoothing of saws.

He built the Clark Building in 1879 and the Cunha Saloon on Merchant Street in 1881, and the 2-story brick Lincoln Block on King Street and Spreckels Bank on Fort Street in 1884.

GEORGE W. LINCOLN,

Contractor & Builder!

86 KING ST., HONOLULU.

DESIRES TO INFORM HIS FRIENDS and the public generally, that he is now prepared to accept Contracts for

Buildings, Cottages,
                  Stores or Dwellings,

After AMERICAN, FRENCH, ITALIAN, SWISS or GERMAN STYLES, and from NEW DESIGNS, which combine all the necessary requisites for health and comfort, in a warm climate.

Orders Respectfully Solicited for
   Designs, Plans and Specifications,
      For Dwellings, Stores,
           Public Buildings, Halls, Hotels,
Mills and Works of Every Description,
          — IN EITHER —

Wood, Brick, Iron or Stone Constructions.

I pledge ACCURACY and COMPLETENESS in all respects, and will visit any of the Islands in person to examine SITES, LOCATIONS, etc., upon payment of travelling expenses.

My arrangements enable me to supply competent men to superintend the construction of Buildings and Works on any of the Islands. Having formed a business connection with one of the

Principal Mills on the Coast,
I AM PREPARED TO DO

First-Class Work!
AT MODERATE RATES.

Satisfaction Guaranteed.

☞ One of the Latest Inventions for retoothing SAWS has been brought by me from the Coast, and old Customers and new ones, are invited to call on me with their old and worn-out SAWS and I will make them as good as new, and at moderate rates.

☞ **GIVE ME A CALL.** ☜
oct8 1y*

Right Side UP.

That's the way the sign at the new shop reads, and the business is right side up, and in the new quarters I have more room to work in, consequently feel that I can do more satisfactory work in both planning and executing.

If you have any serious intention of building a home or business block, economy demands that the work should be the best and that's the kind I prefer to do.

It's more satisfactory to you, and to me, to do work that will stand as a landmark.

LET ME DO YOUR FIGURING.

GEORGE W. LINCOLN,
Contractor and Builder,
King Street, near Alakea.

1885 was a particularly busy year – he built a large icehouse for James Campbell, the new mansion for Judge McCully at "Pawaa-on-the-plains", and the Pacific Commercial Advertiser Building on Merchant Street.

He built the S.M. Magnin Building at 941 Nuʻuanu Street and the Quong Sam Kee Building at King and Maunakea streets in Chinatown in 1886, and briefly partnered with George Kavanagh in 1887.

Lincoln built the Von Holt Building in 1895 and the new Opera House in 1896 with Thomas B. Walker and Archie Sinclair as subcontractors. He ran his last newspaper ad in 1912, selling his saw-filing business.

LORD-YOUNG ENGINEERING CO.

Edmund Joseph Lord (1868-1938) was born in Canada and as a young boy worked in the logging camps.

He later worked in the Duluth, Minnesota, city engineer's office, going to San Francisco in 1899 and Honolulu in 1900 as with Vincent & Belser, working on the city's first sewer system.

He formed Lord & Belser in 1901 which became Lord-Young in 1910. J.L. Young left in 1915 and E.J. Lord went out on his own in 1918 after the firm was purchased by the Dillingham interests. Lord sold his business to E.E. Black in 1930.

LORD-YOUNG ENGINEERING CO., LTD.
E. J. LORD, President   F. E. THOMPSON, Vice-President
J. L. YOUNG, Manager and Treasurer

Architects, Engineers
General Contractors

CONSULTING, CIVIL, ELECTRICAL, SANITARY, MECHANICAL, BIOLOGICAL, CHEMICAL, PHYSICAL AND TESTING LABORATORIES

EXAMINATIONS   APPRAISEMENTS   ESTIMATES

CAMPBELL BLOCK

P. O. Box 592   Telephone 2610

Lord specialized in roads and utilities and was estimated to have done more than one-half of the public works in Hawaii.

Lord-Young built the University Club (1910), Pearl Harbor Marine Barracks (1910), Judiciary Building Renovation (1911), Library of Hawaii (1911), Bishop Hall Annex (1911), Palm Building (1912), Star Building (1912), Union Building (1912), Hilo Wharf (1912), E.W. Quinn Building (1913), Kauikeolani Building (1914), McCandless Building 5th floor (1914), Mission Memorial Hall (1915), plus ammunition houses at Fort Shafter and Piers 2, 8, 9 and 10.

GEORGE LUCAS

George Lucas (1821-1892) was born in County Clare, Ireland. His father was one of the English guards who watched over Napoleon during his banishment to St. Helena, and Lucas's parents later moved to Australia where he met and married Sarah Williams from Limerick, Ireland.

He and his wife spent three weeks in Honolulu in 1849 on their way to the California Gold Rush. Not having much luck as a miner, he turned to carpentry and worked in San Francisco for six years.

On July 10, 1856, they arrived in Hawaii on *Maria,* and in 1859 he founded the Honolulu Steam Planing Mill on the newly reclaimed land called the Esplanade in front of the former fort. The mill employed 20 people housed in a "shapely stuccoed brick structure".

He worked on the Custom House with Robert Lewers, and his first major building was a large Templar Hall on Hotel Street near Nuʻuanu Street in 1869 with Albert Wiggins. He built the Keystone Saloon at Fort and King streets and the Masonic Hall at Fort and Queen streets in 1878.

Lucas provided all the carpentry, cabinetry, and woodwork for ʻIolani Palace in 1882, including the Grand Staircase, using imported woods like American walnut and white cedar plus Hawaiian woods like koa, kou, kamani, and ohia. He also built the new YMCA Building at Hotel and Alakea streets.

In 1883 he built a landmark clock tower adjacent to his shop that was an official timepiece for mariners and King Kalākaua, and it was also an important range marker for ships entering and leaving the harbor. Lucas's mill also provided steam power to Laine's feed shop and J.T. Chayter's Blacksmith Shop. A steam whistle announced 7, 12, 1, and 5 o'clock.

Lucas also built the Coronation Pavilion, Brunig Building, Campbell Block/Knights of Pythias Hall, interior of the Hawaiian Hotel, Mutual Telephone Building, Cosmopolitan Saloon, Bickerton Block (Club Hubba Hubba), Holt Block, Yim Quon Building, Mendonça/Encore Saloon, Friend Building, Damon Building, Brewer Block, Honolulu Iron Works Storage Building, Chilton Block, Robinson Block, and a stone bridge on Nuʻuanu Street.

Lucas was a proud and active member of the Honolulu Volunteer Fire Department and was their chief engineer for many years. He was also the first president of the old Mechanics' Library which became the Honolulu Library and Reading Room.

His funeral in 1892 was one of the largest seen in Honolulu, with over 60 carriages and large musters of firemen and members of benevolent societies he had helped, plus the Royal Hawaiian Band.

HENRY W. MCINTOSH

Born in County Meath, Ireland, Henry W. McIntosh (1840-1892) first came to Hawaii around 1872 as a visitor. After spending a few years in Oregon he returned to Hawaii to stay in 1880.

The first major building that we know he designed was the McInerny Block at Fort and Merchant streets building in 1888 by E.B. Thomas. Michael McInerny was so pleased with his work that he gave McIntosh "a magnificent gold watch and chain in recognition of the architect's efficient work on the new block, and as a token of esteem and friendship".

In 1889 McIntosh designed the Saint Paul's Church in Makapala, Maui, for its mostly Chinese congregation.

McIntosh drew the plans for the 2-story brick A.L. Smith Building on Fort Street that was built by Fred Harrison in 1890. That same year he was appointed Superintendent of Public Works where he reviewed plans, inspected projects, and supervised the construction of a large bridge at Kaneohe consisting of two spans of 60 feet each.

After a day about the town "in his usual healthful appearing condition and cheerful spirits", McIntosh died suddenly that evening of apparent heart failure in 1892 at age 53.

> **FOR SALE!**
>
> **Attention, Mechanics!**
>
> **A RARE OPPORTUNITY.**
>
> An A1 Collection of Mechanic's Tools, the Property of the late HENRY W. McINTOSH, comprised as follows:
>
> 1 Turning Lathe, complete; with Tools Suitable for Lock or Gunsmith.
>
> 1 Complete Set of Wood Carver's Tools.
>
> Chest of Carpenter's Tools, comprising some Fine Planes and Saws, Drawing Boards and Trestles for same.
>
> 1 Hart Patent Duplex Die Stock, size AA.
>
> 1 Wiley and Russell Lightning Die Stock, 3-32 to 9-32.
>
> Callipers, Drills, Levels and numerous other useful Tools.
>
> ☞ The above mentioned Articles can be seen at the shop of Mr. F. Wilhelm, King Street.
>
> ☞ For further particulars enquire of
>
> M. McINERNY,
> Administrator Estate of H. W. McIntosh.
> 594-ts

MERRILL, SIMMS, & ROEHRIG

Associates of C.W. Dickey Associates since 1941, with some having worked at the firm since 1929, William Merrill, James Simms, and Kenneth Roehrig took over the firm after Dickey's death in 1942. They kept the company name until 1948 when they rebranded as Merrill, Simms & Roehrig.

William Dickey Merrill was born in 1909 in Honolulu and was C.W. Dickey's nephew. He obtained his Masters in Architecture at Harvard University, and a PhD at Edinburgh University. After working in Jerusalem for two years, he was with C.W. Dickey Associates and its successors from 1936 to 1965.

James Clyde Simms (1892-1959) was born in Lewiston, IL, and moved to Honolulu from Los Angeles in 1929 to work for C.W. Dickey. **Kenneth William Roehrig** (1907-1969) was born in Oakland, CA, and came to Hawaii in 1937.

They designed the Cooke Trust Building (1949), Kamehameha Elementary School (1954), Capital Investment Building (1955), Marks Garage (1957), Seabord Finance Building (1957), and the C.S. Wo Building (1957). The firm became Merrill Roehrig Onodera and Kinder in 1960.

ISAAC MOORE

Isaac M. Moore (1841-1904) was born in Balbriggan, Ireland, and came to Honolulu about 1881. He worked for many years as draughtsman and architect in the employ of George Lucas and the Honolulu Planing Mill.

He designed the Gazette Building (1882), YMCA (1882), the interior of the 'Iolani Palace (1883), Campbell Block (1883), Honolulu Library and Reading Room (1883), Spencer Building (1883), McInerny Block (1884, not built), P.C. Jones residence, James Campbell residence (1884), and the J.T. Waterhouse residence remodel (1885).

ISAAC MOORE,

ARCHITECT

Office at present: Corner King and Fort Street, with Dr. R. I. Moore.

Plans, Specifications details and Superentendence given for all description of Buildings.   3317-tf

In 1888 he was reportedly the heir to $40,000 ($1.25M today) and moved to San Francisco. He returned in 1893 and opened an office in the Chilton Block.

LOUIS CHRISTIAN MULLGARDT

Louis Christian Mullgardt (1866-1942) was born in Franklin County, MO, and studied architecture in St. Louis and at Harvard University. He initially worked in Chicago and started his own practice in St. Louis in 1895. After working in Manchester and London in the UK, he moved his office to San Francisco in 1905.

In addition to buildings and houses in the San Francisco Bay area, Mullgardt prepared preliminary designs for a multi-building complex in downtown Honolulu in 1915, but the only one that was built was the massive T.H. Davies building on Bishop Street, completed in 1921.

WILLIAM MUTCH

Born in Scotland, William Mutch (1845-1920) was the Superintendent of Buildings for the Bishop Estate. He provided the woodwork for the original Bishop Museum in 1892 and designed the new $30,000 wing to the Bishop Museum built in 1893. Mutch was also the head carpenter at Kamehameha Schools.

Mutch built the Kamehameha School for Girls, Waverley Block, Model Block, Hospital for Incurables, Colusa Building, Armstrong Building, Moana Hotel Addition, and the Alexander Young Hotel which at that time was the largest construction project ever undertaken in Hawaii. He was the first foreign-born naturalized American citizen in the Territory of Hawaii.

E.A.P. NEWCOMB

Edgar Allen Poe Newcomb (1846-1923) was born in Boston, MA. After working in his father's firm for five years he traveled through Europe and became a member of the "Artist's Colony" in Paris.

He designed the Carpenter Memorial Library and the Frank Pierce Carpenter House in Manchester, NH, The Edward Wells House in Burlington, VT, the H.S. Chase house in Brookline, MA, the Tuck's Point Rotunda at Manchester by the Sea, MA, the First Baptist Church in Haverhill, MA, First Universalist Church in Boston, and the high altar at the cathedral in Albany, NY.

In 1901 he came to Hawaii from Boston to partner with C.W. Dickey as Dickey & Newcomb. They designed the new convent school for the Catholic Sisters of the Sacred Heart on Fort Street in 1901, the $21,000 F.M. Swanzy residence and 2 brick stores on Beretania in 1902, and in 1903 they were one of two firms submitting designs for proposed new wings on the Capitol Building ('Iolani Palace).

Dickey & Newcomb designed the 1904 Royal School, Bishop Hall at Punahou, Hale Paahaua, St. Clement's Chapel and Parsonage, and residences for Arthur C. Alexander, P.M. Pond, H. Waterhouse, T. Clive Davies, and Judge Humphries.

After spending 2-years on Samuel Strong Spaulding's "Mohican Manor" in New York, Newcomb returned and worked with Dickey on the Territorial Normal School, Wailuku School, and residences for Alfred Hocking, C. Du Roi, and Mrs. Fanny Lane. Newcomb designed the Sacred Heart Church at Punahou in 1914, the Nichiren Sect Mission Administration Building in 1918, and in 1920 the Knights of Columbus Hall and Sacred Heart Catholic Sisters residence on Union Street that incorporated the old coral building of Stephen Reynolds.

Newcomb was also a poet and musician, composing the music to "Slumber Song", "The Sweet Tum Tum", "Hawaii", "Come Unto Me", "A Little Mountain Maid" and 50 others. He wrote the music for two comic operas with W.M. Brown and Arthur Macy – "Betty" and "The Maid of Marblehead".

KENJI ONODERA

Born in Honolulu, Kenji Onodera (1911-1998) initially studied civil engineering at the University of Hawaii before getting his architecture degree at the University of Illinois in 1935. He worked with C.W. Dickey until World War II, opened his own office in 1946, and joined Merrill Roehrig Onodera & Kinder in 1960.

Onodera designed the Pier 15 Fire Station, UH Men's Dormitory, Hansmann Building, Kenneth Goto House, Honpa Hoongwanji Mission Expansion, Kyo-ya Restaurant, Kobaayashi Hotel, Kokusai Theater (Empress Theater), Maili Elementary School, Kalaheo Intermediate School, and the Medical Arts Building.

J.G. OSBORNE

Very little is known about J.G. Osborne, especially his time before or after he was in Honolulu. We don't even know what the "J.G." stands for. There are two conflicting sources about his origins – one said he was an Englishman from Yorkshire, and another said he was a German from New Zealand.

Osborne first appears in the Honolulu newspapers on March 3, 1866, in an article about potential brickmaking with Osborne, "a mason by trade", proposing to "erect machinery to manufacture them on as large a scale as may be required."

The first building of his that we know of is the 2-story 60' x 90' Bonded Warehouse built adjoining the Custom House in 1867. That same year he "made a draft" for a proposed hotel for Charles Woolley. Osborne was severely injured in 1868 when blasting for stone in Waialae but recovered to dismantle the old William French store on Ka'ahumanu Street to build a new 2-story building for Godfrey Rhodes.

Osborne built the brick E.O. Hall Building in 1869 and made major additions and improvements to the Castle & Cooke store that same year. His next project was the Post Office Building, completed in 1871. He built it with concrete made from "volcanic rock of the hills, reduced to a proper size and mixed with cement". It was the first use of structural reinforced concrete in Hawaii. He had also used concrete on the Castle & Cooke Building and made curbstones of concrete which he sold for 75 cents each.

Osborne drew the plans for the Hawaiian Hotel in 1871 and built the concrete foundation. In 1872 he built a 2-story 50' x 70' concrete store for Dillingham & Co. on King Street and might have also built the new concrete building for C.E. Williams on Fort Street. He sailed to San Francisco on August 7, 1872, on the steamship *Idaho* and seemingly disappears from history.

VLADIMIR OSSIPOFF

Born in Vladivostok, Russia, Vladimir Nicholas Ossipoff (1907-1998) grew up in Tokyo and came to Hawaii in 1932 shortly after graduating from the University of California at Berkeley.

Ossipoff initially worked with Charles W. Dickey and founded his own firm in 1936.

He was Hawaii's foremost Modernist architect, mixing Modernism with Japanese and Hawaiian Territorial elements. Many of his houses and buildings incorporated large informal indoor/outdoor living spaces through open walls and multiple lanais.

Ossipoff designed over 1,000 buildings, including the University of Hawaii Administration Building (1949), Hawaiian Life Insurance Building (1951), the Liljestrand house (1952), Liberty Bank (1952), The Pacific Club (1959), IBM Building (1962), and the Outrigger Canoe Club (1963). Described as both "charming and cantankerous", he waged a "War on Ugliness" against Hawaiian architecture that was neither regional nor climate-friendly. Ossipoff bequeathed 66 boxes of drawings and papers to the University of Hawaii at Manoa. For more, see *Hawaiian Modern: The Architecture of Vladimir Ossipoff* by Karla Britton (Yale University Press, 2015).

JOHN OUDERKIRK

A native of Colchester County, Nova Scotia, John Ouderkirk (1846-1914) came to Hawaii in 1881.

He built the A.P. Fernandez House (1884), North Pacific Missionary Institute (1889), OR&L Wharf (1890), Irwin Block (1897), Henry E. Cooper House (1898), US Coal Depot (1898), C. Brewer Warehouse (1899), Dr. McGrew Cottage (1899), InterIsland Steam Navigation Wharf (1903), Odd Fellows Building (1903), Queen's Hospital Expansion (1904), Elks Building Remodel (1906), Cooke Library at Punahou (1908), Makee/Grinbaum Building Remodel & Addition (1909), Robert W. Shingle House 16-Room Addition (1910), George Isenberg House (1910), Schuman Carriage Company Building (1911), California Feed Co. Warehouse (1913).

In September 1900 he bought Arlington Hotel main building for $180 and Dr. McGrew's old house for $70, to be demolished in 30 days. He sold the lead from the roof of the McGrew house for $63 and the carved redwood staircase for $15, and it was estimated Ouderkirk would clear $2,500 from the salvage.

> "His character was forthright and dealings always above board, so that those engaging or contracting his services were assured of their money's worth."

PACIFIC ENGINEERING COMPANY

John Mason Young (1874-1947) was born in Lewisburg, Tennessee. He served in the Spanish American War as a master machinist at the U.S. Naval Station in Key West, FL, and earned two masters degrees in engineering from Cornell University.

After working for American Bell Telephone Company, Purdy & Henderson, and Westinghouse, he came to Hawaii in 1908 to be professor of engineering at what would become the University of Hawaii. He also created the Pacific Engineering Company in 1908 to design and construct private buildings.

In addition to planning and engineering buildings on the university campus, Young built Castle Hall at Punahou School, Theo H. Davies block, Empire Theatre, S.M. Damon Building, Christian Science Church, Scottish Rite Cathedral, Bank of Hawaii, Alexander Young Annex, Hawaii Theater, Blaisdell Hotel, and the Central YMCA.

When he retired from the university in 1940, he was the last of the original thirteen faculty members.

ISAAC A. PALMER

Born in St. Clairsville, Ohio, Isaac A. Palmer (1835-1908) served in the Wisconsin 30th Regiment as Principal Musician in the Civil War. He moved to Seattle, Washington in 1871 and by April of 1872 was advertising as an "Architect and Builder". He designed the county courthouse and jail, several houses and commercial buildings, plus the towering 12-room 1883 Central School on Sixth Street with French mansard roof, clock tower, and tall central belfry.

By 1887 he was in Honolulu and was the architect of the new Hoffschlaeger Building. Palmer also designed the Perry Block (1888), T.H. Davies Building (1888), Cartwright Building (1889), Robinson Block (1891), J.A. Cummins Building (1891), Hawaiian Hotel Lanai (1891), British Club (1891), Daily Bulletin Building on Merchant Street (1892), and John S. Walker House (1897).

In 1891 Palmer teamed up with former USS *Benecia* ship's carpenter W.W. Richardson to form Palmer & Richardson, advertising "Eastlake, Queen Anne, Renaissance, Gothic, Italian, Classic and Norman" styles of architecture in "stone, brick, iron or wood".

Based on stylistic similarities with the Perry Block, along with his interest in Eastlake architecture, there is little doubt he was also the architect for the Hopper Warehouse (1889), Royal Saloon (1890), Chilton Block (1890), T.R. Foster Building (1891), Pacific Mail Warehouse (1891), and maybe the E.S. Cunha Republic Building (1894). While in Honolulu, Palmer also played violin in Palmer's String Band.

Apparently catching "gold fever", Palmer was in southern Oregon by 1896 where he designed at least 20 downtown buildings and houses in Medford and Grants Pass until he died there in 1908.

CARL H. PATZIG

Carl Hugo Patzig (1858-1908) was born in Dresden, Saxony, Germany, emigrated to the United States at age 17, and came to Hawaii in 1893.

He worked for William Mutch as the head builder of the Waverley Block in 1896, built the Progress Block and the Central Fire Station in 1897, the Palama School in 1899 and the Elite Block in 1900. Other than having 8 children, not much else is known about Carl Patzig.

GEORGE W. PERCY

George Washington Percy (1847-1900) was one of the best-known architects in California. He was born in Bath, ME, studied architecture under Francis Henry Fassett in Portland, ME, and went to Boston to work for Bradley & Winslow.

He went to California in 1869 and built the Insane Asylum buildings. He went to Chicago after the great fire to help rebuild, and also to Boston after the fire there where he built the Equitable Life Building. He returned to California in 1876 and lived in Oakland.

He was selected by Alexander Young to design the Alexander Young Building in downtown Honolulu. Upon his sudden death on December 14, 1900, Oliver G. Traphagen took over as the supervising architect of Percy's plans.

HARDIE PHILLIP

The famous New York architect Bertram Grosvenor Goodhue was working on several Honolulu projects when he suddenly died in 1924. The firm continued as Goodhue Associates and later Mayers, Murray & Phillip with Francis L.S. Mayers, Oscar Harold Murray, and Hardie Phillip.

Hardie Phillip (1888-1973) took over the projects in Hawaii and went on to design several of Honolulu's largest homes and iconic buildings.

His projects included the Honolulu Academy of Arts (1927, now the Honolulu Museum of Art), Lester McCoy House (1928), Bank of Hawaii (1927), the $3M Kamehameha Schools Campus with Dickey & Wood as local architect (1928), Bank of Hawaii Annex (1928), George R. Carter House "Paliku" (1928), Harold K.L. Castle House (1929), Dillingham Hall at Punahou (1929).

Phillip was also the architect for the C. Brewer Building at Fort and Queen streets, completed in 1930.

The Church of the Heavenly Rest (1929) in New York City is perhaps Phillip's most famous building.

MARK POTTER

William Mark Potter (1896-1966) was a descendant of Christopher Wren and was born in London, grew up in New Zealand, and came to Hawaii in 1914 at age 18. By 1923 he was partnered with architect William C. Furer as Furer & Potter, and he opened his own practice in May 1928 in the James Campbell Building.

Potter designed the Mrs. J.L. Harding house (1928), Henry Bredhoff house (1928), Makiki Hotel 1929, with Furer), Lester M. Fishel house (1929), Mrs. Edna C. Taylor house (1929), James Gardner House (1929), Honolulu Bible Training School (1929), Roswell M. Towill House (1929), C.G. Harrington House (1930), Oahu Ice Plant Expansion (1930), Dr. Richard Wrenschall House (1930), Otto F. Heine House (1931), Kokokahi Amphitheater (1931), Liberty Bank/Yim Quon Remodel (1931), Eaton H. Magoon House (1931), W.T. Vofeld House (1934), N. Aoki Store (1934), Waialua Hospital Administration Building (1936), Arlington Building Remodel (1937), UH Women's Dormitory "Hale Laulima" (1940), Ideal Finance Building (1940), UH Castle Memorial Hall (1941), Waikiki Aquarium (1945), Dairymen's Association Hilo Plant (1946), Hawaiian Trust Expansion (1948), UH Chemistry Building (1949), First Federal Building (1949), Frank Cooke Atherton Memorial Chapel (1950), Hawaii State Archives Building (1953), Boston Building Remodel (1954), Bunny's Building in Kailua (1954), Hartfields Star (1956), Manufacturer's Shoe Store Remodel (1957), Central Union Church Buildings (1963). His last project was the Lloyd B. Osborne House in Kailua, built in 1966.

FRED H. REDWARD

Born in Peckham, Surrey, England, Frederick Henry Redward (1849-1924) came to Honolulu in 1880. He teamed up with Thomas B. Walker and built the Damon Building in 1887, a reservoir in the Nuʻuanu Valley, and an addition to the Armstrong Building at Punahou in 1889. In late 1889 they bought the old wooden Royal Saloon buildings for $100 and built the new Royal Saloon for $6,127. In 1890 he partnered with James Howell, owning the Excelsior Planing Mill and advertising in January 1891 of having a "local architect of considerable knowledge and experience"– very likely Isaac A. Palmer. But the mill was sold in bankruptcy to Ah Hee for $4,850 in July 1891.

Redward was arrested along with many others on January 7, 1895, for complicity in the Wilcox Rebellion and jailed for 38 days. Claiming innocence, he and eleven others chose to leave Hawaii instead of facing trial. After intervention by the British Foreign Office, Redward was allowed to return in March 1896.

He built the Merchants' Exchange Cellar in 1901, the F.M. Swanzy House in 1902, suffered another bankruptcy in 1906, was the foreman for the Yokohama Specie Bank in 1908, built the Schuman Carriage Company Building in 1915, and was the architect for the Miss Daisy Smith House in 1923, his last project.

CLINTON B. RIPLEY

Clinton Briggs Ripley (1849-1922) was born in Peru, ME, and worked in Chattanooga, Nashville, and Los Angeles before moving to Hawaii in 1890.

His first job here was working as the architect for Peter High's Enterprise Planing Mill. In 1891 he teamed up with English architect Arthur Reynolds (1863-1925).

C. B. RIPLEY, ARCHITECT.
OFFICE: Room 5, Spreckels' Block.
Mutual Telephone 208.

New Designs ! Modern Buildings !

Complete plans and specifications for every description of building. Contracts drawn and careful superintendence of construction given when required. Call and examine plans. apr 29 1y

Ripley & Reynolds designed the Hawaiian Hotel Music Pavilion (1892), Safe Deposit Building (1893), Masonic Temple (1893), Queen's Hospital Addition (1893), Sailors Home (1894), Healani Boat Club House (1895), Von Holt Building (1895), Senator Waterhouse Building (1895), Pauahi Hall (1896), and the Waverley Building (1896).

When Reynolds left Hawaii to tour the world in late 1895, Ripley then partnered with Charles W. Dickey from 1896 to 1900 and they designed Bishop Estate Building (1896), Love Building (1896), Central Fire Station (1896), Sailor's Home (1896), Irwin Block (1897), Mott Smith Building (1897), Fisher Building (1897), Emmeluth Building (1897), E.O. Hall Building (1898), Progress Block (1898), Brewer Warehouse (1899), Alana Block (1899, not built), Honolulu Brewery (1900), Austin Block (1900, not built), and the Stangenwald Building (1901).

Ripley & Dickey also built houses for L.A. Thurston, S. Wilder, Harold Mott-Smith, William G. Ashley, Paul R. Isenberg, F.R. Day, H.P. Baldwin, E. Kopke, S.N. Castle, H. Von Holt, E.D. Tenney, F.B. Auerbach, G.P. Castle, and the Kamehameha Alumni Association.

Ripley developed a strong interest in concrete buildings and started The Concrete Construction Company in 1900 after investigating techniques on the mainland and returning with specialized machinery. He sold his house and moved to Manila to do concrete construction from 1902 to 1907, afterwards moving to Oakland from where he designed Honolulu's First Methodist Church (1910), then moving back to Hawaii in 1910 when he got the contract for the YMCA Building.

He teamed up once again with Arthur Reynolds from 1910 to 1912 as Ripley & Reynolds, and they designed the YMCA (1911), Palm Building (1912), Union Building (1912), and Star Building (1912).

In March 1912, Louis E. Davis joined the firm, and it was briefly Ripley, Reynolds & Davis until Reynolds departed in September and it then became Ripley & Davis. They designed the Honolulu Iron Works warehouse (1912), Hocking Building (1914), Kauikeolani Building (1914), Campbell Block Remodel (1916), Methodist Parsonage (1917), Love's Bakery (1917), and the 5th floor of the Judd Building (1922).

Ralph A. Fishbourne became a junior partner in late 1921 and the firm became Ripley, Davis & Fishbourne. When Ripley passed away in February 1922 it became Davis & Fishbourne.

LINCOLN ROGERS

Herbert Lincoln Rogers (1878-1944) was born in Topsham, Sagadahoc County, ME, studied at the Pratt Institute of Architecture and the Masqueray Atelier in New York City. He was the architect for some "76 monumental buildings" for the New York Board of Water Supply. During WWI he was a commander in the U.S. Navy Corps of Civil Engineers, in charge of planning and designing camps and naval training stations at a total cost of $100,000,000.

After the war he went to San Diego to design the $3M naval training station in the Spanish colonial style of architecture. He later designed the multi-million-dollar amusement center at Mission Beach, and was the architect of the 6-story $500,000 Army and Navy YMCA in San Diego. He also designed YMCA buildings in Los Angeles, San Pedro, and Glendale, CA. Rogers also designed the San Diego Senior High School Auditorium with seating for 2,500 students.

He designed the Army and Navy YMCA in Honolulu in 1928, and the Dillingham Transportation Building in 1930 with Marshall Webb as the supervising architect.

GUY N. ROTHWELL

Guy Nelson Rothwell (1890-1971) was born in Honolulu, went to Punahou, attended high school in Seattle, and graduated from the University of Washington with a degree in architectural engineering. In 1911 he became a Navy employee at Bremerton, WA, and took a post at Pearl Harbor.

After two years of active duty in the Navy he returned to Hawaii and worked with several local firms before starting his own consulting firm in 1922 after previously working for Charles Ingvorsen.

Rothwell's projects include: Robinson Block Remodel (1924), Love Building (1924), New Palama Settlement (1924). John H. Kangeter and Marcus C. Lester became partners in 1925. Rothwell, Kangeter & Lester were the supervising architects for the construction of the First National Bank (1925), M.C. Harris Memorial Japanese Church (1925), Oahu Railway Depot (1925), Patten Building (1927), and Burgess & Johnson Building (1928).

In 1929 the partnership became Rothwell & Lester. They were supervising architects for City Hall (1929), Advertiser Building Remodel (1931), Bank of Hawaii third floor (1937), American Legion Building (1938), Sears Roebuck Store (1940), Mutual Telephone Building (1941), St. Francis Hospital Expansion (1941), Liberty House Reconstruction (1951), Jemal Building (1951), and Long's Drugs on Bishop Street (1954).

E.B. THOMAS

Born in Liverpool, England, contractor and builder Edwin B. "Ted" Thomas (1850-1908) came to Hawaii in 1877 on the steamship *Zealandia* as a tourist to see the volcano and decided to stay. He teamed up with Alfred Foster for one year in 1878 as Foster & Thomas, and quickly became one of the most prominent and respected builders in Honolulu.

He provided the brickwork for 'Iolani Palace (1880-1882), the Music Hall (1880), Lunalilo Home (1881), Wilder Building (1881), Honolulu Library (1883), Love's Bakery (1884), Bishop Hall of Science (1884), and the Kalakaua Police Station (1885).

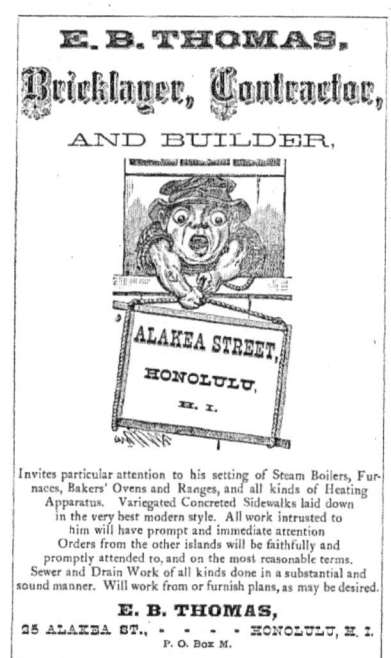

1886 was a particularly busy year for Thomas: United Chinese Society Building, John F. Colburn Building, Aswan Building, brickwork for Quong Sam Kee Building, Uyeda Building, Sing Chong Building, Anchor Saloon, Magnin Building, a 300' breakwater in Waikiki for C. Afong, and a building for Mrs. Thomas Lack. In November of 1886 the bark *Forest Queen* from San Francisco delivered to Thomas 400 barrels of lime and 83,240 hard bricks plus iron and wood mill work.

In 1887 he built the McInerny Block, Pacific Saloon Building, W.E. Foster Building, Hoffschlaeger Building, the brickwork for the Judd Building, plus a new front the King's Court (Yat Loy) Building. In 1888 he built the T.H Davies Building and the Perry Block, followed by the Cartwright Building in 1889. He built the British Club Building and the Wong Kwai Building on Nu'uanu Street in 1891, and the T.R. Foster Building in 1892. Thomas also built the Hawaiian Hotel Music Pavilion and Masonic Temple in 1892, laid some of the granite sidewalk on King Street below Maunakea Street, and did the brickwork for the Von Holt Block (Hawaiian Gazette Building) in 1895. He laid the foundation for the Central Fire Station (1896) and developed and built the Katsey Block (1900).

He was known as "Kamaki" to the Hawaiians and was described as a man of "a genial and sociable nature, though a man of firm opinions and outspoken expression". On January 7, 1895, he was arrested for conspiracy in the Wilcox Rebellion, something do with 50 pounds of gunpowder he had hidden on the *Haleakala*. He was imprisoned for 3 months until finally pardoned.

On October 30, 1900, Thomas left for South Africa via Liverpool, but after two years wrote that it was "the most awful country" and returned to Hawaii in 1908.

GEORGE THOMAS

Very little is known of "accomplished and skillful mason" George Thomas who only appears in the Honolulu newspapers between 1857 and 1861. He was the superintendent for the construction of the Oahu Prison in 1857. In 1859 he built the Odd Fellows Building and the C.L. Richards Building with Charles W. Vincent, and he was also the superintendent for the Customs House in Lahaina.

In 1860 he did the mason work on the Custom House in Honolulu and "broke the first ground" for the Queen's Hospital. The following year he built the ovens for Love's Honolulu Steam Biscuit Bakery and did the mason work for the 1-story Castle & Cooke building. And that's the last we hear of him.

OLIVER G. TRAPHAGEN

Tony Diercxkins, Zenith City Press

Born in Tarrytown, New York, Oliver Green Traphagen (1854-1932) moved with his parents to St. Paul, Minnesota in the 1870's and became a carpenter and later an apprentice with architect George Wirth.

He moved to Duluth in 1882 and worked on his own as well as partnering with Wirth and Francis Fitzpatrick and built a number of prominent public and private buildings in Duluth: First National Bank, Turner Hall, Wieland Block, City Hall and Jail, Fire Station No. 1, First Presbyterian Church, Duluth Central High School, and the landmark Oliver G. Traphagen House called Redstone. Many of his designs were in the Richardsonian Romanesque style.

Traphagen moved his family to Hawaii in November 1897 due to his daughter's health and he quickly became "the most prolific and highly regarded architect in town". He designed the Judd Building (1899), Elite Block (1899), James B. Castle House (1899), Peacock Block in Hilo (1899), McChesney Warehouse (1899), Thomas McTighe House (1899), Gerrit Wilder House (1899), A.W. Meyer House (1899), four houses for E.M. Walsh (1899), Haleiwa Hotel Additions (1899), Kakaako Pumping Station (1900), Boston Block (1900), Hawaiian Hotel Alterations (1901), Moana Hotel (1901), Palama Fire Station (1901), two large Mendonça Buildings (1901), local architect for Alexander Young Building (1901), Senator George Carter House (1901), Collins Building (1901), T.H. Davies Building (1901), Hackfeld Building (1902), E.O. Hall Building (1902), Lewers & Cooke Building (1902), McIntyre Building (1902). Waity Building (1902), O'Neill Building (1903), Odd Fellows' Building (1904), Hilo Jail (1904), Hawaiian State Archives Building (1906), and Punahou School president's home (1907).

> O. G. TRAPHAGEN,
> ARCHITECT.
> 223 MERCHANT ST., HONOLULU.
> Between Fort and Alakea.
> Telephone 743.

In 1902, Traphagen buildings were on three of the four corners at Fort and King streets: O'Neill, McIntyre, and E.O Hall buildings.

Traphagen was incredibly prolific and was only in Hawaii ten years before moving to Alameda, California in 1907. He retired in 1925.

CHARLES W. VINCENT

Not much is known of the early life of Charley Vincent, one of Honolulu's first builders. Reportedly a native of New York, he first appears in the newspapers in 1844 and is listed as a house carpenter in the 1847 Register of Foreigners.

Vincent employed a sizable workforce and was the premier builder in town in the 1840's and 1850's in stone, brick, adobe, wood, or thatch. He built the Robert Wyllie house and the Sailors' Home and was also known for several house-moving projects. In 1847 he took out an ad for 4,000 coral stones, perhaps for the construction of Liberty Hall.

He was also a dealer in lumber, hardware, paint, and builder's supplies. His lumberyard was located on Maunakea Street just mauka of King Street, and at one time he stocked as much as 140,000 feet of Astoria pine timber, plus a huge stock of windows, sashes, doors, nuts, bolts, etc.

Vincent founded Honolulu's first theater, The Thespian, in 1847, and married a Hawaiian woman named Mauli in 1848. In 1849 he teamed up with his neighbor across the street, Isaac Montgomery, in the Puuloa Salt Works.

For the 1854 Fourth of July parade, he displayed a small mahogany center table that was an heirloom from his grandparents, upon which George Washington and the Marquis de Lafayette had often taken tea together in 1778.

Vincent built The Bungalow (1847), Courthouse (1952), Swan & Clifford Building (1854), Sailors' Home (1855), and the C.L. Richards Building (1859) and undoubtedly many other early Honolulu buildings.

The last newspaper reference to C.W. Vincent in Honolulu is in 1864 where he is listed as a "foreign juror".

The *Pacific Commercial Advertiser* on September 9, 1865, reported: *"By the Polynesian, particulars of the death of C.W. Vincent, Esq., were received. It appears that he was murdered at Guaymas"*. Perhaps he was there for the Baja California silver rush since fellow builder R.A.S. Wood had gone there in 1863.

THOMAS B. WALKER

Born in Syminorthic, Norfolk, England, Thomas Beresford Walker (1847-1932) came to Hawaii in 1877 after serving with the British Army in Afghanistan and Abyssinia in 1868.

Stopping in Cheyenne, Wyoming, on his way to San Francisco in 1875 he helped build the Inter-Ocean Hotel. He knew Wild Bill Hickock and General George Custer, and fought with the Third Cavalry against the Sioux and was wounded at the Battle of Powder River in 1876.

In San Francisco he met E.B. Thomas who convinced him to come to Hawaii in 1877. By 1880 he was a bricklayer teamed up with W.K. Metcalfe and by 1883 with H.G. Treadway.

Insolvent by 1884, he worked at the Keystone Saloon and was manager of the Royal Saloon in 1886 when he was arrested in a highly publicized burglary of a safe at the post office. The trial captivated the town and he was eventually acquitted by the Hawaii Supreme Court.

He was married to Mathilda Kaumaka Walker, the eldest daughter of Hawaiian statesman John A. Cummins.

In 1887 Walker teamed up with fellow Englishman Fred H. Redward as Walker & Redward and they built the Damon Building in 1887 and the new Royal Saloon at Merchant and Nu'uanu streets in 1890.

By 1891 the firm was Bertelmann & Walker, building the Brewer Block (J.J. Williams Building) on Fort Street for $12,200. Walker also built the 200' tall smokestack at the Makaweli sugar mill.

A staunch royalist, he was arrested in 1893 with Archibald Sinclair for conspiracy to overthrow the Provisional Government and spent 2 months in jail before being acquitted. He was arrested again in the 1895 Rebellion and was pardoned after being sentenced to 30 years imprisonment and a $5,000 fine for organizing and making hand grenades.

Described as "a very popular but at times erratic man", he was an accomplished performer on the English concertina, but one day in 1897 he also took a rifle and shot at building owner John Emmeluth in broad daylight, apparently upset over the construction schedule.

As Sinclair & Walker he worked on the Von Holt Building in 1895.

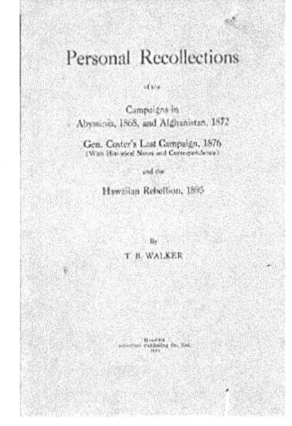

He provided patrol and security services in the 1910's and in 1929, at 82 years old, he rehabilitated the smokestack at the Waianae plantation, and in 1931 he wrote a 100-page book titled "Personal Recollections" that was published by Advertiser Publishing Company.

FRED W. WILLIAMS

Frederick W. Williams (1883-1925) was from Great Britain and came to the United States in 1908 and then to Hawaii after briefly living in San Francisco. His first project that we know of here was a 1-bedroom bungalow designed in 1922. Two years later he led the campaign to create the Hawaiian Humane Society Animal Home and drew the plans for free. In 1927 he became associated with the Home Building Department of Allen & Robinson, Ltd.

Other designs: James R. Judd House (1924), Latter Day Saints Community Hall (1925), Sacred Heart Auditorium & Classroom (1926), R.W. Atkinson House (1926), F.W. Williams House (1927), C. Marshall House (1927), A.A. Weissberger House (1928), Catholic Mission Rectory (1928), F. Dickson Nott House (1928), Colonel Reuben Miller House (1928), William Cross House (1928), Monsarrat Building (1929), Piggly Wiggly Store in Kalihi (1929), Crucifix Statue at Diamond Head Memorial Park (1929), Kalihi Orphanage (1930), Mystic Lodge No. 2 of the Knights of Pythias (1930), Mrs. W.L. Frazee House (1930, Wailuku Parish House (1931), Chrones Store (1931), Harold L. Houvener House (1931), Borthwick's Undertaking (1932), Nuʻuanu Catholic Chapel (1932), F.V. Reynolds House (1937), Melcher Building Alterations (1936). Last mention of Williams is the completion of his own house on Huelani Drive in Manoa in 1941.

Williams was also a boxing enthusiast and former titleholder, and he was the official coach and trainer of the City-Wide Boxing Club.

WIMBERLY & COOK

George J. "Pete" Wimberly (1914-1995) was born in Ellensburg, WA, and came to Hawaii in 1940 to do architectural work at Pearl Harbor. He teamed up with Howard L. Cook (1915-1974) from Great Falls, MT, in 1945 and their first big job was the rehabilitation of the Royal Hawaiian Hotel.

Other designs include: Don the Beachcomber Restaurant (1948), Capital Investment Building (1948), Royal Hawaiian Market (1950), Kaimuki Bowl (1950), Surfrider Hotel (1951), Bishop Bank in Waikiki (1951), Motor Supply Showroom (1952), Canlis Restaurant (1954), Gasco  Building (1954), US Navy Commissary (1956), International Marketplace (1956), Waikikian Hotel (1956), Hawaiian Trust Building (1957), Finance Factors (1958), Kapiolani Bowl (1958), C.S. Wo Building (1958), Jean Charlot House (1958), Bishop National Bank (1959), McInerny Department Store (1959), Windward Shopping Center (1959), Hawaiian Memorial Park Building (1960), Kailua Baptist Church (1960), Hotel King Kamehameha (1960), Princess Kaiulani Hotel Addition (1960), Home Insurance Building (1960), Pali Lanes (1961), Chilton Building Remodel (1961), and the First National Bank on University (1962).

Cook left in 1962 and the firm became Wimberly, Whisenand, Allison and Tong, now known as WATG.

R.A.S. WOOD

Born in Boston, MA, Robert A.S. Wood (1815-1877) came to Hawaii c.1840. He was one of the founding members of the Excelsior Lodge of Odd Fellows in 1846, and by 1847 was advertising as a cabinet maker and upholsterer with William C. Parke. In 1850 he teamed up with William Brandon to buy C.W. Vincent's "stock and stand" and sold the cabinet business to William H. Stuart and Gustave W. Rahe.

Wood & Brandon prepared preliminary plans for a combined courthouse and jail, and it is very likely their design was used for the standalone Court House completed in 1852.

Wood built a large 14-room house on Beretania between Fort Street and Dr. Rooke's house in 1851. He was appointed Superintendent of the Bureau of Public Works in 1855 and oversaw the development of the Market Wharf, the Esplanade "wharf lots", and the demolition of the Honolulu Fort. He was the architect for the Oahu Prison in 1855, and he "perfected" Theodore C. Heuck's plans for the Fort Street Church in 1856.

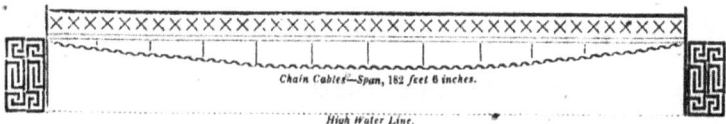

The Pacific Commercial Advertiser, June 23, 1859

Wood designed the first suspension bridge below the falls of the Wailuku River in Hilo in 1859 as well as the Custom House in Lahaina. He designed and supervised the construction of the Honolulu Custom House in 1860 and was the contractor for the rebuilding of the Lahainaluna Seminary in 1862.

Wood left Hawaii in 1863 to become the superintendent of the Baja California Silver Mine in San Antonio, Mexico, and in 1871 he ended up in Hayward, CA.

RALPH E. WOOLLEY

Ralph Edwin Woolley (1886-1957) was born in Grantsville, UT, and graduated from the engineering department of the University of Utah. His father was the first president of the Hawaii Mission of the Latter Day Saints.

Woolley built the Alexander & Baldwin Building, Castle & Cooke Building, Bishop Trust Building, Bishop National Bank building (S.M. Damon Building), Hawaiian Electric Building, Dillingham Transportation Building, C. Brewer & Co. Building, Liberty House Remodel, Laie Mormon Temple, Royal Hawaiian Hotel, Outrigger Canoe Club, S.H. Kress Store, and the Sears Roebuck Store.

Woolley spoke fluent Hawaiian and often helped Native Hawaiians.

He was the chairman of the Public Utilities Commission from 1921 to 1927 and was elected to five terms in the Territorial House between 1933 and 1943.

YORK & SAWYER

Based in New York City, Edward York (1863-1928) and Philip Sawyer (1868-1949) formed their own firm in 1898 after working with McKim Mead & White. Their first project was for a building at Vassar College for which they used drawings prepared for a completely different project. The project came in below budget by $1.75 and they gave a check for that amount to the president of the college who passed it on to the donor, John D. Rockefeller.

York & Sawyer specialized in institutional buildings like banks and hospitals, and were famous for magnificent buildings in Classical, Florentine, Renaissance, and Beaux Arts styles of architecture. They designed the Brooklyn Trust Company Building (1916), Greenwich Savings Bank (1922), Bowery Savings Bank (1923), Central Savings Bank (1928). Their largest design was the Federal Reserve Bank of New York, completed in 1924.

In Honolulu, they designed the classical First National Bank (1925) at the corner of Bishop and King streets, with the Federal Building & Post Office (1922) and the New Hawaiian Electric Building (1927) across the street both being in the "Spanish Mission Colonial" style. Louis Ayres was the company's architect responsible for the designs of the Post Office and Hawaiian Electric buildings.

One of their last projects was the design and construction supervision for the $40M Tripler General Hospital built in 1948, now known as Tripler Army Medical Center.

J.L. YOUNG ENGINEERING CO.

James Lenderman Young (1867-1936) was born in California, KY, and attended the Clermont Academy in Ohio, the University of Kentucky in Lexington, and the University of Lebanon, Ohio. He initially did railroad construction work and private consulting in Cincinnati, OH, before becoming a civil service engineer. His first assignment was remodeling buildings, fortifications, and the sanitation system in Havana, Cuba. He also worked in the Philippines.

Young came to Hawaii in May 1905 and built Ft. Shafter, and started construction of Ft. Ruger, Ft. Kamemeha, and Schofield Barracks. He also built 36 ordinance buildings on Magazine Island in Pearl Harbor and five hangars at Luke Field.

He co-founded the Lord-Young Engineering Company in 1910 but left in 1915 to start the J.L. Young Engineering Company.

As J.L. Young Engineering he built the Pearl Harbor Naval Radio Station (1915), Royal Hawaiian Garage (1918), Patten Building (1923), UH Library (1925), Patten Building (1927), YWCA (1927), Burgess & Johnson Building (1928), Catholic Rectory (1928), in addition to many street and utility projects.

Young built the first steel bridge in Hawaii and fabricated all the steel girders in the Army Navy YMCA. The company had its own steel fabricating plant, cement products plant, and tile and brick factory.

SOURCES & ACKNOWLEDGEMENTS

A very special thanks to these people and places for their most welcome and gracious assistance:

Adam Jansen, Diane, and Troy at the Hawaii State Archives

The many volunteers of the Historic Buildings Task Force

Cynthia Engle, Hawaiian Historical Society

DeSoto Brown and Krystal Kakimoto, Bishop Museum Archives

Don Hibbard

Linda Louie

William Bixler

Tony Dierckins

Barry Lawrence Ruderman Antique Maps, Inc.

Photographers Isaiah W. Tabor, J.J. Williams, Frank Davey, Henry S. Chase, R.W. Perkins, et al.

Kay Ueda and Dawn Webb at the Hawaii Times Photo Archives Foundation, Nippu Jiji Photo Archives. Copyright holder: Hawaii Times Photo Archives Foundation; digitization: Densho; and bilingual metadata: Hoover Institution Library & Archives and National Museum of Japanese History; From the Scenery-Hawaii Collection.

The many newspaper reporters and chroniclers who have documented Honolulu's history of Chinatown through the years, including Stephen Reynolds, Gorham Gilman, Warren Goodale, Richard Greer, Nancy Bannick, Bob Sigall, Peter Young, and many many others.

And especially all the uncredited archivists who have digitized thousands of historical newspapers, maps, photographs, and other primary sources that were so invaluable to this research.

Websites:

newspapers.com

chroniclingamerica.loc.gov

digital.library.manoa.hawaii.edu

digitalarchives.hawaii.gov

findagrave.com

hawaiinuiakea.contentdm.oclc.org

hmha.missionhouses.org

Publications:

Lion Fire Insurance Maps (1879)

Dakin Fire Insurance Maps (1885, 1891, 1899, 1906)

Sanborn Fire Insurance Maps (1914, 1927, 1955)

Honolulu: The Cross-Roads of the Pacific, Lewis Garrison with photos by R.W. Perkins (Hawaiian Gazette Co. Ltd., 1913)

Honolulu Town, Laura Ruby and Ross W. Stephenson (Arcadia Publishing, 2012)

Thrum's Hawaiian Annual (1876-1936)

History of Later Years of the Hawaiian Monarchy and the Revolution of 1893, William DeWitt Alexander (Hawaiian Gazette Company, 1896).

Hawaiian Historical Society Journals

Newspapers:

Daily Herald
Daily Honolulu Press
Evening Bulletin
Hawaiian Gazette
Hawaiian Star
Honolulu Advertiser
Honolulu Republican
Honolulu Star-Advertiser
Honolulu Star-Bulletin
The Independent
The Pacific Commercial Advertiser
The Polynesian

THE AUTHOR

Trained as a licensed site civil engineer, Gary R. Coover has long had a keen interest in history and the built environment, and especially in those who have done the designing and building.

When Gary was much younger he enjoyed working on 1,000-piece jigsaw puzzles but little did he realize at the time that these same skills would apply to historical research. The pattern recognition is similar except the pieces are scattered all over the place, some will be missing, some will be wrong, some will be broken, and then there is the multidimensional aspect of different pieces fitting different places at different times.

He has previously rediscovered the histories and works of several long-lost architects and has identified the builders and construction dates for over a thousand buildings in Texas and Arkansas.

Gary created the Historic Downtown Fayetteville Walking Tour and Virtual Marker Program that was the winner of a 2017 Preservation Award from Preservation Arkansas for its innovative use of QR codes to enhance the visitor experience with additional information and historical photographs.

A featured presenter in HGTV's "Dream Drives" and "If Walls Could Talk" television programs, and lecturer for many years in the Historic Neighborhoods series at the Rice University School of Continuing Studies, he also created the Historic Neighborhoods Photography Contest in conjunction with Houston FotoFest as well as the controversial "Godzilla Award" for demolished structures that was featured in *Preservation* Magazine.

Gary now lives in Honolulu and can often be found wandering around imagining historical Honolulu and Chinatown. His history of every building in Chinatown, *Honolulu Chinatown: 200 Years of Red Lanterns and Red Lights*, was published in 2022 by Rollston Press.

INDEX

1

1882 James Campbell Building, 311

A

A.B. Howe Building, 349
A.L. Smith Building, 206, 578, 586
A.W. Peirce & Co., 521, 526, 542
A.W. Peirce Building, 542
Advertiser Building, 118, 435, 436, 577, 583, 595
Alakea Building, 51
Alana Block, 83, 575, 594
Aldrich, William A., 468, 533
Alexander & Baldwin, 120, 121, 142, 378, 493, 499, 575, 601
Alexander & Baldwin Building, 120, 499, 575, 601
Alexander Young Building, 133, 134, 138, 140, 592, 597
Algaroba Tree, 82, 294
Allen Block, 527, 530
Allen, Samuel C., 434, 439, 440
Aloha Grill Building, 110
American Mutual Life Building, 71
Amweg, Frederick J., 492, 579
Andrade & Co., 215
Arcade Building, 435
Architects Hawaii Ltd., 549
Arlington Block, 317, 319
Arlington Hotel, 133, 317, 414, 415, 590
Arlington House, 410, 417
Associated Oil Service Station, 149
Austin Building, 198, 204, 205

B

B.F. Bolles & Co., 402, 521
B.F. Ehlers, 211, 216, 218, 219, 299, 519
B.F. Ehlers / Campbell Building, 216
B.F. Ehlers store, 211, 218, 219
B.F. Snow Building, 478, 481
Bailey Furniture, 142
Bailey, Harry B., 142
Baker, Thomas J., 193, 235, 239, 403, 467, 473, 521, 543, 568
Bank of Bishop, 97, 120, 129, 425, 533
Bank of Hawaii, 182, 197, 367, 407, 417, 420, 489, 590, 592, 595
Bay Horse Saloon, 306
Beardslee, Frederick W., 53, 538, 569
Beaux Arts, 492, 602
Beaver Block, 183, 184
Beck, Martin, 103
Bell Tower, 324
Benson Smith Building, 239
Benson Smith Drug Store, 214, 242
Benson, Smith & Co., 236, 242, 389, 391
Bernhardt, Sarah, 413
Bertelmann, Henry F., 233, 570, 599
Bertram Grosvenor Goodhue Associates, 417
Bethel-Pauahi Building, 109
Bijou Theater, 104, 107
Bishop Bank, 97, 129, 351, 370, 462, 467, 468, 600
Bishop Estate, 349, 355, 415, 472, 575, 577, 587, 594
Bishop Estate Building, 472, 575, 577, 594
Bishop National Bank, 131, 428, 600, 601
Bishop Trust Building, 420
BIshop, Bernice Pauahi, 61, 411, 466, 472
Bishop, Charles R., 12, 61, 410, 411, 467, 468, 472, 533
Black Cat Café, 336
Black, E.E., 141, 196, 201, 202, 584
Blaisdell Hotel, 276, 282, 283, 286, 577, 590
Blaisdell, Cora Ammie Shaw, 283
Bolles & Co., 521
Booth, Joseph, 300
Boston Block, 215, 226, 229, 332, 403, 597
Bowler, John F., 150, 212, 216, 217, 294, 453, 471, 555, 570
Bradley, Henry, 392
Brandon, William, 171, 172
Brannan, Samuel, 552
Brewer Block, 77, 233, 236, 568, 585, 599
Brewer Estate, 215, 226, 229, 315, 317, 319, 406, 559, 575
Brewer, Charles, 80, 189, 226, 227, 406

Brickwood House, 44
British Club, 44, 65, 67, 146, 591, 596
Burgess & Johnson, 69, 433, 434, 595, 602

C

C. Brewer & Co., 187, 189, 227, 233, 517, 601
C. Brewer Company, 182
C.L. Richards Block, 524, 526
C.M. Cooke Company, 196
C.M. Cooke Estate, 202, 283
C.M. Cooke Ltd., 207
California Feed Co., 548, 590
California One Price Bazar, 254
Camp Boston, 414
Campbell Block, 241, 474, 477, 581, 585, 587, 594
Campbell Estate, 189, 217, 222, 238, 477
Campbell Estate Building, 189
Campbell, James, 183, 187, 216, 219, 221, 232, 235, 258, 311, 312, 368, 382, 474, 483, 577, 583, 587, 593
Canton Hotel, 12, 245, 304, 307
Carson, Mervin B., 504
Cartwright Building, 456, 533, 591, 596
Cartwright, Alexander J., 72, 73, 112, 427, 456, 470, 530, 533, 543
Castle & Cooke, 101, 103, 130, 193, 355, 360, 408, 508, 534, 575, 589, 597, 601
Castle & Cooke Building, 358, 495, 508, 575, 589, 601
Castle, Samuel N., 359, 495
Catholic Rectory, 153, 602
Catton, Neill & Co., 49, 50
Catton, Robert, 49, 50
Catton-Neill Building, 49
Cayton, Herbert Cohen, 107, 129, 322, 323, 367, 429, 571, 575
Central Building, 381
Central Fire Station, 84, 88, 324, 575, 592, 594, 596
Central Pacific Bank, 55, 434, 578
Century Square, 155
Chambers Drug Co., 389
Chang, Annie Lan Nyuk, 144, 145
Charlton, Richard, 11, 348, 513
Chase, Henry L., 234, 237
Chase, Robert S., 55, 108, 234, 235, 237, 550, 570, 588
Chayter Building, 164
Chayter, John T., 164, 585

Chilton Block, 8, 219, 242, 389, 585, 587, 591
Chilton, William R., 389, 392
Clark, D.W., 469
Clemens, Samuel, 464
Cliff, John L., 142, 205, 408, 409, 571
Club Stables, 244, 248, 268, 503
Collins Building, 376, 580, 597
Collins, Charles R., 376, 382
Commercial Trust & Bank Building, 375, 570, 577
Conrad, Conrad W., 59, 135, 144, 145, 383, 387, 572, 573
Cooke Trust Co., 202
Cooke, Amos S., 359, 495
Cosmopolitan Restaurant, 102
Court House, 171, 172, 173, 174, 175, 519
Criterion Saloon, 261, 262, 299
Cummins, John A., 193
Cunha, Emanuel S., 371, 471, 591
Custom House, 162, 463, 578, 585, 589, 597

D

Dahl & Conrad, 144
Dahl, Bjarne C., 144, 145, 383, 387, 556, 572, 573
Dahl, Conrad & Preis, 572
Daily Bulletin Building, 498, 501, 591
Dall, George L., 47, 273
Damon Building, 356, 362, 585, 593, 599
Damon, Rev. Samuel C., 12, 97, 98, 109
Damon, Samuel Mills, 97, 129
Davey, Frank, 255
Davies, Theo H., 114, 124, 126, 128, 130, 142, 347, 351, 500, 527, 533, 587, 588, 590, 591, 596, 597
Davis & Fishbourne, 406, 407, 550, 574, 594
Davis, Louis E., 205, 399, 454, 455, 550, 574, 594
Day Block, 88
Day, Francis R., 88
Denver Grill, 73
Desky, Charles S., 77, 293, 295
Dias, Frank M., 45, 454
Dickey, Charles W., 83, 84, 120, 129, 196, 201, 202, 253, 256, 273, 275, 277, 293, 295, 299, 383, 396, 400, 408, 409, 421, 472, 491, 492, 495, 518, 571, 572, 575, 578, 581, 582, 586, 588, 589, 592, 594
Dickson, J.S., 376
Dickson, Joshua G., 204
Dickson, Meinizies, 234
Dillingham & Co., 193, 377, 378, 568, 589

Dillingham Transportation Building, 115
Dillingham, Benjamin F., 117, 207
Dillingham, Walter, 118
Dimond Block, 377, 396
Dodd, James, 245
Dowsett House, 562
Dowsett, James I., 142, 146, 147, 181, 200, 368, 550, 562
Dowsett, Samuel, 562
Dunn, Francis R., 430, 576

E

E.O. Hall & Son, 378, 395, 396, 399
E.O. Hall Building, 394, 397, 409, 574, 575, 580, 589, 594, 597
E.W. Quinn Building, 508
Eastlake Victorian, 165, 193, 356, 371, 389, 447
Ehler's Block, 382
Ehlers, Bernhard F., 218, 519
Eli Jones House, 155
Elite Block, 315, 323, 325, 569, 578, 592, 597
Elite Ice Cream Parlor, 254, 261, 313, 315, 325
Elks Building, 377, 590
Emmeluth Building, 132, 421, 423, 424, 575, 594
Emmeluth, John, 421, 422, 599
Emmert, Paul, 66, 80, 90, 155, 253, 278, 332, 475, 478, 479, 513, 521, 523, 562
Emory & Webb, 55, 104, 193, 212, 235, 238, 282, 283, 311, 343, 349, 375, 381, 435, 441, 499, 576, 577
Emory, Walter L., 55, 104, 193, 212, 235, 238, 282, 283, 311, 333, 343, 349, 375, 381, 435, 441, 499, 576, 577
Empire Theater, 305, 306
Executive Center, 141, 215, 242, 319, 407

F

F.A. Schaefer & Co., 458
F.L. James Building, 550, 574
Fashion Stables, 320, 322
Fayerweather, Abraham, 142, 149
Financial Plaza of the Pacific, 205, 399, 409, 425, 497
first electric passenger elevator, 256, 488
First Hawaiian Center, 51, 131, 428, 502
First National Bank, 401, 409, 424, 425, 508, 570, 575, 595, 597, 600, 602
Fishbourne, Ralph A., 550, 574, 594

Fishel, Charles J., 241, 254, 313, 380
Fisher Building, 275
Flitner, David N., 533, 560
Fong Hing, 511
Fort Street Church, 98, 295, 296
Foster, Thomas R., 196
Foster, William E., 195, 196, 201, 202, 596
Fowler's Yard, 106
Fred Harrison Block, 79
Freitas, Henry J., 399, 561
French Hotel, 204, 253, 263, 264, 266, 561
French, William, 66, 210, 307, 308, 350, 470, 473, 475, 478, 568, 589
Friend Building, 97, 585
Fujioka, Fred Y., 110, 361, 577

G

Galen Building, 95
Geddes, Charles Herbert, 527
Gertz, Frank, 200, 219, 254, 261, 313, 469
Gibson, Walter Murray, 455
Globe Hotel, 218, 219, 358, 382, 532
Goodhue, Bertram, 189
Government Printing Office, 460
Gray's Block, 298
Grosvenor Center, 549
Grunwald & Schutte, 235, 237
Gulick, Charles T., 427
Gunst-Eakin, 383

H

H. Hackfeld & Co., 165, 174, 218, 382
H.E. McIntyre & Brother, 402
Hackfeld, 165, 174, 175, 218, 219, 225, 382, 519, 523, 578, 597
Hackfeld Building, 175, 219, 578, 597
Hackfeld, Heinrich, 519
Hale Alakea, 66
Hale Mahoe, 530
Haleakala, 410, 411, 596
Halehui, 186
Hall, E.O., 378, 394, 395, 396, 397, 399, 402, 408, 409, 574, 575, 580, 589, 594, 597
Hall, Edwin O., 395
Hamilton House, 413, 414
Hammer, Charles, 386

Hansmann Building, 271, 588
Hara, Ernest H., 55, 109, 326, 434, 574, 578
Harding, Thomas G., 450, 451
Harmony Hall, 45, 132
Harriet Bouslog Building, 468
Harrison Brothers, 124, 192, 193, 197, 221
Harrison, Arthur, 226, 366
Harrison, Fred, 79, 114, 165, 175, 206, 207, 216, 275, 326, 371, 381, 383, 397, 436, 453, 487, 491, 492, 578, 586
Hawaii Building, 108
Hawaii Hochi Sha (Hawaii Herald), 514
Hawaii Theater, 104, 105, 107, 508, 577, 590
Hawaiian Contracting Co., 417
Hawaiian Dredging & Construction Company, 48, 150, 153, 409, 458
Hawaiian Electric Building, 437, 441, 577, 582, 601, 602
Hawaiian Engineering & Construction Co., 77, 277, 278, 322, 370, 426, 579
Hawaiian Gazette Building, 469
Hawaiian Hotel, 66, 135, 138, 230, 245, 253, 338, 340, 344, 377, 413, 447, 472, 575, 578, 582, 585, 589, 591, 594, 596, 597, 600, 601
Hawaiian Trust Building, 440, 600
Hawaiian Trust Co., 198
Hayden, Isaac N., 251, 268, 580
Heuck, Theodore C., 296
Hobron, Neuman & Co., 389
Hoffman & Riley, 272, 322, 376, 580
Hoffman, Dr. Edward, 468, 473, 519, 533
Hoffman, Victor, 322, 396, 580
Hoffschlaeger Building, 356, 574, 591, 596
Hoffschlaeger, Elard, 475
Hollister Drug Co., 164, 230, 232, 236, 238, 242, 251, 312
Holmes, Hannah, 358, 382
Holmes, Oliver, 210, 221
Home Insurance Building, 408, 409, 571, 600
Honolulu Fort, 12, 157, 467
Honolulu Hale, 461, 463, 466, 574, 575
Honolulu House, 463
Honolulu Library and Reading Room, 330
Honolulu Planing Mill, 169, 221, 222, 587
Honolulu Savings and Loan Building, 502
Hopp, John, 363
Horn, Frederick, 200, 214, 304, 309, 355
Hotel Baths, 328

House of Mitsukoshi, 361, 577
Howard & Train, 216, 251, 272, 540, 569, 581
Howard, George A., 56, 216
Howe, Aaron B., 349
Hudson's Bay Company, 146, 184, 185, 186, 189, 329, 350
Hummel, Frederick G., 43, 64
Hunnewell, James, 348
Hustace Block, 76
Hustace-Peck Building, 537
Hyman Brothers, 479, 542

I

Ideal Finance Building, 554, 593
Ingvorsen, Charles F., 150, 216, 217, 294, 375, 383, 400, 405, 406, 407, 424, 487, 489, 570, 595
Inter-Island Steam Navigation Building, 540
Inter-Island Steam Navigation Company, 120, 181, 504, 520, 521, 536, 540
International Hotel, 103, 300
Irwin, William G., 112, 114, 187, 461, 464, 543
Italian Renaissance, 226, 325, 370, 396, 400, 425, 467, 487, 492
Ives, Albert Ely, 73

J

J.A. Cummins Building, 192, 193, 591
J.H. Fisher Building, 272
J.J. Williams Building, 233, 570, 599
J.L. Young Engineering Co., 129, 151, 153, 433, 556, 602
J.T. Waterhouse Buildings, 512
J.T. Waterhouse Warehouse, 449
Jade Building, 142, 144, 145, 146, 573
Janion, Robert C., 348, 349, 513, 539
Jemal's, 274
John Hopp Store, 363
Johnson, Hamilton, 413
Jones, Eli, 155, 478
Judd Building, 417, 487, 488, 489, 578, 582, 594, 596, 597
Jun Hee, 102

K

Kalakaua Police Station, 453, 596

Kamehameha V Post Office, 460
Kapiolani Building, 52, 53, 54, 401, 569
Kauikeolani Building, 406, 574, 584, 594
Keawe, Auntie Genoa, 111
Kekuanohu, 157
Kerr, Harry L., 49, 62, 76, 77, 88, 100, 221, 222, 243, 244, 305, 306, 341, 377, 379, 437, 452, 483, 487, 489, 502, 540, 548, 561, 582
Kerr, Laurence B., 56, 135, 469, 538, 539, 581
Keystone Saloon, 392, 585, 599
King Theater, 367, 571
Knights of Columbus, 294, 570, 588
Knights of Columbus Building, 294, 570
Knights of Pythias, 45, 79, 132, 221, 585, 600
Kohn Pedersen Fox, 51, 131, 428, 502
Kraft, August, 373
Kress Building, 266, 561

L

L.B. Kerr Building, 56
Laine, Richard W., 141, 167, 168
Lathrop, Dr. George A., 523
Lee Wai, 505
Lewers & Cooke, 203, 204, 205, 273, 406, 409, 426, 428, 485, 495, 579, 597
Lewers & Dickson, 203, 234
Lewers, Christopher H., 181, 204, 296
Lewers, Robert, 162, 204, 485, 585
Lincoln Block, 429, 583
Lincoln, George W., 187, 366, 429, 471, 583
Long's Drugs, 141
Lord Young Engineering Company, 344
Lord, Edmund J., 129, 559, 584
Lord-Young Engineering Company, 49, 100, 101, 313, 406, 407, 494, 508, 559, 570, 584, 602
Love Building, 273, 274, 278, 575, 582, 594, 595
Love, William A., 273
Lucas Brothers, 47, 52, 222, 243, 244, 365, 439, 440, 451, 521, 527
Lucas Clock Tower, 166
Lucas, George, 97, 162, 166, 167, 169, 183, 221, 235, 253, 255, 311, 317, 331, 389, 451, 453, 469, 483, 500, 512, 543, 585, 587
Lucas, John, 260
Lucas, Thomas, 251, 474

M

M.P. Robinson Building, 538, 569
M.S. Grinbaum & Co., 533
Magoon Building, 501, 502
Makee & Anthon, 478, 479, 523, 532, 560
Makee Block, 467
Makee Residence, 93
Makee, James, 93, 155, 349, 519, 523, 532, 533, 590
Market House, 516, 517
Masonic Hall, 526, 543, 585
Masonic Temple, 61, 66, 577, 594, 596
Matson Navigation Company, 546
Maxey, John, 446, 447
May Building, 211, 228
Mayers, Murray & Phillip, 417, 592
McCandless Building, 100, 582, 584
McCandless, William, 51
McChesney & Sons, 526
McChesney Building, 521
McChesney Coffee Company, 449
McCorriston Building, 260
McCorriston, Hugh and Daniel, 260
McGrew Building, 70, 71
McGrew, Dr. John, 138
McInerny Block, 193, 481, 482, 586, 587, 596
McInerny Bros., 401
McInerny, Michael, 482, 586
McInerny's, 264, 405
McIntosh, Henry W., 206, 207, 482, 483, 586
McIntyre Building, 53, 400, 401, 405, 424, 597
McIntyre, Hugh, 402
McKibbin, Dr. Robert, 490, 523
Melchers Building, 457
Melchers, Gustave C., 457, 458
Mellis, Alfred M., 241, 254
Merchant's Exchange, 470
Merrill, Simms, & Roehrig, 586
Metropolitan Meat Building, 368
Model Block, 293, 581, 587
monkeys, 415
Monsarrat Building, 142, 571, 600
Monsarrat, Marcus C., 142, 147
Monsarrat, Marcus D., 142
Moore, Isaac M., 48, 330, 331, 469, 474, 483, 587
Morgan, James F., 351, 538, 539
Morgan, Julia, 556, 572
Mott-Smith Building, 253, 262, 488

Mott-Smith, Dr. John, 253, 254
Mrs. Lack Building, 196, 201
Mullgardt, Louis Christian, 124, 128, 587
Murphy's Bar and Grill, 448
Mutch, William, 133, 293, 299, 515, 587, 592
Mutual Telephone Building, 43, 64, 500, 585, 595

N

National Building, 12, 310
Newcomb, E.A.P., 150, 277, 294, 575, 588
Nicholson, Charles H., 358
Nolte, Henry J., 510, 511
Nott, John, 378, 379
Nunes and Sons Ukulele Factory, 53

O

O'Neill Building, 211, 383, 387, 409, 578, 597
O'Neill, Jeremiah, 385
Oahu Builders, 431
Occidental Hotel, 430, 431, 506, 576
Oda, George J., 73
Odd Fellows Building, 208, 211, 218, 219, 222, 377, 578, 581, 590, 597
Onodera, Kenji, 271, 588
Oregon Block, 315, 322, 323, 571, 579, 580
Osborne, J.G., 230, 340, 350, 358, 360, 377, 394, 460, 461, 589
Ossipoff, Vladimir, 71, 589
Ouderkirk, John, 208, 377, 379, 392, 400, 415, 499, 518, 532, 548, 590
Our Lady of Peace Cathedral, 288

P

Pacific Construction Co., 54, 144, 409, 440, 554
Pacific Engineering Company, 95, 104, 124, 283, 435, 540, 590
Pacific Guardian Center, 549
Pacific Hardware Company, 193
Pacific Land & Improvement Company, 70
Pacific Mail Warehouse, 165, 591
Page, George W., 53, 543, 569, 581
Pākī, Abner, 410
Pākī, Bernice Pauahi, 410, 411
Palm Building, 313, 315, 559, 584, 594
Palmer & Richardson, 498, 591
Palmer, Isaac A., 67, 165, 192, 193, 348, 356, 371, 389, 446, 447, 456, 591, 593
Pan Pacific Plaza, 266, 280, 561
Pantheon Building, 243, 244, 252, 582
Pantheon Saloon, 244, 250, 251, 261, 580, 581
Parke, William C., 312
Patten Building, 151, 595, 602
Patzig, Carl H., 84, 295, 299, 325, 592
Pauahi Tower and Tamarind Park, 140
Peacock, Walter C., 351, 447, 448, 597
Peirce, Abraham W., 526
Percy, George W., 133, 134, 592
Pettit, Edwin C., 49, 582
Phillip, Hardie, 189, 417, 420, 592
Philp, Fred, 382
Pioneer Plaza, 202, 207, 372, 375, 380, 391, 471, 481, 486
Podmore Building, 435, 505
Podmore, Joseph W., 505
Polynesian Building, 461
Poppleton's Home Bakery, 275
Portland Building, 320, 322
Potter, Mark W., 207, 212, 215, 225, 229, 317, 319, 322, 389, 391, 407, 554, 593
Preis, Alfred, 144, 145, 572, 573
Princess Roller Skating Rink, 107
Princess Victoria Kamamalu Building, 440
Progress Block, 77, 293, 295, 326, 488, 575, 578, 582, 592, 594
Pulaholaho, 513, 517
Punchard's Store, 510

Q

Quinn, Edward W., 508

R

R.W. Wood Building, 519, 523, 533
Redward, Fred H., 61, 62, 362, 368, 446, 447, 452, 503, 593, 599
Republic Building, 193, 371, 591
Reynolds House, 150
Reynolds, Stephen, 150, 237, 446, 447, 588, 603
Rhodes Building, 350, 351
Rhodes, Godfrey, 350, 589
Richards, Charles L., 524
Richardsonian Romanesque, 400, 472, 597

Ripley & Davis, 216, 217, 333, 406, 487, 489, 547, 574, 594
Ripley & Reynolds, 313, 315, 329, 365, 494, 515, 559, 574, 594
Ripley, Clinton B., 47, 48, 61, 62, 83, 84, 197, 216, 217, 253, 256, 273, 275, 293, 295, 299, 313, 315, 329, 333, 365, 383, 396, 406, 407, 421, 451, 472, 487, 489, 491, 494, 515, 518, 547, 559, 574, 575, 582, 594
Ritz Store, 280
Robinson Block, 585, 591, 595
Robinson Warehouse, 535
Robinson, James, 157, 196, 307, 535, 536, 538
Rogers, Lincoln, 115, 117, 343, 595
Rose Lane, 12, 102, 103
Rothwell, Guy N., 43, 64, 65, 141, 151, 274, 424, 425, 433, 435, 575, 595
Royal Credit Jewelers, 387
Royal Hawaiian Garage, 336, 344, 345, 602
Royal Hotel, 447
Royal Saloon, 446, 447, 448, 591, 593, 599
Russian-American Trading Company, 10

S

S.C. Allen Cottage, 439
S.M. Damon Building, 129, 132, 425, 590, 601
Sachs Building, 77, 283, 582
Sacred Heart Convent, 149, 150, 570, 575, 579
Sacred Heart Convent School, 277, 575
Safe Deposit Building, 197, 205, 417, 575, 594
Sailors' Home, 47, 48, 447, 450, 598
Schäffer, Georg Anton, 157
Schnack Building, 75
Schuman Carriage Co., 498, 499, 503
Schuman, Gustav Adolph, 503
Seamen's Bethel, 12, 97, 98, 129, 296, 362
Security Diamond Company, 387
Senator Waterhouse Building, 515
Shillaber, Theodore, 552
Silent Barber Shop, 318
Silva's Toggery, 380
Smith, Augustus L., 207
Snow Cottage, 335
Snow, Benjamin F., 335, 479
Sociedade Lusitana Beneficente de Hawaii, 55
Sociedade Portugueza de St. Antonio Beneficente de Hawaii, 55

Spalding, Josiah C., 564
Spanish Mission Colonial, 553, 602
Spreckels Block, 187, 189
Spreckels, Claus, 187, 494
Stangenwald Building, 193, 360, 491, 492, 493, 501, 575, 579, 594
Stangenwald, Dr. Hugo, 492
Star Building, 494, 547, 584, 594
Star-Bulletin Plant, 547, 574
Steiner, James, 323, 325, 326
Stephenson, Stanley, 423
Stettin, H. Richard, 108
Stevenson, Robert Louis, 50, 578
Stiehl, Claude A., 286, 370
Stuart & Rahe, 312
Swan & Clifford, 530, 532, 598

T

T.H. Davies Warehouse, 114
Tani Contracting Company, 110
Territorial Tavern, 118
Thayer, Leonard E., 315
The Bungalow, 552, 553, 598
The Old Corner, 510, 511
Theo. H. Davies Buildings, 347
Thomas / Yat Loy Building, 353
Thomas, E.B., 61, 62, 67, 180, 195, 196, 201, 330, 348, 353, 354, 356, 366, 453, 456, 482, 483, 490, 498, 568, 586, 596, 599
Thomas, George, 162, 210, 358, 359, 513, 524, 597
Thrum, Thomas G., 80, 90, 155, 241, 312, 358, 468
Title Guaranty Building, 550
Tom Moore Tavern, 211, 385
Tom, Al, 431
Train, Robert F., 216, 581
Traphagen, Oliver G., 66, 133, 134, 175, 208, 226, 325, 335, 370, 376, 383, 397, 400, 426, 487, 498, 521, 580, 581, 582, 592, 597
Tregloan Building, 235, 236, 238, 242, 311, 312
Tregloan, Henry S., 236
Triangle Auto Supply Building, 566
Tsugawa, James K., 438, 468, 493
Twain, Mark, 109, 464

U

Union Building, 315, 559, 560, 584, 594

Union Grill, 373, 375, 578
Union Plaza, 564
Union Saloon, 469, 471
Union Trust Building, 55, 570
Usborne, Gordon, 64, 104

V

Varieties Theater, 101, 365, 373, 447
Vincent, Charles W., 171, 172, 450, 451, 470, 524, 530, 552, 597, 598
von Hamm-Young Company, 59, 135, 284
Von Holt Block, 365, 367, 596

W

W.E. Foster Building, 195, 596
W.M. McChesney & Sons, 521
Waity Building, 370, 579, 597
Walker Park, 174, 537, 539, 540, 543
Walker, Thomas B., 233, 353, 362, 392, 421, 422, 570, 583, 593, 599
Wall, Charles J., 568
Wall-Nichols Co., 193, 372
Warren, Major William R., 307
Waterhouse, John T., 44, 59, 212, 214, 378, 403, 448, 449, 505, 512, 520, 587
Waterhouse/Andrade Building, 212, 229
Watumull Building, 286
Waverley Block, 103, 299, 300, 587, 592
Way's Block, 132
Webb, Marshall W., 115, 333, 435, 576, 577, 595, 603
Whitney, Henry M., 460, 463, 464
Wichman Building, 218, 219, 221, 225, 582
Wichman, Henry F., 222
Wilder Building, 180, 182, 596
Wilder Steamship Company, 181, 520
Wilder, Samuel G., 181
Williams, Charles E., 225, 230, 232, 235, 312, 589
Williams, Fred W., 45, 142, 153, 600
Williams, James J., 233, 234, 241, 570, 599
Williams/Hollister Building, 230, 238
Wimberly & Cook, 51, 389, 391, 440, 600
Wm. French Residence, 66
Wm. S. Anner & Co., 378
Wolter, Edward H.F., 92, 430, 431
Wolters Building, 266, 561, 582
Wong, Gin D., 266, 561
Wood, Dr. Robert W., 138, 468, 519
Wood, George, 564
Wood, John H., 476
Wood, R.A.S., 75, 162, 171, 172, 296, 312, 598, 601
Wood/Spalding House, 564
Woolley, Ralph E., 115, 120, 129, 266, 286, 349, 441, 589, 601
Woolworth's, 234, 242
Wou, Leo S., 409, 477, 497
Wyllie, Robert C., 44, 75, 264, 329, 513, 598

Y

Yat Loy, 355
Yee Chan & Co, 361
YMCA, 106, 329, 330, 331, 332, 333, 335, 336, 343, 450, 570, 575, 577, 579, 585, 587, 590, 594, 595, 602
YMCA Building, 329, 579, 585, 594
YMCA Building (Old), 331
Yokohama Specie Bank, 452, 582, 593
York & Sawyer, 424, 441, 602
Young, Alexander, 56, 59, 134, 135, 138, 140, 328, 415, 576, 582, 587, 590, 592, 597
Young, James L., 129, 151, 153, 243, 244, 433, 556, 584, 602
Young, John Mason, 129, 590
YWCA, 145, 326, 333, 508, 556, 572, 602
YWCA Building, 145, 556

Z

Zupplein, Henry, 355

GEOGRAPHICAL INDEX

For histories and information on downtown Honolulu buildings between Nuʻuanu Street, Beretania Street, River Street, and Nimitz Boulevard:

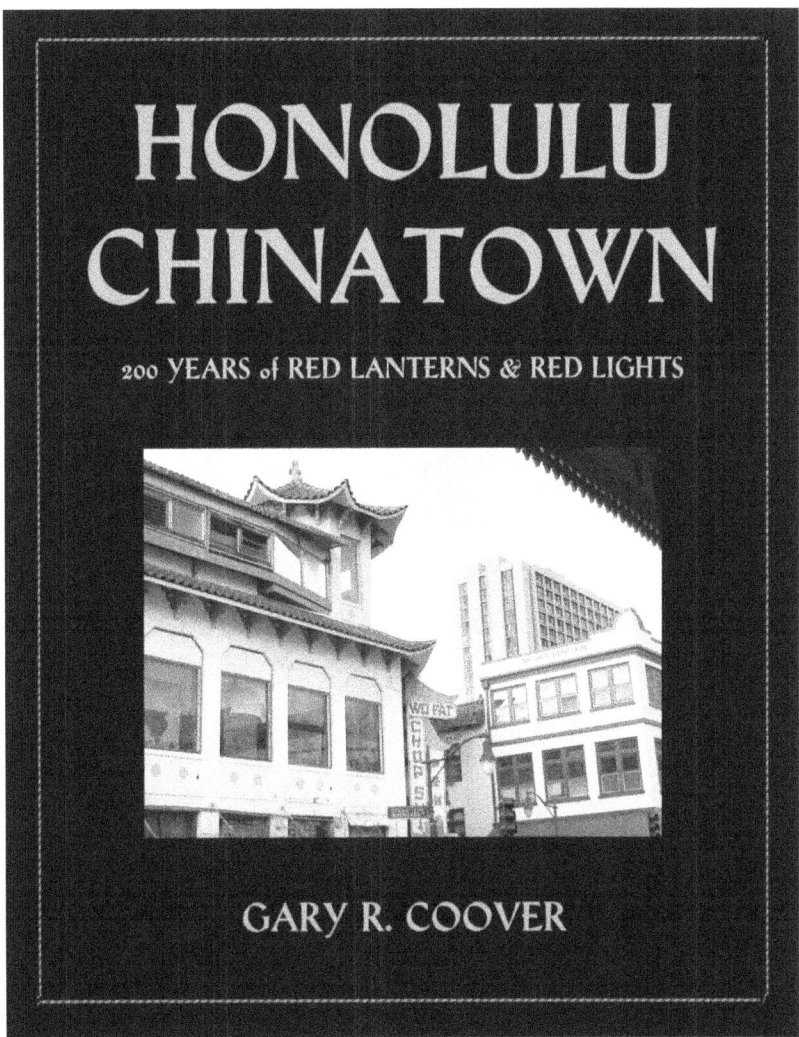

458 pages, 8 x 10 paperback and Kindle

ISBN-13: 978-1-953208-01-0

Rollston Press (2022)

2022 Preservation Award from Historic Hawaii Foundation

www.ingramcontent.com/pod-product-compliance
Lightning Source LLC
Chambersburg PA
CBHW080537230426
43663CB00015B/2623